W9-BZA-909

Bower

Teaching the Language Arts

Expanding Thinking Through Student-Centered Instruction

CATHY COLLINS BLOCK
Texas Christian University

ALLYN AND BACON
Boston London Toronto Sydney Tokyo Singapore

Dedicated to
my loving husband, Stan Block;
my wonderful family, JoAnn Zinke, Wanda Zinke,
Michael Donegan, Mary Block, Michelle Block,
Randy Block, Rosalyn Block, and Maury Block; and
John Mangieri, whose courage, character, and wisdom
assists me to help others.

For permission to use copyrighted material, grateful acknowledgment is made to the copyright holders on pages 552–553, which are hereby made part of this copyright page.

Copyright © 1993 by Allyn and Bacon
A Division of Simon & Schuster, Inc.
160 Gould St.
Needham Heights, Massachusetts 02194

Editor-in-Chief, Education: Nancy Forsyth
Series Editor: Virginia Lanigan
Editorial Assistant: Nicole De Palma
Cover Administrator: Linda Dickinson
Manufacturing Buyer: Louise Richardson
Editorial-Production Service: The Wheetley Company, Inc.

Library of Congress Cataloging-in-Publication Data

Block, Cathy Collins.
   Teaching the language arts: expanding thinking through student-centered instruction / Cathy Collins Block.
       p.   cm.
   Includes index.
   ISBN 0-205-14209-5
   1. Language arts.   I. Title.
LB1576.B499   1993
428'.0071--dc20   92-37823
                                                              CIP

Printed in the United States of America

10 9 8 7 6 5 4 3 2 1   97 96 95 94 93 92

CONTENTS

Chapter 6   *Reading Instruction in A Student
Communication Center   176*

Chapter 7   *Writing to Communicate and Think   210*

Chapter 8   *Revising: Using Grammar, Rewriting, and Rephrasing
as Tools to Clarify Meaning   248*

Chapter 11 *Creative Expression: One Step Beyond Integration* **346**

Chapter 12 *Teaching Students to Communicate with
High Level Thinking* **376**

Teaching the Language Arts was written to describe the numerous changes that have occurred in language arts instruction within the last few years. *Teaching the Language Arts* explains these changes, as well as modern concepts, materials, and instructional techniques to assist your teaching. It does so in a step-by-step manner. That is, in Chapter 1 you will come to understand how thinking and communication abilities can develop rapidly in a classroom fashioned as a student communication center—a place where students' speaking, listening, reading, and writing needs are the central concern. In Chapter 2, you will discover the research that supports new approaches to instruction in speaking, listening, reading, and writing. In each subsequent chapter you will discover how this research can be applied to daily lessons you teach. This text was also organized to present the scope and sequence of language arts instruction from the beginning to the end of the school year.

Teaching the Language Arts describes several innovative approaches to instruction, such as how to teach phonics and compare/contrast strategies in an integrative, whole language based program; how new middle school language arts programs can be built; and how to build students' higher level thinking and creativity through language arts instruction and real-world assessments.

Teaching the Language Arts is divided into fifteen chapters. Each chapter opens with the themes and objectives of that chapter. After these introductory comments, the discussion is divided into three sections: Theoretical Foundations, Putting Theory into Practice, and Strategies that Teach.

Theoretical Foundations describes the principles, research data, and theory that support innovative instructional concepts, classroom practices, and daily lessons.

Putting Theory into Practice depicts how teachers translate this theoretical knowledge into different approaches to instruction.

Strategies That Teach sections are comprised of the following practical features: (a) "Creating Lessons" supply the materials and ideas to create daily or week-long lessons which implement the theory and approaches that individual teachers value, and that specific student populations need, and (b) "Critical Thinking Activities" demonstrate how you can develop your students' higher level thinking and communication competencies through a student-centered curriculum.

Because your competencies as a teacher are the most important elements that will determine your students' success as communicators and thinkers, each *Strategies That Teach* section concludes with "Professional

Development Opportunity" which describes how you can perform a new teaching act that will expand your students' capabilities. Once you have completed this text, these professional development opportunities will have increased your ability to grow throughout your career.

The "Try It: Challenges" contains activities you perform alone or with a colleague, and/or elementary and middle school students to enlarge your competency with the objectives in each chapter. These activities occur outside of the college classroom, and will be completed after you have read each chapter. "For Your Journal" was created for two purposes. First, it helps you generate and maintain a professional development journal, as doing so will increase your teaching abilities. Second, it provides activities where you create new types of journals and journal entries that function as models for your students. These models will become samples as you teach your students how to use their journals in new and evermore effective ways.

The last professional development strategy appears on the last pages of each chapter. It is the "Building Your Professional Portfolio" section. This section has resources, addresses, and forms that you can use with students, parents, and colleagues throughout your professional career. *Building Your Professional Portfolio* is constructed to be duplicated and placed inside separate file folders. After finishing this textbook, you will have the most current information concerning each topic in the professional portfolio sections. You can add new materials to each folder as it becomes available. Together these folders can become professional resources. This text also enables you to practice using journals and portfolios as new instructional and assessment tools. Through this practice you will be better prepared to demonstrate their use to your students.

The main body of each chapter also contains two special boxed features: *Notecards* and *The Challenge of Diversity*. *Notecards* are 3" × 5" notecard sized listings of children's literature that can be duplicated and placed in your own file box for future reference. Each notecard presents literature that can be used to teach your students the language arts concepts described in each chapter. These listings are not available in other texts. Several teachers worked diligently so your student communication center could be equipped with many captivating books concerning 31 different student needs. If you make the titles from all notecards available, your students will have new selections of children's literature to read each week of their school year!

The *Challenge of Diversity* boxes are equally valuable. Each box relates to the discussion that immediately precedes it in the text. The box describes one or more strategies to use with multicultural students, students with learning needs, or students who have exceptional competencies in the area portrayed in the discussion that precedes the box. These boxes assist you in addressing the diverse multicultural needs and learning styles of students in your class.

As you begin this textbook, I wish you every success in your career as an educator. My intent is that this text will assist you in reaching the many goals you envision.

Table of Contents of Notecards

Teaching the
Language Arts

1 Language and Thinking Development in the Elementary School

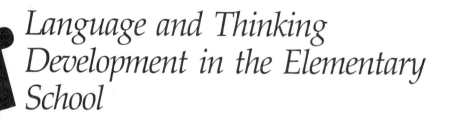

The language arts classroom you create will be strikingly different from those in which you were taught. These differences arise from a more complete understanding of the significant role students play in learning and using their language.

The beginning is the most important part of the work.

—Plato, *The Republic*

The time you spend reading this chapter may be the most important step you will take to become the best language arts teacher that you can be. Through this reading you will have the opportunity to image your ideas and learn the most recent knowledge concerning language arts instruction.

Before you opened this textbook you may have heard many new terms related to language arts instruction (e.g., whole language, writing workshops, invented spelling, heuristic speaking, sentence combining, and DLTA). When you were in elementary school such concepts did not exist. As you may recall, your language arts program likely contained separate textbooks for reading, spelling, and handwriting. You drilled on rules of grammar, participated in plays, read orally, and answered questions. Your teachers probably kept all students together, as a large group, to work one exercise at the same time.

Federal, state, and local school district administrators as well as publishers of textbooks prescribed what you were to learn. Your teachers were "curriculum managers" who told you when to combine language "rules" that were to become your language. When told to work a new page of language drills, you likely did precisely as you were told because of the desire to please your teacher. In this educational system, you may not have gained the confidence or competencies to express your own unique ideas.

More recent understandings of learning will lead you away from asking your students to follow such prescriptions and memorize rules. Such memory work is impractical because we now know that language and thinking abilities are not rote knowledge (Piaget, 1966; Vygotsky, 1978; Kozulin, 1990). Language and thinking abilities are continuously expanding awarenesses. They develop through the initiatives students will take to use new communication principles or thinking processes they discover to reach a goal that is important to them.

Throughout this chapter you will learn new philosophies and principles of teaching language arts. This knowledge may enable your students to reach higher levels of communication and thinking capabilities than you did at their age. With your assistance, today's students can become exceptionally talented speakers, listeners, readers, writers, and thinkers whose communication expands their world and unlocks its mysteries.

By the end of this chapter, you will have learned:

1. Principles that guide successful language arts instruction;

2. Eight content areas of the language arts;

3. Eight dimensions of thinking your students can develop;

4. A lesson plan that builds thinking and language arts abilities simultaneously;

5. An instructional activity that introduces you to "scaffolding" instruction;

6. To conceptualize your own personal philosophy of language arts instruction.

Each chapter in this book is divided into three sections:

1. **Theoretical Foundation** which describes the theoretical foundation and research bases upon which language instruction is built;

2. **Putting Theory into Practice** which describes how theoretical principles can be placed into practice in the classroom; and

3. **Strategies That Teach** which suggests ways in which these practices can be scheduled as daily lessons. This third section is marked by a red side bar in the right margin of the textbook. It is highlighted in this way because it contains many lessons, critical thinking activities, ideas, and methods that you can use in field experiences and in your classrooms throughout your teaching career. Look for this red bar as it will be easier for you to reference each of the following types of teaching strategies: (1) *Creating Lesson Plans* which teaches you how to use different materials in your classroom; (2) *Critical Thinking Activities* which demonstrate how to integrate speaking, listening, reading, and writing to expand preschool through eighth-grade students' thinking; (3) *Professional Development Opportunities* which enable you to learn new teaching skills; (4) *Try It* questions which allow you to reflect upon and self-assess how much you have learned; (5) *For Your Journal* which contains journal writing activities you can use in your classroom; and (6) *Building Your Professional Portfolio* which contains additional resources and teaching aids that you can copy and place in file folders for future reference for the rest of your professional life.

Each chapter also contains **Notecards** that you can copy and place in your own file box. Each notecard contains titles of numerous children's books and magazines that can be used to develop specific language and thinking competencies. Throughout this textbook you will also find **The Challenge of Diversity** boxes. These boxes provide information about teaching strategies to meet the special needs of students who have a multicultural heritage, exceptional learning ability, and/or unique learning modalities.

THEORETICAL FOUNDATION
WHAT PRINCIPLES DETERMINE SUCCESSFUL LANGUAGE ARTS PROGRAMS?

You may have been apprehensive when you opened this language arts textbook. Teaching students to communicate and think effectively and to express their unique ideas is an enormous responsibility. You know that you want to meet your students' language needs, but how can you? Is it your job to just sit back and let students tell you what they want and need to learn? How can they? Some won't communicate their needs well; others will require new knowledge before they realize their potential. Should you become a charismatic leader who rallies the "troops" into action? And if you do, will students be able to motivate themselves to "rise to greatness" without you later in life?

You will find answers these questions in the next few pages. Before you do, it is important that we define a few terms. The term *Language Arts* consists of three equally important concepts. **Language** *is the structured system of rules used to communicate with others.* Language is created when two or more people agree upon, and understand, a word or phrase to represent a single idea, object, emotion, and/or experience. **Arts** *is the use of acquired skill, knowledge, and imagination in producing works.* **Thinking** *is the ability to organize language, and explain ideas so as to conceive, analyze, infer, or resolve* (Barrell, 1991; Collins, 1992; Lippman, 1988; Resnick, 1989).

Language operates in concert with thinking in both known and unknown ways. When listening and reading, the mind continually translates language so it can be stored. It categorizes information according to merit, weight, and personal worth; discards incongruencies; and enriches previously known concepts. When speaking and writing, the mind takes stored language and ideas and reworks them. It searches for experiences and examples with which to create, relate, and evaluate new thoughts. Moreover, for your students to use language as a vehicle for thought, they must translate their ideas into the subsystems that govern English.

English is comprised of the following subsystems: **phonology**—*the sound system of our language;* **morphology**—*units that carry meaning in print;* **syntax**—*the principles of grammar that place meaning into sentences;* and **semantics**—*the different understandings, connotations, and denotations of individual words.* Therefore, **language arts instruction** can be defined as the section of the educational program that *assists students to use an ordered system of symbols and principles to transmit ideas and information.*

Through your instruction students can advance their abilities to read, write, speak, listen, think, spell, punctuate, use fitting grammatical structures, operate technology, and choose appropriate communication for different situations and audiences. Your **philosophy of language arts instruction** directs the ways in which you teach communication symbols and principles to students. Your philosophy is *the convictions you hold regarding language learning; and the criteria you use to select between equally attractive instructional alternatives that compete for your attention.*

PRINCIPLES OF LANGUAGE ARTS INSTRUCTION

The first step in developing your language arts philosophy is to learn the new principles that guide today's most successful language arts classes.

Principle 1: Language arts classes must be positive, comfortable, and challenging environments. In these classes students learn concepts that they will value and refine throughout their lives. A student-centered communication center is one in which all speakers, listeners, readers, and writers share their work while communicating with, and learning from one another. Within this community, cooperation is championed and competition is moderated (Mason & Au, 1990). Students are surrounded with good literature as well as many peers and adults who serve as role models (Decker, 1985; Harste, Woodward, & Burke, 1984).

In your classroom *each* person is significant. Their contributions will be celebrated, their limitations will be braced, and their differences shared. Your students will ask questions, admit confusion, and chance making mistakes. You will grant them permission to do so through statements such as "I'm glad you took a chance," "What are you thinking?" and "I like your question." Through your leadership, students will begin to realize that they can produce meaningful ideas in the minds of others (Costa, 1989).

As the teacher in this student-centered environment, you also assure that elements in the classroom favor risk-taking. You will demonstrate that in order to be right most of the time, students have to risk being wrong some of the time. Less successful efforts need not be final. Through restructuring their inadequate solutions, your students will learn that "trying again" is an effective strategy for life. You show in your teaching that you are not afraid to leave your safe "harbor" and explore new seas. Your students become your captains. In your class, the curriculum serves as a compass that merely sequences the activities. You establish the ultimate goal and land to be explored. The school district determines the "type of boat" in which activities are formed. However, it is the students who operate the compass, steer the boat, calculate the ports of call, and map the explorations that will occur. You assist them to alter their course to comply with their emerging strengths, weaknesses, needs, and curiosities, in language and thought. In other words, in your class thoughts are continuously emerging and being nurtured. Your students spark new needs for growth.

Furthermore, because you want your students to become good sailors (communicators and thinkers), you will not limit their education to on-ship drills, with their boat docked at port. You will not ask them to perform isolated maneuvers all day (i.e., worksheets of fill-in-the-blank exercises). Instead, you go with them to sea, tell them stories about how you surmounted important communication obstacles, and perform tasks with them so that your modeling, coaching, and strategies elevate confidence in their own independent sailing (communication) abilities. They must have your support, guidance, and encouragement in times of trial before they believe greater ports of understanding are open to them. Some will never leave the harbor without your instruction. Some must also see you fail in your communicating and thinking, but get up undaunted, and be successful again, before they will overcome their fear of communicating. You and your students will discuss newly developing ideas, and describe your and their thinking. You will relay to them when you are perplexed about something, and explain how you take a communication problem, connect it to a new thought, and establish a higher level of understanding.

As Harste, Woodward, and Burke (1984) state: "Only when things go wrong, when the expected relationships or known rules do not hold, is the language user forced to develop new rules and new responses in order to cope. To live within existing rules and predictable patterns is not to grow. It is only under conditions in which all of the relationships are not known that language users must scamper to outgrow their current selves" (p. l36).

In addition to the challenges and stimulation you provide, the classroom climate is influenced by physical elements such as space, noise, light, air, colors, and activity. Appropriate and necessary materials should be easily accessible to students. Desks and chairs are arranged to heighten student interaction, and yet grant places for privacy and independent concentration (Collins, 1987; McNeil, 1980).

You will fill your class with challenges students ask to conquer, and sensory stimuli, materials, and vicarious experiences that push the limits of your students' language and thinking. Students can easily repeat what you tell them, memorize information, move their eyes across the page as their minds wander, copy from the board, and think what you want them to think. However, if they are required to enact their own initiative, they will have to speak up, listen actively, read purposefully, write messages, and think about ideas in their classes.

Principle 2: Student communication centers are places where students' needs are the central concern of the curriculum. In essence, in your language arts classroom, students will learn that their successes and needs are as important to you as they are to them.

To illustrate how you can create a needs-based classroom, think of the last time you improved your ability to communicate or think. That educational incident likely contained some of the following features: (1) you learned the information because you knew you would use it again; (2) you made a conscious choice to think or use language in a way you wanted; (3) you discarded other ways of communicating or thinking because they were not as comfortable or successful as the one you selected; (4) you expressed a thought or reached an intended goal with more precision than ever before; (5) you ventured to try because you were in a supportive environment with people you trusted. Moreover, your learning may have emerged even though you hadn't set an earlier goal to learn this new skill. Perhaps you faced a challenging and engaging task where the need arose to add something to your language.

Presently at least half of our students exert little or no effort to learn because school doesn't address their learning needs in these ways. The old theory that " 'We can make 'em work; all we have to do is get tough' has never produced intellectual effort in the history of the world" (William Glaser, as interviewed in Gough, 1987, p. 605). In your class, students will satisfy their belonging needs for power, caring, sharing, as well as creating and cooperating with others.

Principle 3: Speaking, listening, reading, writing, and thinking are highly complex, intricate, and interactive systems. Students can improve their language through appropriate classroom procedures, technological learning aids, and rewards from the products they produce. You can ensure that students receive the maximum when these elements effectively integrate the language arts and thinking processes. Your students should understand why they are good speakers, readers, writers, listeners, and thinkers. Their answers should also demonstrate a regard for the complexities and interrelationship of language and thinking. For example, in a field-test of activities contained in this book, students were asked: "How do you know when you are reading and writing well?" Molly Sausan, a second grader in Fort Worth, Texas, said, "I know I'm a good reader when what I think follows what the writer was thinking. I *know* I'm a good reader, writer, *and thinker!* I know by the way it sounds when I do it. You know, does it have some sort of pattern? Does it flow?"

The ways in which you enable students to integrate language arts brings us to the fourth principle of effective instruction.

Principle 4: Language arts teachers know they are an important force in their students' lives. They continuously work to nurture characteristics that correlate to high student achievement (Ruddell & Kern, 1986).   As Haim Ginott stated in his book *Teacher and Child*, "I have come to a frightening conclusion. I am the decisive element in a classroom. It is my personal approach that creates the climate. It is my daily mood that makes the weather" (p. 16).

What makes a good language arts teacher? Bruner (1986) stated that such educators do not present knowledge as a set of facts but allow students to draw conclusions. They also have a high level of commitment to, and enthusiasm for, the language arts; they ask for multiple explanations; and they invite students to challenge points.

Research has identified nine ways that such teachers engage students' highest levels of capabilities.

1. Effective language arts teachers allow students to set learning goals, and explain why they are important (Good & Grouws 1975; Porter & Brophy, 1988; Rosenshine & Furst, 1971). Their directions are unusually clear and informative.
2. A good language arts teacher will develop pupils' positive attitudes toward school, and promote high self-esteem (Berliner & Tikunoff, 1976; Medley, 1977).
3. Most successful teachers establish class rules that permit pupils to attend to their personal and procedural needs, without having to check with their teacher (Collins, 1987; Gage, 1978).
4. Productive teachers keep students actively involved, vary the difficulty of the lesson as necessary, give credit for partially correct answers, encourage question-asking, and provide adequate pupil response time (Borick, 1979; Brophy & Evertson, 1974).
5. Effective language arts teachers provide variety in work, and negotiate a number of classroom goals simultaneously (Porter & Brophy, 1988).
6. Such teachers explicitly model and potentially instruct pupils in

"sense making" and problem solving to foster their higher level thinking (Porter & Brophy, 1988).

7. Productive language arts teachers are reflective. They think about what, why, and how they are teaching (Porter & Brophy, 1988). They have consistently high expectations of themselves and their students.

8. Most successful teachers show one or more sample end products of communication before students begin to create their own. They also engage in the same activities they assign students, such as pursuing their own reading in view of students, and talking about speaking problems they overcame.

9. Successful teachers model active listening. These teachers are so attentive that their listening skills communicate that they believe that their students' next sentences could be the most important they have ever created.

Are there other characteristics that your language arts teachers possessed that you appreciated? Reflect about what a specific teacher in your past did to increase your communication or thinking abilities.

Principle 5: Students need to work on tasks they will use in the world; activities that are authentic and intrinsically motivating.   For the rest of their lives your students will read books; therefore, they should read children's literature in your room. Because students will not circle "verbs" or identify pictures on worksheets later in life, they will not do so in your room. Your students will learn to read for their own purposes as well as to identify books, thoughts, and discussions they value, which they will do as adults. As Rigg and Allen (1989) state: "If you and I were in my car . . . and we got stuck in rush-hour traffic, and while sitting there I nudged the car forward a little so I could read the bumper sticker on the car in front of me . . . you'd think my behavior perfectly normal. But if, as we sat there, I whipped a set of flashcards out of my purse and started reading each one in my announcement voice—*can, close, if, too, this*—you'd think me strange (Stranger still if I started giving definitions for each one.)" (p. 44).

In essence, if you are implementing Principle 5 effectively you will answer yes to this question: "Will my students have to do the assignment we've just created sometime in their real life outside of school?"

Such real-life experiences interest them and students remember them better (Pauk, 1989). Through meaningful activities, students' thinking and language abilities are incessantly learned, elevated, and churned. In conjunction with this doctrine, silence does not always equate to intense thinking. Students' intrinsic motivation will increase when their communication helps someone who is important to them (Collins, 1990a; Langer, 1991).

Intrinsic motivation is also built when your instruction matches the student's **zone of proximal development** (*the difference between a student's ability to solve a problem without any assistance or with some assistance;* Vygotsky, 1962). Your job is to take children beyond what they can not do unaided, to what they can learn. You do so by structuring goals and intentions in ways that use students' talents to support new growth (Kozulin, 1990; Vygotsky, 1962, 1978).

Principle 6: Language arts teachers evaluate students' communication differently than your teachers did when you were in school. They use multiple measures of communication competence, and evaluate communication competencies in action, as demonstrated in Chapter 15. Many assessments will be made during, rather than after, instruction since assessments now document how students communicate and think while they are in the process of doing so. Best evaluations do not compare the amount of effort or the results of one student's work to that of another. Instead they compare each student to his or her own learning history (Bandura & Schunk, 1981; Goa, 1973; Schunk & Rice, 1989).

In closing this section of the chapter, recall the six principles that effective teachers follow. In the future, to evaluate your language arts program, pause at the end of the day and recount these principles in light of that day's events. How often did your students tell you what they wanted to learn next, and why? How many times did you require students to pose their own questions? Did you revert to asking questions for which you already knew the answer? And, was your class a place where students *really lived*, where important, "life-changing" events occurred?

PUTTING THEORY INTO PRACTICE
HOW DO YOU TEACH THINKING AND LANGUAGE ARTS?

Aristotle believed that the depths of one's thinking governed the types of language one could use (Anderson, 1985). This intricacy and interconnection between thinking and language was also revealed in Helen Keller's (1956) encounter:

> As the cool stream gushed over one hand, Anne Sullivan finger spelled into my other hand the word "water," first slowly, then rapidly. I stood still, my whole attention fixed upon the motions of her fingers. Suddenly I felt a misty consciousness as of something forgotten—a thrill of returning thought; and somehow the mystery of language was revealed to me. I realized then that water meant the wonderful cool something that was flowing over my hand. That living word awakened my soul, gave it light, hope, joy, set it free . . . I left the well-house eager to learn. Everything had a name and each name gave birth to a new thought (p. 36).

We now believe that language abilities and thinking competencies shape each other. Both are of equal intensity in fostering learning. Through the power of language use, the quantity and quality of students' thoughts can be improved. Through reading, writing, speaking, and listening, transitory thoughts can be transformed into lasting principles. This transformation occurs because single ideas enter the mind as **cognitive entries,** capable of bonding with collective categories of former thoughts. These categorical thoughts are then stored as a *dense cognitive structure* called **schema**. Each schema is *the collection of learnings, experiences, emotions, and values one has about a topic*. Nerve endings of schema in the brain expand in length and breadth as one discusses, writes, and reads about a concept. This depth and breadth eventually become wisdom as more and more dendrites (branches from nerve endings) are forced to intertwine (Rosenblatt, 1978; Smith, 1978). Thus, if you do not ignite students' thinking, writing, reading, speaking, and listening, you regularly limit their wisdom (Collins, 1992c). As Gardner and Hatcher (1989) state, "the relationship between language and thinking has been a topic of debate for a very long time. However, nearly every program we have considered acknowledges the importance of language facility to effective thinking in one way or another . . . [Students] must become an adroit manipulator of language, logical forms, computer programs, or other symbol systems that, in effect, can serve as vehicles for thought" (p.48). Therefore, since students' thinking abilities and language development are of equal value and influence upon the depth of their communication, you should develop both competencies if your students' potentials are to be reached.

The union of cognitive entries and schema explains how new information is acquired and combines with previously learned knowledge (Loban, 1976). Research has also demonstrated that even kindergartners come to school with well-established schema about life and language. Our job is to refine their less accurate ideas, embellish schema that are less nurtured, and fashion new bodies of understanding to unite schemata. As Rigg and Allen (1989) state:

> It is not simply a matter of having taken something in and mapping it onto our old self; [our] new thinking [about language and learning] is to relate [new learning] to everything else we have, in an individual way. Indeed, each aspect of learning is unique because of previous schema we possess; those schema predispose us to see the world in a certain way, and they also provide the boundaries, so to speak, of where [our] learning will fit (p. 35).

While each child is a unique individual, children pass through similar stages in thinking and language development (e.g., most children's brains increase to about 90 percent of adult brain size by age five, about the same time as they master oral language competencies). However, each person has distinct cognitive inclinations and communication modality preferences (Brown & Campione, 1986; Gardner & Hatcher, 1989; Sternberg, 1985).

DEVELOPING THE THINKING PROCESS

Some psychologists suggest that thinking development should precede language instruction. A leader of this position is Jean Piaget (1886–1980), a Swiss psychologist (Duckworth, 1987; Piaget, 1960). Piaget professed that students learn language by translating thoughts (notions, natural inclinations, and tendencies) into words. He emphasized the need for teachers to deliver instruction that was rapidly paced; students were to explore materials and discover labels and names for concepts they found (Duckworth, 1987).

Piaget (1960) supported this theoretical framework with evidence that young children learn to talk through their own initiative and curiosity, without formal instruction if they are immersed in a language-rich environment. In a period of only three or four years, for example, children acquire a vocabulary of 5,000 words, and internalize major grammatical rules of their spoken language. Piaget proposed that schools should use immersion and exploration as learning tools throughout the high-school years.

On the other hand, some psychologists believe that thinking processes should be developed as the language labels of a concept are presented. Leaders in this research are Bruner (1986), Kozulin (1990), and Vygotsky (1978). Vygotsky theorized that through the use of specific words and language patterns, thinking is shaped. He and other psychologists reason that the degree and direction of thinking will be related to the breadth of one's language development. Thus, if you teach language arts from this perspective, you will develop thinking simultaneously with language. You will assist students to translate ideas, feelings, and experiences into words, as soon as a mental image appears. At the same time, the accuracy and specificity of this translation will be determined by the depth and precision of thinking that students learned outside of school and have been taught. For example, when students state their thoughts aloud, they may realize that their thinking is not clear. As a result, they may call upon a novel example to state the point in a slightly better way, and thus evolve a deeper sense of it for themselves. When students have to convince their classmates, they will provide themselves with the reasons for the thinking they did. Likewise, when classmates misunderstand parts of an argument, they may think through it again, which improves and advances their understanding and communication.

There are several additional reasons why you should improve students' thinking as you build their language abilities. First, teaching strategies that strengthen thinking competencies increase language arts achievement (Collins, 1991b). A myth exists that as people mature, their thinking and reasoning naturally escalate. Unfortunately, critical and creative thinking abilities *do not* develop automatically. Adults who were not taught to think critically and creatively exhibit cognitive abilities that are no more advanced than the thinking processes they used when they were in the sixth grade (Gardner & Hatcher, 1989).

Another reason to build students' cognitive and language competence is related to our society. Prior to the twentieth century, after-school apprenticeships increased students' analytical reasoning abilities. Every day children worked with adults. They observed and questioned their mentors as they made decisions concerning the work and world events they both experienced side by side. In addition, students were active partners in conversations and asked questions about the stories their parents and grandparents told and read by the fireplace. These elders often explained the thought processes they used which led to their wisdom. Through the activities and instruction in this book, you can re-create these thinking and language learning opportunities for your students through a classroom communication center.

Also, knowledge in our world increases 15 percent per year; many jobs our students will hold in the year 2000 have not been invented; and our present information about technology will represent less than 10 percent of that which today's kindergartners will need when they become adults (Duffy, 1992). Therefore, much of the *content* in language arts your students learn will become obsolete by the time they become adults; however, while the communication competencies students need will change in the future, the strengths in thinking they develop in your class will be retained.

Finally, students in America are not performing as well on measures of higher level thinking as students in other countries (Kutscher, 1989). If your students are to continue to rise to international leadership positions, you must teach them how to think, how to use fair-minded flexibility in groups, how to create ideas cooperatively, how to encourage multiple options, and how to select among equally attractive alternatives. To be literate now requires that students know more about how to think; not just how to read. Students must learn to identify problems in, and reason effectively with, printed information. For example, as Beck (1989) states, "Reading and language arts are the perfect vehicle for developing higher order thinking because literature—perhaps more than any other source of information—provides powerful models of problem-solving processes. It is full of characters who engage in effective and ineffective attempts at solving problems, who use incisive or fuzzy reasoning, and who rely on adequate or inadequate evidence. . . . What is needed is to move the activities that involve higher order thinking into the core of our lessons, to move our concern toward developing higher level thinking into the mainstream of instruction" (pp. 680, 682). To help students develop these abilities, we need to relegate more time to instruction concerning high-quality thinking with printed and spoken material.

A major difference between thinking and language, however, is that psychologists do not yet know the "rules" thoughts follow in their creation. Linguists have identified many "rules" of language. To give ideas to others, students *must* translate them into a standard communication unit, through the rules of language. Throughout this book, you will learn ways your students can translate their reflections into these language standards. Your language arts program *can shift from instructing students about things to teaching them to think and communicate ideas.* You will shift from helping students gain knowledge to showing them how to form ideas. As you foster critical thinking, your teaching will change. If you now have a tendency to lecture others, these **didactic** habits will diminish.

DIMENSIONS OF LANGUAGE ARTS AND THINKING ABILITIES IN INSTRUCTION

There are eight components of language arts instruction: oral language, listening, reading, writing, grammar, writing conventions, language arts used across the curriculum, and creative expression. Methods of teaching these components are presented in Chapters 3 through 12. Figure 1-1 outlines major competencies within each of these language arts.

There are eight dimensions of thinking competencies that are amenable to instruction (Baron & Sternberg, 1987; Beyer, 1987; Collins, 1991b; deBono, 1970). These dimensions of thinking affect the quality of communication students can create; they are depicted in Figure 1-2. Dimension 1 contains *basic cognitive operations,* including the ability to clarify ideas, examine relationships, see errors, summarize, and remember. Dimension 2 includes *thinking processes* that call upon more than one operation, including inferencing, interpreting, thinking like an expert, and making multiple comparisons. In Dimension 2, concepts, literal elaborations, and connections between ideas are also developed.

Dimension 3 consists of *decision-making abilities* where one selects from competing alternatives that may or may not be obvious to the decision maker, uses decision-making tools, and recognizes critical points when making a decision will eliminate problems before they begin. Dimension 4 is comprised of *abilities one uses to solve problems,* resolve perplexing situations, assess the quality of ideas, eliminate biases, establish criteria, and judge the credibility of sources. Dimension 5 contains *metacognitive thinking,* involving control of self; assessing one's current knowledge relative to individual tasks; and identifying barriers that interfere with one's talents, projects, and goals.

Dimension 6 is *creative and innovative thinking,* including shifting frames of reference; and using models, metaphors, substitutions, humor, risk-taking, curiosity, as well as forecasting to create new thoughts and products. Dimension 7 is comprised of the abilities one uses for *thinking effectively in groups,* such as understanding the nature and quality of thinking in group settings; exercising power/authority/influence appropriately; using talents interactively; and developing analytical listening abilities. Dimension 8 includes the *abilities to think effectively when alone,* such as setting goals, establishing redirection, taking action, and eliciting self-motivation to increase productivity.

FIGURE 1-1
Components of Language Arts Instruction

ORAL LANGUAGE

Informational speech
Instrumental speech
Regulatory speech
Heuristic speech
Imaginative speech
Interactive speech
Personal speech
Dialectical differences
Cultural variations
Vocal qualities
Oral performances
Valuing speech as an important
   communication tool to inform,
   persuade, and entertain

WRITING

Prewriting tools
Drafting and composing
Revising
Editing
Sharing and publishing
Writing to different audiences using a
   variety of genre
Valuing writing as an effective
   communication tool to inform,
   persuade, and entertain

READING

Decoding meaning of words
Vocabulary and concept development
Comprehending literal and inferential
   meanings
Applying information read to life
Using reading to create
   understandings
Appreciation for reading as an
   important, self-selected, lifetime
   pursuit to receive information,
   opinions and enjoyment

GRAMMAR

Sentence building
Transformational grammar
Traditional grammar
Structural grammar
Story grammar
Oral grammatical variations
Valuing the use of grammatical rules
   to improve communication

WRITING CONVENTIONS

Invented spelling
Traditional spelling
Punctuation
Capitalization
Penmanship
Valuing the use of writing
   conventions to improve
   communication

LANGUAGE ARTS ACROSS THE CURRICULUM

Parallel scheduling
Thematic units
Interdisciplinary instruction
Topic integration

CREATIVE EXPRESSION

Brainstorming, Brainwriting
Creative dramatics
Plays
Puppets
Poetry
Imagery

LISTENING

Receiving auditory input
Discrimination
Auditory messages
Attention to spoken meanings
Listening comprehension
Applying spoken messages to life
Listening critically and imaginatively
Valuing listening as an important
   modality to receive information,
   opinions, and enjoyment

FIGURE 1-2
Thinking Dimensions Developed Through Instruction

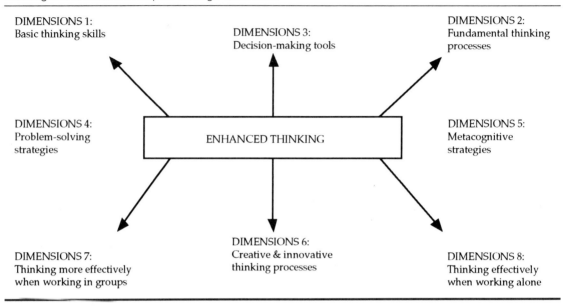

DIMENSIONS 1:
Basic thinking skills

DIMENSIONS 3:
Decision-making tools

DIMENSIONS 2:
Fundamental thinking
processes

DIMENSIONS 4:
Problem-solving
strategies

ENHANCED THINKING

DIMENSIONS 5:
Metacognitive
strategies

DIMENSIONS 7:
Thinking more effectively
when working in groups

DIMENSIONS 6:
Creative & innovative
thinking processes

DIMENSIONS 8:
Thinking effectively
when working alone

STRATEGIES THAT TEACH
TRANSFERRING PRACTICES INTO DAILY LESSONS

You can use the following lesson plan format to build thinking and language simultaneously. This basic format can be adapted to complement any type of material or children's literature that your students need or want.

Typical Lesson Plan Format

Step l: Introduction. It is important to open students' minds and engage their language arts/thinking competencies with your introductory comments. You do so by telling students why you chose the lesson, and what types of objectives they can expect to reach from this lesson.

Step 2: Stating Clear Objectives. In order to clarify objectives for students, you suggest a goal, method, and assessment they can use to advance their language and thinking. You suggest what they need to learn, ways they can learn it, and how they will know that they have learned it. For example, if your school district were to require mastery of noun and verb agreement, you and your students would decide upon an objective to learn, and an activity that they could do to apply this objective to their lives. For instance, your class could decide that the objective they wanted to reach was to eliminate errors in noun and verb agreement that interfere with their spoken and written messages. The method that students select to eliminate their errors is to write rules they will follow to permanently remove agreement mistakes from their writing and speaking. Then they decide that to measure how much they learned, they will teach their mastered "rules" to a younger group of schoolmates. Through Step 2 you will open lessons with a dual purpose of building language and thinking. By doing so, students will bring higher quality ideas and purposes into play as they plan their day's activities.

Step 3: Dispelling Misconceptions About the Lesson Objective. In the third step of your lesson plan, you ask students to recall what they already know about the lesson's objective. If students have limited background *about that objective*, explain problems former students have had with the topic, and how they overcame them. In this step of the lesson plan, students also state their strongest belief about the objective, and you correct their incorrect facts. In addition, students ask themselves questions about the objective that they want to answer by lesson's end (Beck & Dole, 1992; Collins, 1992c; Many, 1990; McCaslin, 1991).

Step 4: Study a Thinking Guide or Strategy Sheet. In this step, you introduce a thinking guide. Each thinking guide is a one-page chart or diagram of a specific language arts or thinking ability. You will see several thinking guide samples throughout this book.

Step 5: Examples. After the thinking guide and/or communication strategy is presented, students share three examples of how they can use this strategy to meet the lesson's objective. These examples are real-world situations students face or may encounter in their lives (Collins 1992c). It is important that these examples are used *only as samples* of the types of thinking and language objectives that students can establish for themselves in the lesson.

Step 6: Students Select Their Objective. After studying these examples, a book is read (or a real-world activity begins) and students apply the thinking guide to the characters and events in the story (or to the activity).

Step 7: Students Then Complete a New, Second Objective. At the beginning of the year, students may have difficulty selecting their own objective, and deciding on an activity to meet it. You can assist by giving choices from which they can select. These choices are designed to appeal to different learning styles. For example, you can design objectives that ask students to either (1) understand the relationship between _____ and _____; (2) receive the reward of . . . ; (3) gain the result of . . . ; or (4) understand the reason for . . . . During the beginning of the year, you can also complete Step 7 by asking the class, as a whole, to select an objective that they complete as a large group activity, under your direction. By the middle of the year, students should be able to divide into small groups and work on different objectives and activities in ways that they judge to be valuable. Near the end of the year students may even suggest activities they want to do alone to reach their own objectives.

Step 8: Rethink, Restate, and Reformulate Their New Understandings. In this step, students apply what they've learned to their lives. For example, instead of memorizing a poem to recite for a grade, students create their own way to (a) explore their ideas about poetry, (b) determine where and how much information to gather, and (c) create their own presentations concerning significant poetry in their lives. Rewards students receive from this rethinking step are an increased eagerness to learn, an ability to generate alternatives in order to recover from incomplete understandings, confidence to share their own expertise, and a desire to reconsider others' opinions.

Step 9: Self-Selected Assessment. The last step in the lesson is for students to choose how they will demonstrate what they have learned about the thinking/communication strategy that appears on the thinking guide in Step 4. Such self-selected assessments include:

- Exercises in applied citizenship. Students make real choices in the world relative to the strategy depicted on the thinking guide. Exercises come from current, real-world problems in business and society. Once students assess their ability to use the thinking/communication strategies through solving the real-world problems in these exercises, they compare their demonstration to the decisions made by authorities responsible for these problems in the real world.
- Students make tests for themselves or others.
- Students generate their own "back-up strategy" in case a communicating/thinking strategy did not work in the way they intended.
- Pairs, or small groups of students, demonstrate what they learned for the class.
- Students report ways they have transferred what they learned to their lives.
- Students teach and diagram the communication and thinking strategy under study to groups outside the classroom.

CRITICAL THINKING ACTIVITY I
How to Scaffold Instruction

Recommended Grade Levels: Preschool–8th Grade

At this point in each chapter you will read about an activity you can lead that follows the basic lesson plan format above and integrates eight dimensions of language arts and higher level thinking. The first critical thinking activity that does so is scaffolding.

Scaffolding is *an instructional strategy which supports students as they attempt to use a competency for the first time.* Scaffolding provides the freedom but adds direction and clues so a child can begin a new task. You gradually reduce your support as the student becomes more self-directed and self-sustained. This approach works much as a temporary scaffolding does in building multistory skyscrapers. You place temporary "scaffolds" around students' learning to structure students' construction of ideas. As the task progresses and students' thinking becomes more substantial, the scaffold (your support) is removed.

You can scaffold or support individual instruction in a large group lesson. Notice how Julie Brenegan allows one student to begin as soon as he understands the concept.

You scaffold instruction by (1) modeling the entire strategy first, before the student begins; (2) inviting students to engage in a new task with you, such as holding a student's hand when writing manuscript letters for the first time; (3) clueing specific elements in the new process a student is trying to learn as the child watches, e.g., "Try using Step 1 that I just completed"; (4) listening to and then replicating specific strategies you cue, such as saying, "Which decoding strategy do you want to try?"; (5) providing two models a student can choose between (Collins, 1992a; Reed, Hawkins, & Roller, 1991). An example of a scaffolding lesson follows. A student, Stan, may ask, "Would you help me? I can't think of a title for the story I wrote."

You respond, "What have you tried?"

He answers, "I want a short title, but I don't want it to begin with the word 'My,' like all my other titles."

This answer documents what you suspected: Stan already uses summarizing thinking well. What he needs now is a way to increase his creative thinking. You scaffold by giving him two creative processes to select between: "In the future when you want to create something new, like a title, you can use either of these thinking strategies. First, you can begin with old ideas and *substitute* parts of them with new words. Then you can add slightly different ideas. For example, you don't want your title to be "My Trip," so you substitute words similar to "my," such as "Stan's," "Our," "Mine," "Me," or "The." The second strategy is to *rearrange* your thoughts. For example, instead of making your title "My Trip," you can rearrange your ideas by putting the last part (the trip) first, and the first part (you) last, such as "The Trip I Took," "A Trip That Took Stan by Surprise," or "The Most Important Trip."

Once you've delivered this mini-lesson (scaffold), you ask Stan which strategy he wants to use. Because you've demonstrated both, he can more reliably select the one he judges will be most successful for him.

To pause and restate major points in the chapter thus far, language is a system of patterns and rules that enables one to communicate thoughts. The principles that govern how language is used are phonological, morphological, syntactical, and semantical. Through your instruction students learn and refine these principles to create and transmit ideas as they think, read, write, speak, listen, spell, act, and use technology.

There are also several principles that guide successful language arts programs: (a) students must satisfy their needs, and have a valuable place in the classroom community; (b) lessons must be self-generative, integrative, and based upon research concerning language learning; (c) classroom learning experiences must be authentic with students completing processes and products that will be used in the real world; (d) processes of language and thinking are learned simultaneously as students implement their ideas and ask their questions; (e) assessment occurs through teacher evaluations, grading, measuring progress, student self-assessments, and testing; and (f) teachers must possess characteristics that hold a high correlation with student literary achievement. Critical Thinking Activity 1 helps develop language/thinking processes through scaffolding. The mission of this chapter will culminate in the Professional Development Opportunity that follows where you formalize your philosophy of language arts instruction.

PROFESSIONAL DEVELOPMENT OPPORTUNITY
Identifying Your Teaching Philosophy of Language Arts Instruction

At the end of each chapter you will have a Professional Developmental Opportunity in which to engage. These are designed to assist in your application of material in the chapter and to establish a new teaching competency.

Sir Frederick Banting said, "You must begin with an ideal and end with an ideal!" To become the language arts teacher you desire to be, you must formalize your philosophy of instruction. Your philosophy becomes apparent in many ways as you answer parents' questions about your instruction; decide how much time you will spend with a single student on a specific day, and select material for your students.

Today you can make your philosophy less nebulous by composing a philosophy statement through the guided exercise below. You can repeat these steps when your philosophy is challenged by new research or when you have trouble establishing instructional priorities. To formulate your teaching philosophy, reflect upon or write your answers in each of the following steps. If you write your answers, you can reference them throughout your career to see how your philosophy has changed.

Step 1. Visualize what your ideal language arts classroom looks like. Picture your room as it will look when you open the door. Complete the following sentence: "As I walk in my room, I see . . ."

Step 2. Mentally project a typical day in action, with your students engaged in successful language learning experiences. Picture the materials your students are using, the number of adults in the room; and the talents you are engaging. Complete the following:

"My students are . . ."

"Other people are . . ."

"Three talents I am using are . . ."

Step 3. Describe how you will feel on the last day of school, after all of your students have left, if your students have had a successful year. Now complete the following statement:

"I picture my students leaving me on the last day of school and they are . . ."

"When my students are successful, I will have . . ."

"On the last day of school, I will know my language arts program has been successful because . . ."

Step 4. Because great visions often start with small dreams, the fourth step in defining your philosophy is to actualize small goals. To do so, write the following professional goals. If you write them, you can return to your list in subsequent days to see if they were accomplished.

   a. What three values (beliefs) about language arts instruction will you never abandon?
   b. What will your students do in your language arts class that would make you most proud?
   c. If _____ isn't occurring in your class, it will bother you. What will you do to ensure that _____ will always be present in your class?
   d. What types of support do you need? What actions will you take to ensure that these supports are available?
   e. Think of someone who has a very different instructional philosophy from yours. What strength in that person's teaching style do you need to incorporate so your program becomes more effective?

Step 5. Compose your teaching philosophy statement now. Do so by writing one to three sentences. Each sentence is a three-part objective. The first part describes a goal you seek. The middle section of the statement delineates the first method that comes to mind as to how you will reach that goal. The last part describes how you will feel; how you will know you have reached the goal. As Roger Mager (1977) stated:

To rise from a zero,
To become a big campus hero
The answer to three questions I must surmise.
Where am I going?
How will I get there? and,
How will I know I've arrived?

The four activities that follow enable you to assess your understanding of the information in this chapter.

TRY IT

1. List the characteristics of the best language arts teachers. Rank in order your own capabilities according to this list.

2. Notecard 1 is a list of books that you can read on the first day of school. Notecard 2 provides selections you can share during the first week of school. These books assist students to overcome school-related anxieties. Select one of the books from Notecard 1 or 2 and practice reading it aloud.

NOTECARD 1:   BOOKS TO READ THE FIRST DAY OF SCHOOL

PRESCHOOL–THIRD GRADE

Me at Preschool by Jan Godfrey
The Kindergarten Book by S. Calmenson
Berenstain Bears Go to School by
   S. Berenstain and J. Berenstain
The My Getting Ready for School Book by
   Eric Hill
Starting School by Muriel Stanek
Curious George Goes to School by
   H. A. Rey
Toad School by Cathy Bellows

Time for School, Nathan! by N. Alexander
When You Go to Kindergarten by J. Howe
Starting First Grade by Miriam Cohen
Starting School by K. Petty and L. Knopper
Morris Goes to School by
   Bernard Wiseman
Pete's First Day at School by J. Clenen
First Day of School by K. Jackson
First Day of School by Helen Oxenbury
Back to School with Betsy by C. Haywood

FOURTH GRADE AND UP

Charlie Brown Goes to School by
   Charles Schulz
The New Teacher by Miriam Cohen
Miss Nelson is Missing by
   H. Allard

Louis James Hates School by
   Bill Morrison
I like Books by Jared Lee
The Teacher from the Black Lagoon and
   other books by M. Thaler

NOTECARD 2:   BOOKS TO READ THE FIRST WEEK OF SCHOOL

First Grade Takes a Test by Miriam Cohen
See You in Second Grade by Miriam
   Cohen
Sometimes I Hate School by Barkin and
   James
A Hippo Ate the Teacher by Mike Thaler
When Will I Read? by Miriam Cohen
Will I Have a Friend? by Miriam Cohen
Miss Nelson is Missing by H. Allard
The Best Teacher in the World by
   B. Chardiet and G. Maccarone
Leo the Late Bloomer by Robert Krause
Frosted Glass by Denys Cazet
The Flunking of Joshua T. Bates by
   Susan Shreve
Ramona Quimbly, Age Eight by
   Beverly Cleary
Teach Us, Amelia Bedelia by P. Parish
Fourth Grade Rats and other books by
   Jerry Spinelli

The Truth About Sixth Grade by
   C. O'Shaughnessy
Homesick: My Own Story by Jean Fritz
Ramona the Pest by Beverly Cleary
The Latchkey Kids by C. Anshaw
Class Clown and other books by J. Hurwitz
School by Emily Arnold McCally
Josie Smith at School by Magdalen Nabb
What Mary Jo Shared by Elizabeth Sayles
Sometimes I Don't Like School by P. Hogan
This is the Way We Go to School by
   Edith Baer
Moog-Moog, Space Barber by M. Teague
One of the Third Grade Thonkers by
   P. Naylor
Rent a Third Grader by B. Hiller
Nothing's Fair in Fifth Grade and other
   books by Barthe DeClements
Kid in the Red Jacket by Barbara Park
Scrawny, the Classroom Duck by S. Clymer

3. Devise a system whereby you can regularly receive suggestions for improvement by students, peers, parents, and administrators. For example, one teacher wrote a letter to each of the above constituencies over the Winter Vacation. The letter asked for suggestions for her improvement in five areas.

4. Ask a group of students to discuss, or write, characteristics of a good language arts teacher. Ask them to defend their positions. Then inquire as to how they will feel and how much they learn when they set their own goals for language arts and thinking development, and when they are allowed to pick books or topics about which they want to read, write, discuss, or analyze.

FOR YOUR JOURNAL

You can experience the benefits of journal writing activities by performing this and subsequent FOR YOUR JOURNAL activities at the end of each chapter. The purpose of this section of the textbook is to encourage you to create a professional/personal journal to enhance your productivity. This journal can become a diary, your teaching history, or a tool by which you reflect on your teaching philosophy and resolve professional/personal difficulties.

A second purpose is to provide examples of journal entries to share with your students. FOR YOUR JOURNAL activities in this book enable you to practice ways to use journals with your students to stimulate thinking, evoke talent, and foster creative expression. To begin, purchase a journal or design a section of the notebook you use for this course as your journal. On the first page write today's date. Read the following, and write your response on this first page.

If you are to become the language arts teacher you desire, you will devote time to continuously improve your skills. One of the most effective ways of doing so is to develop a self-improvement plan whereby you can maneuver your time and resources to enhance your professional abilities. Include information you learned from the principles of this chapter and the philosophy you developed as you write your professional development plan. For example, your program could include an entry in your journal each week to note insights you have about your development as a teacher, communicator, reader, writer, speaker, listener, and thinker. You could also set aside a specific time each week to learn a new teaching skill.

Figure 1-3 may assist as you think. In the left-hand column is a list of principles for effective language arts instruction covered in this chapter. In the middle column you can note methods that come to mind to implement each principle. In the right-hand column you can specify aspects of your teaching ability that you want to improve in order to use each method effectively.

FIGURE 1-3
Personal Plan to Implement the Principles of Effective Instruction

PRINCIPLES FOR EFFECTIVE LANGUAGE ARTS INSTRUCTION	METHOD TO IMPLEMENT THE PRINCIPLE	TEACHING ABILITY I WANT TO USE/DEVELOP TO REACH THIS PRINCIPLE
1. My program must include challenging, positive, and comfortable learning experiences for my students.		
2. The needs of my students are the basis for lessons I plan.		
3. I am an important force in my students' lives. I work to nurture teaching characteristics that correlate with high student achievement.		
4. Students work on intrinsically motivating real-world tasks.		
5. I use assessment tests that my teacher did not use when I was in school.		

BUILDING YOUR PROFESSIONAL PORTFOLIO

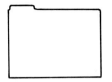

At the end of every chapter you will receive information and resources that can be filed in a professional portfolio. Each contains information to use in parent conferences and to upgrade instruction. Each can be copied and made into a permanent "file folder" to which you can add updates for the rest of your career. Start your portfolio with the list of resources below.

Resources and Additional References to Teach Language Arts

The New Reading Teacher's Book of Lists by Edward Fry, Donna Fountoukidis, and Jacqueline Kress Polk. Englewood Cliffs, NJ: Prentice-Hall, 1985. This book can provide many word lists for parts of speech, irregular verb forms, spelling patterns, reference words, homophones, survival words, spelling demons, synonyms, compound words, prefixes, phonically irregular words, and many other types of reading materials and teaching aids for easy reference.

Read With Me Books and Cassettes, which contain books and audiotapes for students. New York: Mulberry Books, William Morrow and Company.

Semantic Mapping: Classroom Applications by Joan Heimlich and Susan Pittelman. Newark, DE: International Reading Association, 1986. This book features ten classroom applications of the semantic mapping procedure in a variety of content areas in Grades 1 through 8.

Teaching Vocabulary to Improve Reading Comprehension by William E. Nagy. NCTE and IRA, 1988. Describes effective methods of using integration, repetition, and meaningful word contexts to increase comprehension.

Children's Literature in the Reading Program by Bernice Cullinan (Editor). IRA, 1987. Provides a wide array of practical ideas to draw K–8 students into reading.

Fairy Tales, Fables, Legends, and Myths by Bette Bosma. New York: Teachers College Press. Many ideas and more than 50 complete lessons to enhance students' reading, thinking, writing, speaking, and listening skills through fairy tales, fables, legends, myths, and folk literature.

The following books provide additional ideas for literature-based reading instruction:

Books Appeal: Get Teenagers Into the Library. Upstart, Box 889, Hagerstown, MD 21741.

Share It If You Read It. Upstart, Box 889, Hagerstown, MD 21741.

An ABC of Children's Book Activities. Upstart, Box 889, Hagerstown, MD 21741.

Back to Books: 200 Library Games to Encourage Reading. Upstart, Box 889, Hagerstown, MD 21741.

Book It! National Reading Incentive Program. Pizza Hut, P.O. Box 2999, Wichita, KS 67201.

Helping Young Minds Bloom on Literature. The Teacher's Touch, 1909 West Avenue G, Muleshoe, TX 79347.

For an annotated listing of children's magazines to include in your reading program, see Donald Stoll's book entitled *Magazines for Children* (1990), co-published by Educational Press Association of America and the International Reading Association, Glassboro State College, Glassboro, NJ 08028; 800 Barksdale Road, P.O. Box 8139, Newark, DE 19714-8139.

2 Putting Your Philosophy Into Action: Designing Your Student Communication Center

"The single most important activity to build the knowledge required for eventual success in reading is reading aloud to children." (Report to the United States Congress by the Commission on Reading)

Here is Edward Bear, coming downstairs. Now, bump, bump, bump, on the back of his head, behind Christopher Robin. It is, as far as he knows, the only way of coming downstairs, but sometimes he feels that there is another way, if only he could stop bumping for a moment and think of it.

—A. A. Milne, *Winnie the Pooh*

The purpose of this chapter is to give you the time to think about and build a new and better way of teaching the language arts. How can you implement the principles of effective instruction in a 50-minute period? How can you maintain a positive attractive room; support students' risk-taking; conference individually; allow student selection in planning; maintain discipline; monitor student-led, small group discussions; and advance students' communication and thinking abilities daily?

This chapter describes how your language arts classroom can be organized as a student communication center. You will select between three organizational systems, analyze your teaching style, and identify your students' strengths and weaknesses.

By the time you finish this chapter, you will know:

1. How to establish student communication centers and the research base that supports this concept of instruction;

2. How to make multiple plans, schedules, and activities for a communication center;

3. What types of materials facilitate learning;

4. How to assess your students' communication strengths and weaknesses;

5. How to group your students as a community where low and high achievers are respected.

THEORETICAL FOUNDATION

A STUDENT COMMUNICATION CENTER IN ACTION

It will be helpful to have a vicarious experience in a student communication center before you build such a room for your students. To provide this exposure, in the next few pages you will become a member of a college course that follows the principles of student-centered instruction. As you read, note how you feel (and how your students are likely to feel) in a class where language and learning needs are the focus.

And now you will be placed in a student communication-centered college class.

YOUR STUDENT COMMUNICATION-CENTERED CLASS

The semester begins! You are excited and slightly nervous about your language arts methods course. You registered for an experimental course—a course designed to teach the principles of a student-centered classroom by *placing you in one* rather than *telling you about one*. The Dean hired a new professor. You know nothing about her, but you want her to be a really good teacher.

As you enter the class, you are struck by the beautiful decorations. The room is filled with print: books, posters, signs, charts, and book jackets. There are five tables around the room with signs on the wall that label them as the "Publishing Center," "Editing Resource Center," "Free Writing Center," "Research Center," and "Free Reading Corner."

A mini-library, three computers, and a standing chart easel are at the front of the room. Your professor is seated on a large rug, labeled "Our Sharing Area." Students are taking chairs and forming a circle around the edge of the rug. The chalk ledge is lined with hard- and soft-covered books about language arts instruction. As you scan the titles, you find a place in the group.

The professor speaks: "As you make your decisions about language arts instruction, I want you to experience what it is like to learn through a student-centered approach. Materials in our room are displayed in the same way you can arrange them in your classroom. We will begin our class in a similar manner to which you will begin yours. I will model the newest principles of language arts instruction. My teaching will center around your needs, and start with concepts you already know. To begin our first day, tell me what you know and what you want to learn about language arts instruction."

Your classmates speak up, and your professor writes their comments on the board. When your class's ideas cease, your professor reads the following book excerpt aloud:

Virtually all human babies learn to speak their home language remarkably well in a very short time, without any formal teaching. But when they go to school, many have difficulty, particularly with written language, even though they are instructed by diligent teachers using expensive and carefully developed materials.

We are beginning to work out this seeming paradox. Careful observation is helping us to understand what makes language easy or hard to learn. Many school traditions seem to have actually hindered language development. In our zeal to make it easy, we've made it hard. How? . . . We took apart the language and turned it into words, syllables, and isolated sounds. Unfortunately, we also postponed its natural purpose—the communication of meaning—and turned it into a set of abstractions, unrelated to the needs and experiences of the children we sought to help. (Goodman, 1987, p. 369).

FIGURE 2-1
Class Chart of Student Learning Needs

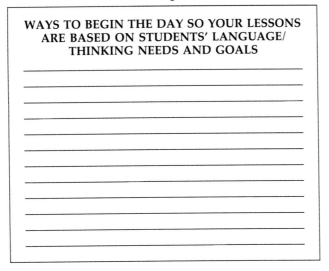

**WAYS TO BEGIN THE DAY SO YOUR LESSONS
ARE BASED ON STUDENTS' LANGUAGE/
THINKING NEEDS AND GOALS**

Your professor stops reading, points to a chart on the bulletin board. She says, "I want to model ways to open a student-centered lesson. What are some of these ways?" (Figure 2-1 provides a class chart.)

One student says, "We can either ask students what they know or want to learn, or read them some new information to think about."

"Correct. I'm pleased that you see how teachers can do both of these," your professor responds. "Would you mind listing these ideas on our chart? We'll add more to our list as we learn them."

Your professor tells the class that Dr. Donald Graves (1986) is an expert on writing instruction; he wrote: "If our classrooms are to be effective, they should be filled with stuff, the stuff of what children know, and what they want to know more about. This is how children learn at home" (p. 3). She then asks everyone to describe, in individual paragraphs, materials they want to include in their language arts classroom. You write the following on your paper:

> In my language arts class there will be many library books, and other materials students want to read. I want to create a room where students have a lot of writing papers, notebooks, freshly sharpened and long pencils, felt-tip markers of many sizes and shapes, and more than one activity from which to choose. My students will write individual responses to material they read.

Your professor interrupts the writing. "Would you pass your writings forward? I want to read them this evening. I will use this writing as a way I can learn more about your competencies in written communication. I want you to collect a similar writing sample (or a drawing) from your students during your first language arts class period."

Most days your students will select their own books to read that are different from those of their classmates. They will talk with classmates, work at their own pace, set goals, conference with you about their work, share projects, and make decisions about what to learn next.

As soon as your professor stops talking, you ask, "How will I know what to teach in my student-centered class? How can I determine what my students need? I have heard that many teachers do not use a textbook or a teacher's manual."

Your professor responds: "Let's all think about the answer to your question tonight as we only have a few minutes left today and that question deserves more time. We'll address it first thing in our next class; during the time remaining, I'd like you to choose what you want to do before we meet again. You can choose a book to read, write something you want me to know about you, or sit with me to list other subjects you want to answer in our next class. If you choose to write, select a spiral notebook at the Free Writing Table, as that will become your journal this semester. If you elect to read a book, take it with you at the end of class and read at least one chapter from it before we meet again. We need a system so I and others know what you are learning, what you take home, and how you will share what you are learning with us. What system do you want?"

After a discussion, the professor writes our decisions on a chart board, titled "Sharing Record." What was decided was that each of us would work on something for the class, write what we are doing, and when we would share it. Only two people a day would share.

With these decisions in mind, you look at something on the bulletin board that catches your eye. Above four book jackets is the question: "What is a student-centered classroom? These books describe different types!" You scan the book jackets, and take the one that seems the most basic. After all, you know very *little* about new language arts methods. You sign up to tell what you learned from this book, *Living Between the Lines* by Lucy Calkins (1991). You sit down at the Free Reading Center where others are reading silently. As you peruse the first chapter, you imagine how Lucy organized her class. You find that most teachers read to their students daily. When they call the entire class together, they teach a mini-lesson, share their own readings and writings with their students, or teach by using students' reading and writing. They listen carefully as students share what they want to learn next. How teachers and students relate and communicate is very similar to the real world, responding to each other's expressions and needs.

The more you read, the more you were impressed. Students not only make choices about the topics which they want to read, but they decide what they will write, say, think, or do with what they've read. In this way, Calkins (1991) explained, students learn they have unique interpretations. They are graded upon having chosen something to read based on a valid criteria, effectively listening and speaking to others, and asking questions that aid someone else's thinking.

In the next class, someone brought in big books that they had made and showed how to use them.

You began reading how **big books** (*books that are two feet tall*) and **wordless picture books** (*books that have no words, but stories are carried through pictures*) can be used in kindergarten and first grade. You read that these big books enable students to see and decipher words as you read to them. In this way, students learn to decode and comprehend early, in their "reading" careers. **Skinny books** are *single chapters from multichapter books that are separated into individual books.* They help children transport to reading multichaptered books.

Your professor interrupts your concentration. She tells you that in the next class you will see and discuss a videotape segment from several teachers' classes, including Ms. Dawn Martine, a second-grade teacher at Mahalia Jackson Elementary School in the Harlem area of New York City, and Ms. Jayne Hayes, a first-grade teacher in Salem, Oregon. They have developed student-centered classes. You are looking forward to seeing such classrooms in action. As you leave, a friend asks if you know how you award grades in a language arts program. "I don't," you reply, "but if I find anything in this book, I'll tell you." You walk to the student union together.

When the next class opens, your professor asks if anyone has found answers to the five questions asked at the end of the last class meeting. You say, "Yes. I read that the way you decide what you need to teach is to collect samples and to note students' speaking, listening, reading, and writing (which also shows their spelling, grammar, and punctuation) needs. Then you identify objectives common to many children and let them work in groups on those they choose to improve. I still don't understand why the new approaches to language arts use library books in addition to, or as replacements for, textbooks, more than in the past. Why do teachers not assign short stories and ask students to answer questions after reading them?"

Your professor replies, "I wondered the same thing until I read Chapter 4 in Nancy Cecil's book, *Freedom Fighters: Affective Teaching of the Language Arts* (1989). In this chapter, Nancy says that if we were asked to describe our most pleasant reading experience, we recall specific, full-length novels. Few of us recall a specific story from our elementary textbooks. There is something special and endearing about a multichaptered story. The author carefully crafts very real characters in a specific setting with a set of problems and resolutions. Similarly, through full-length books, your students will feel as if they are sharing their lives with the characters. As Nancy states, it is the length of the novel, as compared with the shorter genres, that allow us the greater time to get to know the characters, and makes the reading experience all that much more intense. That's why we try to use whole books with children."

One classmate adds, "In a book that I really liked, by Donald Halliday, I read that the language found in quality children's literature helps students express ideas, interpret and organize their experiences and create schemas about the world around them (Halliday, 1982). In Charlotte Huck's book, *Children's Literature*, it says, "Literature records the depths and heights of the human experience. It develops compassion by educating the heart as well as the mind. It helps children entertain new ideas, develop insights, stretch their imagination, create new experiences, and develop a sense of what is true and just and beautiful" (p. 317).

You were so glad you asked that question. You also reflected about how the principles of Chapter 1 occur in a student-centered community, and how you are integrating your language and thinking in this course. You are anxious to learn about as many children's books as possible. You vowed that you would select books for your students that had lasting charm; those that had a sort of magic. What you want are books that contain beautiful language and meanings that students can reuse in their own language and thinking. Your professor gives you Notecards 3 and 4 to help you build a personal repertoire of favorite selections of children's literature. You decide to set a goal to read one book a week from each of these notecards.

NOTECARD 3: CALDECOTT AWARD-WINNING BOOKS

1938 *Animals of the Bible* by D. P. Lathrop
1939 *Mei Li* by T. Handforth
1940 *Abraham Lincoln* by I. and
 E. P. d'Aulaires
1941 *They Were Strong and Good* by
 R. Lawson
1942 *Make Way for Ducklings* by
 R. McCloskey
1943 *The Little House* by V. L. Burton
1944 *Many Moons* by L. Slobodkin
1945 *Prayer for a Child* by E. O. Jones
1946 *The Rooster Crows* by M. and
 M. Petersham
1947 *The Little Island* by L. Weisgard
1948 *White Snow, Bright Snow* by
 R. Duvoisin
1949 *The Big Snow* by B. and E. Hader
1950 *Song of the Swallows* by L. Politi
1951 *The Egg Tree* by K. Milhous
1952 *Finders Keepers* by N. Mordvinoff
1953 *The Biggest Bear* by L. Ward
1954 *Madeline's Rescue* by L. Bemelmans
1955 *Cinderella* by M. Brown

1956 *Frog Went A-Courtin'* by
 F. Rojankovsky
1957 *A Tree Is Nice* by M. Simont
1958 *Time of Wonder* by R. McCloskey
1959 *Chanticleer and the Fox* by B. Cooney
1960 *Nine Days to Christmas* by M. H. Ets
1961 *Baboushka and the Three Kings* by N. Sidjakov
1962 *Once A House* by M. Brown
1963 *The Snowy Day* by E. J. Keats
1964 *Where the Wild Things Are* by
 M. Sendak
1965 *May I Bring a Friend?* by
 B. Montresor
1966 *Always Room for One More* by
 N. Hogrogian
1967 *Sam, Bangs and Moonshine* by
 E. Ness
1968 *Drummer Hoff* by E. Emberley
1969 *The Fool of the World and the Flying Ship* by
 Uri Shulevitz
1970 *Sylvester and the Magic Pebble* by William Steig
1971 *A Story—A Story* by G. E. Haley

(cont'd)

NOTECARD 3 (cont'd)

1972 *One Fine Day* by N. Hogrogian
1973 *The Funny Little Woman* by B. Lent
1974 *Duffy and the Devil* by M. Zemach
1975 *Arrow to the Sun* by G. McDermott
1976 *Why Mosquitoes Buzz in People's Ears* by Leo and
 Diane Dillon
1977 *Ashanti to Zulu: African Traditions* by Leo and
 Diane Dillon
1978 *Noah's Ark* by P. Spier
1979 *The Girl Who Loved Wild Horses* by P. Goble
1980 *Ox-Cart Man* by B. Cooney
1981 *Fables* by A. Lobel
1982 *Jumanji* by Chris Van Allsburg
1983 *Shadow* by M. Brown
1984 *The Glorious Flight* by A. and
 M. Provensen
1985 *St. George and the Dragon* by Trina Schart Hyman
1986 *The Polar Express* by Chris Van Allsburg
1987 *Hey, Al* by R. Egielski
1988 *Owl Moon* by J. Schoenherr
1989 *Song and Dance Man* by
 Stephen Gammell

1990 *Lon Po Po* by Ed Young
1991 *Black and White* by David Macaulay
1992 *Tuesday* by D. Wiesner
1993 (Fill in as the award is made each year)
1994
1995
1996
1997
1998
1999
2000
2001
2002
2003
2004
2005
2006
2007
2008

NOTECARD 4: NEWBERY AWARD-WINNING BOOKS

1922 *The Story of Mankind* by H. W. Van Loon

1923 *The Voyages of Doctor Dolittle* by H. Lofting

1924 *The Dark Frigate* by C. Hawes

1925 *Tales from Silver Lands* by C. J. Finger

1926 *Shen of the Sea* by A. B. Chrisman

1927 *Smoky, the Cowhorse* by W. James

1928 *Gay-Neck* by D. G. Mukerji

1929 *The Trumpeter of Krakow* by E. Kelly

1930 *Hitty, Her First Hundred Years* by R. Field

1931 *The Cat Who Went to Heaven* by E. Coatsworth

1932 *Waterless Mountain* by L. A. Armer

1933 *Young Fu of the Upper Yangtze* by E. Lewis

1934 *Invincible Louisa* by C. Meigs

1935 *Dobry* by M. Shannon

1936 *Caddie Woodlawn* by C. Brink

1937 *Roller Skates* by R. Sawyer

1938 *The White Stag* by K. Seredy

1939 *Thimble Summer* by E. Enright

1940 *Daniel Boone* by J. H. Daugherty

1941 *Call It Courage* by A. Sperry

1942 *The Matchlock Gun* by W. D. Edmonds

1943 *Adam of the Road* by E. J. Gray

1944 *Johnny Tremain* by E. Forbes

1945 *Rabbit Hill* by R. Lawson

1946 *Strawberry Girl* by L. Lenski

1947 *Miss Hickory* by C. S. Bailey

1948 *The Twenty-one Balloons* by W. P. du Bois

1949 *King of the Wind* by M. Henry

1950 *The Door in the Wall* by M. de Angeli

1951 *Amos Fortune, Free Man* by E. Yates

1952 *Ginger Pye* by E. Estes

1953 *Secret of the Andes* by A. N. Clark

1954 *And Now Miguel* by J. Krumgold

1955 *The Wheel on the School* by M. De Jong

1956 *Carry On, Mr. Bowditch* by J. L. Latham

1957 *Miracles on Maple Hill* by V. Sorensen

1958 *Rifles of Watie* by H. Keith

(cont'd)

NOTECARD 4 (cont'd)

1959 *The Witch of Blackbird Pond* by E. G. Speare

1960 *Onion John* by J. Krumgold

1961 *Island of the Blue Dolphins* by S. O'Dell

1962 *The Bronze Bow* by E. G. Speare

1963 *A Wrinkle in Time* by M. L'Engle

1964 *It's Like This, Cat* by E. Neville

1965 *Shadow of a Bull* by M. Wojciechowska

1966 *I, Juan de Pareja* by E. Trevino

1967 *Up a Road Slowly* by I. Hunt

1968 *From the Mixed-up Files of Mrs. Basil E. Frankweiler* by E. L. Konigsburg

1969 *The High King* by L. Alexander

1970 *Sounder* by W. H. Armstrong

1971 *Summer of the Swans* by B. Byars

1972 *Mrs. Frisby and the Rats of NIMH* by R. C. O'Brien

1973 *Julie of the Wolves* by J. C. George

1974 *The Slave Dancer* by P. Fox

1975 *M.C. Higgins the Great* by V. Hamilton

1976 *The Grey King* by S. Cooper

1977 *Roll of Thunder, Hear My Cry* by M. D. Taylor

1978 *Bridge to Terabithia* by K. Paterson

1979 *The Westing Game* by E. Raskin

1980 *A Gathering of Days: A New England Girl's Journal, 1830–32* by J. W. Blos

1981 *Jacob Have I Loved* by K. Paterson

1982 *A Visit to William Blake's Inn: Poems for Innocent and Experienced Travelers* by N. Willard

1983 *Dicey's Song* by C. Voigt

1984 *Dear Mr. Henshaw* by B. Cleary

1985 *The Hero and the Crown* by R. McKinley

1986 *Sarah, Plain and Tall* by P. MacLachlan

1987 *The Whipping Boy* by S. Fleischman

1988 *Lincoln: A Photobiography* by R. Freedman

1989 *Joyful Noise: Poems for Two Voices* by P. Fleischman

1990 *Number the Stars* by L. Lowry

1991 *Maniac Magee* by J. Spinelli

1992 *Shiloh* by P. R. Naylor

As your professor prepares to show the video, students list on the class chart two new ways they learned to begin language arts lessons: student sharing from work done at home, and having demonstrations, such as a videotape. When your professor showed the videotape of student communication-centered classrooms in action, it was great. The teachers were flexible. Their students admired them, and worked hard. You want to have that much classroom management and learning in your room. You want to organize materials and desks to maximize student communication. You ask the professor if she has any books about how to set up the classroom. She gives you several and allows the class to choose groups and find answers to the remaining four questions listed on the class chart.

You and three classmates consolidate what you have learned, and prepare a sample classroom layout. Three people meet with your professor. You pick up folders to take home that your professor had labeled *Strengths of the Student-Centered Approach; State of the Art in Language Arts Instruction; Planning;* and *Sample Classroom Designs.* You can hardly wait to read them.

RESEARCH ON STUDENT COMMUNICATION CENTERS

Now let's reflect upon your two days' experience. Did you use the principles from Chapter 1? Were you in a room where reading, writing, thinking, speaking, and listening were tools for living and growing, rather than subjects? Did your teacher create lasting learning experiences that you needed for your career? Let's analyze how this occurred and describe the research concerning reading, speaking, and writing upon which such student communication centers revolve.

Reading. The research base that underscores a literature-rich, student-centered approach to reading rests upon the work of Clay (1979), Goodman (1970, 1987), Smith (1989), Rumelhart (1984), as well as Teale and Sulzby (1986). These researchers are among the leaders in language arts theory. DeFord (1981) and Blount (1973) also found that positive experiences with reading and sharing literature in student-centered classes motivates pupils to read more frequently. Furthermore, students who read frequently write better than those who read less often. Without a student centered climate, poorer students will read less than their higher achieving peers.

Correlational studies have also found that children who read voluntarily, or show an interest in books, achieve higher scores on standardized tests (Bird, 1987). Similarly, voluntary reading correlated with higher levels of reading achievement, increased comprehension, vocabulary development, and reading fluency (Anderson et al., 1985; Heath, 1983; Morrow, 1987). One of the reasons for this correlation is that students in literature-rich classrooms read significantly more words than students in traditional classrooms (Anderson, Hiebert, Scott, & Wilkinson, 1985; Mervar & Hiebert, 1989). In addition, students in a literature-rich classroom take nine minutes longer to select a book they want to read than students who had learned to read through basal readers. "Without exception, children in the literature-based classroom sampled text from one or more books before making their selections, either by reading parts of books to themselves or to another child. They also employed strategies like using the card catalog to find books on a desired topic or author" (Armitage & Peck, 1985, p. 174).

Speaking.   **Peer conferencing,** *when two students meet to discuss and improve work they did separately,* heightens students' abilities to write messages for audiences (Collins, 1992b). Such meetings expand young language users' awareness of the balance necessary to match or extend speakers'/ writers' communicative intentions and listeners' expectations (Calkins, 1991).

Writing.   The research base that informs teachers about the writing process rests, in part, on the work of Graves (1975), Calkins (1986), and Clay (1979). For example, Stuart and Graves (1987) found that children who write more produce better writing when they are given control of topics and are encouraged to use their own developmental spelling. Research also demonstrates that **journal writing,** *where students write about topics of importance to them on a regular basis,* increases their ability to take risks and write more specific and original thoughts when they communicate (Stanton, Shuy, Kreeft, Peyton, & Reed, 1988). Another study found that young writers who write in journals regularly become more sophisticated writers (use more effective and complex syntax) than peers who do not write in journals (Nystrand, 1989).

Other studies demonstrate that writers benefit from peer reviews of their work (Calkins, 1991; Collins, 1991b, 1992b; Nystrand, 1989). These benefits occur in part because when teachers respond to student writing, they often do so as an evaluator, measurer, and copy editor. These changing roles are not as consistent as the one played by peers, who generally approach each writing only as an interested reader.

Students in student-centered communication classes also appear to shift their perceptions of reading and writing from a skill to a meaning-emphasis process. Such a change does not occur in traditional classes. For example, students in one second-grade, literature-rich classroom authored an average of 18 books of 20 pages or more. In traditional classrooms, students authored few books, and when they did, the manuscripts tended to be composed of one-page compositions from each member of the class (Hagerty & Hiebert, 1989).

In summary, a student communication center contains many discussion periods, pupil compositions, self-selected reading, and expressions of students' creative/critical thinking. Children's literature is a major instructional tool as it affords ever so many opportunities for in-depth cultivation of students' communication and thinking competencies. Research has documented the benefits of a student-centered program. The purpose of our discussion up to this point has been to increase your understanding of the theory that supports a student-centered approach to instruction of the language arts. Our next discussion will assist you to plan 36 weeks of instruction so you can effectively transfer this theory to practice. Implementing theory on a daily basis occurs through a thoughtful plan and effective schedule.

PUTTING THEORY INTO PRACTICE
PLANNING AND SCHEDULING

A student communication center requires a master plan, daily schedules, grouping systems, and effective activities.

DEVELOPING A MASTER PLAN

There are three procedures that construct a master instructional plan. Your **master plan** (*your yearly programmatic goals*) began as you contemplated, reflected upon, and refined your philosophy of instruction in Chapter 1. This philosophy is already guiding your yearly, weekly, and daily instructional decisions. It will be modified each day, as students' needs are evidenced from the previous day's work. Each morning, before students arrive, it will be helpful if you visualize the work you and they want to accomplish, based on your philosophy and the organizational principles that enhance learning, planning, grouping, and classroom management, presented in this section of this chapter. Your instruction will also adhere to the natural process by which speaking, listening, reading, writing, and thinking develop, which you will learn in Chapters 3–12.

Your second planning action is to develop the thinking habit of asking yourself: "How will I know and measure the amount my students have learned?" By planning the evaluation actions you will take before you start instruction, your students will accomplish more.

The third planning step is to obtain a copy of your state's and district's objectives for language arts and become familiar with the specific content and communication competencies within the K–12 scope that are your responsibility. These objectives are likely to be similar to the following, which are practiced in one state:

- Students become considerate, effective speakers who express innovative ideas, and insightful commentary that adds to others' thinking;
- Students elect to read widely, for pleasure, and learn to use printed materials to improve their lives;
- Students influence others through skillful and effective writing;
- Students listen actively and increase their listening vocabularies to more fully appreciate thoughts that others share in discussions;
- Students are comfortable and effective in thinking creatively and analytically.

There is no magic number of goals to create, as long as you address each of the language arts and focus upon maximizing students' thinking capabilities. Once you have written your goals, you can spend a few hours reflecting upon past and present students, their needs, and the goals you want to reach more successfully than in the past. Finally, you translate these goals into semester-long and weekly activities.

For students to put forth maximum effort, they need a consistent and effective daily schedule—a schedule they can understand that minimizes unnecessary interruptions in the class's work. While your schedule will alter occasionally, this established procedure provides the daily security and structure students need to reach their goals and take risks.

DEVISING DAILY SCHEDULES

Equally effective communication centers can be scheduled in many ways. Various amounts of time can be allocated to separate activities. The daily schedule you create to open the school year will not have as much student input as you would like. Therefore, during the second, and subsequent, grading period(s) you and your students will alter this schedule as deemed necessary to better meet their needs.

To establish a daily schedule, you can personalize one of the models that follow. You can develop learning centers plan (Sample Schedule 1) where students spend equal time in each center. Alternatively, you can

---

Sample Schedule I: Centers

[The room is organized in centers as illustrated in the college classroom scenario]

9:00–9:15 *Opening:* Morning Message where the class generates two or three paragraphs about ideas they had since the day before; goals for the day or week are posted; and important events in students' lives are noted. Alternatives for this opening section appear in Figure 2-2 (students write in their journals, meet in pairs to share books to read, or share individual projects/proposals with classmates).

9:15–9:45 *Centers:* Students select (or are assigned) to one of these centers each day but no one spends more than one day a week at each center. The types of centers you can elect to use are Writing Center; Publishing Center; Silent Reading Loft; Library Center; Teacher Assistance Center; Reading Center; Shared Reading Center; Listening Center; Research Center; Working in Pairs Center; or Working Alone Center.

9:45–10:00 *Sharing:* Teacher or classmate reads to the class. This can also be the time for author's chair (students read to the class), a sharing time, and a time to set purposes for tomorrow's work.

Sample Schedule 2: All Subjects Each Day

9:00–9:10 Students share and participate in a mini-lesson. At the end of this lesson, students refer to the class chart to see where they have been placed in groups based on their needs and the information in the mini-lesson. A chart to use for this placement appears in Figure 2-3.

9:10–9:40 Students complete their responsibilities in small groups. Group compositions change as new goals are set, e.g., during this time students may be assigned to edit a peer's paper, evaluate and work in their portfolios, participate in a teacher-student conference, or work as the leader of a group.

9:40–10:00 *Sharing:* Teacher and students evaluate progress on learning the objectives of the mini-lesson and select groups from the chart for the next day's work.

Sample Schedule 3: Emphasizing Different Language Competencies on Specific Days

This schedule changes during the week. Three days a week students meet in the same heterogeneous group to discuss and use language arts and thinking objectives they have set, and to produce real-world products. Keegan and Shake (1991) recommend that group discussions center around two open-ended questions: one that you provide, and one that students select. For example, you can ask students to discuss how the author shows that Peter really cares for his sister, despite all the trouble she makes for him, in *Peter's Chair* by Ezra Jack Keats. Then students raise and answer their own questions as the second, open-ended question. At the end of these discussions students make entries into their literature logs which become a portion of their language arts grade. You note examples of good thinking and oral/group skills.

The two remaining days of the week are less structured, and allow time for deeper reflections. During these days, students plan their own day's work, reread previous writings, and schedule time with you and peers to work on authentic, individually designed language/thinking objectives. You have the freedom to spend as long as necessary with individuals and groups; you can even spend an entire hour conferencing with one child. You don't have to feel guilty that your remaining 24 students will not receive your individualized attention during that hour; they are secure in the fact that in the days that follow their individual needs will be met completely when they need you.

allocate different amounts of time to separate types of instruction and grouping arrangements (Sample Schedule 2). A third possibility is to follow one schedule three days of the week, and a different schedule on the remaining days (Sample Schedule 3). Once your schedule is in place you will spend about three days teaching students to follow the plan. You will note things they do well on their first trials and patterns in their movements and behavior that they can improve in days 2 and 3 of their practice runs.

A growing body of research suggests that ability grouping does not increase students' achievement, and is likely to have detrimental effects upon self-concept and achievement for weaker students (Berghoff & Egawa, 1991). One reason for the detrimental effect of homogeneous grouping is that less-proficient students are those in most need of developing ways to organize new information, make valuable contributions to conversations, and write or read challenging words. Peers who can model these processes are absent in most homogeneous groups. (See Figure 2-2 for additional classroom ideals.)

Figure 2–2 provides additional activities for each time period within sample Schedules 1–3. The benefits of Sample Schedule 1 are that students work in their areas of need, because they can choose their centers. One caution relative to this plan is to be sure that you do not neglect instruction in the more difficult skills. Some students could elect to repeat an easier, fully developed competency than to assume a new challenge.

In Schedule 2, the time to meet students' individual needs is briefer than in the two other daily schedules. Mini-lessons provide time to demonstrate language and thinking strategies, and address group needs. To better address single student needs, and to praise new language growths, the following rules should be in place for schedules that follow an all-subject plan, such as Sample Schedule 2:

- No one interrupts individual reading conferences;
- Student-group leaders resolve group needs or put unresolved issues in writing so time can be reallocated during another class period to address them;
- Students are responsible for assessing their day's work in their portfolios at 9:35 each day;
- Everyone stays with only one activity for the full selection period (9:10–9:40);
- Individual reading conferences are approximately 10 minutes in length, (with two being held each day from 9:10–9:30). Those not involved in conferences will work in small groups.

The strength of Sample Schedule 2 (see Figure 2-3) is that students receive equal instruction in each of the language arts and each student receives the same amount of your individual attention. The weakness of this daily schedule is that the language arts can become compartmentalized, and less integrated into real-world outcomes unless special care is taken to select small group work and projects that can serve a real-world purpose in students' lives.

FIGURE 2-2
Student-Centered Instruction by Grade Levels

	BELOW 2ND GRADE	2ND–3RD GRADES	ABOVE 3RD GRADE
BEFORE THE BELL	Calender Weather chart Introduce a word	Conference	Students write what they want to share with the group later in the day.
MORNING MESSAGE	Morning message is less than 5 sentences. Students can copy it.	Morning message can be as long as desired. Each student composes a last paragraph at their desk.	Students write the morning message. Each day one student selects a topic and writes a paragraph before class begins.
LARGE GROUP ACTIVITY	Reading readiness activity or other readiness skill	A comprehension, decoding, or thinking development activity	A personification, concept map, mediation, or brainstorming activity to introduce new concept
SMALL GROUP MEETINGS	Individual follow-up of readiness skill tests for understanding	Teacher/students share their readings and writings. Author studies	Thematic units: Leadership, love, courage, idealism, heroes, war, etc. Author studies
CHORAL READING	Finger plays Jump rope rhymes Poetry Choral chants Music	Poetry Music, including current songs Reciprocal readings	Poetry Music, including current songs Short student writings are read chorally.
SHARING GROUP/ AUDIOTAPE	Share favorite story book Listen to audiotape story	Read their own writing, read from a favorite book, read peer's writing. Student-lead reading or	Author's chair Ten-minute writes are written and read. writing groups
WRITING PERIOD & INDIVIDUAL CONFERENCE	Draw pictures of words, learn to write new words, learn to write longer stories.	Journals, letters to teacher and others, mailboxes in the room Writing new genres	Journals, letters to others, community projects, six-week topic studies, write their own books, SSW
SHARED READING TIME	Wordless picture book, listening center Older tutors read with students.	Small groups read together, SSR, listening center, dramatized reading	Give particular assignments: find a description, key words, opening paragraph, book reports, peer conferencing

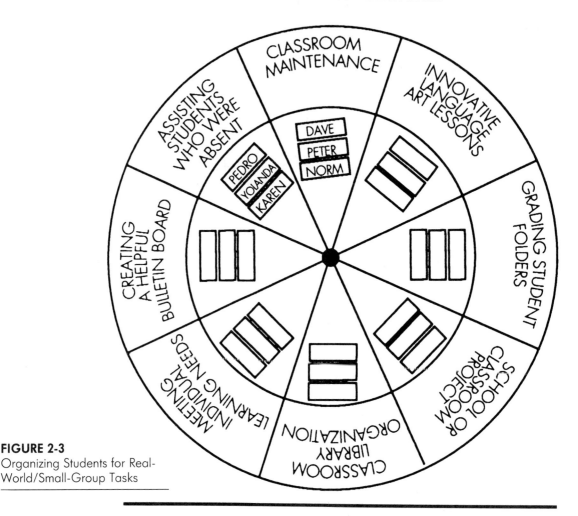

FIGURE 2-3
Organizing Students for Real-World/Small-Group Tasks

Materials and additional ideas for Sample Schedule 3 appear in Figure 2-4. The benefits of this organizational plan are that for two days students have the opportunity to engage in high quality **academic learning time** (*amount of time a student spends attending to relevant tasks while performing those tasks with a high rate of success*, [Caldwell et al., 1982; Bruner, 1986]. Students are also likely to experience **eustress** (*a state of being where they are so immersed in an activity of interest that they loose a sense of time*). One caution is to ensure that depth of study does not minimize their breadth of knowledge. You may need to refer to your yearly goals more frequently in this scheduling system to ensure that time is available to study each.

As you view the daily schedule Ms. Janice Hays (White City, Oregon) follows in Segment 2 of the video that accompanies this text, you can think about the daily schedule you desire. Recall aspects of the classroom registry that you liked when you were an elementary-age student. What was important to you? In what periods of the day did you learn the most?

Once your schedule is in place, you can begin to select the group size and activities you and your students will use.

FIGURE 2-4
How to Organize People, Space, and Materials in Student Communication Centers

LARGE GROUP ACTIVITIES	SMALL GROUP ACTIVITIES	INDIVIDUAL ACTIVITY

teacher reading aloud
sustained silent reading
sustained silent writing
independent practice—teacher
  monitoring
storytelling
choral reading
reader's theatre
dramatic/role playing
singing/chanting
	teach "mini" lessons
	listening station
	groups sharing or editing
	cooperative reading groups
	pairs sharing, reading and
	  writing triads working
	student dictating language
	  experience
	Directed Reading Thinking
	  Activity (described in
	  Chapter 13)
		sustained silent reading
		sustained silent writing
		independent practice centers
		one-to-one teacher conference
		editing/revising
		reading aloud for assessment
		retelling/summarizing for
		  assessment
		dictating language experience

WRITING MATERIALS	READING MATERIALS
paper—all kinds and sizes tablets—student, chart, legal pads notebook paper newsprint tagboard—lined and unlined chalkboards—classroom and individual posterboard sentence strips index cards transparencies pencils—regular and colored pens markers—regular, transparency, hi-lighters chalk—regular and colored crayons and chalkolas scissors, glue, staplers paints	trade books—variety of genres and reading levels big books resource books—thesaurus, encyclopedias, dictionaries books of lists, almanacs magazines—variety of interests and levels newspapers student-made books—individual and class charts/graphs/maps menus/transportation schedules catalogues brochures/bulletins/advertisements phone books logos junk mail instructional bulletin boards bulletin boards displaying student work

SPACE FOR READING AND WRITING ACTIVITIES AND PRODUCTS		OTHER IDEAS
boxes and shelves for supplies boxes for student word banks pocket charts folders for student writing boxes/files for student work bulletin boards to display student work	bathtubs/bean bags/special chairs rugs and throw pillows easels racks bookshelves chart racks	

SELECTING GROUPING SYSTEMS FOR INSTRUCTION

When it comes to grouping, there is no "best" group size in a student communication center. There is one *incorrect grouping arrangement*, however. Students should never stay in the same size group each week because no grouping system is powerful enough to address all of their language needs. Moreover, in your class community, as in society, those who learn through identity with only one group will have limited development opportunities. In addition, when students are allowed to choose whether to work in pairs, small groups, or alone, they can identify their best learning styles through their choices.

The following types of groupings should be used in your class:

1. *Paired Groupings.* Paired instruction provides more intense, personal work than other grouping systems because there is less negotiation of agenda and more opportunities for creative thinking. Paired groupings can be self-chosen (or teacher assigned) between stronger/weaker, same sex, mixed sex, or older/younger students. Such partnerships are also well suited for sharing work, performing "think alouds," revising compositions, asking questions for clarification, grading individual spelling tests, practicing active listening, and learning to speak more effectively. Essentially, whenever students need critiques or assessments of their own unique communication, pairs work well.

2. *Small Groups.* Small groups are best when students need longer than 10–15 minutes to share more than one person's opinion about a work, or explore a wider variety of perspectives. Special types of small groups are: (1) Interest groups, where students develop a communication tool or thinking ability for which they are curious; (2) Project groups, where each student is an expert or in charge of different aspects of a project; (3) Homogeneous groups, where pupils of comparable ability meet to work to advance that competency; (4) Heterogeneous groups, where students of different ability levels are purposely placed together; (5) Task or Process Specific groups, where students rotate from center to center to concentrate on a single task or step in a process.

Before students break into small groups, ensure that they clearly understand the objective, the tasks, and the activities in which they are to engage. The students (or teacher) appoint a group leader and assign special responsibilities to other members, e.g., secretary (records group accomplishments and future goals); resource materials manager (locates new materials, books, and writings); and field note recorder (takes "field notes" documenting effective speaking strategies, incidents of active listening, and effective group thinking skills during work). With these actions in place, small groups will run smoothly and you can meet with individual students or meet with only one group during small-group working sessions.

3. *Large Groups.* Large groups can promote a community climate. As a whole class, students make decisions, develop class plans, resolve issues, see "expert" demonstrations, and become real audiences for student sharings. Large groups can also meet many belonging needs, establish bonding,

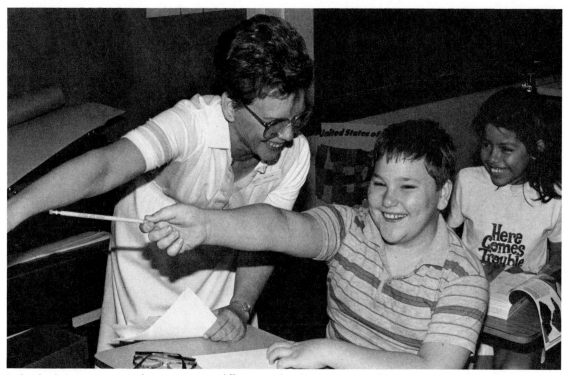
Individualization is more than assigning different tasks to separate students. It is caring for and supporting each individual in the best way for that person. It is also realizing when students need your assistance.

formulate goals, and review knowledge common to the whole. This grouping is also best when communicating needs to the entire group, and for "celebrative experiences." As demonstrated in videotape segment 2, when Karen read her book to her mother in a paired setting, a celebrative moment did not occur. However, sharing the same book a few moments later with the entire class created an event Karen cherished.

4. *Learning Centers.* Learning centers are often a combination of individual and small group instruction. In learning centers, explicit instructions are posted so students who seek assistance know what to do during and after tasks are finished. Instructions also state how to record progress and store materials, as well as the number of people who can use the center at one time. Centers build students' self-directed work skills, initiate new ideas, and create a value for exploring. Different types of centers are shown in the video and described through the remainder of this textbook.

5. *Independent Work.* Independent work allows sustained reading, writing, thinking, and reflection. Students can enjoy learning without reducing or increasing their speed of learning to meet the needs of others. Independent work provides maximum time to develop ownership over projects and learning. Independent work is also among the best occasions for you to individualize instruction. **Individualization** means that you have *identified the needs of your students so well that you provide opportunities for students, even working on the same objective to meet different needs.*

Individualization is riveted focus upon single student needs at one time. It is not a specific type of material. Such personalization occurs through a variety of ways, e.g., learning centers, contracts, bibliotherapy, and student-teacher conferences. One of the most important methods of individualization is to prepare multiple means for students to learn through personal learning styles (Dunn, 1990).

A second purpose of independent work sessions is to enhance your abilities to help students in one-to-one settings, and assist them to work more independently and effectively alone. An example of this grouping system's potential to spark students' instant improvement is demonstrated in the following interaction between a teacher and student:

> One 12-year-old student, Paul, had worked hard from September to January and had successfully mastered many reading strategies and had progressed from primer level to third-or-fourth grade text. He was still extremely slow in his reading, however, paying laborious attention to each word as he read. His teacher discussed his slow reading with him before he read one day, mentioning that although she was proud of this improvement, she wished he could read more smoothly. She asked if he thought he could read a little faster. He replied, "Sure I can!" and proceeded to double his reading speed from 30 to 60 words per minute without any increase in miscues. . . . Once the teacher clarified her expectations, Paul was able to show his abilities (From *Teaching Reading to the Student with Reading Difficulties*, p. 454).

CREATING EFFECTIVE ACTIVITIES

Throughout this book you will learn many instructional lessons that adhere to the principles you've internalized thus far. Because each lesson will assist your students, it is important to checkmark those that most appeal to you. In this way, intuition becomes one criteria in activity selection. Intuition is important because it attracts activities that use both you and your students' present talents and strengths. For example, when you read an activity or lesson plan in this book and say, "I can't wait to try that with my students!" that is an indication that it appeals to your talents and complements your teaching philosophy. Later in the school year, you will return to this book and select unmarked activities as your instructional repertoire expands and student needs dictate.

In brief, planning a year-long instructional program requires devising a master plan of instructional goals, developing a daily schedule, selecting group sizes, and choosing activities. Once these choices have been made you can turn your attention to developing effective daily lesson plans to open the school year.

STRATEGIES THAT TEACH

LESSONS TO USE EARLY IN THE SCHOOL YEAR

It is in the creation of daily lessons that you will realize your power to set theory and practice in motion to advance students' language and thinking competencies. In the lesson plans that follow you will learn strategies to (a) teach on the first day of school; (b) implement on the first week of school; (c) identify your students' talents; and (d) develop effective group work habits.

CREATING LESSONS FOR THE FIRST DAY OF SCHOOL

M	T	W	Th	F

The language arts lesson for the first day of school begins before the opening of school. By completing the following ten activities a few days before school begins, your language arts program will get underway with fewer disruptions.

1. Move your desk to a corner of the room, away from the door, so as to create an inviting, open passage into the room. By doing so, students sense that you are not the sole owner of the class.
2. Put materials on open shelves, and have a chart ready where students will write classroom rules, consequences, and rewards.
3. Secure 100 or more reading materials and library books, ranging from wordless picture books, magazines, newspapers, novels, and poetry, which are appropriate for your students' age (for reference see Figure 2-2 and the Notecards in this book). Borrow books from public libraries, and join a children's book club.
4. Make decisions about which thematic units, learning centers, or community improvement events requiring in-depth thinking and literate behaviors that you wish to make available to students (see Chapters 10–13 for ideas about each).
5. Prepare methods to inform parents of your student communication center, and plan ways they can become involved. Harste (1989) found that in most successful programs there was a conscious effort to keep parents involved and informed. Students can plan ways their parents can become involved in their class. The letter in the BUILDING YOUR PROFESSIONAL PORTFOLIO section can be used as a model for the first letter you send to them.
6. Design ways students can self-monitor, self-correct, contemplate, rebuild confidence, and persist when discouraged, e.g., identify a special location where students can leave important notes to you that no one else will read.
7. Develop a systematic record-keeping system, and allocate times in the year where individual student talents are identified and used in the classroom (see ''Helping Students Identify Their Learning Styles'' (p. 53).

STRATEGIES THAT TEACH

8. Design how to teach the rules for discipline and classroom management. Set aside three days during the first week of school to practice class rules and movement patterns. At the end of each practice session, have students review what they did well, and how they can improve. Then practice again. Have students dedicate themselves to responsibilities they want to assume for their room, especially students who presently see themselves as failures (Collins, 1987).

9. Decorate the room. Create something special that helps students feel that they are very exceptional (such as a large pocket apple tree for library book check-out cards). Then in October, have students design and build something distinctive they want to add to their room; such as a mock TV/puppet stage, flannel boards, or a platform for role plays, plays, and impromptu speeches. This enables them to contribute to making their room extraordinary.

10. Identify resource people and coordinate activities with them. For example, Richek and Glick (1991) recommend that teachers collaborate so students who go to the federally funded Chapter 1 classes and resource rooms read a book or story you plan to share with the class the day before you introduce it in yours. In this way, slower learners have a double exposure and more chances for success.

On the first day of school you will institute a positive climate through the following actions:

1. Read a book from Notecard 1: "Books for the First Day of School" (Chapter 1).

2. Learn students' names through peer interviews, and individual student writing/art samples which you differentiate and associate with the names before the second class period.

3. Show students that they are important (e.g., design a way for them to bring an item or idea to school the second day that means a lot to them. They will share these during "morning message," or at another point on the second day).

4. Begin a *Most Important People* bulletin board whereby you announce that students have an 8 1/2" x 11" section on the bulletin board to fill with whatever they wish to show who they are and what they want the class to know about them. Each space has a background of one sheet of construction paper so colors of construction paper are varied.

CREATING LESSONS THAT IDENTIFY STUDENTS' SPEAKING, LISTENING, READING, WRITING, AND THINKING APTITUDES

The next six activities are the content for the first week of school. Schedule them according to Sample Schedule 1, 2, or 3 as you choose. These activities, along with *Critical Thinking Activity 2,* build your abilities to assess students' language knowledge and deficiencies. During the first week of school include at least three of the following diagnostic lessons.

1. *Journal writing and reading evaluations.* Students write or read for 20 minutes and then talk to you and classmates about the content of their reading and writing. Students then note new and special things about the writing and reading abilities that their classmate's work, helped them understand.

2. *Free writing and free reading.* Students are free to select which books and types of writing they want to do. They write why they choose that book so you learn the depth and direction of their literacy tastes.

3. *"Important to Me" papers.* There is a special place in the room where students display an item that is important to them. Before the object can be placed on the table, however, students write a 1–5 page report to describe the object and why they consider it important.

4. *Morning message ideas.* Begin your morning messages with a famous quotation. Such quotations are available in *Thoughts to Begin Students' Day K–2* and *Thoughts to Begin Students' Day, 3–8* (Collins, Block, & Zinke, in press).

5. Diagnose students' preinstructional language strengths and needs as described on pages 57–58.

6. Allen, Michalove, Shockley, and West (1991) recommend that curriculum during the first weeks of school be filled with experiences, such as hikes in the woods, cooking activities, class-made stories, and field trips. Such experiences help students feel valued and loved. For example, select a book like *A Taste of Blackberries* or *Charlotte's Web* and read the full book in three days, allowing students to talk together for long periods of time. Alternatively, plan a field trip where every person in the class has a job to do. This builds a familylike environment. Building this group unity is as important as the time spent establishing classroom routines if students are to have the security they need to grow cognitively, socially, and emotionally.

As mentioned earlier in this chapter, it is important that you spend up to three days "practicing" the procedures and guidelines for effective small group work. Before you explain the process of moving to and from groups or centers, students benefit from having been taught the following lessons that facilitate group learning.

CREATING LESSON PLANS THAT TEACH STUDENTS TO WORK COOPERATIVELY

This lesson is written as you would conduct it in your class. You begin by telling students the objective: "Today, I will read you a story about Bambi" (*Friends of the Forest*, Racine, WI: Western Publishing Co, 1975) or about _____ [the main character] from one of the following books:

1. Brett, Jan. *Beauty and the Beast.*
2. *Goldilocks and the Three Bears.*
3. Bemelmans, Ludwig. *Madeline.*
4. Seuss, Theodore G. *Are You My Mother?*
5. Cohen, Miriam. *Starting First Grade.*
6. Freeman, Don. *Corduroy.*
7. Hutchins, Pat. *Changes, Changes.*
8. Turkle, Brinton. *Deep in the Forest.*
9. Milne, A. A. *Winnie-the-Pooh.*
10. Piper, W. *The Little Engine That Could.*

You continue: "We are going to listen and discover the ways that Bambi [or another main character from the above list] made friends. We are also going to see how Bambi and his friends worked together to make sure everything was safe and okay for all of their friends. Throughout your life, you will continually make friends and need to work together in groups with one another. Put yourself in Bambi's place and think of the ways you could work together better with your friends.

"As I read this story to you, I want you to raise your hand if I say a word you do not know. At that time, I will write the words you do not know. After the story, I will help you learn the new words. It is important for you to know what all the words mean. They will help you understand all of the story and it will make more sense to you. We will go over each word and I will give you the definition of the word and a synonym (a word that means the same)." [Read book to students]

Dispelling Misconceptions

You might think to yourself, "I could never have made as many friends as Bambi [or the main character from one of the other books] in one day," or you might think you could not have been as brave as Bambi to help save his friend Thumper. However, if you were in Bambi's position, you would have thought to save your friend, especially since your friend Thumper had helped you. Put yourself in Bambi's place. After I finish reading, explain how you would make friends and work effectively in groups.

Thinking Guide Instructions

When we work together this year we will improve how much we can learn in groups. (Then insert three rules you want the class to follow when working in groups; for kindergarten you might describe the following rules and have pictures on a chart to remind students of each.) First, we will look around the classroom to see if there is anyone that does not have a workmate. If you find such a person, go over and invite him or her to work with you or in your group. Second, once you add a new friend to your group, ask him or her to help on something that was difficult for you or the group. Third, when working in groups, you should be cooperative and share. Everyone has a turn. This will help you keep friends and have a good time when working in groups. You will have more fun if you cooperate.

Objective Choices

Now, choose one of the following to do:

1. Think about our three rules and the Thinking Guide (posted on the wall) while you work in the teacher's center today. You will add a fourth rule to our thinking guide that you want us to follow. At the end of center time we will discuss new ideas we have to improve our group work.
2. Put yourself in Bambi's position and tell what you would have done if you were in his place. You can tape your suggestions at the listening center today.
3. Draw a picture of how you would show people making friends or working in a group. Write about it at the reading corner today.

Rethink and Reformulate

After center time, say: "Think of other ways you would benefit from working in groups and explain why you think groups will help you in the future. Tell me why you think working together is important for you. Tell me all the places you will work in groups in the future."

Students evaluate their group work skills and add new procedures to the chart after they have practiced working in groups for three days.

CREATING LESSONS THAT HELP STUDENTS IDENTIFY THEIR LEARNING STYLES

Day 1: (Approximately 50 minutes)

Suggested Books and Genre for This Lesson

Presidents' Biographies: *John Adams* by Marlene Targ Brill; *John Quincy Adams* by Zachary Kent; *George Bush* by Zachary Kent; *Ulysses S. Grant* by Zachary Kent; *Herbert Hoover* by Susan Clinton; *Andrew Jackson* by Alice Osinski; *Thomas Jefferson* by Jim Hargrove; *John F. Kennedy* by Zachary Kent; *Abraham Lincoln* by Jim Hargrove; *James Madison* by Susan Clinton; *James Monroe* by Christine Maloney; *Ronald Reagan* by Zachary Kent; *Franklin D. Roosevelt* by Alice Osinski; *Theodore Roosevelt* by Zachary Kent; and *George Washington* by Zachary Kent.

Hispanic-American Biography: *Roberto Clemente: Baseball Superstar.*

African-American Biographies: *Martin Luther King, Jr.: A Man Who Changed Things; Jackie Robinson: Baseball's First Black Major Leaguer.*

Other Biographies: Set #1—*Crispus Attucks, Clara Barton, Albert Einstein, Lou Gehrig, Dorothea Lange, Robert E. Lee, Abraham Lincoln, Our Golda: The Story of Golda Meir, Jim Thorpe, The Wright Brothers;* Set #2—*Story of Alexander Graham Bell, Christopher Columbus, Story of Walt Disney, Thomas Jefferson, Mikhail Gorbachev, Harry Houdini, Lincoln—A Photography, Sally Ride, Teddy Roosevelt, Harriet Tubman.*

Language Arts Thinking Objective Presented to Students

One of the most important keys to success in life is identifying your talents. When you do so you will place yourself in situations that more often call upon your talents and enhance your choices for success. You can learn to identify your talents by comparing yourself to a person you admire and by reflecting upon the type of environment that supports your highest achievements. You will know you have identified some of your learning talents and are successful when you select talents and environmental preferences you have from Thinking Guide 2-1.

Dispelled Misconceptions

Write what you would most like to learn about yourself and your talents at the bottom of Thinking Guide 2-1.

Thinking Guide Instructions

Each person has preferred environmental, emotional, sociological, physical, and psychological preferences. Before you circle your preferences on your Thinking Guide, reflect upon the answers to these questions and facts:

Motivation has to come from within or it won't work. You can't have somebody want something for you more badly than *you* want it. If you work *hard* and develop your talent you can become one of the best. You need something to strive for that inspires you. You have to learn the process and mechanics of achievement and have a million little goals. Don't set monstrous goals that are too far out of reach. Take pride and succeed in doing every little thing well. [Students answer each of the following orally or in writing.]

- How valuable is your imagination to accomplish important goals?
- Do you think it is as valuable as your sense of humor?
- Are these two "senses" related? How? Why not?
- What activity requires more of your imagination than anything else you do?

Now identify and circle your preferences for learning and the environmental factors that contribute to your success on Thinking Guide 2-1.

Three Examples of the Thinking Guide in Use

To give examples of the Thinking Guide in use, ask the students to name (or create in advance) three extremely different types of people. You can

THINKING GUIDE 2-1
Identifying Your Talents

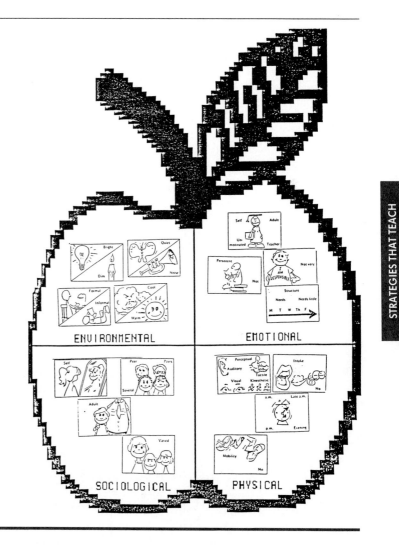

ask students to describe main characters from the biographies they are reading. If you and students wish to be creative and learn more about the differences that identifying one's talents and preferences can make, have students role-play each character as he or she would look, act, and speak in discussing a topic students select. Students then select the preferences or talents each character used well and defend their selections.

Students Select and Complete Their Own Objective

In this section of the lesson, students become more aware of their individual talents and increase the use of metacognition while thinking, listening, and reading. Each student selects a famous person born on his or her birthdate from the lists available in *126 Strategies That Build the Language Arts* (Collins, 1992a). Students read a biography (and autobiography, if possible) about the person selected. Students record personality traits of the famous persons, compare these traits to their own, and list talents each possesses. A journal entry describes what it might have been like to be the famous person's best friend. Each student identifies activities the two might have enjoyed in the student's community.

Day 2: (50 minutes or longer if student projects or extensions across the curriculum are implemented)

Rethink and Reformulate

In this final section of the lesson, students write autobiographies that focus upon their self-perceived strengths. Each student is then paired with a friend and writes about that friend's strengths, without conferring with the friend. Afterward, students compare their autobiographies and biographies. They write explanations as to why differences in perceptions and self-perceptions exist. After this activity, students choose from the following:

Tell the students: "If you want to practice relating your personal experiences to what you read and learn how to do so more effectively, meet with me before you begin reading."

Students may also elect to meet in groups with those who have similar preferences and design a realistic plan to modify classroom activities so as to call upon more of their talents and preferences. Each group submits their plans to you and then the class as a whole discusses ways in which all plans could be implemented.

Alternatively, you can elect to construct a test to identify other talent and preference areas such as the following:

1. What is you dream?
   What do you want?
   Who do you want to be?
   Why?
2. What are the things that make your dream unable to come true?
   What are the limits or the "roadblocks?"
3. What are your strengths?
   What are you good at?
   When do you do your best?
4. Do your strengths outweigh your limitations?
   How?
5. Do you believe that your plans or dreams are possible?
   Why?

Some students may read sections from Kathy Balsamo (1987), *Exploring the Lives of Gifted People* (Carthage, IL: Good Apple) and identify if these people have common characteristics. Students also suggest ways they can use their talents to better the class.

In summary, through these lessons you will have implemented the principles in Chapter 1 and 2, planned for a productive first week in a student communication center, learned many aptitudes of your students, helped students work together more effectively, and taught the importance of identifying one's talents and learning styles. Through the Critical Thinking Activity that follows you will take the first step toward using individual student's strengths to eliminate their communication and thinking weakness.

CRITICAL THINKING ACTIVITY 2
First Week of School: Diagnosing Students' Preinstructional Language Strengths and Needs

Recommended Grade Levels: Preschool Through Grade 8, with Drawings Used at Grades Preschool Through Grade 2

During the first week of school administer an Attitude and Interest Inventory, as shown in Figure 2-5, or one you design.

FIGURE 2-5
Attitude/Interest Inventory

Name _____ Date _____

1) Does anyone read to you at home? How often?
2) Do you like reading by yourself?
3) Finish this sentence: "When I read, I feel . . ."
4) Make up a title for the most exciting book you have ever read.
5) Name your favorite book or story. What makes it your favorite?
6) Do you have a hero or favorite person? Who is it and why do you admire this person?
7) What do you want to do or be when you grow up?
8) If you could live anywhere in the world, where would it be?
9) Is reading important to you? Why or why not?
10) What kind of stories make you feel bored?
11) Tell me about a favorite story you've written.
12) Do you like to read these types of stories?

1 means a lot, 2 means sometimes, 3 means not usually, and 4 means never.

Historical Fiction	1	2	3	4
Animal Stories	1	2	3	4
Mysteries	1	2	3	4
Encyclopedias	1	2	3	4
Sports Stories	1	2	3	4
Science Fiction (space, aliens, etc.)	1	2	3	4
Fairy Tales	1	2	3	4
Poetry	1	2	3	4
Humorous Stories	1	2	3	4
Romances	1	2	3	4

* Created by Ms. Sara Falstad, Graduate student, TCU

FIGURE 2-6
Example of Informal Reading Inventory

Jack looked at the little dog. "Oh, yes," he said. "We take care of all pets." _____ main idea All day Ned and Jack took dogs. They took big dogs. And they took many little dogs. _____ detail Ned looked at the dogs. Then he looked at Jack. "We have many dogs," said Ned. "How many do we have?" _____ detail "Let's see," said Jack. "One, two, three . . . One, two, three . . . Oh, Ned. I don't know. Let's say we have fifteen dogs." _____ sequence "Look, Jack," said Ned. "Here is a man with a big cat. We don't want to take care of a cat, do we?" "Oh yes," said Jack. "We take care of all pets." _____ inference	**COMPREHENSION** **QUESTIONS** 1. What were Jack and Ned doing all day? (They were taking care of big and little dogs.) 2. How many dogs did they think they had? (fifteen) 3. Did the boys know exactly how many dogs they had? (no) Why do you say that? (They gave up counting and Jack said he didn't know.) 4. What was the last pet that was brought to Jack and Ned? (a big cat) 5. Why might Ned not want to take care of a cat? (Dogs don't like cats and they had many dogs; Ned thinks they have enough pets to care for.)

You will also collect a writing (drawing) sample where students describe things they want you to know about their listening, speaking, writing, and reading needs and strengths, and about themselves as people.

Then, call individual students to your desk, one-at-a-time, to read into a tape recorder. Students read from a selection of children's literature, or from a page in a basal reader. Record the counter numbers on the tape before that student begins to read. During the reading, mark the errors they make on a copy of the page the student reads. Mark the following errors as they read, as shown in Figure 2-6:

1. Circle the words they omitted.
2. Write words they say incorrectly above the words they should have read.
3. Insert words they say that are not printed.
4. Place an "R" above words repeated.

5. Place a "P" above words you pronounce for the student because they do not attempt to decode it after a six-second pause.
6. Place a // after words where students pause for less than five seconds before continuing to read.
7. Write "SC" above words in which the student self-corrects the pronunciation.

FIGURE 2-7

Comprehensive Assessment of Grade Level Reading Ability and Enjoyment

Name _____   _____ Six Weeks

Comprehensive Assessment of Grade Level
Reading Ability and Enjoyment

One to One Conferences:

Reading Selection:

Decoding Skills: Comprehension:

No. of Miscues _____   Teacher Remarks _____

Comments _____
_____
_____
_____

Assessment/Recommendations: _____
_____
_____

Reading Selection: _____

Decoding Skills: Comprehension

No. of Miscues _____   Teacher Remarks _____

Comments _____
_____
_____
_____

Assessment/Recommendations: _____
_____
_____

LEARNING CENTERS FOR MAKING READING AUTHENTIC

	1st	2nd	3rd	4th	5th	6th

FREE TIME RECORD

WEEK				
1	2	3	4	5

WEEK	BOOK TALLY
ONE	
TWO	
THREE	
FOUR	
FIVE	
TOTAL NO. READ	

After you turn off the tape recorder, ask the students to retell what they learned from their reading. Make notes of the students' comprehension strengths, and any evidence of students' reading, listening, and speaking abilities, and difficulties, as shown in the example (Figure 2-6). Prompt students and ask questions for additional evidence of reading comprehension to expand their retellings.

When each student returns to his/her seat, analyze why the student made the decoding and comprehension errors and indicate your thoughts on that student's form. Make note of these analyses on the sheet where you noted beginning counter times. Fast forward the tape recorder, so as to leave a blank space that is the same length of time as the student's reading just completed. This space will be used at the end of the year for a rerecording of the student's reading. You then begin a comprehensive assessment of grade level reading ability and enjoyment record for that child (see Figure 2-7). Complete this using all the diagnostic activities you have made during the first week of school. Then call the next student to your desk. This student then engages in each of the above steps. Continue until all students have been assessed.

At the end of the year, students choose any selection they wish to read into the tape recorder, but the requirement is that they may not have read the piece previously. After each student reads into the recorder, rewind the tape so students hear their beginning-of-the-year reading and their end-of-year reading side by side. This tape is a documentation of the student's reading growth. An alternate plan is to use a separate audiotape for each student. In this way students have their own tape to put in their portfolios, and they can state their goals for the year on this tape as well. After their end-of-year reading, students can replay their goals to hear if they reached those they set for themselves. This tape could then be passed to subsequent teachers.

Once you have prepared these lessons, you are ready to arrange your classroom furniture to invite students' self-initiated learning. You will build your professional expertise in room design through the following professional development opportunity.

PROFESSIONAL DEVELOPMENT OPPORTUNITY
How to Arrange Your Class So It Becomes a Student Communication Center

The next discussion assists you to arrange your classroom so that it provides for maximum student psychological security. You will also view many classroom arrangements in the videotape that accompanies this textbook. As you view these rooms in action and the sample floor plans in Figure 2-8, you can create key elements that facilitate students' communication in your room design. Identify and list items you want in your room from Figure 2-8. Cut out and arrange objects that you desire to use in your room. Place these objects from Figure 2-9 on the blueprint in Figure 2-10 as you would like. Modify your blueprint until all your organizational needs are met. By midyear, you could give the grid to your students and they can submit plans for redesigning their communication center.

FIGURE 2-8
Sample Floor Plans

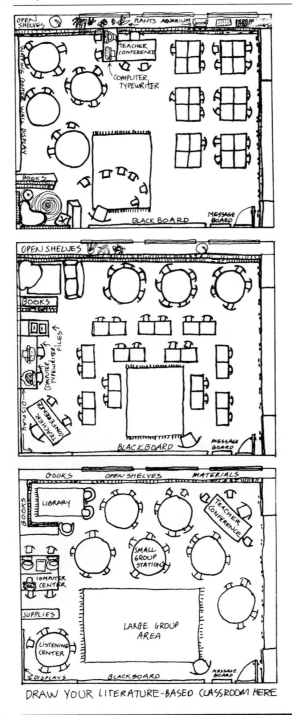

DRAW YOUR LITERATURE-BASED CLASSROOM HERE

FIGURE 2-9
Designing Your Classroom: Part 1

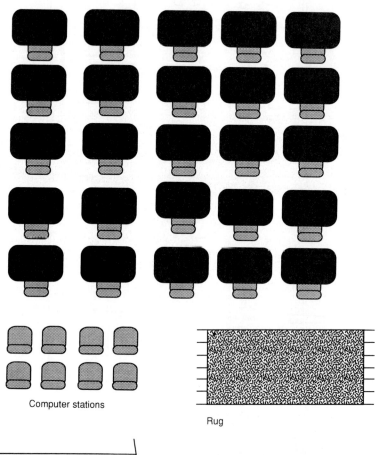

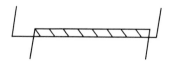

Computer stations

Rug

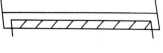

Project table

FIGURE 2-10
Designing Your Classroom: Part 2

Measure the size of the room on the grid at the bottom. Cut the pieces that are models of things in your room. Arrange the room as you'd like it.

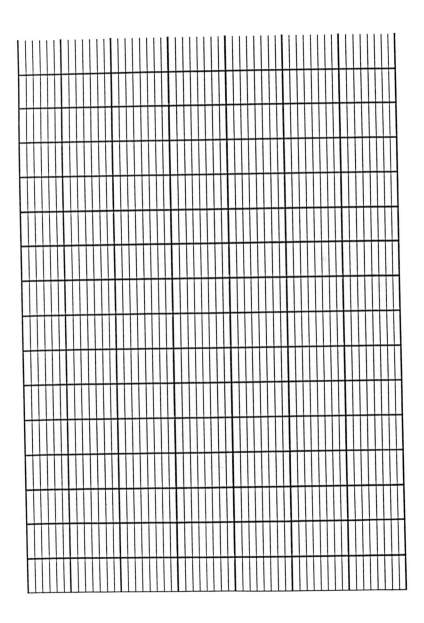

STRATEGIES THAT TEACH

FIGURE 2-11
Book Review Cards

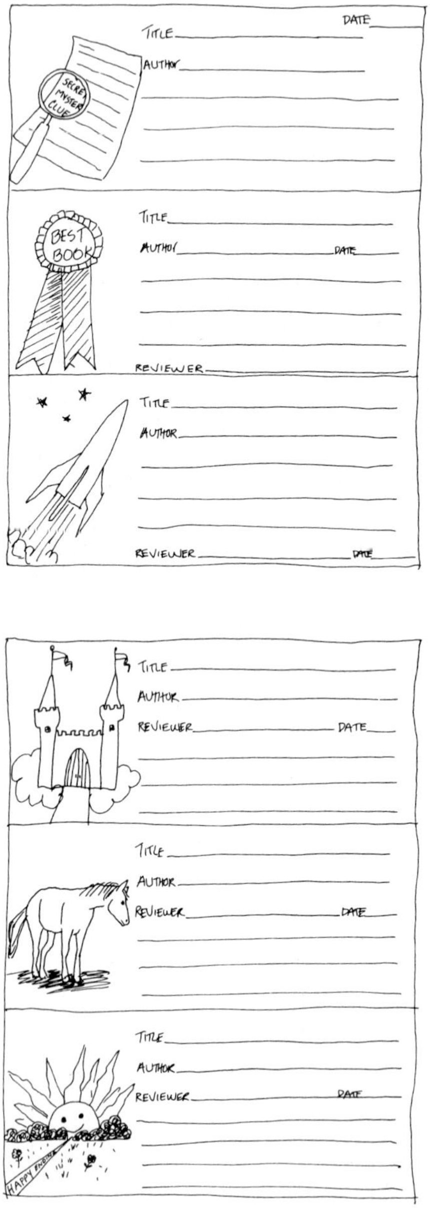

As we close this chapter, you probably thought of many essential elements that add to the success of your language arts program. All of these reflections will have taken place before the first students walk into the classroom. With the information learned in Chapters 1 and 2 you are now ready to meet your students. In Chapter 3 you will learn how their lives, needs, and present levels of communication will guide your instruction.

TRY IT

The four activities that follow enable you to assess and implement your understanding of the information in this chapter.

1. Reflect upon the dimensions of thinking that are important to instruction and the eight language arts you will teach. If you are not teaching, observe a language arts lesson in an elementary school or reflect upon your favorite language arts class when you were a child. List the principles of language learning from Chapters 1 and 2 that were in operation. If possible, interview the teacher about the principles he/she follows in instruction. Compare these principles to those cited in Chapters 1 and 2.

If you are presently teaching, in the coming week, practice increasing your students' ability to take risks. Say to your students, "I'm glad you took a chance," "I like to hear that you have several alternatives in mind that you want to try," and "I like your question." Model how to say, "I don't know but I'm going to find out." You might also thank your students for the effective lessons you have together.

2. You can make colorful copies of the "Book Review" cards (see Figure 2-11). These cards can be used by students who will serve as book reviewers. Some book review cards have pictures that depict the type of literature they convey. Students select a card that represents their book and they write their critique on the card and place it before the first page in their book. In this way classmates can have an editorial review before selecting that book.

3. If you are presently teaching, share a book you are reading with your students. Tell them why this book is important to you. Describe the results of this sharing. If you are not yet teaching, identify one of the most important books you've ever read, and reflect upon why it was important to you. Visualize yourself sharing this book and its importance with future students. Describe how you will share it.

4. Select three children's books you can use for the assessments in Critical Thinking Activity 2.

FOR YOUR JOURNAL

Design a system by which you will read children's literature on a regular basis. Enter the plan in your journal. You may also like to begin a list of instructional aids and titles of children's books to suggest to relatives as presents for your birthday. Fashion a program to read the Caldecott and Newbery Award Books on Notecards 3 and 4 (pp. 35–36). Mark your journal in some way to remind you that it is time to read another Caldecott and Newbery Award Book.

STRATEGIES THAT TEACH

BUILDING YOUR PROFESSIONAL PORTFOLIO
Parent Letters

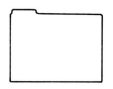

The following letter can be mailed to parents/guardians to originate a two-way communication system to continue throughout the school year.

Date

Dear Parents:

The next nine months will be a time of growth and exploration for your child. I look forward to sharing these exciting times and helping your child through challenging ones. I will use my professional background to teach and guide your child to the best of my ability.

As a parent, you are your child's first and most important teacher. I encourage you to become actively involved in your child's education. I am seeking ways in which you can share time with your children at home and in our classroom. Please take a moment to help me by filling out the enclosed sheet.

I would also like to meet you during this first month of school. If you can come to my room (#___) at any of the following times, please indicate the time you prefer.

Parent-Teacher Conference Times from September 1–30

Monday:	3:30, 4:00, 4:30	Date _____
Tuesday:	7:45 A.M., 3:00, 3:30	Date _____
Wednesday:	3:30, 4:00, 4:30	Date _____
Thursday:	7:45 A.M., 3:00, 3:30	Date _____
Friday:	3:00, 3:30, 4:00	Date _____

I cannot come during the hours listed, please call me at _____ .
I prefer a home visit, please call me for a time _____ .

Our class would enjoy and benefit from your expertise. The following form suggests several activities in which you could participate. Please feel free to add ideas of your own.

Name _____

Address _____

Phone _____

1. I am willing to help in the following areas:

   _____ room mother/father/grandparent
   _____ assistant room mother/father
   _____ phone committee
   _____ sewing
   _____ cooking for holiday parties
   _____ carpentry
   _____ drama
   _____ music

   _____ dancing
   _____ arts and crafts
   _____ physical education
   _____ field trips
   _____ contacting people or resources for lessons

2. I would enjoy working with you and the class at school in the following ways:

   _____ working with individual students in these subjects:
   _____
   _____
   _____
   _____ working with small groups
   _____ preparing learning centers

   _____ making games
   _____ typing
   _____ library assistant
   _____ reading stories
   _____ ordering new books

3. I have the following special interests, talent, hobby, occupation, or materials I would be willing to share with the class: _____
   _____
   _____

4. The best time for me to help in the class is on _____ Monday _____ Tuesday _____ Wednesday _____ Thursday _____ Friday at _____ o'clock.

5. Is there any type of special information concerning you and/or your child that would help me to advance your child's learning?
   _____
   _____

Again I am looking forward to having your child as a student, and I am looking forward to meeting you.

Sincerely,

[*Note*: Before parents begin their in-class volunteer work they need to conference with you. During this conference you teach them the strategies they will use with students, and establish a subsequent time to meet (in three weeks) to assess how valuable their volunteer work has been. By limiting volunteer periods to three weeks' duration, you can more easily reassign parents who are not as effective, or satisfied, with their work as they/you desire to other areas of responsibility. At the same time, you can increase the challenge for those who are highly successful within their areas of responsibility.]

STRATEGIES THAT TEACH

3
The Students Arrive: Developing Students' Oral Communication Abilities

Although "teacher talk" constitutes as much as two-thirds of all speaking in past language arts programs, this time was not closely related to high student achievement. What proved to be highly correlated to students' success was the amount of time students were allowed to talk about the important tasks in which they were engaged (Durkin & Biddle, 1974).

The thinking human being not able to express himself stands at the same level as those who cannot think

—Pericles

In this chapter you will learn to teach students to express themselves. As you will read below, such instruction begins on the very first day of school!

Once again it was time to prepare for battle as summer's drowsy magic drew to a close. We had lived such a short time in bliss. Children once again, we fished and swam and played for hours under the green shade trees, only to flop exhausted in the wind-ruffled seas of tall grass. Haircuts were received, new clothes were bought, return we must. As all great heroes, we had to rise again to meet the enemy who stalked silently every year in that most beautiful and yet wicked month of September. All around the room you could hear the sound of various battle preparations as old traps were set for a new teacher. We were stronger this year; the summer had made us sleek and fast. Older and wiser now, we would be no match for an unseasoned veteran. A hush fell over the room.

Footsteps approached. We tensed in preparation for the onslaught. He stood before us, powerful and confident, a worthy opponent, no doubt. Smiling, he said, "I would like to begin today by just getting to know you."

We were stunned.

"Why don't you start by telling me a little bit about yourselves and the kinds of things you like to do." Something was very different here; could this be a sneak attack designed to lure us into complacency? **We had never been permitted to talk so freely, and what was even more surprising was that he really seemed to be interested in what we had to say** (Newman, 1987, p. 166).

The purpose of this chapter is to assist you to develop students' speaking abilities in a student communication center, refine and improve their oral communication, and eliminate their speaking deficiencies.

By the end of this chapter you will know:

1. Six reasons why students need oral language instruction;

2. Five theories that explain how their speech develops;

3. Speaking difficulties that you can assist students to overcome;

4. How your students can make artful oral presentations, and use their speaking to ritualize, inform, regulate, interact, image, and share personal feelings (which are the functions of oral language).

THEORETICAL FOUNDATION

STUDENTS' ORAL LANGUAGE NEEDS

Leonard Bloomfield (1933) once wrote that language learning is, "doubtless the greatest intellectual feat any one of us is ever required to perform" (p. 29). There are six reasons why students need your help to reach their oral languaging potential.

WHY YOU NEED TO DEVELOP STUDENTS' SPEAKING ABILITIES

Reason 1: *Many students will enter your room with experiences beyond their years, if we use the milestones in your life, as the standard.* They need your assistance to talk about their experiences and to place them in proper perspective. They will likely have won more Nintendo battles, built more intricate "castles," explored more creeks (and cities, vicariously), watched more MTV, listened to more rap music, and solved more difficulties in daily life than you had at their age. However, when they arrive at your classroom, many will have also "lost" much more than you had as well. They will have mislaid the belief that what they have to say is important to others. Many will avoid voicing their thoughts. They may have survived *so much life* they are afraid to venture.

McClure (1989) and Collins (1992a) have evidence that your students can learn to persuade, inform, or entertain others orally. They also have evidence that in a student communication center pupils can distinguish their individuality, cease worries about what they cannot communicate, and discover what they know. The activities in this chapter will increase students' desire to express themselves. Through these activities students will learn to communicate deeply felt emotions and thoughts, which will be acknowledged and appreciated by classmates. Once these expressions are understood, students lose their fear of sharing ideas.

Reason 2: *Students need to speak effectively and frequently, because in the future (if not in the present) oral communication will become the medium by which most people receive information.* If these two facts *alone* were the *only* reasons to develop students' speaking ability, they would be sufficient. Educators are becoming more aware that an increasing proportion of students' successes, professionally and personally, will depend on their effective use of speech. Unfortunately, the emphasis in many schools is still on "reading, writing, and 'rithmetic." The need for a rich, oral language developmental program is so overshadowed by these priorities that students talk more at home than at school, even though the average time spent in exchanges with adults at home is only seven minutes a day. When pupils do talk at school, they tend to give truncated answers to teacher questions, asked at the rate of one every eleven seconds (Wells, 1986). In your student communication center, students *will tell* what they know, connect the "familiar" to the new, and use ramblings and questions to originate schemas/patterns for new knowledge. Daily, you can improve students' oral language by: (1) not wanting everyone in a discussion to reach the same conclusion; (2) requiring students to find new information about the world, others, and themselves; and (3) encouraging students to question as well as to give reasoned opinions. Your class will contain student-centered discussions because you end comments with invitations for student talk. For example, you will say, "Who has a good question to ask about what Jacqueline said?" You will extend students' abilities to look at both sides of an issue by saying, "What if . . . ?" You will increase their higher level thinking by turning questions asked of you back to the students, e.g., a student asks "Why did Chris Van Allsburg name his book *The Polar Express* instead of *The Christmas Bell*, or something else?" Your answer will be, "Class, what do you think Mr. Van Allsburg's rationale might have been?"

Reason 3: *Research has demonstrated that students who have less well-developed oral abilities will have limited reading, writing, and overall scholastic success* (Loban, 1976; Sampson, 1986). This correlation exists because of the following:

1. The words they speak become the first that they recognize and use in reading or writing. Therefore, when you build students' speaking vocabularies, you simultaneously increase the number of words they can attempt when reading and writing independently;
2. Students who speak comfortably will more quickly recognize the graphemes that represent phonemes. Such students will more frequently interact with friends who point to printed words during conversations. Similarly, such students will not feel self-conscious about asking friends the meaning of unfamiliar words as soon as friends say them;
3. The rich context of a personally relevant conversation creates the schema necessary to store new word meanings. Moreover, the definition students receive through conversations will probably be in terms they can understand. Then, in the course of that same conversation, students will likely say the new word they just learned. This immediate application further ensures that these terms will become a part of students' permanent speaking, reading, and writing vocabulary.

Reason 4: *Concepts employed at school are different from those used at home.* Words such as "sentence," "recess," and "assessment" are infrequently used in students' home-based experiences. If students are to become successful speakers in school, and throughout life, they need your instruction and practice to appropriately adjust their speech for various settings and purposes.

Reason 5: *A strong oral language program increases the pleasure of learning.* Most people enjoy conversing above other leisure pastimes. Sharing with others and the spontaneity that speech provides brings unique pleasures to the school day. In addition, expressing themselves to others fashions new memories for students, which will be relived in future conversations. As discussed in Chapter 1, when your class becomes a place where students learn from their life-related experiences, schools become establishments of high appraisal and praise!

Reason 6: *Without your help students may not have a path to follow in acquiring an effective oral language.* Students pass through similar stages in oral language development. When this developmental path is known, you can help individuals rewalk that road and discover important landmarks they missed. The most prominent theories concerning this developmental path of language acquisition follow (Stockard, 1992).

Behavioristic Theory. Behaviorists contend that children learn to speak through **shaping** (*the positive reinforcement of desired behaviors and the negative reinforcement of undesirable ones*). Bloomfield (1933), Owens (1984), Skinner (1957), and Wardhaugh (1971) explain language learning as a process of imitating sounds, words, and phrases that are rewarded or scolded by adults. These reinforcements direct students to duplicate acceptable English speaking patterns. While many researchers support the behavioristic theory, others believe it does not explain how children learn to say sentences. They propose alternate theories for oral language development (Ferreiro & Teberosky, 1982; Pflaum, 1986). These researchers note that imitation or selective reinforcement cannot explain how students form sentences they have never heard before. Their research suggests that learning to speak is more complicated than behaviorists anticipated.

Nativistic Theory. In 1975, Noam Chomsky conceived language learning as an active interaction between a child and the environment. This interaction occurs through use of a part of the mind he labeled the **language-acquisition device** (*the section of the brain that receives information from the environment, analyzes it, and generates language rules*). According to Chomsky and other naturalistic theorists, the language-acquisition device organizes graphemes, phonemes, syntax, grammar, and semantic features into separate categories. These theorists propose that students learn to speak naturally when they are exposed to speech (Chomsky 1975; Watson 1979). Opponents to this theory, however, posit that a language acquisition device fails to explain why some of the more complex language forms must be taught before students understand and use them appropriately.

Cognitive Field Theory. Cognitive field theorists believe that students acquire language by creating hypotheses and restructuring their thinking as they learn. These theorists posit that students choose words to label new learnings according to their level of thinking ability (Canady, 1977). Cognitive field theorists claim that students create their own meanings, which explains why (1) each produces a different mental image when hearing a word (e.g., "dog"); (2) mental pictures change over the years; and (3) single words hold multiple connotations. Cognitive theorists state that rather than having innate "language acquisition devices," students make rules about language subconsciously. Therefore, language learning is accelerated through an instructional program which erects subconscious rules to a conscious level where they can be intentionally used (Boomer, 1984; Page & Pinnell, 1979; Piaget, 1966).

Psycholinguistic Theory. Alternatively, psycholinguistic theorists argue that language use, learning, and thinking are driven by students' innate capacity to seek and reflect upon the meanings gained through seeing, feeling, and doing. Psycholinguistic theorists recommend that language ability is best developed through the language experience approach (see Chapter 4), personal letter writing, plays, debates, counseling, conversations that engage active listening, and problem-solving lessons that build an appreciation for the worth of clear-thinking. These theorists posit that articulating and examining beliefs, sharing and exploring ideas, and talking through plans/problems are important to learning (K. Goodman 1987; F. Smith, 1988).

Mastery Learning or Subskill Theory.   Subskill Theory proposes that language use, and learning/thinking maturity is attained by the sequential mastery of basic skills (Bloom, 1956). Subskill theorists believe that different working systems (skills, subskills, abilities, preferences, inclinations, dispositions, and prior knowledge) interact when one encounters material of variant difficulties. This theory relegates as much as 30 percent of overall learning and thinking power to the attitudes, beliefs, and values one holds, and supports a need for continuous instruction throughout adulthood.

STAGES OF LEARNING TO SPEAK

Regardless of which theory (or theories) most accurately explains language development, knowing them helps you understand what students must do to say a new word or thought. It is possible that future research will uncover that one ideology explains how certain words are learned and another describes how thoughts emerge. On the other hand, it might be that some students learn through one means and others through another process. While research seeks a more definitive explanation for language acquisition, we now know that most students pass through the following stages as they learn to speak.

Birth to Age Two.   Most children say their first, recognizable English words at about one year of age. (However, children differ; Albert Einstein did not say his first word until age 4!) These first words students say are called **holophrastic speech.** *One word is meant to convey the same meaning as complete thoughts and sentences relay for adults.* Most children begin to put two words together by age two (e.g., "Mother come" . . . "All gone" . . . "Daddy toast"). However, when these two-word statements are used, they mean different things at different times. For example, when a baby says, "me milk" at breakfast, it means "I want some milk." When said at lunch it means "I don't want any more milk." At the evening meal it means "I can't reach my milk."

Two to Five Years.   Speaking vocabulary expands rapidly during these ages. At this stage *students acquire the ability to associate words with mental images and past experiences,* an ability Piaget (1966) labeled **symbolic function** or **telegraphic speech.** Such speech received its name from the telegraph which *uses content words to convey meaning.* With telegraphic speech, children use single words to signify events, experiences, and things that are not present in the child's immediate environment, e.g., "Daddy

TABLE 3-1

Major Stages of Oral Language Development

APPROXIMATE AGE	ORAL LANGUAGE ACCOMPLISHMENTS
5–6 years	*Uses pronouns and verbs in present and past tense *Uses complex sentences more frequently
6–7 years	*Speaks in complex sentences with adjectival clauses *Begins to use conditional dependent clauses
7–8 years	*Uses relative pronouns as objects in subordinate adjectival clauses *Uses gerund phrases as objects of the verb
8–10 years	*Uses connectors to relate concepts to general ideas *Begins to use present participles active, perfect participles, and the gerund as object of the preposition
11–13 years	*Uses complex sentences with subordinate clauses of concession introduced by connectives to frame hypotheses and envision their consequences *Uses auxiliary verbs more often *Uses longer communication units and subordinate adjectival clauses *Uses nouns modified by participle or participle phrases, gerund phrases, adverbial infinitives, and compound predicates more frequently
14 years	*Includes details in important message ideas
15 years	*Uses strategies in learning vocabulary
16 years	*Uses strategies in learning grammatical constructions
17 years	*Makes changes in elaborations based on illustrations
18 years	*Makes interesting questions and comments

Adapted from Walter Loban, *Language Development: Kindergarten Through Grade Twelve* (Urbana, IL: National Council of Teachers of English, 1976), pp. 81–84; and Christine C. Pappas, Barbara Z. Kiefer, & Linda S. Levotik, *An Integrated Language Perspective in the Elementary School* (White Plains, NY: Longman, 1990).

gone bye-bye." Soon, the need to use "function words," such as *is, to, the, that, of,* and *and* arises. Only when children acquire function words will they move beyond a dependence on nouns and verbs to communicate. Most children also learn to use endings on verbs and nouns (-ed, -s, -tion) before age five.

At some point between two and five years of age, children begin to organize language into typical English sentences. Chomsky (1975), a nativistic theorist, suggests that this reorganization results from a neurological development that causes maturation in the language-acquisition device. He hypothesizes that this device metamorphosizes in a manner similar to the transformation of larvae into butterflies. By age three, children's speaking vocabularies reach 1,000 words and, in their next three years of life, their vocabularies increase fivefold. Thus, by the time children enter first grade, most will have a speaking vocabulary of 6,000 words.

Ages Six to Seven.   When children are placed in the social setting of school, they begin to use language to ritualize, instrumentalize, regulate, personalize, heuristicalize, imagine, and inform. Instructions you provide during these ages extend students' sentences so they convey more accurate meanings, e.g., when they say, "Cinderella is happy," you add to their language by responding, "Yes, Cinderella has a bright future and overcame problems, didn't she?"

Many students in first and second grade, however, still mispronounce words that contain *v*, *th*, *ch*, and *sh*. Many also substitute *w* for *r* and *l* in some words (Reed, 1978).

Ages Eight Through Thirteen.   From second through eighth grade, the quality of oral language is greatly reliant upon the types of instruction students receive. While wide ranges of development can be expected during these years, the major oral language accomplishments to be expected from good language programs appear in Table 3-1.

In brief, there are six reasons why you must teach students to speak more effectively; five major theories to explain how speech evolves: behavioristic, nativistic, cognitive field, psycholinguistic, and mastery learning or subskill; and four stages your students will pass through as their speaking ability matures. You will now read how your instruction can assist students to make more effective requests, gain control, relate, express feelings, give information, imagine, and investigate. You will also learn the "daily dozen discussion strategies" that advance oral communication, redirect students' incorrect answers, and eliminate students' speaking deficiencies.

PUTTING THEORY INTO PRACTICE
TEACHING STUDENTS TO SPEAK MORE EFFECTIVELY

You will teach students to express themselves effectively by employing the following dozen actions on a daily basis.

1. *Extend students' vocabularies, deepen their connotations, and enhance their delivery daily.* As Michael Halliday (1982) stated: "A child doesn't need to know any linguistics in order to use language; but [you] need to know some linguistics to understand how the process takes place . . . [and] what is going wrong when it doesn't" (p.11). **Linguists** (*researchers who study language*) have analyzed all the tools that oral language provides effective speakers. Through your diagnoses, students' facility with each of the following "tools" can be developed so their thoughts become more explicitly and effectively communicated. You will teach students to use language in seven ways.

Instrumental.   Productive speakers use oral language to make requests that satisfy their needs. By school age, children should use instrumental language appropriately, easily, and nonabrasively, e.g., "I would like . . ." "I want . . ." and "I need." If students are unable to make such requests, model how to do so. Also, ask students what they want, like, and need, and place them in groups with peers who assert themselves appropriately.

Regulatory.   Effective speakers use oral language to control others, and to receive as well as issue commands. One strategy that improves students' use of regulatory language is to stop periodically, when reading orally (or discussing a topic in class), and describe the regulatory strategy a book character (or peer) used skillfully. Describe why this oral language statement influenced you so positively, and suggest ways others could use similar regulatory expressions in their interactions with others.

Interactional.   Impressive speakers use oral language to build strong personal relationships. For many students, speaking in school will become their first use of interactional language. They need your help to learn to (1) establish rapport, (2) include others, (3) build status, and (4) persuade more than one person at a time. You can strengthen their interactional language skills by praising students who do so in their small-group work sessions, and by engaging the class in activities that are described later in this chapter.

Personal.   Competent speakers use speech to express their feelings, talents, attitudes, concerns, and worries. As students progress through the grades they become more adept in expressing these thoughts and feelings. In the process they create their own identity and begin to realize their point of unity with and uniqueness from others. You may employ two strategies to assist this process: (1) model personal language by telling students your feelings, attitudes, and concerns; and (2) honor students' concerns by asking follow-up questions as well as paraphrasing, such as, "If I understood you correctly, you feel . . ."

Informational.   Informational oral language is the ability to give and receive new knowledge. Critical Thinking Activity 3 builds students' skill in relaying information and asking questions (p. 98).

Imaginative.   Convincing speakers know how to use oral language to stimulate an invention and the imagination. Developing students' creativity through oral language is increasingly important because our world is becoming exponentially more complex and competitive. If students are to succeed they must have new ideas and pass them on to others through oral descriptions. Moreover, they must learn to adjust to rapid changes in patterns of communication, thinking, and life-style because these become outdated rapidly. While there will be many activities to develop this imaginative function presented in Chapter 11, you begin to enhance students' imaginative language by asking them to imagine scenes from books you read before you show the pictures from them.

Heuristic. Forceful speakers use language to explore and investigate reasons. Because today's students can more easily access large volumes of current and past knowledge, they have more opportunities to talk about relationships among these knowledge bases than we did at their age. Through instruction on posing useful questions, students can better employ their innate curiosities to increase their knowledge (e.g., They learn to ask "why," "what is . . ." and "I wonder why . . .").

To sum up, oral language performs many functions for effective oral communicators. The first step in your oral language program is to assess and improve your students' abilities to use oral language to: (1) make requests that satisfy their needs; (2) express their feelings and opinions; (3) perform rituals and engage in culturally determined discourse with social grace; (4) imagine and "field-test" new ideas (where students' voices become the chisels and paint of new creations); (5) offer information; and (6) regulate. By reading books (or your reading of books to them) from Notecards 5 and 6 students can develop these functions, as characters in these books manifest appropriate use of each function.

NOTECARD 5: FOLK TALES, TALL TALES, FAIRY TALES, LEGENDS, AND MYTHS FOR SHARING, READING, AND STORYTELLING

The Gingerbread Man by Paul Galdone
British Folktales by Katherine Briggs
Iroquois Stories: Heroes and Heroines, Monsters and Magic by Joseph Bruchac
Italian Folk Tales by Italo Calvino
Best-Loved Folktales of the World by Joanna Cole
Mexican Fairy Tales by J. H. Cornyn
Legends of Earth, Air, Fire, and Water by Eric Handley and Tessa Handley
One Potatoe, Two Potatoe: The Folklore of American Children by Mary and Herbert Knapp
World Tales by Idries Shah
How Davy Crockett Got a Bearskin Coat by Wyatt Blassingame
Big Sixteen by Mary Calhoun
Lion and the Ostrich Chicks and Other African Tales by Ashley Bryan

The Night of the Stars by Douglas Gutierrez and Maria Hernandez
The Snow Child by Freya Littledale
Strega Nona by Tomie DePaola
Canadian Wonder Tales by C. Macmillan and E. Cleaver
World Folktales: A Scribner Resource Collection by Atelia Clarkson and Gilbert Cross
Tales from Indian Classics by Rupa Gupta
The People Could Fly by Virginia Hamilton
Scandinavian Legends and Folk-Tales by Gwyn Jones
Tokoloshi: African Folk Takes Retold by Diana Pitcher
Sally Ann Thunder and Whirlwind Crockett by Caron Lee Cohen
Old Stormalong by Adele Deleeuw

(cont'd)

NOTECARD 5   (cont'd)

The First Morning by Margery Bernstein and Janet Kobrin

Why the Sun and Moon Live in the Sky by Elphinstone Dayrell

Giant Treasury of Brer Rabbit by Anne Hessey

Paul Bunyan Finds A Wife by Adele Deleeuw

Febold Feboldson by Ariane Dewey

Mike Fink by Harold W. Felton

John Henry by Erza Jack Keats

Casey Jones by Glen Rounds

American Tall Tales by Adrien Stoutenburg

Why Mosquitos Buzz in People's Ears by V. Aardema

The Tale of the Bluebonnet: An Old Tale of Texas and *The Legend of the Indian Paintbrush* by Tomie dePaola

Stories to Solve: Folktales from Around the World by George Shannon

Such a Noise! by Aliana Brodmann

Pecos Bill by Ariane Dewey

What Happens Next? by Janina Domanska

"The McBroom Series" by Sid Fleischman

Paul Bunyan by Steven Kellogg

Heroes in American Folklore by Irwin Shapiro

Hush Up! by Jim Aylesworth

Rip Van Winkle by M. Gipson

The Fool and the Fish by Aleksandr Nikolayevich Afanasev

The Little Match Girl by H. C. Andersen

Favorite Greek Myths by Mary Pope Osborne

How the Ox Star Fell from Heaven by Lily Toy Hong

For additional stories, see:

Handbooks for Storytellers by Caroline Bauer

In the Storyteller's Soucebook: A Subject, Title, and Motif for Children by Margaret McDonald

Fairy Tales, Fables, Legends, and Myths: Using Folk Literature in Your Classroom by B. Bosma

---

2. *Your language arts program should diagnose students' oral grammar needs.* By age eight most students will have created their own linguistic speaking system, even if it contains nonstandard grammatical structures. It takes time and patience before some students replace less effective linguistic patterns with more powerful sentence structures and word choices. You accelerate students' progress through lessons that include unison/choral readings, chants, and songs containing standard English sentence patterns. Such activities also minimize any student's embarrassment as he/she may struggle to learn standard English. As you watch such activities in section 3 of the videotape, notice how many students (even in the reduced-risk settings that group oral recitations provide) struggle as they replicate basic sentence patterns that are not a part of their personally created linguistic system.

Because new words are continuously invented and standards for acceptable grammar are constantly changing, celebrate your students' personal speaking system and their innovative uses of English. Such attention emphasizes that the goal in speaking is to communicate. In your student-centered program, dialectical diversity is honored as the illustrations they are of our language's infinite and multifaceted nature and beauty.

When students' dialects interfere with their ability to communicate or comprehend, identify which nonstandard features are causing problems and use activities in Chapter 8 to overcome them. Because incorrect word choices and inappropriate expressions are interpreted as an absence of background knowledge or education, oral grammar errors can often lead those listening to your students to an incorrect inference. Without your direction, students' messages may be demeaned as their listeners think: If this person has limited information or education [inappropriate grammatical usage], I'm not going to support his/her idea. He/She may lack the

Instead of correcting students' oral grammar errors in public, model standard phrases in private conferences. Notice how Dina Mahoney is teaching Homer to say "There are four . . ." instead of "There is four . . ." during a conference where she asks Homer to repeat after her, "There are 3, there are 4 . . ."

strength to actualize it. I don't want to be judged "dumb" because I believed in a loser. Therefore, while you accept students' present speaking patterns, strengthen their power of communication by making them aware of how variations in oral language could influence their listeners. Oral grammar and language differences can also transfer to students' writings as shown in Figure 3-1.

Deciding what to do about students' oral language usage is a complex problem. To illustrate let's turn to the most obvious language variation, **dialect** (*characteristics of speech peculiar to a region, community, social group, or occupation that deviates from standard speech, including jargon, slang, and coined words*). Just determining which items of dialectical usage are unacceptable is difficult enough, since there are 25 different dialects in the American version of English (see Figure 3-2).

3. *Eliminate distracting vocal qualities in students' speech that limit their communicative effectiveness.* Students need your help to develop a melodic pitch, tone, speed, and appropriate juncture. Students' voices that are monotone, nasal, gruff, or whiny are improved through activities described on pages 93–98. Enlist the assistance of a speech therapist, if necessary.

You may assist students to create a volume that makes hearing their messages easy and enjoyable, and to eliminate "crutch words" (e.g., "O.K.," "ah," "you know," and other words used as "fillers of silence" for students uncomfortable with the time it takes to transfer inner thoughts to words). Crutch words are eliminated by teaching students to construct sentences they can say to replace a "crutch word." For example, if a student uses the word "O.K.," teach that student to substitute the following sentence as soon as he hears himself say the "Oh" in "OK": "Oh, the next thing I want to say is . . ." Soon, the crutch word and substitute sentence will disappear from the student's speaking.

4. *Intentionally plan lessons that improve students' selection of content and vocabulary in speech.* You can do so by providing in-class opportunities for individual students to study a topic no one else has examined. This student's vocabulary expands as he/she shares this experience with classmates and explains the content words relative to the topic. Second, ask students to read their writings or children's literature aloud in small groups. In the discussions that evolve, most "student readers" will use the exact words they read to answer questions. This self-initiated use will likely transfer these terms to their personal speaking vocabularies. Books for kindergarten through grade 3 that work well for this activity are included on Notecard 6.

FIGURE 3-1
African-American Dialect Reflected in Written Language

Filimon   Oct 10/30/90
Mrs McCann
One day dewos a girl name Lisa and Lisa
was por and she gad tow sisters day
wer men tow Lisa and One day
Lisa fund a bare god moter and she
tolder to maicer a dres for she can
go to the ball and at the ball she
faund a pries is name was Bortman
and he tolder if he wonsto dans and
she sed yes and Lisa sed to look
at the wendow and Lisa wint run in
home and gat mere

The End

FIGURE 3-2
Dialectical Regions in the United States

NOTECARD 6: CHILDREN'S LITERATURE TO DEVELOP STUDENTS' READING, SPEAKING, WRITING, AND LISTENING VOCABULARIES

The following books begin a vocabulary development program for students in Kindergarten through Grade 3. The number in the parenthesis after the titles is the total number of words in the books.

A Woggle of Witches (139) by Adrienne Adams
I Sure am Glad to See You, Blackboard Bear (133) by Martha Alexander
Cloudy with a Chance of Meatballs (419) by Judi Barrett
So Do I (75) by Barbara Bel Geddes
My Red Umbrella (68) by Robert Bright
Arthur's Tooth (311) by Marc Brown
Good Night Moon (54) by Margaret Brown
Two Dog Biscuits (254) by Beverly Cleary
Miss Rumphius (418) by Barbara Cooney
The Robbery at the Diamond Dog Diner (390) by Eileen Christelow
Mr. Murphy's Marvelous Invention (441) by Eileen Christelow
The Chick and the Duckling (32) by M. Ginsburg
Have you Seen my Duckling? (9) by Nancy Tafuri

Grandpa Bear (352) by Bonnie Pryor
If You Give a Mouse a Cookie (122) by Laura Joffe Numeroff
A Three Hat Day (340) by Laura Geringer
The Story Grandmother Told (147) by Martha Alexander
Animals Should Definitely Not Wear Clothing (65) by Judith Barrett
Hester (128) by Byron Barton
Pelle's New Suit (158) by Elsa Beskow
Arthur's Nose (150) by Marc Brown
Once a Mouse (156) by Marcia Brown
The Purse (272) by Kathy Caple
Jim's Dog Muffins (232) by Miriam Cohen
Nothing Ever Happens on My Block (80) by Ellen Raskin
Blackboard Bear (64) by Margaret Alexander

THE CHALLENGE OF DIVERSITY

The most recent census reported that two million students in the United States cannot speak, read, or write English. If you speak their first language, you can develop these students' oral and aural vocabularies by "code switching" from English to their first language as you give directions and lead discussions. For example, you can provide an in-depth description in English, followed by a brief description in the first language of your second language learners. At the end of lessons you distrubute a sheet with all the English questions you want second language students to ask each other. If they ask their partners appropriately, they place a checkmark beside the question. The pair then works together to write, in English, the answer given to that question. If the pair finishes early, they can write new questions they will ask a second pair.

Similarly, shy students often take longer to develop effective oral language than their more aggressive peers. You increase their risk-taking abilities by scaffolding as Lisa Harding demonstrates in the photo, and by giving them one-to-one speaking responsibilities with classmates. These responsibilities include showing a new student "the ropes" at school, becoming a classroom monitor, and explaining assignments to a classmate who arrives late.

5. *Discussion periods are preceded with time to explore a topic to be canvassed.* By establishing this precedence students will have a depth of information to share. One of the benefits of creating such informative and interactional discussions is that classmates will increase their appreciation and value for their classmates' oral exchanges. They will *learn from each other.* A second informative and interactional discussion is to engage students in a "conversation club." (Students list topics they want to discuss and attend a small group to discuss the topic for which they have the strongest opinion or facts to report.) During self-initiated conversation clubs, note which people (a) extend the discussion without coaxing; (b) hold listeners' attention; (c) check for accuracy without being told to do so; (d) ask questions for clarification; (e) state novel but provable points; (f) give solutions or compromises for conflicting data; and (g) have inviting vocal habits. Mark this information on the *Individual Student's Oral Language Needs Monitor* (Figure 3-3) and select new objectives to teach other students who do not exhibit these informative and interpersonal language uses.

6. *Meet the needs of all your students, regardless of their present level of speaking ability, and their familiarity with English.*

Once you've taken these steps, both shy and second language learners should become eager to share their thoughts. (To further assist shy students you can employ the strategies in *Bring Out the Talents and Oral Expression Skills of Shy Students,* Collins, 1989b, Educational Research Dissemination.)

One of the reasons it is important to develop shy students' speaking confidence is that they should graduate from school able to explain their thoughts. With your help, shy students can overcome timidity of thought. No student should leave your class believing that "If I don't say anything, I won't be called upon to repeat it" (Calvin Coolidge).

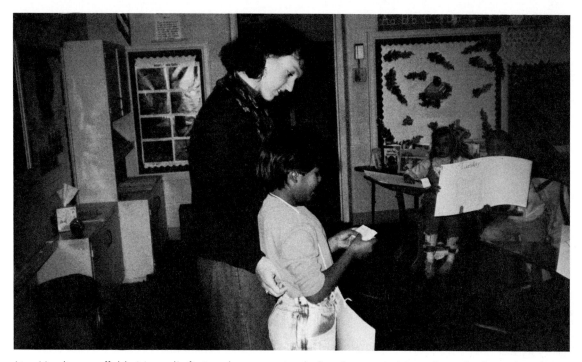

Lisa Harding scaffolds Manuel's first oral presentation before his peers. Manuel's smile shows how he is overcoming his inhibitions under Lisa's direction.

7. *Your oral language program will include "celebrative experiences."* **Celebrative experiences** *are events where students exert extraordinary effort and invest strong emotions to reach a personally important goal.* These goals are usually shared with an audience (e.g., giving a play at school or a speech to the community). When students have the oral skill and responsibility to map language so as to create vivid, celebrative experiences for others, their desire to perfect oral expressions intensifies. In addition, through celebrative experiences, students create positive and successful experiences with oral language that transfer into pleasurable lifetime memories.

Celebrative experiences are so powerful because, in their creation, students use all functions of oral language: they imagine, inform, command, share, identify, relate, and satisfy needs as they perfect their "performance." Through these experiences students also learn to self-evaluate, and have a voice in the world. Students internalize that language in school is like language in the real world; their speaking is not followed by correcting or grading. Their language is used to make a difference, to connect, and to further others' knowledge, just as they will do in the world.

While celebrative experiences occasionally occur serendipitously, it is helpful to allot time each grading period for at least one celebrative experience. During the first grading period, you can design the activity. In subsequent periods students fashion their own experiences and use their own innovative thinking processes. In segment 3 of the videotape, you will view a group of fifth-graders practicing a celebrative event. You'll notice the intensity of their work as they read *Sick*, by Shel Silverstein. You'll also watch how students' intonation, stress, and pitch are being refined, which was the oral language objective for this activity.

FIGURE 3-3
Individual Student's Oral Language Needs Monitor

Student's Name _____ Date _____

___ 1. Speech problems: substitutions ("w" for "v"), omissions ("member" for "remember"), insertions, and distortions.
___ 2. Pitch
___ 3. Tone
___ 4. Speed
___ 5. Volume
___ 6. Crutch words
___ 7. Good content
___ 8. Good vocabulary
___ 9. Instrumental: "I want"
___ 10. Regulatory: "Do this"
___ 11. Interactional: "We . . ."
___ 12. Informational: "This is"
___ 13. Imaginative: "I wonder"
___ 14. Heuristic: "What is?"
___ 15. Overcoming shyness
___ 16. Celebrative experience
___ 17. Extend small-group discussions without coaxing
___ 18. Check for accuracy of spoken statements
___ 19. Ask questions for clarification
___ 20. State novel but provable points
___ 21. Give solutions or compromises for conflicting data
___ 22. Dialect does not interfere with meaning
___ 23. Stuttering, malocclusions, cleft palate are absent

8. *You will question often.* You will ask questions, design discussions, and correct a wide variety of speech difficulties daily. Hilda Taba (1975) stated that *constructing effective questions* is "by far the most influential teaching act." When your questions are built upon the following principles, you will encourage maximum thinking and language development (Aulls, 1978; Durkin 1978–1979; Collins, 1989). Good questions, prepared in advance, elicit different thinking/language abilities (see Bloom's Taxonomy of Cognitive Development, Figure 3-4, to assist in the preparation of the variety of questions you ask).

You also narrow or expand students' thinking by using different types of verbs in your questions. Some verbs (see page 103) build students' accuracy; others expand students' elaborative skills.

Your questions will be *respondent-centered rather than text-centered.* **Respondent-centered** questions are those that do not have *one correct answer, but enable students to defend the validity of their personal response.* Alternatively, **text-centered** questions ask for only one answer, and that answer is usually *given in a book or by the speaker. Text-centered questions merely elicit recall of previously stated information.* Respondent-centered questions broaden the range of possible responses, and teach that *most questions and problems in life* *do not have only one answer*. Likewise, such questions elicit longer responses and students' deeper thinking. To illustrate, contrast the following respondent-centered questions to the subsequent, and less powerful, text-centered one:

1. Respondent-centered: "Do you agree or disagree with the author of this poem, and why?" or, "What do you think the author meant by . . . ?"
2. Text-centered: "Who is the author of this poem?" or "What does the author mean by . . . ?"

Two ways you can create respondent-centered questions are to *not ask a question for which you know the answer*, and to *place the word "you" after the verb in your question*. By asking such questions, discussions are authentic (e.g., in life we most often ask questions to find answers we do not know). Examples of such questions appear in Figure 3-5.

FIGURE 3-4
Bloom's Taxonomy of Cognitive Development

The following levels of thinking can be used to develop objectives or to design activities, questions, or learning centers.

Use the web below to select verbs (processes) and nouns (products) when asking questions at the various levels of thinking. Each pie shape represents one thinking level. They are sequenced from 1 to 6 in order of complexity.

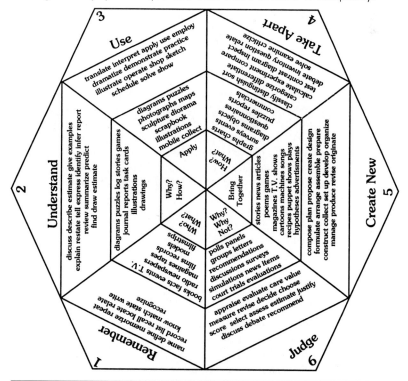

FIGURE 3-5
Types of Respondent-Centered Questions

QUESTIONS OF CLARIFICATION

What do you mean by _____ ?

What is your main point?

How does _____ relate
   to _____ ?

Could you put that another way?

What do you think is the main issue
   here?

Is your basic point _____
   or _____ ?

Let me see if I understand you; do you
   mean _____ or _____ ?

How does this relate to our discus-
   sion/problem/issue?

What do you think John meant by his
   remark? What did you take John to
   mean?

Jane, would you summarize in your
   own words what Richard said? . . .
   Richard, is that what you meant?

Could you give me an example?

Would this be an example: _____ ?

Could you explain that further?

Would you say more about that?

Why do you say that?

QUESTIONS THAT PROBE ASSUMPTIONS

What are you assuming?

What is Karen assuming?

What could we assume instead?

You seem to be assuming _____ .
   Do I understand you correctly?

All of your reasoning depends on the
   idea that _____ . Why have
   you based your reasoning

on _____ rather than
   _____ ?

You seem to be assuming _____ .
   How would you justify taking this
   for granted?

Is it always the case? Why do you
   think the assumption holds here?

QUESTIONS THAT PROBE REASONS, EVIDENCE, AND CAUSES

What would be an example?

What are your reasons for saying that?

What other information do we need to
   know?

Could you explain your reasons to us?

Is that good evidence for believing that?

Are those reasons adequate?

Is there reason to doubt that evidence?

Who is in a position to know if that is
   the case?

What would you say to someone who
   said _____ ?

What do you think the cause is?

By what reasoning did you come to
   that conclusion?

How could we go about finding out
   whether that is true?

Can someone else give evidence to
   support that response?

How do you know?

Why did you say that?

Why do you think that is true?

What led you to that belief?

Do you have any evidence for that?

How does that apply to this case?

What difference does that make?

What would convince you otherwise?

What accounts for that?

How did this come about?

QUESTIONS ABOUT VIEWPOINTS OR PERSPECTIVES

You seem to be approaching this issue
   from _____ perspective. Why
   have you chosen this rather than
   that perspective?

How would other groups/types of people respond? Why? What would influence them?

How could you answer the objection
   that _____ would make?

Can/did anyone see this another way?

What would someone who disagrees
   say?

What is an alternative?

How are Ken's and Roxanne's ideas
   alike? Different?

QUESTIONS THAT PROBE IMPLICATIONS AND CONSEQUENCES

What are you implying by that?	What if that happened, what else
When you say _____ , are you	would also happen as a result?
implying _____ ?	Why?

9. *You will assist students' participation in discussions.* There are five instructional steps to develop your students' discussion skills. First, at the beginning of the year read Diane Stanley's *How to Carry on a Discussion* (New York: Macmillan, 1983). Through this book, students see how Peter Fieldmouse learned the importance of good listening skills in group work. Second, you open your first discussion periods of the year with a "polling technique," i.e., ask students to choose which of two responses they support. Ask, "How many believe William Armstrong should have allowed Sounder to die? How many believe that that was the best ending to the book? How many believe that William Armstrong would have built a stronger ending if Sounder had lived?"

The third step also occurs early in the year. You assist students to create their own rules for large and small group discussions (e.g., when will it be necessary to raise hands, how will peers' comments be analyzed, and how will disputes be resolved). A sample list of rules they could use in fashioning their own appears in Figure 3-6.

Fourth, tell students that you do not want immediate answers to questions you pose. You prefer that they take a moment to think before they speak. Request more than one student's opinion or point of view (e.g., "Give me another interpretation"; "What do you think another reason could be?"; and "I'd like to hear two points of view about . . ."). You respond to their answers by stating how much you appreciate the time they took to reflect on these answers. If they ask you to repeat your question, restate it as closely as possible to the original wording because students report that a loose paraphrase confuses them (Collins, 1988). Similarly, refrain from restating student answers, as doing so is interpreted that an answer is not adequate unless you add your authority by repeating it. It is valuable to tape-record your discussions periodically; listening to them isolates your (and your students') speaking needs.

Last, in selecting items for discussion, relate topics to the needs and world of your students (e.g., in discussing "Huck Finn" instead of asking for author's purpose for writing the story, state, "I told you a list of things Mark Twain was 'making fun of' about his society in the story of Huck Finn. Is this book an accurate mirror of our society today, and the people you know?"). By asking questions in relevant ways, you not only establish topics of interest, but encourage students to treat them on their own terms. The topic choice may be yours or theirs, but the elaborations belong to the

FIGURE 3-6

Rules for Good Group Discussions

RULES FOR GOOD DISCUSSIONS:	RULES THAT LEAD TO GOOD DISCUSSIONS IN OUR GROUP				
	Name				
1. Listen to each other.					
2. Think before you talk.					
3. Talk in a normal voice.					
4. Stick to the subject.					
5. Do not put down someone's idea.					
6. Take turns.					
7. Encourage everyone to practice.					
8. Use person's name when speaking to them.					
9. One person speaks at a time.					

Note to Teacher: This is the progress I think our group made today in our discussion: _____

_____

_____

_____

students. Nystrand (1991) has found that such co-constructions increase student average oral response length from 5 to 17 words. In such discussions, students frequently introduce contradictions and complications they notice.

10. *You will use* **deliberate silence.** Sollon (1983) stated that "deliberate silence is *the most intriguing alternative to questions and one of the most effective to build student's oral speaking abilities*" (p. 38). He suggests that when students finish a response, or falter, you assist their thinking by being deliberately quiet:

Sam: "I think Dave got tricked. Does anyone agree?"

[Your deliberate silence]

THE CHALLENGE OF DIVERSITY

Johnston (1992) has found that some teachers are likely to wait longer for a response when they call upon more able than less able students. If you are quick to call upon a second child for the answer, it can reduce the first student's self-esteem; because the student begins to believe that he/she can't come up with answers.

To draw less able students into a discussion, ask a question with multiple possible responses, where all possibilities can be correct, e.g., "How do you feel about . . . ?" "Do you prefer _____ or _____ ?" "What do you see as the future for . . . ?" If you prefer additional strategies for building productive class discussions, refer to Collins (1987, 1992a).

Troy: "If I had him here I'd say, "Mr. Dodds, let me take you aside and give you a piece of advice." [Your deliberate silence].

George: "Maybe he could be a little more tactful."

11. *Once students have had several successful discussion periods, they benefit from more advanced discussion formats.* These include **exploratory, fishbowl, integrative,** and **paired discussions. Exploratory discussions** deal with complex issues. *Students choose aspects of an issue that they want to explore. Then students meet in small groups to have "issue-specific" discussions, and share their separate analyses and evaluations.* **Fishbowl discussions** *occur when one-third of the class sits in the center of the room to discuss a topic.* The rest of the class circles this group. Those who observe the discussion note oral expression improvements that could have been made, gaps in thinking about the topic that occurred, and new connections that the discussions caused them to make between topic ideas.

Integrative discussions are those that *end with each student's written or oral responses to points made during the exchange.* Integrative discussions can be completed in several ways, but Osburg (1989) has had success in using two student leaders to begin integrative discussion. These leaders come to the front of the room with differing responsibilities. One is the *journal-assigner.* This student writes his/her starter topic/thought on the board. Classmates then make a ten-minute journal entry concerning that student's opinion over a topic under study. When the class finishes, the second student (the *sharing-moderator*) guides the sharing of entries, as both students seek as many diverse positions as possible. Finally, the sharing-moderator is responsible for summarizing, and bringing the discussion to a close.

Another type of integrative discussion is when students turn to a partner to define a new term, construct summaries, or share personal anecdotes. When pairs have discussed their viewpoints, one member of the twosome shares their thinking with the entire group. This type of pairing is demonstrated in videotape segment 4.

12. *Handle "off-the-track answers" and eliminate your students' inappropriate discussion habits.* During class exchanges, students have two problems. They lead discussions in counterproductive directions, and give answers that bore classmates. When students lead discussions in ancillary directions, you can redirect their comments by saying:

1. "That's a different thought, and an interesting idea. It relates to the next point in our discussion by . . ."
2. "I've not thought of that before. How do you relate that to the point we just discussed?"
3. "I think I understand what you mean. Are you saying that . . . (tying students' comments to the main part of the discussion)?"
4. "That's a possibility. Are there other interpretations?"
5. "That's a college-type idea!"
6. "I like it when you tell us what you are thinking. This time when you did so you . . . (pointing out an improvement in the students' oral speaking abilities)."
7. "It sounds like you have done some original thinking. How does _____ fit with the conclusions we have drawn thus far?"
8. "That causes me to wonder about . . ."

When students dominate a discussion, and lose their audience, you need to diagnose the cause. Such students may have an unfulfilled need for attention, or are unaware of their distracting speech habits. If students ramble due to a need for attention, you help by detecting and acknowledging feelings they express in recitations. For example, if the class is discussing how to include more effective adjectives in their writings and one student injects that his uncle is a very good writer, and is coming to visit soon, and drives a red truck, and so on, you detect this student's feelings about, apprehension over, or longing for his/her uncle's visit, and acknowledge those feelings. You ask a yes/no question concerning the feeling, such as, "I think you are fond of your uncle. Am I correct?" Once the student answers, you direct the discussion toward the topic at hand, and the student is better able to listen. This type of response also addresses the student's need to be understood, without causing embarrassment for his/her extraneous statements.

If students' problems stem from distracting speech habits, teach them to state their main idea first. Then they are to stop after that sentence. If other students ask questions, they add the information desired. If classmates do not ask for more information, the speakers are to interpret the silence positively. It likely means that their statements were effectively made and communicated so completely that supplemental comments were unnecessary.

13. *Limit the times you tell students they are wrong.* "When children give a wrong answer, it is not so often they are wrong, as they are answering another question. It is our job to find out what question they are in fact answering" (Bruner, 1986). You can use the strategies in Figure 3-7 as responses to students' incorrect answers.

THE CHALLENGE OF DIVERSITY

African-American students make more episodic- than topic-centered responses. They also talk about topics out of the sequence in which they were introduced. Being aware of the value these personally embellishing statements hold for these students increases your understanding; e.g., when you state, "I'm just going to start this story on Martin Luther King" and a student interrupts to answer to a repondent-centered question you asked earlier. The student says, "My mama was 19 when he died." You will better understand when the student is responding out of sequence. He is responding to the question you asked 15 minutes ago, i.e., "What do you already know about Martin Luther King?" (Cazden, 1988)

---

14. *You can help students* **articulate** *(the ability to make speech sounds correctly).* This is done in a one-to-one conference by showing them how a sound is made and having them watch your lips and imitate you as they examine their trials in a mirror.

Occasionally, articulation errors are interpreted as reading errors. To avoid this misdiagnosis, write a familiar but short word and ask the child to say it. If the student gives the meaning of this word, but mispronounces it, the problem is probably related to articulation, not decoding difficulties.

Stuttering is *speaking with involuntary pauses, spasms, and repetitions or prolongations of sound and syllables.* It is among the most misunderstood of speech difficulties. While the difficulty may relate to a psychological problem, it is not necessarily so, nor may correction be possible. If students ask how to overcome the difficulty, advise them not to pressure themselves, and refer them to an adult who overcame stuttering. This adult can teach diaphragm movements and other techniques that they used to overcome stuttering. You can also secure books for the students to read concerning stuttering in your Professional Portfolio (see Chapter 14).

Malocclusion is *a failure of teeth to meet properly, causing gaps in alignment.* Problems with speech that result from such gaps often correct themselves, but you will need to monitor the ramifications these gaps have upon speaking habits. **Cleft palate** is *a pathological problem caused by the roof of the mouth failing to close before a child is born.* Surgery corrects the palate, and children must relearn to move the air in their mouth to form sounds. During the period of reeducation, you can explain to classmates how sounds are made and why someone is having difficulty speaking.

As a review, your responsibilities to advance students' oral expression are exercised in many ways each day. You will also alter aspects of their language that interfere with their potential to have their speech understood and appreciated by others. Such alternatives most often occur through private one-to-one conferences. You will now discover four powerful daily lessons that target specific oral language competencies.

FIGURE 3-7
Responses to Students' Incorrect Answers

1. *Think again.* When students have sufficient background to answer a question, respond to their first "less than correct attempts" by asking them to "think again." This response reassures students that they can produce an effective response, if only allowed a little more time and thought. Use this strategy to respond to a student's insufficient answer when you are 99 percent certain that the student can respond more effectively with a second try.

2. *Give a relevant prompt.* If students give a partial answer, provide a relevant fact about the topic, and then reask the question (e.g., "Why do you think Cinderella didn't run away from her wicked stepmother and stepsisters?" Students do not answer. You prompt: "Placing yourself in Cinderella's shoes will help you understand what she could have thought.").

3. *Reword the question.* When you ask a question, and a student's answer suggests that your wording was vague, acknowledge this student's attempt and say, "Good try. Let me clarify my question. I think it confused you."

4. *Could you expand your answer for us? Why do you think so?* When students' answers appear to be off the point, ask them to explain their thinking. In many incidents the answer is relevant when the thoughts that support it are explicated.

5. *"Remember that. I'm going to return and ask for this information again."* When several answers students give demonstrate that they misunderstand major concepts in a discussion, provide more information. Once you provide this added material, tell students to remember it because you will call upon them to state thoughts about it before the class is over. Then as the class ends, you ask their thoughts about that information and the original concepts again.

6. *That would have been correct if . . .* If you recognize the reasoning behind a student's answers, follow the insufficient answer with, "That would have been correct if I had asked . . . but I am asking . . ." (restating your original question). For example, if you ask, "What do you do to organize paragraphs when you write?" and a student answers, "Combine sentences to make them less redundant," you respond by saying, "That is an effective sentence-revising strategy, but what I was asking for was a strategy you use in the drafting stage."

7. *Examples and nonexamples of possible solutions.* This discussion strategy can be used to close a lesson or as a review of possible information. It is based upon a multiple choice testing format, in that you supply several answers to a question you asked, and students select one of the choices, or generate a better solution. To illustrate, you are reviewing a student's language arts portfolio at the end of a grading period. You suggest three future goals, and ask the student to decide which he/she most values.

    Nonexamples are used to stimulate students' thinking by stating what a discussion is not designed to cover. For example, you begin a class dialogue by stating, "Yesterday we covered some of the ways you can decode words. Today we want to extend our discussion. I do not want you to tell me the names of the decoding strategies on your thinking guide. Instead, I want you to tell us a word you used one of the strategies to decode."

THE CHALLENGE OF DIVERSITY

Some speakers of nonstandard English and bilingual students have cultural traditions that dictate when it is acceptable to speak or remain silent. For example, Asian, Vietnamese, or Amish students may not answer you because they have been taught not to speak to adults. It is important that oral language instruction be sensitive to such psychological needs, social acceptability, and standards of propriety.

STRATEGIES THAT TEACH

DAILY LESSONS THAT IMPROVE STUDENTS' ORAL LANGUAGE

As you will notice, each of the following lessons incorporates principles from Chapters 1 and 2, culminates in real-world products, builds thinking, addresses student needs, and integrates the language arts.

CREATING LESSONS WITH AUDIO AND VIDEOTAPE RECORDINGS

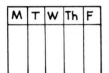

You can tape-record a practice session of a speech that students are to give in a public forum (such as a presentation to a boy or girl scout meeting). Students then critique this tape themselves or ask others to assist in noting areas for improvement, which makes the assessment authentic. This lesson also develops informative language items 1–6 and 23 in the *Individual Students' Oral Language Needs Monitor* (Figure 3-3, p. 84). Similarly, class discussions and formal presentations can be videotaped. A first tape recording can enable students to judge which discussion skill they want to improve; a second can be taped during a "dress rehearsal" to refine their performance prior to "opening night," or as a posttest.

CREATING LESSONS WITH PANEL DISCUSSIONS/DEBATES

Panel discussions *are formal discussions to present information.* **Debates** *are formal presentations that present opposing viewpoints.* In panel discussions, participants are assigned different topics to research. They discuss their topics before an audience who is less knowledgeable about the topic, and who asks questions.

Often local access cable television networks welcome student panel discussions on talk shows. Through such broadcasts, students' work becomes authentic. They learn to use facts (from their research) to support their opinions, and develop interactional, heuristic, and informative language functions (Items 11–14 and 16–23 on the *Individual Students' Oral Language Needs Monitor* and group thinking skills). Figure 3-8 can be used to evaluate speeches, debates, show-and-tell lessons, and panel discussions.

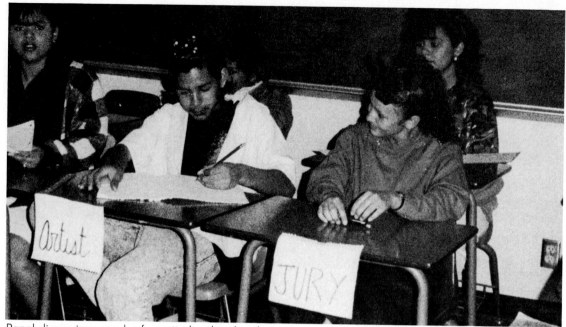

Panel discussions can be formatted as legal trials to increase students' experience with the speaking skills employed in our legal system.

Some children in grades 4–6 are attracted to, and benefit from, "formalized" discussions of opposing viewpoints. During debates two pupils present one position concerning an issue and two present the opposite position. Each speaker states a proposition, and then takes notes for a rebuttal. An opposing speaker states the propositions and then prepares notes for rebuttal. There is a time set for each proposition and rebuttal. Team members are allowed to confer with partners during the debate. A typical time frame for a debate follows:

First speaker, "pro" position of the issue	3–5 minutes
First speaker, "con" position of the issue	3–5 minutes
Second speaker, "pro" position of the issue, who can also include points of rebuttal for the first speaker for the "con" position	3–5 minutes
Second speaker, "con" position of the issue, who can also include points of rebuttal for the first speaker of the "pro" position	3–5 mi-
First Rebuttal (Pro position)	1/2–1 minute
Second Rebuttal (Con position)	1/2–1 minute
Third Rebuttal (Pro position)	1/2–1 minute
Fourth Rebuttal (Con position)	1/2–1 minute

Debates can be used to develop and assess all items on the *Individual Students' Oral Language Needs Monitor* (Figure 3-3, p. 84). They also develop students' problem-solving thinking, especially when these abilities are taught prior to the debate. Videotaping debates for presentation at Rotary Clubs, PTO/PTA meetings, or city council meetings increases this activity's authenticity. Encourage students to anticipate opponents' arguments before the debate begins.

FIGURE 3-8
Form to Grade Speeches

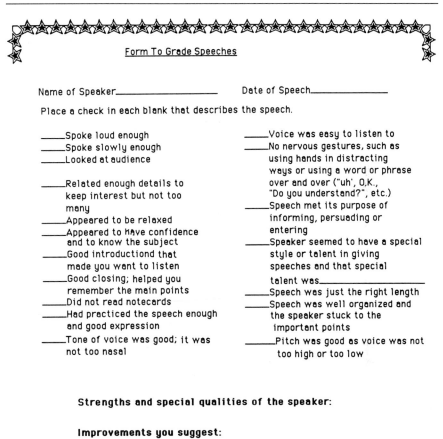

Form To Grade Speeches

Name of Speaker_____   Date of Speech_____

Place a check in each blank that describes the speech.

_____Spoke loud enough
_____Spoke slowly enough
_____Looked at audience

_____Related enough details to
keep interest but not too
many
_____Appeared to be relaxed
_____Appeared to have confidence
and to know the subject
_____Good introductiond that
made you want to listen
_____Good closing; helped you
remember the main points
_____Did not read notecards
_____Had practiced the speech enough
and good expression
_____Tone of voice was good; it was
not too nasal

_____Voice was easy to listen to
_____No nervous gestures, such as
using hands in distracting
ways or using a word or phrase
over and over ("uh', O,K.,
"Do you understand?", etc.)
_____Speech met its purpose of
informing, persuading or
entering
_____Speaker seemed to have a special
style or talent in giving
speeches and that special
talent was_____
_____Speech was just the right length
_____Speech was well organized and
the speaker stuck to the
important points
_____Pitch was good as voice was not
too high or too low

Strengths and special qualities of the speaker:

Improvements you suggest:

Methods to improve that you suggest:

_____
Rater's Signature

CREATING LESSONS WITH THE TELEPHONE

Telephoning teaches students to use effective oral skills and has a built-in
application to the real world. If possible, teach these skills by using real or
simulated telephones that telephone companies provide. Prior to instruction, students brainstorm skills necessary for specific situations that occur
in telephone conversations, such as taking messages and communicating

clearly. Skills identified in this brainstorming session are then taught. Students also practice these skills at home and report on their success.

Sample telephoning skills are:

1. Before making calls, list points you will address.
2. Identify yourself when making or receiving a call.
3. Speak courteously as if you were involved in a face-to-face conversation, e.g., ask questions of clarification, and summarize to be sure both parties agree upon key points.
4. Be prepared to leave a message on an answering machine and speak slowly when doing so; repeat your phone number in the message if you desire a return call.
5. Ask permission before using another person's telephone.
6. Ask people for the most convenient time to return their call.

The functions of language that telephoning develops are regulatory, instrumental, interactive, personal, and informative. Telephoning skills are especially valuable for students who speak English as a second language, or who need practice on standard English patterns. Telephoning builds items 9–12 of the *Individual Students' Oral Language Needs Monitor* (see p. 84).

One method of authenticizing this activity is to solicit parents' aid. Send parents a checklist of telephoning skills in advance and have each student in the class call a classmate's parent to describe something about a future class event (e.g., what to bring, when, where, etc. for a special classroom project). Parents make comments on the checklist of skills concerning that student's performance on the telephone and places it in a envelope to be returned to you the next day. After reviewing parents' comments, summarize and share them with students as a whole class performance assessment.

CREATING LESSONS USING STORYTELLING AND SHOW-AND-TELL

Wordless Picture Books (see Chapter 13) and books that appear in Notecards 5 and 6 can be used to build students' creative thinking through storytelling. The first storytelling lesson should teach the following steps:

1. Teacher or librarian models storytelling;
2. Students select the story they want to tell from Notecards 5 and 6;
3. Students read the story three to four times until they know the feel and flow of the story;
4. Students memorize their opening lines which can be an imaginative, fanciful, or fictitious reason for telling the story;
5. Students practice telling the story to a small group, or before a mirror, and use the checklist in Figure 3-8 to evaluate this practice session (students can develop fluency if they practice their story twice a day for a week);
6. Choose the day they want to tell their story, allowing one story per day until all have told their first story.

One of the first indications that your oral language program is successful will occur when students bring *more and more* of their lives into the classroom. As Ms. McClure (1989), a fifth-grade teacher, demonstrated by October of the school year, she has to keep a pencil and pad in her morning robe because she becomes so overwhelmed with insights she wants to tell her class! As she moves from room to room, busily getting ready for school, she has to jot her thoughts on the pocket pad. Her students are beginning to do the same! If your oral language program is successful, your students will similarly burst into class with many stories to tell: these stories will be alive with ways they experimented at home with the new thoughts and language they created at school.

Show-and-Tell.　This is an activity where students tell about important thoughts and events in their lives. It develops students' personal (and, if structured in the following way), informative as well as interactive language functions. Before "show and tell," students make rules, which could include these: (1) speakers bring something they judge to be of interest to a lot of people (students are less self-conscious when they have an object to "show and tell"); (2) prepare three points to make and two questions to ask listeners at the end of the sharing; (3) listeners should ask questions; and (4) listeners should state something they enjoyed or appreciated about each presenters' speaking, preparation, or thinking. After several presentations, listeners develop the ability to give more specific compliments and suggestions for improvements. Skills to teach students include these:

1. Give a critique and personal opinion by opening with the intent of helping, and saying, "I have a suggestion, if you'd like"; "You seemed to . . . which I do sometimes too"; or, "I really enjoyed your talk, and I'd like to suggest something you may want to add next time."
2. Begin a critique by pointing to the positive aspects already mastered, and one aspect that could be improved, e.g., "I really enjoyed how you listed several things, and if you use shorter sentences in the future I can remember your main points better."
3. Suggest a method to eliminate the difficulty. When students recommend strategies for improvement, they can state ones they've used to overcome a similar speaking problem.

Even with preplanning, two difficulties can arise during show-and-tell lessons. First, students could direct their talk only to you rather than their classmates. You limit this difficulty by taking a seat at eye level with students near the back of the group. You also give two directives before show and tell begins. You tell students the order of presenters and that each student is responsible for calling the student after his/her presentation. The second assignment is that as soon as a speaker is seated, the previous presenter aids that presenter with objects and provides verbal prompts if that person loses a train of thought. With these directives in place, show and tell becomes a real-world setting, one in which the speaker is in charge and speaks to an entire group.

Second, students may have trouble deciding what to discuss. You assist them by sending a list of topics home that will be studied in other content areas. Parents can plan show-and-tell topics related to new information the class is learning. Students can also create their own Flannelboard stories to show and tell, show and tell in partners, or take roles in a commercial, display, or model demonstration they create.

Show and tell increases students' abilities in items 6–12 and 22–23 on the *Individual Students' Oral Language Needs Monitor* (p. 84), as well as Division 1 and 2 thinking abilities (see Chapter 12).

If a few of your students are afraid to speak before the class, read to the class Joan Detz's book, *You Mean I Have to Stand Up and Say Something.* Her humorous treatment of this fear decreases student fears. When students have completed the above lessons, they are ready to learn to ask questions to clarify meanings and develop deeper levels of understanding. Critical Thinking Activity 3 below demonstrates how oral language instruction can expand students' thought processes.

CRITICAL THINKING ACTIVITY 3
Asking Questions to Clarify

Language Arts/Thinking Objective Presented to Students

"Today you will learn how to reduce confusion when you read, listen, speak, and write. You will do so by asking questions. At the end of our work, you will see how much you have improved your ability to ask good questions. Scientists have discovered that successful people have a few things in common. One is that they ask questions when they are confused. Because they do this, they better understand others and others better understand them. When you learn to ask questions, you will not misunderstand as many things. If you are successful in this lesson, within two weeks you will find yourself asking more questions when you are confused about something. Today you will learn eleven types of questions that many people ask."

Dispelled Misconceptions

Students answer the question, "When have you benefited from asking someone else or yourself a question? What caused that question to be helpful? When you asked questions and they did not help, what caused them to not help you?" Following this discussion, ask students to write their feelings about asking questions of themselves and others (e.g., if they are shy they write how they feel about it; if they think people don't like them because they ask too many questions in class, they write what they want to learn to overcome this problem). After recording these feelings, students write something they want to learn as they work on this lesson. They will return to this objective at the end of the lesson to determine if they learned what they desired.

THINKING GUIDE 3-1
Asking Questions to Clarify

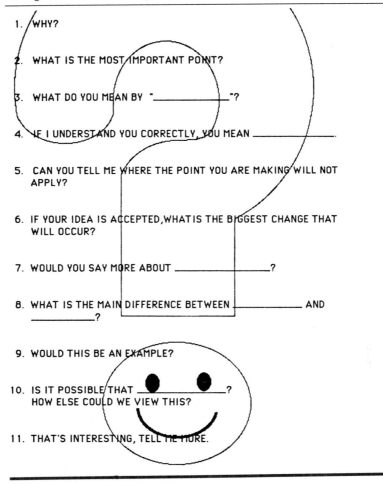

1. WHY?

2. WHAT IS THE MOST IMPORTANT POINT?

3. WHAT DO YOU MEAN BY "_____"?

4. IF I UNDERSTAND YOU CORRECTLY, YOU MEAN _____.

5. CAN YOU TELL ME WHERE THE POINT YOU ARE MAKING WILL NOT APPLY?

6. IF YOUR IDEA IS ACCEPTED, WHAT IS THE BIGGEST CHANGE THAT WILL OCCUR?

7. WOULD YOU SAY MORE ABOUT _____?

8. WHAT IS THE MAIN DIFFERENCE BETWEEN _____ AND _____?

9. WOULD THIS BE AN EXAMPLE?

10. IS IT POSSIBLE THAT _____? HOW ELSE COULD WE VIEW THIS?

11. THAT'S INTERESTING, TELL ME MORE.

Thinking Guide Instructions

Ask students to take out Thinking Guide 3-1. Tell them that they will lay it beside their notebooks so that they may refer to it as they read. At this point, go over each question on the Thinking Guide. Give examples to students of each question type and when it is most appropriate. Ask students to place a checkmark beside the two questions they like best and want to learn to use in conversations this week. You can also ask for examples where students have used a specific question type successfully (see Thinking Guide 3-1).

Examples of the Thinking Guide in Use

Keri, Natasha, Steven, and Nic are three eighth graders and one seventh grader who shared four examples of how they used the information in this lesson to help them. When they finished the lesson, they wrote about four important things they had learned:

Keri said, "I am now able to ask questions to anyone and not feel stupid doing it."

Natasha said, "I want to learn how to be even more specific when I ask questions."

Steven said, "When I asked about a question I had, the teacher gave me ideas about it. I wasn't confused for the rest of the period. I was able to keep up with what the class was thinking. It felt good to be with everyone else. I understood and had my own ideas about President Roosevelt, too!"

Nic said, "I learned that the harder my problem is the better questions I need to ask."

Students Select and Complete Their Own Objective

You tell students: "There are several ways to improve your reading and thinking abilities as you read today. Suggested objectives are on the board. Select the one that will help you the most, or create your own objective and submit it to me for my approval. With either choice, write why this objective will benefit you most. When you've written your reason, raise your hand. I'll discuss it with you."

Suggested objectives are:

1. If you have trouble reading big words, practice breaking these words into smaller parts as you read today. Circle the big word you read and use structural analysis to decode. When you finish, go back over your reading and write what you think about structural analysis. Is it a useful strategy for you? Why or why not? When and/or when not?

2. Today's story is true. If you enjoy comparing what you think to those of other people, pretend you are the reporter in the story. Describe what you would have done had you truly been the reporter. You will then read what the reporter actually did and describe why your actions were the same or different from the reporter's.

3. If you like to challenge other people's thinking, create three questions that you will ask the class after you finish reading.

Students Read the Following Story and Complete Their Objective

President Roosevelt was campaigning to be reelected for his second term. During this campaign he gave speeches from a train that traveled from the east to the west coast. Then, as now, newspaper reporters traveled with the President. They reported news from the trip to their newspapers and wrote stories about the President's speeches. Pretend you are one of these reporters, and you represent a Chicago, Illinois, newspaper.

By the time the President had finished his third speech he knew who you were. You were the reporter who always eased your way to the front row for each speech. When his speeches were over you pointed out mistakes in what he said and wrote unfavorable reports. You did not believe the President was correct in his plans for the country, and your newspaper stories said so. You were becoming famous for the stories you wrote about the President.

About two weeks later, as the President was speaking, it began to rain. As soon as it began to rain the President moved to the front of the platform. He looked across the crowd, and then at you. He noticed you did not wear your raincoat. He politely leaned over the rail, took off his raincoat, and handed it to you.

What do you say or do next?

Before you read the rest of the story, be sure you have written what you would have done, in detail. You can even write about two different things you might have done.

Let's finish the story now. Compare what you just wrote to what actually occurred.

The reporter was shocked. The reporter had learned a characteristic of successful people, and he used what he had learned to help him now. This is what actually happened:

Stunned, the reporter took the coat. He then asked, "Mr. President, you know I am your biggest critic. Why do you want to give me your coat?"

The President looked at the reporter, and with a kind voice said, "I know how smart you are. I know how strong you are in your opinions. I respect that. I'm also sure that if you could feel what it is like to be President you would better understand me and that some of your opinions are not correct. I thought if you wore my coat for a while you might understand what it feels like to be President. I thought this would help you."

If you selected objective 2, stop reading now, and tell what you think happened next. Then describe why you think as you do. When you finish your writing, read the ending and tell why your answer was the same or different from what really occurred. If you did not select objective 2, read the rest of the story now.

Soon after this incident, President Roosevelt and the reporter grew to become close friends. Upon his reelection, the President made the reporter his Press Secretary. They worked closely together until the President died.

Rethink and Reformulate

(Student self-assessments, planned assessments, and extensions across the curriculum)

1. Students write an essay to recount times in their lives when it was difficult for them to ask questions. They outline a plan to overcome this difficulty in the future.

2. Students read one of the following books that contain vivid characters: *Dear Mr. Henshaw; Graciela: A Mexican Child Tells Her Story; The Girl Who Loved Wild Horses; Jacob Have I Loved; The Whipping Boy;* or *Isamu Noguchi: The Life of a Sculptor.* As they read they record incidents where one of these characters asked questions for clarification. They write the effects these questions had upon the plot. They also note characteristics of the more and less effective communicators in the book, and why they judged each character as they did. Alternatively, students can return to a book where one of their favorite characters appeared. They reread that book, noting pages where their favorite characters did or did not ask questions for clarification, and the effect of having done so, or not having done so, upon other characters and the plot.

In summary, most variations in oral language will be altered through private conferences with individual students. Specific lessons that build oral language competencies include audiovisual tape recordings, show-and-tell, telephoning skills, debates, and storytelling. By cultivating students' abilities to ask questions, you can advance their thinking abilities. Before the discussion about the oral language program ends, it is important that you develop the ability to model and perform think alouds frequently in your class. The Professional Development Opportunity that follows will instruct you in how to do so.

PROFESSIONAL DEVELOPMENT OPPORTUNITY
How to Do a "Think Aloud"

Modeling is one of the most effective ways to demonstrate thinking and communication processes. **Modeling** means *to demonstrate how to think by talking about it immediately before or after it occurs in your class.* Modeling is one of the most **powerful** think alouds. A think aloud demystifies successful thinking, writing, reading, speaking, and listening, as it describes thought-in-action; for instance: "Boys and girls. I want to share with you how I think when I read. Open our books to the chapter entitled 'Hearing Ear Dog.' Before I read a story, an article, or a book, I do a number of things. Think about them as I do them. First, I look at the title. The title usually tells me a lot about what is going to be in the story. Second, I look at the pictures, or maps. Third, I read the captions under the pictures or any notes that appear in the margins. Fourth, I look at the headings and subheadings that break up the text. Fifth, I make a prediction about what the overall big idea of this selection is. Sixth, I look once more at the title and first heading and/ or subheading. For instance, there is a beginning heading here that says, 'How Penny Puts Her Ears to Work.' I then make a prediction about how Penny puts her ears to work. I begin reading, checking what I read against the prediction I have in my head about what Penny will do with her ears. After I find out whether my first prediction was right, I make another one about what will happen next. And I keep doing that until I finish reading. So, I always have a prediction in my head about what will happen next. Finally, after I finish reading, I think again about the main idea of the text and try to restate it" (paraphrased from Ripley & Blair, 1991, pp. 211–212). You should do think alouds frequently in your class because this is among the best methods of showing an end product before the class tries to replicate the thinking or language arts process to be learned.

TRY IT

1. As you studied in this chapter, to mold precision and elaboration in thinking, you will ask questions that refine as well as expand students' thinking. To improve your ability to ask both types of questions, study the list of verbs below. Select four that you want to include in your questioning repertoire. Two you select should narrow, and two should expand students' thinking when they are used as the verb in questions you ask. Once your selection is complete, check to see if you placed the verbs in the correct type of thinking they elicit students to perform (elaborating or refining). [Answers appear on p. 512.]

name	elaborate
cite an example	justify
predict	be more specific
create	give us an illustration
imagine	give us a nonexample
explain	demonstrate
recall	wonder
cause—effect	resolve
compare—contrast	apply to your life
summarize	analyze differences between two things
pretend	infer

2. How do students learn language by imitating others?; How do students learn language through a "language acquisition device?" Why does an effective oral language program increase achievement in reading, writing, and other scholastic areas?

3. If you are teaching, it is important that your oral language program invites students to express higher level thoughts. To assess your program, audiotape yourself as you teach Critical Thinking Activity 3 or as you lead a whole-class discussion. Analyze the tape to identify specific strengths you have and improvements you can make to encourage more effective student communication and thinking. Also, set a specific three-part objective to improve one of the following areas in your own speaking ability:

- pitch, speed, volume, crutch words
- questioning
- diagnosis of students' speaking problems
- use of a new instructional activity

Reassess your improvement at the end of the month. If you are not teaching, practice doing a think aloud (the Professional Development Opportunity) and tape-record it. Analyze it as described above.

4. The first story you tell to your students may be a difficult, and risk-taking challenge for you. If you are like I, when you see how effective storytelling can be as an oral language model and teaching tool, you will be thankful that you ventured to do so. Select a book from Notecard 5 or 6 and follow the preparation steps for storytelling outlined in this chapter.

Set a specific oral language/thinking development objective for your story-telling lessons, tell students the objective, and then the story. Evaluate your effectiveness as a storyteller. If you do not teach presently, complete this challenge with a group of peers and ask for their feedback.

FOR YOUR JOURNAL

Assigning homework is sometimes a policy of the school and desired by many parents. If you wish, journals can be used for homework. Give each child a journal called a language arts log. The homework assignment would be the same Monday through Thursday: Read a self-selected book, discuss a topic, reflect or write about a goal you set for the week, and work on it for at least 20 minutes each day at home. Record the starting and stopping times of your work and have it initialed by an adult (so parents would have some contact with the homework), and write a brief evaluation of your day's work. On the first day send home a letter to parents explaining this procedure.

It is an abiding problem to find the time to write responses in numerous language arts logs. One solution is to buy a 5-tier stand in which students place their folders. The first tier contains one-fifth of the students' journals that you grade on Monday; the second tier contains one-fifth that you grade on Tuesday, etc. Students can turn in their journals each day so that they will write every night. You spotcheck some journals in the tiers that you do not grade that day.

To practice using your journal in this way, set a communication goal for yourself for this week. Every night, work, read, or discuss your goal for 20 minutes. Record your work as described above as your journal can become an example to share with your class before they engage in this activity for a six-week period.

BUILDING YOUR PROFESSIONAL PORTFOLIO
Journals About Language Arts Instruction

There will be several occasions when you will reference new research in language arts. These are some journals and publishers to contact to continue your professional development and to improve your language arts program:

1. *CBC Features*
   Children's Book Council, Inc.
   67 Irving Place
   New York, NY 10003
2. *Childhood Education*
   Association for Childhood
   Education International
   11141 Georgia Avenue,
   Suite 200
   Wheaton, MD 20902
3. *The Elementary School Journal*
   University of Chicago Press
   P.O. Box 37005
   Chicago, IL 60637
4. *The Good Apple Newspaper*
   P.O. Box 299
   Carthage, IL 62321
5. *The Horn Book*
   Park Square Building
   31 Saint James Avenue
   Boston, MA 02116

6. *Language Arts*
   National Council of Teachers
   of English
   1111 Kenyon Road
   Urbana, IL 61801
7. *Learning*
   530 University Avenue
   Palo Alto, CA 94301
8. *The Middle School Journal*
   National Middle School
   Association

P.O. Box 14882
Columbus, OH 43214
9. *Teaching K–8*
   P.O. Box 912
   Farmingdale, NY 11737
10. *The Reading Teacher*
    International Reading
    Association
    800 Barksdale Road
    P.O. Box 8139
    Newark, DE 19711

4 Listening: Beginning to Build the Student Communication Center

Periodically giving good listeners' awards to students who use critical listening skills keeps listening development on the forefront of students' minds. Similarly, when students watch peers who are good listeners, they gain confidence in becoming good listeners as well (Rodgers & Couvillon, 1992).

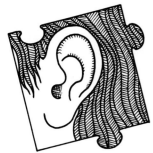

Know how to listen and you will profit even from those who talk badly.

—Plutarch

One of your major responsibilities is to help your students know how to listen. To learn how to do so, imagine for a moment that you have been invited to observe a class at a university laboratory school. Students in this class are involved in a research study to develop listening abilities. You arrive before school begins and as you enter the classroom you are struck by the differences between the oral interactions these students have and those of other elementary pupils you have seen. In-depth discussions are in progress and there are no "put-downs." Listeners are asking questions.

The bell rings as the teacher greets you. When the teacher begins to introduce you to the class, without being asked to do so, the students stop talking to each other. After the introductions, students are asked to gather for the class circle. Students arrange themselves in a large circle, sitting on a rug. Two students reach for your hands and invite you to join them, at a spot they've prepared. On the other side of the circle, the teacher states: "Let's move from left to right today. Everyone can share something good that happened to them since we last talked. You have the right to pass if you wish."

One by one students share: "My dad played catch with me last night for a really long time"; "Colin is coming to my house after school today"; "Our Editing Committee invented a new game that we'll show you today"; "My puppy isn't sick anymore"; "I brought some *real* bamboo for our project!" Everyone listens carefully, nodding their heads in affirmation several times.

A few students pass their turns. No one pressures them to participate. As it grew close to the time you are to speak, you aren't nervous like you usually are when you have to speak before a group. You have something good you *wanted to tell them.* Then students' eyes suddenly fall upon you, and you say: _____ .

Unless you were a part of a listening development program when you were in school, you may not understand how these students could make you feel so comfortable, and how they learned to listen so attentively and actively. The purpose of this chapter is to help you develop your pupils' listening abilities so exchanges such as these occur often inside their classrooms.

By the end of this chapter, you will know:

1. Research relative to listening instruction;

2. How to help students think while they listen;

3. How to develop students' abilities to recognize propaganda and listen more effectively in groups;

4. Activities that strengthen five levels of students' listening abilities;

5. How to build students' listening, speaking, writing, and thinking abilities through interviews, oral histories, and simulated newscasts.

THEORETICAL FOUNDATION

STUDENTS' LISTENING NEEDS

Listening is a *highly complex* and *interactive process defined as "the process by which spoken language is converted to meaning in the mind"* (Lundsteen, 1989, p. 1). Leland Jacobs calls instruction to increase listening ability the "Johnny-come lately of the language arts program" (1990, p. 35). Pflaumer (1971) further defines ideal listeners as those who "keep an open, curious mind. They listen for new ideas everywhere, integrating what they hear with what they already know. They also know how to evaluate many points of view."

To become a good listener, students must become personally involved with what they hear. By becoming aware of this, students will be unwilling to blindly follow the crowd. Students will look for ideas, organization, and rationales as they discern the essence of things. Knowing that no two people think the same, students will learn to stay mentally alert by outlining, objecting, approving, and adding illustrations of their own. Good listeners also ask questions which assist speakers to analyze their thoughts.

One of the major reasons you will allocate more time to listening instruction is that without it students remain confused about certain language patterns (Chomsky, 1969), and process only 25 percent of material in a 10-minute speech (De Haven, 1988). Moreover, as researchers have found, most students and adults spend 50 percent of their communicative time listening, 25 percent talking, 15 percent reading, and 10 percent writing (Lundsteen , 1989). However, by the time students graduate from high school, they will have received approximately 12 years of writing instruction; 1,274 hours of reading instruction; 141–283 hours of oral language development and *less than six hours* of instruction to improve their listening abilities (Burley-Allen, 1982).

One of the reasons listening was not instructed in the past was that many teachers were not taught how to teach listening methods as it was not emphasized in college textbooks. Swanson (1986) found that from a total of 3,704 pages in nine preservice language arts textbooks in 1985, only 12 percent of the text was allocated to methods of developing listening ability. In this chapter you will learn 35 strategies to develop your students' listening abilities. Through this chapter, you will learn three times the number of methods to teach listening than did teachers prior to the 1990s.

PURPOSES FOR LISTENING

There are five purposes for listening: (1) *to distinguish sounds;* (2) *to understand messages;* (3) *to assist speakers and dismantle problems;* (4) *to comprehend and evaluate what one hears;* and (5) *to enjoy, appreciate, and respond emotionally* (Wolven & Coakley, 1979). Students pass through phases as they develop competence in each of these listening purposes (Jacobs, 1986). For example, infants have limited consciousness when they are listening, and appear only to distinguish sounds when immediate needs demand. Gradually, students begin to **half-listen**, choosing to hear what is important to them. By providing the following instruction you can change your students from half-listeners to active and effective critical listeners.

One of the most important concepts students should know is that listeners understand twice as fast as speakers can talk. Because people understand speech so rapidly, most listeners only half-engage their mental capacity to comprehend what they hear. To more effectively listen, your students must engage their remaining mental processes productively, and think as they listen. There are five levels of thinking students can engage as they listen: receiving, auditory discrimination, paying attention, listening comprehension, and critical listening. It is important to plan classroom activities devoted to learning or improving each of these thinking and listening skills. Students need opportunities to listen to you and to practice new listening strategies during classroom discussions. Not only do you serve as a good role model when you listen actively to students' comments, but students learn about the needs and interests of classmates through their active listening.

Among the activities that build listening competencies and strategies are listening guides, conversation clubs, radio broadcasts, guest speakers, directed listening-reading-thinking activities, detecting propaganda, interviews, oral histories, and TV news broadcasts. You will now learn how to incorporate these into your student communication center.

PUTTING THEORY INTO PRACTICE
TEACHING STUDENTS TO LISTEN MORE EFFECTIVELY

The following instructional strategies teach students how to comprehend and learn from what they hear. Strategies are divided into the five types of thinking and listening abilities they strengthen: receiving messages, discriminating auditorially, attending to messages, building comprehension, and listening critically.

LEVEL 1: RECEIVING: ENSURING STUDENTS CAN HEAR

With the increased noise in our society, more and more students are purposely choosing not to listen, or suffering hearing losses (Moffett & Wagner, 1983; Lundsteen, 1989). For this reason it is important to determine if students hear what is said. An activity to make this determination appears in Figure 4-1. Through this activity you can note individual student's ability to attend to details/main ideas, and to summarize. Once these notes are made, you and your students can decide upon a program to overcome their individual difficulties in receiving messages.

Students who need instruction in specific listening skills are taught in small homogeneous groups. Each group includes an expert listening peer who performs a "think aloud" about an already perfected ability to listen in a specific way.

FIGURE 4-1
Diagnosing Students' Abilities to Receive Messages

FACING LINES
Seat half the class with their backs to a book, the other half facing it.

Book shown to Bs from here

As

Bs

Students who can see the book read two pages silently and then tell two pages to their partners. Once the entire book is finished, each storyteller asks the partner to retell the story. The storyteller writes down everything the partner says. These pages are collected and analyzed for listening comprehension.

For older students, each pair selects a book from those they have never read or heard. Once the story is told, and the retelling is complete, the pair looks at the book and compares it to the retelling. The listener tells the storyteller why certain parts were not included in the retelling (e.g., "not important," "didn't hear it," "didn't remember that part"). The parts omitted from the retelling are noted on the back of the retelling record, along with the listener's explanation for each part's absence. Partners then switch roles and repeat the process. You collect each of these papers and analyze each student's instructional needs.

In the event you suspect a student has hearing difficulties, stand a short distance behind the student and call his/her name. Ask a question. If the student is not deeply concentrating, and has no hearing difficulty, he/she will turn to face you. If the student does not turn around you can contact the school nurse who will secure auditory testing through the following instruments:

1. The Sequential Tests of Educational Progress
2. The Stanford Achievement Test Series
3. The California Achievement Tests/Listening Test
4. The Brown-Carlsen Listening Comprehension Test
5. The Detroit Tests of Learning Aptitude

LEVEL 2: AUDITORY DISCRIMINATION: INSTRUCTION TO DISTINGUISH SOUNDS

Two activities increase students' auditory discrimination. First, divide students into partners. Pairs sit side by side and each has a sheet of paper and a pencil as he/she listens to a story you read. Prior to reading the story, you will have identified words that contain consonants which frequently begin English words (b, d, f, g, h, l, m, n, p, r, s, t, v), words that contain short vowel sounds, or words that have one of the most frequently appearing consonants at the end of the word (d, g, l, m, n, r, s, t). As you read, you stop at the end of a sentence that contains one of the key words you've identified. Ask students to write the word they heard that had the sound of a consonant (at the beginning or end) or the long or short vowel you specify. Students write the word they think they heard and a second word that they know contains the same sound. After you've read the book and asked for several words, correct words are given, and students check a partner's paper (misspellings do not constitute errors). Partners give a word they thought had the same sound or ask their partner to help them think of a word. If they think of a word unaided they place a capital *A* (for alone) after the word they wrote. If they asked their partner to help them think of a word, they place a capital *P* (for partner) after the word. If neither partner can think of a word, they both write *N* (no additional word) after the words they had written. There are two purposes of asking students to tell each other a second word that contains the same sound. First, generating words to match a spoken sound strengthens auditory discrimination. Second, students have an opportunity to hear other words from their partner with the same sound immediately following a stimulus sound, which highlights the unique sound of each consonant and vowel. You collect the papers. Through them you have a record of the types of sounds each student does and does not discriminate well.

After you have analyzed the discriminations that need improvement, place students in homogeneous groups according to their needs. They then listen for 10 words that begin with their particularly difficult sound and watch your mouth as you say this sound. Then read a book into a tape recorder that has several words containing the sound they need to discriminate (e.g., students who need to discriminate the /b/ sound will read *Brown Bear, Brown Bear* orally). When you play the tape back for these individuals, they should say and hear the differences between the /b/ and all other sounds. They demonstrate that they can hear it by closing their eyes and raising their hand each time they hear the sound on the tape. If students cannot yet read, you will have read the story into the tape for them before the lesson begins.

THE CHALLENGE OF DIVERSITY

Bilingual students and second language learners learn English letter sounds more rapidly if they repeat tongue twisters and then invent their own to challenge classmates.

LEVEL 3: ATTENDING TO A MESSAGE: TEACHING STUDENTS TO PAY ATTENTION

Many students need to be taught how to pay attention during listening. To teach this skill, select a cassette tape of someone reading a favorite selection of children's literature. Before you use this tape, teach students **to set a purpose for listening.** You do so by telling them that for the first three times you read a story this week, you will show them how you set a purpose

FIGURE 4-2
Steps to Becoming a Good Listener

Now we are going to learn six steps to improve your listening ability. When we are finished you will draw a second picture to see if it looks more like the intended object than the picture you just completed from my oral description. If it does, your listening skills have improved.

SIX STEPS TO IMPROVING LISTENING SKILLS

In the future you can improve your listening ability by doing the following six things:

1. As soon as you begin to listen, try to hear the sentence that tells what the subject is; ask yourself what the total focus of the person's talk is. Pick the most important details the person will say.
2. Pay close attention to all words that tell directions such as north, south, east, west, or up, down, here, there, over, under, above. As soon as you hear such a word picture it in your mind.
3. Listen for the words that signal order, such as first, second, last, after, before, and also. Try to put yourself in the place of the person speaking, and in your mind, perform the order of the activities he/she is describing.
4. As you listen, picture what is described. This mental picture will help you distinguish the most important details and how they relate together. As you hear each detail tie it to the detail immediately preceding it. The person talking had a very important reason for putting these details together and you have to be thinking what that reason is.
5. Pay special attention to words such as and, or, but, yet, and because. These words tell you how two ideas are related to each other.
6. Ask questions of the person talking to clarify the points being made.

Now to practice using good listening skills, find a picture in your textbook and describe it to your partner. Your partner will do the same for you. Draw what is described. Compare to the picture.

---

for listening. You perform this "think aloud" for three consecutive days. Then you give students a choice as to the purpose they want to set before you start the tape on the fourth day. On the last day of the week students will write or tell their own purposes for listening to a different tape or book you read and describe why/how they set that purpose.

Purposes for listening that you can model include answering a question about the topic; preparing a question to use in future conversations; evaluating the piece; or predicting the ending and justifying that prediction. You tell them that giving oneself a reason for listening increases how much they learn (listening comprehension). For older students, you can advance their attending skills by introducing the "Steps to Becoming a Good Listener" in Figure 4-2.

You discuss why each of the six steps in Figure 4-2 improve listening ability. You then ask students to use one of the six in a second activity to build their abilities to pay attention. Divide the class into six groups. People in one group can choose to use the first step of Figure 4-2 as they listen to the main idea and then relate details; people in another group can choose to use step 2: picturing what they heard in their minds, etc.

Then you either play a videotape of the previous evening's news broadcast, give a speech on a topic that contains many details, or invite an upperclassmate to talk about an unusual hobby or interest area in which he/she is an "expert." Students are to use the listening strategy they selected and write (or diagram) how they used this strategy as they listened. When the speech is finished, group members collect individual members' writings (or diagrams) to best demonstrate the use of that group's listening strategy. Then the group's combined product is shared with the class and they describe how their abilities to listen improved.

A third lesson to increase students' ability to pay attention is featured in videotape segment 7. Tell students that there are times when listening that their thoughts interfere with what the speaker has to say. Teach that if they find themselves thinking of what they want to say when they should be listening, they are to "bracket" these thoughts. **Bracketing** means *to put some thoughts away to hold them to think about at a later time.* It enables people to concentrate more on the task at hand. Do a think aloud of one method of bracketing that you use, such as making notes when your mind wanders. In this way you will be sure not to forget the thoughts you had. The note frees your mind so you can concentrate more on the speaker's message. Ask students to create their own method of bracketing. Then request that they listen for 20 minutes and discuss the effects of bracketing upon their ability to pay attention.

A fourth lesson to build attentive thinking and listening was created by Danielson (1992). It increases the students' ability to attend to spoken messages by blending listening and writing objectives into a single lesson. Danielson uses the following books to teach the importance of listening for and writing graphic descriptive words: *Gobble, Growl, Grunt,* and *Crash! Bang! Boom!* by Peter Spier, *Pigs Say Oink* by Alexander, *Sound Words* and *More Sound Words* by Hanson. As students listen to one of these books, they write ten words they "liked" the best that they wish to incorporate into their speaking and writing vocabularies.

> **THE CHALLENGE OF DIVERSITY**
>
> If some of your students speak nonstandard English, they may need extensive instruction in auditory discrimination. These exercises help students hear differences between initial, medial, and final sounds in words. Such exercises begin by asking students which of the words you said began or ended with a sound you specified. When your students are comfortable performing this listening task, couple the activity with meaning clues by creating riddles, such as: "I'm thinking of something we all wear. The name of these articles begins like *shine*. Everyone has these objects on today. What word am I thinking of?"

LEVEL 4: BUILDING LISTENING COMPREHENSION ABILITIES

As shown on segment 7 of the videotape, Ms. McCall builds her students' abilities to comprehend by listing the actions students take to be good listeners. She then models how to attend to key words to follow directions. Students then place books between themselves and a partner. Using five or six pieces of paper of various sizes and shapes, one student describes how to put those pieces together. When the speaker has finished, the pair compares their finished products to assess the listeners' comprehension. At lesson's end, students add to the list of actions they can take to become even better listeners. Mize (1992) follows this activity with one of increased difficulty. She places directions on an audiotape. These directions are an authentic extension of the above learning experience, as they concern how to go from the classroom to another location outside or inside the school. At the end of the tape students must have discerned where the directions would have taken them.

Another activity to build listening comprehension uses listening guides (Castello, 1976). A **listening guide** is *a partially complete outline created by a speaker to show listeners the relative importance of the speaker's points.* Before the speaker begins, the listening guide is distributed so students' listening comprehension can be more focused. Students complete missing parts of the outline during or immediately following the speech. Listening guides can be used in a wide variety of ways, including students creating their own listening guides to accompany talks they give to a small group of their classmates. The classmates complete the guide while the speech is being delivered. When the speech is finished, the speaker shows the completed listening guide he/she made prior to the speech. Students compare theirs to it and then discuss what they can do to improve their listening abilities.

The "Conversation Club" is another activity that builds listening comprehension. As mentioned in Chapter 3, to initiate this activity, students submit topics they wish to discuss. You select from them and place students in groups based upon the topic they choose to discuss. Students converse freely for a few minutes about the topic and then write what each person did to be an effective listener. At the end of the "conversation club," students also write objectives they want to achieve to strengthen their own listening ability in future "conversation club" meetings. These objectives are stored and referenced prior to the next club meeting.

A fifth method of developing listening comprehension is to use video-tapes or records that accompany children's literature. Sources of or such recordings are: (1) *All Ears* (a record series to develop listening comprehension published by Penguin, 375 Hudson Street, New York, NY 10014-3657); (2) records by Weston Woods, Weston, CT 06883; (3) multimedia materials by Random House, 400 Hahn Road, Westminster, MD 21157; (4) Pied Piper, P.O. Box 320, Verdugo City, CA 91466; (5) The Listening Library, Inc., 1 Park Avenue, Old Greenwich, CT 06870-9978; (6) *Read with Me Books and Cassettes* (books and audiotapes for students), Mulberry Books, William Morrow and Co., 105 Madison Ave., New York, NY 10016; (212) 889-3050; and (7) Additional references in *Films and Filmstrips for Language Arts: An Annotated Bibliography*, National Couuncil of Teachers of English, Urbana, IL.

A sixth activity to develop listening comprehension is Radio Broadcast Listening, or mock trials. Many students have never heard stories as they were told on radio years ago. To begin, order a set of tapes of old radio broadcasts from Cassette Library, P.O. Box 5331, Baltimore, MD 21209; or the *Tune-In Series*, Sunburst Communication, Pleasantville, NY 10570. The broadcasts include Sherlock Holmes's Adventures, Superman Episodes, Two Thousand Plus, The Shadow, Hopalong Cassidy/Gene Autry/Lone Ranger Western Episodes, George Burns and Gracie Allen Specials, and Jack Benny Shows. Small groups of students listen to one broadcast and then enact it (and embellish it) for classmates who did not hear the original version.

THE CHALLENGE OF DIVERSITY

When students are monolingual in a language other than English, their listening comprehension improves greatly when you or an aide teaches them about multiple meanings of words in their native language. When they hear, see, and talk about these concepts in their own language, they learn to express and interpret them completely. Once this schema is in place, learning English connotations and multimeaning words is simplified.

LEVEL 5: DEVELOPING CRITICAL LISTENING ABILITIES

One of the first steps in developing critical listening abilities is to invite a guest speaker to class. Prior to the presentation, teach students (1) how to listen for the goal the speaker is trying to accomplish; (2) three ideas that are important to that goal; (3) how to summarize; and (4) how to develop questions to ask the speaker. To teach such integration, introduce students to Figure 4-3. They are to use it as they listen to a prerecorded video or live speech. After students complete the five items in Figure 4-3, they discuss their responses and list strategies they can use to strengthen their own critical listening abilities in the future.

FIGURE 4-3
Listening Guide

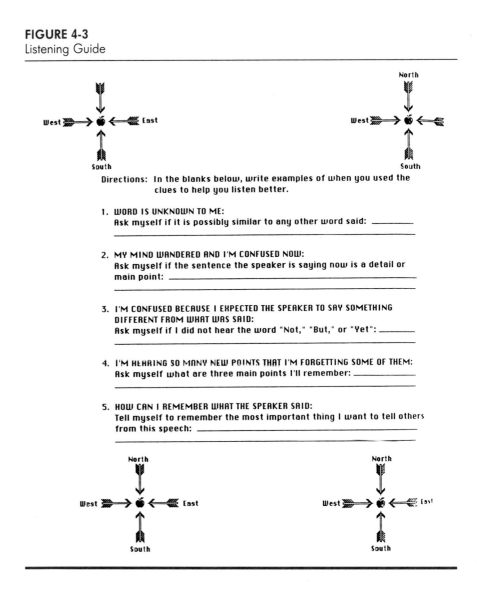

Directions: In the blanks below, write examples of when you used the
clues to help you listen better.

1. WORD IS UNKNOWN TO ME:
   Ask myself if it is possibly similar to any other word said: _____
   _____

2. MY MIND WANDERED AND I'M CONFUSED NOW:
   Ask myself if the sentence the speaker is saying now is a detail or
   main point: _____
   _____

3. I'M CONFUSED BECAUSE I EXPECTED THE SPEAKER TO SAY SOMETHING
   DIFFERENT FROM WHAT WAS SAID:
   Ask myself if I did not hear the word "Not," "But," or "Yet": _____
   _____

4. I'M HEARING SO MANY NEW POINTS THAT I'M FORGETTING SOME OF THEM:
   Ask myself what are three main points I'll remember: _____
   _____

5. HOW CAN I REMEMBER WHAT THE SPEAKER SAID:
   Tell myself to remember the most important thing I want to tell others
   from this speech: _____
   _____

Critical listening abilities also improve when you ask interesting and challenging questions. To demonstrate the impact such inquiry can have, place yourself in the following scenario. Pay attention to the level of your thinking both of the following teachers' questions elicit:

After reading the book *Cinderella,* teacher *A* asked students the following: "What did the Fairy Godmother use to make the carriage?" "What did Cinderella lose at the ball?" and "What time was Cinderella supposed to leave the party?" Teacher *B* asked questions that built critical listening: "Why do you think Cinderella did not run away from her wicked Stepmother?" "What is the difference between love at first sight and real love? Which type do you think the Prince had and why?" Teacher *B* then opened the discussion to allow students to ask their own questions. Margarietta asked: "If everything else the Fairy Godmother gave to Cinderella turned back into its original form, why didn't the glass slipper change back as well?" Students in the second class were listening intently because they wanted to know the answers. They wanted to listen.

In closing our discussion of the five levels of thinking and listening developmental activities, we come full circle. We have reemphasized a point made in Chapter 1: You are the most important element in building students' listening ability! Include each student in "your audience." When all students know their listening is important to you, they give ideas, feel supported in their work, and learn to value that their classmates listen to their opinions and information. As Duckworth (1987) stated, "It is a matter of being present as a whole person with your own thoughts and feelings. It is a matter of working very hard to find out what those thoughts and feelings are, as a starting point for developing a view of a world in which people are as much concerned about other people's security as they are about their own"(p. 120). The following formal lessons move students closer to reaching higher levels of critical thinking and listening abilities and make it easier for them to learn from others for the rest of their lives.

STRATEGIES THAT TEACH
LESSONS THAT IMPROVE STUDENTS' HIGH LEVEL LISTENING ABILITIES

The following lessons use all five types of listening in authentic settings. Each lesson also integrates listening with other language and thinking competencies.

CREATING LESSONS USING THE DIRECTED LISTENING (READING) THINKING ACTIVITY (DLTA)

M	T	W	Th	F

Russell Stauffer (1969) created this lesson which incorporates divergent thinking and listening. Students predict story events prior to hearing or reading them. Students read or listen to prove or modify their prediction by using logic, induction, and the structure of the genre to be read or heard. The first steps in this lesson are to *survey and set a purpose for reading/listening*. Then students make predictions about the story's ending. For more advanced students you can cover the title of the story and pictures in the book to reduce the context clues available to them. Students are encouraged to generate alternative outcomes and to justify their preferences. Then, students complete a *silent reading of the first part of the selection* to prove or modify their prediction. They are asked to stop at a preselected point, before an important event is to occur. Students then predict this upcoming event, reevaluate their prior prediction, and describe the thinking processes they used to combine new information to previous projections. *If the story is short students read to the end and prepare for a postreading discussion.* This discussion begins with points students consider important. It concludes with identifi-

---

NOTECARD 7:   CHILDREN'S LITERATURE THAT DEMONSTRATES THE NEED FOR AND METHODS OF LISTENING EFFECTIVELY

Listen Rabbit by Aileen Fisher
Sounds of a Summer Night by
   Mary Garolick
Henry and the Monstrous Din by
   Russel Hoban
Morning, Noon, and Nighttime Too by
   Lee Bennett Hopkins
The Silent Concert by Mary Leister
If You Listen by Charlotte Zolotow
A Friend Can Help by Terry Berger
That Man is Talking to His Toes by
   Jacquie Hann
The Silly Listening Book by Jan Slepian
   and Ann Seidler
*The City Noise Book, The Country Noise
   Book,* and other noisy books by
   Margaret Wise Brown
Sounds of Home (Series) by Bill Martin, Jr.

Kartusch by S. Cosgrove
Gossip by Jan Pienkowski
Horton Hears a Who! by Dr. Seuss
The Other Way to Listen by B. Baylor and
   P. Parnall
High Sounds, Low Sounds by
   Franklin Branley
Is Anyone Listening? by Wayne Carley
Listen! And Help Tell the Story by
   Bernice Carlson
Noisy Nancy Norris and other books by
   Lou Ann Goddert
What Is That Sound? by Mary O'Neill
The Listening Walk by Paul Shower
The Listening Book by Don Safier
Kermit's Mixed-Up Message by J. Barkan
Effie by Beverley Allinson
Small Boy Is Listening by H. Zemach

---

cation of skills they have developed to become better listeners, readers, and thinkers, and how they improved their predictive thinking. First person narratives are a powerful genre for this lesson, as you will experience if you read and subsequently use Figure 4-4 with your students. Students can rethink and reformulate what they learned by reading a book of their choice from Notecards 7 and 8. Once students have completed their selection they discuss different methods their books suggested to improve listening abilities. [The answers to Figure 4-4 appear at the end of the book.]

CREATING LESSONS BY USING INTERVIEWS THAT BUILD STUDENTS' LISTENING, SPEAKING, WRITING, AND THINKING ABILITIES

When students learn to interview effectively, their speaking, listening, and writing abilities improve simultaneously. A good interview is a blend of planned and spontaneous questions posed by an interested person who is an expert on a topic. If you read *Mana and Her Boys* by Lee Hopkins aloud before students begin their first interview, they will learn from the young boy who interviews the school's custodian for the school newspaper. From this encounter a special relationship develops. Another book is *The Kidnapping of Aunt Elizabeth* by Barbara Parte. In it a girl interviews and listens to the tales her relatives share about their youth for a social studies report.

Students learn not to ask general questions in an interview. ("What do you think is the biggest problem in our school?") Instead, they ask force-choice, or comparative questions, such as "Which of the following situations are most troublesome to you and why?" They ask comparative questions, such as "In what way was _____ better than now?" and "How is this different from _____ ?"

FIGURE 4-4

DLTA Story: Read a Clue and Then Predict

**C
L
U
E**

#1

Lunch made me sleepy, so I curled up to take a nap. With sleep came a wonderful dream. I was stretched out on a lovely green lawn with the sun warming my body. Birds were singing gaily overhead, and little yellow daffodils peeked out through the grass. I reached out to touch one—and suddenly there was no sun.

A heavy shadow had shut out the light. Something grabbed me and I cried out, fighting to get free. It was no use; I was travelling through space. This was no dream. It was real. I had been captured, and there was nothing I could do about it.

**C
L
U
E**

#2

Soon I felt something solid at my feet. I could move, but it was hard to stand. My legs felt limber. Where was I?

Cautiously, I stepped forward, OUCH! I bumped into a wall and again in the other direction, but every time there was a wall. Four walls and no door. I'm in a cell!

All of a sudden there was a blast of cold air from above. I looked up but could see nothing. Where was the air coming from? Suddenly I knew: there was no roof on my cell! I had discovered a way out.

**C
L
U
E**

#3

Stepping carefully toward a wall, I attempted to reach the opening. I wasn't tall enough, so I sat down again to think. The cell was still rocking. Maybe I could throw myself against one of the walls and tip the cell over. Again and again I rushed at the wall, but I finally gave up, defeated.

Sitting down, I tried to gather the energy for one more try. If that didn't work—Wait, the movement stopped!

A minute later I heard an earthshaking bang as I felt a different motion. My cell was moving up and down, not back and forth. I couldn't keep my balance. I said to myself I'd conquer whatever it was. I'd be ready. In an instant there was a horrible crunch, and the wall nearest me was ripped away. Beyond the opening I could see a dazzling light.

**C
L
U
E**

#4

"Now's your chance," I told myself, cautiously crawling to the opening. At first, I saw nothing but a shiny wood floor. Then I saw *them*!

Feet! Giant feet! They seemed about to surround me, so I quickly retreated. I could be ground to smithereens out there! Of course, that's what they were planning—that's why they made it easy for me to escape! Well, I'd fool them; I wouldn't move.

No, I couldn't stay. I had to try to get out.

**C
L
U
E**

#5

Once again I crept to the opening, but the feet were still there. Then I noticed something else. Near two of the feet, four round posts rose from the floor. The posts were topped by a thick, low roof. I could easily squeeze under it, but those giant feet couldn't.

I took a deep breath and moved quickly. Racing out of my cell, I skidded under the thick roof. I made it! My legs felt like rubber again, but I was safe for the moment.

**C
L
U
E**

#6

What would happen next? I wondered. I didn't have long to wait, however, for I heard voices high above the roof.

"Oh, Donald, she's afraid of us!"

"Well, naturally," came the reply. "That must have been a very frightening trip for such a little _____ ."

NOTECARD 8:   PICTURE BOOKS TO DEVELOP LISTENING, SPEAKING, READING, WRITING, AND THINKING VOCABULARIES FOR YOUNGER STUDENTS

Dinnertime by Jan Pienkowski
Giorgio's Village by T. dePaola
Look Again! and other books by T. Hoban
The Most Amazing Hide-and-Seek Counting Book by R. Crowther
Lavinia's Cottage and other books by J. Goodall
Arthur's Prize Reader by L. Hoban
Bobo's Dream and other books by M. Alexander
Do You Want to be My Friend? and other books by Eric Carle
King Bidgood's in the Bathtub by A. Wood
Tadpole and the Frog by S. Knobler
Martin's Hats by Joan Blos
Mr. Archimedes' Bath by P. Allen
Bunny Rabbit Rebus by D. Adler
Anno's Medieval World by M. Anno
Building a House by B. Barton
I Wish I Was Sick, Too! by F. Brandenberg
Lost in the Museum by M. Cohen
The Knight and the Dragon by T. dePaola
Oops by M. Mayer

The Mixed-Up Chameleon by Eric Carle
Jamberry by Bruce Degen
Pigs in Hiding by Arlene Dubanevich
Round Trip by Ann Jonas
Pet Show by Erza Jack Keats
The Relative Came by Cynthia Rylant
Horton Hears a Who! by Dr. Seuss
Truck Song by Diane Siebert
Brian Windsmith's Birds by B. Windsmith
A My Name is Alice by Jane Bayer
Alfie Gets in First by S. Hughes
The Story of Ferdinand by M. Leaf
Mama One, Mama Two by P. MacLachlan
Mommies at Work by E. Merriam
The Lazy Dog by J. Hamberger
Lily at the Table by T. Heller
In My Garden and other books by E. Cristini
Frank and Ernest (Series) by A. Day
The Sleeping Beauty by Trina Schart Hyman
The Wish Card Ran Out! by J. Stevenson
Jeff's Hospital Book by H. L. Sobol

(cont'd)

NOTECARD 8   (cont'd)

The Lady Who Saw the Good Side of Everything by P. D. Tapio
I'm Not Oscar's Friend Anymore by M. Sharmat
My Dentist and other books by H. Rockwell
What a Good Lunch! and other books by E. Watanabe
One Step, Two . . . and other books by C. Zolotow
Peter's Long Walk by L. Kingman
Owliver by Robert Kraus
Out! Out! Out! and other books by M. Alexander
The Package: A Mystery by L. Anderson
The Wrong Side of the Bed by E. Ardizzone
Elephant by B. Barton
The Blue Balloon by F. Asch
Franklin in the Dark and other books about Franklin by Brenda Clark
Busybody Nora by J. Hurwitz
Rosie's Walk by P. Hutchins

Where the Wild Things Are by Maurice Sendak
Noisy Word Series: Cluck Baa, Jangle Twang, Slam Bang, Skip Trip, Sniff Shout, Wobble Pop by John Burningham
Dig, Drill, Dump, Fill by Tana Hoban
Kitten Can . . . a Concept Book by B. McMillan
Busy Day: A Book of Action Words and other books by Maestro and Maestro
I'm Frog and other books by Jan Pienkowski
Frog Medicine by Mark Teague
Nathan's Balloon Adventure by Lulu Delacre
The Moon Clock by Matt Faulkner
Aligay Saves the Stars by Kazuko G. Stone
Is Your Mama a Llama? by Deborah Guarino
The Watching Game by Louise Borden
Zoo Song by Barbara Bottner
Caps, Hats, Socks, and Mittens: A Book About the Four Seasons by L. Borden
You Don't Need Words by R. Gross

See Carolyn Lima's *A to Zoo: Subject Access to Children's Picture Books* for a listing by subject content of 4,400 picture books appropriate for students in preschool through grade two.

You teach students to also use a narrow questioning format such as: "What kind of . . . ?" "What was expected of you as . . . ?" "What does _____ mean to you?" You also teach them to ask, "Did you like _____ ?" and to probe for details about a specific incident that occurred. Students select a person of their choice to interview.

A second type of interview students enjoy is oral histories. **Oral histories** *are interviews to explore ideas of individuals who have similar backgrounds or who shared the same historical event.* Students begin by researching a subject such as the Holocaust, the Civil Rights Movement, the Vietnam War, or the history of their hometown. Individuals living in the area who have had personal experiences with the topic are then interviewed. This interview of the community member is based on no more than twenty questions about the person's personal experiences with the topic under study. Students add these firsthand data to the research they have done. Through these steps, students view history as a living subject, one that involves not only the famous but average people from all walks of life.

Before students begin their oral histories, they can read *Canon in the Courtyard Square/A Guide to Uncovering the Past* or *My Backyard History Book* by David L. Weitzman. It demonstrates how they can use their oral history data to improve their community. In planning an oral history, students work in groups and assume different responsibilities such as:

- Who will create the questions for the interviews?
- Who will make copies of the surveys?
- Who will conduct the interviews?
- Who will collect the completed surveys and write the first draft of the oral history?
- Who will design the proposal to present our results and plan for improvement to appropriate community officials?

CREATING LESSONS USING TELEVISION TO IMPROVE LISTENING ABILITIES

Television can be used in many ways to improve listening and thinking abilities. These are described in the many free materials you can order from the broadcasting companies listed in the Professional Portfolio (p. 130). Another creative lesson was developed by Beary, Salvner, and Wesolowski (1977) in *Newscast*. *Newscast* provides in-depth scripts for students to become their own anchorpersons, news reporters, science reporters, sports reporters, on-the-road reporters, education reporters, human interest reporters, music reporters, business reporters, comment writers, ad personnel, and international reporters. After completing one newscast students are prepared to create their own.

CREATING LESSONS USING THE LANGUAGE EXPERIENCE APPROACH

The language experience approach began in the late 1950s and early 1960s in southern California (Lee & Van Allen, 1963; Van Allen, 1974). The philosophy of this approach is that children can say what they think; you or

STRATEGIES THAT TEACH

students can write what children say; and children can read what you or they write. Nessel, Jones, and Dixon (1989) have written a book that describes ways in which the language experience approach can build higher level communication and thinking abilities. They recommend the following steps in the lesson:

Mondays: Discuss a stimulus event and take students' dictation on a story chart about their thoughts and questions over that event. Students illustrate or read more about the event, and follow up the activity by reading the dictated story on the story chart to strengthen their reading and listening vocabularies.

Tuesdays: Students reread the story they created Monday. Depending upon the grade level, they either underline known words, circle new words, or revise/use a thesaurus to improve sentence structure.

Wednesdays: You and the students design an instructional lesson they need based on the story.

Thursdays: Older students are allowed to design their own independent activity to build individual strengths by using the story as a common theme. Younger students practice an activity to demonstrate that they have learned and can independently complete Tuesday's and Wednesday's objective.

Fridays: This day is used for an alternative activity, such as preparing new word cards, creating challenges for classmates, and reviewing the week's work.

Gregory (1990) demonstrates with this dialogue how you can challenge students' thinking through the questions you use during the language experience approach.

Teacher: Once, a long time ago, when your grandparents' parents were children, fish had feet. How many feet did they have?

Students: Four! Five! Six! [pause, teacher grins] Eight!

Teacher: No fish had seven feet?

Student: Nope. How would they walk?

Teacher: [As she writes on the chart] Once, a long time ago, when your grandparents' parents were children, fish had feet. Some fish had four feet, some fish had five feet, some fish had six feet, no fish had seven feet, and some fish had eight feet.
   What did these fishes wear?

Student: Shoes . . .

Teacher: Right, shoes. What kind?

Students: Colors. Yellow ones. Blue ones because of the ocean that fishes like. Orange.

Teacher: They like colors. I never saw blue, yellow, and orange shoes for fishes. What were they made out of?

Students: Scales. And when they walked, they sounded *tick-tick*.

Teacher: I've heard that sound before. What else goes *tick-tick*?

Students: Clock. Yup. Sounds like clocks. And them too.

Teacher: [checking] The fish sounded like clocks?

Student: Yeah, when they walked, *tick-tick*. [giggles]

Teacher: OK. [As she reads and writes on the chart] Once, a long time ago, when your grandparents' parents were children, fish had feet. Some fish had four feet, some fish had five feet, some fish had six feet, no fish had seven feet, and some fish had eight feet. The fish wore yellow, orange, and blue shoes made out of scales. When they walked they sounded like this: *tick-tick-tick*. They sounded like clocks.

Teacher: But! [dramatic pause; teacher gasps; students gasp] But!

Student: One didn't.

Teacher: Huh? One what? Didn't what?

Student: One fish didn't wear those shoes. Those scales on his feet. [long silence; thinking]

Teacher: Why?

Student: Different kinds of feet. Round ones.

Teacher: Hmmm. Fish with round feet. Hmmmm.

Student: Oh! Hey, listen to me! They were round like a horse foot. No, they were round like something else; it's my answer. No, they were! He wore horse's shoes and when he walked he sounded like a brontosaurus walking. When he walked, he sounded like thunder!

CRITICAL THINKING ACTIVITY 4
Learning to Detect Propaganda

One of the most important critical listening and critical thinking abilities is to detect propaganda devices. Critical Thinking Activity 4, which follows, describes how you can assist students to recognize these devices.

Recommended Grade Levels: Grades 3 Through 8

In the *Platonic Dialogue* Plato wrote, "Seeking truth through discussion is better than persuasion." When your students understand persuasive devices they can circumvent these devices' harmful effects. Begin this lesson by telling students the objective that they will learn ways in which propaganda can be written and why it is important to recognize these devices in oral and written communication. Tell students that it is important to recognize when someone is trying to convince someone else that something is true. The way people most frequently attempt to persuade others is through propaganda. As a matter of fact, TV advertisements and public speakers use at least ten different propaganda statements that you can learn to recognize. (Share Figure 4-5 with the class, either as an overhead transparency or a handout. Once students have discussed these devices, tell them as much of the following information as you desire.)

FIGURE 4-5
Propaganda Devices That Can Mislead You

1. **Name Calling:** Using labels instead of discussing available information, e.g., calling a politician a "crook" and a person whose ideas are unpopular a "fascist" are two examples of unfair labeling.

2. **Glittering Generalities:** Vague phrases that promise much, e.g., "That act will benefit all Americans . . ." or "Everyone should . . ." or "Our way is the American way."

3. **Transfer:** Applying a set of symbols to a purpose for which they are not intended, e.g., an antigovernment group might display the American flag and pictures of Washington and Lincoln at a meeting. These positive symbols help conceal the basic purpose of the group and help gain public support. A second example occurs when an incongruous image is coupled with an idea, such as a picture of a mother and child accompanying the idea of buying a particular vehicle so readers or viewers transfer the feelings of tenderness (evoked by the picture) to the second concept (buying a specific type of car).

4. **Testimonials:** Getting some prominent person to endorse an idea or product, such as Linda Evans endorsing Crystal Light or a sports figure being pictured on a box of cereal.

5. **Plain Folks:** Pretending to be "one of the folks," to win the regard of the general public, such as using a folksy way of talking, kissing babies, posing for pictures with fishing poles, and so forth. For example, some people might try to persuade you by saying, "Howdy, neighbors, y'all remind me of the friendly folks in my home town."

6. **Bandwagon:** Claiming that "everyone is doing it." A second type of bandwagoning is to claim that something is "common knowledge" (so everybody should believe it).

7. **Card Stacking:** Presenting only parts of the facts that favor one side. This can occur when someone uses a quotation out of context, omits a key word from a quotation, references supportive statistics (while omitting unfavorable ones), and states half-truths that cannot be denied or whole truths that sound good but do not really apply to the argument at hand.

8. **Snob Appeal:** Trying to convince you that if you agree with them or purchase a certain product, you will be better than other people or that the product will help you gain status. Examples include designer clothes (especially those with a label or identifying mark openly displayed). Manufacturers use snob appeal to suggest that wearers of their garmets will be better liked and admired by peers who are important because they wear their products.

9. **Slanted Words and Phrases:** Using phrases or words to make someone think that the position being proposed is unbiased and objective. For example, many people use phrases like "It's been scientifically proven" or "laboratory-tested," but they do not have actual data.

10. Emotional Appeal: Using emotionally laden pictures to influence someone's opinion. For example, some greeting card manufacturers attempt to attach sentimentality to their cards through commercials that bring tears to viewers' eyes or remind them of a loved one far away.

Propaganda is a way of trying to change people's ideas and behavior. It can involve the spread of ideas and information deliberately slanted to further one's own cause or damage an opposing cause. This usually occurs subtly, by the propagandist's choice of words which have good or bad connotations. For example, "conversationalist" and "chatterbox" have the same dictionary meaning, but the first is more positively interpreted than the second.

A fact is something you personally experience or something that has been or can be tested. A fact is something which reliably occurs when conditions are right (and to other people, under the same conditions). Facts can be tested (available to be noticed by human senses) or can be tested through scientific, experimental conditions. When someone is proposing a reasoned judgment or an opinion, because factual data is not enough, propaganda can be used to gain an advantage for themselves or to gain others' support. Under these conditions, persuasive devices are used to gain personal advantage, and the devices employed are often illogical and are usually used deliberately.

Once students are familiar with the types of propaganda, they can complete one or more of the following activities:

1. Examine articles from the editorial pages of various newspapers, and discuss each in terms of personal opinion versus facts, biases, radical ideas, and attempts at sensationalism. The same procedures can be used with magazine articles, pamphlets, and books.
2. Explore several books or articles by the same author to trace the origins of or changes in this author's interests, viewpoints, and feelings.
3. Compare two biographies about the same person. Check facts each source gives, and compare them with other sources. Which facts are historically true, and which seem legendary?
4. Watch TV commercials to detect which type of propaganda device is used.
5. Hold elections where students develop campaign speeches avoiding the use of propaganda. The offices for which they campaign can simulate past (or present) political races they research, or may be actual positions they seek as classroom officers.

When a peer makes a suggestion, it is not interpreted by students as a punitive evaluation, as is often the case with critiques from teachers.

PROFESSIONAL DEVELOPMENT OPPORTUNITY
How to Use Paired Instruction

Paired instruction builds listening, speaking, and thinking abilities. "He who teaches others teaches himself." While paired instruction has been used since the time of the Spartans, only recently has research documented its benefits. We now know that paired learning is an effective means by which students grow academically and socially. This lesson can be completed either as a **dyadic** (*in which two students' work is graded as one collaborative piece*) or as a **peer tutoring lesson** (*where older or more advanced students work with younger or less advanced ones and students receive separate grades for their work*). The reason teaching others increases thinking and language learning is that as teachers, students constantly evaluate and increase their critical listening to generate alternatives to communicate and rephrase the same idea to their partner. Other benefits paired listening activities afford are these: (1) both rapid and slow learners have an attentive audience; (2) students are sharing and developing skills by managing greater responsibilities, which enhances their self-images and maximizes their chances for success; (3) often students develop higher level thinking patterns; and (4) students experience greater enjoyment than working alone. One of the best means of understanding the dynamics of paired learning is to analyze a session in progress. As you read the following excerpt from one paired learning session, reflect on the benefits that accrue from this activity:

In dyad tutoring sessions, tutors make notes, organize knowledge in new ways, and talk about concepts with new examples.

Child 1: "Bad." I don't think it should be there. Maybe you could find a better word to describe them.

Child 2: Or maybe leave "bad" out?

Child 1: That might sound better. Why don't you put "cosmetics" instead of "stuff"? It sounds kinda . . . a little babyish or something.

Child 2: OK. Let's see. "Cosmetics. Only the best cosmetics would do." How do you spell cosmetics?

Child 1: C-O-S-M-E-T-I-C-S. I think you need to indent here to make another paragraph. She could give a name, like a designer label. It could be anybody. You know, it's sorta . . . How about using adjectives to describe them?

Child 2: OK.

Child 1: You need a comma in the middle here. This looks sorta like a period or something.

The benefits of this type of activity can occur in only a few minutes. Moreover, the sharing that exists in duo sessions is likely to be more authentic than that which occurs in teacher-student conferences, i.e., students are free to choose to act upon suggestions they receive or not to act upon them. In setting up this style of instruction, students must be at ease, be taught how to listen, ask questions of clarification, take notes, read together, and evaluate their learning sessions. The following guidelines will increase the benefits of paired learning:

1. Assign two students who normally do not work together, blending weaker with stronger students. Acquiring knowledge from peers is very beneficial and meaningful to both ability levels.
2. Before the paired activity begins, decide upon the grading standard, discuss this with the students in advance, and decide whether each student will be graded individually or will be graded as a pair.
3. Paired learning experiences should be scheduled for approximately six weeks, with an option to continue.
4. An important part of this procedure is what you do during the activity. This may be the time you set aside to individualize instruction and meet with a student. You may use this time to jot notes of concern that you want to discuss, or observe, with single students using the record form in Chapter 15 designed for this purpose. You may also monitor pairs to ensure that their work will progress.

Mrs. Strong, a first-grade teacher in Arlington, TX, succeeds in using paired learning 15 minutes each day, with pairings under her control Monday through Thursday; students then select their own partners and materials on Friday. Students read to their partner for ten minutes, discuss, and then change roles. Mrs. Strong found that paired students increased their reading speed to about 37 to 40 words per minute in five weeks' time. Students also reported that getting to read with a partner was their favorite part of their class.

You can stay abreast of new research in paired learning by subscribing to the *Paired Reading Bulletins*, available through ERIC/RCS microfiche, or being placed on the mailing list of Paired Reading Project, Oastler Centre, 103 New Street, Huddersfield HDl 2UA, Yorkshire, United Kingdom.

TRY IT

1. If you are teaching, design two activities, one to be completed as a peer tutoring session; the second as a dyad. Ask students to determine the ways they learned and different communication and thinking abilities they developed in each. Students evaluate which approach was most beneficial to them and why.

If you are not teaching, read a book of your choice from Notecards 7 and 8. Describe how that book can be used to develop your future pupils' listening skills.

2. Select one of the activities in this chapter. Before you teach it to a group of elementary students, administer an informal pretest. Ask children how much they know about a listening objective you select. Teach the

activity and, if possible, wait one day before the posttest. On the posttest ask students how much they know about that same objective. Once these tests are complete, you and the students analyze the value of their instruction.

3. What proportion of your language arts program should you relegate to developing listening abilities, in your opinion? Defend your position.

4. Complete Critical Thinking Activity 4 if you are a teacher, or prepare materials necessary to teach it when you become a teacher. Learn about sample propaganda devices, list classroom offices for which students can run, and collect statements about facts that do not employ propaganda devices. Also write to as many of the television agencies in the Professional Portfolio as you desire, and ask to be placed on their mailing list to receive free teaching aids.

FOR YOUR JOURNAL

In this journal entry, you will practice another strategy to use with your students. Write three key questions on the board about a reading/listening experience that you will assign. In their journals, students will write as complete an answer to each question as they can, prior to their reading/listening experience. They leave space after each answer. This space is used to record facts they gained from their reading/listening, and to summarize what they learned. After the reading/listening is completed, students embellish their first answers and also write how thinking about things they know about a topic *before they listen/read* aids their learning.

In order to experience the power of using journals in this way, write answers to the following questions about topics in Chapter 5 in your journal. Write as much as you know about each before you read Chapter 5. After you've read Chapter 5, return to your journal and summarize other points you learned. When finished, write how this prereading experience aided your thinking and learning.

1. What was your most memorable experience about learning to read? What principles of instruction do you suppose were in operation to make this experience so important to you? (Write your answer and then leave space.)
2. What do you expect to appear in Chapter 5? READING INSTRUCTION IN A STUDENT COMMUNICATION CENTER: PART I.
3. List as many strategies as you use to **decode** (*pronouncing and assigning meaning to unknown words*). Do you know how to teach these strategies to students? Should you teach all of these strategies to students?
4. Think of a lesson you can teach that integrates oral language, reading, and thinking development. Select a grade level of your choice. Write the outline of that lesson in your journal.

BUILDING YOUR PROFESSIONAL PORTFOLIO
Television Teaching Aids

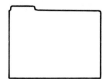

The following agencies and television broadcasting companies provide free teaching aids to build listening and other language arts through television viewing. You can write and ask to be placed on their mailing lists to receive their periodic updates and free materials.

1. Action for Children's Television
   46 Austin St.
   Newton, MA 02160
2. Children's Advertising Review Unit
   Council of Better Business Bureaus
   845 Third Ave.
   New York, NY 10022
3. Federal Trade Commission
   Pennsylvania Ave. at Sixth St. NW
   Washington, DC 20580
4. Zillions Ad Complaints
   256 Washington St.
   Mt. Vernon, NY 10553
5. International Listening Association
   366 North Prior Avenue
   St. Paul, MN 55104
6. Agency for Instructional TV
   Box A
   Bloomington, IN 47401
7. Material Distribution Dept.
   Texas State Learning Resource CT.
   1912 Speedway EDB 348
   Austin, TX 78712

8. ABC
   1330 Ave. of the Americas
   New York, NY 10019
9. Capital Cities Communication
   4100 City Line Ave.
   Philadelphia, PA 19131
10. Cultural Information Service
    P.O. Box 786
    Madison Square Station
    New York, NY 10159
11. Teachers Guide to TV
    699 Madison Ave.
    New York, NY 10021
12. CBS TV Network
    51 West 52nd St.
    New York, NY 10019
13. Cultural Information Service (NBC)
    P.O. Box 92
    New York, NY 10156
14. Prime Time School TV
    120 S. LaSalle St.
    Chicago, IL 60603

5. Reading Instruction In A Student Communication Center: Part I

As with all the language arts, when students read, they will work in more than one type of group. Some groups will be ones that students select, based on interests and needs.

Dear Mrs. Whalen,

I think our new reading program is execellent.
I have read 4 time as much as I used to.
I think that we should stick with this program, it is the best
we have had in the 8 years I been at Saint Marys.

—Ben Grimes
 Seventh Grader
 St. Mary of the Mills School
 Maryland

The purpose of this chapter is to describe the type of reading program that precipitated the above, unsolicited letter from Ben. Now that you know features and activities you will use in your oral language and listening programs, we'll examine ways you can integrate reading into your instructional plan. Before we begin, let's define reading.

What Is Reading?

We need not burn books to kill our civilization; we need only leave them unread for a generation.
—Robert M. Hutchins

Every reader reads himself. The writer's work is merely a kind of optical instrument that makes it possible for the reader to discern what, without this book, he would perhaps never have seen in himself.
—Marcel Proust

Reading makes possible the living of thousands of lives instead of only one.
—G. Robert Carlsen

What is a great love of books? It is something like a personal introduction to the great and good men of all past time.
—John Bright

Students Reflect on What Reading Means to Them

When I first learned to read I loved it and I still do. I would always want to know what the next word would be so I would read on and on. I love reading books that make your mind jump with ideas for the ending.
—Debi Eudaly
 Grade 7

I can remember when I was in the first grade library looking for as many horse books could find. I learned *so* much from the books that when I went to my first riding lesson, I already had most of the

material memorized from the books and pictures I found. I own a horse and show her every once and a while. In the shows I have competed in I have scored in the upper category. I don't know what I would do if I couldn't read.
—Lindsey Trice
 Grade 7

I hadn't really started learning how to read until the second grade. It was kind of late to start learning to read but I hadn't really been taught very good until the second grade. I always wondered

cont'd

Students Reflect on What Reading Means to Them (cont'd)

what those things were that people wrote down. I was so happy when I could read those things.
—Jacean Mallory
Grade 7

Reading has had many changes for me over a period of time. I used to love to read but not now.

I would much rather go to a friend's house or go see the movie. So I guess you could say that if someone makes me read I think its boring but if I do it on my own I think it is a lot of fun.
—Lauren Reed
Grade 7

Why does one student accurately decode a page and comprehend 95 percent of the information while another only 10 percent? The purpose of this chapter is to describe ways your students can learn to enjoy reading. In the last fifteen years more literacy research has been conducted than in the prior 50 years (Harste, 1989). Through this research we have come to define **reading** as the *construction of meaning from coded messages through symbol decoding, vocabulary awareness, comprehension, and reflection* (Manzo & Manzo, 1990).

By the end of this chapter, you will know:

1. The research that preceded new reading instructional strategies;
2. Strategies that lead students to become independent "decoders";
3. How to build students' vocabulary in student-centered classes;
4. How to use surveys and reading/writing samples to demonstrate reading growth to students and their parents;
5. What to do when readers come to words they can't decode;
6. How to integrate oral language, listening, reading, and thinking development into daily lessons.

THEORETICAL FOUNDATION
STUDENTS' READING NEEDS

Reading is a complex mental process. It is influenced by the factors we will discuss in this section:

1. *The level of a student's reading ability is influenced by the level of that student's oral language development.* Students' level of oral linguistic and literary sophistication will affect the types of materials they can read easily (Ruddell & Haggard, 1985; Ripley & Blair, 1989). Similarly, the dialect with which a student speaks also determines the ease with which that student can handle formal features of printed English; and students with pathological speech problems will also require special reading instruction. Because of these cause-and-effect relationships, lessons in this book ask students to integrate speaking, listening, and reading, to talk about what they read and read about new terms they hear.

2. *The experiences a student brings to reading strongly affect that student's reading ability.* Reading comprehension is a **socio-psycholinguistic constructive process**, *a process where the people, setting, state of mind, and level of language knowledge brought to the reading by the reader* are equal in importance the printed words in creating communication between reader and author (Harste, 1989; Rosenblatt, 1978; Tierney, Readence & Dishner, 1990). These multiple variables interact continuously to variant degrees during each reading activity as students create their own meanings (Anderson & Pearson, 1984; Singer & Ruddell, 1985).

3. *This is the first time in history that full-length children's books are used for large and small group decoding and comprehension lessons.* Students read selections of their own, and their teachers' choice, in student communication centers. Unlike the past, a single selection of children's literature can often be read several times during a single year. These rereadings are used to build students' appreciation for literature; to emphasize basic English language patterns, story structures, genre and themes; as well as to increase students' listening and reading vocabularies. Moreover, because literature is a powerful conveyor of culture, its use during reading instruction transmits values to our youngest members of society. Through literature, students learn society's "oft-quoted" lines, values, and concepts.

4. *In the past,* **decoding instructions** *(methods of translating printed words into the auditory words they represent), were taught as separate lessons, removed from comprehension activities. Today, decoding strategies are taught while students comprehend material they select to read.* You will teach students several decoding strategies. You will encourage them to combine what they expect the author to "say" with the letters and sounds in the words they see. Because students select what they read, they more actively add their thoughts to the printed words. As a result, words are more rapidly learned because their meanings are more personally relevant. When individual meanings are discussed, the connotations and subtleties of meaning classmates assign to the same word can be learned and understood.

5. *Reading involves complex strategies and higher level thinking.* Pressley, Harris, and Guthrie (1992) have identified several reading strategies that improve reading comprehension and recall: *summarizing* (as described in Chapter 6); *imagery* (see Chapter 9); *story grammar* (see Chapter 8); *prior knowledge activation; self-questioning;* and *question answering* (see Chapter 6). You can teach your students to use these strategies through activities and lessons that appear in this textbook.

6. *Reading should be a rewarding experience that answers students' questions, satisfies their needs, provides momentary escape, expands creative thinking, increases personal self-worth, and develops empathy through identification with characters.* Such high-level goals place a large responsibility upon you, especially if you teach grades K–4, because, in large part, children's literary tastes have crystallized by Grade 5. Therefore, primary teachers need to expose students to as many genres and literary themes as possible in hopes of nurturing a breadth and depth of literary favorites for students' reference and appreciation throughout their lives. Your ability to expand individual students' literary repertoires is becoming easier because more children's books are being written than in the past. For example, in 1960 fewer than 1,000 children's books were written annually. Now, more than 2,500 children's books are published each year.

7. *In the past, "silent reading" from a library book was most often used as a time filler for early finishers. Now, students regularly and frequently read children's literature silently and alone.* As noted by seventh grader, Debi Eudaly, in the introduction to this chapter, the chance to include more independent silent reading opportunities in language arts has risen from the fact that reading itself is among the best methods of learning new words. For example, if your students choose to read silently for twenty minutes a day during the school year, they can increase their speaking, listening, and reading vocabularies by 2,000 words annually (Baker & Brown, 1984).

8. *Goals and activities in reading instruction are not that different from the goals of your oral language program.* The purpose of these goals is to: (1) develop students' abilities to analyze, interpret, and evaluate literary works and become more comfortable with the power of words; (2) increase students' desire to use reading as a tool for learning and pleasure throughout their lives; (3) use reading to create students' insight about themselves and others; and (4) expand students' knowledge of their multicultural, pluralistic heritage.

To sum up, within the last fifteen years several changes have occurred in reading instruction. These changes have resulted in the more frequent use of children's literature as instructional tools; more varied and heterogeneously constructed reading groups; use of a multiple-decoding strategies approach for learning new words; and an integration of reading/speaking/ thinking/writing/ listening activities to develop reading abilities. In the next section of this chapter you will learn the multiple-decoding strategies that you will teach your students so they become good decoders. You will teach your students to use sight words, phonics, structural analysis, context clues, compare-and-contrast strategies, asking others, and the dictionary to decode words.

PUTTING THEORY INTO PRACTICE
TEACHING STUDENTS TO READ NEW WORDS

You will teach your students seven ways to **decode** new words. While you will introduce each strategy separately, students will learn to use them integratively and interactively as they read. You will make students aware that some strategies are effective for certain words, while others unlock different types. Then you will teach the seven decoding strategies and the types of words they "unlock" to students who are not using the strategies appropriately and independently. You will call students together who need instruction on a specific decoding strategy during small group working times in your student communication center. Because you teach the following decoding strategies only to those who do not yet use them indepen-

FIGURE 5-1
Basic Sight Words

These are the most common words in English, ranked in frequency order. The first 25 make up about a third of all printed material. The first 100 make up about half of all written material. This is the reason that all students must learn to recognize these words instantly and to spell them correctly also.

THE INSTANT WORDS*
FIRST HUNDRED

Words 1–25	Words 26–50	Words 51–75	Words 76–100
the	or	will	number
of	one	up	no
and	had	other	way
a	by	about	could
to	word	out	people
in	but	many	my
is	not	then	than
you	what	them	first
that	all	these	water
it	were	so	been
he	we	some	call
was	when	her	who
for	your	would	oil
on	can	make	now
are	said	like	find
as	there	him	long
with	use	into	down
his	an	time	day
they	each	has	did
I	which	look	get
at	she	two	come
be	do	more	made
this	how	write	may
have	their	go	part
from	if	see	over

Common suffixes: -s, -ing, -ed

* For additional instant words, see *3,000 Instant Words, 2nd Ed.,* by Elizabeth Sakiey and Edward Fry, Jamestown Publications, Providence, RI, 1984.

dently, the membership in your "decoding group" will change with each strategy you introduce.

DECODING STRATEGIES

Sight Words. **Sight words** is a decoding strategy whereby your students memorize *words that are short and/or appear frequently in our language and that may not follow basic phonetic rules.* A list of sight words your students need to learn appears in Figure 5-1. The first 25 make up about a third of the words that students read. The first 100 words comprise approximately half the printed words elementary students will read. As you read Figure 5-1 you will more readily understand why some students have trouble decoding sight words; many are similar in length and in their visual **gestalts** (*the word's total image*).

Because many sight words use the same consonants and vowels (e.g., *there, the, their)*, the first instruction you offer is to make students aware of the differences between similar words. Students are to attend to the gestalts of similar sight words as you outline and contrast them (e.g., *there* vs. *the* to show the relationship of the shape of the word to its meaning. For example, *there* is a longer word because it refers to places; *the* is a short word because it means *only one* of something).

Presenting the same sight word repeatedly in different sentences is another effective method to introduce and assist students' memory of sight words. Create repeated exposures by using the language experience approach and require students to say and/or write a sight word several times, such as in the following lesson.

Design a lesson where students observe a bees' nest; read to them about bees, and invite a sixth grader to tell about his job on a bee farm. Then hold a small group discussion with students who need sight word instruction, asking them to tell all they learned about bees. Most students will begin their sentences with the word "they." Write these sentences, one after the other, on a chart until the list of students' thoughts is complete. Students will then read their thoughts aloud together, resulting in a reading where the sight word "they" will be read repeatedly in a context that has meaning to the students. The resulting reading experience will be analogous to the following:

    Bees

They were busy.
They were noisy.
They were different sizes.
They don't want to hurt people.
They are magical.
They make honey.

The next day students experience a similar activity featuring the word *the;* the following week the lesson emphasizes the word *that*. With each consecutive lesson, students review the previous weeks' charts. At the end of the week they teach these sight words to younger students to make their work more authentic.

A third method to build students' strategic decoding of sight words is to identify a sight word that appears several times on a page in a book that a student(s) has chosen to read during a silent reading (or working alone) period in your student communication center. Before the student(s) read that page, call attention to the sight word and what meaning it adds to each sentence. After they finish reading, ask for the meaning of that sight word.

FIGURE 5-2

Definitions of Terms Commonly Used in Phonic Analysis

TERM	DEFINITION
Vowels	Letters **a, e, i, o,** and **u.** Letters **y** (when in the middle or final position in a word or syllable) and **w** (when in the final position of a word or syllable).
Consonants	Letters other than **a, e, i, o,** and **u.** Letters **w** and **y** when in the initial position in a word or syllable.
Consonant Blend or Consonant Cluster	Two or three adjacent consonant sounds that are combined, although each retains its separate identity; for example, **pl**ay, **str**ike, a**sk**, **br**ake, **dr**ove, **sm**ell, **sw**ing, **tw**ig.
Consonant Digraph	Two adjacent consonant letters that are combined into a single speech sound; for example, **sh**ip, **ph**one, **th**is, **wh**at, ne**ck**, ri**ng.**
Vowel Digraph	Two adjacent vowel letters that are combined into a single speech sound; for example, d**ay**, **ea**ch, f**oo**t, r**oa**d, f**ai**r, m**ee**t.
Diphthong	Two vowel sounds combined, beginning with the first and gliding smoothly into the second; for example, **oi**l, t**oy**, **ou**t, pl**ow.**

Phonics.   **Phonics** is *the science of matching speech sounds to printed letters in reading and spelling.* Phonics is comprised of generalizations that correlate sounds to letters, and divide English words into syllables. Definitions of terms commonly used in phonetic analysis appear in Figure 5-2.

In 1986, Congress decreed that the United States Department of Education was to study the effects of phonics instruction upon reading achievement. After four years of work, *Beginning to Read: Thinking and Learning About Print* (Adams, 1990) was published. The report described the importance of teaching phonics as an important decoding strategy for words with regular English patterns:

> Programs for all children, good and poor readers alike, should strive to maintain an appropriate balance between phonics activities, and the reading and appreciation of informative and engaging texts. As important as it is to sound words out, it is important only as an intermediate step. Sounding words out should not be the end goal, but a way of teaching what they need to know to comprehend text. The only reason for reading words is to understand text. Many teachers downplay the teaching of phonics, or relegate it to seat work, in an attempt to introduce students to texts as early as possible. But treating phonics as a poor relation is poor strategy, particularly for children who have little experience with reading before they start school. Only through explicit phonics instruction will such children learn to sound out words on their own, and be able to read independently without difficulty—a key factor in determining whether they can understand what they read. These children need to be exposed to meaningful, written text as soon as possible so that they will begin to notice and have an interest in reading all of the things that are around them

that there are to be read. The study also recommends that teachers use writing and spelling activities to reinforce knowledge of spelling-sound patterns, as well as a deeper appreciation of text comprehension. Finally, it suggests that teachers should encourage "invented spelling"—letting children spell words phonetically, even if the spelling is wrong—to help children develop knowledge of spelling patterns (Adams, 1990, p. 248).

Phonics instruction has been criticized by some because, in the past, it was taught incorrectly or overemphasized. As you may recall, when you were in elementary school, your teacher probably taught many phonic principles as rules to be memorized and you could have been taught as many as 100. You completed worksheets by matching sounds of letters and words you heard to pictures. Then, you learned exceptions to phonic "rules." Because so many phonic "rules" were taught, when you came to an unknown word often you either did not remember the "rule" it followed, or the word you needed to decode was "an exception to that rule." Today, you will teach your students only 17 phonic generalizations because these are the most prevalent in our language. That is, the 17 phonic generalizations you will teach enable students to decode English words with that pattern eight out of ten times. This is because the letter-to-sound correspondence specified by these generalizations is contained in 80 percent of phonetically regular English words. The generalizations you will teach are presented in Figure 5-3. They will be taught during small group work times just as the sight word strategy was taught.

Phonic Generalizations.   To begin to teach phonic generalizations, stress that phonic generalizations will often *not be the first strategy* students should use to decode all words. Instead, they will recall phonic generalizations when a word looks very similar to another word they can already read (e.g., phonics should be used to decode *hat*, because it looks very similar to *cat, rat, bat,* and *sat* that students already recognize). After you teach and give examples of one phonic generalization, demonstrate how you can use that generalization in conjunction with context clues and structural analysis to decode many new words. Then read a sentence from a book and perform a think aloud to decode one phonetically regular word in that sentence that adheres to the phonics generalization you are introducing. Demonstrate how you use phonics, context clues, and structural analyses interactively to derive the word's meaning. (Big books work very well for this section of the lesson.) Next, the group of students reads orally, or one member reads aloud until he/she comes to the next word on that page that adheres to the same phonetic generalization. A group member explains the thinking the group would use to decode that word if it was unfamiliar. Reading continues in this way until all students have had a chance to verbalize applications of the phonics generalization you were introducing.

A necessary step in introducing phonic generalizations is to model how to select from all the generalizations that have been taught. To do so, make an overhead transparency of a page from a book, stop at a difficult word, and do a think aloud of how you decoded that word. Tell how you also

FIGURE 5-3
Phonic Generalizations That Occur in 80 Percent of English's Regular Words That You Will Teach Your Students

GENERALIZATION	PERCENT OF UTILITY
1. When a vowel is found in the middle of a one-syllable word, the vowel is _____ .	62
2. If the only vowel is at the end of a word or syllable, the vowel will usually have a sound that is _____ .	74
3. When a word ends with the silent final *e*, the first vowel in the word is _____ , and the *e* is _____ .	63
4. An *r* gives a vowel which precedes it a sound which is neither _____ nor _____ . It is called an _____ .	78
5. When a *y* ends a word, it usually has the vowel sound of _____ or _____ .	84
6. All single consonants say their name except _____ and _____ which have the sound of _____ when followed by *e, i,* and *y;* and the sound of _____ when followed by *a, o,* and *u*.	96
7. When a word begins with *kn* or *pn*, the _____ are _____ .	100
8. When a word begins with *wr*, the _____ is _____ .	100
9. When a word contains *ght*, the _____ is _____ .	100
10. When *ph* come together, they will make the sound of _____ .	95
11. When a vowel appears in an unaccented syllable, the sound is most often the sound _____ .	87
12. At times two different consonants (consonant blends) and two different vowel sounds (dipthongs) come together and make _____ .	95
13. Which positions make an /a/ long?	95
14. Which positions make an /e/ long?	95

References used in compiling this list of phonic generalizations: Hanna, P. R. et al. (1966). *Phoneme-Grapheme Correspondences as Cues to Spelling Improvement*. Washington, D.C.: US Department of Education; Clymer, T. (1963). "The Utility of Phonic Generalizations in the Primary Grades." *The Reading Teacher* 16(5), 252–258.

think about meanings of the words you know that are around the unknown word. Then model how you selected and applied one of the sound-to-letter generalizations in Figure 5-3 to decode that difficult word. Reiterate this modeling repeatedly until students volunteer to do a think aloud for you when you stop at a difficult phonetically regular word. Without this oral modeling, students may never learn how to select a generalization on their own, apply it to a word, and use the sounds of letters to trigger meaning from their listening vocabularies. Through your modeling, however, this oral/written language and thinking connection in decoding is made explicit.

The last step in this instructional series is for your students to learn to use the 17 generalizations rapidly and independently. As Adams (1990) states, skilled reading is the result of a reader's speed and competence in perceiving the individual letters in words as well as the spelling patterns that make up words. To this end, and as a priority for beginning readers, Adams and other researchers advocate sufficient practice in the following:

- learning letter names and phonemes;
- learning recurring spelling patterns;
- learning the most common sequence of letters within words.

Realizing that you must know phonic generalizations in order to teach them, you now have the opportunity to test your knowledge. Complete the phonics generalization in Figure 5-3 to check your present level of knowledge concerning phonics.

After grading your paper (answers on page 512), if you scored lower than you desire, you may wish to reference *Programmed Word Attack for Teachers, 5th Edition*, by Wilson and Hall (Merrill Publishers, 1990); *Strategies for Identifying Words*, by Durkin (Allyn and Bacon, 1976); and *Word Identification for Teachers*, by Oliver (High Impact Press, 1990).

Total Reading.   In California, another type of phonics program is being used, called *Total Reading*. It integrates oral language with vowel code markings to teach phonics. In this program students say the words as they appear in vowel code, as shown in a sample page from the program in Figure 5-4. A more complete description of this program is available on videotape (Total Reading, P.O. Box 54465, Los Angeles, CA 90054).

THE CHALLENGE OF DIVERSITY

To diagnose reading needs of bilingual students, ask them to write several English words they know in sentences. Analyze the vowel inaccuracies of the words and the syntactical errors of their sentences. Spanish-speaking students will benefit from instruction in phonic rules 1–5 (see Figure 5-3) because the vowel sounds represented by /a/, /e/, /o/, and /u/ appear less frequently in Spanish than English. Spanish speakers will also benefit from direct instruction of the following English sounds and letter correspondences because they do not exist in Spanish: /v/, /th/, /z/, /h/, /p/, /t/, /K in car/, /r/, /tt as in cotton/, /y/, /w/, and /sh/. Chinese students benefit from repeated instruction in long vowel sounds because they appear very infrequently in many Chinese dialects. Similarly, because there are no letter-sound correspondences in Chinese for /ch/, /sh/, /lf/ as in "calf," and /sw/, students may need special instruction in these spelling patterns. Vietnamese children may have difficulty pronouncing consonant clusters and blends, vowel diagraphs, and dipthongs. They also may need instruction to comprehend negative statements because all Vietnamese sentences are affirmative, i.e., "Yes, I don't agree with you" or "Yes, I do agree with you."

FIGURE 5-4
Sample from the Total Reading Program

6

Just then they saw rain.
It began up on top in the
  woods.
It fĕll on the treeš and
  the ground.
It fell on the mouse and the
  squirrel and the deer.

Unlocking words through Dictation & The Vowel Code

Reprinted by permission of the publisher.

Compare and Contrast. This decoding strategy augments phonics instruction. Comparing and contrasting spelling patterns assists students to use **English phonograms** (*frequent letter combinations*) to decode new words. For example, you teach a key word, such as *cat* for the *at* phonogram, and then say: "If this word is *cat,* then this word is *hat;* if this word is *blue,* then this word is _____ (true)." "Cat" and "blue" are written for students, and said by you. "Hat" and "true" are written by you or appear in a book, which is read aloud by the students. The major and minor phonograms you will teach, with a few sample words you can use for instruction, appear in Figure 5-5.

FIGURE 5-5
Major Phonograms: Kindergarten–Grade 8

-ab	-ace	-ack	-ad	-ade
cab	face	back	bad	fade
tab	pace	hack	dad	made
crab	race	lack	had	wade

-ag	-ail	-ain	-ake	-all
bag	fail	gain	bake	ball
tag	hail	main	cake	call
shag	jail	rain	lake	fall

-am	-ame	-amp	-an	-and
ham	came	camp	can	band
jam	fame	damp	fan	hand
slam	game	lamp	man	land

-ane	-ank	-ap	-ar	-are
cane	bank	cap	bar	care
lane	drank	map	far	dare
plane	rank	nap	car	share

-ark	-ash	-at	-ate	-ave
bark	cash	cat	date	cave
dark	dash	fat	gate	gave
mark	trash	gnat	hate	pave

-aw	-ay	-eak	-eal	-eam
law	clay	leak	deal	seam
paw	gray	peak	meal	team
raw	play	weak	real	cream

-ear	-eat	-ed	-ell	-en
dear	beat	bed	bell	den
hear	heat	fed	cellar	hen
near	neat	red	fell	mention

end	-ent	-est	-et	-ew
bend	bent	best	bet	dew
blend	cent	guests	get	fewer
mend	dent	jester	letter	knew

-ice	-ick	-id	-ide	-ig
mice	kicker	bid	abide	biggest
nicely	lick	did	hide	dig
rice	pickle	hidden	rider	giggle

-ight	*-ill*	*-im*	*-ime*	*-ind*
fight	bill	dim	dime	binder
knight	refill	himself	lime	find
light	hill	rim	chimes	kind

-ine	*-ing*	*-ink*	*-int*	*-ip*
line	bingo	link	flint	dip
mine	king	pink	hint	hip
nine	ring	rink	tint	slip

-it	*-ive*	*-ob*	*-ock*	*-od*
bit	diver	cobbler	dock	God
hit	five	job	knock	nod
kitten	lively	sob	lock	pod

-og	*-oke*	*-old*	*-one*	*-ong*
cognate	joke	bold	bone	bong
fog	woke	cold	cone	long
jogger	broke	hold	tone	song

-op	*-ope*	*-ore*	*-orn*	*-ot*
hop	cope	core	born	got
mop	hope	before	morning	hotter
popular	slope	more	torn	knot

-ow	*-ump*	*-un*	*-ut*
know	bump	bunny	butter
blow	jump	fun	cut
show	slump	shun	hut

Analogy Decoding Approach to Phonics Instruction. Irene Gaskins and Marjorie Downer (Media, Pennsylvania) developed a detailed program called the analogy decoding program that uses comparing and contrasting of spelling patterns as a decoding strategy. You can incorporate this approach into your small group instruction as follows:

The first day you introduce five words that each represent a different phonogram such as *day, flew, flag,* and *red,* and an irregular "glue word" (sight word) such as *the.* You then model the compare-and-contrast strategy, by reading a page from a book that contains a difficult word that is underlined. As you perform a think aloud to demonstrate the compare and contrast strategy, students read along with you. An example follows and the difficult word, *incumbent* (that would be covered), is underlined:

"The senator was an *incumbent,* and so won the election easily." I can't think of a word that would make sense in this blank, so I think I'll try the compare/ contrast strategy. I need to look for spelling patterns. I know a spelling pattern is the vowel and what comes after it. So, the first spelling pattern in this word is *i-n. I-n* is a word I already know, *in,* so I'll move on to the next spelling pattern. In this case that will be *u-m*. We have talked about the key word *drum*, so I will use that to help me with the second chunk. The third spelling pattern is *e-n-t. tent*. I know the word *tent*. I already know the first chunk is *in*. And, if I know *d-r-u-m* is drum, then *c-u-m* is cum. And, if I know *t-e-n-t* is *tent*, then *b-e-n-t* is *bent*. The word is *incumbent*. Let's see if that makes sense in the sentence. "The senator was an incumbent and so won the election easily." Yes, that makes sense. I have heard that word on the news. I'm not exactly sure what it means though. I'll look it up. It says that an incumbent is a person who holds an elective office or position (Gaskins, Gaskins & Gaskins, 1991, p. 216).

Students then complete a structured language experience approach and use all six words you introduced in a story they compose, as a class, on chart paper. Students suggest sentences for the story as shown in videotape segment 5. Students then perform a chant and check spelling exercise (which will be described on page 147), using the five words introduced to reinforce their awareness of the spelling pattern in the five key words. Students then write the six words of the lesson from memory or copy them from the chart. Then they write a word that has the same word part but one that they have not been taught, e.g., *bed* is written and taught, and then students must write *red* without having being taught that word that day.

Right before you conclude this small group activity, students play "What's In My Head." To begin "What's In My Head," select one of the words from the five you've introduced. Then you give a compare-and-contrast clue, a fact about the word students are to identify. For example, you say, "This word is a one syllable word. Students then try to guess "What's in your head" by writing which of the six words taught today you are describing.

This process continues until four clues have been given. After each clue, students write a word on their papers. The first three clues you give apply to at least three of the six words taught. The fourth describes only two of the words. The last clue only applies to one word. Sample clues you can use are:

   a. "My word is on the chartboard."
   b. "My word begins like 'flower' or 'fancy.'"
   c. "My name begins with a consonant blend."
   d. "If you fly a flag on the next day, you can say, I _____ a flag."

On the next day, you continue to teach the analogy decoding approach by asking students to blend consonants and vowels. You model how students can add their knowledge of phonics to their compare-and-contrast strategy to decode many new words (e.g., *rat* = r + *cat*). Students then read five tongue twisters to practice blending consonants and vowels. Students make three flash cards. Each one has a phonetic element, such as *scr, spi,* and *spl* written on the front. Students listen to a word you say that contains one of these word parts. Then you say "Ready, Set, Show." All students hold up one of the three flash cards that they believe represents the beginning consonant sounds as they would appear in print. If a student holds up an inappropriate letter combination, you give an easier word that contains the correct letter combination, and ask that student to identify which of the two remaining cards he/she has might appear in the written form of that word. For example, if a student holds up the word card with "spl" in response to the word *scramble*, you would point to the word *scream* on the board, and say "if this is *scream*, then this is *scramble*. The student has a second chance to hold up the appropriate word card. You praise the student for rethinking and revising the selection.

On the third day your students take a special test called "chant and check." The test is similar to the one the students completed Monday except it is comprised of all the major phonograms and sight words you have taught to this point in the year. During the test students are free to look at the words you've introduced, which are printed on charts. When students hear the word you dictate, they write it. Then you dictate a second word with the same spelling pattern, but the second word is not printed in the room nor has it been taught. For example, you might dictate the word *black*, a word from the lists on charts that you have taught your students. Then you ask them to spell the word *shack*, which can be encoded through comparing/contrasting thinking and phonic knowledge even though you have not taught it directly. "Chant and Check" ends after you have dictated up to ten words representing different spelling patterns. Students grade their work immediately to provide instant feedback. This activity integrates oral language and writing to increase students' decoding skills.

THE CHALLENGE OF DIVERSITY

Reading accuracy may be significantly delayed for slower learning kindergarten through second grade students. These students tend to reverse the letters in words they read and write. To assist with this problem, create a clever way for a student to remember the correct form of the letters they frequently reverse, e.g., if "b" and "d" are reversed, tell the child that "b" comes at the head of a bed, and "d" at its foot. In this way children can image a bed each time they try to write a /b/ or /d/. If special remedial reading teachers can come to your room to work with slower readers in the heterogeneously grouped work of the student communication center, two important results can occur. Less able readers can receive 10-minute individualized mini-lessons on a real-world project at the moment the reading need occurs. Second, you and the special teacher can model and perform demonstrations of the language arts not possible without the two of you.

Structural Analysis.   Teach students to use structural analysis as the first decoding strategy when they need to decode long words. **Structural analysis** is *a method of dividing longer words into morphemes to determine meaning.* **Morphemes** *are the smallest units in written words that carry meaning.* While morphemes can combine to form words, some words, such as *apple*, cannot be reduced into smaller morphemes without loss of meaning, so it is a morpheme in and of itself. Structural analysis is the decoding strategy students use when they divide words into prefixes, suffixes, and root words. When readers combine the meanings of these word parts, they often recognize the total word's meaning. For example, if students do not know the word "repeatedly," they should think, "This is a long word so I should use structural analysis. I know the prefix 're' means to 'do again,' 'peat' is the root word, 'ed' means 'in the past,' and 'ly' means the action is continuing so the word *repeatedly* means something is being done over and over." You teach the following morphemes as students need them (see Figure 5-6), in the same small group setting used to introduce the previous decoding strategies.

FIGURE 5-6
Components of Structural Analysis*

INVARIANT PREFIXES

apo	— apologize, apogee	intro	— introspection, introvert
circum	— circumnavigate, circumvent	mal	— maladjusted, malady
		mis	— misapply, misunderstand
equi	— equidistant, equilibrium	non	— nonentity, nonprofit
extra	— extracurricular, extrasensory	syn	— synagogue, synapse, synonym
intra	— intravenous, intramural		

VARIANT (MORE THAN ONE MEANING) BUT COMMON PREFIXES

bi	— a) bicycle
	   b) biannual
		pro	— a) pro-war, pro-life
			   b) proceed, project

de	— a) dethrone, deactivate
	   b) demerit, devalue
		re	— a) redraw, rearrest
			   b) recall, reaction

fore	— a) forewarn, forecast
	   b) forward, foreleg
		semi	— a) semicircle, semiannual
			   b) semiabstract, semiautomatic

in	— a) inept (also *ir*responsible, *il*legal, *im*material)**
	   b) indoors
		un	— a) unable, unbecoming
			   b) unlock, untie

pre	— a) preschool, preadolescent b) precaution, prearrange		

Deighton discovered that of more than 100 common suffixes, 86 indicate invariably the part of speech of the word to which they are afixed, and most of these 86 provide additional clues to word meaning.

From Johnson, D., & Pearson, P. D. (1978). *Teaching Vocabulary*. Fort Worth, TX; Harcourt Brace Jovanovich, pp. 84–86.

* *Com*, while invariant, was not included because there are so many words in which the introductory letters c = o = m occur, but do not form the prefix *com*, e.g., combination, come, comatose

** Note that the prefixes *il, ir,* and *im* are only phonological variants of in-. They occur essentially because it is more natural to say *ir*responsible than *in*responsible.

NOUN SUFFIXES

Fourteen noun suffixes which indicate part of speech:

-ance, tolerance -ment, judgment
-ence, violence -acity, tenacity
-ation (tion, ion), starvation -hood, manhood
-ism, relativism -ness, wholesomeness
-dom, freedom -ty, loyalty
-ery, drudgery -tude, solitude
-mony, harmony -ship, friendship

Eight noun suffixes which indicate agent:

-eer, auctioneer -ist, cellist
-ess, governess -ster, mobster
-grapher, photographer -stress, seamstress
-ier, financier -trix, aviatrix

Twenty-three noun suffixes with specific meanings:

-ana, Americana -ics, gymnastics
-archy, monarchy -itis, gastritis
-ard (art), drunkard -latry, idolatry
-bility, susceptibility -meter, speedometer
-chrome, ferrochrome -metry, geometry
-cide, suicide -ology, biology
-ee, payee -phor, metaphor
-fer, conifer -phobic, claustrophobic
-fication, glorification -ric, meteoric
-gram, telegram -scope, telescope
-graph, photograph -scopy, bioscopy
-graphy, photography

In addition to noun suffixes, Deighton lists 17 suffixes to form adjectives which have invariant meanings.

Seventeen adjective suffixes:

-est, brightest -less, careless
-ferous, odoriferous -able, laughable
-fold, tenfold -most, foremost
-form, uniform -like, humanlike
-genous, autogenous -ous, humorous
-scopic, telescopic -ose, cellulose
-wards, backwards -acious, tenacious
-wise, clockwise -ful, beautiful

Students in kindergarten through grade 2 should learn the meanings of endings "s," "ed," and "ing," and to decode compound words using structural analysis. Older students can learn to use Greek, Latin, and other foreign root words, as well as prefixes, and suffixes to decode new words.

Context Clues.   Context clues are decoding strategies where students use the *position a word holds in the sentence* (**syntactical context clues**) *and the meanings of other words in the sentence* (**semantic context clues**) *to determine the meaning and pronunciation of unknown words.* For example, you teach students to use context clues if they do not know the word *sputtered* in the following paragraph: "The car started the trip when it was low on gas. After one hour's drive the car sputtered to a stop." You model how they could use context clues in conjunction with phonics to decode the word.

By looking at syntactical context clues you can determine that "sputtered" is a verb. Then, using semantic context clues you predict what the word means in reference to a car that is low on gas. Then, rereading the sentence, you say the sounds of the first letters in the word *sputtered*. You think of words you have heard as well as a meaning that would make sense in that sentence. You add phonics or compare/contrast, by sounding the remaining letters of the unknown word, as you think about the context in which it appears.

When students use context clues, they use hypothesis thinking. If their first attempts at decoding are inaccurate, you say, "That's a possibility. Go back and reread the sentence putting that word and meaning in the proper place. Tell me if the word you just said makes sense or not, and why."

Contextual Wedges.   Another method of introducing the context clues decoding strategy was created by De Santi (1992). This lesson is called *Contextual Wedges*. To make a Contextual Wedge lesson, select a vocabulary word you want students to learn, or students can construct a contextual wedge for partners. A wedge is a three- to four-sentence paragraph where the first sentence gives a general clue for the word's meaning. The second gives a slightly more specific clue, so students who used the context clues in both sentences come closer to recognizing the word you have selected. By the time you write the third and fourth sentences, students who used all the context clues will recognize that only one word could fit all syntactical and semantic clues in the passage. Once you've created the wedge, you tell readers that sometimes an unknown word can be decoded by using the words around it, both their meanings (semantics), and the grammatical function (syntax) they serve. Then students read the first sentence. Students use the words they read, and the order in which they appeared, to decide the blank's meaning. Accept three or four words which would "make sense" in that blank and write these in that sentence. Ask students to describe the thinking processes they used to think of each word. Students read the second sentence and revise their list of words that could fill the blank. Repeat this process with each sentence, until by the end of the passage, only one word makes sense of all combined clues. An example to use with your students follows. (Test your context clues' knowledge by marking the point at which you recognize the word being described.)

Some things are both beautiful and useful. We use
_____ to build many things. It is best when
they are straight and tall. Many people
will travel very far to see groups of
_____ . Throughout the year they
are always changing color.
When a lumberjack cuts
down _____ he
always yells
"Timber."

Spoiling the Context.   A third method of teaching context clues, "spoiling the context," was created by Tang (1992). In these lessons, you rewrite a passage so some words are not related. Students read the passage, use context clues to identify words that spoil the context, and substitute words that "make sense," as in this:

Last Saturday, Mrs. Donaldson went out to do her shopping. At the park, she looked carefully at the prices on all the packets because she's a good mother. She bought some bread, some meat, and then some books for her supper. She almost forgot that she needed a quart of meat and, of course, some liver for the pony. At the display counter, she was given some cheese. She knew that her husband would enjoy the color of this particular kind of sandwich. Later she decided to buy some ice cream because it was a cold day. Finally she was ready to line up and look for what she had in her cart. She had to wait for a long time because there were few people waiting in line. She was anxious to be on her way home to prepare breakfast for her family.

Cloze Exercises.   Another method of teaching context clues is called **cloze exercises** (*passages where some words are replaced by blanks and students write the words they think should appear in the blanks*). With each cloze activity, students write their rationale for words they placed in each blank.

There are four types of cloze passages: *selective word deletions, systematic word deletions, partial word deletions,* and *mazes*. Each can become an impromptu or a mini-lesson to build student(s) contextual awareness.

Selective word clozes are passages where one type of word (such as verbs) are deleted. Students learn the function that word serves by making meaning from selective word cloze exercises, such as: I ____ at the ceiling. I ____ the beams clearly.

Systematic word clozes are passages where every fifth or tenth word is deleted. Systematic word clozes demonstrate that all decoding strategies interact during reading to "make sense," e.g., I looked at the _____ . I saw the beams _____.

Partial word clozes are passages where the first letter of each deleted word is provided. Partial word clozes teach students to use phonic generalizations in concert with context clues, e.g., I looked a____ the ceiling. I saw t____ beams clearly.

Definitions added to deletions clozes are passages where the definitions of words are written below the blanks. I _____ at the ceiling. I
(to see)
_____ the beams clearly.
(past tense of see)

In closing, other activities that help students to use context clues is to: (l) print the words to their favorite songs, and have students sing them in class; and (2) ask them to translate the following nonsense story and explain how they used context clues, other decoding strategies, and their listening vocabularies to derive meaning.

Gloopy and Blit

Gloopy is a borp. Blit is a lof. Gloopy klums with Blit. Gloopy and Blit are floms.
   Ril had poved Blit to a janfy. Lok lo had not poved Gloopy. "The janfy is for lofs," Blit bofd Gloopy. Rum are a borp.
   Gloopy was not klorpy. Then Blit was not klorpy.

(The answers to this nonsense story appear on page 170.)

Ask a Friend or Teacher.   Students need to know that *asking another person the meaning of a word is a valuable decoding strategy and that they are not "cheating" when they use it. This strategy is one that students will use frequently throughout their adult lives.* Students learn that they should use sight words, phonics, structural analysis, context clues, and compare/contrast strategies first, and if these techniques have not unlocked the word's meaning, students can ask you or a friend what a word means. By doing so they can continue reading, learn a new word, and have the least amount of interruption to their train of thought as they read.

Dictionary Use.   Research indicates that direct instruction in dictionary use builds vocabulary (Anderson & Pearson, 1984; Beck & Dole, 1992). This instruction needs to be delivered as lessons in a unit. The following skills comprise these separate lessons. Once students can use these skills the dictionary can become a valued decoding tool:

- different meanings for a word, and how definitions are ordered from most general to most specialized, instead of most common to least commonly used definitions;
- using a word's first letter to open the dictionary (open at the beginning for A–G; middle for H–R; or end for S–Z;
- alphabetical order;
- guide words;
- diacritical markings;
- parts of speech a word can serve;
- skimming the page to locate words quickly;

- pronunciation keys and primary/secondary/tertiary accents;
- selecting most appropriate definitions;
- syllabication;
- preferred spellings;
- information in preface and appendices of dictionaries;
- synonyms and antonyms in word definitions.

Once you've spent approximately two weeks teaching students these skills, students should be allowed to select the dictionary they want to use (e.g., some students like soft-covered/hard-covered; picture/nonpicture; thick/thin; 8 1/2" x 11" and smaller). They can choose from a wide variety of types and sizes of dictionaries that you bring to class from the public and school libraries. A list to begin your collection follows:

Picture Dictionaries

My First Dictionary (600-plus words), Oftedal and Jacob (Grossett and Dunlap).

Picturebook Dictionary (1,000 words), Hillerich, English, Bodzewski, Kamatos (Rand McNally).

Beginning Dictionaries

The Ginn Beginning Dictionary, William Morris (Ginn).

My First Dictionary (Houghton Mifflin).

Beginning Dictionary (Houghton Mifflin).

Scott Foresman Beginning Dictionary, Thorndike and Barnhart (Scott Foresman).

Webster's Beginning Dictionary (G. & C. Merriam [distributed by Ginn]).

Intermediate Dictionaries

Scott Foresman Intermediate Dictionary, Thorndike and Barnhart (Scott Foresman).

Webster's Intermediate Dictionary (G. & C. Merriam [distributed by Ginn]).

The American Heritage School Dictionary (Houghton Mifflin).

Advanced Dictionaries

Webster's Third New International Dictionary (G. & C. Merriam).

Webster's Ninth Collegiate Dictionary (G. & C. Merriam).

The American Heritage Dictionary of the English Language (Houghton Mifflin).

Practice sessions in using the dictionary can include small-group, dictionary "sword drills." In "sword drills," a small group leader calls out a word and members of the group try to be the first to locate the word. The first person to find the word tells the dictionary skills used to locate it, reads the definition, and the leader calls out the next word.

If your unit on learning to use dictionaries, guide words, and diacritical markings is scheduled during November, your students receive an added benefit. At the end of the unit you could ask students to write the title, author, publisher, place of publication, and publication date of their favorite dictionary on a piece of paper. Unbeknownst to students, you mail this information to their parents/guardians. You explain that this is the dictionary their child prefers and suggest that they consider purchasing it as a Christmas, Hanukkah, or Kwanzaa gift. In this way students would have their favorite dictionary available for home use.

As a final note, students should not be required to reference a dictionary unless they choose to do so. Through the writing activities in Chapters 7–9, most students discover for themselves (and internalize) the importance of referencing a dictionary to express their thoughts more exactly. By leaving dictionaries at Revising and Editing Centers, these tools become students' permanent partners for decoding and writing. When this "student-initiated partnership" occurs, it also increases students' appreciation for the hard work their favorite authors did to select "just the right word" for their readers.

By third grade, students should also be introduced to a thesaurus. Five popular thesauruses are: (1) *In Other Words: A Beginning Thesaurus* (for students at third grade level and above) by Schiller and Jenkins (Glenview, IL: Scott Foresman and Company); (2) *In Other Words: A Junior Thesaurus* (for students at fourth grade level and above) by Schiller and Jenkins (Glenview, IL: Scott Foresman and Company); (3) *Roget's International Thesaurus* (for students with a sixth grade reading level and above) published by Thomas Y. Crowell Publishers; (4) *My First Thesaurus* (for students in grades 2–4) published by McDougal, Littel; and (5) *Young Writer's Thesaurus* published by McDougal, Littel.

In the next section of the chapter you will learn how to develop decoding skills and students' speaking/reading vocabularies as an important aspect of a student communication center. You will learn to create lessons that build students' speaking, reading, and thinking vocabularies and decoding abilities through singing, reciprocal teaching activities, choral reading, and exercising decoding strategies independently. The books in Notecards 9 and 10 can be used in each of these lessons. Critical Thinking Activity 5 is a two-week study to build pattern and principle recognition and thinking abilities, which integrate speaking, listening, and reading activities. The Professional Development Opportunity will build your ability to effectively read aloud to your students.

NOTECARD 9: LANGUAGE PLAY BOOKS TO DEVELOP YOUNGER STUDENTS' VOCABULARY

Did You Ever See? by W. Einsel
A Chocolate Mouse for Dinner by F. Gwynne
The King Who Rained by F. Gwynne
The Carsick Zebra and Other Animal Riddles by David A. Adler
Monica Beisner's Book of Riddles by Monica Beisner
A Riddle-iculous Rid-Alphabet Book by Jerry Warshaw
News Breaks, School Daze, and other books by Charles Keller
Giants: A Riddle Book by J. Sarnoff and R. Ruffins
Tyrannosaurus Wrecks. A Book of Dinosaur Riddles by Noelle Sterne
What Do You Call a Dumb Bunny? And Other Rabbit Riddles, Games, Jokes, and Cartoons by M. Brown
Put Your Foot in Your Mouth by James Cox
From the Horse's Mouth by Ann and Dan Nevins
Eight Ate: A Feast of Homonym Riddles and other books by Marvin Terban

Amelia Bedelia by P. Parish
Gobble, Growl, Grunt and others by P. Spier
Snake In, Snake Out by Linda Banchek
The Twisted Witch and Other Spooky Riddles by Victoria Chess
Hello, Mr. Chips by Ann Bishop
Monster Knock Knocks by W. Cole and M. Thaler
Mogwogs on the March! by Oliver Dunrea
King Midas Has a Guilt Complex by Roy Doty
Monster Madness by Jack Stokes
Out to Lunch! Jokes About Food by Peter and Connie Roop
Soup With Quackers by Mike Thaler
Socko! Every Riddle Your Feet Will Ever Need by Stephen Manes
Sniglets by Rich Hall
In My Bedroom by Carol Thompson
What's a Frank Frank? Tasty Homograph Riddles and other books by Giulio Maestro
Words, Words, Words by Mary O'Neill

NOTECARD 10: PREDICTABLE BOOKS TO DEVELOP YOUNGER STUDENTS' VOCABULARY

Why Mosquitoes Buzz in People's Ears by Verna Aardema
Bringing the Rain to Kapiti Plain: A Nandi Tale by Verna Aardema
This Old Man by Pam Adams
One, Two, Three, Going to the Sea by Alain
Go Tell Aunt Rhody, Hush Little Baby and other books by Aliki
Shoes for Grandpa by H. Fox
Bertie and the Bear by Pamela Allen
Monkey Face by Frank Asch
Millions of Cats by W. Gag
What Good Luck! What Bad Luck! by R. Charlip
Goodnight Moon by M. W. Brown
Rosie's Walk by P. Hutchins
Roll Over! by M. Peek
There's a Dragon in My Wagon by J. Nelson
Alexander and the Terrible, Horrible, No Good, Very Bad Day by J. Viorst
Over in the Meadow by E. J. Keats
The Animal by Lorna Balian
Where in the World is Henry? by Lorna Balian

Ten, Nine, Eight by Molly Bang
I Was Walking Down the Road by Sarah Barchas
Animals Should Definitely NOT Wear Clothing by Judi Barrett
Buzz, Buzz, Buzz by Byron Barton
I'm Going to Build a Supermarket One of These Days by Helen Barten
Old Mother Hubbard by Aurelius Battaglia
One Bright Monday Morning by Arline and Joseph Baum
Brown Bear, Brown Bear, What Do You See? by B. Martin
Ask Mr. Bear by M. Flack
Have You Seen My Duckling? by N. Tafuri
The House That Jack Built by R. Peppe
The Judge and other books by H. Zemach
Seven Little Monsters by M. Sendak
Seven Little Rabbits by John Becker
Lisa Cannot Sleep by Kaj Beckman
A First Book of Sounds by Melanie Bellah
The B Book by Stanley and Janice Berenstain
I Know an Old Lady by Rose Bonne & Alan Mills

(cont'd)

NOTECARD 10   (cont'd)

When I First Came to This Land by Oscar Brand
I Once Knew a Man by Franz Brandenbert
The Three Billy Goats Gruff by Marcia Brown
The Friendly Book by Margaret Wise Brown
Where Have You Been? by
  Margaret Wise Brown
A Dark, Dark Tale by Ruth Brown
Mr. Grumpty's Outing by John Burningham
I Can't Said the Ant by Polly Cameron
Do You Want To Be My Friend? by Eric Carle
The Very Busy Spider by Eric Carle
The Very Hungry Caterpillar by Eric Carle
The Grouchy Ladybug by Eric Carle
Jesse Bear, What Will You Wear? by
  Nancy White Carlstrom
Fortunately by Remy Charlip
10 Bears in My Bed by S. Mack
The Little Fish That Got Away by Bernadine Cook
Jimmy Lee Did It by Pat Cummings
When Everyone Was Fast Asleep by
  Tomie dePaola

The Shopping Basket by John Burningham
Poor Esmé by Victoria Chess
Busy Monday Morning by Janina Domanska
Drummer Hoff by Barbara Emberley
Klippity Klop by Ed Emberley
As I Was Crossing Boston Common by
  Norm Farber and Arnold Lobel
This Is The Bear by Sarah Hayes
A House is a House for Me
  by Mary Ann Hoberman
I Unpacked My Grandmother's Trunk by
  Susan Hoquet
Don't Forget the Bacon! by Pat Hutchins
You'll Soon Grow Into Them, Titch by
  Pat Hutchins
When You Were a Baby by Ann Jonas
Whose Mouse Are You? by Robert Kraus
Where Are You Going, Little Mouse by
  Robert Kraus

STRATEGIES THAT TEACH

IMPROVING STUDENTS' DECODING ABILITIES AND SPEAKING/READING VOCABULARIES

You will learn four lessons that integrate thinking processes, oral language, listening, and decoding (reading) abilities. In subsequent chapters, you will discover how to also incorporate students' writing abilities into the student community. As you read the following, order the lessons as to those you will want to teach first, if you are not presently teaching; or, order them as to those your present students need most, if you are teaching.

CREATING LESSONS THAT TEACH STUDENTS WHAT TO DO WHEN THEY DON'T KNOW A WORD

To this point, we have discussed how to teach individual decoding strategies. While your grade level placement will determine the depth and speed with which you introduce each of these strategies, you will have taught at least two before you schedule the following lesson plan. You begin this lesson by reviewing (teaching) the decoding strategies in Figure 5-7. Figure 5-7 should be given to each student and made into a classroom chart. By reviewing this chart, students learn that as a general rule, frequently occurring words should be memorized; words with familiar spelling patterns should be analyzed phonetically, or through compare-and-contrast methods; and, long words should be decoded through structural analysis. Demonstrate how students should ask themselves the following questions when they come to a word they do not know:

FIGURE 5-7
When I Don't Know a Word

Use Sight Words if the word is short.

Use Phonics and Compare/Contrast if the word follows a regular English pattern.

Use Structural analysis if the word is a long word.

Use Context Clues if the other words in the sentence give me a clue to the word's meaning.

Quietly ask a friend if the above strategies do not work.

Ask the teacher if he/she is available.

Look in the dictionary if the above strategies do not work.

Reread the word in the sentence if I'm not sure I understand the meaning.

1. "What type of word is this?" (e.g., if it's a long word I know I should first try the structural analysis decoding tool)
2. "Which strategy should I try first to decode this word?"

Once you feel comfortable that students understand these thinking steps, allow them to practice asking themselves these questions. Students practice by pairing with a classmate. Both read a book of their choice silently. When they come to a word they don't know, they interrupt their partner's reading. This partner helps them to ask the above questions, and reference Figure 5-7 to decode that word. You move from pair to pair listening to students model for their partners.

Following this lesson, whenever students ask a friend or you to assist them in decoding a new word, they (or you) can ask:

1. "What strategy do you think is the best for this word? Why?"
2. If students cannot answer these questions, ask which strategies they have already tried, and if they worked.
3. If students can't remember a specific strategy, help them by reviewing Figure 5-7. If this still doesn't help, perform a think aloud to model which strategy (strategies) you would use to decode that word, and tell why you chose it. In such a sharing episode, students gain confidence that they soon will learn to apply these decoding strategies independently and effectively.

THE CHALLENGE OF DIVERSITY

Bilingual students and less able readers can underline five words in a book that they don't know that they want you to teach them. Then at the end of this lesson or any silent reading period, you can meet with them individually and model the above lesson four times with the first four words the student selected to learn. After your repeated think alouds, the student should feel comfortable applying decoding strategies for his/her fifth word independently. As students attempt this independent decoding exercise, scaffold as they work, so they successfully decode the fifth word.

Once students master this lesson, work to authenticize it by scheduling times for them to teach this lesson to a small group of students in another class, one or two grade levels below your students' grade placement.

Students can also learn how to select library books they will enjoy. In doing so, they will relate oral and written language in a unique way. You will teach students to use what they do when they "meet new people" to "meet" new books. Show students how getting to know people is very similar to "getting to know a book." Show how similar interests is the first step in selecting new friends just as being attracted to a topic of interest or a title of a book is the first step in getting to know a book. Model that to get to know a new person (or book) you observe people; flip through books to get to know their character/format. Model how they should analyze if the person/book will answer questions and satisfy needs in a way that they will enjoy (i.e., people talk the same language as the student; a book has paragraphs about the length they enjoy reading). You then determine how much work the relationship/reading will take (e.g., use the "five-finger" method whereby you count the number of words you don't know on a single page. If that number is five or more the book may require more work to comprehend than you may wish to exert). Five decoding words per page is difficult for your students because the average elementary library book only has 50–100 words per page. Because adult books contain 350–450 words per page, a book that contains five unknown words per page for your students is comparable to a book you would read that has 20–25 words you don't know per page!

Last, you model how a friendship is solidified by sharing thoughts and discovering that you agree. You also discover how much you enjoy talking to that person. It is the same in selecting book "friends." Some books will become your favorites because the thoughts the author shares are like your own, the words the author chooses are similar to those you would have selected and they have a beauty and rhythm you appreciate, and the author's writing style was on your "thinking wave length." You want to tell others what your new book taught you. Help students see that when they discover "a new book friend" they can increase their chances of finding more favorite books when they analyze what they appreciated about that book.

THE CHALLENGE OF DIVERSITY

More able students can add examples of other strategies they use to select good books. These students could also inference as to why some of their textbooks are more difficult for them to read than others, and what they can do to build a "friendship" with their least favorite texts.

CREATING LESSONS THAT TEACH STUDENTS TO USE MORE VIVID WORDS WHEN THEY SPEAK, READ, AND WRITE

M	T	W	Th	F

Through your instruction, students can increase their speaking, listening, reading, and writing vocabularies. It is important that they do so. Vocabulary knowledge affects the number of items students remember from reading (Stahl, Hare, Sinatra, & Gregory, 1991). Furthermore, without instruction, students will not gain more than about 2,000 new vocabulary words per year (Blachowicz & Lee, 1991).

The English language has more than 450,000 words, with an estimated 3,000 new words added each year. Because of this, it is impossible to teach students each word separately that they might be required to read. Let's assume that we tried. To realize that goal, each teacher in kindergarten through twelfth grade would have to introduce 20 words from the present corpus of English words every day, and 18 words from the 3,000 words that originated within that year. If each teacher spent only one minute a day per word, and never talked about any word a second time, 76 percent of their language arts program would consist of teaching isolated single word pronunciations and meanings.

Moreover, even if such direct instruction were possible, students would become so dependent upon being told the pronunciations and meanings of new words that they might be unable to learn the thousands of words that would be added to the English lexicon in their lifetimes. By teaching the vocabulary activities through the following lessons, however, students can develop their own richer vocabularies and increase precision in thinking and word choices.

Building Vocabularies.   The following types of instruction have an added importance when we realize that presently, because vocabulary development was not emphasized in the past, half of all words high school graduates use are those they learned in grades 1–3 (Collins & Mangieri, 1992; Nagy et al., 1989). Anderson and Pearson (1984) state that vocabulary lessons should not "get these words into students' heads," but rather, find what students already know and use this knowledge as anchors to learn a new word. The following methods can be used in whole class, small group, and individual student lessons to expand the listening, speaking, reading, and writing abilities in your student communication center.

1. *Find the new vocabulary terms as I read.* The first method of building vocabularies occurs when you read aloud to the class. When you select literature from Notecards 9 or 10, and write their vocabulary words on the chalkboard prior to reading, students hear and see new words as you read. If you wish, they can write the words from the board in the order in which they appeared in the story as you read it.

2. *Teach words that relate to each other.* Before introducing a unit or a reading, ask students to anticipate words they may encounter. For example, if they are to read a story about Thanksgiving, they suggest words that are likely to be in the story (e.g., *turkey, cranberries,* and *dinner*). Thus, when a new word appears, students learn to anticipate how that new word might relate to the theme of the reading (or speech being heard); e.g., new words in a Thanksgiving story probably *will not be* "tunnel," but "turkey," and *not* "dimmer" but "dinner."

3. *Help students learn words before and after school hours.* Games and motivational activities help students learn many words they hear and see outside the classroom. For example, once a week, students can challenge each other to read and define words they've learned through television. Such activities have the bonus of moving students toward independence in expanding their own vocabularies throughout their lives.

4. *Writing the new words we say.* Because word boundaries are almost impossible to identify in oral language, writing new words you say for students to view immediately after saying them increases their vocabulary. For example, let's assume that Wanda responds to the end of your reading of the last chapter of *Bridge to Terabithia* by saying, "Do you think the author chose the name 'Terabithia' for a particular reason?" In your answer, you tell Wanda how much you liked her use of the word "particular," and write that word on the board. You give its meaning, and use it in your response to her question. Then you ask other classmates to give their answer to Wanda's question, selecting classmates who need to build their speaking vocabularies. Very often these students will begin their responses with a phrase similar to "The particular reason I think she chose the name 'Terabithia' is . . ." Using a new word as soon after it is heard increases the

FIGURE 5-8

Sample of Keyword Method of Developing Students' Vocabulary

Contextually explicit keyword illustration (Experiment 1).

PERSUADE (PURSE) When you talk someone into doing something

From Levin, McCormick, Miller, Berry, Pressley (1986).
Copyright 1986 by the American Educational Research Association. Reprinted by permission of the publisher.

likelihood that the word will become a part of that student's speaking, reading, and writing vocabulary.

5. *List-group-label strategy.* Students associate terms related to the topic they are to read. This association can be through connecting a new word to a person who reminds them of the word's meaning (e.g., *philanthropist* = Andrew Carnegie; *generous* = my mother), or to an experience they have had as demonstrated through the Individual Association Paragraphs (IAPS) by Samson (1992). IAPS are designed to tie something new to something familiar. To begin, students choose five words they want to learn. They list the words, their part of speech, and their definitions. Students then use their experiences, imagination, and these words to create a story.

6. *Keyword method.* This vocabulary strategy involves students associating a keyword, which looks or sounds like a word to be learned, with an unknown word in a creative cartoon they design. Students make a cartoon where the characters use the words to be learned. These cartoons create a mental image to aid recall of the visual gestalt and meaning of words. An example of using the keyword method to learn "persuade" appears in Figure 5-8.

7. *Students generate their own examples of a word's definition.* You can provide the definition for a word the class has come across and that you have written on the board. After hearing the definition, each student is to

FIGURE 5-9
Samples of Students' Use of Vocabulary Development Strategies

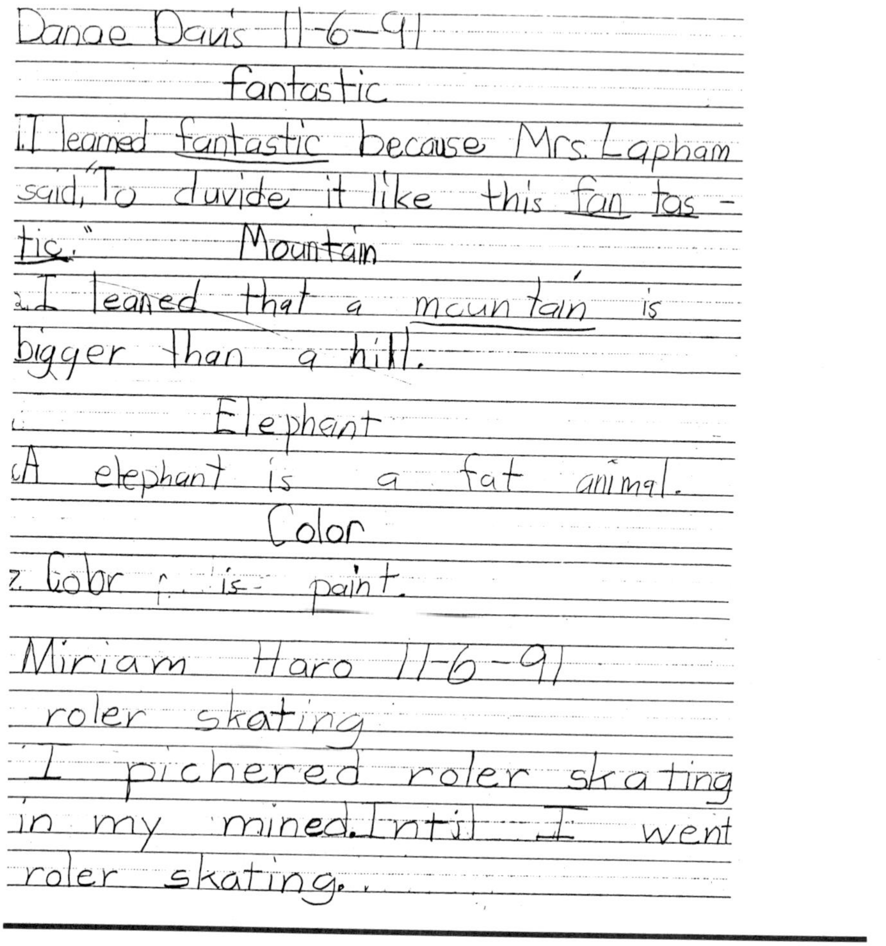

Danae Davis 11-6-91

fantastic

1.I learned fantastic because Mrs. Lapham said, "To duvide it like this fan tas - tic."

Mountain

2.I leaned that a mountain is bigger than a hill.

Elephant

A elephant is a fat animal.

Color

2. Color is paint.

Miriam Haro 11-6-91

roler skating

I pichered roler skating in my mined. Intil I went roler skating.

---

think/write an example. If students think of examples, several can volunteer to share theirs with the group. To illustrate, during a history project a student asks, "What does courage mean?" You write that word on the board and say: *Courage* is a quality when someone has the strength to meet danger or hardship. Someone who has courage is firm in purpose and overcomes fear. An example is . . . (You pause and wait for students to reply.)

8. *Describing their thinking processes.* When students have used any of the above strategies prior to reading materials where the word will appear, you strengthen their writing vocabularies and retention of words learned by asking them to tell you what they did as they read to remember the new vocabulary words' meanings. Responses of second graders in Mrs.

Lapham's class, shown in Figure 5-9, illustrate this lesson and how these students reported their thinking processes.

After teaching several of the above lessons, you may wish to duplicate Figure 5-10 to review the principles you want students to use as they work independently to increase their own vocabularies.

CREATING LESSONS THAT BUILD ORAL LANGUAGE, LISTENING/READING COMPREHENSION, AND INDUCTIVE/DEDUCTIVE THINKING THROUGH SINGING SONGS, CHANTS, AND CHORAL READING

Fox (1988), Calkins (1991), McIntyre (1991), and Barclay (1992) attest to the power of singing and chanting to build vocabularies and thinking abilities. Students can sing from records like the following where a printed version

FIGURE 5-10
Principles of Vocabulary Development

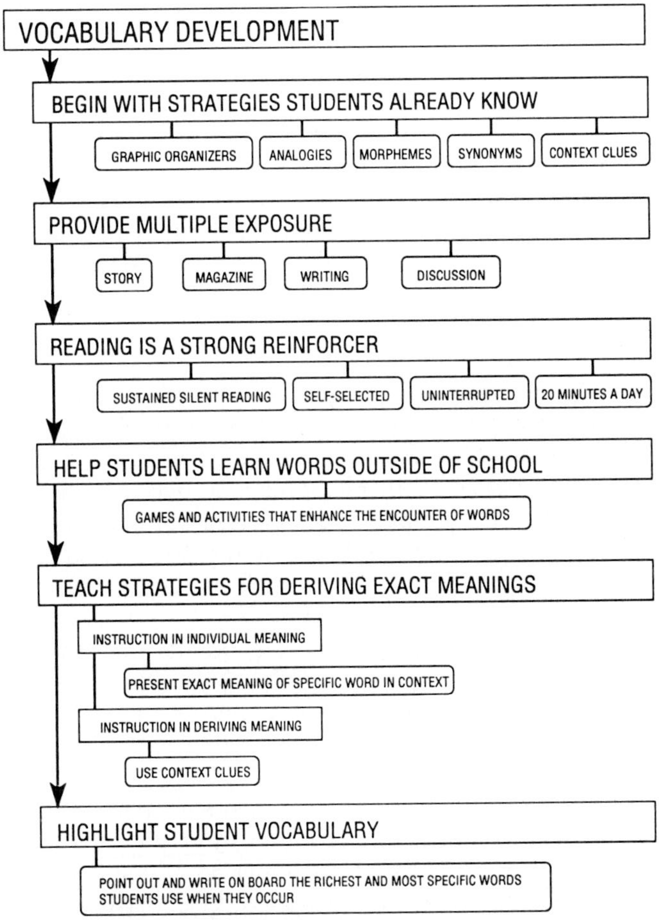

of each song is included, or they can sing songs recorded by their favorite recording artists.

Rock-A-Doodle-Doo with Steve Allen and Jayne Meadows. Kids Matter, Ashland, Oregon 97520.

Sing Along With Oscar Brand. Peter Pan Industries, 88 Saint Frances Street, Newark, NY 07105.

Everything Grows! with Bruce McMillan, photo illustrator (Crown Publishers, 1989). This rendition of the popular Raffi song will probably be an instant hit with Raffi fans, and the repetitive and predictable text allows everyone to join quickly in the reading of this delightful book.

Five Little Ducks with José Aruego and Ariane Dewey, illustrators (Crown Publishers, 1989). Aruego and Dewey's vivid colors and uncluttered illustrations bring this popular Raffi song to life.

There's a Hole in the Bucket with Nadine Bernard Wescott (Harper & Row Publishers, 1990). Wescott's illustrations bring the story to life and provide a humorous ending to a classic children's song.

Frog Went A-Courting with Wendy Watson (Lothrop, Lee, and Shepard, 1990). Watson uses this traditional song as a vehicle to transport readers to a miniature world she creates with her illustrations.

The Vivian Vinn method, demonstrated on the fourth segment of our video, is another powerful way to build logical thinking, oral literary/linguistic sophistication, and decoding strategies. McIntyre (1991) discovered that making "Martian Songs" (repeating the sounds of vowels to rhythm) of the long and short vowel sounds for her first grade students increased the number of vowel/sound-letter correspondences they learned.

Another strategy is to ask students to create a second verse to a rap song you begin, as Angela Powell (fifth grade teacher, Fort Worth, TX) demonstrates (see Figure 5-11). Students then perform their rap for other students.

The beauty of this lesson is that decoding, thinking, and oral literary/linguistic development become fun. Students often repeat the refrains on the playground and at home, and gain self-esteem if they are the first "to know all the words" of the most popular songs on MTV and the radio.

Choral Reading.   When students interpret prose and poetry as a group (choral reading), they experiment with different vocal inflections and increase their interpretive thinking/reading skills.

Choral reading begins by selecting a piece of prose or poetry that relates to a recent experience the class has had. This selection is divided into parts and small groups of students read each part. Choral readings can also be completed as a whole class unison reading, by assigning pairs/groups of students a specific part (as shown in videotape segment 3), or, in rounds (e.g., having each row read a line from "Three Blind Mice" at a different time).

FIGURE 5-11

Sample of Using "RAP" Music to Develop Students' Listening, Speaking, and Reading Vocabularies

PRETEND THAT A SPACE TRAVELER HAS COME TO VISIT YOU. HE IS FRIENDLY AND LOVES TO RAP. HELP HIM COMPOSE A RAP SONG ABOUT HIS VISIT TO EARTH THAT YOU WILL PERFORM TO INTRODUCE HIM TO THE PEOPLE OF EARTH.

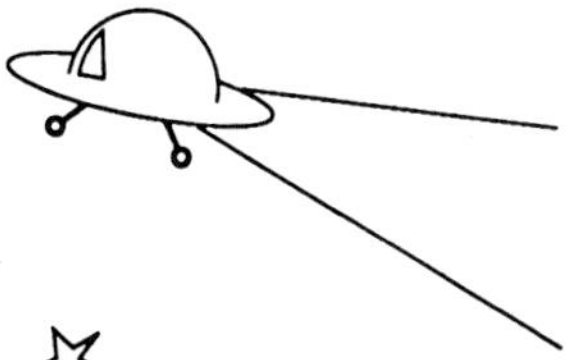

THE FOLLOWING LINES WILL GET YOU STARTED! GOOD LUCK!

This is a story about a dude who was good,
Traveled, round planets...stopped at my neighborhood.

He traveled round the stars a rockin, through the land,
Rappin, to the cool beat of his space time band.

He came to my house and jumped onto my bed
Wiggled his ears...said, "Hey man, I'm Fred."

NOW CONTINUE THE RAP SONG WITH YOUR OWN LYRICS! HERE ARE A FEW BEGINNINGS FOR SUGGESTED STANZAS.

His ears... _____

His skin... _____

He sang... _____

He saw... _____

He said... _____

He ate... _____

He left... _____

So that's how it went with my kookie space friend,
The story's all finished and this is THE END !!!!

Before choral readings are begun, students set a personal objective for their own speaking, reading, or thinking development. Then they evaluate their success.

CREATING LESSONS THAT USE RECIPROCAL TEACHING AND RECIPROCAL QUESTIONING

Reciprocal teaching integrates speaking and listening with the processes of questioning, summarizing, clarifying, and predicting during reading. The lesson begins when you model the strategies students must use as they complete a reciprocal teaching episode (Palincsar & Klenz, 1992): (a) summarize the content of the few paragraphs; (b) question and think about material read; and (c) predict what the next section of reading will contain. Students are then assigned a section of a chapter or story where they are to ask prereading questions for classmates, summarize the reading when all have finished, and make a prediction about the next section to read. Students take turns leading such reciprocal teaching discussions.

With repeated practice students enhance their summarizing skills, create good questions, integrate information, and fashion more logical predictions. A modification of this strategy is to engage in paired reciprocal readings (students take turns reading a page, summarizing it, asking their partner a question about the material on that page, and predicting the next page's content).

Reciprocal questioning is often called the **ReQuest Procedure** (Manzo & Manzo, 1985), and is also designed to build students' questioning minds. Students are told that the purpose of instruction is to improve their thinking and reading ability. Students read a section and ask questions of others, and of their teacher, who has read the same book. These questions are "wondering questions" rather than ones that call for facts in the text, e.g., "What if _____ and _____? I wonder why the author didn't ____ ?"

King (1992) reports that one power of reciprocal questioning arises from students having to both give and receive explanations.

CRITICAL THINKING ACTIVITY 5
Teaching Students to Recognize Patterns and Principles While They Listen and Read

Recommended Grade Levels: Grades 2–8

This one- or two-week activity improves students' ability to perform oral heuristic functions, recognize written patterns so as to improve reading comprehension, and identify patterns in people's actions and speaking. The first day of Critical Thinking Activity 5 begins when students list issues they face that they want to resolve through reading. Then teach the following steps in pattern and principle recognition thinking (which are later transposed into a Thinking Guide):

1. To learn principles and patterns in speech and writings, notice how one concept relates to another concept. Think of how similar concepts relate to one another in laws of science, religion, other content areas, codes of conduct, or rules of stated behavior. Give several examples of concept relationships from content units students are studying.

2. Ask students to think of times in the past when seeing a relationship formed new understandings. Then you model, using a relationship between two concepts students have recently experienced as a class.

3. Read a paragraph as a group and discern a pattern or principle by showing how each piece is placed in a sequence, according to importance, relevance, size, level of specificity, or temporal order. Read a second paragraph and have students tell you the principles being explained and their thoughts to arrive at that answer.
4. Tell students that they will know that a principle or pattern has been identified when they can give examples, and nonexamples of items that adhere to the principle/pattern, and when they can use the principle to categorize, sequence, or analyze new information. Ask them to read a series of content-area paragraphs until they have identified the principle being explained and give an example not in the book. *Where's My Mother* (for grades 2–3), and *The Velveteen Rabbit* (for grades 4–8) can be used for this purpose.
5. Students recognize patterns (and write how they recognized them) in a selection of their choice.

Before the next day, select books where protagonists address problems students listed at the opening of the lesson. See, for example, *The Bookfinder* (Dreyer, 1984), *Adventuring With Books* (Crosbey & Hurely, 1960), *High Interest–Easy Reading Lists* (White, 1979), and *Your Reading* (Walker, 1975). Students select (or you assign) a book to read whereby the protagonist faces a problem similar to the one the student faces. Then, for the rest of the week, students list principles, values, and actions the protagonists followed in their book. As students complete their readings, they meet with you in small groups to discern common and dissimilar thinking patterns between themselves and the protagonists. They also discuss how they can use pattern and principle recognition to face this and other issues when they arise in their lives.

PROFESSIONAL DEVELOPMENT OPPORTUNITY
Developing Speaking, Reading, Writing, Listening, and Thinking Competencies in a Single Setting

Reading Aloud to Students

Reading aloud to students is among one of the best methods of advancing their communication and thinking abilities, as well as developing appreciation for literature. For example, when students are read to, they see the connection between what they hear and symbols that make meaning in print (Sticht, Beck, Hawke, Kleiman, & James, 1974).

A large part of the power of this instructional activity is that for one section of each day, you become "faceless." As you read, students befriend an author they come to love. These "authorial friends" have a closeness to your students that you and others do not; "authorial friends" have not corrected students' errors or asked them to take risks. These friends always see students at their very best. Authors then unconditionally transport their new friends to places they've never been, especially when the following books are shared: *Indian in the Cupboard, The Book of Three, The Black Cauldron, Corduroy, Goodnight Mom, Ira Sleeps Over, Make Way for Ducklings, Sylvester and the Magic Pebble,* and *The Very Hungry Caterpillar* (for younger students); along with "cliff-hanging" chapter endings in *Summer of Fear* and *The View from the Cherry Tree.*

Also, when you read to students, slower readers are on equal footing with better, fluent readers. Moreover, in sharing the beauty and power of the written word, each student experiences the effects that precise, well-chosen words have upon thinking. Often, through this realization, students become convinced that the hard work required to create such language is worth it.

The Bookfinder (Dreyer, 1974), *The New Read Aloud Handbook* (Trelease, 1989), and the Notecards throughout this book aid in selecting dynamic read-aloud books.

How to Read a Book Aloud

Step 1: *Select and practice.* Become a good oral reader. Read the book, preferably out loud, before you share it with students. Vary the genre selections you read to build your students' literary tastes, as through your choices students have access to stories and poems they could not, or might not, read on their own.

Step 2: *Edit the selection.* Before you read, mark descriptions you will eliminate that are unnecessary for your objective, or ones students may not appreciate or understand.

Step 3: *Decide upon an objective you want to achieve in your reading.* The objective can be to call attention to an aspect of the author's style that students can use to improve their writing. The objective can be to strengthen a listening comprehension skill such as to ask students to describe what was happening in their thinking as they listened. It could be to increase students' speaking abilities by having them note particularly vivid phrases they want to use in their conversations. It could be to build reading vocabulary, as new words and semantics (see Chapter 8) are placed on the board at the reading's end.

Step 4: *Create a captivating introduction for your reading.* The introduction can be an interesting fact about the author of the story (see the list of books that describe authors' lives in Chapter 13), an insight that you gained through reading the book, or a description of the first time you read the book when you were a child and what it meant to you.

Step 5: *Prepare how students will give a response to the reading.* Before you read, prepare how you will elicit students' responses when the oral reading is finished.

   a. Sample questions you can use are:

   • Was there anything in the story that troubled you?

- What images, feelings, or memories did the reading stimulate?
- What was there about the reading that influenced you most? Why?
- Were you disappointed or surprised by what was read?
- What questions/comments come to mind?
- Don't worry about how important the details or issue may be, if it's on your mind, it's important enough;

b. Instead of asking students to retell the story to assess their listening and reading comprehension, select a crucial detail and ask students what role that detail played in establishing meaning;

c. To help students demonstrate cause-and-effect thinking processes, ask them to explain why characters behaved as they did. Older students can also discuss whether character actions were prudent/imprudent; appropriate/inappropriate, or rational/irrational;

d. To build students' interpretive thinking and to help them articulate connections, ask them to state the theme or point of the book read. You also ask them to state generalizations that are not adequately supported in the story;

e. Younger students can re-create the story on flannelboards, as a group or in pairs;

f. Use student writings to introduce a story or use a child's composition as the reading.

Step 6: *If you are going to read a multichaptered book, read from this book daily until it is finished, so students are not left hanging.* In multichaptered books, however, you do not necessarily stop at a suspenseful spot—read one full chapter a day. Instead, each day you ask students to share ideas and feelings about events and ask, "What is likely to occur in tomorrow's reading?"

Step 7: *When you read, sit down.* Pull students close. Make sure that everyone is comfortable. Put a sign outside the room asking people to come back to the room at a specified time (when the oral reading time is over). In this way interrruptions of the time between students and their "authorial friends" are reduced.

As a closing note and to reemphasize the importance of reading orally, Beverly Cleary and Russell Baker stated that the turning point in their lives (the point when they decide to become a writer) occurred when a teacher of theirs read something they had written aloud to the class. Both writers said that for the first time, through this activity, they realized that others could and did enjoy their writing.

TRY IT

1. If you are presently teaching, this week begin the practice of writing vivid and melodious phrases the class hears on the board so students see the printed version. Write at least one of these on the board for students to read, by the end of the week.

If you are not presently teaching, listen to others and make a journal entry of three words/phrases used in an especially influential or lyrical manner. Try to use these words or phrases yourself, either in speaking or writing, to increase your vocabulary. In so doing you will strengthen your awareness of the beauty of words, which will be one of your best means of building your future students' vocabularies.

2. Check your answers to the nonsense story on page 152 with the following answer key. Once you have finished, reflect on how your use of context clues and schema influenced your reading. Translate this knowledge to the importance of students having the freedom to give their unique and personally generated response to the material they read.

Answer Key:

Gloopy and Blit

Gloopy is a girl. Blit is a boy. Gloopy plays with Blit. Gloopy and Blit are friends.

Ril had invited Blit to a party. But he had not invited Gloopy. "The party is for boys," Blit told Gloopy. You are a girl.

Gloopy was not happy. Then Blit was not happy.

3. If you are not teaching, observe a reading program in action in an elementary school. What principles are in action? If you are teaching, videotape yourself instructing a reading lesson. Review the principles for reading instruction in this chapter and decide which principle you want to improve upon in your class in the next two months.

4. If you are presently teaching, teach one or more of the Creating Lesson Plans with elementary students. Share results with one or more colleagues or classmates. If you are not presently teaching, read one of the books from Notecards 9 & 10; using the procedures of the Professional Development Opportunity, design a method to use that book in reading instruction.

FOR YOUR JOURNAL

1. One of the most valuable uses of journals for your students is as places where reflections can be recorded. So that you understand the benefits of such assignments: Reflect upon the reading instruction you received in elementary school. How many of the principles and strategies in this chapter were you taught? How do you think that the instruction you received could have been improved? Describe a plan by which you can add this improvement to the reading instructional program you build for your students.

2. Return to the journal entry you made at the end of Chapter 4. Add to the answers you wrote at that time concerning information in Chapter 5. Summarize what you have learned now. Also, answer what writing questions, before you read, did to increase your comprehension.

BUILDING YOUR PROFESSIONAL PORTFOLIO
Holiday Books

This portfolio is designed as information you can share with parents and your students. Many parents ask for books they can read or buy for their children to celebrate the holidays. These are books you can also recommend that parents read aloud to their children. You may also reference this list for books you want to share with your class on holidays.

BOOKS FOR SPECIAL OCCASIONS
For Use With Students In Kindergarten Through Third Grade

January

New Year's Day:

Let's Find Out About New Year's Day by Martha and Charles Shapp
Pinatas and Paper Flowers: Holidays for the Americas in English and Spanish by Alma Flor; Spanish revision by Lila Perl

February

Chinese New Year:

The Chinese New Year by Cheng Hou-Tien

Valentine's Day:

Happy Valentine's Day by Carol Barkin
Valentine's Day by Gail Gibbons
The Festive Year: Secret Valentine by Catherine Stock

March

St. Patrick's Day:

Little Bear Marches in the St. Patrick's Day Parade by Janice
Jeremy Bean's St. Patrick's Day by Alice Schertle
Mary McLean and the St. Patrick's Day Parade by Steven Kroll

April

April Fool's Day:

April Fool's Day by Dorothy Les Tina
April Fool's Day by Emily Kelly

Arbor Day:

Arbor Day by Diane L. Burns
Arbor Day by Aileen Fisher

Easter:

The Festive Year: Easter Surprise by Catherine Stock
The Golden Egg Book by Margaret Brown
Miss Suzy's Easter Surprise by Miriam Young
The World in the Candy Egg by Alvin Tresselt
Cranberry Easter by Wende and Harry Devlin
Easter Treasures by Diane Arico
The Easter Bunny That Overslept by Adrienne Adams
Danny and the Easter Egg by Edith Kunhardt
Peter Cottontail's Easter Book by Lulu Delacre

May

May Day:

May Day by Dorothy Les Tina

Mother's Day:

Happy Mother's Day by Steven Kroll
Mother's Mother's Day by Lorna Balian

June

Father's Day:

Happy Father's Day by Steven Kroll
Hooray for Father's Day by M. Sharmat

Flag Day:

Flag Day by Dorothy Les Tina

September

Labor Day:

Labor Day by James Marnell

October

Halloween:

Space Witch by Don Freeman
Dinosaurs' Halloween by Liza Donnelly
Scary, Scary Halloween by Eve Bunting
In the Haunted House by Eve Bunting
Tilly Witch by Don Freeman

The Witch Kitten by Ruth Carroll
The Terrible Trick or Treat by Edith Battles
Berenstain Bears Trick or Treat by Stan and Jan Berenstain
A Halloween Mask for Monster by Virginia Mueller
Boo by Laura Cecil
Dorrie and the Halloween Plot by Patricia Coombs
It's Halloween by Jack Prelutsky
The Legend of Sleepy Hollow by Diane Wolkstein
Pumpkin Pumpkin by Jeanne Titherington
Real Rubber Monster Mask by Miriam Cohen
Scared Silly by James Howe
Spooky Night by Natalie Savage Carlson
That Terrible Halloween Night by James Stevenson
A Tiger Called Thomas by Charlotte Zolotow
Trick or Treat, Danny! by Edith Kunhardt
The Trip by Ezra Jack Keats
Wobble the Witch Cat by Mary Calhoun
Let's Find Out About Halloween by Paulette Cooper
Halloween by Gail Gibbons

November

Thanksgiving:

OH, What A Thanksgiving! by Steven Kroll
Sometimes It's Turkey—Sometimes It's Feathers by L. Balian
Arthur's Thanksgiving by Marc Brown
Silly Tilly's Thanksgiving by L. Hoban
Mousekin's Thanksgiving by Edna Miller
'Twas the Night Before Thanksgiving by Dau Pilkey
One Terrific Thanksgiving by Marjorie Sharmat
Thanksgiving at the Tappletons' by Eileen Spinelli
Fried Feathers for Thanksgiving by James Stevenson
It's Thanksgiving by Jack Prelutsky
Tiny Turtle's Thanksgiving Day by Dave Ross
Thanksgiving Day by Robert Merrill Bartlett
Let's Find Out About Thanksgiving by Martha and Charles Shapp
Thanksgiving by Gail Gibbons
The First Thanksgiving by Linda Hayward
Thanksgiving Treat by Catherine Stock
1, 2, 3, Thanksgiving by W. Nikola-Lisa

December

Christmas:

Carl's Christmas by Alexandra Day
A Gift From Saint Nicholas by Carole Kismark
Little Bear's Christmas by Janice

Amahl and the Night Visitors by Gian Carlo Menotti
Angel Mae by Shirley Hughes
Christmas Gift Bringers by Leonard B. Lubin
The Fright Before Christmas by James Howe
How the Reindeer Saved Santa by Carolyn Haywood
It's Christmas by Jack Prelutsky
It's Really Christmas by Lillian Hoban
Merry Christmas Ernest and Celestine by Gabrielle Vincent
The Nativity by James Stevenson
The Night After Christmas by James Stevenson
The Secret Keeper by Jamake Highwater
Spirit Child by John Bierhorst
Wake up, Bear . . . It's Christmas by Stephen Gammell
The Family Christmas Tree Book by Tomie dePaola
Christmas Time by Gail Gibbons
Children of Christmas by Hertha Paul

BOOKS FOR SPECIAL OCCASIONS No Specified Age

Holidays

Pinatas and Paper Flowers: Holidays for the Americas in English and Spanish Adapted by Alma Flor, Spanish Version by Lila Perl

Hanukkah:

The Hanukkah Book by Marilyn Burns
Light Another Candle: The Story and Meaning of Hanukkah by Miriam Chaikin

Kwanzaa:

Kwanzaa: Origin, Concepts, and Practice by Dr. Maulana Karenga

Reading Instruction in a Student Communication Center: Part II

An oral reading experience can become a "safe" first step for students who fear speaking before a group, as they do not have to memorize material to be presented.

Interestingly, whatever the reason for a book's appeal, seldom is readers' memory consciously associated with its degree of literary merit. More often than not, readers remember the insights it provided, and the growth it stimulated in themselves.

—G. Robert Carlsen and Anne Sherrill,
Voices of Readers: How We Come to Love Books

In this chapter you will learn how your reading instruction can assist your students to "come to love books." To begin, ask yourself: Do you enjoy reading? Do you comprehend as much as you would like when you read? Another serendipitous benefit of this chapter is that you can also increase your ability to comprehend when you use the strategies you will teach your students (Abartis & Stallard, 1977). More than any period in history, researchers are coming closer to unlocking the mysteries of how the mind comprehends and remembers. In this chapter you'll learn some of these processes.

By the end of this chapter, you will know:

1. How to increase students' comprehension of printed and spoken messages;

2. How to teach decision-making skills, build oral reading skill, and motivate students to use reading throughout their lives;

3. How to employ most recent computer-based and technologically related aids to enlarge students' comprehension.

THEORETICAL FOUNDATION
STUDENTS' READING AND LISTENING COMPREHENSION NEEDS

In the eighteenth century comprehension lessons consisted of asking students to recall information printed on two sides of paper-covered paddles, called Hornbooks. These first "reading textbooks" had the *Lord's Prayer* and alphabet lessons printed on one side. The opposite side contained Bible verses and proverbs, as shown in Figure 6-1.

The purpose of comprehension instruction during this period was to assist students to memorize words. It was not important that students understood what they read. They were learning to read so they could interpret the printed words in the Bible, hymnals, and signs on buildings for their nonreading parents. By "reading" (word calling) words accurately, and with proper phrasing, students assisted their parents' worship and survival. After "successfully calling words," these students' parents could interpret the meaning of the readings to their children.

Since the 1800s, reading and listening comprehension instruction has changed dramatically. It now includes lessons whereby students increase their independent ability to understand, interpret, and use what they read. As Rosenblatt (1978) and Weaver (1988) state, comprehension involves a

FIGURE 6-1
Eighteenth-Century Hornbook

Facsimile of an Early Hornbook

transaction and interaction between the mind of the reader and the language of the text in a particular, situational social context. Weaver (1988) depicts this interaction in the Transactional Model of Reading Comprehension (see Figure 6-2).

Today's students are guided to develop strategies that cultivate their independence in thinking about the text they read. Your instruction will teach comprehension strategies that are more sophisticated than many students would discover on their own, even when they are exposed to the richest of literary materials. Before we describe these strategies, several definitions will be given.

COMPREHENSION DEFINED

Comprehension is *the process of a reader's [or listener's] interaction with printed or oral material* (Brown & Palincsar, 1990; Duffy & Roehler, 1989; F. Smith, 1988). Through schema and previous personal vicarious experiences, students reconstruct the sender's message.

FIGURE 6-2
Transactional Model of Reading Comprehension

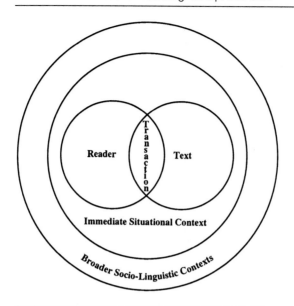

Reprinted with permission from Constance Weaver; *Reading Process and Practice* (Heinemann Educational Books, Portsmouth, NH, 1988).

Literal comprehension is defined as *"reading the lines" or understanding what the author stated, such as recalling details and main points.* To comprehend literal information, students must remember what was explicitly stated. **Interpretive comprehension** is defined as *"reading between the lines."* *Readers process ideas based on what was not stated, but implied by the author, including points the author intended the reader to deduce.* To interpret, students must translate, rephrase, and infer relationships among explicitly stated information. **Applied or critical comprehension** is defined as *"reading beyond the lines" which occurs when the reader evaluates, integrates, and uses information and ideas read/heard in life experiences to make decisions* (Raphael, 1989). To apply what was read, students must relate information in the text to their lives through original/creative/evaluative thinking.

These comprehensions are improved when your instruction builds bridges that provide an in-depth connection between the author's ideas and students' lives. You will "fill students' gaps" in their background knowledge, expand concepts during reading and listening instruction, and alert students to the schemas they already possess prior to reading or listening (Prawat, 1991). The degree to which students transfer new information from exploratory schemas through format schemas is a direct function of how well *connected* the ideas are—both to the specific phenomena they explain (i.e., the reading) and to students' past stored knowledge.

Substantial research suggests that prior knowledge of genres, as well as syntactical features of English, significantly influences students' comprehension (Anderson & Pearson, 1984). As an example, in two research studies, students who had extensive prior experience with a genre and topic misunderstood fewer pieces of information when they read than students who had less prior knowledge. This occurred because the later group used their own rather than the author's structure to organize information (Marzano et al., 1988; Yochum, 1990). It is important that students learn to select appropriate types and depths of thinking before and while they read.

A **strategy** is *an action (or series of actions) employed in order to construct meaning* (Garner, 1987). When readers encounter obstacles to comprehension, they need strategies to overcome their difficulties. Students should be taught a repertoire of comprehension strategies. For example, Pressley et al. (1991) and Weisberg and Balajthy (1991) recommend teaching students to simultaneously predict while reading, to construct images when content can be visualized, to seek clarification, and to summarize at appropriate breaks in the text. Duffy and Roehler (1989), and Pressley, Harris, and Guthrie (1992) have concluded that most successful instructional programs include:

1. Extensive explanation and elaboration of how to use comprehension strategies to gain meaning;
2. Teaching only a few reading and thinking comprehension strategies at one time;
3. Modeling of strategies so students hear a thinking process or a syntactical, genre schema;
4. Reasons why strategies are important and these are explained to students;
5. Feedback about progress that is provided as students apply the strategy;
6. Tailored re-explanations that are given until students can use a strategy independently;
7. Cues for students throughout the year to help them recognize opportunities for a strategy's use.

Researchers have evidence that it takes many years for students to internalize some comprehension strategies (Collins, 1992c; Ogle, 1992). During the 1980s a difference in philosophy developed as to the prominence direct instruction should hold in comprehension instruction. By the beginning of the 1990s, a middle-ground philosophy concerning comprehension instruction became fashionable (Hillerich, 1985). Proponents sympathetic to the position that students can learn to read by reading and being read to began to acknowledge the need for more direct comprehension instruction if students are to become effective readers and listeners (Pressley et al., 1992).

Recent studies by Kletzien (1991) and Zabrucky and Ratner (1989) demonstrate the power of such comprehension instruction. Kletzien discovered that while good and poor comprehenders use similar strategies to understand what they read, good comprehenders differ in their willingness to persist in using them. Moreover, without your instruction, poorer readers tend to reuse only a limited set of reading/listening comprehension strategies.

Real-life comprehension is self-initiated and involves student planning and decisions. Comprehension *evolves* in real life. Information to be understood rarely is given in order of preference, or proper sequence. Further, when one is asked to understand something, the information at hand is rarely complete. In the real world, thinking is spurred when students face a problem, or new information that they are to act upon, not merely when they passively receive facts. For these reasons, comprehension instruction first begins when students misunderstand something. You then teach them strategies they can actively employ to overcome their difficulty.

In summary, the goal of teaching decoding strategies and vocabulary building is for students to independently decode new words; the goal of comprehension instruction is to increase the enjoyment, knowledge, reflection, and personal growth possible through reading. Comprehension is a complex process requiring students' engagement, use of schema, and interpretation of authors' messages as it relates to their life experiences. In the next section you will learn how to teach these components at the three levels for which students can comprehend: literal, interpretive, and applied. Metacomprehension will also be discussed as well as how you can help students orchestrate and monitor their own reading strategies.

PUTTING THEORY INTO PRACTICE
COMPREHENSION STRATEGIES

The comprehension strategies and activities to develop them that students need are: (1) predicting; (2) constructing images when content can be visualized; (3) seeking clarification; (4) prereading planning; (5) summarizing at appropriate points in text; (6) identifying details; (7) sequencing; and (8) metacognition. Instructional activities are presented below.

EIGHT ESSENTIAL COMPREHENSION STRATEGIES

The following prereading and during reading activities teach students to use and organize their thinking and prior information to anticipate what they need for maximum comprehension (Langer, 1991).

1. Free Association. You assist students to learn to ask themselves what comes to mind when they first look at a passage to be read, e.g., "What are you thinking about as you look at this picture and first page of

The Old Man and the Sea or *Make Way For Ducklings*?'' To practice using this strategy, students say (aloud, to a partner, or to themselves) or write what comes to mind when they see or hear key concepts to which their reading will be related. If this free association step is conducted in a group setting, student ideas are listed or mapped on the chalkboard (see Chapter 8 for description of semantic maps). Key concepts can also be outlined in the order in which they occur in the reading/listening experience. Students benefit from this prereading group discussion because classmates' ideas and words embellish their own format schemas before they read/hear new information.

2. Skim Before You Read or Listen.   Teach students to survey a textbook to determine its general character and features so as to project the author's probable purpose. For example, introduce this strategy by asking students to pick up a newspaper and think that the reading will probably begin with a thesis or main idea sentence, followed by most important details. Students next practice skimming a chapter in a book. Afterward, students state something new that they learned about determining the general character of something before reading about it, such as:

> Today I noticed that when I skim and set a real specific purpose for reading something, and if the text isn't talking about it right then, I can still *read* and also *think* about my purpose simultaneously. I remember what I read better this way.

3. K-W-L and K-W-L PLUS.   These strategies enable students to have a graphic aid and ''record keeper of thoughts'' before and during reading and listening (Ogle, 1992). Before students read, they receive a copy of Figure 6-3. Students complete the first two columns before they read and the last column and #2 and #3 during as well as after reading. KWL Plus teaches students that successful reading means asking questions and thinking about ideas while they read.

4. Summarizing.   Students can develop strategies of summarizing while they read when you describe how they can delete redundant or trivial information and relate main ideas to three or fewer supporting pieces of information to better comprehend (as shown in Figure 6-4). Santa (1992) recommends that you do so by asking students to fold a sheet of paper into six parts. Students reopen it and number each section to correspond to the first six paragraphs they will read. As students read each paragraph they describe the thinking they used to delete redundancies and to identify the central idea. All students write one summary sentence in rectangle l to record paragraph l's main point and do the same for the five remaining paragraphs. They share their summarization strategies with classmates.

FIGURE 6-3
The K-W-L Comprehension Strategy

What We Know	*What We Want to Find Out*	*What We Learn—Still Need to Learn*
1.		

2. Categories of Information We Expect to Use

   A.

   B.

   C.

   D.

   E.

   F.

   G.

3. Summary of What We Learned ______________________________

____

____

____

K-W-L Strategy Sheet from "K-W-L: A teaching model that develops active reading of expository text," Donna Ogle, *The Reading Teacher,* February 1986, 564–567. Reprinted with permission of Donna Ogle and the International Reading Association.

FIGURE 6-4
Ways in Which Ideas Can Be Related in a Reading Passage

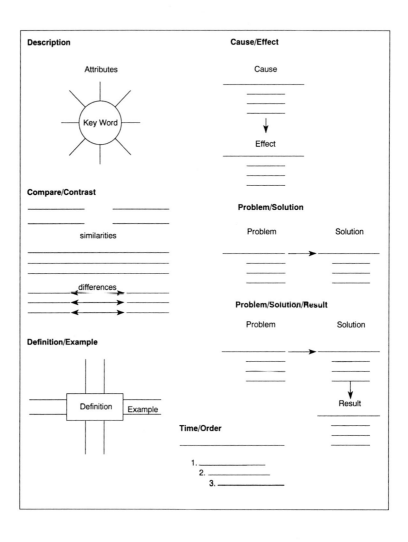

You can also model summary thinking visually by writing a summarizing paragraph as students watch (e.g., summary of a paragraph from *The Velveteen Rabbit* demonstrated in Figure 6-5).

FIGURE 6-5
Summary Thinking: *The Velveteen Rabbit*

There was a velveteen rabbit, and ~~in the beginning he~~ *Who* was really splendid. ~~He~~ *Delete redun dancies* *was* (fat and bunchy), ~~as a rabbit should be~~; his coat was spotted brown and *Combine Ideas* white, he had real thread whisker's and his ears were lined with pink sateen, on Christmas morning, when he sat wedged in the top of the Boy's stocking, with a sprig of holly between his paws, the effect was charming.

There were other things in the stocking, ~~nuts and oranges and a toy engine, and chocolate almonds and a clockwork mouse,~~ but the Rabbit was quite the best of all. For at least two hours, *[^]* the Boy loved ~~mi, and then Aunts and Uncles~~ *the rabbit best* ~~came to dinner, and there was a great rustling of tissue paper and unwrapping of parcels, and~~ In the excitement of looking at all the new presents the Velveteen Rabbit was forgotten, *however*.

Invent
could restate in less wrds
e.g. His body was beauti and adorned with Christmas decorations.

Add summative words.

The following books are excellent for teaching summarization because chapters have clear but implied summaries.

Historical Fiction and Nonfiction

1. *The Courage of Sarah Noble* by Alice Dalgliesh. Scribner, 1954.
2. *A Weed Is a Flower: The Life of George Washington Carver* by Aliki. Prentice-Hall, 1965.
3. *Jack Jouett's Ride* by Gail Haley. Viking, 1973.
4. *The Drinking Gourd* by F. N. Monjo. Harper Junior Books, 1983.
5. *The White Stallion* by Elizabeth Shub. Greenwillow, 1982; Bantam, 1982.
6. *Little House in the Big Woods* by Laura I. Wilder. Harper Junior Books, 1953, 1986.
7. *And Then What Happened, Paul Revere?* by Jean Fritz. Coward, 1973.
8. *Columbus* by Ingri D'Aulaire & Edgar P. D'Aulaire. Doubleday, 1955.
9. *Sarah, Plain and Tall* by Patricia MacLachlan. Harper Junior Books, 1987.
10. *Johnny Appleseed* by Carol Beach York. Troll Associates, 1980.

FIGURE 6-6
Teaching Sequential Reasoning Strategies

5. Detail Recognition Strategies.   You will tell students that details identify who, what, where, and why single events occur. You read sample sentences from intact literature passages that you display on the overhead. You do not ask students to locate specific details you gave prior to a reading because this is not an authentic task. Instead, you ask students to point out details that they found interesting, effective, suspenseful, creative, humorous, or vivid. As a class you analyze differences between detail types and what characterizes the most effective details. Students are encouraged to use such details in their writing, and in the books they read to attend to the subtleties of meaning that authors intended their details to convey.

6. Sequential Reasoning Strategies.   To teach the importance of sequential thinking during reading, listening, and speaking, introduce clue words that indicate order (e.g., *first, next, then*). One method of doing so with older students is to demonstrate a recipe without giving directions or the demonstration to one-half of the class. These students then attempt to duplicate your recipe in writing, as shown in Figure 6-6.

Each of these pupils then gives his/her recipe to a classmate who did not watch your demonstration. That classmate is to read that recipe and

FIGURE 6-7
Teaching Sequential Reasoning to Younger Students

see if he/she knows what you made. Afterward, the pair discusses their success and reads a story using reciprocal teaching. They stop at each sequential clue word in their book and describe what it triggered in their sequential reasoning. Younger students can complete a similar activity by putting clue words on pictures that depict a story's order, as shown in Figure 6-7.

7. Metacognitive Comprehension Strategy Instruction. Garner (1987) recommends that you develop students' metacognitive strategies after they read. You can do so by asking students to describe: (1) a comprehension process they used; (2) something new they learned; (3) a plan to improve their reading comprehension. Duffy and Roehler (1989) illustrate how students report such metacognitive thinking:

Teacher: I'm going to erase from the board the steps of my strategy, and you see if you can use a strategy of your own that is like mine. [puts new word on board] . . . Now, Sam, what would you do first to figure out this word? Can you show me how you'd figure out the word?

Student: [Sam responds by just pronouncing the word.]

Teacher: You said the word correctly, Sam, but I don't know whether you were doing the thinking correctly. What did you do first? Talk out loud so I can hear how you figured that word out.

Student: [Sam responds, stating the steps he used.]

Teacher: That's good, Sam. You stated the steps you used to figure out the word correctly. This strategy doesn't work all the time, because some of our words look like words with prefixes but really aren't. [Illustrates the word *under*] See if this word can be pronounced using our prefix strategy. [Leads students through the process showing them where the strategy doesn't work and why] (Adapted from Example 13.1, pp. 228–229)

8. Students Select Comprehension Strategies to Match Personal Purpose.   When you have taught one or more of the above strategies, you remind students of the strategies they have learned. Before they read their next book they choose one they wish to practice or you alert them to ones that would assist in comprehending a specific body of information they are about to read or hear. For example, you say:

The depth of this story lends itself to full use of your prediction and visualization strategies. The reason I know this is because . . .

With these strategies in mind, students can more effectively use the following lessons, materials, and activities to further build their comprehension abilities.

STRATEGIES THAT TEACH
LESSONS AND MATERIALS TO BUILD STUDENTS' COMPREHENSION

Basal readers, children's literature, reading kits, technology, and oral reading activities can be used in many lesson plans to build comprehension abilities.

CREATING LESSONS WITH BASAL READERS AND CHILDREN'S LITERATURE

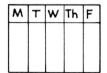

Basal Readers

Basal readers are *textbooks that contain stories taught through a DRA (directed reading activity)*. The DRA contains four steps: prereading activities (to build schema and vocabulary); directed silent reading; oral sharing/reading; and oral rereading or responding to decoding/comprehension activities related to the story. In the late 1970s a debate concerning the value of basal readers intensified. Some argued that basals were excellent teaching tools and provided a core for curriculum. Others argued that basals become the curriculum, and limit students' abilities to develop a lifelong love for reading and writing. Still others claimed that the quality of instruction does not depend upon basals or children's literature. Rather it depends upon a teacher's ability to incorporate the principles of reading instruction to all materials. If you use a basal, most teachers' manuals suggest activities that develop students' comprehension strategies. You will likely modify their suggestions to adhere to the principles of effective instruction you've read in this textbook.

Children's Literature

As shown in videotape segment 4, students can improve reading comprehension through children's literature. You assist students to think before, during, and after they read by teaching the strategies described previously in the chapter. Moreover, research has demonstrated that pupils who examine differences between genre become better readers and writers (Langer & Applebee, 1987). Genres of children's literature as well as suggested titles to build students' comprehension appear below.

Folk Literature.   This is a large body of literature preserved and transformed by generations of storytellers from times when voice and memory alone bound one generation to the next. Folk literature passed from country to country through storytelling. Guide students to discover that folktales are a distinct genre form:

1. They have simple stories that involve "good" over "bad," and begin with "once upon a time."
2. Characters' problems are similar to those of people around the world.
3. Endings are positive and happy, i.e., characters "live happily ever after."

Folk literature includes folktales, fairy tales, myths, legends, parables, tall tales, legends, and proverbs. It is designed to speak to the child in all of us, and symbolizes deep feelings and serious thoughts through fantastic figures and events. Through fairy- and folktales students can use their imagination to create a different world. Moreover, because fairy tales are predicaments being overcome by forces of good, readers receive consolation and courage to pursue positive actions. *Gods, Stars, and Computers: Fact and Fancy in Myth Science* is an excellent book to use in introducing distinctive features of myths. Many popular myths come from Greece, Norway, and the Hindu religion; Kipling's *Just-So Stories* is an example.

Fairytales, Fables, Legends, and Myths by Bette Bosma has more than fifty lessons that develop comprehension through folk literature. Tomie dePaola's *Mother Goose* and Michael Hague's *Mother Goose: A Collection of Classic Nursery Rhymes* are excellent folk literature for younger students. Older students enjoy folktales that represent the following cultures:

Foreign Folktales: *Anansi the Spider* by G. McDermott; *Who's in Rabbit's House?* by V. Aardema; *Why Mosquitoes Buzz in People's Ears* by V. Aardema;

The Village of Round and Square Houses by A. Grifalconi; *Bringing the Rain to Kapiti Plain* by V. Aardema; *The Calf of the November Cloud* by H. Ruben; *Mufaro's Beautiful Daughters* by J. Steptoe; *African Myths and Legends* by K. Arnot; *Not So Fast Songololo* by N. Daly; *African Animals Through African Eyes* by J. and A. D'Amato; *Jambo Means Hello; Mojo Means One;* and *Zamani Goes to Market* by M. Feelings; *Africa* (*A New True Book*) by D. V. Georges; *The Baby Leopard* by L. and C. Goss; *African Dream* by E. Greenfield; *How the Leopard Got His Spots* by D. Glover; *The Elephant's Child* and *How the Rhinoceros Got His Skin* by R. Kipling; *How Many Spots Does a Leopard Have? and Other Tales* by J. Lester; *Jungles* (*A New True Book*) by I. Podendorf; *Safari Adventure* by Troll Associates Publishers; *Endangered Animals* by L. M. Stone; *I Am Eyes: Ni Macho* by L. Ward; and *Africa Counts: Number and Pattern in African Culture* and *Count on Your Fingers African Style* by C. Zaslavsky.

A Russian Folktale by Eric A Kimmel; *The Greatest of All: A Japanese Folktale* by Eric A. Kimmel; *Clockboard Clock Square* by Leoniel Yokhuin, Raduga Publishers, Moscow, which is a collection of 27 Russian folktales; and Sergei Mikhalkov: *A Choice for Children—Poems, Fables, and Fairy Tales*, which is Russian literature, published by Raduga Publishers in Moscow. Penguin provides free teacher's guides, objectives, and activities to lead instruction of major myths from around the world (Penguin Publishers, 375 Hudson Street, NY, NY 10014-3620).

Native American Folktales: *The Fire Bringer* by R. Hodges; Paul Goble's *The Gift of the Sacred Dog;* Olaf Baker's *Where the Buffaloes Begin;* G. Grinnell's *The Whistling Skeleton: American Indian Tales of the Supernatural;* B. Baker's *Rat Is Dead and Ant Is Sad;* B. Baylor's *God on Every Mountain;* E. Coatsworth's *The Adventures of Nanabush: Objibway Indian Stories;* and *Dancing with Indians* by Angela S. Medearis.

Myths: *Adventures of the Greek Heroes* by McLean; *Tales of Greek Heroes* by Green; *Greek Gods and Heroes* by Graves; *Heroes and Monsters of Greek Myth* by Evslin; *Myths of the Norseman* by Green; and *Tales of Ancient Egypt* by Green.

Fables.   Fables are the second category of literature. They are single incident stories with a moral. Examples include: *Fables* by Arnold Lobel; *Twelve Tales From Aesop* by Eric Carle; *Aesop's Fables* by Michael Hague; *Doctor Coyote: A Native American Aesop's Fables* by John Bierhorst; *Spin a Fable, Famous Fables for Little Troopers,* and *Once Upon A Wood: Ten Tales from Aesop* by Rice. Students can select a phenomenon in which they are interested (e.g., origin of the world, seasons of the year) and then create their own fable to explain the phenomenon. Then, since fables were written to represent the cultural values of a society, students can compare their fables to those from Greece and other cultures in order to uncover the beliefs and values each portray.

Students should be led to discover that fables involve a single event between a few characters and usually end with a moral. Not all fables have animal characters (e.g., *Fables in Slang,* and *Fables of Our Time*). Students can test a fable they have written by taking off the moral and asking other people what message the fable was to convey. Tompkins and Hoskinson (1990) recommend that students compare Australian, Native American, Nigerian, and Polynesian explanations of the sun and the moon in *Legends of the Sun and Moon* (Hadley & Hadley, 1983).

Fantasy and Science Fiction.   A third category of literature is fantasy and science fiction. Fantasy includes stories involving personified/imaginary toys, animals, and inanimate objects, such as *Charlotte's Web*. Science fiction involves stories that project people into future scenarios including scientific inventions that did not exist at the time the book or story was written. Concerning science fiction, Carl Sagan stated: "The greatest human significance of science fiction may be as experiments on the future, explorations of alternative destinies, and attempts to minimize future shock. This is part of the reason that science fiction has so wide an appeal among young people—it is *they* who will live in the future" (Sagan, 1990, p. 7). Another value of fantasy and science fiction is to build students' creative thinking as they transcend from literal to imaginary versions of reality, and consider "what-ifs." Older students appreciate the genius of some science fiction writers who correctly predicted the future, e.g., Jules Verne's *2,000 Leagues Under Sea* (prophesied submarine travel) and Isaac Asimov's *Robot* (foresaw the role of robotics in modern societies).

Historical Fiction.   This is a fourth category of literature. It contains descriptions of past events, and tales related to that event that are likely *not* to have occurred. Its value rests in representations of the language and values of historical periods (e.g., *Little House in the Big Woods*, *Mr. Revere and Me*, *Johnny Tremain*, *I'm Deborah Sampson*; also see books on Notecard 22, Chapter 10).

Animal Stories.   This is a fifth category of children's literature. Animal stories are among children's perennial favorites. Students enjoy magical animal tales as well as stories that bond children/characters to their pets. Classic examples include *Black Beauty* by Anne Sewell; *The Yearling* by Marjorie K. Rawlings; *Gentle Ben* by Walther Morey; *Call of the Wild* by Jack London; *Charlotte's Web* by E. B. White; *Rabbit Hill* by Robert Lawson; *The Tale of Peter Rabbit* by Beatrix Potter; *The Wind in the Willows* by Kenneth Grahame; *Sounder* by William Armstrong; *Rascal* by Sterling North; *The Black Stallion* by Walter Farley; *Big Red* by Jim Kjelgaard; *Old Yeller* by Fred Gipson; *Where the Red Fern Grows* by Wilson Rawls; and *The Incredible Journey* by Sheila Burnford.

Adventures and Mystery Stories.   These are the sixth category of literature, and are also among children's most loved. Students enjoy the main characters, fast pace, and survival skills they contain. Younger students enjoy: *The Island of the Skog* by Steven Kellogg; *Madeline's Rescue* by Ludwig Bemelmans; *Create Your Own Mysteries* Series; *Liza Lou and the Yeller Belly Swamp* by Mercer Mayer; *Encyclopedia Brown* by Donald Sobol; *Captain*

Grey by Avi; and *Little Tim and the Brave Sea Captain* by Edward Ardizzone.

Older students enjoy: *The Adventures of Huckleberry Finn* and *Tom Sawyer* by Mark Twain; *The Hardy Boy Mysteries* Series; *The Nancy Drew Mysteries* Series; *Treasure Island* by Robert Louis Stevenson; *My Side of the Mountain* and *Julie of the Wolves* by Jean George; *The Witch of Blackbird Pond* by Elizabeth George Speare; *The House of Dies Drear* by Virginia Hamilton; *Funny Bananas* by Georgess McHargue; and *The Mysterious Disappearance of Leon (I Mean Noel)* by Ellen Raskin.

Fiction Chronicles.   This is the seventh category of literature. Chronicles are books like *The Lottery, Martian Chronicles, The Ark, The Incredible Journey, The Plague, The Wall,* and *Lord of the Flies.* They differ from fictional biographies in that they are relatively impersonal and focus upon communal experiences. Such books focus upon a group of people who engage in the same event, suffer, and survive in their own way (e.g., people in crisis involving natural disasters, expeditions, and team sports).

Autobiographies/Biographies.   This eighth category of literature can be fiction and nonfiction. Fictional autobiographies and biographies are invented stories about a main character who actually lived, but the story about that person is not true. One type of fictional autobiographies/biographies that students enjoy are fictional memoirs. These memoirs are colorful and often humorous styles of storytelling where one person is talking about another person to which the author was close. Examples are: *Ben and Me, A First Biography Series* by Davie Adler; *A Picture Book of John F. Kennedy; A Picture Book of Martin Luther King, Jr.;* and *A Picture Book of Eleanor Roosevelt.* Fictional autobiographies are designed to depict a period of time through the eyes of a main character who grows up or lives during that period, but the main character is fictional, such as *Jane Eyre, Great Expectations, A Farewell to Arms, Catcher in the Rye, The Chosen, The Cool World, In Watermelon Sugar, Heart of Darkness,* and *Spoon River Anthology.* Fictional diaries and letters enable authors to illustrate the charm and wealth single events bring to shaping life and history.

Ghost Stories.   This is a special category of literature that assists students to feel awe, thrill, fear, wonder, curiosity, and amazement. When children read a good ghost story or hear one read aloud, they often retell or write this or a new ghost story, re-establishing the oral and written tradition of storytelling.

Nonfiction and Poetry.   The nonfiction category includes informational books or trade books, which will be described in Chapter 10; poetry will be discussed in Chapter 11.

Among the best ways to build students' literary appreciation is to structure this lesson plan so students have intense and satisfying interactions with many genres. A second step is to teach students to analyze why they prefer one genre above others. Boyd (1992) found that periods of

FIGURE 6-8

The Reading Wheel

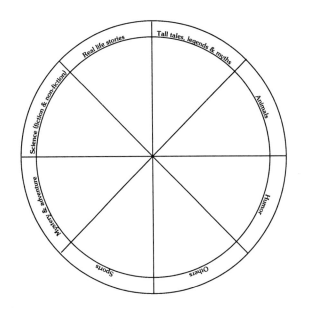

sustained silent reading and the Reading Wheel in Figure 6-8 assist in implementing these steps. To use the Reading Wheel, students complete a book of choice and record its title/author under the category of genre it represents. Students may use more than one wheel per year and carry the record from teacher to teacher, year to year.

Another value of creating lesson plans with literature is that students will be surrounded with varied types of literature and the first stories they write will borrow from these many genres just as their "play-acting" reflects real-life adult role models. The following books contain vivid, heroic, adolescent role models that build middle school students' comprehension through literature: *Books Appeal: Get Teenagers into the Library*, Upstart, Box 889, Hagerstown, MD 21741; and *Writers' Voices* and *New Writers' Voices*, Literacy Volunteers of New York City, Inc., 1221 Avenue of the Americas, New York, NY 10013.

The following sources contain excellent lesson plan ideas that build elementary students' comprehension strategies with selections of children's literature: *Share It If You Read It*, Upstart, Box 889, Hagerstown, MD 21741; *An ABC of Children's Book Activities*, Upstart, Box 889, Hagerstown, MD 21741; *Back to Books: 200 Library Games to Encourage Reading*, Upstart, Box 889, Hagerstown, MD 21741; *Book It! National Reading Incentive Program*,

Pizza Hut, P.O. Box 2999, Wichita, KS 67201; *Helping Young Minds Bloom on Literature*, The Teacher's Touch, 1909 West Avenue G, Muleshoe, TX 79347; and *Improving Reading and Thinking Abilities*, Addison-Wesley, P.O. Box 10888, Palo Alto, CA 94303.

THE CHALLENGE OF DIVERSITY

Research indicates that slower learning students can be paired with their parents or other adults to improve their reading comprehension. Topping (1987) found that such tutoring improved slower learning students' reading accuracy five times their base level. It also increased their reading speed threefold. Rasinski and Fredericks (1991) also found that five minutes of paired reading by remedial readers with their parents each night was effective in advancing comprehension.

CREATING LESSONS WITH READING KITS AND SUPPLEMENTARY MATERIALS

Among the most effective and popular lessons for reading comprehension involve supplementary programs such as kits, high interest–low vocabulary series, multimedia packages, and current event weekly magazines (see Notecard 11). Samples of such materials are described below.

Great Books Series. The Great Books Series is a paperback series of classical and modern literature for grades 2 through 12. Special training is available for this program by writing to The Great Books Foundation, 40 East Huron Street, Chicago, IL 60611. An example of it in use appears in videotape segment 1 when a principal leads a Great Books discussion in his office. Although Great Books are traditionally used as extension material for gifted readers, it has recently been used very effectively to improve comprehension abilities of learning disabled and average readers. Through using the Great Books, students study the classics as a text, learn valuable cultural knowledge, and vicariously experience many lifestyles.

Reading Is Fundamental (RIF). This organization was founded to provide free paperback books for students to take home and make their own. Information concerning this distribution is available through Reading Is Fundamental, Smithsonian Institution, Washington, DC 20560. By 1985, RIF had distributed over 57 million books to students. If you are interested in beginning a RIF program for your students, you may find *The RIF Book of Ideas: Raising Funds, No. 2* and *RIF Book of Ideas: Activities to Motivate Reading* valuable. These books can be ordered from the above address.

Reading Kits. Publishers place a wide variety of reading materials in kits, such as novel units (as discussed in Chapter 10), self-instructional stories, high interest but low level vocabulary materials, and Treasure Boxes with a wide variety of individualized extension activities to develop reading/thinking abilities.

CREATING LESSONS THAT USE TECHNOLOGY TO STRENGTHEN READING COMPREHENSION

You can use the computer in many ways during reading instruction. With your help, students can turn to the computer to overcome several difficulties in comprehension. Research is presently under way to understand all the ways that computer-supported lessons improve students' communication and thinking abilities. Already many forms of technology are a part of many language arts programs. These include videocassette cameras, telephone conferencing networks, international computer databases, word processing, word processing with voice synthesizers, spelling checkers, computer thesauruses, editing programs, and branching software to provide opportunities for students to create their own story endings and plots. With computers your students can be exposed to high quality examples which improve their communication competencies. Technology experts and educators outside your classroom take several months of concentrated work to develop each piece of software. Such instructional materials would not be available for your students without them because you would not have the time to create and do the research connected with their creation.

Another important contribution technology makes to language arts programs is that through it information becomes more vivid. Research has demonstrated that the more vivid the information one receives the more permanent it becomes in long-term memory (French, 1990). Technology also enables current events to be viewed and discussed in the classroom; it adds variety and a change of pace, and increases motivation for language learning. Technologically supported communication tools also have the potential to change the purpose, process, and products of students' communication activities.

A recent study demonstrated that grouping students in computer-based activities cost no more than traditional instruction (Fletcher, Hawley, & Piele, 1990). As a matter of fact, when two students work at one computer, the number of literal comprehension errors decreases. There is also better support for higher level comprehension in pairs than when students work individually at the computer (French, 1990). This appears to occur because two students are likely to have different skills. By working together and dividing the labor, their separate strengths interact to build greater understanding to accomplish more complex tasks. When group size is increased to three or more, however, the organization of the work breaks down and more off-task behavior results. Because there are both high and low quality software, the following assists you in evaluating the software you are considering buying. Most successful software will do the following:

- Capture students' interest and intellect;
- Provide immediate feedback;
- Enable students to control the rate and depth in which text is advanced;
- Have directions that students can easily read and understand;

- Have graphics that contribute to instruction rather than merely stimulate students' attention;
- Require students' use of specific communication/thinking competencies to complete each task instead of allowing random choice;
- Judge student success through comparisons of their present to past performances, rather than comparing their results to those of other students;
- Have documentation in a teacher's manual that provides information concerning the program's objectives, target populations, prerequisites, language and thinking competencies, introductory and follow-up activities, as well as results of field tests and validation studies;
- Enable students to engage their minds and language in ways that would not be possible without it;
- Allow time for reflection;
- Have several options by which students practice the program's objectives, so they can use the software repeatedly without becoming bored.

FIGURE 6-9

Sample from *Kittens, Kids, and a Frog* Computer Software Program

(a)

(b) Jan has a blue car.
Jim has a red car.
Jan's car can go fast.
Jim's car can not go
    fast.

Press <RETURN>.

(c) What car will win?

   a. Jill's car
   b. Jim's car
   c. Jan's car

answer : _

(d)
```
STUDENT :ED
LESSON :CARS 1        <50%>
---------------------------------
THERE ARE 6 QUESTIONS IN THE LESSON.
STUDENT ATTEMPTED ALL 6.
STUDENT HAD 3 CORRECT ON 1ST TRY.
BREAKDOWN BY QUESTION TYPE:
    MAIN IDEA               0 OUT OF 1
    DETAIL                  1 OUT OF 2
    VOCABULARY              1 OUT OF 1
    SEQUENCE                 (NONE)
    CAUSE/EFFECT             (NONE)
    INFERENCE/DRAW CONC.    1 OUT OF 1
    MAKING JUDGMENTS         (NONE)
    PREDICTING OUTCOMES     0 OUT OF 1
    PRONOUNS                 (NONE)
---------------------------------
PRESS <RETURN>
```

Reprinted by permission of the New Horizon Publishing Co.

The following software reach these criteria:

1. *Easy Writer* (Harcourt Brace Jovanovich); *Reading Workshop* (Mindscope); *Communication Computer Programs* (Sunburst); *A Newbery Adventure: Charlotte's Web* (Sunburst); and *Electronic Bookshelf* (Electronic Bookshelf). All enable students to involve characters from favorite literature in a wide variety of plots students devise.

2. *Kittens, Kids, and a Frog* (Hartley Publishers), as shown in Figure 6-9, develops higher level thinking/comprehension abilities for first and second graders.

3. *Storybooks* and *Storylords* (Wisconsin Educational Network) builds higher level thinking and inferential comprehension by interfacing computer simulations with fantasy-based strategy lessons on videotape.

4. *Where in the World Is Carmen Sandiego?* and *Dilemma: Which Ending Will You Choose?* build reading and thinking skills through interactive text adventures where a full-sized World Almanac and Facts book assists students to solve crimes that Carmen and her fugitives commit. In some computer programs, when students make mistakes, the program recycles their incorrect thinking; students view a strategy they could use to overcome the incorrect answer and then they can proceed and experience success.

5. Computer voice synthesis. Through programs such as *The Reading Comprehension Early Reader Series* (Houghton Mifflin), students answer high-level comprehension questions about popular children's stories. Similarly, *Kidtalk* (First Byte Software) enables pupils to create their own stories, and voice synthesis reads it to fellow students. A parrot tells how to use features on the screen and verbal assistance is available when desired. Students who hear their sentences read aloud on *Kidtalk* become more aware of the need to rewrite awkward ones. Other voice synthesized software include *Student Stories* (Minnesota Educational Computing Corporation) and *Scary Poems for Rotten Kids* (Computer Tree) which are predictable chants for choral readings. Students' names from the class are programmed to appear in the chants. *Scary Poems for Rotten Kids* simulates poetry readings, complete with spooky music and a variety of voices. The program pauses and provides pronunciations as well as meanings of words a student references. Other voice synthesizing programs appear in second languages, including Spanish, French, and Cantonese.

6. Computers can also function as databases for reading comprehension activities. For example, *Bookbrain* is an annotated bibliography of children's literature by title, author, and subject. *Explore-A-Story* (Collamore Educational Publishing) enables students to write, edit, illustrate, and print their own books.

7. *Writing Adventure* (DLM) has an adventure-game format where students make decisions that influence the outcome. They also can accept the challenge to construct a story, recount the adventure, and formulate a successful, appropriate conclusion.

8. *Experience Recorder* (Teacher Support Software) prepares word banks for word recognition activities from stories written by classmates.

9. *The Puzzler* (Sunburst Communications) contains two story activities for the overhead projector. Students make predictions about something in a story on the computer. Then more of the story is revealed, and students confirm or reject their predictions. Students describe the comprehension strategies they used.

10. *Winnie the Pooh in the Hundred Acre Wood* (Sierra On-Line, Inc.). This adventure begins with messages, presented in disarray, from all the animals in Hundred Acre Wood. Only by attending to sequence clues, using rereading strategies, and thinking critically can students return items to their rightful owners.

11. *Solve It* (Sunburst). Students are detectives using a database search. Through this program, students use exploratory and problem-solving thought processes to unlock mysteries.

12. *Bookmate* (Sunburst). This program has four options: students can reference books (a) about special events, (b) made into movies, (c) by a special author, or (d) that fit "their mood."

13. *Reading Realities Elementary Series* (Teacher Support Software). This is a reading comprehension program where 1,400 students throughout the United States have written stories about issues they face, such as "So What If I'm Fat?" "My Parents are Divorced," and "Do I Have To Do Math Again?" Programs are color-coded for reading levels, and have vocabulary previews. In addition, skimming strategies are built as a picture is shown and students are to type what they think the story will be about. The story then appears. Students have the option of having it read to them orally. Comprehension checks are also available as is a printout of student responses. *Team* (Davidson & Associates, Inc.) is a similar program except that its units are about current events and famous people's advice. Both of these software packages build students' appreciation of using reading as a tool to solve personal problems.

14. *PRODIGY* (445 Hamilton Avenue, White Plains, NY 10601). This fixed-cost telecommunications service has many features designed by teachers for children and parents. PRODIGY has extended a concept called Videotex to combine high-resolution color pictures with text in an interactive storyline. Regular educational features on PRODIGY include stories, games, and puzzles from National Geographic, NOVA, Carmen Sandiego, Weekly Reader, and a constantly updated on-line encyclopedia. Features for reading include interactive "LapWare" designed to be read by a parent to a young child. This service uses expert authors to help parents understand ways to help their children develop improved study and comprehension abilities while increasing their self-esteem and motivation. With over a million members, PRODIGY is available nationwide; most areas can access the service with a local phone call.

15. *America Tomorrow Leadership Network* (P.O. Box 2310, Bethesda, MD 20827-2310). This fixed-cost service is designed for leaders in education, community-based programs, and business. America Tomorrow offers a broad range of information services including education news, promising comprehension practices, legislation/litigation affecting education, and other topics of concern to leaders dealing with restructuring and educational reform. Information is developed under the guidance of an advisory board formed from a coalition of educational professional associations. Although America Tomorrow is a separate network, it uses the PRODIGY service software and nationwide on-line communication system as a "closed" network for America Tomorrow subscribers.

16. *LinkWay and LinkWay Live* (IBM). LinkWay is an interactive program that enables students to make discoveries and combine information in their own way. Students navigate through history from multiple points of view, engage in studies of the arts, and exercise creativity to enhance comprehension.

CREATING LESSONS THAT USE ORAL READING TO DEVELOP COMPREHENSION ABILITIES

Effective oral reading instruction occurs when one reader presents material and the audience cannot read along. Oral readings are practiced before being delivered to audiences, and the literature is at students' instructional or independent reading levels. Effective oral reading instruction serves five important purposes, as described below:

1. *Diagnostic Function.* When students read orally to you in one-to-one conferences, you can diagnose reading deficiencies that cannot be detected from silent reading tests (Palardy, 1992; Welker 1991). You can detect: (a) students' decoding of all words as they read as well as the kinds and frequency of their word attack errors; (b) their use of the nuances of language to comprehend interpretively; (c) if their reading speed and phrasing is appropriate and facilitates comprehension/retention; and (d) students' use of proper intonation and expression to indicate appropriate reliance on context clues during reading. For example, if students do not have proper intonation they may not be employing context clues to derive meaning. Alternatively, if they overrely upon punctuation markers and context clues, you will notice that they are repeatedly making miscues and substituting words that "make sense" in a sentence but are not the word the author used.

2. *Provide repetition that builds students' schema, vocabulary, sight word knowledge, and listening comprehension.* These abilities are strengthened by oral reading in two ways. First, oral reading provides an added incentive for students to learn new words and interpret exact meanings because they know they are going to perform before an audience. Second, few students reread words and sentences as frequently in silent reading as they do in oral reading. Vocabulary, sight words, and comprehension are strengthened through the repeated exposures to new words that oral reading provides. Oral reading also enriches students' schema because the rhythm and cadence of our language become apparent and can be used as decoding and comprehension tools when oral readings are shared. Research indicates that oral reading also strengthens shy students' self-esteem (Collins, 1991b). Moreover, when an upperclassmate reads orally to your students, a richness of language and vocabulary above your students' independent reading level is shared, and appropriate phrasing is modeled.

3. *Prepare students for times in life when they will have to read aloud to entertain and share information.* Oral reading teaches students to use punctuation and read with proper expression. It also develops their poise in reading before an audience. Oral reading also teaches students the value of distinct enunciation, deliberate pausing, and appropriate speed/pitch/volume when speaking.

Two oral reading lessons that are particularly beneficial follow. *Author's Chair* (Calkins, 1986; Stuart & Graves, 1987) occurs when students come to the front of the room to read their own story or a selection from children's literature. As demonstrated in videotape segment 2, author's chair not only develops students' confidence, but has the potential to become a celebrative experience that enhances self-esteem. The student who is reading sits in the "author's chair." After reading, classmates ask questions about the author's decisions in the writing, or how the "author" generated specific ideas or wordings. Students can also tell stories similar to the one told by Maurice Sendak in videotape segment 11.

A second type of oral reading lesson is for students to do the daily book reading from a selection of children's literature that you normally do. Such student-led readings are enhanced when you select students who have read and enjoyed a genre most of their classmates have not yet read. You invite that student to select his/her favorite excerpt from that genre; he/she practices reading it with you (or a parent volunteer); together you prepare a captivating opening and a suspenseful closing for the oral reading. When such an oral reading occurs, many students become inspired to select new genre (such as science fiction, poetry, or adventure) for their own silent reading.

In closing, your students will mature in their speaking, reading, listening, and writing abilities when you teach Critical Thinking Activity 6. This activity invites students to apply new things they learned about language to their speaking, reading, listening, and writing. It assists students to cluster words they heard but have not yet incorporated into their own speaking, reading, and writing repertoire. Semantic mapping is one of the best methods of introducing vivid and semantically rich expressions to students.

CRITICAL THINKING ACTIVITY 6
Using Semantic Maps to Strengthen Comprehension

Recommended Grade Levels: Preschool Through Grade 8

Semantic mapping (or concept mapping and webbing) is a *visual organizational process where thoughts and ideas are diagrammed according to the way they relate to one another* (Bercik, 1992). It will likely take several months before

To vary the "author's chair" activity, students can pretend that they are their favorite author. They come to the "author's chair" and talk as if they are that author, sharing why and how they write as they do.

students install semantic mapping in their language/thinking repertoires. While it increases comprehension, its newness necessitates your repeated instruction before students unlock its potential unaided (Pressley et al., 1989; Collins & Mangieri, 1992). To begin this integrative instructional activity, model the mapping process by showing different connections ideas can have in writing (see Figures 6-4 and 6-10). Explain how semantic maps make visible the schema authors followed as they made decisions in their writings. Then ask students to select to use a semantic map either before, during, or after they complete their next reading, writing, listening, or speaking assignment. By identifying the author's organizational structure, students better interpret complex concepts embedded in the reading. Also, by visually outlining stories, students become familiar with story grammar (see Chapter 8). They can apply these same formats to their own compositions (see Figure 6-10).

Students need to understand that there are endless possibilities to visually represent relationships among ideas. You can show a variety of concept maps and relate how each can be used. Students could then be asked to think about a decision relative to school or real life. They would then use semantic mapping to connect all the factors that effect that decision. They would select the best semantic map from Figure 6-4 to facilitate their thinking.

FIGURE 6-10
Why Semantic Maps Work

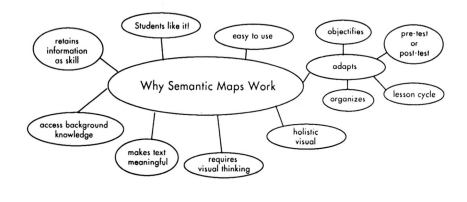

Mapping can also be used effectively as a thinking strategy for large group, content-area instruction, as demonstrated in videotape segment 11. Pressley et al. (1992) found that semantic maps can be used as reviews for content-area tests:

> For an exam about colonial America, students were provided the topic of the in-class examination essay questions. In anticipation of this test, students prepared semantic maps and practice essays. Rather than all students reading the last three chapters of the energy text, the labor was divided, with individual students and pairs of students reading separate chapters and creating semantic maps for each chapter. The students brought their maps back to the reading group and provided a summary using their map prompts. They received before-the-exam feedback from the teachers about these products. The actual exam required an hour and a half of writing (p. 7).

Creative students also enjoy "mind mapping" which turns linear notes into images, key words, codes, and symbols students themselves create, which will increase their retention. A mind map from Marguilies (1991, p. 7) appears in Figure 6-11.

In summary, semantic mapping is a key that brings schema used in *reading, writing,* or *thinking* into a visual arena where they can be organized and comprehended. For further activities with semantic mapping see: Karen D'Angelo Bromley (1991); *Webbing with Literature* (Allyn & Bacon); and *Semantic Mapping: Classroom Applications,* by Joan Heimlich and Susan Pittelman (International Reading Association).

FIGURE 6-11
Mind Mapping to Improve Listening and Reading Comprehension

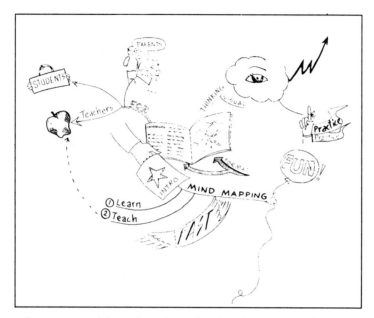

- Create a map and then walk another student through your map, explaining each element of your map.
- Read a story, make a map from it, and then give your map to another student, without telling the name of your story or discussing it. The other student then reads your map and from it writes his or her idea of what the story might be about.
- Ask students to map plans for a field trip. After the trip, map what actually occurred.
- Ask older students to map situations that they find difficult to manage such as moving to a new school or dealing with the presence of drugs or alcohol at a party. Each person can add coping strategies to the maps as ideas are shared in small group discussions.

Reprinted by permission of the New Horizon Publishing Co.

PROFESSIONAL DEVELOPMENTAL OPPORTUNTIY
How to Conduct Effective Reading Response Groups

Reading response groups are *small groups of students who meet to discuss their ideas and reactions to material they have read.* There are several types. The first is where you assign students to a response group. This type was demonstrated in Mrs. Hayes's first grade class on videotape segment 2. As illustrated, Mrs. Hayes meets with one response group a day. Students in each group have comparable reading abilities. They select the book they wish to read. All students spend the next two days reading their books and finishing them at home so reading is completed by the next response group meeting time. Any student who has difficulty with words meets with a partner the first ten minutes of class each day to learn new words.

The second type of reading response group is where students select the response group in which they want to meet. In this system, group members can read the same or different books and share their most significant learnings and impressions. Members analyze authors' styles and learn why they prefer one author above others. When students read the same book, they choose the one they want their group to read. They can also select the topics to be discussed from that book.

Another type of response group was suggested by Calkins (1986) and is a combination of the previous systems. In these response groups, students select the book they will read. Each group receives a common question, even though each has read a different book, e.g., "How did the author of your group's book capture your attention?" Students spend two (or more) days reading their books. Each student returns to the response group with an individual answer to the question. The group mediates until a single, well-written, paragraph-long answer is constructed. One member reads his/her group's work to the class, and students compare group answers orally or in writing. Following this comparison, students select a goal for their group's next day's discussion of their book. All students prepare a ten-minute oral report of their prediscussion ideas for their next day's discussion. Then the next response group meeting is chaired by a group-selected student leader, and covers points of choice. Summaries are written of the discussions, and these are shared with the class.

Such sharings strengthen comprehension and retention, especially when divergent points of view are posited (Many, 1991). Through such discussions students learn that their comprehensions are unique and to trust that their comprehension can be correct even if different from peers. Reading response group sharings also encourage students to construct their personal understandings rather than to look for *the correct theme* or agreed-upon meaning of a story (Many, 1991). For this reason it is often best to begin response groups by calling for expressions of their thoughts rather than by first stating your response to a reading.

One of the easiest ways to vary response group activities is for students to enact their responses to a book instead of discussing them. One group can role-play the ending of a book that they would have preferred for the class, as an example. Because two response groups rarely finish their books at the same time, the group that finishes their book first can select the funniest (or saddest or most exciting or most beautiful) section and practice reading it aloud in pairs, so they can tantalize other groups to select their book in the future.

TRY IT

1. If you are presently teaching, teach one of the comprehension strategies in this chapter. Describe the results of this teaching experience. If you are not yet teaching, prepare the materials and design lessons for one of the comprehension strategies in this chapter by visualizing yourself teaching it. Describe how you will teach it to your future students.

2. Complete Critical Thinking Activity 6 if you are presently teaching. Once the lesson is complete, ask students to "semantically map" themselves. Once maps are completed, ask students to share theirs with a partner. The partner modifies or adds other characteristics his/her partner possesses to the concept map.

If you are not yet teaching, design a semantic map of yourself that you will use at a later date to introduce the above activity to your students. Also design a blueprint for reading instruction. In this plan, designate specific times of the year that you will use the strategies, activities, and lesson plans in Chapters 5 and 6 that you included. Specify two goals per month for this reading component of your language arts program.

3. If you are presently teaching, complete a Lesson Plan in this chapter. Evaluate your success. If you do not have your own classroom, describe how one of the Lesson Plans differs from the lessons you had when you were in elementary school.

4. Secure a magazine from Notecard 11 or a hobby book from Notecard 12. Design a lesson that would use semantic maps to make a decision relative to that reading material. Incorporate an oral language objective from Chapter 3 in the lesson you design. Also, use your CD/RM for 20 minutes to learn how computers can assist in developing students' reading abilities. With what types of objectives and students would this software be effective?

STRATEGIES THAT TEACH

NOTECARD 11: MAGAZINES FOR CHILDREN

These can be used in language art centers, creative dramatics, libraries, and thematic units in a variety of ways. Addresses and subscription information can be found in the current editions of *Magazines for Libraries* or *The Standard Periodical Directory* under the heading <u>Children and Youth-For</u>. These books are availble for use in the reference section of the public library. Recommended age range for magazines is in parenthesis following most of the titles. *These magazines are highly recommended.

GENERAL INTEREST

Turtle (2–5)
Sesame Street (2–6)*
Children's Playmate (5–7)
Wee Wisdom (6–12)
Highlights for Children (2–12)*
Muppet (7–13)
Bear Essential News for Kids
Mickey Mouse (4–8)
Snoopy (4–8)
Jack and Jill (6–8)

Children's Magic Window (6–13)
Child Life (7–9)
Children's Digest (8–10)
Children's Own-The Newspaper for Kids
Peanut Butter (4–6)
Humpty Dumpty (4–6)
Kid City (6–10)*
Creative Kids (6–14)
Hot Dog (7–9)
New York News for Kids

MATH/SCIENCE/NATURE

Your Big Back Yard (3–5)*
Super Science I (6–9)
Dolphin Log (7–15)
3-2-1 Contact (8–14)*
Super Science II (9–12)
Chickadee (4–9)*
Ranger Rick (6–12)*
Odyssey (8–14)*

Zoobooks (5–14)
National Geographic World (8–14)*
Scienceland (5–8)
Naturescope (6–14)*
Owl (8–14)*
Kind News
Dynamath (9–14)*

(cont'd)

NOTECARD 11 (cont'd)

HISTORY/SOCIAL STUDIES

Cobblestone (8–14)*
Think, Inc. (8–12)
Buried Treasure
Weekly Reader
Faces (8–14)*
Skipping Stones

Streetwize Comics
National Geographic World*
Zillions (8–14)*
Calliope (9–12)
Scholastic News

WRITING/LITERATURE

Stone Soup (6–13)*
Sprint (8–12, low reading level)
Shoe Tree: The Literary Magazine by and for
  Children (8–14)*

Cricket (6–12)*
Plays (8–18)*
Short Story International: Seedling Series (10–12)
Creative Kids (6–14)*

SPORTS/HOBBIES/CRAFTS

Kidsports (8–14)
Sports Illustrated for Kids (8–14)

Pack-o-Fun (5–13)
Children's Surprises (5–12)

AVAILABLE IN BRAILLE

Wee Wisdom (6–12)

Children's Friend

OF INTEREST TO GIRLS

Barbie (4–12)
Hopscotch (6–12)
American Girl

Young Miss (8–12)
Teen (13–18)

OF INTEREST TO BOYS

He Man and Master of the Universe (4–12)
G.I. Joe (8–12)

Boy's Life (8–17)

NOTECARD 12: BOOKS ABOUT HOBBIES

PRIMARY LEVEL

You're a Good Dog, Joe: Knowing and Training
  Your Puppy by K. Unkelbach
Exciting Things To Do With Color by Janee Allen
The Little Pigs First Cookbook by N. C. Watson
Coins You Can Collect by Burton Hobson
How to Draw Silly Monsters and other how-to-
  draw books by Frank Smith

Splodges by Malcolm Carrick
Create-a-Kite by Editors of Consumer's Guide
Easy Origami by Dokuohtei Nakano
How to Draw Cartoons by Syd Hoff
Insect Pets: Catching and Caring for Them by
  Carla Stevens

INTERMEDIATE LEVEL

Paint a Rainbow by John Hawkinson
Introducing Needlepoint by Donna Lightbody
Cookie Craft by B. Williams and R. Williams
Getting Started in Stamp Collecting by
  B. Hobson
How to Paint with Water Colors by
  A. Zaidenberg
Creating with Burlap by M. J. Fressard
Know Your Game: Baseball and other sports
  books by Marc Bloom
The Drawing Book by John Deacon

Children's Plays for Creative Actors by
  C. Boiko
Collage by Mickey Klar Marks
Drawing and Painting with the Computer by
  Don Bolognese and Robert Thornton
Easy Weaving by D. M. Lightbody
Jewelry from Junk by Helen R. Sattler
Rock Collecting by Thomas Y. Crowell Publisher
Model Cars and Trucks and How to Build Them
  and other books by H. Weiss
Indoor Gardening by D. Fenton

(cont'd)

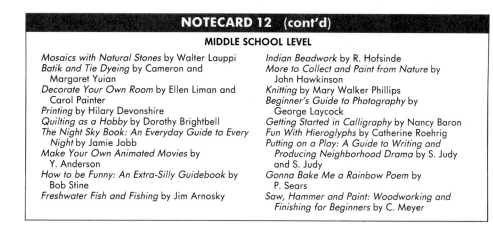

NOTECARD 12   (cont'd)

MIDDLE SCHOOL LEVEL

Mosaics with Natural Stones by Walter Lauppi
Batik and Tie Dyeing by Cameron and
  Margaret Yuian
Decorate Your Own Room by Ellen Liman and
  Carol Painter
Printing by Hilary Devonshire
Quilting as a Hobby by Dorothy Brightbell
*The Night Sky Book: An Everyday Guide to Every
  Night* by Jamie Jobb
Make Your Own Animated Movies by
  Y. Anderson
How to be Funny: An Extra-Silly Guidebook by
  Bob Stine
Freshwater Fish and Fishing by Jim Arnosky

Indian Beadwork by R. Hofsinde
More to Collect and Paint from Nature by
  John Hawkinson
Knitting by Mary Walker Phillips
Beginner's Guide to Photography by
  George Laycock
Getting Started in Calligraphy by Nancy Baron
Fun With Hieroglyphs by Catherine Roehrig
*Putting on a Play: A Guide to Writing and
  Producing Neighborhood Drama* by S. Judy
  and S. Judy
Gonna Bake Me a Rainbow Poem by
  P. Sears
*Saw, Hammer and Paint: Woodworking and
  Finishing for Beginners* by C. Meyer

STRATEGIES THAT TEACH

FOR YOUR JOURNAL

Another way to use student journals is for pupils to write a question or concern they have about a topic the class will explore. Students exchange journals and research (or write their own opinions) to address their classmate's concern. This approach can be expanded by dividing students into groups of three so each student receives two opinions concerning his/her entry.

For you to experience the value of using journals in this way, reflect upon one aspect of teaching reading, not covered in this chapter, that you want to learn later in the textbook. If the topic appears later in the text, return to your entry and hypothesize about why it might have appeared at that point in the text, rather than in this chapter. If it does not appear later in the text, reflect upon what its absence may indicate about differences between your philosophy of reading instruction and the textbook's philosophy.

BUILDING YOUR PROFESSIONAL PORTFOLIO
Textbook Selection Guidelines

Throughout your career you will be asked to select and purchase curriculum for your students. You may even serve on the school district's textbook selection committee. For these reasons, it is valuable to file guidelines and criteria for textbook/material selections in language arts. You can begin your file with the following *Guidelines for Judging and Selecting Elementary Language Arts Textbooks,* created by the National Council of Teachers of English, March 1991.

GUIDELINES FOR JUDGING AND SELECTING
ELEMENTARY LANGUAGE ARTS TEXTBOOKS

*from the Committee on Elementary Language Arts Textbooks
National Council of Teachers of English*

The English language arts textbook is a familiar volume in the desks of many students across the country. Some educators look to the text as the basic tool for language arts instruction, the organizer for most of the language arts curriculum. Others deplore the presence of a text series in the classroom, charging that it prescribes the language curriculum, seriously narrowing students' possibilities for language learning.

To help educators sort through the conflicting points of view on the potential of textbooks and to help them validate their judgments about the teaching materials they choose to use, the NCTE Committee on Elementary Language Arts Textbooks offers eight guidelines that summarize current theory and research on language learning. These guidelines provide substantive criteria upon which text materials can be judged.

1. **Language arts textbooks should center on children's own language.**
   Student language, ideas, and purposes are primary in language arts instruction. Textbook lesson ideas should help teachers keep the focus of instruction on students' real purposes for communication. Information that the textbook may present about the language itself or individual skills related to listening, speaking, reading, or writing should clearly demonstrate its significance for students' interest in language and their knowledge of its importance and use. Textbooks, therefore, should supplement and enrich students' active use of language in listening, speaking, reading, and writing.

2. **Language arts textbooks should emphasize activities that focus on social uses of language.**
   Lessons suggested by textbooks need to present communication as both a method of learning and as a valued outcome. They should encourage students to be genuine, responsive audiences for the speaking and writing of peers and of adults; they should help students value their own speaking and writing efforts and help them learn to make their communication clear and appropriate.

3. **Language arts textbooks should reflect the integrated nature of listening, speaking, writing, and reading.**
   Language is oral and written, receptive and expressive. Its skills are interrelated and interdependent, not collections of discrete skills or separate bits of information. Language use is powerful when reading, writing, speaking, and listening are used together. Textbooks should help teachers and students achieve greater integration of language in the classroom by focusing clearly on a limited number of major goals, by providing provocative literature and language activities, and by emphasizing how students of varying interests and abilities can use reading, writing, speaking, and listening together toward the accomplishment of goals.

4. **Language arts textbooks should recognize broad patterns of developmental language growth.**
   Language development seldom follows a definite scope and sequence. At best, there appear to be broad developmental patterns in language growth. The goals of language arts instruction, therefore, are more similar across grade levels than they are different; and textbooks should

emphasize this continuity. Students cannot be expected to master the major goals of language growth at a particular grade level but should learn to use their knowledge, skills, strategies, and awareness with increasingly complex samples of language and in more sophisticated contexts.

5. **Language arts textbooks should help teachers assess students' use of language.**
   Assessment of language needs and growth is very complex. Textbooks should guide teachers in developing assessment procedures for all the major goals of the language arts curriculum and should also provide help in interpreting observations of students' daily use of language for a variety of purposes. Textbooks should help students make judgments about their own growth in all language areas and help them determine their needs for instruction.

6. **Language arts textbooks should stimulate children's and teachers' thinking.**
   Textbooks need to promote inquiry about language: its purposes, its origins, its growth and change. They can help students and teachers to develop a variety of systematic ways to think about experiences and to develop strategies for extending and deepening reflection. Rather than replacing teachers' thinking and planning, textbooks should help the teacher to think about the abilities, needs, and interests of students and their language development and learning.

7. **Language arts textbooks should be equity balanced.**
   Language is one of the most obvious indicators of cultural differences. Language arts textbooks should help students become aware of the cultural aspects of their own language and help them achieve a sensitivity toward and understanding of the cultural aspects of the language of others. Issues such as dialect and body language need to be examined in the context of communications. Emphasis should be placed on valuing the cultural contributions of all groups in a pluralistic society, and the literature in the text should be selected from a wide range of world cultures.

8. **Language arts textbooks should reflect the centrality of listening, speaking, writing, and reading for learning in all subject areas.**
   Learning in all subjects depends upon language. Language arts textbooks should help students and teachers see English language arts instruction not only as a special area of study but as foundational for all learning. Examples and suggested activities in the textbook need to be selected from a variety of subject areas. Language skills and attitudes are central to living outside the schoolhouse as well as in it, so textbooks should help students appreciate the significance of language competencies for family life, occupations, citizenship, and leisure time.

"Guidelines for Judging and Selecting Elementary Language Arts Textbooks," from the NCTE Committee on Language Arts Textbooks, *Language Arts,* March 1991. Copyright 1991 by the National Council of Teacher of English. Reprinted with permission.

STRATEGIES THAT TEACH

7 Writing To Communicate and Think

"When student and teacher become partners in inquiry and learning through the writing process, no one stands still for long. Just as a canoeist learns to read and respond to the energy of a river, the teacher learns to read the child's energy and guides it. It is a tricky art . . . one learned . . . in the living of it" (Deborah Sumner, 1986, p. 158).

The most important sentence of all is the first! It must pique your readers' interest so they read on. The next most important sentence is the second. It must so intrigue that readers don't want to leave your ideas. Your writing skills must capture them!

The purpose of this chapter is to develop your students' writing abilities. In addition, you will learn how to use journal writing, assisted writing, and student conferences to overcome student writing problems.

After reading this chapter, you will also know:

1. The four principles of writing instruction;
2. The stages students pass through as writers;
3. The authoring cycle;
4. Computer aids for your writing program;
5. Specific lessons that develop writing and thinking abilities.

THEORETICAL FOUNDATION

STUDENTS' WRITING NEEDS

"In many current reading programs, writing is no longer seen as a separate subject. Writing, like reading, is viewed as a tool for thinking . . . as a vehicle for sorting out and clarifying thinking" (Harste, 1989, p. 29). Presently students are deficient in higher order thinking and writing skills (Applebee, Langer & Mullis, 1988). However, many educators believe that the 1990s are finding students exercising more types of writing (and possibly fashioning new genres themselves) than at any other time in history (Nystrand, 1989; Collins, 1991b).

Writing evokes specific types of thinking: questioning, citing evidence, making assumptions, validating previous hypotheses, evaluating, and using schema (Langer & Applebee, 1987). The more students reformulate content, the more their thinking and writing abilities build. In the process your students play with words, organize thoughts, and compose to increase their own personal significance and understanding. Through writing they will bring information to *the world* in a way that is much more permanent than possible from even the most skilled orator, avid reader, or speed listener! Moreover, through a well-constructed writing program, students grow to command a tool that can sculpture their own thinking. Specifically, good writing skills enable students to examine their ideas and discern if they can sustain critique.

A good writing program also strengthens students' self-image, as the following journal entry demonstrates:

> I was astounded when the teacher read *one of my paragraphs* in class. Until then I didn't know I could write, *or that I had anything to say.* [When she finished reading it and talked about my ideas,] I began to think I could do something right for a change (Stuart & Graves, 1987, p. 89).

This power that writing has to increase students' self-esteem is attributed to the fact that most pupils are more courageous in their compositions than in their speech. Writing affords the time necessary to cultivate confidence and ideas. Therefore, thoughts communicated through writing more often express students' deepest convictions which, when appreciated, expand their self-worth.

Also, through creating their own aesthetically pleasing narratives, students strengthen their appreciation for other people's writing. Similarly, when students craft their work argumentatively, persuasively, and descriptively they learn to express more effective ideas, and to stimulate others to action (Collins Block, in press; Temple et al., 1988).

Finally, writing creates knowledge for others. When students translate their insights, experiences, and memories into written words others can read and grow.

PRINCIPLES OF WRITING INSTRUCTION

Several principles guide effective writing instruction, as discussed below.

Principle 1: "The problem with writing is not poor spelling, punctuation, grammar, and handwriting. The problem with students' writing is no writing"   (Stuart & Graves, 1987, p. 34). Students need to write often if they are to learn to communicate more effectively through the written word. In most successful writing programs, pupils complete 15–30 minutes of writing each day, and have 30–45 minutes of whole-class instruction a week (e.g., completing language experience stories on topics of interest). They also engage in full class periods of small group writing projects for community/school improvements; and select free writes when they finish other work.

The advantage of daily writing has been demonstrated in several studies that compared students who drilled on worksheets over spelling, punctuation, and grammar to students who did not practice such isolated exercises but wrote daily instead. Those who composed regularly performed better on tests over writing conventions than those who did worksheet drills (Calkins, 1986; F. Smith, 1988).

Composing with your students is a successful strategy to teach writing. By writing at the same time they write, you will (1) experience "writer's block" just as your students do; (2) feel writers' "good days" and "bad days" (which heightens your one-on-one conferencing abilities); (3) model writing abilities, so you become more credible to your students; (4) demonstrate that sometimes if you just write long enough and think "hard enough" you can express truly important ideas for others; and (5) have opportunities to add to your professional journal so that it becomes a more complete record of your insights.

Principle 2: If students are to master writing they must not only compose regularly but their writing must be found interesting by readers. When students write for peers, even those at a distant school, the quality of their work will be significantly greater than if they write solely for their teachers (Cohen & Riel, 1989). Moreover, when students personally relay important information to significant audiences, they produce more variety, present information more cogently, and eliminate irrelevant details. Because young writers flourish when parents, community members, and peers read their texts, your students' writings could be framed and hung in school hallways, corporate offices, central administration buildings, public libraries, hospitals, storefront windows, and doctor or dentist waiting areas. Students could also make *handmade books* for classroom/school libraries or as gifts for nursing homes and churches. They can create *student publications* (such as school newspapers, yearbooks, literary magazines, and classroom anthologies) as another means of writing for peers.

Principle 3: Your interest, enthusiasm, and belief that students' are *real writers* is what they need to become *real writers*. As was true with speaking, listening, and reading development, writing abilities heighten when you surround students in a world of factual, opinion-based, practical, expressive, narrative, and poetic writing. You will also use strategies that motivate students who are slow starters, and/or those who are disinclined to write. You will *give honest responses to students' work,* and explain which parts of their writing you most enjoyed and why.

Principle 4: You know and recognize the stages your students pass through as they grow as writers. A description of these stages follow. Although stages are labeled by grade levels, these labels are general as students vary in their rate of writing skill.

Preschoolers and Kindergartners. Writing is a normal form of expression for preschoolers, even though their expressions are unintelligible. Preschoolers write by scribbling, drawing, and lettering. For example, at age 1, children are communicating when they make one long mark on a piece of paper (or wall)! By age 2, children scribe a single letter, which to them is the written version of their entire name. By age 4, children spend several minutes scribbling below a picture, and these scribbles "tell all about the picture." By age 5, students form real letters, use invented spellings, and write only a few words to represent many sentences, as demonstrated in Figure 7-1 (Bridwell, 1980; Hawisher, 1987; Halliday, 1982; Maynor, 1982).

First Graders. First graders are "noisy" writers. They talk as they write, rehearsing what they want to say. Likewise, when compositions are complete, first graders read them aloud to "hear how it sounds." To them, writing is a pleasurable activity. They value writing more as an enjoyable process than for the fact that it creates finished products. Because of this perspective, first graders most often compose for themselves rather than for an audience. They also prefer designing something new to reworking yesterday's work. As a matter of fact, if required to revise (without their initiative), they can become inhibited and digress in their writing (Salinger, 1992).

Second Graders. Second graders move from scribing for personal pleasure to writing for an audience. They also become more interested in final products, spending considerable time revising and editing. Because they have had only a few years of writing experience, and because they are concerned with other people's perception, they frequently destroy many drafts before they report that one writing "is just right!"

Interestingly enough, 7- and 8-year-olds tend to be less creative than first graders (Calkins, 1986). This decreased inventiveness is *not a regression* in composition ability. Rather, it is a compensation these young students make to learn how to write for a real audience. Many second graders face two problems: they need instruction before they can expand their topics and use more vivid adjectives; and they compose stories which imitate plots in their favorite books (e.g., they devise "John and the Three Dogs," which replicates "Goldilocks and the Three Bears").

Third Graders. Third-grade students become more concerned about spelling, punctuation, capitalization, handwriting, and grammar. In addition, third graders tend to choose giant, all-inclusive topics such as "My Life," "My Family," and "The World."

Because third graders concentrate upon global concepts, they are likely to overlook important details. They need your assistance during the prewriting stage to narrow their topics. Once they've finished their first draft, they also need to be taught revising and editing strategies.

Fourth, Fifth, and Sixth Graders. In these upper grades students' writings become increasingly more sophisticated. Pupils also develop their own stylistic features. They read and reflect on their writings. When taught revising strategies, they usually apply them rapidly. Through your instruction, they learn to eliminate unnecessary details, narrow to a singular purpose, and select from many genre and sentence structures as they draft to their final work.

During fourth through sixth grades you introduce high level revising strategies that move beyond the word level. You teach sentence combining strategies (see Chapter 8) and paragraph types (Bridwell, 1980; Hawisher, 1987; Maynor, 1982). Throughout these upper grades, students enjoy reading about peers their age. To use this interest to advantage, you will encourage students to read books from Notecard 13. Characters in these books use writing to improve their thinking and contribute to the world. After reading a book, ask students to explain the value writing held for the main character, who is about their age. It is your intent that by reading about a peer's use of writing, your students' esteem for it will increase.

In summary, writing will become students' most disciplined and precise expressions of thought. Through instruction, students learn to scrutinize compositions until they accurately depict their ideas. There are five principles that guide writing instruction; students should become skillful in prewriting, drafting, revising, editing, and sharing their work. Young writers pass through stages as they grow. In the next section you will read how students can be taught the writing process.

NOTECARD 13: CHILDREN'S BOOKS WHERE MAIN CHARACTERS USE WRITING TO IMPROVE THEIR THINKING

The Burning Questions of Bingo Brown by Betsy Byars

Journal of a Teenage Genius by Helen V. Griffith

Boy by Roald Dahl

Long Ago When I Was Young by E. Nesbit

Judy Blume's Story by Betsy Lee

Return to Sender by Whitaker Murphy

The Ramona Quimby Diary by Beverly Cleary

The Limerick Trick by S. Corbett

Bad Boy, Good Boy by M. H. Ets

Me and My Mona Lisa Smile by S. Hayes

Diary of a Rabbit by Lila Hess

Hold On to Love by Mollie Hunter

Penny Pollard's Diary by Robin Klein

Tough-Luck Karen by J. Hurwitz

The Bat Poet by R. Jarrell

Anastasia Krupnik by Lois Lowry

I Write It by R. Krauss

The Anne of Green Gables Diary by S. Tanaka

Libby on Wednesday by Z. K. Snyder

Diary of a Frantic Kid Sister by Hila Colman

Harriet the Spy by Louise Fitzhugh

Dear Mr. Henshaw by Beverly Cleary

Little by Little: Education of a Writer by Jean Little

Starting from Home by Milton Meltzer

A Girl from Yamhill by Beverly Cleary

A Gathering of Days by Joan Blos

Eaton Stanley and the Mind Control Experiment by D. A. Adler

Daphne's Book by Mary Downing Hahn

Zed by Rosemary Harris

Perfect or Not, Here I Come by K. D. Hall

God, Mrs. Muskrat and Aunt Dot by I. Holland

Up a Road Slowly by J. Hunt

Penny Pollard's Letters by Robin Klein

Anastasia, Ask Your Analyst by Lois Lowry

The Trumpet of the Swan by E. B. White

(cont'd)

NOTECARD 13 (cont'd)

Miss Tibbett's Typewriter by E. Merriam

Write a Tale of Terror by R. Peck

The Last of Eden by S. S. Tolan

Invincible Louisa by C. Meigs

Rag Doll Press by E. J. Taylor

Slim Down Camp by S. Manes

The Witch of Blackbird Pond by E. G. Speare

Loretta P. Sweeny, Where Are You? by Patricia Reilly Giff

Nabby Adam's Diary by M. A. Bourne

The Death of Evening Star: Diary of a Young New England Whaler by L. E. Fisher

The Diary of Trilby Frost by D. Glaser

The Devil in Vienna by D. B. Orgel

Dorrie's Book by M. Sachs

On the Way Home by L. E. Wilder

Are You There God? It's Me, Margaret by J. Blume

Airmail to the Moon by Tom Birdseye

Linda's Air Mail Letter by N. Bell

Frog and Toad are Friends by A. Lobel

Carry on Mr. Bowditch by J. Latham

The Birthday Door by E. Merriam

Rapscallion Jones by J. Marshall

I, Trissi by N. Mazer

Mysteriously Yours, Maggie Marnelstein by M. W. Sharmat

Joshua's Westward Journal by J. Anderson

My Journals and Sketchbooks by R. Crusoe

Anne Frank: Diary of a Young Girl by A. Frank

My Side of the Mountain by J. C. George

The Diary of a Church Mouse by G. Oakley

Diary of the Boy King Tut-Ankh-Amen by J. Reig

Three Days on a River in a Red Canoe by V. B. Williams

Sarah, Plain and Tall by P. MacLachlan

Arthur's Pen Pal by T. Hoban

Dear Dragon by Lesyle Joslin

A Letter to Amy by E. J. Keats

FIGURE 7-1
The Writing Cycle

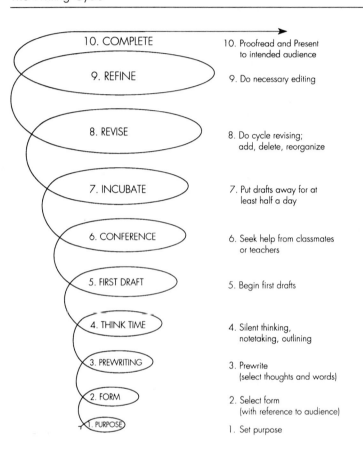

10. COMPLETE	10. Proofread and Present to intended audience
9. REFINE	9. Do necessary editing
8. REVISE	8. Do cycle revising; add, delete, reorganize
7. INCUBATE	7. Put drafts away for at least half a day
6. CONFERENCE	6. Seek help from classmates or teachers
5. FIRST DRAFT	5. Begin first drafts
4. THINK TIME	4. Silent thinking, notetaking, outlining
3. PREWRITING	3. Prewrite (select thoughts and words)
2. FORM	2. Select form (with reference to audience)
1. PURPOSE	1. Set purpose

PUTTING THEORY INTO PRACTICE
COMPOSITION INSTRUCTION

As you will detect in the following discussion and in Figure 7-1, teaching writing includes instruction before and during students' **prewriting, drafting, revising, editing,** and **sharing stages of composing.**

STEP 1: PREWRITING

Prewriting is the section of composing instruction in which students explore ideas, consider options, and corral their thoughts. If students are taught to use this prewriting step they will take time to find something to say and consider ways of saying it. Murray (1984) and Rose (1992) recommend that students pick their own subject about which to write: "It is not the job of the teacher to legislate the student's truth. It is the responsibility of the student to explore his own world, with his own language, to discover his own meaning" (Murray, 1984, p. 13).

In the prewriting stage, students also envision an audience and consider its purpose. Through your guidance, they will learn several prewriting strategies such as "drawing out" ideas; discussing vocabulary with a peer; reflecting and outlining alone; listening/observing/reading to find new ideas; brainstorming; freewriting; interviewing; and asking for critiques as they work.

Early in the year, you will model how to prewrite by verbalizing your own prewriting thoughts. You will recount examples of how you (and they) can select a purpose, topic, genre, audience, and tone for writing.

Some students need your guidance so as to not spend too much time in the prewriting stage. Before you make suggestions, discern if students' hesitancy to draft is due to the necessary "germination of ideas" or "writer's block." If the "germ" of their idea is so big they need more time to think, you will suggest that they use the prewriting strategies stated above. On the other hand, if students are "afraid" to begin (writer's block), the following instructions will assist.

Prewriting Strategies. Writer's block comes from unorganized ideas. The problem is overcome by advising students to write from what they know, what they care about or wish to learn. When students write about topics they know well, the organization evolves easily. Facts become more specific and events are chronologically relayed (Linden & Whimbey, 1990). Students can achieve this level of organization through the following strategies:

1. *Listing:* Students label a page in their journals with a topic's name. For five minutes they write every idea that comes to mind about that general subject and specific interest areas. They then select an issue to write about from the list they brainstormed.

2. *Semantic mapping:* Students put their thoughts on paper and then connect them subordinately, categorically, or graphically. This semantic map graphically displays their areas of greatest interest and expertise.

3. *Referencing journal entries:* Students make a special page in their journal where ideas are recorded about which they'd like to write in the future, and they select one idea from this list when they feel they have nothing of importance to say.

4. *Doing unfocused and focused freewriting* (Elbow, 1981): Unfocused freewriting is when students write, rambling from topic to topic, for 5 to 10 minutes until they find an intriguing idea. Focused writing develops and expands one idea by writing in a stream of consciousness about that idea. Donald Murray, researcher of the writing process, reports that this is the prewriting strategy he uses to overcome his writer's block: "These [freewriting] paragraphs provide no earth-shaking revelations, but they give me the opportunity to relive part of my life and to understand it better than I had before" (Murray, 1984, p. 14).

5. *Questioning:* Ask the student, "Read to me what you have so far," and ask, "What can you tell me about what you've written or why you think you're stuck now?"

6. *Prompt a starter sentence for students:* Suggest several leads for their story, e.g., tell them that sometimes a different lead can get you going in a different direction. Ask, "Why don't you turn your paper over and write two new leads. I'll be back in a minute, and we'll see which one we like the best."

THE CHALLENGE OF DIVERSITY

Dysgraphic students benefit from using a typewriter. Fitzgerald and Markham (1987) and Stotsky (1989) discovered that poorer writers spend less time and do shallower thinking during the prewriting stage than good writers. Often, poorer writers can improve their writing by selecting to read an "All About _____" book at the outset of their writing period.

Higher achieving students' writing abilities expand when they select a problem in their writing or in the world that they can use their composition to solve.

FIGURE 7-2
Master Concept Spin Example

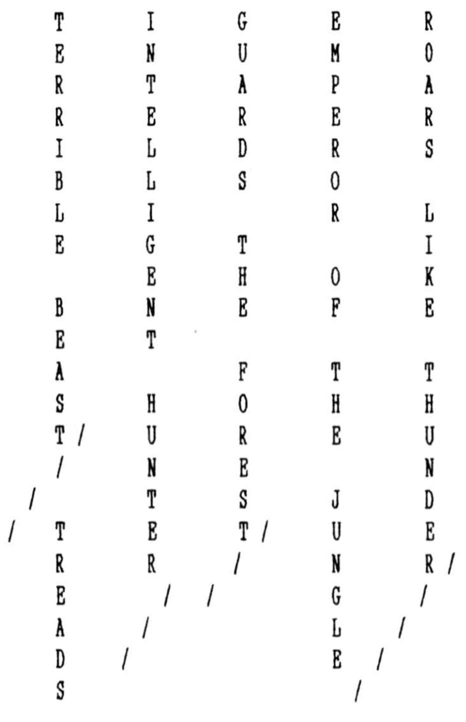

```
T       I       G       E       R
E       N       U       M       O
R       T       A       P       A
R       E       R       E       R
I       L       D       R       S
B       L       S       O
L       I               R       L
E       G       T               I
        E       H       O       K
B       N       E       F       E
E       T
A               F       T       T
S       H       O       H       H
T /     U       R       E       U
/       N       E               N
        T       S       J       D
T       E       T /     U       E
R       R       /       N       R /
E       / /             G       /
A       /               L       /
D     /                 E     /
S                       /
```

7. *Present an on-the-spot mini-lesson* over the concept causing the problem, such as when a student says, "I can't decide how to describe the setting," teach strategies for creating good settings (as described in Collins, 1992a).

8. *Tell the student:* "Let me be your secretary; you tell me what you want to write and I'll write it down." Because words are easier to organize orally, many writing blocks can be broken if you write the first few sentences as a student composes orally. This "secretarial assistance" frees students to focus solely upon connecting their thinking to their speaking, and eliminates the need to simultaneously restructure their thinking to adhere to the grammatical principles of written language.

9. *Engage a lesson early in the semester* whereby students create a chart of starter sentences to "jump start" them over future writer's block. Post this chart in a prominent place for student reference as they write. A sample of sentences students might sugggest are:

"I really don't know what I want to write next because . . ."

"I remember a time in my life that is similar to [this part] so I'll add things I thought, wished, or occurred then, which can make this part of the story better."

"I know a person like this or if my main character were just like _____ , this is what he/she would do next."

10. *Concept spins* created by Pritchard (1992) are a divergent thinking strategy to break writer's block. In a concept spin, students produce many ideas clustered around a central theme. Students make a concept spin by using individual letters of a word from a subject of interest. Those letters trigger new ideas. The concept spin strategy can also be productive when the entire class combines individual concept spins into a master—one that relates several concepts. An example for the concept "tiger" is shown in Figure 7-2. This spin was used as a prewriting assignment after students saw tigers on film and in the zoo. The concept spin was to prompt writing as to why tigers are so apt a symbol for power.

In addition to these strategies for overcoming writer's block, tell students an important truth about writing: Most often, inspiration comes during the exertion rather than before it. Your students will soon learn that by simply beginning to write, apprehensions frequently end. Murray (1984) also suggests that students think of a person to whom they wish to tell their story and list ideas that person would want to read. Then put the writers in pairs. They ask their partner which of these ideas they find most interesting. The partner's answer will increase the writer's confidence that his/her idea is a good one, and provide a reason to begin composing.

In closing, Murray (1989) encourages students to take the time necessary to collect "warehouses" full of information; so much information that its sheer abundance makes the need for meaning and order insistent. "We must teach students to avoid the vague and general; to seek the hard-edged and precise. The more particular or more specific people are the more universal they are. We must learn to treasure the informing detail, the revealing specific, the organizing fact, building potential significance from abundant fragments. An insight is a fragile relationship between facts, a sketch, a hint, a feeling, a guess, a question. It takes time for the key question to appear" (Murray, 1984, p. 14).

THE CHALLENGE OF DIVERSITY

What if these strategies do not work? Special needs students often progress in their writing ability if they use a tape recorder (Meltzer & Solomon, 1988). Slower learning students profit because they can organize their information orally and reformulate it as they transcribe. Bilingual students also benefit because they can hear their thoughts in their native language.

STEP 2: DRAFTING

The drafting step involves writing a first draft. Students erase, cross out, and insert ideas as they write. Drafting allows students to clarify meaning, add new ideas, and make better connections in their messages. You might ask students to experiment while writing their first drafts and leave a blank line between handwritten lines (double-spacing their drafts) so revising will be less difficult.

It is during the drafting stage that the most direct writing instruction occurs. Teaching occurs through one-on-one conferences as well as whole class mini-lessons which precede the silent drafting period. Mini-lessons contain: (1) examples of stylistic features from peer writings; (2) models of vivid phrases from children's literature; and (3) how to increase precision in vocabulary. Mini-lessons originate when one or several students exhibit a specific writing weakness. For example, you observe that during the last month students have created only one-dimensional characters. To construct devices that fashion more memorable characters, read selections from Note-card 14 (or ask students to read their favorite sections), and discern how these authors' characters became memorable. Strategies students detect are listed on a chart, and students use one in their next composition.

Another instructional method to increase the quality of first-draft writing is for the class to experience an event, audiovisual presentation, guest speaker, or field-trip. After the shared event, each student turns a sheet of notebook paper lengthwise and uses the left-hand margin line as a "fact-line." This factline notes the flow of the "story" in which they participated. Once the incident is over, students place a sheet of paper below their factline, and write their first draft. An equally effective teaching method, "The Ten Minute Write," developed by Ms. Marjorie Downer, Benchmark School, Pennsylvania. Ms. Downer allows students ten minutes after a classroom event to (1) write comparisons of that event to their lives, (2) explain the moral or message as they interpreted it, or (3) invent an imaginative sequel. Then they read their writing to the class.

NOTECARD 14: BOOKS THAT MODEL HOW MEMORABLE CHARACTERS ARE CREATED

To provide instruction in developing strong, believable characters, students can read excerpts from three of the following books. Students compare these authors' strategies to create memorable characters with their own writings:

Did You Carry the Flag Today Charley? by R. Caudill

Blue Skye by L. Littke

Shoeshine Girl by Clyde Robert Butler

Queenie Peavy by Robert Burch

After the Goat Man by Betsy Byars

Ramona the Brave and other books by B. Cleary

Inside Out and other books by A. M. Martin

Bridge to Terabithia and other books by K. Paterson

Terror on the Mountain by Philip Viereck

Harriet the Spy by L. Fitzhugh

Something Special for Me by Vera Williams

Johnny Tremain by E. Forbes

My Side of the Mountain by J. C. George

Thank You, Jackie Robinson by B. Cohen

Class President by J. Hurwitz

Anastasia Krupnik by Lois Lowry

Caddie Woodlawn by Carol R. Brink

Best Friends for Frances by R. Hoban

Frog and Toad are Friends by A. Lobel

Winnie the Pooh by A. A. Milne

The Tale of Peter Rabbit by B. Potter

Like Jake and Me by M. Jukes

Call It Courage by A. Sperry

Brave Irene by W. Steig

Roll of Thunder, Hear My Cry by M. Taylor

Willie Bea and the Time the Martians Landed by Virginia Hamilton

Henry Huggins by Beverly Cleary

The Haunting by Margaret Mahy

Summer of My German Soldier by B. Greene

Mary Poppins by P. L. Travers

Blowfish Live by the Sea by Paula Fox

The Sign of the Beaver by E. Speare

A strategy that builds persuasive writing skills is to hold a poll. Students are asked to take a position about current events or issues at school such as, "How many think . . . ? How many would . . . ?" Once they express their opinion orally it is easier for them to write their rationale and cite evidence of support. Then, their persuasive writing draft is off and running!

Teach students to begin descriptive writings by jotting the scene, incident, or detail that first triggered their thinking about a topic. Explain to students that this initial thinking will be very vivid and thus occasion deeper meanings. This first description may be subsequently moved to a later section of the writing. As Calkins (1991) explains, "the reason for putting concrete details on the page first and lingering long enough to capture the vivid, sensory particulars of a scene or an experience is that only then will we begin to know the fullness of the experience for ourselves and make our own new meaning from it" (p. 279).

Last, in some drafting activities students should self-select spaces in the room where they want to write. Through this choice, students feel more in charge, have a greater sense of solitude, and can more rapidly move into a still and concentrated state of reflection to begin writing (Calkins, 1991).

STEP 3: REVISING

Revising is a reworking of the first, and subsequent, drafts. Revising occurs during, and immediately following, the drafting process. The revising step is the point in the writing process where students craft their art. Students "chisel and polish" meaning. They ensure that they have communicated exactly what they wanted to say. Pupils reorganize content, and insert or delete details. They do not focus on grammar, spelling, and writing conventions. You assist students to make better revisions by teaching, and then posting the following revising questions:

Revising Questions to Ask Myself

1. Can I change a word so my ideas become clearer?
2. Does each paragraph contain vivid details and a main idea?
3. Can I shorten any sentence?
4. Can I make the connection between ideas, phrases, sentences, and paragraphs better?
5. Can I use an example to make it easier for readers to understand?

You also assist students' revision thinking by asking classmates to describe how they do a revision. A third strategy is to teach a lesson so students begin to consciously use two levels of revision: *Level 1: Total Text Revisions* and *Level 2: Microrevision*. In doing *Total Text Revisions*, students decide if a total or partial rewrite is necessary. Total rewrites should occur when students believe a change of content, emphasis, purpose (e.g., changing a persuasive piece to an informative one), genre, audience, and/or point of view will improve their writing. In *Microrevision*, students move, delete, substitute, add or expand phrases, sentences, and paragraphs. With your instruction in revision groups, students can learn to use both levels. Following this instruction students who work in revising groups are not allowed to bring pencils to their meeting. Without pencils, revisions will more likely focus upon total text/microrevisions, rather than grammar and spelling changes. Also, when group members use discussion as their only communications media, enriching opportunities are created where meanings conveyed in individual compositions are improved.

Moreover, during the first two grading periods, students benefit from reaction guides, such as that displayed in Figure 7-3. Subsequently, advanced revising strategies can be practiced when students become members of an "editorial board." As a board member they make very specific suggestions concerning classmates' "best works." As compositions pass through the board, specific notes are made beside each paragraph such as, "This is where the piece works well"; "This is where I found the main ideas coming together well"; "We sort of see this part but it's not very attention-getting"; "What kind of doll did she have?" "Great simile! We like it!" and, "Fantastic ending sentence. It tied all your main points together."

Students can also learn to improve their *tone, clarity, variety, writing style*, and *texture*. They can measure their creations against the yardsticks in Figure 7-4. Once students are skilled in suggesting revisions orally, group members can read their writings aloud, while peers write improvements on notecards. In closing, more detailed information about teaching students how to make more specific revisions will be discussed in the next chapter.

FIGURE 7-3
Individual Student Evaluation Form

RESPONSE GROUP ASSIGNMENT

Paper number _____

Score _____

Write a brief comment explaining why you gave the paper the score you did. For example: Did the author use colorful, vivid language? Was the paper exciting? Did the paper follow a logical sequence?

Scorer's Name _____

ADDITIONAL QUESTIONS (for older students)

What is the best sentence or word?

What is strong about this piece?

What do you like about it?

What don't you understand?

Are there good descriptions, effective use of words?

Are there words inappropriately used, or words that could be stronger?

Does the story have a clear beginning, middle, and end?

Does the story make sense?

What needs to be clarified?

Which part of the paper needs more specific descriptions?

What questions are left unanswered?

Find a good or weak example of a recently studied aspect of writing.

FIGURE 7-4
Qualities That Improve Students' Writing

QUALITIES THAT IMPROVE WRITING CLARITY

Reality	Affect	Coherence	Humanity
clear	stark	logical	plain-speaking
simple	candid	intelligible	frank
obvious	transparent	comprehensible	undisguised
plain	bold	unambiguous	
positive	mysterious		
direct	plausible		
forthright			
effective			
sharp			
distinct			
vivid			

QUALITIES THAT IMPROVE WRITING TONE

Reality	Affect	Coherence	Humanity
true	candid	exact	open
realistic	frank	correct	honest
actual	delicate	rigorous	pure
certain	fine	sophisticated	sincere
accurate	faithful	sound	just
natural	perfect	logical	right
plausible	excellent	accurate	scrupulous
			reliable
			trustworthy
			satirical

QUALITIES THAT IMPROVE VARIETY IN WRITING

Fiction	History	Criticism	General
fairy tale	journal	discussion	scripts
fable	diary	commentary	writing—
legend	log	criticism	popular
parable	anecdote	essay	magazine
folktale	memoirs	editorial	technical
allegory	autobiography	manifesto	scholarly
romance	journalism	leaflet	learned periodicals
novel	annual	tract	minutes
short story	chronicle	sermon	petition
		satire	summary
			precis
	Drama	*Exposition*	abstract
	monologue	report	letter
	tragedy	article	epitaph
	comedy	manual	proverb
	farce	treatise	parody
	spoof	lecture	fiction

burlesque	nonfiction
extravaganza	advertising copy
musical	advertisements

QUALITIES THAT IMPROVE WRITING STYLE

Reality	Affect	Coherence	Humanity
content	style	middle	incident
form	point of view	climax	dialogue
mode	setting	anticlimax	slice of life
theme	plot	crisis	monologue
tone	subplot	crux	parody
mood	flashback	ending	satire
atmosphere	introduction	episode	symbol

QUALITIES THAT GIVE WRITINGS A FINER TEXTURE

	Vocabulary		Usage
abstract	setting	inflection	intonation
concrete	diction	emotive	grammar
general	common	sentimental	syntax
particular	formal	tired	context
literal	colloquial	overworked	tense
figurative	informal	cliché	number
metaphorical	slang	synonym	agreement
ambiguous	vulgarism	antonym	standard English
idea	euphemism	alternative	dialect
concept	technical	spellings	levels
notion	scholarly	derivation	register
generalization	Anglo-Saxon	etymology	pronunciation
abstraction	Latinized	syllable	stress
dialogue	foreign	stem/root	
punctuation	hip/mod	affixes	

STEP 4: EDITING

Students eliminate errors in spelling, punctuation, and capitalization. Throughout the year you build editing skills with the following methods.

1. *Peer editing.* Students select a revising partner. They edit each other's drafts. Before they begin, model how to edit by reading one of your writings and showing on the overhead projector the editing changes you made.

2. *Class "experts."* Students skilled in specific editing skills check classmates' drafts (e.g., a punctuation "team" edits for punctuation).

3. *Minimal mark.* Editors (you, or student editors) place a dot or checkmark at the end of a line on a classmate's paper that contains an error. Authors then find their own errors in marked lines and make corrections.

4. *Sentence/Paragraph of the week.* You identify a noun/verb or capitalization/punctuation error many students need to learn. Demonstrate how to make the correct form. Students then reference their past writings and correct any incidents where this capitalization, punctuation, or tense error occurred. During the week you praise students who correctly use the principle in a new writing. Alternatively, or in addition, you develop the practice of writing one student's beautifully written sentence or thoughts on the board for classmates to read, and possibly add that writing style to their own writing repertoires.

5. *Skill charts.* Work with small groups or with individual students on a specific writing problem. Then you and/or the student records improvements on student record forms.

6. *Computer editors.* Students use word processing and then use *Ghost Writer, Editor,* and other computer error detection programs to edit their writing.

7. *Editing groups.* Small groups edit each others' writings: (a) students give one-sentence suggestions as to ways their friends might edit their writings; (b) students note words and phrases from a peer's paper that make a particularly vivid impression; and (c) students tell writers what they thought as they read (e.g., how the writing style assisted comprehension).

As this editing step continues throughout the year, students evidence growth in their (1) use of more interesting words; (2) variety of sentence styles; (3) more captivating leads; and (4) correct spelling/punctuation.

STEP 5: SHARING

Since writing is indeed a public act, it is meant to be shared with others. The last stage in the writing cycle is to arrange for a genuine audience for student writings. Methods of doing so were demonstrated in Sample Schedule 3 in Chapter 2, where time is set aside each day for voluntary sharing. A second method is for students to make class or individual student books. The procedures for doing so are presented in Professional Portfolio. Also, you can open the writing period by asking for the names of those who need someone to listen to their work or who want to sign up to share later in the week.

Finally, you can institute a program through the school librarian where students write their comments about the book on a book marker. Markers are large enough for several students to write on the same one. In this way students can see schoolmates' comments as they select a book.

You can assist some students to have a national audience for their works by referencing *Helping Students' Creative Writing to Be Published in National Journals* (Educational Research Dissemination, P.O. Box 161354, Fort Worth, TX 76161).

THE CHALLENGE OF DIVERSITY

Remedial writers benefit by being told the criteria for identifying problems and strengths in their writing and how to correct or avoid specific problems. After using the process writing approach in this chapter, remedial writers can be shown specific sentences which illustrate the strengths and weaknesses in their writing. As Diederich (1991) stated: "I believe very strongly that noticing and praising whatever a student does well improves writing more than any kind or amount of correction of what he does badly, and that this is especially important for less able writers who need all the encouragement they can get" (p. 24). Johnston (1992, p. 23) suggests that you give a reason for students for your confusion rather than ask them a question about their writing. For example, respond to a weaker student's writing by saying, "The part in the middle about the horse made me feel very sad, but I feel a bit confused about the part where you were going home." This statement will have a more helpful effect on the student's writing than asking, "Why did you write the part about going home in that way?" or "I really liked the part where . . ." Some slower writers may prefer drawing a picture as a means of rehearsing their ideas (Gaskins, Gaskins, & Gaskins, 1991).

STRATEGIES THAT TEACH

BUILDING STUDENTS' WRITING ABILITY

As you will now read, students of all ages benefit from collaborative computer activities, writing in various formats, progressive dinner exercises, and writing workshops. Many computer programs are available to assist students in composing, selecting more precise words, constructing clearer sentences, obtaining data for writing, and creating several genres for varied audiences.

CREATING LESSONS THAT USE WRITING WORKSHOPS

M	T	W	Th	F

Descriptions of writing workshops appear in several full-length books (see Calkins & Harwynne, 1987; Calkins, 1991; Stuart & Graves, 1987). This approach is usually conducted in three to four centers through which students rotate to complete the writing stages specified earlier in this chapter. A sample workshop schedule follows:

9:00–9:10   Mini-lesson on some aspect of writing;
9:10–9:25   Sustained silent writing time (you and every student);
9:25–9:50   Writing Stations: Students go into the writing centers.
9:50–10:00   Sharing time for students to read self-selected pieces to the class.

You conference and students draft, revise, edit, and share/publish in separate centers. Students rotate between centers as you assign or as their writing needs dictate. Other types of centers students can create follow.

STRATEGIES THAT TEACH

A *Conferencing Station* is for students who need help with drafting their writing. Activities students can schedule at this center include brainstorming, webbing of major points, talking about their pieces, or asking questions of peers. "Staff" at this center is a student who likes to help other students.

A *Research Station* is for students who need help in finding information, or who desire additional data on their subject. Sample resources available at the center are dictionaries, grammar handbooks, an encyclopedia, and a spelling rules chart. "Staff" at this center is a student who feels confident about knowing where to find answers, and enjoys answering detail-oriented and editorial type questions.

An *Illustration Station* is for students who seek advice on illustrations or graphics to accompany their work, or want someone else to illustrate it. Materials at the center are markers, crayons, colored pencils, and art books to show professional illustrators' use of media. "Staff" at this center is an "artist in residence" available for advice. Authors credit this artist if they illustrate the manuscript.

A *Creating Station* is for students who want to improve their ideas before they write or revise. Resources at this center include encyclopedias, atlases, and tradebooks. "Staff" is a student who enjoys listening and collaborating to invent ideas.

CREATING LESSONS THAT TEACH COMPOSITION SKILLS USING A PROGRESSIVE DINNER FORMAT

This lesson is patterned after progressive dinners. Its purpose is to provide samples of different writing styles (Wepner, 1992). To begin, place students in five-member groups at tables. Five objects (e.g., box of cereal, wooden spoon, old sneaker, hat, flashlight) are placed on each table, with five pieces of large chart paper. One person per table volunteers to be the recorder for each group.

Step 1 (Prewriting): Each group of students jots ideas (i.e., prewrite) related to the objects on their table for five minutes. Then the entire group moves to the next table.

Step 2 (Writing): At the next table each group writes a separate story (related to the objects on that table), using the ideas created by the previous group. They employ as many varied and vivid sentence patterns as possible (20 minutes). The group moves to the next table.

Step 3 (Revising): Each member of the group revises (add/delete/reorganize) the story written by a member from the previous group (10 minutes), then moves to the next table.

Step 4 (Editing): Each group member edits (mechanics/grammar/spelling) a revised story from the previous group (7 minutes), and then moves to the next table.

Step 5 (Creating final copy): Each group member creates a final copy of the edited piece written by a previous group (7 minutes), and sketches an illustration if desired. The group returns to the table where they did their

Word processing can improve the amount and quality of students' revisions (Kurth, 1987). In a survey conducted by IBM, it was also discovered that more than 82 percent of teachers reported that computer use improves students' motivation, creative thinking, and self-confidence (*T.H.E. Journal,* 1991).

writing. They study how their original thoughts were revised and improved by others. Then they identify one of their sentence structures represented in their revisions that they want to incorporate into their writing styles. They write a title for their story (to practice summative thinking).

Step 6 (Sharing): Some students share their stories with the entire class and highlight new sentence structures they want to use in the future. This activity also can be used to help students write about books they have read. Each group could be given a different object from the same book (e.g., *It's Not the End of the World* by Judy Blume, 1972) and these objects are used to begin their drafts. A third use of the progressive dinner lesson is to begin with concepts about which students want to write, such as divorce, "middle children," fighting, reconciliation, or happiness.

CREATING LESSONS THAT USE THE COMPUTER IN WRITING INSTRUCTION

Initial research indicates that the nature of peer collaborations and feedback in writing programs that use computers differs from programs without computers (Sulzby, in press). For example, when computers are used in paired writings, students collaborate significantly more, and the amount/ quality of students' revisions increases. Computers can serve several other important functions for young writers.

1. *Compupoem* (South Coast Writing Project, University of California, Santa Barbara) assists students to experiment with poetry and increases their understanding of how poems are written.

2. *Stories and More* and *Writing-to-Read* (IBM) build emergent literacy skills by combining a modified alphabetic system with word processing. These programs assist students to develop and articulate their ideas in a variety of written forms. In *Stories and More,* human voices are a part of the computer program so children's literature can be read aloud while students read the screen.

3. *Bank Street Writer* (Scholastic, Inc.), *Story Tree* (Scholastic, Inc.), *Tales of Discovery, Tales of Adventure,* Microsoft Works, WordPerfect, Express Publisher, Magic State, Muppet State (IBM), *The Print Shop* (Tandy), and similar word processing programs build students' ability to create their own stories. *The Writing Notebook* (Humanities Software, P.O. Box 590727, San Francisco, CA 94159) offers creative ideas for using word processors in a wide variety of ways. A second way word processing interrelates reading/writing/thinking processes is illustrated in *Explore-A-Story* and *Language Experience Recorder* (Teacher Support Software). These programs begin with pictures from computer graphics. Students follow an animated story on the computer until the story stops and students become the writers. Students use the characters and opening events of the computer story (which have been programmed by the students' teacher to meet individual comprehension needs) to complete the stories which are printed and made into a book. Instructions for programming are provided in the manual of these packages.

4. *Language Master 4000,* an electronic dictionary/thesaurus/phonetic spelling corrector, pronounces words typed into the computer to build students' written/spoken vocabularies.

5. *Immigrant* is a computerized project in which students work with historically accurate information about the Irish immigration in 1850 (Harvard Graduate School of Education, Cambridge, MA) to improve their writing of descriptive narratives.

6. *Writer Rabbit* (Apple) and *Sentence Combining* (Miliken) build students' writing abilities by teaching sentence parts that answer the questions who did what, when, where, why, and how.

7. *ABC-Optical Data Bank* is a program through which students gain information from news broadcasts from the 1940s to the present. After viewing these on videodisc, students write about them to reach a variety of purposes and audiences.

8. *Networking with the Library of Congress* and the *National Geographics Kids Network* (Department 1001, Washington, DC 20077-9966) provide multiple sources of data on a subject. Other on-line networks include *Compuserve* (Computer Service), *GEnie* (General Electric), *World Classroom* (GTE Education Services), and *Long Distance Learning Network* (AT&T).

9. *Project World Link* (Tandy Corporation and McGraw-Hill Information Exchange) enables students and teachers to access peers in other states/countries.

10. *Show Time* (MECC) enables students, collectively, to write short plays following program directions.

11. *Game Show* or *Tic Tac Show* (Advanced Ideas Software Co.) is a program that enables students to prepare review questions so that other groups, in a play format, may use the computerized questions as reviews for tests or as comprehension checks on selections from children's literature.

12. *Logo* and *Logowriter* (LCSI Educational Services) are programs through which students learn language while experimenting and creating with a "turtle" on the screen that students direct. Gifted students particularly benefit from learning computer languages, such as *Logo*, and how to program computers.

13. *Great Reading–Great Writing Series* (Scholastic, Inc.). These software packages contain four selections of children's literature. Experiences in poetry, news story, interview, and letter writing build students' reading, writing, and thinking skills simultaneously.

14. *Computer-based Telecommunications:* Computer-based telecommunications are *the processes of connecting two computers by telephone so information can be exchanged in digital form.* Many school districts use telecommunication units to develop writing skills. Programs include the following:

a. *Great Pumpkin Letter Writing Campaign*: Fourth and seventh graders from different cultures and geographic regions write to each other, serving as big and little brothers and sisters.

b. *MeLink*: This system links students in remote classes to instructors and students in larger districts, so that smaller districts can increase the available real audiences for student writings.

c. *Kidwire*: This telecommunication system produces student-written journalism; and maintains a "riddle collection," a series of brain teasers, and student-created trivia contests.

d. *Quill*: Quill was one of the earliest writing projects to make use of telecommunication networking. The planner component of this system organizes ideas on a specific topic. The library component stores draft copies and finished documents. Quill also has a mailbag which is an electronic bulletin board service. This system also links college students to elementary students in many innovative and effective ways.

e. *DeOrilla a Orilla* (*From Shore to Shore*): This telecommunication system connects students in Spanish so that they improve their writing skills in Spanish. The system publishes a Spanish newspaper, a data bank of Spanish proverbs from parents and relatives, and other materials that enable Spanish-speaking students to communicate with one another.

15. *Interactive Videos and Computers* (LInkwayLive by IBM) incorporates video, newscasts, audio, and text displays on the computer screen about a wide variety of topics.

Don Beauregard, principal at King's Canyon Middle School, reported that interactive video computers raised achievement scores of his high-risk students, and "the computer program, which integrates reading and writing, does more for kids than any other method I have seen" (*T.H.E. Journal*, 1991, p. 81).

STRATEGIES THAT TEACH

Barone (1989) found that children as young as six benefit from keeping journals. The written dialogue they produce helps them move beyond literal comprehension of stories.

CREATING LESSONS THAT TEACH STUDENTS HOW TO COMPLETE LARGE WRITING PROJECTS

In this lesson you teach students eight strategies that can be used to complete long-term projects.

Introduction of the Lesson

Describe to students how they will learn to more successfully complete the many different types of tasks that are placed before them. You tell them that they will know they have been successful if they begin to vary the strategies they use to complete large writing tasks.

Dispelled Misconceptions

Introduce the project: Prior to today you may have thought that you can perform all big tasks with the same method. However, tasks are completed faster and more effectively when you match characteristics of the task with an approach that complements those features, as you will learn today.

Thinking Guide Instructions

As I describe each of the approaches on our Thinking Guide (see Thinking Guide 7-1), make notes about key ideas you want to remember. Write these in your own words on a separate sheet of paper.

THINKING GUIDE 7-1
Eight Methods to Complete Projects

EIGHT METHODS TO COMPLETE A "MASTERPIECE"

1. Begin now but not at the beginning
2. Leave it lying around
3. Make a deadline
4. Do it better the second time around
5. Chip away with 7 and 11
6. Make an assembly line
7. Seek expert assistance
8. Change the working procedure to capitalize upon your talents

---

1. Whenever you face a brand new or big task that you dread, you will produce higher quality products in a shorter amount of time if you begin with either clearly defined sections or ones you know you can do well. When you begin with a section you can do, you will build your knowledge and momentum to tackle more difficult and less-well defined sections. (Give students an example from an incident that occurred earlier in the year or from your own life when you began a difficult writing task by starting a section you already knew how to complete instead of trying to begin with something less familiar or more difficult. Give an example following each of the remaining seven descriptions as well.)

2. When you have a task that you are anxious to complete but will take longer than one setting to complete, leave it lying around in a location that is clearly visible so you can work on it in bits and pieces when you have a few moments. This strategy works well because when you see a task often, your commitment to complete it increases.

3. Whenever a task "nags" at you continuously, or you are beginning to feel guilty that you have not completed it, you can set a deadline and that will encourage you to complete the task more rapidly.

4. Whenever you have to complete a task in less time than it would normally take and the task is one that you have done previously, before you begin, use a creative thinking strategy (see Chapter ll) and create a new method of doing the task with equal quality in the time available.

5. Whenever a task is monotonous and/or you have several little tasks to do before the project is finished, set aside a few minutes (like seven minutes in the morning before school; and eleven minutes the very first thing when you get home from school) to work on that task. Because you only work on it for a short time, the task will not as easily bore you.

6. Make an assembly line if the project has several objects that require the same, repeated actions. In this way you will get faster at completing one task of the project than you would if you moved from one section to the next on each object. Once you have completed the same action for all objects, then you can move on to the next action required of all objects.

7. When a task is routine, important, and difficult, or if a project may be a little beyond your level of unassisted ability, find people or resources to help you.

8. When a task becomes more difficult the longer you work on it, change the working procedure to better suit your working style and the characteristics of the task itself (see Thinking Guide 7-1).

Students Select and Complete Their Own Objective

Students select a project and a method of choice to complete that writing project by the end of the week. They evaluate their success on the task and their selection of an effective thinking strategy to complete it.

Rethink and Reformulate

(For student self-assessments, and planned extensions across the curriculum)

Students use the fishbowl method to summarize what they have learned in this lesson (see Chapter 3). The fishbowl strategy is where a few students sit in a circle and discuss the thinking strategies they used and demonstrate how they refined or used the methods in Thinking Guide 7-1. In the fishbowl method, the rest of the class sits in a larger circle around that smaller group and listens to their comments, asks questions, and learns new ways to use the methods of Thinking Guide 7-1.

Extensions Across the Curriculum

- Students write letters to someone they admire to ask if he/she uses one or more of the thinking strategies of this lesson.
- Students select a group project, dramatic activity, display, audience reading, or interview in which they implement one of the methods learned in this lesson. They defend why the method they chose to use is the best for the type of project in which they engaged.
- Students call a doctor, lawyer, teacher, religious leader, homemaker, secretary, construction worker, artist, and other professionals to determine if projects within their professions most often adhere to one of the eight thinking strategies of this lesson.

CRITICAL THINKING ACTIVITY 7
Using Journal Writing to Increase Students' Problem Solving Abilities

To this point, Critical Thinking Activities have integrated the language arts to build students' thinking abilities through (1) scaffolding; (2) diagnosing; (3) asking questions of clarification; (4) recognizing patterns in oral and written form; (5) detecting propaganda; and (6) semantic mapping. In this activity you will learn how journal writing increases students' abilities to

FIGURE 7-5

Learning Log Example

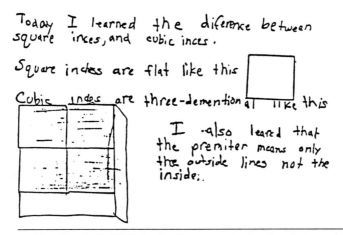

Today I learned the diference between square inces, and cubic inces.

Square inces are flat like this ☐

Cubic inces are three-demention al like this

I also leared that the premiter means only the outside lines not the inside:.

From Weaver, C. (1988) *Reading Process and Practice: From Socio-psycholinguistics to Whole Languages.* Portsmouth, NH, Heinemann, p. 245.

solve problems and explore ideas. Problem solving journal entries often enable students to do their best thinking. Some students may wish to guarantee the privacy of some of their problem-related journal entries. They can do so by folding (and even stapling) entries they prefer that no one reads.

Types of Journals

Introduce students to journals by explaining the following purpose for which they will use their journals. Demonstrate each type before students begin. Allow students options as to which type of journal they will keep for each grading period. Make the following options (in addition to the types of journal entries demonstrated in the FOR YOUR JOURNAL sections at the end of each chapter in this text), available to your students.

   1. **Learning Logs.** Students use their journals to summarize a day's lesson and to react to what they learned. Learning logs are also used as a source book of ideas, and collection of facts to be combined later. A separate page in a learning log can be set aside to record questions prior and during reading, conferences, and response groups. Learning logs can also become tracking devices, so students see how much they've read, learned, written, said, or accomplished in a specific period of time, as shown in Figure 7-5.

   2. **Simulated Journals.** In this type of journal, students assume the role of another person and write from that person's point of view. Simulated journals are also called literary portraits in which students write within the role of a historical figure they admire.

STRATEGIES THAT TEACH

FIGURE 7-6
Sample of Student-to-Teacher Response Journal

Dear Mrs. Whalen,

"Sounder" is a very good book. I think I like it because it tells about hardtimes for a slave family. I like how realistic William H. Armstrong's caracters are. One word I couldn't undersand is in this sentence - His eyes began to <u>smart</u> what does this mean. I am about halfwai through this book and I am looking fowar to the rest.

Ben Gaines

Dear Ben,

"Sounder" is a classic that stands the test of time!

"His eyes began to smart ..." <u>Smart</u> can have other meanings besides the common one relating to intelligence. It can mean to experience a stinging sensation. Have your eyes ever smarted?

Please reread your journal entry. Could you tell me what kind of hardtimes the family experienced, and, <u>how Armstrong's characters are realistic?</u>

If you like this book, you might enjoy Cynthia Voight's "Homecoming." We don't have it in our library yet, but I bet Laurel has it.

Mrs. W.   Date!

FIGURE 7-7
Double Entry Diary (DED)

SOMETHING IN THE STORY THAT TOUCHED YOU	PARENTS' RESPONSE
Instead of piles of leather there were tiny suits of clothes.	This reminds me of my mom because she laid my clothes on the heater so they'd be warm for school.

TEACHER'S RESPONSE

Sally,

   Your response reminds me of something from my childhood. In the winter, I used to get dressed in the living room by the stove since there was no heat in our bedrooms.

   Mrs. Jones

3. Private Journals. Students have a section in their spiral notebook in which they write what is important to them. As the name implies, these are the student's private entries; their own diaries. Rarely are private journals graded.

4. Response Journals. Students dialogue with others about thoughts and questions. These journals are similar in format to the private journal, but are accessible to teacher and peers who write their responses to students' ideas, as demonstrated in Figure 7-6.

5. Buddy Journals. This type of journal, which can also become a separate section of students' spiral notebooks, involves students trading journals with one another. One buddy writes an entry, and the other buddy writes a response. To begin buddy journals, allow interested students to choose someone with which they want to communicate for a two-week period. These students write in their journals two times a week, making entries two days of the week, and responding to their buddy's entries for two days. On the last day of each week they discuss each other's comments to their initial entries.

6. Three-Way Interactive Journals. These journals involve both the parents and teacher responding to a child's journal entry. Three-way interactive journals are not only effective in building strong relationships with the parents and teacher, but enable parents to observe and understand new dimensions of their child's thinking, as shown in Figure 7-7 (Wiseman, 1992; Young, 1992).

7. Focus Journals. In focus journals, students have a number of entries that relate to the same issue. Students are free to choose their topic, and to write for a number of sessions on this topic/issue. Bishop (1992) reports that students prefer to share focus journals after one week's writing has ended.

8. Problem-Finding/Solving Journals. One of the most valuable uses of journal writing is to teach the problem-solving process. As Ricardo illustrates in Figure 7-8, problem-finding/solving journal entries is often where students do their best thinking. Problem-finding/solving journals begin by teaching a creative problem-solving process. Students keep this process thinking guide before them as they replicate the process in writing about problems they face. Once the process is complete, students use one of the problem-solving tools to be described in Chapter 12 to select solutions.

PROFESSIONAL DEVELOPMENT OPPORTUNITY
How to Conduct Effective Conferences

Conducting effective conferences is difficult because each is an entirely different and new event having its own combination of goals and constraints. Through one-to-one conferencing, you advance student's abilities in whatever areas are most important at that point in time for that student, whether you have an idea of the area of need before the conference begins or not. There is no script to follow. While there are many equally effective methods of conferencing, the following principles underlie each:

1. Conferences are one of the best times to "tell stories" and invent analogies to help students learn difficult concepts. Conferences provide opportunities to scaffold intensively in a student's zone of proximal development. The most important functions of a conference are: (1) to give each child the opportunity to share a personal experience of listening, speaking, reading, and/or writing with the most influential person in his/her school experience; (2) to give you an opportunity to interact with each child personally, to monitor his/her reading experience, diagnose difficulties, offer guidance, and set practice where necessary; (3) to check the reading/writing log of each child and make appropriate records in the conference log (Holdaway, 1990).

2. Conferences can be scheduled: (l) when the student signs up for a time to meet with you because they need your help on a specific problem or task; (2) when you schedule times to meet with all students for approximately 20 minutes each month while the rest of the class is doing silent writing and reading; (3) daily, as demonstrated in sample schedules in

FIGURE 7-8
Student Testimonial About the Value of Journal Writing

> Ricardo G,
> I like when we wrote in our Jurnl.
> I like it begose we wraght about
> our persenl lives and what we
> wont for our birthday. the thing I
> like is when we had to right comvencm
> somebody to buy a car or to go to a new
> band that boully came to town.
> and they wont you to go that was
> my best think

Chapter 2; (4) impromptu to overcome specific problems; (5) when two (or more) students meet with you to discuss similar needs; (6) when you need to know the thinking that led to specific decisions a student made while speaking, reading, writing, or listening, e.g., "Why did you decide to cross out those words in the first paragraph of your first draft?"; (7) when you check a set of objectives for a grading period (printed on a chart) and each student adds something new he/she wants to learn; for example, in writing, do they want help in "overcoming writer's block"; tightening their main theme; creating vivid details; using sequence creatively; incorporating varied sentence structures; or identifying their own writing style; (8) as an assembly-line conference (Clark, 1987), e.g., at the end of class if there are five to six students who signed up for a conference but you were unable to meet with them, they line up beside you as classmates prepare to end the period. You answer individual questions so all students in the line benefit from hearing the answers, and each student has a suggestion to overcome a personal difficulty before the next class begins.

3. Some conferences are scheduled because students have a need they identified, and they begin with their specific questions. Others are scheduled because you have something to share with a student; some are scheduled with no clear goal in mind (e.g., you and a student spontaneously share something together). Each student conference you hold, however, focuses upon identifying something to assist a student to speak, read, write, listen, or think more competently in the future. Doing so means that you care and share ideas and feelings, as well as laugh and experiment together until students "know they know" what they want to do to grow.

4. To open a conference, generally, you can ask students what they want to discuss. Before all conferences begin, however, take time to *think*

FIGURE 7-9
Student Conference Evaluation Form

CONFERENCE LOG

Name

Room   Sheet number _____

Level

Conferences	Date	Publishing conferences	Date
1		1	
2		2	
3		3	
4		4	
5		5	
Small teaching groups		**Folder check**	
1		1	
2		2	
3		3	
4		4	
5		5	

---

about what you want to say so as to initiate a new course and path of thinking. To become their trusted mentor, you cannot rush from one student to the next. You will know you are a successful conference mentor when you *do not* say to yourself, "Only five more conferences to go"! When conferencing becomes a way of instructing/assessing in the life of your classroom, you will restructure the time demands you place upon yourself so you can *really* help students change. You may spend up to 1–1/2 hours with one student, and 30 seconds with a second, yet give both what they need. Equal giving will no longer equate to a standard time spent each day with each child. At the end of the week, you will also note the number of times each student had your undivided attention, so next week's conferences begin with those with whom you did not spend time the previous week.

5. If at any point during the conference you feel tempted to take a child's pencil out of his/her hand and begin writing the answers for that child, and you see the student slump back in the seat as you take ownership over his/her thinking, stop yourself. At such times you are asking the student to change to fit what you are teaching ("making" him/her understand). Instead of providing answers for students who cannot proceed alone, schedule a second conference, within the same week, to meet with

that student again. This rescheduling gives you time to think of a new method of instruction to assist this student in overcoming his/her difficulty.

6. The most important part of a conference is near the end because it has the greatest potential to amplify the knowledge/strategies students have learned during the conference. It is at the end of the conference when you ask students to summarize what they learned and how they plan to think/communicate better in the future. During conferences avoid the temptation to correct a student's thinking. Instead when you are certain you understand the student's most important concern, suggest a strategy to improve it, and then add, "Try it, if you want, and then come see me if it doesn't work." As Henri Amiel stated in 1864: "To know how to suggest is the great art of teaching."

7. Evaluate each conference, mentally or literally, by noting aspects that worked and didn't work well for you and that child. The conference form in Figure 7-9 assists in this reflective/assessment process.

8. Tape-record some of your conferences. When you replay the tape you can assess your growth as a mentor, and refresh your memory of specific reflections students made during a conference.

TRY IT

1. If you have an available group of students, ask them how they feel about having their writing evaluated. Discuss with them how they would evaluate other students' writing, if they were teachers. Share your findings in class.

2. If you are teaching, work with two or more students or adult writers, ask them to describe what makes a good writer and analyze characteristics of good writing they value. Have these older students or adult writers come to class to share a list of writing tips they follow. Prior to their visit have your class brainstorm tips they use to write. Once speakers finish, students determine if their tips agree. Why or why not?

3. If you are not teaching, answer the following questions: How will you respond to a student who is just sitting there "looking into space" while others are freewriting? How will you help a student who experiences writer's block? If you are teaching, begin a new type of journal activity for your students using one of the types in Critical Thinking Activity 7. Make a photocopy of either your or a student's entry. In class the next day, with that student's permission, edit the photocopied version on the overhead. Write the main point of the story (or your story) or the most important thing you want your readers to gain from these stories on a second sheet of paper. Have the class make the type of journal entry you illustrate. If you are not teaching, prepare a buddy journal entry and ask a friend to respond, ask the friend to write the most important thing he/she thought about your writing and to suggest how you can improve it. Make these revisions. Describe what you have learned about the editing process and how you will help students in your class use editing and buddy journals more productively.

Model bookmaking by showing a completed version you made, and by making a second during the class period.

4. If you are not teaching, select a book from Notecards 13 and 14 (pp. 215, 221) and design a lesson described in this chapter to which that book would contribute. If you are teaching, this week practice telling your students: "Let me be your secretary; you tell me what you want to tell others and I'll write it down." Analyze the effects of this strategy in overcoming your students' writing blocks. If you are not teaching, conduct a mock conference and tape record it. You can conference with a classmate, and analyze the tape to see if you followed the principles in Professional Development Opportunity.

FOR YOUR JOURNAL

You have now learned about many types of journals. You have also made six types of entries in your professional journal. The journal entry for this chapter is designed to demonstrate the power of journals in solving problems. To use this journal writing activity with your students, pose reflective questions at your students' level that are similar to the following that are posed for you. Write your answers to the following in your journal:

What do you feel comfortable in doing and teaching to improve students' writing and thinking processes? What things do you want to learn to do better, and how do you propose to do so?

Reflect upon how you write. Do you write single drafts? Do you ask colleagues or family members to edit and revise? Note ways you can improve your writing based on the principles in this chapter.

BUILDING YOUR PROFESSIONAL PORTFOLIO
Bookmaking

There are nine steps that assist students to write their own book. Before you teach these steps, students can choose the type of book they want to make from those presented in Figure 7-10. The steps in bookmaking you will teach follow.

1. The first book your students write should be 16 pages long so that the text can be combined into the books described in Figure 7-10.

2. Students do not have to write the title first, but instead write an outline of the beginning, setting, conflict/problem, and end of their stories. Then students decide if their stories will be humorous or serious.

3. They should illustrate their stories with clear, simple pictures when the book is in the revising stage.

4. Students rewrite sections so as to "grab readers' attention" by making characters more whole and complete; establishing the sense of time and place quickly in the first two pages; showing the thinking processes of the characters so the story becomes more action-filled; adding richness in details to create a better mood; making the dialogue believable; utilizing a stylistic feature from one of their favorite authors; and taking chances to write a great opening sentence (see Figure 7-4).

5. Students discover their book's visual identity by laying every two pages side by side, and overlapping a single picture between two pages. Any student having trouble drawing pictures should be told "to draw faster" because the more creative side of the brain will likely take over when speed increases. Students should complete two drawings a period, at least. Once drawings are complete, students can improve them merely by making most important lines heavier and wider. You can also hold up best drawings as samples to stimulate students' ideas for the next day's work.

6. When books have been assembled, you need 10 minutes to describe how to design the book's front cover. The book title should be easy to read and the cover design should suggest the book's contents without crowding the space. After you've given these guidelines, and shown students a few samples, allow only 20 minutes for students to make their covers. With such a tight time limit they won't have time to tell themselves they can't do it. Tell students that they must show their cover at the end of this class period.

7. Students complete the backs, flaps, and spines of their books by bringing a picture of themselves, and asking another student in the room to read their stories and write a review for their front flap. The front flap tells just enough of the story to intrigue a reader. The back flap describes a few sentences about the author and is where the photograph is placed. The spine has the author's last name at the top, the title of the story in the center, and the title of the "publishing company" (the class) at the bottom.

8. Host an "unveiling of the books" with refreshments. Invite parents, principal, librarian, and students from other classes. Each student holds up his/her book, and gives a one-minute synopsis. While refreshments are

STRATEGIES THAT TEACH

FIGURE 7-10
Types of Books Students Can Make

There are many ways to publish a book, here are a few suggestions ranging from the very simple to more complicated methods.

SCROLL

Book is written on a long sheet of paper, one page at a time is revealed. Dowels can be fastened at each end.

ACCORDIAN

A long sheet of paper is folded fanlike to make pages or individual sheets of paper are joined with tape. When pages are folded together, shapes can be cut paperdoll style so the pages are not severed. Stiff covers can be added.

RING BOUND/YARN BOUND

Covers and inside pages are gathered and holes are punched—various yarns or rings are inserted. Revisions or additions are easy to do.

BRASS BRAD BOUND

Covers and inside pages are gathered and brass brads are inserted. If the book is thick, prepunch the holes. Revisions or additions are easy to do.

STAPLE BOUND

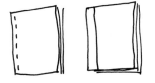

Covers and individual pages are gathered and stapled down the edge. Opaque tape covers the staples and reinforces the spine.
Variation: Folded cover and folded pages are collated and stapled down the middle using a long-arm stapler to reach the fold.

STITCH BOUND

Folded cover and folded pages are collated and stitched down the middle using one of a variety of string types. Fabric can be used instead of paper for soft books.

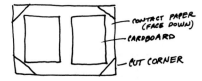

CONTACT PAPER (FACE DOWN)

CARDBOARD

CUT CORNER

LIBRARY BOUND

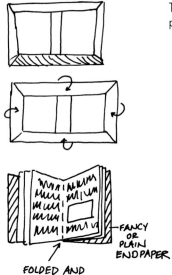

The inside pages are stitched and then the end papers are glued into stiff covers. (A, B, C, D, E)

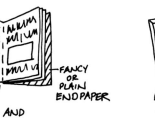

FOLDED AND
SEWN
BOOKLET

FANCY
OR
PLAIN
ENDPAPER

GLUE ENDPAPERS
TO COVERS

COMB BOUND

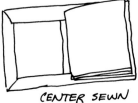

Covers and individual pages are gathered and brought to a comb binder which a library or copy center might have.

CENTER SEWN
BOOKLET ON
INSIDE COVERS.

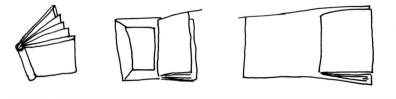

eaten, books are displayed on the chalkboard ledge for all to see. Books are then placed on display in the school library or public library for a week before students are allowed to take them home as gifts or to keep for themselves. The day books go off display, students select the class in the school in which they would like to read their book, and they do so.

8 Revising: Using Grammar, Rewriting, and Rephrasing as Tools to Clarify Meaning

These girls are refining their grammar usage by meeting in a revising committee, responding to their favorite parts of their peer's writing, and describing what it was about the grammatical structures that made the language so effective.

When Confucius was asked what he would do if he had the responsibility for administering a country, he said he would improve language. If language is not correct then what is said is not what is meant; if what is said is not what is meant, then what ought to be done remains undone; if this remains undone, morals and arts would deteriorate, justice would go astray; if justice goes astray, the people will stand about in helpless confusion.

—Confucius, 551–479 B.C.

The purpose of this chapter is to help you improve your students' language. In the process you will learn new methods of teaching grammar, revising, and rephrasing to clarify students' meanings. Your students can influence other's ideas if they use appropriate word orders, sentence structures, paragraph functions, and story grammar. The strategies in this chapter will assist your students to use these language principles independently.

By the end of the chapter you will know:

1. Ways to include grammar instruction in students' self-selected reading, writing, and speaking activities;
2. Strategies students can use to build more effective sentences;
3. How students can make more appropriate grammatical choices;
4. Definitions of traditional, structural, and transformational-generative grammar;
5. How to intensify students' use of idioms, personification, metaphors, and figurative language to clarify and strengthen their spoken and written communication.

THEORETICAL FOUNDATION
STUDENTS' NEED FOR GRAMMAR INSTRUCTION

Grammar is *the description of the structure of our language.* It is comprised of principles that govern word choice, word order, usage, sentence structure, sentence type, dialect, paragraph form, paragraph function, and story structure. By using these principles appropriately our students can fashion an infinite number of unique communications.

Why teach grammar? In 1963, and in a recent follow-up report of the National Council of Teachers of English, *"the teaching of formal grammar* [emphasis added] was found to have a negligible or even harmful effect on the improvement of writing because it usually displaces some instruction and practice in actual composition" (NCTE, 1987). Other studies show that papers written by students who studied *traditional* grammar for two years had more errors than students who merely wrote daily instead of working exercises in grammar textbooks (e.g., Noyce & Christie, 1983; Elbow, 1981; Linden & Whimbey, 1990). With results such as these, why do we continue to teach grammar?

REASONS FOR TEACHING GRAMMAR

Researchers interpret these data to mean that the *traditional method of teaching grammar* is the reason for the limited self-initiated use of grammatical principles. The principles are important; the method of teaching them needs revision (Combs, 1975; Howie, 1979). Past instructional methods violated the principles of learning described in Chapter 1. These methods asked students to memorize rules through isolated textbook exercises which is comparable to asking students to become better runners by solely studying leg muscles on anatomical charts. You will not teach your students the power of verbs by asking them to conjugate "see." Rather, students will learn to use stronger verbs when they revise their own or a partner's paper, and in the process they notice (or you teach them) that the way to strengthen weaker sentences is to increase the precision of the verb used. Then students reference thesauruses to find more vivid and effective verbs.

There is evidence that the methods presented in this chapter increase students' use of effective grammar as they speak and write. These methods appear to make students' subconscious knowledge explicit as they use conversation and revising to internalize grammatical principles. The new methods assist students to translate their experiences more explicitly, and to make decisions about the grammar they use as they select between a variety of grammatical structures (Applebee et al., 1988; Stuart & Graves, 1987). Without this instruction, students seldom reword or combine sentences, rearrange material, or improve meanings (Paul, 1990).

What type of grammar should be taught? While educators agree that students must possess a knowledge of grammatical principles, there are different sets of rules they can learn. You may elect to teach one or more of these sets of principles or theories of language structure which follow.

Traditional Grammar.   Traditional grammar is *the sorting of English words into categories, or parts of speech,* as shown in Figure 8-1. Traditional grammarians posit that students will learn to speak and write grammatically when they combine these parts of speech correctly. Traditional grammar was the first type of instruction offered in American public schools. It is based on the rules that govern Latin, and is modeled after instruction offered in Great Britain. New traditional grammatical theory treats English as an **inflected language,** one whose words signal meaning through word endings. While Latin and Old English were inflected languages, modern English is not. Meaning in our language is not communicated through the endings of words (aside from the meanings of plurality/verb tense). Moreover, with the increasing frequency of individual words which have multiple meanings (e.g., *run, tire, read,* and *bat*), the principle that Modern English words can represent only one part of speech is invalid. Today, single English words can describe an action (verb = *run* home); things (noun = home*run, run* in a stocking, 6K *run*), a gerund (*run*ning the race, *run*ning the campaign), or an adjective (the *run*ning faucet).

FIGURE 8-1
Parts of Speech

Nouns

Traditionally, a noun is defined as the name of a person, place, or thing.

I. *Derivational Affixes*

-age	coverage, village
-ance	clearance, importance
-ee	trustee, employee
-er	employer, dancer
-ment	pavement, government
-ce	independence, insolence
-cy	democracy, lunacy
-ity	vanity, scarcity
-ness	stillness, silliness
(also:	-ster, -ism, -ist, -ship)

II. *Inflectional Affixes*
To make plurals:

-s	coats, pigs
-es	dishes, ditches

But note the irregular plural forms:
children, women, oxen, men, deer, geese, feet

Also, *mass nouns* are not commonly pluralized:
communism, milk

III. *Sentence Test Frames*
The _____ couldn't hide its _____ .
One _____ had many _____ .
Sharon was in _____ .

Verbs

Traditionally, verbs are defined as words that name actions, or states of being.

I. *Derivational Affixes*

-ize	socialize, criticize
-ify	classify, mystify
-en	darken, lighten
-ate	hesitate, navigate
en-	enlist, enlarge
be-	belittle, bedazzle

II. *Inflectional Affixes*

-s	runs, moves
-ed	flagged, started
-ing	flagging, starting
to . . .	to run, to fall

III. *Auxiliary Verbs*

be/is/am/ are/was/were	is going, was talking
have/has/had	have taken, has talked
might/may	might run, may rain
shall/should	shall fight, should speak
will/would	will run, would stall
can/could	can find, could lose
must	must begin

IV. *Sentence Test Frame*

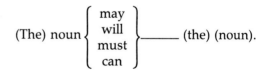

$$(\text{The}) \text{ noun} \left\{ \begin{array}{l} \text{may} \\ \text{will} \\ \text{must} \\ \text{can} \end{array} \right\} \underline{\quad} (\text{the}) \,(\text{noun}).$$

Note that parentheses ( ) mean "may choose this element." Braces { } mean "must choose one of these elements."

Examples:
The aardvark *whistled* the tune.
Rain must *fall*.

cont'd

Adjectives

Traditionally, adjectives are defined as words that modify nouns.

I. *Derivational Affixes*

-y	funny, crazy
-ive	active, passive
-able	comfortable, agreeable
-ful	bashful, cheerful
-less	helpless, thoughtless
-ar	regular, circular
-ary	ordinary, legendary
-ic	civic, terrific
-ish	childish, fiendish
-ous	fabulous, hideous
*-en**	wooden, woolen
*-ed**	beloved, aged
*-ing**	charming, interesting

II. *Inflectional Affixes*

-er	fuller, smaller
-est	biggest, tallest

III. *Sentence Test Frames*

A _____ noun seems very _____ .

Examples:
A *stingy* person seems very *stingy*.
But not
A *telephone* man seems very *telephone*.

*Not to be confused with verb inflectional affixes.

Adverbs

Traditionally, adverbs are defined as words that modify verbs.

I. *Derivational Affixes*

a-	ahead, away
-ly	slowly, happily
-ward	backward, skyward
-where	somewhere, nowhere
-wise	clockwise, likewise

II. *Sentence Test Frame*

_____ the noun _____ verbs the noun _____.

Examples:
Sometimes the clock disturbs the baby.
The clock *greatly* disturbs the baby.
The clock disturbs the baby *now*.

Prepositions

Traditionally, prepositions are rarely defined.

Sentence Test Frames for Prepositions

The first frame identifies all but nine of the forty-two prepositions.

1. The ant crawled _____ the door.

Those prepositions that will fit this slot are:

about	behind	from	round
above	below	in	through
across	beneath	like	to
after	beside	near	toward
against	beyond	off	under
along	by	on	underneath
around	down	opposite	up
at	for	over	with
before			

Prepositions that will not fit the slot are these:

among	except
but (meaning *except*)	of
concerning	regarding
during	since
	until or till

Some of the second group will fit the slot in this test frame:

2. The old man was silent _____ the war.

The others—*among, but, except,* and *of*—will fit the slot in this one:

3. No one was talking _____ the girls.

A second weakness with traditional grammatical principles is that modern English has more than the eight categories of words (e.g., articles are "noun markers"; prepositions and conjunctions can also function as "connectors," "phrase markers," and "noun markers"). Because of these weaknesses you can supplement students' knowledge of the roles and functions of words by teaching common sentence patterns and pointing out how their favorite authors use vivid paragraph structures to convey meaning. Students enjoy identifying and comparing their author's most frequently used word orders, sentence structure, and paragraph organization to other authors and to their own writing.

Structural or Descriptive Grammar. This principle helps students understand subtle differences in meanings of our language as it is used. Structural or descriptive grammar is a *theory of grammar that does not prescribe a "correct" form, but reports language as it is used today* (Bloomfield, 1933; Fries, 1963). In descriptive/structural grammar, words are divided into functions, with many words serving more than function. For example, students are taught that while all sentences contain subjects, all subjects are not always nouns as traditional grammar might lead them to believe. If you teach structural grammar, you will introduce word functions within basic sentence patterns, as demonstrated below:

Noun markers	*The* birds fly.
Verb markers	The mailman *is* coming.
Negatives	He is *not* sad.
Intensifiers	He is *very* happy.
Conjunctions	The trees *and* flowers are signaling spring has arrived.
Phrase markers	The rain caused Rover to run *for* shelter.
Question markers	*What* is the proper way to teach grammar?
Clause markers	The party will be held *before* we leave school.

According to structural grammarians, modern English is comprised of word patterns, sentence orders, word classes, functions, and inflectional changes. Figure 8-2 delineates the principles that depict English "structure."

An effective strategy to demonstrate descriptive grammar is to transcribe an oral story and give it to students. Then you distribute a second account of that same story as it was originally recorded in a printed form. Students are to compare the grammatical differences between oral and written language. As they describe these differences, they chart the principles they believe to govern written English. You also ask students to select their favorite sentence from one of the following books: *Where in the World Is Henry?; Goodnight Moon; A Dark, Dark Tale; The Cock, The Mouse, and the Little Red Hen; What Good Luck!; Millions of Cats; The Little Red Hen; The Three Billy Goats Gruff; The Chick and The Duckling; Where's Spot?; Good-night Owl!;*

FIGURE 8-2
Sample of Grammatical Rules That Govern Sentences

Noun (subjects)-verb (predicates)	Dogs eat.
Noun-verb-adjective	Flowers are fragrant.
Noun-verb-adverb	John walks slowly.
Noun-verb-noun	I eat hamburgers.
Noun-verb-noun-noun	Daddy threw Susie the ball.
Noun-linking verb-noun	Martha is a policewoman.
Noun-linking verb-adjective	The mountains are awesome.

Brown Bear, Brown Bear, What Do You See?; Roll Over!; Have You Seen My Duckling?; Alexander and the Terrible, Horrible, No Good, Very Bad Day; Do You Want to Be My Friend?; Elephant in a Well; Ask Mr. Bear; The Gingerbread Boy; Rosie's Walk; There Was an Old Woman; The House That Jack Built; The Great Big Enormous Turnip; I Know an Old Lady Who Swallowed a Fly; Mommy, Buy Me a China Doll; and *The Judge.* They analyze why the sentences they select were so memorable. Most often these analyses lead students to appreciate how rephrasing can change the emphasis and clarify meaning.

Transformational-Generative Approach.   This theory of grammar explains how English speakers generate sentences they have never heard or read before. The theory of **transformational-generative grammar** *explains what we do when we invent and change sentences* and why the same thought takes on slightly different meanings in separate sentences. Transformational-generative grammarians pose that sentences have a deep structure and a surface structure. *Deep structure* refers to the meaning of the sentence and why that meaning can be conveyed in several forms. *Surface structure* is the form selected to communicate the deep structure. The surface structure is what is spoken, written, or sung.

To help students understand the difference between deep and surface structure, ask them to picture a white, furry rabbit. Then ask students to describe the rabbit in one sentence. Their sentences are written on the board, and will likely resemble the following: "The rabbit is furry and white." "The furry rabbit is white." "The white rabbit is furry." "The rabbit I see is furry and white." "The rabbit I see is white and furry." "The rabbit is white and furry." Once several samples have been written, describe that each is a way that the *same* meaning can be communicated in *through a different* sentence to be expressed. Then explain how transformational grammar enables us to understand how people can create a wide variety of active sentences, passive sentences, negative sentences, questions, and imperatives to show their own connotations (see Figure 8-3).

FIGURE 8-3
Transformation of Sentences

TRANSFORMATION *Simple Transformations*	DESCRIPTION	SAMPLE SENTENCE
1. Negative	*Not* or *n't* and auxiliary verb inserted	Lions roar. Lions don't roar.
2. Yes-No Question	Subject and auxiliary verb switched	The lion stalked the jungle? Did the lion stalk the jungle?
3. *Wh-* Question	*Wh-* word (*who, what, which, when, where, why*) or *how,* and auxiliary verb inserted	Lions roar. Why do lions roar?
4. Imperative	*You* becomes the subject	Lions give cubs meat. Give cubs meat.
5. There	*There* and auxiliary verb inserted	Lions are cautious. There are cautious lions.
6. Passive	Subject and direct object switched and the main verb changed to past participle form	Lions make cubs hunters. Cubs are made hunters by lions.
Complex Transformations 1. Joining	Two sentences joined using conjunctions such as *and, but, or*	Lions roar. Tigers roar. Lions and tigers roar.
2. Embedding	Two (or more) sentences combined by embedding one into the other	Lions are animals. Lions are cautious. Lions are cautious animals.

Another set of grammar rules apply to oral English. Students need to learn how stress, juncture, gestures, body language, and pitch carry meaning, and how, in written language, capitalization, punctuation, and story grammar substitute for these oral rules so meaning is accurately conveyed.

When students have been introduced to these four sets of English-language principles they need to learn how to generate them independently. You will next read about how you can nurture this independence for your students.

Sentence order can be learned when students "make sentences" in a line-up.

PUTTING THEORY INTO PRACTICE

HOW TO TEACH GRAMMAR

The goal of grammar instruction is for students to elect correct usage. For this reason, in teaching, you aid students to self-correct their grammar. You provide this assistance through the following instructional approaches.

SENTENCE BUILDING AND COMBINING APPROACH

Because students as young as five years old have mastered the sentence patterns of spoken English and have thousands of words in their listening vocabulary, your job is to raise their intuitive knowledge to a conscious level which will aid meaning generation as they read and write. The sentence combining approach develops students' greater awareness of what language is, and cultivates a flexibility in constructing more powerful sentences (O'Hare, 1973).

THE CHALLENGE OF DIVERSITY

Students who speak a different language must be taught the structure of the English sentence, the order of adjectives and adverbs, and the noun and verb agreement. An effective method is to introduce several concepts orally with objects. For example, bilingual students hear and then say the words *under, up, on, beside, table, chair, book, in, over, behind* as they place a book in appropriate locations to a chair and table.

Begin sentence combining with the students' own writings. You also explain why grammar principles are so complex, e.g., "Verbs are complicated to study, not because some ancient, devious grammar teacher conjured conjugations to confuse students, but because as English was used over the centuries, people adopted words from other languages in an unplanned way." You can also ask older students to create selective cloze paragraphs in their writings with white-out or post-it notes, where the only words deleted are the verbs. Students exchange these selective clozes with a partner. Once partners have filled in blanks in the sentences, their words are compared to classmates' originals. Students discuss how each can improve verb choices in future writing. They commit this goal to a written contract. Students' writing samples are assessed in the future to note increased grammatical strength and if their goals were met. This lesson develops decoding, grammar, and thinking abilities simultaneously.

Similarly, younger students can be taught the positions, power, and functions of words through chants, choral readings, nursery rhymes, and language experience stories. As you read books, pause at a powerful sentence and ask why its order is so memorable. Young students also learn by making compound subjects, predicates, and sentences. For example, ask them to read two sentences where all words are the *same* but one. They are to combine single words from both of these sentences to make one. ("Rover eats dog food." "Rover eats beef." = "Rover eats dog food and beef.") Moreover, a major difficulty with students before reaching third grade is that they will either "overcombine" or "undercombine" sentences as they write. In one-to-one conferences you can correct the improper emphases students are placing upon overly short or long sentences in their writing.

Phrase Placements.   Once students are skilled in word choice and sentence length they can be taught to combine phrases more effectively, e.g., "Fluffy is my little kitten. Fluffy is my pet. = Fluffy is my little kitten and pet." Books that use illustrations of vivid phrase placements, for younger students, include: *Where the Wild Things Are; The Snowy Day; Madeline; Blueberries for Sal; The Biggest Bear; Sam, Bangs, and Moonshine; The Happy Owls; A Bear Called Paddington; Mother Goose; Crow Boy; The Dead Tree; If I Found a Wistful Unicorn; Find the Cat;* and *At Marry Bloom's.*

After these lessons have been taught, you build grammatical awareness by asking students to write a report of the steps they followed in a science experiment.

When you receive this report, you can improve students' grammatical awareness through the following sentence combining activity: First, write their opening two sentences on the board. You model how meaning is clarified and made interesting when redundant words and phrases are eliminated. Also remind them of the phrase placement rules. Then students work in small groups to combine the remaining sentences of their report. To illustrate, to report their experiment, a group of your scientists might record the following in their learning logs:

We put dirt in cups. We put seeds in the dirt. We put the seeds one inch deep. We watered the seeds once a week. We watered the seeds on Mondays. We watered the seeds six times. The seeds made stems. The stems made leaves. Flowers came out this Wednesday!

After grammar instruction the final report would be similar to the following:

After putting six inches of dirt in small paper cups, we planted pansy seeds one inch deep. We watered seeds each Monday for six weeks. During the fifth week, stems sprouted, and leaves developed. On the Wednesday of the seventh week, flowers bloomed!

Students then practice combining sentences from their own writings, explaining their use of subordinate phrases that adhered to the following rules:

1. *Adverbs and Adverbial Phrases.* When they appear at the end of the sentence, they are subordinate to the main point, add detail, or enhance the flow and beauty of the total message: e.g., "The deer leaped gracefully and gently over the brook," versus "Gracefully and gently the deer leaped over the brook!"

2. *Adjectives* make images more vivid and convey relative importance, such as, "The fragile, budding gardenia bush grew," versus the emphasis given through a different adjective placement in, "The fragile gardenia bush was budding."

3. *Prepositional phrases* added to the beginning, middle, and end of sentences embellish images, and reveal substitutes of meaning, e.g., "For the longest time I have yearned to move west," versus "Moving west has been my deepest yearning."

Refining Meaning.   When students are skilled in all three aspects of sentence combining (word, phrase, and sentence levels), they are ready to alter and expand sentence patterns to refine meaning. For younger children, this part of instruction can begin by embellishing basic sentence patterns in a language experience story. After writing several sentences, demonstrate how two sentences (with different subjects and verbs) can combine to make a more powerful statement. Explain to young students that it is important for them to do so if their writing is to become more interesting.

For older students, refined meanings can be taught through a "cued format" (O'Hare, 1973). In "cued" refining activities, students learn to improve the meaning in four weak sentences. They are shown how the same meaning can be communicated more effectively in one stronger sentence, for example: (1) the main sentence is presented, e.g., They ate fruit; (2) word(s) to be inserted from a second sentence are underlined, e.g., The fruit is an <u>orange</u>; (3) word(s) to be deleted are crossed out, e.g., ~~They~~ ate an apple; (4) connecting words, such as *and*, are written in parentheses after the sentence they connect, e.g., (AND). Students then combine these four parts into one sentence, "The boy and girl ate an orange and an apple."

They then discuss how the combination improved meaning. Once students are skilled in combining "cued" sentences, they learn to add prepositional phrases to sentences, e.g., "JoAnn went" is the sentence, and "to the store," "in the van," and "to buy *Velvet Lady*" are the phrases. "JoAnn went to the store in the van to buy *Velvet Lady*" is the resultant combined form.

You can also project a **kernel sentence,** *a sentence with only a noun and a verb,* on the overhead projector. This kernel sentence concerns a topic or experience the class has just completed, such as "We sang." Several students are asked to come to the board and add to this sentence. Once statements are complete, each is analyzed. Beneath the statements, students write where the sentences could be combined (students put grammatical rules and sentence expansion concepts they followed to create the statement in their own words). Students then meet in cooperative groups to create a chart of these self-generated grammatical rules which are posted above the editing committee table for future reference.

Another refining meaning activity begins when you copy a page of children's literature that has a particularly powerful message. As you read the page orally, students read silently. Students check sentences they like, and discuss why they prefer the sentences that they do. They write (in their own words) the grammatical rules that governed each sentence they selected. They add these rules to the chart described above. Then students are assessed on their use of these rules in their next composition.

This activity has been called "writing imitations" (Linden & Whimbey, 1990). Students read one of the following literature sources and replicate a sentence/phrase from that book so as to integrate its appealing nature and communicative power in their writing and speaking (e.g., *The Polar Express* can illustrate effective compound sentences). Other books that illustrate these advanced grammatical principles include: *The Borrowers; The Twenty-One Balloons; The Cricket in Times Square; A Wary Snake in a Fig Tree; The Space Child's Mother Goose; Jump or Jiggle; A Chocolate Moose for Dinner; The King Who Rained; How a Horse Grew Hoarse on the Site Where He Sighted a Bare Bear; Ask Mr. Bear; One Was Johnny; Drummer Hoff; Mommy, Buy Me a China Doll; The Rainbow of American Folk Tales and Legends; Tall Tale America; Heroes in American Folklore;* and *Whoppers, Tall Tales and Other Lies.*

Finally, give students an increasing number of ideas and transformations to make, using varied sentence types. Teach them the purposes of words such as *though, but, yet,* and *in this case.*

In closing, students can assess their own growth in grammatical awareness. They can write a pre- and then a post-instructional story. They compare their prewriting to their post-writing and describe how their increased conscious knowledge of grammatical principles affected their writing ability. The benefits of the sentence combining approach can be immediate, even for first graders (as shown in Figure 8-4, which was written after only one grammar lesson). Figure 8-4 is the postinstructional writing. These are results of sentence combining lessons in writing samples from first grade students (lessons were taught by Ms. Susan McMurray, Fort Worth Independent School District).

FIGURE 8-4
First Grade Post-instructional Writing Sample of Sentence Combining

THE MODIFIED TEXTBOOK APPROACH

Language arts textbooks are the traditional material used to teach grammar. The way in which these books are used is crucial, however. No longer should you ask students to memorize rules in artificial contexts and complete isolated, end-of-chapter drills. Instead, you and students will reference pages in the text that describe specific grammatical principles needed to improve students' writing or speaking. Lessons will be on an individual or small group basis and determined by the errors individual students make in their speaking and writing. In the modified textbook approach textbooks are rarely referenced for large group instruction. Grammar textbooks serve as reference manuals, much like dictionaries and encyclopedias. When students lack a certain grammatical principle, mini-lessons are developed and students can reference examples in the text as a source of internalizing the principle they need. The principle is then practiced in student-fashioned messages rather than through the drill and practice exercises of the book. Ask students to use that principle in their writing that day and assess their skill.

GRAMMAR INSTRUCTION IN REVISING COMMITTEES

The third method of teaching grammar follows an "impromptu" mode of instruction, providing grammar instruction as needed, such as during rehearsals for oral presentations, or in revising committees. A form that assists students in developing grammatical awareness is shown in Figure 8-5. Students check the description within each category of the entire class's writing evaluation form that best depicts a peer's level of competence. You can also use Figure 8-5 as an assessment form for your entire class by writing students' names across the top.

FIGURE 8-5
The Entire Class's Writing Evaluation Form

	WRITING OVERVIEW																								
ORGANIZATIONS	SPECIAL FLAIR																									
	VERY CLEAR																									
	GAPS IN MEANING																									
	CONFUSING																									
MEANING	EFFECTIVE																									
	APPROPRIATE																									
	IRRELEVANT																									
	NO FOCUS																									
CONVENTIONS	ADDITIONAL MEANING																									
	CORRECT MECHANICS																									
	SEVERAL ERRORS																									
	ERRORS INTERFERE																									
THOUGHT QUALITY	ACCURATE																									
	LOGICAL																									
	ILLOGICAL																									
	INACCURATE																									
WORD SELECTION	EVOCATIVE																									
	COMPLETE																									
	SOME PRECISION																									
	LACKS PRECISION																									
STORY STRUCTURE	CAPTIVATING																									
	SMOOTH																									
	SOME CONFUSION																									
	LACKS STRUCTURE																									

When students discover a new and effective sentence structure or word choice in a peer's paper, they can ask their peers what they thought in order to create that structure. In this way, they learn to incorporate this structure into their future compositions. The revising committee approach works well because students come to understand that "any time anyone says anything or jots down something, some of what is said or written is luckier than the rest" (Stafford, 1986, p. 97). All students can work to identify grammatical principles that can turn these chance performances into writing tools for which they have permanent, self-selected access.

Last of all, the revising committee approach utilizes students' self-initiated discussions about grammar. An example of one such discussion among three second graders appears below. As they disagree about the use of a single grammatical time frame in which they want their story to occur, they internalize verb tense knowledge.

Barbara: (reading) "In Lancaster, Wisconsin, a small eight-year-old boy found a lost cat." *Found* is past tense. Is he finding him right now?

Faith: Are we telling the story over again or is it really happening right now?

Barbara: Half the story is past tense and half the story is present tense.

Faith: I think it's present tense because, see, he says, "How long will I have to stay?"

Barbara: How about "While they're gone, Tommy started walking around"?

Faith: (sarcastically) Yeah. That's what we put on the draft you lost. (She makes a face at Lillian in front of Barbara.)

Barbara: (upset) No we didn't. It doesn't matter, Faith. You don't have to look at Lillian that way.

Faith: (to Lillian) What do you like, past or present?

Barbara: (aloud to herself) She's going to say present.

Faith: Present tense. Just keep it present tense (Nessel, Jones, & Dixon, 1989, p. 235).

STRATEGIES THAT TEACH
WAYS TO STRENGTHEN STUDENTS' GRAMMAR

As a final note, you can teach all of these approaches. Rather than being mutually exclusive, when combined, they complement each other. The four lessons that follow illustrate how such integration can occur. These plans demonstrate how to teach impromptu oral grammar lessons, how to increase students' sensitivity to point of view and sentence structure, as well as how to use students' writing samples in grammar lessons.

CREATING IMPROMPTU LESSONS THAT DEVELOP STUDENTS' ORAL/WRITTEN GRAMMATICAL AWARENESS

M	T	W	Th	F

Developing students' ability to use correct oral sentence structures and word choices is important. Many researchers support the position that such instruction should begin when a student asks a question about spoken or written English (O'Hare, 1973; Veatch, 1991). Some researchers recommend that students as young as five years old learn to clarify their ideas. They suggest impromptu teaching begins by responding to students' questions with mini-grammar lessons.

For example, if a first grader asks, "What is a noun?" you provide the definition. Following this explanation, the student can read one of the books concerning grammatical awareness in Notecard 15. After reading, you conference and identify that child's favorite nouns in the story, emphasizing the importance he/she can place upon selecting specific nouns when speaking and writing.

As a second illustration, study the following incorrect example of an impromptu lesson. As you read the scenario, identify why this teacher's response did not assist the student to improve her oral grammar.

Loretta, a student in Mrs. Henson's class says, "I ain't got no pencil." Mrs. Henson replies: "You do not have a pencil."

This correction is not effective because Mrs. Henson's reply did not model the appropriate grammatical structure. Mrs. Henson used the second rather than first person. Loretta would have benefited more from a model of how the correct grammatical principles in her sentence would have sounded, e.g., "I don't have a pencil either. Let's find one." Without such an explicit, first-person example Loretta will likely be unable to apply the following advanced grammatical principles that would have been necessary if she was to learn from Mrs. Henson's impromptu lesson:

1. Omit "ain't";
2. Select the verb "do" and add it to the predicate, in the proper location to indicate present tense;
3. Change the negative contract from "ain't" to the noncontracted form of "don't";
4. Change the verb tense from present to present perfect;
5. Eliminate a double negative, e.g., change *no* pencil to *a* pencil.

Furthermore, aside from the number of transformations Loretta would need to learn the correct grammatical structure from Mrs. Henson's impromptu lesson, Mrs. Henson's instruction did not adhere to the principle of authenticity. That is, rarely in Loretta's life will she have to say, "You do not have a pencil." However, she will have many opportunities in life to say, "I do not have a pencil," which could have been learned through a different impromptu lesson that Mrs. Henson could have delivered. With these points in mind, return to the above example. What would you have done to better assist Loretta?

Did you consider responding in this manner:

NOTECARD 15:   CHILDREN'S LITERATURE THAT DEVELOPS STUDENT'S GRAMMATICAL AWARENESS

Hot and Cold and Other Words That Are as Different as Night and Day by Joan Hanson
Push-Pull, Empty-Full: A Book of Opposites by Tana Hoban
Fast-Slow, High-Low by Peter Spier
Opposites by Richard Wilbur
On the Go—A Book of Adjectives by Betsy and Guilio Maestro
Lollipops: All About Adjectives by Ruth Heller
Fishes by Brian Wildsmith
Anno's Britain by Mitsumasa Anno
A Cache of Jewels and Other Collective Nouns by Ruth Heller
Kites Sail High: A Book About Verbs by Ruth Hellen
The First Crazy Word Book—Verbs by Byron Preiss and Ralph Reese
Action Alphabet by M. Neumeier and B. Glasser

A Snake is Totally Tail by Judi Barrett
Animals Should Definitely Not Act Like People by Judi Barrett
Great Gorilla Grins by Beth Hilgartner
A Woggle of Witches by Adrian Adams
A My Name is Alice by Steven Kellogg
More Than One by T. Hoban
Your Foot's On My Feet! and Other Tricky Nouns by M. Terban
An Amazing Alphabet by John Patience
A-B-Cing: An Action Alphabet by J. Beller
Cluck Baa, Jangle Twang, Slam Bang, Skip Trip, Sniff Shout, Wobble Pop by J. Burningham
Dig, Drill, Dump, Fill by T. Hoban
Kitten Can . . . A Concept Book by B. McMillan
Camping Out by Betsy and Guilio Maestro
Aster Aardvark's Alphabet Adventures by Steven Kellogg

(cont'd)

NOTECARD 15   (cont'd)

The Day Jimmy's Boa Ate the Wash by T. H. Noble
M is for Move by V. Shiefman
I Think I Thought and Other Tricky Verbs by M. Terban
A is for Angry: An Animal and Adjective Alphabet by S. Boynton
Guinea Pig ABC by K. Duke
A Children's Zoo by T. Hoban
Super, Super, Superwords by B. McMillan
Snake In, Snake Out by L. Bancheck
Inside, Outside, Upside Down by S. and J. Berenstain
Bears in the Night by S. and J. Berenstain
Over, Under, and Through and Other Spatial Concepts by T. Hoban
Animalia by Graeme Base
Amazing Animal Alphabet Adventures by Roger and Mariko Chouinard
Slithery Snakes and Other Aids to Children's Writing by W. Petty and M. Bowen

The Very Hungry Caterpillar by Eric Carle
The Z Was Zapped by Chris Van Allsburg
Nice or Nasty: A Book of Opposites by Nick and Mick Inkpen Butterworth
Brown Bear in a Brown Chair by Iriana Hale
Bicycle Bear by Michaela Muntean
Silly Goose by Jack Kent
It's Not Easy Being a Bunny by Marilyn Sadler
Esteban and the Ghost by Sibyl Hancock
Chicken Soup with Rice by Maurice Sendak
If You Give a Mouse a Cookie by Laura Nemeroff
The Vanishing Pumpkin by Tony Johnson
The Important Book by Margaret Wise
Summer Is . . . by Charlotte Zolotow
Hailstones and Halibut Bones by Mary O'Neill
Some Things Go Together by Charlotte Zolotow
Where the Sidewalk Ends by Shel Silverstein
Word Works: Why the Alphabet is a Kid's Best Friend by Cathryn Berger Kaye

Loretta: "I ain't got no pencil."

You reply: "I don't have a pencil either."

Loretta: "Where can I get a pencil?"

You: "When I don't have a pencil I _____ . What are you going to do in the future when you don't have a pencil?"

Loretta: "When I don't have a pencil, I'll _____ ."

You: "Would you like me to tell you what you did to make your meaning clearer?"

Loretta: "Yes."

Then you tell Loretta the rules that changed the sentence and explain that such corrections make her language easier for others to understand because it adheres to "standard English." You then say that less formal language may communicate well in casual settings, but standard English usually communicates better in formal settings. Then you ask Loretta to read a book listed on Notecard 16. The next day she is to tell you at least one new oral grammatical principle she discovered.

Written grammatical errors also respond to such individualized mini-grammar lessons. For example, a successful mini-lesson to eliminate run-on sentences involves peer editors. Such editors make a slash mark between the sixteenth and seventeenth words of any sentence in a classmate's writing that reaches that length. This slash indicates that the sentence has exceeded preferred sentence length, and the two students work together to rephrase the longest sentences. A second mini-lesson to reduce sentence length is for students to read their writings aloud, but to themselves. Any time they take a breath before the end of a sentence, the student has a clue that that sentence may need to be rewritten to reduce its length. Reading their writings aloud is also an effective strategy to assist students in locating inappropriate verb tenses and noun-verb agreements.

To sum up, these lessons demonstrate how the modified textbook, revision approach, and sentence combining methods can be integrated to correct violations of oral and written grammar. The following lessons will

---

NOTECARD 16: BOOKS FOR STUDENTS WITH DIFFERENT DIALECTS OR WHO HAVE DIFFICULTY WITH ENGLISH SPEAKING PATTERNS

The following books increase students' awareness of various dialects and/or demonstrate common sentence patterns and word usage in the English language.

I Hate English! by Ellen Levine
What Do I Say? by N. Simon
Nathaniel Talking and other books by E. Greenfield
His Own Where and other books by J. Jordan
Amelia Bedelia (Series) by Peggy Parish
The King Who Rained and other books by F. Gwynne
A Hero Ain't Nothing But a Sandwich by A. Childress
Animals Should Definitely Not Act Like People and other books by J. Barrett
Amifika by Lucille Clifton
Git Along, Old Scudder by Stephen Gammell
My Brother Fine with Me by Lucille Clifton
Lordy, Aunt Hattie and other books by I. Thomas
Secret Dreamer, Secret Dreams by F. Parry Heide
Victor by C. J. K. Galbraith
Dmitry, A Young Soviet Immigrant by –. Bernstein

Sounder by W. Armstrong
My Special Best Words by J. Steptoe
The Friends by R. Guy
He Who Run-Far by H. Fredericksen
I Met a Man by John Ciardi
The Phantom Tollbooth by –. Justin
Amos and Boris and other books by W. Steig
Annie and the Old One and other books by A. Miles
Cajun Night Before Christmas by H. Jacobs
The Magical Adventures of Pretty Pearl by Virginia Hamilton
What Happened to Heather Hopkowitz? by Charlotte Herman
The Chinese Daughter by E. F. Lattimore
The Night Journey by K. Lasky
Wind in the Willows by K. Grahame

expand your skill in integration by depicting three ways to teach grammatical concepts in small, student need-based groups.

CREATING LESSONS THAT TEACH STUDENTS TO RECOGNIZE DIFFERING POINTS OF VIEW

The purpose of this lesson is to increase students' sensitivity to points of view, methods of discerning the impact points of view have upon ideas, and strategies to resolve conflicts of perspectives. As a language arts teacher, your responsibility is to prepare students to contribute to an international family of human beings. Students' lives will increasingly be influenced by points of view that vary greatly in national and cultural heritage.

To begin this preparation, students learn that facts and events can be explained from four perspectives: first person, using the words "I" and "we"; second person, one person telling another what to do using the word "you"; third person, reporting events for which they were not present, using the words "they" and "he/she"; and omniscient point of view, where a person seemingly sees all and knows all and pronouns are not used.

Then explain how one's perspective alters interpretations. Read a book to the class that has more than one character. After hearing the book, students divide into response groups and retell the story from a different character's point of view. Each group shares the character's rendition that they decided to depict. Then students describe how the character's point of view established a new perspective of story events.

Students then have a second practice session of taking a new point of view. They select a current event involving more than one country. After studying the cultural and societal values of that country, and contacting officials from the ambassadors' or consulate offices, they prepare position papers about the current event from that country's perspective.

In a third session, students role-play situations in their lives where they are in conflict with another person. In these role plays, a student assumes the role (and point of view) of the person with whom they are in conflict. Classmates assume the role of the student and others involved in the difficulty. After the enactment, each student writes what was learned from assessing another person's perspective.

CREATING LESSONS THAT TEACH HOW TO WRITE VARIANT SENTENCE TYPES

You can teach students to write many different types of complex sentence structures by demonstrating how to write with sequential clue words. You can use the prompted outline shown in Figure 8-6. Then you ask students to revise one of their previous writings by inserting clue words, and varying the types of sentences they write.

FIGURE 8-6
Sequential Clue Words That Create Variety in Written Sentences

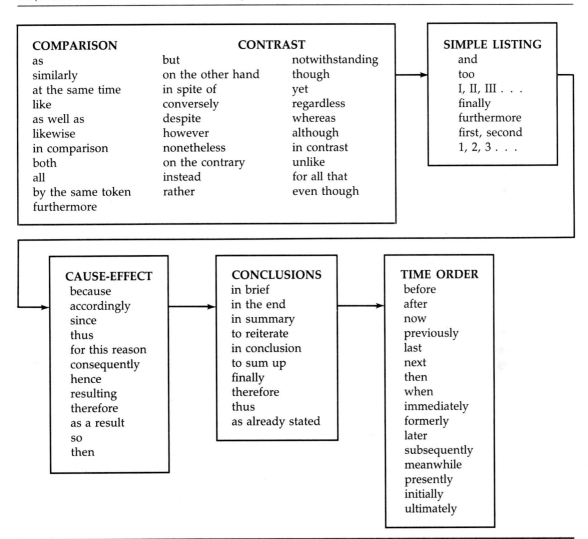

COMPARISON	CONTRAST		SIMPLE LISTING
as	but	notwithstanding	and
similarly	on the other hand	though	too
at the same time	in spite of	yet	I, II, III . . .
like	conversely	regardless	finally
as well as	despite	whereas	furthermore
likewise	however	although	first, second
in comparison	nonetheless	in contrast	1, 2, 3 . . .
both	on the contrary	unlike	
all	instead	for all that	
by the same token	rather	even though	
furthermore			

CAUSE-EFFECT	CONCLUSIONS	TIME ORDER
because	in brief	before
accordingly	in the end	after
since	in summary	now
thus	to reiterate	previously
for this reason	in conclusion	last
consequently	to sum up	next
hence	finally	then
resulting	therefore	when
therefore	thus	immediately
as a result	as already stated	formerly
so		later
then		subsequently
		meanwhile
		presently
		initially
		ultimately

CREATING LESSONS THAT USE YOUR OWN, FAMOUS PEOPLE'S, OR STUDENTS' REVISIONS AS SAMPLES

You can make a transparency of Thomas Jefferson's first draft of the Constitution (see Figure 8-7) to open a discussion of the importance of grammatical principles. Point to each change the author made and do a "think aloud" for each addition, deletion, substitution, and reorganization. Then you follow by doing a revision of one of your compositions on the overhead as students listen and watch. Students then review before-and-after revisions

FIGURE 8-7
Jefferson's First Draft of the Constitution

of their classmates' writings in group settings as each author describes the reasons behind his/her changes. Doing so enables students to recognize new ways others combine sentences, which they are likely to emulate.

Once students are comfortable with basic grammatical principles, you are ready to use their grammatical awarenesses to expand their creative thinking abilities. Critical Thinking Activity 8 demonstrates how the advanced grammatical structures of idioms, figurative language, metaphors, similes, personifications, and proverbs can be used to build creative thinking.

CRITICAL THINKING ACTIVITY 8
Using Idioms, Figurative Language, Metaphors, and Similes to Advance Higher Level Thinking

One of the most effective means to develop students' revising, rephrasing, creative thinking, and to clarify their meanings is teaching them to use images, idioms, figurative language, metaphors, similes, personification, and proverbs in their speech and writing (Manzo, 1992).

An **idiom** is *a complex expression whose meaning can not be derived from the meanings of its individual words.* **Figurative language** is *phrases with words placed together so they convey a feeling or thought characterized by the image painted by the phrase,* such as "soft as silk" to explain how soft something is. **Metaphors** are *figures of speech that make a comparison between two things that have something in common.* **Similes** are *metaphors that make comparisons between two things through the use of the words* like, as, *or* than. **Personification** is *a figure of speech in which nonhuman things are given human qualities.* **Proverbs** are *sayings that describe a truth in living,* i.e., *they are "the daughters of daily experience"* (Dutch proverb).

These advanced grammatical structures occur frequently in literature and in conversational speech. Through Critical Thinking Activity 8 students learn to discern and use these literary devices to communicate more specifically and to better understand other people's literal and inferred meanings. Because each literary device differs in the extent to which its literal meanings relate to its implied meanings, as you would expect, students have an easier time when introduced to those whose literal meanings are closely related to their personal experiences.

This activity is taught through children's literature as it easily illustrates how effective each of these literary devices are in clarifying meanings. As Manzo (1981) reports: "The process of attempting to unravel the collected and codified wit and wisdom of a people seems to be an effective way to build 'social comprehension,' abstract verbal reasoning, dialectical thinking, evaluative thinking, and general oral language abilities"(pp. 411–412).

Once you have read a book that contains several of these devices, develop students' awareness of their power and build their self-selected use of each type. You can begin by describing how such expressions are used (and the importance of learning what they mean) by showing the following cartoon on the overhead (see "Nancy" cartoon).

NANCY © 1973 Reprinted by permission of UFS, Inc.　　　　　　　　© 1973 United Feature Syr

You can also place an idiom, proverb, or figurative language on the board every day for two months. Ask students to reflect upon its meaning and discuss it in a half-minute activity at the end of school as everyone prepares to leave for home. You can also encourage students to use the device in a writing assignment or you can use it in a morning message.

Another effective lesson is to guide students to reconcile opposing positions in proverbs, idioms, and figurative language. As Manzo (1981) found: "Most often this . . . step has the most profound effect upon intellectual growth. Through it students come to realize that most things are set in a dynamic tension to one another. Life and learning are a process of reconciling seemingly opposing positions" (p. 414).

It will be advantageous to teach students as many of the following as appropriate for their age level. In addition to these sayings in Figure 8-8, others are available in *Quotations to Begin Teachers' Day* (Collins & Zinke, in press); *World Treasury of Proverbs; Book of Proverbs, Maxims and Famous Phrases; In a Pickle* and *Mad as a Wet Hen;* as well as *Racial Proverbs.*

If students wish to learn more about idioms, the following books will be helpful: *Hog on Ice and Other Curious Expressions* (Funk, 1948); *Tenderfeet and Ladyfingers; Eight Ate; A Feast of Homonym Riddles; In a Pickle and Other*

FIGURE 8-8

Proverbs, Idioms, Metaphors, Similes, and Personification to Advance Critical Thinking

PROVERBS

"Look before you leap."

"You can't judge a book by its cover."

"A stitch in time saves nine."

"The genius, wit and spirit of a nation are discovered in its proverbs." (English)

"Stretch your feet only as far as your sheet will permit." (Spanish)

"There is no proverb which is not true." (Spanish)

"Speak softly and carry a big stick; you will go far." (Theodore Roosevelt, American)

"No government ought to be without censors; and where there is a free press, no one ever will." (Thomas Jefferson, American)

"Every man has his price." (originally Lord Chesterfield)

"What soon grows old? Gratitude." (Greek)

"You do not teach the paths of the forest to an old gorilla." (African)

"Lend to one who will not repay, and you will provoke his dislike." (Chinese)

"Only in the grave is there rest." (Yiddish)

IDIOMS AND FIGURATIVE LANGUAGE

hold your horses	raise a stink
hit the ceiling	shake a leg
killing two birds with one stone	smell a rat
don't beat around the bush	spill the beans
you don't have a leg to stand on	spread onself too thin
he had me in stitches	tongue-in-cheek
all ears	wet blanket
at the end of one's rope	straw that broke the camel's back
bend over backward	wet behind the ears
cat got your tongue?	under the weather
dressed to kill	between the devil and the
elbow grease	deep blue sea
eyes bigger than your stomach	give someone the cold shoulder
for the birds	keep your shirt on
go to bat for someone	bury your head in the sand
horse of a different color	in one ear and out the other
if the shoe fits, wear it	white elephant
keep something under one's hat	straight from the horse's mouth
knock someone's socks off	chip off the old block
let the cat out of the bag	get into someone's hair
monkey business	paint the town red
out of the woods	thinking cap
play it by ear	feather in your cap

Funny Idioms (Terban, 1983); *Put Your Foot in Your Mouth and Other Silly Sayings* (Cox, 1980); *From the Horse's Mouth* (Nevin & Nevin, 1977); *Chin Music: Tall Talk and Other Talk* (Schwartz, 1979); and *Heaven to Betsy and Other Curious Sayings* (Funk, 1948).

The books listed below contain different expressions commonly used in various regions of our country, or have literal illustrations of idiomatic expressions: *Amelia Bedelia* books by Peggy Parish; *The King Who Rained* by Fred Gwynne; and *The Burning Questions of Bingo Brown* by Betsy Byars. The following books contain vivid examples of figurative language: *The Sixteen Hand Horse* by Fred Gwynne; *As: A Surfeit of Similes* by Norman Juster; *The Dove* by Marvin Terban; *Guppies in Tuxedos* by Marvin Terban; *Mad As a Wet Hen* by Marvin Terban; *Corduroy* by Don Freeman; *The Napping House* by Audrey Wood; *Quick as a Cricket* by Audrey Wood; and *Thirteen* by Remy Charlip and Jerry Joyner.

PROFESSIONAL DEVELOPMENT OPPORTUNITY
How to Teach Story Grammar

This Professional Development Opportunity may be especially profitable because you may not have been taught story grammar when you were in school. Moreover, you may not have observed another teacher teaching it. Because students' reading and writing skills improve when they understand story grammar, completing this Professional Development Opportunity will develop your abilities to teach story grammar to them (Fitzgerald & Speigel, 1983). Story grammar is a rule system that describes the regularities found in stories. It is the episodic ordering of story events. You can teach the basic episodic structure by presenting Figure 8-9 to students. Explain what the setting, problem, goal, climax, and outcome are by giving several

FIGURE 8-9
Story Grammar Map

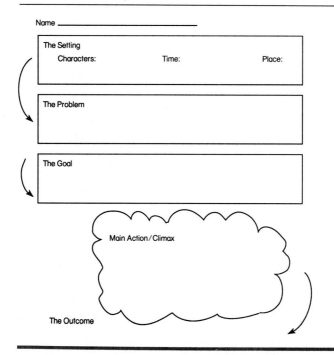

Name _____

The Setting
Characters: Time: Place:

The Problem

The Goal

Main Action/Climax

The Outcome

FIGURE 8-10
Sample of *Charlotte's Web* in Story Grammar

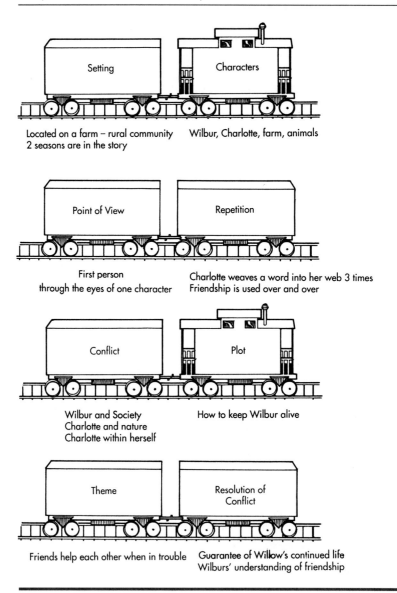

Located on a farm – rural community   Wilbur, Charlotte, farm, animals
2 seasons are in the story

First person   Charlotte weaves a word into her web 3 times
through the eyes of one character   Friendship is used over and over

Wilbur and Society   How to keep Wilbur alive
Charlotte and nature
Charlotte within herself

Friends help each other when in trouble   Guarantee of Willow's continued life
Wilburs' understanding of friendship

examples from books you've read aloud to the class. Then you show the example of how E. B. White used story grammar to write *Charlotte's Web* by sharing Figure 8-10 with students.

Once this lesson is complete, students read one of the following books that have a clear episodic structure. They then complete the story map in Figure 8-9 in response groups using a book of their choice. Each group reads a different book. Groups can also develop a dramatization of the story. Once the story is complete, each group tells their story (or gives their dramatization) to classmates who in turn complete Figure 8-9 for that group's story. The class then compares their work to the story map the group created prior to the storytelling or the enactment.

The following books are excellent for this section of activity. Grades K–3: *Going to Squintum* (Westwood, 1985); *Jumanji* (Van Allsburg, 1986); Wordless Books (presented on Notecard 26); *Little Tim and the Brave Sea Captain* (Ardizzone, 1971); *A Bargain for Frances* (Hoban, 1970); *Rumpelstiltskin* (Zelinsky, 1986); *The Ugly Duckling* (Andersen, 1979); and *Ira Sleeps Over*. Grades 4–8: *Mrs. Frisby and the Rats of NIMH* (O'Brien, 1971); *Julie of the Wolves* (George, 1972); *Call It Courage* (Sperry, 1968); *Tales of Fourth Grade Nothing* (Blume, 1972); *The Summer of the Swans* (Byars, 1970); and *Island of the Blue Dolphins* (O'Dell, 1960).

A second method of teaching story grammar is to introduce each section of story grammar separately. In doing so, you read or have students read one or more of the following books which contain particularly vivid examples of separate story grammar entities, and contain well-defined beginnings, middles, and/or endings.

Plot

The Clown of God by T. dePaola
The Ugly Duckling by H. C. Andersen
Millions of Cats by W. Gag
The Gingerbread Boy by P. Galdone
Sixteen Short Stories by Outstanding Writers for Young Adults by D. R. Gallo
The Island of the Skog by S. Kellogg
The Call of the Wild and Other Selected Stories by J. London
The Tale of Peter Rabbit by B. Potter
Rapunzel by B. Rogasky
Where the Wild Things Are by M. Sendak
The Wreck of the Zephyr by C. Van Allsburg
Duffy and the Devil by H. Zemach and M. Zemach

Setting

Old Arthur by A. Skorpen
Bridge to Terabithia by K. Paterson
Tuck Everlasting by N. Babbitt
Homesick: My Own Story by J. Fritz
Saint George and the Dragon by M. Hodges
From the Mixed-up Files of Mrs. Basil E. Frankweiler by E. Konigsburg
Beyond the Divide by K. Lasky
A Wrinkle in Time by M. L'Engle
Sam, Bangs, and Moonshine by E. Ness
The Witch of Blackbird Pond by E. Speare
The Long Winter by L. Wilder

STRATEGIES THAT TEACH

Theme. It is important that students learn how to discern the underlying meaning of a story. Explicit and implicit themes are presented in the following books:

Charlotte's Web by E. B. White
The Nightingale by H. C. Andersen
Chanticleer and the Fox by B. Cooney
Henny, Penny by P. Galdone
Rabbit Hill by R. Lawson
The Boy Who Held Back the Sea by T. Locker
The Little Engine That Could by W. Piper
The Polar Express by C. Van Allsburg
Hey, Al by A. Yorinks
The Girl Who Loved Wild Horses by P. Goble

Portrayal of Personalities (Characterization). Students should be taught how appearance, actions, dialogue, and monologues of what the character thinks are authorial tools to develop memorable characters. Books that exemplify strong characterizations appear in Notecard 14, and especially vivid demonstrations of individual elements within developing characterizations are found in the following stories: *James and the Giant Peach* demonstrates appearances (Dahl, 1961, p. 7); *The Pinball* demonstrates power of character actions in conveying character (Byars, 1977, p. 4). *Roll of Thunder, Hear My Cry* (Taylor, 1976); *Ida Early Comes Over the Mountain* (Burch, 1980); *Anastasia Krupnik* (Lowry, 1979), and *Dear Mr. Henshaw* (Cleary, 1984) demonstrate how monologues of the characters show their moral fiber.

Conflicts in Stories (Problem/Goal). These are of four types: (1) Conflicts between characters and nature (as seen in *Little Tim and the Brave Sea Captain* by E. Ardizzone, 1971; *Julie of the Wolves* by E. Speare, 1972; *Island of the Blue Dolphins* by S. O'Dell, 1960; and *Call It Courage* by A. Sperry, 1968); (2) Conflicts between the main character and society, such as *The Witch of Blackbird Pond* by E. Speare, 1958; *The Island of the Skog* by S. Kellogg, 1973; and *Zoar Blue* by N. Hickman, 1978; (3) Conflicts between characters, such as *A Bargain for Frances* by R. Hoban, 1970; and *The Westing Game* by E. Raskin, 1978; (4) Conflicts main characters have within themselves, such as *The Cabin Faced West* by J. Fritz, 1958; and *The Cay* by M. Taylor, 1969.

TRY IT

1. Prepare a three-paragraph statement for parents that clarifies the differences between traditional, descriptive, and transformational-generative grammatical theories.

2. Choose one of the selections of children's literature on Notecard 16 (p. 265). Develop a lesson to enhance your students' grammar awareness with that book using the revision group approach. Reflect on the information you learned in this chapter before you create your lesson.

3. Examine a language arts grammar textbook. Identify the theory of grammar upon which it is based. Identify if it uses any activities from this chapter to enhance students' knowledge. Make a list of pages you will reference for mini-lessons with your students.

4. If you are teaching, or if you are assigned to teach first grade in the future, what modifications do you need to make in the information presented about writing, conferencing, and grammar programs to take into account that first graders need to vocalize as they write? If you are teaching (or should teach) in a third grade classroom or above, ask your students to collect, on a special page in their journal, favorite advanced grammatical structures that they read or write. Spend one period at the end of the grading period asking them to share their opinions about why these grammatical structures were so good.

FOR YOUR JOURNAL

You can teach students to use journals as tools to understand themselves better. To practice using your journal in this way, read a section from a work by your favorite author or a selection from a book you are currently reading. Identify what grammatical features are attractive to you as a reader. What does this tell you about your reading style? What does your selection of readings tell you about yourself? What do you want to improve about your oral grammar and which sentence structure is most difficult for you?

THE CHALLENGE OF DIVERSITY

While this journal activity is valuable for all students it is particularly beneficial for slower learning students. Such students tend to be unreflective and impulsive. When such students become frustrated over a task or social situation ask them to write down what they tried right before the frustration and how they felt. After three to five days read the journal and conference with the student. If the student continues to be frustrated, ask him/her to read about one of the main characters in a book from Notecard 13 (p. 215) who uses writing to increase his/her reflectivity, in order to find a new way to use writing to assist the student.

If you practice using your journal to reflect on a problem you face, you will be better prepared with a model for your special needs students in the future.

BUILDING YOUR PROFESSIONAL PORTFOLIO
Ordering Computer Software for Your Language Arts Program

There are many software programs that increase students' revising processes. Many have become "idea processors," and also build students' spelling, punctuation, and sentence combining skills. In addition, grade management packages, such as MECC's Grade Manager, allow you to store and retrieve grades. Some programs either calculate the mean, total average, class rank, and drop the lowest grades, or calculate only the highest grades, print different reports, and permit the creation of back-up

STRATEGIES THAT TEACH

disks. Before you order a specific program you may wish to reference one of the following which provide professional critiques and evaluations of software:

> *The Yellow Book of Computer Products for Education*
> *Only the Best: The Discriminating Software Guide for Preschool–12*
> *MicroSoft*
> *Micro-Courseware PRO/FILE and Evaluation*
> *TESS: The Educational Software Selector*
> *Software Reports: The Guide to Evaluated Educational Software*
> *Educational Software Directory*
> *The Computer Database, Microcomputer Index, Education Resources Infor-mation Centers,* and *Resources in Computer Education* (Databases to reference by computer)

You can stay abreast of new software developments by subscribing to *The Computing Teacher* (Department of Computer and Information Science, University of Oregon, Eugene, OR 97403); *AEDS Monitor,* a publication of the Association for Educational Data Systems (1201 Sixteenth Street, NW, Washington, DC 20036); *Classroom Computer News* (Intentional Educations, Inc., 341 Mt. Auburn Street, Watertown, MA 02171); *Educational Computer Magazine* (P.O. Box 535, Cupertino, CA 95015); *Electronic Learning* (Scholastic, Inc., 902 Sylvan Avenue, Englewood Cliffs, NJ 07632); *School Courseware Journal* (1341 Bulldog Lane, Suite C, Fresno, CA 93710); and by referencing the following directories: *Courseware Report Card* (150 W. Carob Street, Compton, CA 90220); *Swift's Directory of Educational Software for the IBM P.C. or Apple Computer* (Sterling Swift Publishing Company, 7901 South Interstate Highway 35, Austin, TX 78744); *Software Reports Editor* (2101 Las Palmas Drive, Carlsbad, CA 92008); *MicroSIFT Reviews* (Northwest Regional Educational Laboratory, 300 S.W. Sixth Avenue, Portland, OR 97204); *School Microware Reviews* (Dresden Associates, Box 246, Dresden, ME 04342); *Hyperlink Magazine* [News programs in hypertext and hypermedia] (P.O. Box 7723, Eugene, OR 97401); *Only the Best: 1992* (Customer Service, R. R. Bowker Co., P.O. Box 762, New York, NY 10011); and *Educational Software Preview Guide* (Publication Sales, California State Department of Education, P.O. Box 271, Sacramento, CA 95802).

From Texas Christian University Information Services Newsletter, December 1989, p. 5. Reprinted by permission.

9 Editing: Teaching Spelling and Other Writing Conventions

To evaluate spelling, punctuation, and capitalization, you and a student can select student writing samples from the beginning and end of each month and compare the number of correct spellings, punctuation, and capitalizations.

In a time not long ago and a land not far away, students copied "spelling words" ten times each. In a land very near, and a time not unlike our own, students traced alphabet letters with *giant* pencils! In the recent past and in a land like our own, students read sentences in workbooks just to decide whether *?*, *!*, or *.* was to be at their end!

In this chapter you will learn more effective methods of teaching spelling, penmanship, punctuation, and capitalization. You will discover the *word patterning, invented spelling, modified textbook, and basic word lists* approaches to instruction.

By the end of the chapter you will know:

1. Why it is so difficult to spell correctly;
2. How to teach spelling, punctuation, and capitalization as the important editorial skills they are;
3. What special strategies build correct manuscript and cursive penmanship;
4. How to teach handwriting to left-handed students.

THEORETICAL FOUNDATION

TEACHING SPELLING, PENMANSHIP, AND OTHER WRITING CONVENTIONS IS NOT A "TAKE IT OR LEAVE IT" PROPOSITION

The philosophy and strategies for spelling and writing convention instruction changed during the latter part of the 1980s. The change occurred because many teachers were disenchanted with teaching and testing a list of spelling words or writing conventions each week. Their students would complete the activities and spelling tests with 100 percent accuracy on Fridays but misuse and misspell them in their own writings. Researchers explored this phenomenon and identified seven reasons why drilling on spelling and writing conventions wasn't working in our schools.

DIFFICULTIES IN TEACHING SPELLING, PUNCTUATION, CAPITALIZATION, AND PENMANSHIP

1. *Spelling, capitalization, and punctuation are probably the most difficult of all writing conventions to learn.* Their difficulty arises from the fact that they are usually demonstrated in conjunction with other thinking tasks, e.g., when students spell, they are also writing, creating, and paragraphing. Other language arts (reading, speaking, and listening) can occur without the simultaneous execution of other language arts. Further, correct spelling, capitalization, and punctuation are governed by many rules. For these reasons, the Wisconsin Language Arts Curriculum Guide for Spelling begins with the statement that "spelling is the yardstick by which the public often evaluates our students and our teaching" (1987, p. 6).

2. *The ratio of time students spend speaking and listening is three times greater than the time spent in writing.* This difference reduces the opportunities students have to practice spelling, punctuating, and capitalizing. This decreased time in composing reduces students' exposure to the spelling patterns that frequently appear in English.

3. *Young children receive positive reinforcement when they stumble and stutter as they learn oral language. However, when they share their first writings, parent/ teachers often read the many correctly spelled words without lavish praise.* Instead of praising and supporting students' beginning attempts to spell, punctuate, capitalize, and pen correctly, parents and teachers frequently pause at incorrect spellings and improper writing conventions and accentuate the errors. These disapproving reinforcements often inhibit students' desire and ability to learn.

4. *Words in the English language are difficult to spell.* Because our written language is an imperfect alphabetic system, few sounds have unique spelling representation. Specifically, 26 letters must represent 44–46 sounds and more than 26 dialectical variations. To represent these sounds, letters combine to make hundreds of spelling patterns. For instance, to spell *even our single, spoken sounds,* the English language requires 500 different letter combinations (Horn, 1947). The difficulty in learning to spell was most clearly dependent when Hanna et al. (1966) programmed a computer with 300+ English spelling principles. Even though the computer used every English language rule it "knew," it could only spell 49 percent of the 17,000 randomly selected English words correctly. Considering this fact, isn't it a testimony to our educational system that most of our students can spell more than 50 percent of their words correctly! While present instructional methods in spelling are making a difference, through the use of information in this chapter, your teaching can have an even greater impact.

5. *Spellings and writing conventions have been altered by changes from Old and Middle to Modern English.* In the transitions of our language, sounds of numerous words and word orderings in sentences changed but their spellings and writing conventions remained constant. For example, when Old English changed to Middle English, the sound of *p, w,* and *k* at the beginning of words was eliminated but the spelling remained (e.g., *know, wren, wrong, pneumonia*). Therefore, as today's students spell and compose, the reasoning that originally supported the correct forms no longer applies to modern English so students do not understand the spelling of the words that they must memorize.

6. *Presently, as many as 75 percent of the new words added to our language are borrowed from other languages and their spellings are foreign* (Tompkins & Yaden, 1986). For example, when students learn to spell *lieutenant, ballet,* and *chic,* English spelling rules do not apply. Although these words are treated as English words, they are spelled by the rules that govern the French language.

7. *Positioning is an important principle for spelling and writing conventions.* This principle is difficult for some students to learn. For example, spelling a word correctly involves knowing the position in the word in which the letter is to appear (e.g., /f/ is spelled *f* at the beginning of words [*f*ir], *but ff* or *lf* or *gh* at the end of words [bu*ff*, ha*lf*, and rou*gh*]). Students must also know which of the common morphemes (-in, -en, -an, etc.) appear at the beginning or end of words.

8. *Positioning is important in handwriting.* If students are to develop legible penmanship, they must use proper hand position in their grip, place the features of letters appropriately, and position their pencils on the correct starting point of the line. Accomplishing all of these positioning feats is not easy. Moreover, your instruction must not only train these positionings but build students' small muscles while maintaining their desire to improve their penmanship.

9. *During the 1980s the emphasis upon penmanship instruction decreased.* The reduced amount of time elementary teachers spend in developing manuscript and cursive writing skills raised the concern of junior/senior high school teachers and parents. By the 1990s, increasingly larger proportions of our students' writing was becoming illegible.

In brief, there are several reasons why students need to be taught spelling, capitalization, punctuation, and penmanship. Several researchers collected data to explain deficiencies in common methods of instruction during the 1970s and 1980s (Enri & Wilce, 1987; Fitzsimmons & Loomer, 1978; Hillerich, 1985; Hodges, 1981). The data they compiled formed the rationale which fashioned four new approaches to spelling, handwriting, capitalization, and punctuation instruction. As you will read in the next section, you can use students' invented spelling and word patterns to develop their knowledge of orthography. You can also use textbooks and word lists in new ways. And last, you can structure the editing step of your writing program to emphasize the correct use of all writing conventions and principles that govern proper manuscript and cursive penmanship.

PUTTING THEORY INTO PRACTICE
HOW TO TEACH SPELLING, HANDWRITING, CAPITALIZATION, AND PUNCTUATION

Today, students' spellings are defined in two ways. **Traditional spelling** is *when the words they spell correspond to the way adults spell; words are spelled as they appear in the dictionary, and they adhere to the spelling rules that govern them.* Students can also use **invented spelling** *when they spell a word and the spelling they choose is not the correct spelling of that word.* Other writing/conventions you will be required to teach are **penmanship** (*the art or practice of writing with a pen, pencil, or other hand-held writing instrument*), **capitalization** (*the act or process of scripting or printing with capital letters at appropriate points*), and **punctuation** (*the act, practice, or system of inserting standardized marks in written matter to clarify the meaning and separate structural units in sentences*).

HOW TO TEACH SPELLING, PUNCTUATION, AND CAPITALIZATION

There are four new methods of building students' spelling, punctuation, and capitalization skills. As you will read below, each of these approaches has its advantages. You can decide which most adheres to your teaching style and to the instructional needs of your students. Many teachers combine the following approaches, as you may prefer as well.

Approach 1: Invented Spelling and Creative Conventions

Students' invented spellings and creative capitalization/punctuation is a valuable stage in writing development (Adams, 1990). When students are free to spell and punctuate the way they think is "right," they simultaneously develop phonemic awareness and initiate their own learning of language principles (Fehring & Thomas, 1985). Moreover, students who use invented spelling and creative writing conventions are not delayed in learning to traditionally spell or punctuate and capitalize (Silverman, 1989). "It is important that students' invented spellings are valued and that they are interpreted as displays of these students' intelligence and emerging proficiencies. It is [also] clear that instruction in standard spelling can assist the developmental process, and that invented spellings change after exposure to spelling instruction" (Sowers, 1986, p. 246).

Furthermore, when you allow your students to use invented spellings as they write, their higher order thoughts about the content they are creating are unobstructed. They are freed as writers. If you authorize invented spelling (and permit creative use of other conventions), you teach students: (1) different sounds are represented by different letter combinations; (2) there are many orthographic and syntactic patterns; (3) handwriting mechanics become more automatic; and (4) resources can be used to find correct spellings and principles that govern punctuation and capitalization. In the invented spelling approach you require students to transpose their invented conventions and spellings into traditional forms during editing, and when their writings are to be shared with others.

If you follow this approach, the 20–30 minutes a day that would have been relegated to textbook exercises are spent completing an authoring cycle. In essence, students' writings become a textbook for spelling development. Similarly, evaluation of capitalization, punctuation, and spelling shifts from right/wrong answers on dictated tests to an analysis of correct use of spelling and writing convention principles in students' compositions. Such analyses compute the percentage of invented words used and the quality of errors made (e.g., errors begin to more closely approximate traditional spellings, punctuation, and capitalization over time). Such assessment is based on a thorough understanding of the developmental stages that students pass through as they learn written language rules. When you know these stages, you can more rapidly build upon students' present level of lexical mastery, and assist their transport to traditional spelling, punctuation, and capitalization.

FIGURE 9-1

Sample of the Precommunicative Stage in Spelling Development

(For Andy)

Stages in Development of Spelling Skill. Preschool children's invented spellings are governed by a set of principles different from those that guide traditional spelling (Read, 1975). Building upon Read's work, Gentry (1982) classified young children's self-constructed understandings into developmental stages that students pass through to become effective writers and spellers. Students must bridge between the *precommunicative, semiphonetic, phonetic, transitional,* and *correct spelling (writing) stages before they become traditional spellers and writers.*

Precommunicative Stage. The first stage of invented spelling evolves the moment children realize that letters and not lines or numbers are the things that "spell." Students do not know which letters represent which sounds. The sign that students are in the *precommunicative stage of spelling development* is that they write one or more letters to represent a word. Interestingly, the letter they write may not be in any part of the word it is intended to depict. The reason children believe that a single letter represents an entire word (or sentence) is because it takes them so long to write one letter they feel as if they have written their entire thought (Beers, Strickland, & Beers, 1981)! See four-year-old Randy's spelling as an example. He attempted to write a "w" to stand for his entire name (see Figure 9-1).

Semiphonetic or Prephonetic Stage. The second stage begins at about age four when students understand left-to-right orientation. They start to realize that individual letters represent specific sounds. Another characteristic is that students always write in a straight line.

Instruction for students in this stage includes reading a book while you move your finger below the print; labeling objects in the classroom; pointing to the initial letter as you say printed words; bringing environmental print to the classroom; composing "rebus" stories; and chorally reading students' favorite chants.

Phonetic Stage. The third stage begins when students use the basic English phonograms, e.g., /an/, /at/, /in/, /en/, /on/, /up/, and /us/. While students in the phonetic stage will put a letter or word for each thought they want to communicate, their spellings and writing conventions will be

FIGURE 9-2
Sample of Phonetic Stage in Spelling

incorrect. They will only write the sounds they hear, such as writing "u" for "you." Their writings are logical and systematic, however, such as *kr* for car, and *n* for in, as illustrated in Figure 9-2.

Instruction for students at this stage includes internalizing basic word and sentence patterns and the capitalization and punctuation that accompanies them, such as their own name, high frequency words, their friends' names, Mother, and Father. Temple, Nathan, Burris, and Temple (1988) have found phonetic spellers also benefit from segmentation activities where an important word is rewritten several times. Students can cut the strip between each word, such as drawing lines between each word "spell" in a line: spellspellspellspellspellspellspellspellspellspellspellspellspell.

Transitional Stage.   In this stage, pupils learn to pay attention to visual patterns and clues in words and sentences as well as to the letter-to-sound correspondences they represent (Adams, 1990; Hillerich, 1985). When students use all the right letters, but place them in an incorrect order, they have reached this advanced writing level (Wilde, 1989a; 1989b). Students also develop a spelling memory and use a visual coding mechanism, as shown in Figure 9-3. During the transitional stage, students benefit from instruction that emphasizes:

1. Short vowel patterns (cvc), long vowel patterns (cvce and cvvc), and consonant blend/digraph spellings, such as teaching *br, pl, st, th, ch,* and *ph;*
2. Spelling words with *m* or *n* before other consonants, which letter-name spellers usually omit in words such as, *lamp, find,* and *stand;*

FIGURE 9-3
Sample of Transitional Stage in Spelling

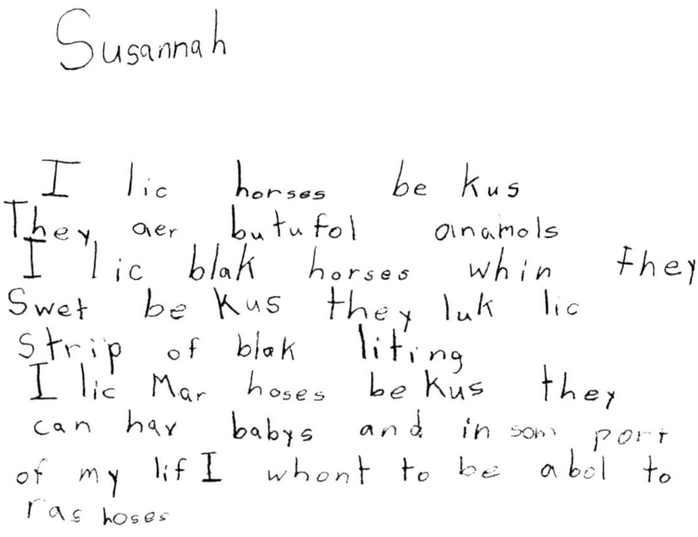

Susannah

I lic horses be kus
They aer butufol anamols
I lic blak horses whin they
Swet be kus they luk lic
Strip of blak liting
I lic Mar hoses be kus they
can hav babys and in som port
of my lif I whont to be abol to
ras hoses

---

3. Spellings at the end of words; words ending in *-ve* (such as *move,* *have,* and *love*) and words that end with a double consonant (such as *ball, fall, miss,* and *pass*);
4. Spelling of past tenses of verbs (*-ed*);
5. Rules that govern capitalization and punctuation that appear in their own writings.

Correct Spelling Stage.   It is at this stage that students understand the idiosyncracies of English orthography. They often self-initiate their own proofing to be sure they have spelled and written sentences correctly. They write prefixes, suffixes, silent consonants, irregular spellings, and complex sentences correctly. Most students reach this stage at about 8–9 years of age. However, many will not use traditional spelling and writing rules for many years beyond third grade, especially if instruction in these rules is not provided.

In summary, you should encourage students to invent. Students' improvisation engages thinking and learning about writing. A child who has been encouraged to progress through the developmental stages of invented spelling and creative use of punctuation and capitalization is more likely to develop a deeper understanding of English orthography and writing principles than a child who lacks these constructive experiences. Inventive spelling frees students to write and integrate the language arts:

The composing of words according to their sounds . . . is the first step toward reading. Once the child has composed a word, he looks at it and tries to recognize it. The recognition is slow, for reading the word seems much harder

FIGURE 9-4
Sample Page from a Spelling Book

than writing it. Often the child works it out sound by sound, the reverse of the process by which he wrote it, and then recognition dawns all at once (Chomsky, 1975, p. 120).

Students' quality of writing also increases as they do not limit their expressions to their written vocabularies and they pen from imaginative thinking (Sowers, 1986). For example, a young girl in Sowers' study was excited as she read her story about the "froshus dobrmn pensr" (translation: ferocious doberman pinscher); her excitement would have not existed had she written only what she could spell, "bad dog."

Approach 2: Modified Textbook Approach

In the past, textbook approaches for spelling, punctuation, and capitalization followed the same process: students were pretested over a set of words or rules, completed four days of drill and practice exercises, and took a posttest over the same words or rules. Students usually studied 36 units which included the most frequently occurring words and punctuation/ capitalization rules in our language. If all the exercises in a series were completed, by the end of sixth grade students would have been tested over 97 percent of all words children and adults use in their writings, and all the rules that govern punctuation and capitalization (Wilde, 1989a). A sample page from a spelling textbook appears in Figure 9-4.

As early as 1947, Horn (1947) identified two strengths with this approach. The first is that the pretest helped students identify words they already knew so they could study only those that were difficult for them. Since the average child knows how to spell 75 percent of the words in his or her grade-leveled text before studying there is no reason to teach the words already known (Hillerich, 1985). Through this pretest procedure, individual students can eliminate known words from their study list. The second strength is that students correct their own tests so they receive immediate feedback.

A weakness with this approach is that many students can score 100 percent correct on their weekly posttests and not transfer these correct spellings to their writing (Johnson, Langford, & Quorn, 1981). A second difficulty is that many practice activities, while using words and rules in the unit, do not teach students *how to spell, punctuate, and capitalize words when they compose.* Teaching students to recognize English language patterns has been found to be important in developing spelling skill (Graves, 1977). Research also indicates that *no more than 12 to 15 minutes a day* should be spent in learning to spell. Additional time does not result in significant increases in spelling ability (Johnson, Langford, & Quorn, 1981).

While most recently published texts incorporate some of the research findings in this chapter, the text you select should not ask students to do nonauthentic writing/spelling tasks. Best texts would include spelling/writing pattern recognition exercises, games, and metacognitive study strategies similar to those in Critical Thinking Activity 9.

If you modify the textbook in the following ways, you can maximize its instructional strength:

1. Use more than one grade-level from the series in your class.
2. Ask students to add words/rules to their weekly writing lessons that they want to learn.
3. Require students to learn words they misspell in their own writing in addition to those described in the text.
4. Integrate the language arts by assigning students to textbooks that contain word and sentence patterns that you will emphasize during your week's reading and oral language instruction.
5. Construct informal tests. For example, if you were teaching third grade, you could give an informal spelling test on Monday that contained 30 words and rules (one from each unit in the spelling and language arts textbooks for Grade l); on Tuesday test 30 words and rules from the spelling textbook from Grade 2 (one item per unit); on Wednesday, test from the third grade speller; on Thursday, test a sample from the fourth grade speller; and on Friday, another test from the fifth grade speller.

Prior to administering the tests, prepare a chart that keys each item on the test to a set of pages in the five spelling/language arts texts students will study if they missed that item on the informal pretest. As soon as students grade their tests, *they* decide upon the types of work they will do to eliminate each error. Students with similar problems group themselves together and work together upon specific objectives using pages in all grade-level textbooks together four days a week. On the fifth day, students break into pairs to test each other by looking at all writing samples their partner wrote that week to see if all rules/words studied during the week transferred.

As an alternative, students can work at their own pace for four days a week, completing as many spelling units during the week as they are able. Then, on the fifth day, students pair and test each other over individualized spelling lists. These lists are comprised of words they have misspelled during the week's writing workshops as well as in the spelling pattern lessons they have chosen to learn. Students who miss few words on the pretest are given word/sentence patterns represented in higher grade-level texts. A second grade is awarded for how many rules were evidenced in the students' writings that week.

Approach 3: Basic Word List Instruction

This approach develops spelling skills by dividing the 3,000 most frequently occurring words of our language into lists. These lists account for 60 percent of all words written by elementary school children (Hillerich, 1985). Each weekly list is introduced with a pretest which is immediately corrected by students. They list words they need to learn, and keep records to measure their own success. To begin this program, administer a test of basic English words to diagnose students' level of spelling ability. Those who correctly spell at least half of the words on this pretest should be given more difficult words (see pp. 310–311). As Hillerich (1985) states:

> A compromise between the ideal and the practical suggests no more than three lists in use in any given classroom. Each group can be given its pretest, either by the teacher or by a student from another group. Even though each pupil in the group may have different words for the check test and mastery test, the entire group can be administered the list once, and each pupil can write only his or her own words. They know which are their words, since they corrected their own pretests and studied those words. Of course, complete individualization can be accomplished by pairing students on a buddy system or by putting the list of words on tape (p. 172).

This approach requires about one hour a week of instruction. Once students spell all the words on the basic list correctly, they are ready to learn the 3,400 other most frequent words in our language (see Hillerich, 1985, for grade-ranked words by spelling patterns which can be used in this approach). When students master these lists, they can spell 98 percent of all the words they will ever write.

Approach 4: Learning to Spell During the Editing Step of Writing

As students edit their writings, they usually learn to spell at least one word they didn't know how to spell on their first draft. Conference with a student and notice which word pattern the student is not spelling exactly correct. (A list of spelling patterns to bring to this conference appears in Chapter 4.) The fact that a student is inventing a pattern demonstrates that he/she

---

THE CHALLENGE OF DIVERSITY

To reduce the difficulty of spelling for multicultural children, write the Spanish word or show a picture of the English word students are trying to read and spell below the English word. Then use post-it notes to scaffold. Here is an example:

Day 1: You go to school.
                    (picture)

Day 2: You go to s

Day 3: You go to school.

(cover the picture with a post-it note)

---

is ready to learn its spelling. For example, if a student writes: "They mak the snak go in the lak," you would show the list of words with the /-ake/ spelling pattern and ask the student to read each word. Then the student returns to the above sentence and adjusts the spelling. You also teach a mini-lesson. A sample follows:

> Mr. Mangieri: You have everything about the trip to the cafeteria, even about eating together. I also like the way you wrote this part at his house. It is very descriptive. I also notice, Catherine, that you remembered to use periods throughout the book, and it's nice to see that. I'd like you to look at the word *said.* Say the letters you used to spell *said.*
>
> Catherine: S . . . A . . . D.
>
> Mr. Mangieri: Those are three of the letters in *said.* You are very, very close to spelling it 100 percent correct. What I'd like you to do right now is draw a line under *said* every time you see it on this copy of page 4 from *Dear Mr. Henshaw* that you are reading. Now, return to your writing. How do you spell *said?*

Let's see if you can use this approach to teach spelling. Study Susie's sample that follows, and describe a rule about spelling you would teach her:

> I brok my ancl. I brok it when I was at mi mapl tre.

What would you teach Susie about spelling? (Check your answer on page 512.) When the editing approach is used, students who are not in conferences can meet in groups to increase spelling skills through the following activities:

1. *Disappearing Lists.* This activity is one section of a larger, experimental program created by Stevens, Madden, Slavin, and Farnish (1987). It begins with words students misspell in their writing. Pairs of students then test each other over the list of misspelled words. Words are taken off the list when a student and that student's partner is convinced that this student can spell the word. Students establish a standard to determine that spelling has been learned (e.g., any word misspelled in the partner's writing must be spelled correctly three times in a row in subsequent writings before it is removed from the spelling list).

2. *Wheel of Fortune Spelling.* In a recent research study, Hall and Cunningham (1988) used the "wheel of fortune game" to teach context and graphemic clues in spelling and reading. Words used in the game could be those on a wall chart in the room, words students select, or words from a content area of study. This game begins by four-member groups of students electing a moderator and three contestants. The moderator writes a cloze sentence on a sheet of paper, with the word to be spelled omitted from the sentence. Contestants spin a wheel for the amount of money each correct guess is worth. Contestants try to guess letters of the missing word until it is spelled correctly.

3. *Friday-Is-Game-Day.* On Friday, a fun activity is scheduled where individuals or teams earn points. Such activities include cloze passages, puzzles, spelling bingo, spelling bees, and having students write their words in pudding, whip cream, or finger paint. To make spelling bees more valuable to students, instead of only one student from each team standing to spell a word, every team member uses an individual blackboard and writes the spelling of the word called. Individual student blackboards can be made from 8 1/2" by 11" cardboard pieces that have been painted with blackboard paint, purchased at a paint store. Each team scores one point for each word spelled correctly by all members of the team.

4. *Look, Say, Cover, and Write.* In this activity, students look carefully at a word to memorize the spelling. In succession they then say the word aloud (or to themselves), cover it, and write the word from memory.

5. *Word Families.* Children learn word *families.* They identify words that contain the same word part and that are related in meaning, e.g., identify and spell words that contain the word *hand.* Students are given two days to collect as many words as they can find relative to their "word family." Students share their words in a creative way with the class, e.g., words with *hand* in them can be displayed within the outline of a hand. Students are also required in their oral presentations to ask questions about the related meanings of their spelling words: Why is it called a *hand* kerchief? Under*hand* ed? *Hand* y? On the day after the presentations, students can be paired and their partner gives them the spelling words they have collected as a test, or the class can elect to spell as many of the word families as they can that the entire class gathered.

6. *Discovering Famous Authors' Use of Conventions.* Basic punctuation and capitalization are traditionally introduced in first grade. After an initial explanation of these conventions, the most effective practice of their use occurs in writing groups, in the revision/editing steps. The reason these times are the most effective is because students want to communicate something. They see the importance of the conventions in doing so. As students progress, you can guide them to discover the more advanced rules

FIGURE 9-5
EDITING CHECKLIST

EDITING CHECKLIST   NAME _____

AUTHOR _____ DATE _____

TITLE _____

_____ SPELLING   (It was a ⟨special⟩ *special* shirt.)

(Watch for homonyms; ⟨Wear⟩ *where* should I ⟨where⟩ *wear* it?)

_____ CAPITALIZATION   (I looked good. l̲et's go! I'm ready to visit d̲octor c̲ollins.)

(Watch for out of place capitals; We went to the /School.)

_____ PUNCTUATION   (The sentences all end with punctuation marks⊙ I've checked for appropriate

use of commas⋏ for example⋏ in listing and for sentence clarity.

Apostrophes are used to show possession and as part of a contraction⊙)

_____ PARAGRAPH INDENTION (⁋ Another idea for.....)
                                   and that is the best...

_____ MARGINS (| and so...)
                  →then...

_____ COMPLETE SENTENCES (Then⋏went home.)
                                we

_____ CLEAR MEANING (They⋏then went to MacDonalds after practice.)
                          band

_____ WHAT COULD MAKE THIS PAPER BETTER? _____

_____

_____

_____

⬭ Spelling or word choice	⊙ Add period	⁋ New paragraph
⚌ Capitalize	⋏ Add comma	⟋ Insert
⟋ Don't capitalize	⌄ Add apostrophe	ℓ Delete

(i.e., possessives, semicolons, dashes, and parentheses) by comparing and contrasting the different punctuation styles of their favorite authors. Students can also use an editing checklist (see Figure 9-5) as they write.

FIGURE 9-6
Handwriting Models

Zaner-Bloser Model

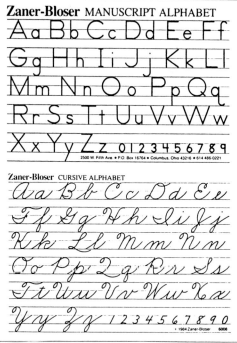

Used with permission from *Handwriting: Basic Skills and Application.* Copyright © 1984 Zaner-Bloser, Inc., Columbus, Ohio.

HOW TO TEACH HANDWRITING

Handwriting instruction is important because "handwriting allows the student to see his own spirit in action" (Laib, 1989, p. 2). There are three types of handwriting that you may be required to teach: **Manuscript**—discontinuous strokes; **Cursive**—flowing writing with continuous strokes; and **Italics**—unconnected, but flowing strokes. There are more than 100 programs or commercially prepared materials that can be used to teach penmanship. There are also four important principles you will follow to make your program most successful.

First, as we have demonstrated with all the language arts, you will integrate oral stimuli with visual practice. For example, as you describe letter formations, you will provide an oral stimulus by modeling how to make each letter as students see the visual features of each letter you are creating. Students will also say the letter strokes as they subsequently write the word.

Second, you will not force students into instruction unless the following readiness skills are developed: muscle coordination; hand/eye coordination; ability to hold writing tools for long periods of time; how to grip a pencil; an ability to form letters; and how to space between letters and words. It is important to remember that without proper instruction, students often devise their own methods of writing, which leads to bad habits. These bad habits interfere not only with legibility but writing speed.

Third, research supports the use of one-on-one instruction to alter individual students' writing errors. Such instruction will be more effective if students view and then replicate a model rather than trace difficult letters. (see sample models in Figure 9-6). However, viewing and trying to copy a letter alone will not significantly change the penmanship of students who are having difficulty. Such students need you to show them how to make each feature of their troublesome letters, such as how to make the down-strokes, circles, and stems it contains (Peck, Askov, & Fairchild, 1980).

Finally, erasers can be a problem for teachers and students. When students get in the habit of erasing, writing speed is slowed, and holes in their papers destroy meaning. You should demonstrate the process of crossing out errors.

Manuscript Writing

While several important readiness aspects of handwriting instruction occur in early childhood education programs, manuscript instruction traditionally begins in first grade. One reason for this is that young students' small muscles are less-well developed than older students'. Therefore, many primary students have trouble guiding their writing utensils to make all the angles required of cursive writing. Another reason manuscript writing is usually taught prior to cursive is because printed letters look more like the typeset letters students have read in books (Askov & Peck, 1982; Duvall, 1986).

Researchers have found that giving beginners "giant" pencils will not improve their penmanship. Students prefer small, adultlike writing utensils. In addition, first and second grade students tend to write longer stories if they use ballpoint or felt-tip pens as opposed to pencils (Askov & Peck, 1982).

The first manuscript letters to be introduced are lower-case letters because large muscles are more involved in their formation than in upper-case letters. Capitals should be taught and practiced one at a time as students learn to write their own and classmates' names. The easiest letters for first-grade students to write, and the suggested order to introduce manuscript letters are: *l, o, h, d, i, v,* and *x.* The most difficult letters for young students to write, and those that should be introduced last are: *q, g, p, y, j, m, k, u, a,* and *g.* Even as late as nine years of age, many children continue to have difficulty in forming *r, u, b,* and *t.* Some students may require that you guide their hand as they first learn to write these letters.

The following activities are effective in teaching manuscript writing:

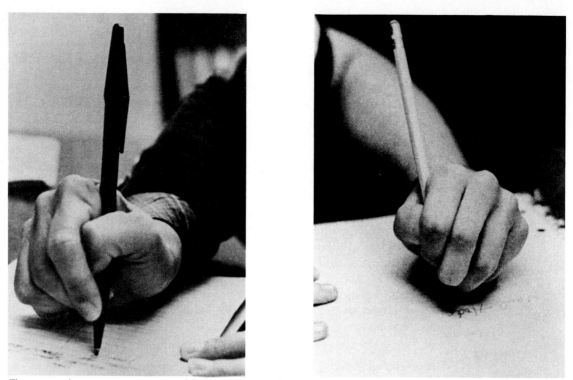

These are the correct posture and paper positions for right- and left-handed students.

1. First, say and then write a letter (with a crayon on paper, or on the blackboard); students observe the process. Students need to see you demonstrate each letter stroke. You verbalize what you are doing and students verbalize after you. Students say the directions for making strokes as they write them. "By talking aloud" as they write, they see their creations, and strengthen their mental images.

2. You and students copy letters (with the index finger) in the air several times before students pick up their pencil.

3. Students practice penmanship at the chalkboard. The chalkboard affords freedom of movement, allows use of larger arm and shoulder muscles to develop smooth handwriting, aids students in developing eye-hand coordination, and provides a kinesthetic experience which speeds learning of letter shapes (Collins, 1992a).

4. Place a model of the alphabet on students' desks in the form of a desktop letter strip, transparent notebook paper overlay, three-dimensional form, clay or hand-held model, or onion-skinned overlay. After students have practiced one or more difficult letters, they compare their letters to those on the model. When they judge their letter forms are accurate, they write a meaningful passage to communicate something important to someone else.

5. As a management tip, you can keep a jar of sharpened pencils and a variety of writing utensils (prepared by a student officer) in the room so students can experiment with new writing utensils.

Cursive Handwriting

Instruction in cursive handwriting usually begins in late second or early third grade. Cursive words are written laterally, formed at a 60-degree angle. The strokes of looping, retracing, rounding, and closing letters are taught separately, following the steps previously described for manuscript writing. Students' most frequent errors in cursive writing are faulty endings, incorrect undercovers, mixed slants, failure to produce letters in the center of a word, incorrect formation of initial strokes, capital letters, and not using appropriate downstrokes.

Students can learn to write cursive easier when they practice less complicated letters first. For example, begin by asking students to write several short words with the same letter:

> *add, all, at, call, cup, cut, dad, did, do, got, go, had, hall, hid, hunt, it, lad, late, little, oat, old, pad, pat, pig, pill, tall, to, tooth,* and *up.*

Once you have completed this lesson, help students recognize that most legibility errors occur through five mistrokes (Hillerich, 1985). Students can identify if they have a problem with any of these through the following activity:

1. Students write the words *darling, good, guide,* and *adding.* Ask them to look at their words and determine if their letters are or are not closed at the top. If they are not, students need to practice circle strokes.
2. They write *nothing, nautical, many,* and *number.* You ask them to look at the letters *m* and *n.* What happens if their tops are not rounded? If students do not like how these words appear, they can practice rounded strokes.
3. They write the words *item, triangle,* and *time.* Have them study the letters *t* and *i* and determine if these two letters are the same size. Students need to practice proper line length if they are.
4. Students write the words *ladder, letter,* and *left.* They analyze if the loops on the letters *l* and *e* are not open. If they are not, students need to practice backstrokes.
5. Pupils write the words *umbrella, underwater, runner.* Then they study each of the letters that they made. They are to describe what would happen if the tops of the *u* are not pointed. If they are not pointed, students would improve their handwriting by practicing upstrokes and subsequent retracings.

The major reasons students have poor cursive penmanship are improper instruction, poor pencil grip, and incorrect posture. You can diagnose if students are holding their pencils improperly by watching their hands as they write. If they are gripping the writing utensil too tightly, the handwriting will be too dark, or writing will be slow. If students are gripping their utensils with proper tension, you should be able to take the pencils from their hands without having to pull hard. Children should also have established a hand preference by first grade.

Tips for Left-handed Writers

Left-handed writers should be told that they may feel self-conscious during handwriting lessons as they are among a minority group. Only 9.7 percent of the girls and 12.5 percent of the boys their age will prefer to write with their left hand (Hawisher, 1987). You can help them overcome their self-consciousness by teaching that hand preference makes no difference in their level of success in life. Writing with one's left hand is no different from choosing to eat *Cheerios* when a friend desires *Captain Crunch*. You can also share a personal experience about a time when you were in a minority group, and what you learned from that experience. If a student expresses that he/she feels less able than students who are right-handed, share names of highly successful left-handed people such as President Bush, President Ford, President Truman, Leonardo da Vinci, and Judy Garland. You can also ask if they know which teacher or administrator in their school is left-handed. Suggest that the reason they don't know is because being right- or left-handed is inconsequential to a person's ability. You can also suggest that there are benefits to being among this smaller group of the population. For example, left-handed pitchers are rare and very valuable to major league baseball teams.

Without your special assistance, left-handed students may write by placing their hand below the writing line or hooking their hand over it. You must teach left-handed writers to place their paper properly, grip their pencil, and slant correctly. You can place a piece of masking tape on left-handed students' desks to mark the position where the upper left-hand corner of the paper should be placed each time students begin to write (see photo for this positioning). The upper right-hand corner of the paper should be in line with the center of the student's body. Once the student has the paper in this position for a few times, remove the tape and have students determine their own paper position, as each will select a slightly variant position from this mean positioning. Once a correct, personalized position is established, replace tape to mark both edges of the upper left-hand corner for at least the next grading period.

Left-handed students should hold their writing instruments at least an inch to an inch and one-half above the sharpened end. This position provides for eye-hand coordination which is necessary to prevent hooking the wrist. If the pencil is held near the end, students tend to move the pencil point to see their work which causes the wrist to hook. The best aid to assist students in remembering to hold the pencil up high is the "gripper." This is a triangular-shaped soft plastic ring that attaches to the pencil, available from Hoyle Products, Inc., 302 Orange Grove, P.O. Box 606, Fillmore, CA 93015.

Additional instructional strategies for left-handed students follow:

1. These students' elbows should be kept close to the body as they write. The blunt end of the pencil or pen should be directed back

FIGURE 9-7
Student Self-Selected Handwriting Practice

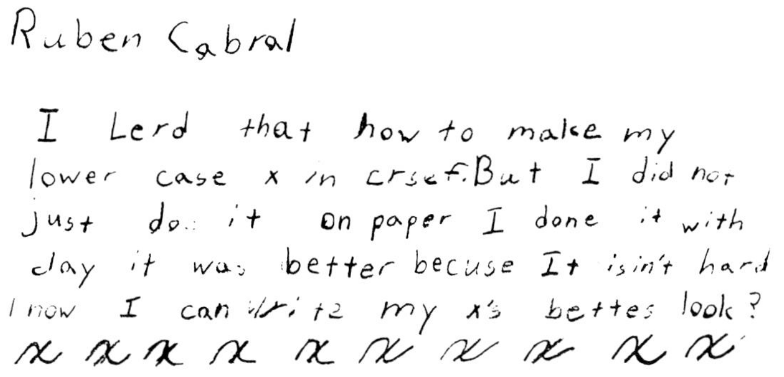

Ruben Cabral

I Lerd that hov to make my
lower case x in crsef. But I did not
just do it on paper I done it with
clay it was better becuse It isin't hard
I now I can write my x's bettes look?
x x x x x x x x x x

---

over the shoulder. The desk should be high enough for the child to see the pencil or pen as it touches the paper. Group left-handed students together for handwriting instruction so you can observe each of these qualities and so left-handed students can help each other during instruction.

2. Correct each first attempt as soon as it is made as learning to write in a right-handed system is difficult for left-handed students. By correcting first attempts, students will avoid developing hand positions, postures, and grips that will make writing uncomfortable for them for the rest of their lives.

3. In manuscript writing, "circle strokes" should be made from the left to the right, counterclockwise instead of clockwise as right-handed writers do.

4. Ask students to write four sentences. They make a tiny vertical line at the point where they place their pencil to begin each letter. Study these markings to analyze if letter strokes are beginning at the proper position for left-handed writers.

5. Demonstrate to students that each upward stroke will be pushing strokes rather than pulling strokes as is the case for right-handed writers.

6. It is becoming increasingly acceptable for left-handed students to use manuscript writing indefinitely when they find it easier than cursive.

7. Lastly, students should compare their writing samples to a handwriting model and identify one letter they wish to improve (see Figure 9-7).

THE CHALLENGE OF DIVERSITY

Gifted students often enjoy using a calligraphy kit. Ask such students if they know anyone who could come to class to teach calligraphy to those who are interested. Place a group of very good handwriters and/or gifted students in charge of solving problems connected with the guest speaker's visit. This group will select a problem solving strategy to resolve issues such as who will contact the guest, who will introduce the speaker, and how all language arts curriculum can be covered during the period the guest will visit, and still allow time for everyone who desires to learn calligraphy.

STRATEGIES THAT TEACH

CREATING DAILY LESSONS TO TEACH SPELLING, WRITING CONVENTIONS, AND PENMANSHIP

To this point in the chapter the importance of teaching spelling and writing conventions, as well as methods of doing so have been presented. In the next section you will learn how to create daily lessons where students: (1) use the computer, children's literature, and student compositions to master writing conventions, (2) use word play and word patterning games to enhance students' spelling abilities, and (3) use imagery to overcome common spelling errors.

CREATING LESSONS THAT USE THE COMPUTER IN SPELLING, HANDWRITING, PUNCTUATION, AND CAPITALIZATION INSTRUCTION

Computer programs such as *Spellcheck, Spelling Checker,* and *The School Speller* assist students to detect error patterns in their writings. There is also a wide selection of spelling practice software, such as *Spell It; Computer Scrabble; See It, Hear It, and Spell It;* and *Taking Test Spell* (Scholastic), which allow students to hear the word being spelled. Other varieties of spelling programs are *S-P-E-L-L* (IBM), a year-long curriculum that also includes word games; and *M-SS-NG LINKS* (IBM) which uses language puzzles to build analytical/predictive thinking and spelling skill. Punctuation skills are built through *Punctuation Put-On* (IBM).

CREATING LESSONS THAT IMPROVE STUDENTS' PENMANSHIP

Students benefit from practicing downstrokes (*i*), upstrokes (*m*), circles (*o*), and slants (*l*) in cursive writing. You can increase the enjoyment in such practice by telling a made-up story, using students' names and descriptions of previous classroom events. Each time you say a student's name, everyone must write one row of the lowercase, cursive letter that corresponds to the capital letter that begins that name. Once everyone has finished the row of letters, you continue the story.

As an aside, some students also find it easier to make letters of proper

Students enjoy and benefit by practicing writing letters in plates of jello, pudding, or whip cream. This practice increases writing speed and correct letter formation. Students also enjoy licking their fingers between letter formations.

size when you tell them that *a, c, e,* and *m* are "one-story letters." "Two-story letters" (such as *b, d, j,* and *l*) are introduced next; and "basement letters" are introduced last (such as *q, j, p,* and *y*). Figure 9-8 provides a checklist students can use to improve their handwriting.

Students who have difficulty with their slant enjoy practice writing on a slant sheet. A slant sheet is a piece of overhead projector acetate that has vertical (for manuscript) or 45-degree slanted lines (for cursive) printed on it. Students place the acetate beneath their lined paper as they write as a guide for the correct slant of their letters.

CREATING LESSONS THAT USE CHILDREN'S LITERATURE AND STUDENTS' COMPOSITIONS TO BUILD PUNCTUATION AND CAPITALIZATION SKILLS

Punctuation and capitalization should not be on students' minds during the brainstorming and first draft stages of their writing, but rise in importance during the editing and revising stages. To begin this lesson, give initial explanation of these conventions. Then students either read their writing to another student or allow several students to edit together. As students read their works aloud, both reader and listeners suggest punctuation according to what they hear. Students can also read books in Notecard 17 that help them develop punctuation and capitalization skills.

FIGURE 9-8
Clues to Improvement in Handwriting

I. RATE THE QUALITY OF YOUR HANDWRITING

Excellent (1), Good (2), Average (3), Fair (4), Poor (5)

_____Neatness
_____Arrangement (margins, indentations)
_____Legibility

II. LOCATE THE TROUBLE SPOTS IN YOUR HANDWRITING

Check (√) one or two areas in which you need special practice:

_____Slant (Do all your letters lean the same way; are your down strokes really straight?)
_____Space (Are the spaces between letters and words even?)
_____Size (Are your tall letters, i.e., *l, h, k, b,* and *f,* about three times as tall as the small letters; the middle-sized letters, i.e., *t, d, p* twice the height of small letters; and the lower loop letters one-half space below the writing line?)
_____Alignment (Are all tall letters evenly tall; all small letters evenly small; and are all letters resting on the line?)
_____Line Quality (Is the thickness of letters about the same throughout the page?)
_____Ending Strokes (Are the endings without fancy swinging strokes; and are they long enough to guide the spacing between words?)
_____Letter Formation   (Are the loops open and equal in size?
　　　　　　　　　　　　Are the hump letters *m, n, h, u,* rounded?
　　　　　　　　　　　　Are the letters *o, d, a, g, p, q* closed?
　　　　　　　　　　　　Have you made long retraces in *t, d, p*?
　　　　　　　　　　　　Are your capital letters well-formed?)
_____Number Formation   (Do you use the correct form?
　　　　　　　　　　　　Do you use the correct slant?
　　　　　　　　　　　　Are the symbols well aligned?)

In essence, as students reference and use the punctuation functions in the following lessons they will discover the importance of correct punctuation in their writing (see Figure 9-9).

1. Make a copy of one or two students' writing samples for the class. Omit the capital letters or punctuation marks relative to the skills you want to teach. As you display this modified sample on the overhead projector, together with you, students discover which capital letters and/or punctuation marks were omitted and how their addition enhances the message their classmate intended.

2. Use whiteout to delete the punctuation marks and capital letters on cartoon strips. Students replace these marks and letters and then compare their versions to the authors' originals. Students compose punctuation and

FIGURE 9-9
Punctuation Mark Skills Checklist

Punctuation Mark Skills Checklist			
Name: _____ Grading Period 1 2 3 4			
Skill	Introduced	Practiced	Applied in Writing
Period at the end of a sentence			
after abbreviations			
after numbers in a list			
after an initial			
Question Mark at the end of a question			
Exclamation Mark after words or sentences showing excitement or strong feeling			
Quotation Marks before/after direct quotations			
around title or a poem, short story, song, or TV program			
Apostrophe in contractions			
to show possession			
Comma to separate words in a series			
between day and year			
between city and state			
after greeting in a friendly letter			
after closing of a letter			
after an initial yes or no			
after a noun of direct address			
to separate a quote from the speaker			
before the conjunction in a compound sentence			
after a dependent clause at the beginning of a sentence			
Colon before a list			
in writing time			
after the greeting of a business letter			
after an actor's name in a script			
Parentheses to enclose unimportant information			
to enclose stage directions in a script			
Hyphen between parts of a compound number			
to divide a word at the end of a line			
between parts of some compound words			

capitalization rules from the cartoon strips where punctuation marks had been whited out, as illustrated in Collins (1992a).

3. Students work in editing committees to develop charts with rules they've discovered that govern punctuation and capitalization; these charts are then displayed at the Editing Center.

NOTECARD 17:   CHILDREN'S BOOKS THAT MODEL/DESCRIBE PRINCIPLES OF SPELLING, PUNCTUATION, CAPITALIZATION AND WORD ORIGINS

The following books and activities increase students' appropriate use of English conventions.

The Chocolate Mouse for Dinner by Fred Gwynne

The King Who Rained by Fred Gwynne

Eight Ate: A Feast of Homonym Riddles by M. Turban

My Tang's Tangled and Other Ridiculous Situations by Brewton, Brewton and Blackburn

The Story of the Dictionary by R. Krause

101 Words and How They Began by Arthur Steckler

Last, First, Middle and Nick: All About Names by Barbara Hazen

Hannah is a Palindrome by M.W. Skolsky

Bunnicula: A Rabbit-Tale of Mystery by J. and D. Howe

Perplexing Puzzles and Tantalizing Teasers by Marvin Gardner

On Your Marks: A Package of Punctuation by Richard Armour

Words Words Words by Mary O'Neill

Finding a Poem by Eve Merriam

Dandelions Don't Bite: The Story of Words by Leone Adelson

Words by Jane Sarnoff and Reynolds Ruffins

What's Behind the Words by H. Longman

Wonder in Words by M. Nurnburg

Teach Us, Amelia Bedelia by P. Parish

---

4. Students explore how each punctuation mark began, and report this information to classmates and younger students.

5. Victor Borge has published a record called the *Audible Punctuation* system. He selected distinctive sounds to communicate each punctuation mark. Students learn the roles each mark plays because the sounds connotate the meanings of the mark (e.g., sound for period is a short plunk and then a pause to denote the ending).

CREATING LESSONS THAT TEACH "SPELLING DEMONS"

In this lesson students learn some of the most frequently misspelled words in our language. Once students are aware of types of errors they are likely to make in their work, you assist them to overcome their problems by posting a "Spelling Demons Chart" (see pp. 310–311). Students add words to this chart that they misspelled in their writing. The day before a test over the "spelling demons" words, the class creates a mnemonic aid or clue to teach themselves how to spell the words from the demons chart, such as imagery as described in Critical Thinking Activity 9. Charlene Peck has written a book entitled *Word Demons* which helps students master 86 "spelling demons" through a game she has devised. A second reference you may find useful is *Graded and Classified Spelling Lists for Teachers* by Celeste Forbes (both books are available through Educators Publishing Company in Cambridge, MA).

STRATEGIES THAT TEACH

FIGURE 9-10
Using Configuration to Improve Spelling

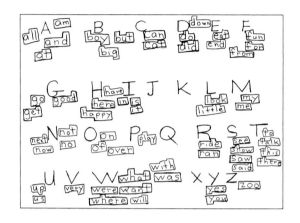

From *PHONICS THEY USE: Words for Reading and Writing*, by Patricia M. Cunningham. Copyright © 1991 by Harper Collins Publishers. Reprinted by permission.

Hall and Cunningham (1988) suggest that students learn to use configuration to build spelling ability. **Configuration** is *using the shape of letters in a word to distinguish that word from others*, such as *the* versus *that*. As shown in Figure 9-10, when students have difficulty with a word, they spell it, cut around it, place it on the "word" wall, study the word's shape, and then are tested on it.

THE CHALLENGE OF DIVERSITY

If you teach bilingual students, Sally Matheson-Mejia's article will be of interest. She describes the six most common spelling errors bilingual students make and the means of helping them overcome them. (See Matheson-Mejia, S. (1989). Writing in a Second Language: negotiating meaning through invented spelling. *Language Arts, 66,* 5, 516–521.)

CRITICAL THINKING ACTIVITY 9
Teaching Students to Image to Improve Spelling, Speaking, Reading, Writing, Listening, and Thinking Abilities

One of the most important skills in creative thinking is imaging. This lesson is designed to build students' creative thinking abilities so as to strengthen their speed of mental processing, retention, and comprehension.

Imagery is *students' ability to form a mental picture in their minds concerning what they think, read, hear, and say*. It aids the brain in making inferences, increases the capacity of long term memory, and matches schematic and textual information (Gaskins, Gaskins, & Gaskins, 1991; Purnell & Solman,

FIGURE 9-11
Using Images to Improve Spelling

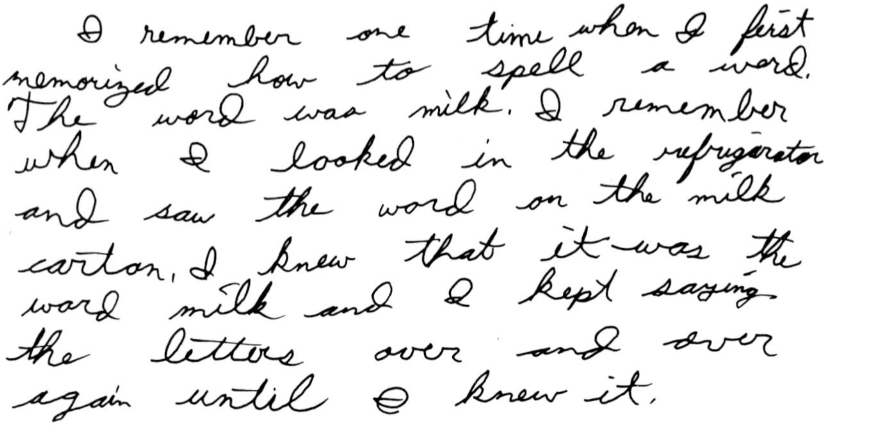

> I remember one time when I first memorized how to spell a word. The word was milk. I remember when I looked in the refrigerator and saw the word on the milk carton, I knew that it was the word milk and I kept saying the letters over and over again until I knew it.

1991; Sadoski, Goetz, Olivarez, Lee, & Roberts, 1990). Students more easily relate unknown to known when they are taught to begin a new chapter or book by constructing a mental image from maps, graphs, chapter summaries, and review questions. Gambrell and Bales (1986) also demonstrate that poor comprehenders seldom image without explicit directions to do so. For these reasons, it is important that you include the following activities to build students' imagery.

1. One of the simplest and most effective methods of building imagery, metacognitive thinking, and spelling skills is to describe thoughts you have as you try to spell. Gore (1992) calls this strategy "Image Modeling." Simply stated, you tell students how and why you create the mental pictures that you do. These images will aid the student to build visions or pictures in the mind as a bridge in learning to read and spell. Sometimes students need more than concrete experiences, lectures, or demonstrations to draw these pictures in the mind, as Courtney Duval, a seventh grader stated, in Figure 9-11.

An example follows of a teacher using image modeling to help a student in the fourth grade having a problem learning to spell.

Teacher to a fourth grade student: "When I was studying to learn to spell a new word, I would listen to the word pronounced, look at the written word, and then picture how the word looked in my mind. I then looked at the word and mentally traced the spelling. Then I pronounced the word silently to myself. Next, I wrote the word following the picture in my mind's vision. As I drew the picture of the word letter by letter in my mind, I made sure I crossed all the *t*'s, dotted all the *i*'s, and looped all the *l*'s. I repeated this process until I was sure I could spell the word I wanted to know.

2. Help students form mental images of the setting, characters, and

NOTECARD 18: BOOKS WITH SURPRISE ENDINGS TO BUILD IMAGERY

YOUNGER READERS

Miss Nelson Has a Field Day by H. Allard
Who Sank the Boat? by P. Allen
Clifford and the Grouchy Neighbors by
  N. Bridwell
The Velveteen Rabbit by M. Williams
The Vanishing Pumpkin by T. dePaola
Pleasant Dreams by A.B. Francis
Hugo and the Spacedog by L. Lorenz
The Mysteries of Harris Burdick by C. Van
  Allsberg

Snow Lion by D. McPhail
Oscar Mouse Finds a House by M. Miller
The Frog Who Drank the Waters of the World
  by P. Montgomery
Bert and the Missing Mop Mix-Up by
  S. Roberts
Dr. Desoto by W. Steig
Something Special for Me by
  V. B. Williams

OLDER READERS

My Dog and the Knock Knock Mystery and
  other books by D.A. Adler
Arthur's April Fool by M. Brown
Judge Benjamin: The Superdog Secret by
  McInerney
Octopus Pie by S. Terris
The Mystery of the Smashing Glass by
  W. Arden
*The Graveyard and Other Not-So-Scary
  Stories* by W. Warren

Christina's Ghost by B. R. Wright
The Castle of the Red Gorillas by
  W. Ecke
The Twiddle Twins' Haunted House by
  H. Goldsmith
The Borrowers by M. Norton
Tom's Midnight Garden by P. Pearce
The Revolt of the Teddy Bears by J. Duffy
A Wizard of Earthsea and other books by
  U. Le Guin

events of a book they are about to read. Making these mental images before they read enhances comprehension more than if they make them after they read (Rasinski, 1992). Notecard 18 contains lists of books that are helpful in building imagery.

3. Begin by showing students an object they can see for less than one minute. Have the students describe the images they create about that object in as much detail as they can. Follow this experience by asking students to recall similar objects, scenes, and past experiences. Next, read a story with high imagery potential. Once the story is finished, students describe their images, and then write the steps they will use in the future to image when they read. After they finish reading, students share their impressions of the story. Through this sharing students will come to understand that everyone's image can be different, based on what is important to them (Cramer, 1992).

4. Students are reminded to refer to their images whenever they are asked questions or challenged to retell events they have read or heard. They can strengthen their recall by looking at a blank spot on the wall as they remember. An activity to practice this strategy follows:

> Let us imagine that there is a boy standing in the corner of this room. Let us give him a hat. What color would you like the hat to be? Let us give him a jacket. What color jacket shall we give him? Let him have some shoes. What color will you let him have?
>
> Now change the color of his hat. What color did you change it to? Change it again. What color this time? Change it again. What color? Look at his jacket. What color is it? Change it to another color. Change it again. Change it again. What color are his trousers now? Change the color of his trousers. Change them again. What color are his shoes now? Change them to another color. Change them again. Change them again. What color are they now?

FIGURE 9-12
Using Personification as a Spelling Tool

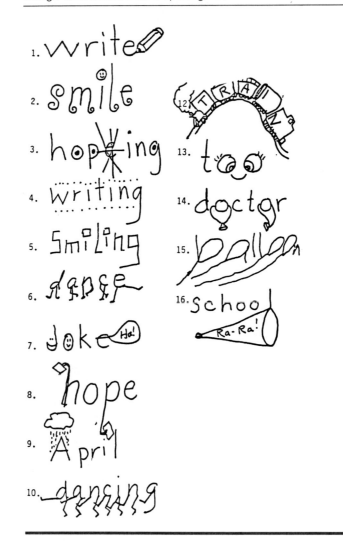

Have him stand on one foot and hold his other foot straight out in front of him. Have him stand on the other foot. Have him walk over to another corner of the room (DeMille, 1981).

5. Students complete a science experiment (Koval, 1992). They are shown a glass beaker filled with a colored liquid (vinegar and food coloring). Sprinkle powder (baking soda) into the beaker, but do not tell the students the ingredients or the purpose of the experiment. Once the powder enters the beaker the liquid will begin to bubble, foam, and expand until it erupts from the beaker. Ask students to use their imaginations, to answer the following questions:

- Who would create such a potion?
- Why would it be created?
- What would it do?
- To whom would it be given?
- How would it be administered?
- What consequences would result?

As small groups brainstorm, their answers are placed in story maps. Story maps must contain a setting, characters, conflict, solution, resolution, theme, and end with a question that another group could explore through a new science experiment they constructed. After stories are shared, students begin research and prepare the requested experiment, as well as a factual report, to provide information about the question their group was asked. These reports and experiments are shared. Scientific principles common to the imagery, stories, reports, and experiments are listed as a culminating review.

6. Personification is to *represent an inanimate object to have humanlike qualities*. It is a powerful teaching aid and form of imagery. Personification can increase students' spelling ability when they turn words into animate objects that convey their meaning (see Figure 9-12).

PROFESSIONAL DEVELOPMENT OPPORTUNITY
How to Teach Word Patterns to Improve Spelling, Reading, and Writing Abilities

Teaching word patterns as a combination of word play and word pattern activities can build students' use of spelling patterns. In the next few pages we will describe a few of these types of activities.

The first type was developed by Culyer (1992) and is called *Word Wizard*. *Word Wizard* is a thinking and spelling activity designed to help students learn to spell. It can be used at two levels of difficulty. In the more difficult version, students are challenged by the word wizard to take two words and change one letter at a time in the first word until it becomes the second word. For example, the word wizard challenges first grade students to change "cat" to "dog." Students could do so by using the following sequence: *cat* to *hat* to *hot* to *hog* to *dog*. Another sequence they could use would be to change *cat* to *cot* to *dot* to *dog*. An easier way the word wizard can challenge students is to use a puzzle format where definitions are given next to the word in each sequence. By attaching meaning to the clues, students can more easily complete the sequence. For example:

cat
_____ headpiece
_____ cold (antonym)
_____ adult pig
dog

The *Word Wizard* also builds metacognitive thinking and problem-solving abilities. A few items you can use appear in Figure 9-13.

FIGURE 9-13
Samples of Word Wizard Lists

1. **cat**	2. **lose**	3. **car**	4. **hate**
hat	lone	bar	have
hot	line	ban	Dave
hog	fine	**van**	dove
dog	**find**		**love**

5. **one**	6. **sick**	7. **dumb**	8. **push**
ore	lick	dump	bush
are	lice	damp	bust
arm	mice	dame	best
aim	mile	dime	belt
dim	mill	dice	bell
Tim	will	rice	bull
tin	**well**	rise	**pull**
ten		**wise**	

9. **city**	10. **soft**	11. **warm**	12. **mean**
pity	sort	ward	lean
pits	fort	word	loan
pots	ford	ford	loon
tots	cord	food	goon
tows	card	fool	**good**
town	**hard**	**cool**	

13. **poor**	14. **fawn**	15. **open**	16. **work**
door	dawn	oven	word
doom	down	even	ward
room	gown	ever	wand
roam	goon	eves	sand
ream	noon	eyes	send
read	neon	ayes	seed
bead	Leon	apes	shed
bend	lion	aped	shad
bond	lien	sped	shay
bone	lies	shed	slay
tone	ties	shod	**play**
tine	tees	shot	
tide	teas	**shut**	
ride	tear		
rice	dear		
rich	**deer**		

Another word pattern strategy is to show how some word parts convey meaning and will be spelled alike even if they sound differently, such as *industry* and *industrial*. Nagy, Anderson, Schommer, Scott, and Stallman (1989) demonstrated that this is possible because there are morphologically based word families. These morphemes dictate the spelling of derivational and inflectional words in their respective word families. Learning to use these morphemes is important in learning to spell. One method of helping students develop this spelling ability is to give them a list of words, such as appears in the left-hand column below, and ask them to find other words that contain the same word part.

photograph	photography
history	historical
govern	governor
microscope	microscopic
literate	literary
culture	culturally
major	majority

When students are proficient with this strategy, you can help them understand the spelling of silent consonants using a procedure first reported by Donogue (1990). Give students words in the left-hand column and ask them to think of related words in which the silent consonants are pronounced, such as those in the right-hand column.

bom*b*	bom*b*ard
sof*t*en	sof*t*
mus*c*le	mus*c*ular
si*g*n	si*g*nal
condem*n*	condem*n*ation

TRY IT

1. Collect writing samples from students of the same age, preferably below Grade 3. Analyze those samples in three ways. First, identify the stage of spelling development that each sample indicates. Second, state one instructional action you will take for each student. If you are not teaching, complete these analyses with the samples that appear in this chapter. Once you've completed your analyses, share your answers with a partner. Check each other's thinking.

Third, analyze these samples to diagnose a need each student has to improve his/her penmanship. Specify the instructional strategy you would use to overcome each student's difficulty.

2. Outline the spelling program you will develop. Include a description of the class and grade level you teach (or are preparing to teach). Tell when and if you will use textbooks in your spelling program. Describe two types of homework assignments you will give for spelling, punctuation, penmanship, and capitalization. Which, if any, of these assignments would you feel justified to give unilaterally to the whole class? Describe a type of homework assignment you will give to a student whose percentage of invented spellings is not decreasing.

3. Explain why it is so difficult to learn to spell and how spelling, reading, and writing are related. Select a book from Notecards 17 or 18 and design a lesson to increase students' awareness of spelling or improve a dialectical interference problem your students could have.

4. How many of the following invented spellings can you recognize? Can you tell the stage of development each represents?

acl	next stordaber
bothring	althawaup
butrfli	lecdrek
yace dodl	rtst
mapl	youmembein
ovr	wereed
revr	vakumklenr
sntcls	jimnozzme
	filisdiler
	plgavalegents

Answers to invented spellings above are: ankle, bothering, butterfly, Yankee Doodle, maple, over, river, Santa Claus, next door neighbor, all the way up, electric, artist, human being, worried, vacuum cleaner, Jim knows me, Phyllis Diller, pledge of allegiance.

FOR YOUR JOURNAL

Students can use journals to record questions they will ask in an interview or as they read. To practice using your journal in this way, throughout Chapters 2–8 you have explored various aspects of reading and writing instruction. Use your journal to write five questions you will use to interview elementary or middle school students who have worked in authoring cycles and reading response groups. Ask them what goals and activities they enjoyed and those from which they learned the most. Ask how speaking, reading, writing, and listening instruction was similar. Write the questions you ask, and the answers you receive, in your journal. What will you add to your language arts program as a result of these interviews?

BUILDING YOUR PROFESSIONAL PORTFOLIO:
Spelling Demons

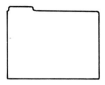

The spelling demons you can introduce at each grade level follow.

Second Grade Spelling Demons

balloon	every	nice	sometimes
birthday	father	off	store
bought	friend	once	teacher

cont'd

boys	goes	party	their
brother	likes	people	there
brought	lots	pretty	train
children	much	Saturday	very
coming	name	snowman	white

Third Grade Spelling Demons

afternoon	didn't	lessons	teacher's
again	don't	letter	that's
along	fine	morning	today
answer	fourth	November	tomorrow
April	from	now	vacation
arithmetic	getting	please	well
because	hello	received	write
close	January	Sunday	writing
cousin	know	sure	yours
daddy			

Fourth Grade Spelling Demons

all right	downstairs	legs	soon
already	earth	meat	spent
autumn	everyone	meet	sudden
been	fight	met	think
bicycle	half	mountains	though
cannot	haven't	noise	Thursday
can't	hide	ocean	tonight
carried	I'll	prince	truly
chose	isn't	puts	walked
church	it's	quite	weather
dead	just	reached	won
doctor	laugh	sea	

Fifth Grade Spelling Demons

address	desert	neighbor	receiving
anyway	shopping	pieces	thinking
awful	different	plain	sincerely
balloon	fourteen	teacher	swimming
schoolhouse	handkerchiefs	quiet	they're
blow	language	quit	tooth
chief	stationery	really	you're
choose	lie		

Sixth Grade Spelling Demons

afternoon	how's	neighbors	scissors
beginning	kindergarten	off	sleigh

course	ladder	pitcher	stiff
dining	loose	pour	tow
flower	lose	route	union
heart			

Seventh Grade Spelling Demons

advise	easier	joined	pleasure
anxious	exercise	knowledge	regular
auditorium	freight	natural	shoulder
believed	generally	necessary	system
choir	hurried	officer	terrible
description	independent	permission	worried
difficult			

From: Clanfield, M., and Hannan, C. *Teach Spelling by All Means*. San Francisco: Fearon Publishers, 1961.

Integrating Language Arts Across the Curriculum

Thematic units provide a multitude of language opportunities through which students grow linguistically, culturally, and cognitively, a powerful combination.

Today the trend in some classrooms as well as in the research community more generally, is to see reading and writing as tools for learning . . . and to learn through [the language arts], to grow, change, and learn (1989, p. 19).

—Jerome Harste

In this chapter you will learn how students can integrate writing, reading, speaking, and listening to comprehend more in content area courses. Through such instruction, students learn to use the thinking patterns that scientists, mathematicians, artists, historians, and public speakers use. In doing so, students also come to assess their aptitudes and interests in future professions in a more realistic fashion. They perform authentic speaking, listening, reading, and writing tasks within each content discipline in ways that they will be required to do so in the real world.

When you complete this chapter, you will know:

1. Several methods of integrating language arts and other content area classes;

2. How to use children's literature in conjunction with science, math, social science, and the fine arts;

3. How to conduct thematic units to organize language arts and content area instruction.

THEORETICAL FOUNDATION

NEED TO INTEGRATE LANGUAGE ARTS AND CONTENT AREA INSTRUCTION

There are several reasons why your content areas instruction should call upon and integrate your students' abilities to ask questions, listen to experts in the field, discuss key issues, and engage in self-selected and purposeful reading and writing activities. The first reason is that such intense participation, as the integrated language arts approach brings to a topic, generates a denser background knowledge for students, and provides multisensory experiences, which students can more easily transfer to their lives (Norton 1990; Beck & Dole, 1992).

A second reason to conduct language arts–related activities in coordination with content area instruction is that there are not enough pages allocated to each topic in social studies, science, mathematics, and other content area textbooks to build students' depth of understanding. For example, in a study of content area textbooks, Greenlaw (1987) found that social studies textbooks included no more than 9–19 pages of information related to every issue concerning World War II. Not only do textbooks of necessity cover many points briefly, but they omit important information about the people, rationale, and emotions behind each event. When students read, discuss, listen, study, and write about tradebooks, people, current events, and other nonfiction books relative to content topics, their activities fill this void. Samples of childrens' literature that can be used to support content area instruction appears in the Notecards of this chapter (see Notecards 19–22).

NOTECARD 19:   CHILDREN'S LITERATURE THAT ADDS TO STUDENTS' KNOWLEDGE OF HISTORY AND THE SOCIAL STUDIES

Being an American Can Be Fun by Munro Lear
Shh! We're Writing the Constitution and other books by J. Fritz
The Judge by H. Zemach
Democracy by D. Lawson
Getting Elected: Diary of a Campaign by J. Hewett
How Many Days to America? A Thanksgiving Story by E. Bunting
Picture Book of Abraham Lincoln (Series) by D. Adler
The Book of Where: How to be Naturally Geographic by Neill Bell
A Weed Is a Flower: The Life of George Washington Carver and other books by Aliki
Sarah Morton's Day: A Day in the Life of A Pilgrim Girl by Kate Waters
New Clothes: What People Wear from Cavemen to Astronauts by Lisl Weil
Where in the World Are You? by Kay Cooper

What's in a Map? by Sally Cartwright
Billy Yank and Johnny Reb by Earl Schenck Miers
Why Do We Have Rules? by C. Arnold
Banking by N. Nunnan
The Fourth of July Story by Alice Dalgliesh
People and other books by Peter Spier
Little House in the Woods and other books by Laura Ingalls Wilder
The Sorely Trying Day by L. Hoban and T. Hoban
Rosa Parks by Eloise Greenfield
A Family in Japan (Series) by J. Elkin
Where the Buffaloes Begin by Olaf Baker
The Obadiah books by Brinton Turkle
America the Beautiful (Series) by Children's Press
The Butter Battle Book by Dr. Seuss
The First Teddy Bear by Kay Helen
Growing Up Amish by R. Ammon
From Path to Highway: The Story of the Boston Post Road by Gail Gibbons

(cont'd)

NOTECARD 19:   (cont'd)

Magic Carpet and other books by P. Brisson
My Backyard History Book by D. Weitzman
The Milk Makers by G. Gibbons
Ice Cream by W. Jasperson
A Long Hard Journey by P. McKissack
This Place Is Cold (Series) by V. Cobb
When I First Came to This Land by O. Brand
A Country Far Away by Nigel Gray
Follow the Drinking Gourd by J. Winter
Call to Glory by Robert Elliot
Johnny Tremain by Esther Forbes
Patchwork Quilt by V. Flournoy
Across Five Aprils by Irene Hunt
The Cay by Theodore Taylor
The Callender Papers by Cynthia Voigt
Bright Fawn and Me by J. Leech and Z. Spencer
Good Night, Mr. Tom by Michelle Magorian
Eating the Plates by L. Recht Penner

Cassie's Journey: Going West in the 1960's by Brett Harvey
Ashanti to Zulu: African Traditions by M. Musgrove
Teammates by P. Golenbock
Weird Parents by A. Wood
Foxfire Books by E. Wigginton
Geography from A to Z by J. Knowlton
Nettie's Trip South by A. Turner
Calico Bush by Rachel Field
Rehema's Journey by B. A. Margolies
You Be the Jury and other books by M. Miller
Father of the Constitution: James Madison by Katherine Wilkie
How Far, Felipe? by Genevieve Gray
Hello Amigos by Tricia Brown
Me and Willie and Pa by F. N. Monjo
One Bad Thing About Father by F. N. Monjo

For additional titles of fiction books suitable for use in the social studies classroom, see *American Historical Fiction and Biography for Children and Young People* by J. Hotchkiss, 1973.

Compounding the problem of limited coverage, logical connectives and transition words to show relationships between topics are omitted in many content textbooks (Irwin, 1991; Beck & Dole, 1992). When reading and writing are combined with content area instruction, these connections become more explicit and achievement on multiple choice and essay questions over content area material also increases significantly (Flood & Lapp, 1991).

Finally, through integration, students read and write from many resources, and discuss several perspectives. Such comparisons are less likely when textbooks are the sole reference during content instruction. With these advantages in mind, we will turn our attention toward specific ways this integration can occur.

PUTTING THEORY INTO PRACTICE
HOW TO INTEGRATE LANGUAGE ARTS INTO CONTENT AREA INSTRUCTION

As noted above, it is becoming increasingly important that students use communication tools and processes as they study content area material. In the process they will also improve their thinking, speaking, listening, reading, and writing abilities. In the next section you will learn how to use the *interdisciplinary, parallel scheduling, thematic units, topic integration,* and *joining bits of information* approaches to reach these goals.

APPROACHES TO INTEGRATION

There are five major ways that langauge arts can be integrated into content area studies. Some involve coordinating activities between teachers and some can be implemented by you alone. Each provides opportunities and time for extended self-selected reading in related subject areas, writing to clarify meaning and extend concepts, and reflecting upon a variety of authorial perspectives.

Interdisciplinary Approach.   The first approach is implemented by a team of teachers and is called the interdisciplinary approach. In this approach, *teachers and students use more than one class period to examine a central theme, issue, problem, topic, or experience,* e.g., English and History are combined into a two-hour block where two or more teachers and classes join together to explore important historical issues from a humanistic perspective. You will view five teachers creating such an interdisciplinary curriculum in video segment 7.

Parallel Scheduling.   This is a second integrative approach, and it also involves two or more teachers working together to achieve integration. In this approach *teachers in several subjects schedule similar topics of study at the same time so curriculum is parallel, but end products are not coordinated to produce single exhibits or performances. Each subject is assessed separately, but students are expected to make connections between concepts from all classes as they think, write, and read.* For example, the study of prehistoric times (in history classes) is scheduled during a unit on dinosaurs/reptiles (in science classes), a unit on the beginnings and history of mathematics (in mathematics classes), and a unit of literature about dinosaurs and prehistoric man (in language arts classes). Jacobs (1989, p. 58) shows how such a parallel structure was created to increase middle school students' understanding of intelligence (see Figure 10-1).

NOTECARD 20:   CHILDREN'S LITERATURE THAT ADDS TO STUDENTS' KNOWLEDGE OF SCIENCE

KINDERGARTEN–GRADE 2

Little Rabbit's Loose Tooth by Lucy Bate
Petunia by Roger Duvoisin
The Carrot Seed by Ruth Krauss
Hi, Cat! by Ezra Jack Keats
Frog and Toad All Year by Arnold Lobel
Me and My Shadow and other books by
   A. Dorros
My Five Senses and other books by Aliki
Ecology by J. Bendick
How to Make a Cloud by J. Bendick
Grouchy Ladybug and other books by E. Carle
The Quicksand Book and other books by
   T. dePaola
A Snake Is Totally Tail by Judi Barrett
Koko's Story and other "Koko" books by
   Dr. F. Patterson
Quiet on Account of Dinosaurs by J. Thayer
How Many Stars in the Sky? by L. Hort

What It Feels Like to Be a Building by F. Wilson
What the Moon Saw by B. Wildsmith
Dandelion by Don Freeman
Owl by Orin Cochrane
Joey by Jack Kent
A First Look at Leaves by M. Selsam
The Beaver Pond by Alvin Tresselt
*Crinkleroot's Book of Animal Tracks and Wildlife
   Signs* by I. Arnosky
Exploring as You Walk in the City by P. Busch
Light and other books by D. Crews
Patrick's Dinosaurs by C. Carrick
A Seed is a Promise by C. Merrill
Exploring Autumn by S. Markle
Tyrannosaurus Was a Beast by J. Prelutsky
Two Bad Ants by C. Van Allsburg
Jacob and Owl by Ada and Frank Graham
The Astronaut Training Book for Kids by K. Long

(cont'd)

NOTECARD 20   (cont'd)

GRADES 3 AND UP

A Bird's Body and other books by Joanna Cole
The Magic School Bus (Series) by Joanna Cole
Jupiter by Seymour Simon
*The Night Sky Book: An Everyday Guide to Every
   Night* by J. Jobb
*Blood and Guts: A Working Guide to Your Own
   Insides* and other books by L. Allison
The Book of the Goat by Jack Scott
Nature's World Records by John Quinn
Storytime Science by Virginia Baekler
Science Teasers by R. Wyler and Eva Baird
Earth Alive by S. Markle
Weird and Wonderful Science Facts by
   Dr. M. Pyke
The Voyage Begun by Nancy Bond
The Cry of the Crow by Jean Craighead George
Mrs. Frisby and the Rats of NIMH by R. O'Brien
House of Stairs by William Sleator
If You Lived on Mars by M. Berger

The Kingdom of Wolves by Scott Barry
*Alligators, Raccoons and Other Survivors: The
   Wildlife of the Future* by Barbara Ford
The Human Body by J. Miller
Machines That Think and other books by
   Isaac Asimov
Science Facts You Won't Believe by W. Gottlieb
Save the Earth! An Ecology Handbook for Kids
   by Betty Miles
Dinosaurs of North America by Helen Sattler
Astronomy Project for Young Scientists by
   Necia Apfel
Mr. Wizard's Experiments for Young Scientists by
   Don Herbert
All Creatures Great and Small by James Herriot
The Far Side of Evil by Sylvia Engdahl
Hatchet and other books by Gary Paulsen

For additional titles, see *The American Association for the Advancement of Science Book List for
   Children,* Deason, 1972.

FIGURE 10-1

Interdisciplinary Model: A Unit on Intelligence

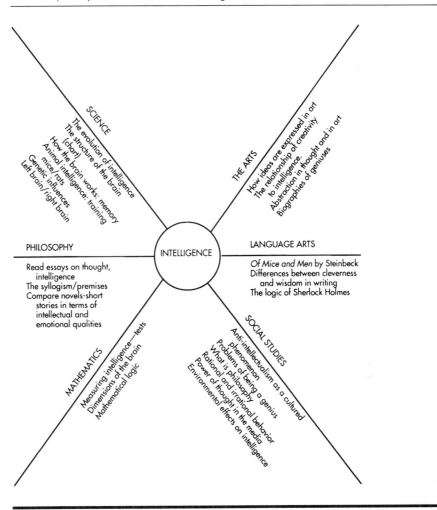

Thematic Units.   Thematic units are the third approach to integration. In thematic units, *reading, writing, speaking, and listening are employed to learn a section of information in one content area.* Thematic units enable children to explore a topic in depth, and to more actively participate in their learning. Such units extend for a week or more. Students approach the topic by seeking multiple definitions; comparing beneficial and detrimental influences; identifying past, present, and future applications of the topic; and reporting their positions about an area of personal interest. Thematic units have four parts: (l) a theme selected by students that they consider important and that can result in a product/process to be presented to people outside the classroom and improve that part of the students' world; (2) eight subtopics with each student working concurrently on two subtopics;

FIGURE 10-2
Samples of Thematic Units for Younger Students

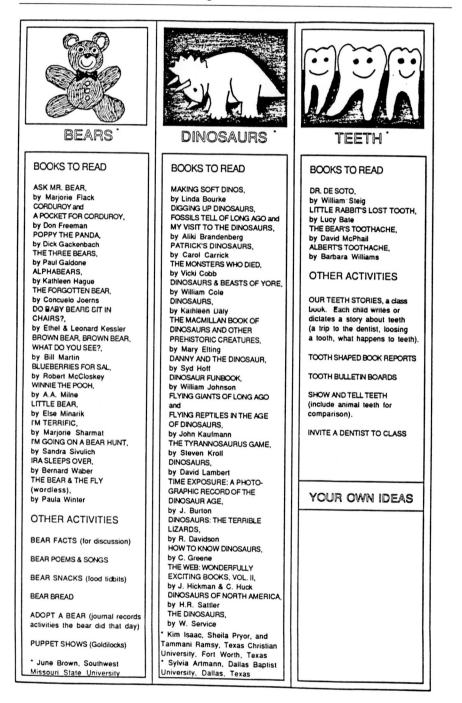

BEARS [*]

BOOKS TO READ

ASK MR. BEAR,
by Marjorie Flack
CORDUROY and
A POCKET FOR CORDUROY,
by Don Freeman
POPPY THE PANDA,
by Dick Gackenbach
THE THREE BEARS,
by Paul Galdone
ALPHABEARS,
by Kathleen Hague
THE FORGOTTEN BEAR,
by Concuelo Joerns
DO BABY BEARS SIT IN
CHAIRS?,
by Ethel & Leonard Kessler
BROWN BEAR, BROWN BEAR,
WHAT DO YOU SEE?,
by Bill Martin
BLUEBERRIES FOR SAL,
by Robert McCloskey
WINNIE THE POOH,
by A.A. Milne
LITTLE BEAR,
by Else Minarik
I'M TERRIFIC,
by Marjorie Sharmat
I'M GOING ON A BEAR HUNT,
by Sandra Sivulich
IRA SLEEPS OVER,
by Bernard Waber
THE BEAR & THE FLY
(wordless),
by Paula Winter

OTHER ACTIVITIES

BEAR FACTS (for discussion)

BEAR POEMS & SONGS

BEAR SNACKS (food tidbits)

BEAR BREAD

ADOPT A BEAR (journal records
activities the bear did that day)

PUPPET SHOWS (Goldilocks)

[*] June Brown, Southwest
Missouri State University

DINOSAURS [*]

BOOKS TO READ

MAKING SOFT DINOS,
by Linda Bourke
DIGGING UP DINOSAURS,
FOSSILS TELL OF LONG AGO and
MY VISIT TO THE DINOSAURS,
by Aliki Brandenberg
PATRICK'S DINOSAURS,
by Carol Carrick
THE MONSTERS WHO DIED,
by Vicki Cobb
DINOSAURS & BEASTS OF YORE,
by William Cole
DINOSAURS,
by Kathleen Daly
THE MACMILLAN BOOK OF
DINOSAURS AND OTHER
PREHISTORIC CREATURES,
by Mary Elting
DANNY AND THE DINOSAUR,
by Syd Hoff
DINOSAUR FUNBOOK,
by William Johnson
FLYING GIANTS OF LONG AGO
and
FLYING REPTILES IN THE AGE
OF DINOSAURS,
by John Kaufmann
THE TYRANNOSAURUS GAME,
by Steven Kroll
DINOSAURS,
by David Lambert
TIME EXPOSURE: A PHOTO-
GRAPHIC RECORD OF THE
DINOSAUR AGE,
by J. Burton
DINOSAURS: THE TERRIBLE
LIZARDS,
by R. Davidson
HOW TO KNOW DINOSAURS,
by C. Greene
THE WEB: WONDERFULLY
EXCITING BOOKS, VOL. II,
by J. Hickman & C. Huck
DINOSAURS OF NORTH AMERICA,
by H.R. Sattler
THE DINOSAURS,
by W. Service

[*] Kim Isaac, Sheila Pryor, and
Tammani Ramsy, Texas Christian
University, Fort Worth, Texas

TEETH [*]

BOOKS TO READ

DR. DE SOTO,
by William Steig
LITTLE RABBIT'S LOST TOOTH,
by Lucy Bate
THE BEAR'S TOOTHACHE,
by David McPhail
ALBERT'S TOOTHACHE,
by Barbara Williams

OTHER ACTIVITIES

OUR TEETH STORIES, a class
book. Each child writes or
dictates a story about teeth
(a trip to the dentist, loosing
a tooth, what happens to teeth).

TOOTH SHAPED BOOK REPORTS

TOOTH BULLETIN BOARDS

SHOW AND TELL TEETH
(include animal teeth for
comparison).

INVITE A DENTIST TO CLASS

[*] Sylvia Artmann, Dallas Baptist
University, Dallas, Texas

YOUR OWN IDEAS

(3) one method/activity that builds international, multicultural understanding; and (4) at least one of the eight subtopics involves controversial, political, historical, economic, human, or environmental issues (Burke, 1992; Brown C, 1992; Brown J, 1992). Samples of thematic units for younger students appear in Figure 10-2 (and on video segment 7). A description of how to create thematic units as well as two samples for older students appear below.

Thematic units contain the same components as daily lesson plans (see Chapter 1) with the difference being that each step takes one or more days to complete. For example, you spend one day setting the objectives, allowing students to include goals they wish to reach. You and students spend a day locating resources, such as those listed in the sample resource lists in Figure 10-2. Students spend several days designing and writing about their projects and completing an in-depth study of a single topic, as the following example shows. This thematic unit was designed for upper elementary or middle school to develop their awareness of and sensitivity to other countries and cultural groups (Hadaway, 1992).

At the beginning of the year, students choose a country or city. This choice becomes the students' adopted "homes" for a specified period of time. Once new homelands are decided upon, the first project is to create or obtain a map depicting each student's new country of origin. This map is displayed in the classroom and referenced throughout the unit so students increase their geographical knowledge. During the first half of the unit, students cultivate and strengthen research skills as they are challenged to constantly stay abreast of information about their adopted countries. Students develop a scrapbook which describes their adopted "country," including its artwork, collages of places and facts about the country, newspaper clippings, magazine articles, travel brochures, geographical information, as well as economic, social, and political facts and figures. Each student's scrapbook is uniquely crafted and is a tool to enhance his/her speaking and listening skills, when it is presented to the class.

Students can also elect to participate in a poster contest. They prepare a poster and slogan which helps to sell *their* adopted homelands to the rest of the class. Students would use persuasive language and factual information to present each adopted country in a positive light.

Part 2 of the unit involves student selection from the following or similar options. Students can elect to perform a role play concerning their country. The role play would add to their study because students would have to create real-world families, schools, interests, events, and activities that occur in their countries. These elements will have evolved from within the cultural parameters of their countries, based on students' growing awareness of how geography and culture impact human behavior. A second option is for students to design a travel brochure for their country. They would become responsible for making an itinerary, transportation arrangements, and daily schedules. With this option, students would not only research the history and geography of their countries, but the exchange rates, weather conditions, and cultural and social expectations (see an excerpt from fourth grader Jon Young's travel brochure in Figure 10-3).

FIGURE 10-3
Fourth Grader's Travel Brochure

Jon Young

Come to Ft. Worth Tx. and have some fun. You mary want to go to the stock yards, there are lots of animals raised there. You might want to go to the Sheraton hotel. You also may want to go to Six Flags, I would go to the Hong Kong restaraunt. I would also go to the museums. We also have a Ft. Worth zoo. We also have a Tandy Center. We have a college called Texas Christian University. We also have a Trinity river. So come have some fun.

FIGURE 10-4

Thematic Unit on the Yellowstone Fires

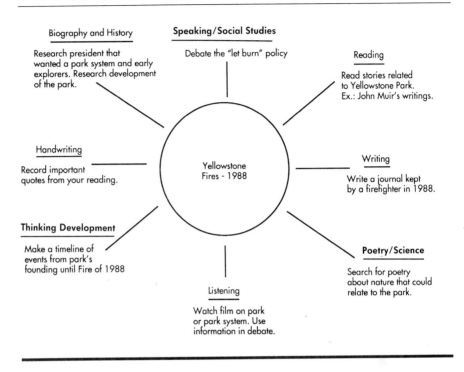

The second example of a thematic unit is offered by Wikstrom (1992) and demonstrates how political events, natural disasters, and ecological studies (such as the California earthquake of 1989, the earthwarming trend study, the fall of the Berlin Wall, or the devastation from the Yellowstone fires) and all current events can be used as thematic topics in grades kindergarten–8 (see Figure 10-4).

In this unit students debated on the "burn" policy of the National Park System and created films as well as poetry to depict their positions. They read books and articles about the people, politics, and events that were important in developing our first national parks. John Muir's *Yellowstone Park* was read aloud to provide background for one objective students chose, which was to create a timeline to depict changes in national parks. Poetry and reports (containing information from outside readings) were also written to portray students' predicted future of the National Park System. When this thematic unit was completed, students suggested other studies that they wished to pursue. Motivation was high, and education was no longer viewed as isolated studies of bits and pieces. The relationships across the curriculum had become the way of learning students preferred.

Additional information about constructing thematic units is available in *I've Got a Project* (by Geoff Ward); *Engaging Children's Minds: The Project*

Approach (by Lillian Katz and Sylvia Chard); *Children's Literature: Springboard to Understanding the Developing World* (by Nancy Pollette); and "Teaching Multicultural Literature" (by Donna Norton, *The Reading Teacher*, 44 (1), September 1990, pp. 31–40).

Topic Integration.   A fourth method of integration, created by Beck (1980), Beck, Perfetti, and McKeown, 1982, is called **topic integration**. Topic integration can be completed in your room without the assistance of other teachers. It *begins students' exploration of a topic in any subject by asking them to think about that topic's relationship to other disciplines.* Once these questions are listed, groups of students or individuals select a question they wish to answer. For example, a topic integration about the Civil War could include the following questions from many disciplines from which students select:

History: What was occurring? When?
Geography: What were the crucial states?
Economics: What products and concerns helped lead to the struggle?
Math: What was the population? Compare it with that of the present.
Civics: What were the implications for civil rights, then and now?
Science: What were the limitations of technology? Compare with those of the present.
Industrial Arts: What tools and weapons were available? Compare.
Home Economics: How might nutrition have related to the war?
Language Arts: Who were some of the important people of the time? What did they contribute?
Music: What tunes were popular at the time? How were they listened to? What instruments were most popular?
Art: What were the effects of the war on creative production?

Once selections and research to answer questions are complete, students report findings to the class.

Joining Bits of Information Guides.   This is the fifth integrative approach. This approach can also be conducted in your classroom without coordination between teachers. In this approach you provide a guide of the organizational structure of a content area textbook and a tradebook before students begin a study. Because these guides make schema and the organizational pattern followed by authors of both books explicit, students can compare their differing perspectives and thinking patterns while they read. Joining Bits of Information Guides can be written (as depicted in the listening guide of Chapter 4) or given verbally: "I want you to study the title of a writing; and the subheadings throughout the chapter. Notice how the subheadings are arranged, and pay attention to the author's use of sequence words as you read. In this textbook, the author uses time order to connect each of his paragraphs. Subheadings are arranged chronologically as well. In the accompanying tradebook you will read this week, notice . . .."

STRATEGIES THAT TEACH

BUILDING INDIVIDUAL LESSONS THAT FOLLOW THESE INTEGRATED APPROACHES TO INSTRUCTION

In this section of the chapter you will become familiar with lessons that use all five types of integration described above. You will learn how to integrate language arts through lessons that take only one day to complete and through week-long projects, museum packets, and newspaper units. In addition, Critical Thinking Activity 10 describes how students can enhance their abilities to think like social scientists, physical scientists, artists, and mathematicians.

CREATING INTEGRATIVE LESSONS THAT CAN BE IMPLEMENTED IN ONLY ONE DAY

M	T	W	Th	F

There are several strategies that integrate speaking, listening, reading, and writing activities into content area instruction on a daily basis. Harp (1989) recommends that you use integrative strategies, such as those that follow, about three hours weekly.

1. *Using Tradebooks to Build Content-related Reading, Writing, and Thinking Abilities.* This method is to use one or more of the tradebooks from Notecards 19–22 to introduce a textbook topic. This strategy might best be described through an example created by P. Smith (1992). Smith used Eric Carle's book, *A House for Hermit Crab* to introduce a science unit on sea life. (*A House for Hermit Crab* describes a crab who is not really a hermit; he loves having others around him and each of his neighbors performs an important function. For example, the snails clean around him. When he locates a bigger shell, he moves in and invites sponges, a clown fish, sand dollars, and an electric eel to live near him.)

Introduce the book by asking students to note the research facts Eric Carle listed on the inside front cover of *A House for Hermit Crab*. Then explain that writers often research a topic to include details in their writing. After you establish a factual background concerning hermit crabs, ask students to listen to the story of a specific hermit crab who decides to move. While you read, students can write the research facts that Carle includes in his story or complete another objective they set such as: (a) after the reading, students decide what help each of his neighbors might offer. They write a creative persuasive invitation for another animal to join the hermit crab, as shown in Figure 10-5; (b) students can read a second tradebook about an animal they choose and describe how that animal would benefit from befriending the hermit crab.

2. *Idea Maps.* Students read different tradebooks. Each constructs an idea map about his or her reading. Once the writings are finished, the class does a "read around." Classmates take notes and combine concepts as they listen or read peers' idea maps. To illustrate the diversity and depth of thought this integrated activity creates, two second graders' idea maps, following a unit on American leaders, appear in Figure 10-6.

FIGURE 10-5

Student Example Using Tradebooks in Conjunction with a Textbook Topic

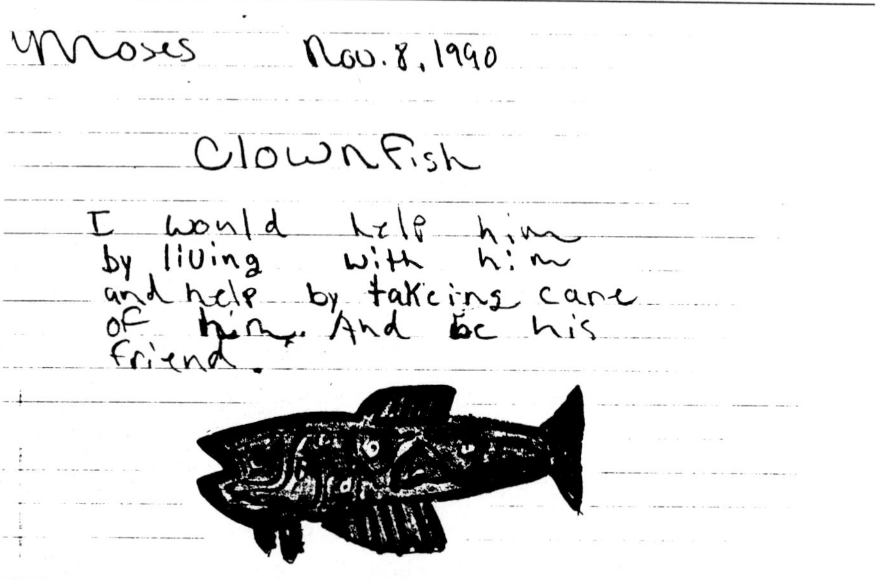

MMoses   Nov. 8, 1990

ClownFish

I would help him by living with him and help by takeing care of him. And be his Friend.

3. *Spin-Off Writing.* A third method to include language arts in content classes is called *spin-off writing.* In this lesson students pose questions about a content area topic that interests them. Students research that topic and then write their thoughts. They leave their reports on their desks. Students rotate from desk to desk, read classmates' reports, and add additional information to each report that they learned from their research. The last step in spin-off writing is for each student to return to his/her original writing, and reflect, accept, or reject additions the classmates made. Then students write the final revision and summary of their report.

4. *Lesson Agendas.* The first day you begin a new unit of study students select which pieces of information they want to learn, people responsible for obtaining each piece of information, and how much time they want to allocate to its study (Petry, 1992). A sample agenda format your class can use appears in Figure 10-7.

CREATING INTEGRATIVE LESSONS THAT BUILD STUDENTS' SKILLS THROUGH WEEK-LONG REPORT WRITING, DISPLAYS, AND PROJECTS

Oral and written reports and projects develop students' study skills, library reference abilities, and creative/analytical thinking abilities. Report writing activities can culminate in broadcast speeches (or displays with props), mini-books, magazine articles for the classroom library, legal briefs, and persuasive posters. As students work on their reports or projects, distribute Figure 10-8, the Progress Report Form. Students complete the form and specify deadlines for their presentations.

FIGURE 10-6
Second Graders' Idea Maps on American Leaders

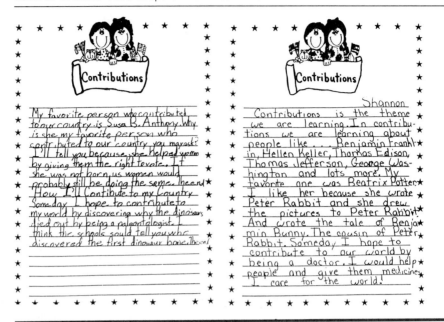

Contributions

My favorite person who contributed to our country is Susan B. Anthony. Why is she my favorite person who contributed to our country you may ask? I'll tell you because she helped women by giving them the right to vote. If she was not born, us women would probably still be doing the same. The end How I'll Contribute to my Country Someday I hope to contribute to my world by discovering why the dinosaurs died out by being a paleontologist. I think the schools sould tell you who discovered the first dinosaur bone. The end

Contributions

Shannon
Contributions is the theme we are learning. In contributions we are learning about people like... Benjamin Franklin, Hellen Keller, Thomas Edison, Thomas Jefferson, George Washington and lots more. My favorite one was Beatrix Potter. I like her because she wrote Peter Rabbit and she drew the pictures to Peter Rabbit. And wrote the tale of Benjamin Bunny. The cousin of Peter Rabbit. Someday I hope to contribute to our world by being a doctor. I would help people and give them medicines. I care for the world!

FIGURE 10-7
Sample Agenda Format

| NAME OF GROUP _____ |
| DATE, PLACE, TIME _____ |
| AGENDA _____ |
| CONVENER _____ |
| RECORDER _____ |
| EVALUATOR _____ |
| SUMMARIZER _____ |

AGENDA ITEMS	PERSONS RESPONSIBLE	TIME ALLOTED
NOTES:		

STRATEGIES THAT TEACH

Displays are particularly valuable. Students hang posterboards for the display's backdrop and create four tasks classmates are to complete relative to the topic.

During the drafting of their presentations, students revise and edit in pairs, until their final draft is submitted for a grade. When students decide their project is ready for assessment, they learn to balance "perfect" end-products with pressures of other, upcoming deadlines, which is a valuable real-world skill. The first time you provide this self-monitoring opportunity give a two-week range of dates within which you will receive final reports (e.g., you can complete your projects from February 3–17). About February 1st you intervene by modeling methods by which quality can be maintained as deadlines approach. You then grade projects on criteria you and students select in advance, with an example shown in Figure 10-9.

CREATING INTEGRATIVE LESSONS USING MUSEUM PACKETS

This lesson includes both written documents and objects or "artifacts," all of which must fit into a manilla envelope (10 × 13) provided to the students (Wyatt, 1992). Students illustrate their concept on the envelope. Choices in topics range from well-known to obscure figures in history, popular figures making history in their lifetimes, or current events.

The two museum examples featured in the above photographs are:

FIGURE 10-8
Progress Report Form

Project procedure checkpoints

- Topic selected and accepted by teacher.
- "What I know/What I want to know" completed.
- Reasons for study understood.
- Parents informed of project topic and deadline.
- Sources of information identified.
- Gathering of information commenced.
- Format for project report accepted by teacher.
- Study of relevant library files completed.
- Letters to outside sources of information drafted.
- Letters edited and sent.
- Notetaking system selected.
- Interviews arranged and proposed questions prepared.
- Information gathering completed and evidence for report identified.
- Headings for report selected.
- Outline of sections drafted.
- Introduction completed.
- Section 1 (etc.) completed.
- Illustrations selected or produced.
- Summary completed.
- Assembly of project completed.
- Oral report prepared.
- Reports presented or community project implemented.

Adapted and modified from an original prepared by Ward, Geoff. (1988) *I've Got a Project On.* Rozelle Australia: Primary English Teaching Association.

Lynette Woodard

Written Documents:
1. Certificate of birth
2. Letter to Coach Merian Washington

3. Flyer of the 1984 Olympics

4. Newspaper article

Significance:
Shows that she was born in Kansas.
Tells she played basketball at the University of Kansas and that she and Coach Washington were good friends.
Indicates that Lynette was on the Olympic team.
Tells that she was the first female player on the Globetrotters' team.

FIGURE 10-9
Criteria Upon Which Projects Will Be Graded

WHAT WE KNOW
WHAT WE WANT TO FIND OUT
WHAT WE THOUGHT/ WHAT WE STILL NEED TO KNOW
CATEGORIES OF INFORMATION WE EXPECT TO USE A. B. C. D. E. F.

5. Newspaper article

Says she was quitting the Globe-trotters.

6. Contract of sale

Shows that she and Coach Washington brought sports to Lawrence, Kansas.

Artifacts:
1. Actual photograph of Lynette

Significance:
Shows that she works with a girl's basketball camp.

2. Medal (a track medal belonging to the student).

Proves she won a Gold medal in the Olympics.

Sources Used:
Newman, M. *Lynette Woodard*. (1986).
Rosenthal, B. *Lynette Woodard: They First Female Globetrotter*. (1986).
Lawrence (KS) *Journal World*, "Woodard to Play in Italy," January 11, 1990.

Lewis and Clark

Written Documents:
1. William Clark's Journal
2. Meriwether Lewis' Journal

Significance:
A record of their travels.
Diary which tells about plans.

Artifacts:
1. Maps of entire route

Significance:
Locates the trail from St. Louis to the Pacific Ocean and important places along the trail.

2. Piece of four firs

Show that this helped to start trading with the West.

cont'd

"Museum Packets" contain a description of objects in the museum and an annotated bibliography for further information about these objects.

3. "Bags" (small plastic) of flour, sugar, coffee, and salt — Representing some of the supplies they took with them on the trip.
4. Horse (plastic) — Lewis and Clark got horses from the Shoshoni Indians to travel over the mountains.

Sources:
Blumberg, Rhonda. *The Incredible Journal of Lewis and Clark* (1987).
Hays, Wilma P. *The Meriwether Lewis Mystery* (1971).
Peterson, David. *Meriwether Lewis and William Clark: Soldiers, Explorers and Partners in History* (1988).

CREATING INTEGRATIVE LESSONS THAT USE NEWSPAPERS IN CONTENT STUDIES

Not only does the newspaper motivate students to read, write, speak and listen to other's points of view, it integrates language arts with social studies, students' life outside of school, and students' critical and creative thinking. There is something of interest for most students, and the reading level is not too difficult for remedial readers. The newspaper's vocabulary is practical. Words are those that students will use over and over throughout their lives. The stories are clear, concise, and simply written. Stories can be cut, pasted, and adapted in a variety of ways (e.g., headlines can be cut from stories and students write their own headlines about the stories, or

write stories from detached headlines). Subsequently, students compare their renditions to the original newspaper headline or story.

In many large cities, local newspapers publish booklets of additional classroom resources they provide for elementary/middle school teachers. For example, the staff of one large city newspaper located people in the community who are willing to pay for a year's newspaper subscription for a classroom. In this program, all students have a daily newspaper of their own. Your newspaper may provide a comparable service if you contact their Public Relations or Education Department. In addition, Newspaper Education Week usually occurs the second week in March, and the American Newspaper Publishers Association provides resources and activities which integrate the language arts into content area instruction at this time each year.

Students can also integrate the language arts with many content areas by creating their own classroom or school newspaper, with an editorial staff which selects individual pieces to publish.

CRITICAL THINKING ACTIVITY 10
Teaching Students to Think Like Scientists, Mathematicians, Social Scientists, and Artists to Increase Their Comprehension of Content Areas

Recommended Grade Levels: Fourth Through Eighth

"Birds of a feather flock together." When students understand differences between the format schema and thinking approaches content area experts use, they better comprehend that discipline. They are also able to identify and appreciate the writing formats different content areas tend to follow. To develop this knowledge, collect as many tradebooks, texts, and reference books as possible relative to mathematics, social science, science, or fine art (see Notecards 19–22). Students examine these books and make journal entries that provide evidence of the following thinking patterns.

NOTECARD 21: CHILDREN'S LITERATURE THAT ADDS TO STUDENTS' UNDERSTANDING OF MATHEMATICS

COUNTING/NUMBER

Counting House and other books by M. Anno
A Hundred Hugs by J. Cowley
Millions of Cats by W. Gag
So Many Cats by B. deRegniers
Too Many Hopkins and other books by T. dePaola
Count and See by T. Hoban
The Doorbell Rang and other books by P. Hutchins
One, Two, One Pair! by B. McMillan
Bunches and Bunches of Bunnies by L. Mathews
One, Two, Three by M. Brown
Two Ways to Count to 10 by R. Dee
How Many Snails by P. Giganti, Jr.
Farm Counting Book by J. Miller
Project 1-2-3 by E. Merriam
Count-A-Saurus by N. Blumenthal
Numbers: A First Counting Book by R. Allen
Count Your Way Through (Series) by J. Haskins
The Story of Numbers by R. Lauira

CLASSIFICATION

Caps for Sale by L. Slobodkin
Rub-a-Dub-Dub. What's in the Tub? by M. Blocksma
Odd One OuT by R. Peppe

PATTERNS

The Ants Go Marching by B. Freschet
If You Give a Mouse a Cookie by L. Numeroff
Sheep in a Jeep by N. E. Shaw
Shoes by E. Winthrop

MEASUREMENT

Who Sank the Boat? by P. Allen
The Enormous Watermelon by J. Parkes and M. Smith
How Much and How Many: The Story of Weights and Measures by J. Bendick
Think Metric! by F. Branley

(cont'd)

NOTECARD 21 (cont'd)

SHAPES

Three-D, Two-D by D. Adler
The Little Circle by A. Atwood
Three Sides and The Round One by M. Friskey
Shapes and Things and other books by I. Hoban
My Very First Book of Shapes by E. Carle
The Missing Piece by S. Silverstein
Straight Lines, Parallel Lines, and Perpendicular Lines by M. Charosh
Are You Square? by L. Kessler and E. Kessler
Angles Are as Easy as Pie by R. Froman
What is Symmetry? by M. Sitomer and H. Sitomer

TIME

One Bright Monday Morning by A. Baum and J. Baum
The Wednesday Surprise and other books by E. Bunting
Charlie Needs a Clock by T. dePaola

MONEY

If You Made a Million and other books by D. Schwartz
Making Cents by E. Wilkensen

A Chair for My Mother by V. Williams

FRACTIONS

Eating Fractions by B. McMillan
Less Than Nothing is Really Something by R. Froman

PROBLEM SOLVING

The First Book of Numbers and other books by V. Wilkes and H. Zeff
Adding Animals by C. Hawkins
Aha! Gotcha and other books by M. Gardner
The I Hate Mathematics! Book and others by M. Burns
What Do You Mean by Average? By E. James and C. Barkin
Sideways Arithmetic From Wayside School by L. Sachar

TEACHER RESOURCES

A Collection of Math Lessons from Grades 1–3 by M. Burns
Children's Mathematics Books by M. Matthais
Arithmetic Teacher (magazine)

1. *Social scientists tend to examine many primary sources and connect them to form a coherent interpretation of places, people, and eras.* Their format schemas and thinking tendencies are to follow deductive thinking, form questions, inference, narrate, summarize, and declare. Social scientists also tend to value information received through social interactions. They prioritize data according to the degree of national/social importance they hold. They enjoy planning for social gatherings more than other types of scientists. You can test students' predilection to social science thinking patterns (and develop them) by asking them to seek independent projects that answer questions relative to social issues. Then students analyze if they enjoyed their projects and if they exerted talents they value. Sample projects students can complete follow:

- Volunteer to role play characters and events in a current figure's life for a local drama society.
- Create a mural or a diorama of the life and times of a famous person to be displayed in a high school history classroom.
- Make a relief map of places important to a group of people to be displayed at a local supermarket. Synergetics (P.O. Box 84; E. Windsor Hill, CT 06028) has such projects in the form of commercially prepared materials. Their projects are *Joust For Fun*, about the Middle Ages, and American history from 1750–1959 called *Pioneer Skills. Joust For Fun* has 27 learning centers, 76 multidisciplinary activities, and culminates in a Knighting Ceremony and a Medieval Banquet. *Pioneer Skills* contains 20 projects where students practice survival skills.
- Evaluate multiple records of an event of interest to find hidden biases and share these in a letter to the editor of the local newspaper.
- Conduct a mock interview of a famous person for a schoolwide presentation on the day in history related to that person's life.
- Make timelines of events to be displayed in the school hallway.
- Create a personal timeline for one's life as demonstrated in Figure 10-10. This timeline could even project into the future and be stored for future reference in individual student journals.
- Respond to an article. Students locate an editorial or critical article appearing in a U.S. publication which focuses on some aspect of a country. Students form groups, analyze the major arguments of the author, and make a chart-diagram which ranks these points, and the evidence the author provides for each argument. Each student in the group writes his or her own *persuasive* response to the author's argument (agreeing or disagreeing), supported by their own evidence and facts. Each group sits as a discussion panel (one student as m.c. and mediator), and the class is the audience. At this point, the chart-diagram defining the original author's argument is presented. Next, each student displays his/her charted response (Fowler, 1992).

FIGURE 10-10
Sample for Teaching Students to Think Like Social Scientists

STRATEGIES THAT TEACH

WRITING ACTIVITY:

Create a personal timeline, telling important events for each year you've been alive.

RELATED BOOK:

The Hundred Penny Box

PROCEDURE:

PREWRITING:

1. Read and discuss the book with students. Focus attention on the fact that Aunt Dew had a special memory for each year of her life.

2. Ask students to think about each year of their lives and something special or significant that happened to them. Give them a prewriting timeline sheet and have them jot down events for each year of their lives. Have sudents take these sheets home and get help and suggestions from parents.
(The prewriting sheet would simply list the years, from birth year to present, and leave space after each year for notes.)

3. Cut white drawing paper into approximately 3″ × 11″ strips. Give each student three strips. Students can tape the strips together and divide the resulting strip into equal-sized sections, one section for each year of their lives. For example:

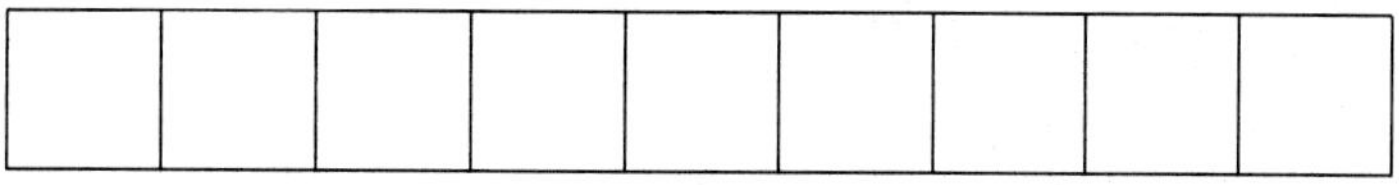

DRAFTING:

4. Have students design a timeline entry for each year of their lives. The entries should include the year, a written account of the event, and a photo or drawing which illustrates this event (when possible).

SHARING:

5. Have students share their timelines in small groups of 3–5 students. Post the timelines for further reading and sharing.

Created and used through courtesy of Dr. Vicki Olson, Augsburg College.

• Interior monologues or diaries. Students examine an expressive picture or read about a person living in another country, complete research, and construct a diary or interior monologue based on that picture/reading. (Interior monologues are use of "I" voice to tell a story of a person's experiences, hopes, and fears.) In doing an interior monologue, the student imagines how another person would tell his/her life story based on the evidence in the photograph and research. Avery (1989) reports how she demonstrated interior monologues for her class by debuting a unit on historical China dressed and speaking as the Chinese emperor who created the *Great Wall of China*. Similarly, students' interior monologues would be used to introduce new topics in content area studies.

- Create at least a three-paragraph long message one character would give another character that would change the ending to a historical account. After students present their messages to the class, students state why this message reflects the change they prefer.
- Make a symbol to characterize chapters and books they read. The symbol is to convey the personal significance the chapter or book held for the student. This meaning is to be conveyed in no more than three spoken or written sentences that are shared with parents and/or classmates.
- Write the speech for the ceremony where a main character in a current event or fictional/nonfictional chronicle was presented an award. Share this presentation at a Rotary Club or Lions Club meeting in the city.
- Describe how a historical character, scientist, or artist might respond to a current fictional/nonfictional crisis without lessening his/her believability. Students disclose the change the figure would implement, its effect on the historical outcome, why the change was made, and defend why the character would have responded in this way. Characters for this project are selected by younger classmates who admire each character suggested. Once the descriptions have been written, they are given to the younger classmates in oral and/or written form.
- Rewrite the most vivid section or the most important chapter of a book so a point of view other than the one taken by the author is represented. This rewriting is inserted at the appropriate point in the book so present and future schoolmates can read both accounts consecutively.
- Students predict the future for a living person described in a content area study. They dispense details of where he or she will be and with whom, and what will happen to this character ten years from today. Then students compare their registers with classmates.
- *Story-starters: Social Studies* (Pelican Publishers, Fairfield, CT) is a software package that provides story openings, clip art, and background information about scenes related to colonial America, the Civil War, and progresses in present day America.

   2. *Scientists in the physical sciences and professionals in the fine arts tend to use the thinking processes of defining, analyzing problems, formulating principles, observing, classifying, hypothesizing, verifying, and creating more than other professionals.* These researchers and artists rely upon information from sensory inputs, they access field trips, cope with elements, and experiment with balance and design more so than other professionals. Students learn and discern their scientific talents, as scientific thinkers, through the following activities:

- Weave cloth or make paper just as historical characters did and donate the finished product to a museum in the city.
- Do a scientific experiment associated with a literature selection and conduct that experiment for younger students whose teacher is reading that selection of literature to the class.
- Hypothesize about how a modern invention might have changed history. Once all students have completed their research and made predictions about the changes their invention would have caused, students group themselves by historical periods, e.g., students projecting changes upon the 1920s would group together, as would students projecting changes upon the 1930s, 1940s, etc. Each group would combine their projections and create a play that demonstrates the new era their combined inventions would have structured. This play is given for another class that is studying that group's historical period.
- Create a shadow puppet show of a story, using inventive lighting effects and ask for the audience's response. Many cities have summer playhouses and churches that allow teachers to borrow their stage during the school year. If such a facility is available, students must read about and learn to use actual lighting equipment before the shadow puppet show is performed. In the process they can determine many areas of interest in the fine arts.
- Graph a topic of choice. Students contact printing sources to enhance the quality of their rendition. They can learn to print with computer graphics, or work in conjunction with a high school that has print facilities. Once graphs are duplicated, students make them into overhead transparencies for class presentations.
- *Story Starters: Science* (Pelican Publishers) is a content-specific, graphics-adorned, "talking" word processing software package. Story openers, clip art, and background information concerning many topics in life science (plants, animals, ecology), physical science (matter and energy), earth science (earth, space, and weather), and the human body are available.

3. *Mathematicians tend to think sequentially more than other professionals.* They depend upon the thinking processes of averaging, computing, projecting, rating, bidding, totaling, allocating, estimating, and dividing. Activities that enable students to assess their mathematical interests and talents follow:

- Students create a barter system and it operates for one week. This system can be one similar to that used in pioneer life, which students come to understand from books on Notecards 19 and 21. Students determine the merits and deficit of bartering for modern America and use this experience to deduce mathematical principles.
- Make recipes in class (e.g., *Stone Soup*), and attend to measuring, fractions, and sequence. Students end the eating experience in a ten-minute write about their self-assessed competencies and preferences for math.

NOTECARD 22:   CHILDREN'S LITERATURE THAT ADDS TO STUDENTS' APPRECIATION OF THE FINE ARTS

The Pottery Place by Gail Gibbons
Scissor Cutting for Beginners by Hou-Tien Cheng
Crayons Paints by Henry Pluckrose
Ed Emberley's Big Red Drawing Book by E. Emberley
Draw 50 Cars, Trucks and Motorcycles by L. Ames
I Did It and other books by Harlow Rockwell
An Artist (Series) and other books by M. B. Goffstein
A Young Painter by Z. Zhensun and A. Low
Pencil, Pen, and Brush Drawings for Beginners and other books by H. Weiss
Picture This: A First Intro. to Painting by F. Woolf
A History of Art by M. B. Davidson

The Art of Colonial America and other books by S. Glubok
Discovering Design by M. Downer
The Magic of Holography by P. Heckman
Easy Origami by D. Nakano
Far Out: How to Create Your Own Star World by R. West
How to Be a Puppeteer by L. Boylan
The First Book of Rhythms and other books by L. Hughes
Do Your Ears Hang Low? and other books by T. Glazer
Golden Guitars, The Story of Country Music by G. Landon and I. Stambler
The Wheels of the Bus Go Round and Round: School Bus Songs and Chants by N. Larrick

(cont'd)

NOTECARD 22   (cont'd)

The Instruments of Music by G. Luttrell
Orchestranimals by I. Eugen and V. Van Kampen
Peter and the Wolf by S. Prokofiev
Mozart Tonight by J. Downing
On Their Toes by A. Morris
Bad News Ballet by J. Malcolm

Of Swans, Sugarplums and Satin Slippers by V. Verdy
My Ballet Class and other books by R. Isadora
The Metropolitan Museum of Art Activity by Osa Brown
Treasures to See: Museum Picture Book by L. Weisgard

- Students write a class "Choose-a-Path Adventure Story" with alternate series of events and various endings. *The Super Storytree* computer program (Brackett, 1989) assists students in doing so. Once the program is perfected, it is programmed into a computer in the school library so schoolmates can read the adventure story they devised. Through this activity students assess their abilities to work in mathematically oriented industries, computer driven jobs, as well as occupations that combine creative and highly technical skills.
- Contract to prepare graphs for community agencies.
- Study one of the mathematical topics from the booklist below and report intriguing facts to classmates:

> Crowley, Thomas H., *Understanding Computers*
> Hartung, Maurice L., *How to Teach Trig Slide Rules*
> Potter, Phillip J., *Slide Rule Problems*
> Sommers, Hobart H., *The Slide Rule and How to Use It*
> Tom, F. S., *How to Use the Chinese Abacus*
> Yoshino, Y., *The Japanese Abacus Explained*
> Anderson, Raymond W., *Romping Through Mathematics*
> Bell, Eric T., *Men of Mathematics*
> Bendick, Jeanne, and Levin, Marcia, *Take a Number*
> Bergamini, David, *Mathematics*
> Friend, J. Newton, *Numbers, Fun and Facts*
> Hogben, Lancelot, *Mathematics for the Millions*
> _____, *Mathematics in the Walking*
> _____, *The Wonderful World of Mathematics*
> Menninger, Karl, *Number Words and Number Symbols*
> Osen, Lynn M., *Women in Mathematics*
> Stokes, William T., *Notable Numbers*
> Stonaker, Frances B., *Famous Mathematicians*
> Valens, Evans G., *The Number of Things*

Now that you have read the approaches, daily lessons, week-long projects, and a critical thinking activity that integrate language arts across the curriculum, you can use the following Professional Development Opportunity to assess your ability to lead these actions in your classroom.

PROFESSIONAL DEVELOPMENT OPPORTUNITY
Assessing Your Ability To Integrate Language Arts Across the Curriculum

Many teachers value a standard by which they can rate their abilities to integrate the curriculum. The following checklist (see Figure 10-11) is such a standard and can assist you to move toward a curriculum in which students process content more deeply and use their communication tools to help others. At the end of this (your first) teaching year, (and in each subsequent year) answer "yes" or "no" to the following questions. You can return to the assessment in subsequent years to evaluate your growth.

FIGURE 10-11
Climbing the Ladder to Effectively Integrate Language Arts
and Content Disciplines

	THIS YEAR	199-	199-	199-
1. Have your students had the opportunity to use the interdisciplinary, parallel scheduling, thematic units, topic integration, and joining bits of information approaches to content area instruction at least once this year?				
2. Have you used a tradebook to introduce a new topic in a content area?				
3. Have students created at least one idea map, spin-off writing, lesson agenda, report, display, or museum packet this year?				
4. Have you exposed students to the newspaper and incorporated at least two of its sections into two content area classes?				
5. Did students ask to design their own thematic units at least once this year?				
6. Are topics of study within content areas chosen by the students and you?				
7. Are students finding that the end of one class period does not necessarily mean they have to stop their work? Are they more frequently using two back-to-back classes to become involved in integrative study from two or more subject areas?				
8. Are students beginning to rework, rewrite, or rehearse many times to satisfy themselves as they learn content area material?				
9. Are students asking fewer questions about what you expect, indicating that they are learning to set and meet more of their own objectives? Are you hearing fewer questions like: "How long does the report have to be?" "Do we have to make a semantic map first?" "How many books do I have to read before I can write my report?"				

	THIS YEAR	199-	199-	199-
10. When students need feedback, do they ask classmates to listen to their ideas and read their works?				
11. Do you wait until students have completed their content area assignments before you provide comments and assessments, or do you have ongoing conferences throughout the creating process?				
12. Have at least one of the class's projects been presented to the community and/or have students taken their content knowledge to improve some part of their community, e.g., contributed to the school library, local newspaper, or PTA/PTO?				

If you answered "yes" to all 12 you are an expert integrative teacher! If you said yes to all but one, you are 92 percent "perfect"; you've more than 75 percent mastery if you answered "yes" to 9 or 10 items; and, you can select several new methods in this chapter to boost your students' learning next year if you answered yes to 8 or fewer items.

TRY IT

1. Ask local restaurants or businesses to display some of your students' best content area reports. In contacting each business, ask if they would be willing to display five of your students' best typed reports if these reports were framed. You would change the reports once every grading period so the business would have new information for their customers.

2. Combine one of the integrated approaches with the Holiday Book list in BUILDING YOUR PROFESSIONAL PORTFOLIO. In this combination, plan an integrated study around a holiday theme. Members in your class can divide into grade-level groups with each group planning an integrated study of a different holiday. In this way when each group's integrated study is shared, you will have methods of building students' knowledge and communication skills for different holidays.

3. Choose one of the five approaches to integration that you prefer. Design a one-week integration of language arts with content instruction. In this plan incorporate one of the books from Notecards 19–22 and decide how the book can introduce or enrich a content discipline for your students. Decide if it should be read by all in conjunction with the textbook; or used as a resource for a selected student who wants more information about its subject. In a three–page position paper, defend the choices you made in each decision.

4. Discuss the importance of student choice in each of the approaches to integration. With a group of elementary or middle school students discuss methods of instruction they would like to add to their content areas that would call upon more of their interests and talents. Which of their ideas do you want to incorporate into your content area classes?

FOR YOUR JOURNAL

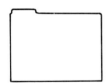

Daybooks are a very specific type of journal where, each day, students record their achievements, activities, and levels of effectiveness from their perspectives. Each student also records his/her interests, thoughts, and ideas generated during the day (Neve, 1992).

Daybooks are very similar to diaries except that they center around cognitive dilemmas students pose or challenges you give them, as opposed to insights they record concerning their personal lives. To demonstrate for yourself the effectiveness of daybooks (and to use as an end product to model for your students) make a daybook entry in your journal from the cognitive challenge posed for you in the next sentences. State your response to the following opinion of John Keats. He wrote: "I am convinced more and more, every day, that fine writing, next to fine doing, is the top thing in the world." Do you agree? Why? Why not? Return to this question each day for a week and add at least one new aspect to your answer each day. At the end of the week reflect on what the daybook revealed about your personal thinking style.

BUILDING YOUR PROFESSIONAL PORTFOLIO
Holiday Books to Recommend to Parents and to Use in Grades 4–8
Books for Special Occasions
For Use with Students in Fourth Through Eighth Grade

January

Martin Luther King Day:

About Martin Luther King Day by Mary Virginia Fox

New Year's Day:

A Holiday Book: New Year's Day by Lynn Groh
Happy New Year Around the World by Johnson

February

Valentine's Day:

Things to Make and Do for Valentine's Day by Tomie dePaola
Valentine Crafts and Cookbook by Gardner Quinn
Valentine's Day by Cass R. Sandak
Valentine's Day by Elizabeth Guilfoile
Happy Valentine's Day by Carol Burkin and Elizabeth James
St. Valentine's Day . . . by Clyde Robert Bulla
Valentine's Day by Joyce K. Kessel

March
St. Patrick's Day:

St. Patrick's Day in the Morning by Eve Bunting
Tim O'toole and the Wee Folk by Gerald McDermott
To Sing a Song as Big as Ireland by Nathan Zimelman
Daniel O'Rourke by Gerald McDermott

April
April Fools' Day:

Look Out, It's April Fools' Day by Frank Modell

Easter:

The Runaway Bunny by Margaret Brown
Easter by Jan Pienkowski
The Country Bunny and the Little Gold Shoes by D. Heyward
Silly Tilly and the Easter Bunny by Tana Hoban

May
Mother's Day:

Mother's Day by Mary Kay Phelan
The Mother's Day Mice by E. Bunting

Memorial Day:

Memorial Day by Geoffrey Scott

July
Fourth of July:

The Fourth of July by Mary Kay Phelan
America's Birthday by Tom Shachtman
The Glorious Fourth by Joan Anderson
The Fourth of July by Charles P. Grave
Parade by Tom Shachtman
Red Letter Days by Elizabeth Sechrist
Fireworks, Picnics, and Flags by James Cross Giblin
America's Birthday, The Fourth of July by Tom Shachtman

September
Labor Day:

Labor Day by Geoffrey Scott

October
Halloween:

Sir Halloween by Jarrold Beim
Wobble the Witch Cat by Mary Calhoun
What Does A Witch Need? by Ida Delage

STRATEGIES THAT TEACH

Trick or Treat Trap by Dirk Zimmer
Hubknuckles by Emily Herman
The Halloween Party by Lonzo Anderson
The Pumpkin Smasher by Anita Benarde

Columbus Day:

Columbus Day by Paul Mier

November

Thanksgiving:

Molly's Pilgrim by Barbara Cohen
Daisy's Crazy Thanksgiving by Margery Cuyler
The Thanksgiving Story by Alice Dalgliesh
Cranberry Thanksgiving by Wende and Harry Devlin
Naughty Little Pilgrim by Wilma Hays
Speak Up, Edie! by Johanna Johnston
Turkeys, Pilgrims, and Indian Corn by Edna Barth
A Holiday Book: Thanksgiving by Lee Wyndham
Squanto by Cathy Dubowski
The Harvest Feast by William Harper
Thanksgiving Is For What We Have by Bettina Petterson
Chester Chipmunk's Thanksgiving by Barbara Williams
The Thanksgiving Treasure by Gail Rock
Fowl Play, Desdemona by Beverly Keller
Happy Thanksgiving by Carol Barking and Elizabeth Jones
Thanksgiving Feast and Festival by Mildred C. Lackhardt
It's Time for Thanksgiving by E. H. Sechrist and J. Woolsey
Thanksgiving by Margaret Baldwin
The Thanksgiving Book by Lucille Recht Penner

December

Christmas:

The Story of Holly and Ivy by Rumer Godden
The House Without a Christmas Tree by Gail Rock
Countdown to Christmas by Bill Peet
Merry Christmas, Amelia Bedelia by Peggy Parish
Plants of Christmas by Hal Borland
Holly, Reindeer, and Colored Lights by Edna Barth
46 Days of Christmas by Dorothy Gladys Spicer
Christmas Tales by James and Lillian Lewick
Christmas on the Prairie by Joan Anderson
Christmas by Cass R. Sandak
Merry Christmas by Robina B. Wilson
Talk Joy by Tasha Tudor
The Sugar-Plum Christmas Book by Jean Chapman
The Christmas Book by James Reeves

Christmas Trees by Dorothy Patent
Christmas by D. J. Heroa
M&M the Santa Secrets by Pat Ross
The Boy of the Bells by Carly Simon
Gus was a Christmas Ghost by Jane Thayer

Books About Holidays

Kindergarten Through Third Grade

Why It's a Holiday by Ann McGovern
Once Upon a Holiday by Lilian Moore
Fiesta by June Behrens
The Holiday Handwriting School by Robin Pulver

Fourth Through Eighth Grade

Holidays by Bernice Burnett
Spring Holidays by Sam and Beryl Epstein
Patriotic Holidays and Celebrations by Valorie Grigol
Winter Festivals by Mike Rosea
The First Book of Holidays by Bernice Burnett
Holidays Around the World by Joseph Gaer
The Book of Holidays by J. Walker McSpadden
Holiday Hullabaloo! by Richard Churchill
Fiesta Time in Mexico by Rebecca and Judith Marcus
A Parade of Soviet Holidays by Jane Watson
Let's Talk About The Jewish Holidays by Dorothy Krifke
Festivals and Celebrations by Roland Auguet

Books About Birthdays

Kindergarten Through Third Grade

Happy Birthday by Gail Gibbons
The Festive Year: Birthday Present by Catherine Stock

Fourth Through Eighth Grade

Everybody Has A Birthday by Caroline Arnold
Birthdays: A Holiday Book by Patterson
Candles, Cakes, and Donkey Tails by Lila Perl
Happy Birthday Around The World by Lois S. Johnson

STRATEGIES THAT TEACH

11 Creative Expression: One Step Beyond Integration

Participating in a classroom play enables students to grasp the aesthetics of an excellent story.

Creative thinking depends upon working at the edge more than the center of one's competence

—Perkins, 1984

As students integrate the language arts with content area knowledge, their creative thinking begins to expand. Students increase their depth of information, exercise options, examine issues with differing ideas and perspectives, and practice flexibility, which are some of the most important components of creative thinking. Students need your guidance, however, before they can consistently use creative thinking tools to make a variety of new connections in real-world situations. Through this chapter you will learn how to promote students' imaginative language, creativity, and inventive expressions, important tools in building original ideas. You will also learn how to support students as they create and make discoveries, which are provinces that are unique to humans.

By the end of this chapter, you will know:

1. What creativity is, why it is important, and how it can be increased in your students;

2. Four lessons that develop students' inventiveness;

3. How to teach predictive thinking, poetry, and plays so they build students' ingenuity.

THEORETICAL FOUNDATION
WHY STUDENTS NEED TO DEVELOP CREATIVE THINKING

There are several reasons why students need to think creatively and require your help to do so. First, creativity does not mature naturally without instruction. As demonstrated in a longitudinal study of kindergarten students, 84 percent of all kindergartners ranked high in aptitude for creative thinking. By second grade, however, when these students had not received any instruction to expand this creative potential, only 10 percent sustained even a significant level of inventive capacity. It seems that unless you devote special attention to creativity in your language arts program, most students will stop their exploratory thinking processes as soon as they create their first answer. Most students will quickly come to accept that *there is only one right answer, and that it is very easy to be wrong.* Their underlying belief is that someone else knows all the answers and they don't. They stop trying to find their answers because their answers are only valuable if they fill someone else's (usually their teacher's) blank. As Paul Messier, Department of Education, observed, before five-year-old children go to school, if they want to cut a string, they cut it wherever they decide. After they come to school, however, they begin to realize that there is only *one* middle. These same children will work feverishly to cut each of the subsequent strings they decide to cut exactly where all strings are supposed to be cut, in the middle, of course (P. Messier, personal communication).

A second reason to increase students' creative thinking is that such augmented abilities enhance their abilities to solve complex problems in life. Unless you assist them to recognize the complexities and relationships between seemingly disparate ideas, many things outside of school will convince them that answers to problems should be simple; that problems do not demand deep, creative reflection. For example, students see that "all you need is one grand shoot-out at the O. K. Corral at high noon and all this complex fuss that they have watched for three hours will be over [and so to should all problems be instantly and simply solved]" (Stuart and Graves, 1987, p. 23).

Third, students need models of how to use creative thinking effectively. In their lives they hear and see numerous examples of language as it functions to criticize, protest, and punish. They have fewer exemplars of it being used to propagate effective ideas, establish long-term innovations, and project new visions. Because they have had infrequent experiences of creative thinking students can assume that criticizing someone else's ideas is a high, "adultlike" level of thinking and communicating. Through your instruction, however, students can discover how their creative thinking and innovative expressions can construct solutions for themselves and others. Through the language lessons in this chapter, students can learn how to generate ideas and incubate ideas until they crystallize into a workable plan of action. When students engage in these activities, they will also learn to use their relaxed mental states, access their imaginations, and complete positive mental images that enhance their depth of understanding.

Last, developing students' creative thinking increases pleasure in, and the amount of, learning. As an example, one group of seventh graders field-tested the problem-solving and decision-making activities to come in Chapter 12. After eight weeks of instruction, these students describe how their future classes could be improved. While they requested that schools continue to develop decision-making and problem-solving abilities, they also wanted activities that allowed them to be creative. They wanted to enact situations in their lives about which they wished to gain more understanding. They reasoned that such experiences are more challenging and meaningful because they enable "desks to be moved back. We can get involved in real-life through hands-on thinking."

You might not have expected these 12–13 year olds to have wanted more opportunities to develop their creative thinking and to be inventive. However, students' needs for such sensory, creative learning is becoming increasingly evident at all grade levels (Adams, 1986; Collins, 1991a, 1991b, 1992, in press).

ADVANTAGES OF INSTRUCTION THAT DEVELOPS CREATIVE THINKING

Creativity is *the act of producing original ideas and products.* Creativity springs from (a) a seemingly simple and surprising event; (b) an ability to generate and recognize undervalued ideas; (c) avoiding joining the crowd; (d) redefining problems; (e) insights; (f) beliefs; (g) ambiguity; (h) a willingness to excel and grow (Sternberg & Lubart, 1991).

While creativity has been a topic of interest to educational and psychological researchers for decades, there has been a phenomenal growth in knowledge in the last forty years (Travis, 1992). For example, during the 100-year period from 1855 to 1955, only 10 studies of creativity and its development were conducted in the world. From 1956–1966, ten additional studies were completed. Now, more than 250 studies are completed each year (see *Annual Review of Psychology*). The previous void of knowledge concerning the nurturing of creative processes helps to explain why teachers in the past did not focus upon developing creative thinking. Fortunately, you can take our new understandings and elevate your students' abilities to innovatively contribute to our world.

Research indicates that creative people maintain high standards, accept confusing uncertainties, and view the higher risks of failure as part of the process for monumental accomplishments. Highly creative individuals also approach what they perceive to be important aspects of their work with considerable intensity and engagement. They exhibit an internalized license to challenge the conventional, and to express their own insights frequently and fervently. As Einstein reported, fantasy was more important than genius in his work. Similarly, Tesla, the inventor of the fluorescent light, the A.C. generator, and the "Tesla" coil, stated that he used creative images and language constantly, to "project before my eyes a picture complete in every detail of a new machine I want to create." He tested devices mentally, by having them run for weeks, after which time he would examine them thoroughly for signs of wear "before he began to create his invention through work and oral/written words!" (Adams, 1986, p. 36).

In the next section of this chapter you will discover how your instruction can develop students' creative thinking. Without such practice opportunities, students cannot estimate the probable consequences of creative actions. Moreover, without this ability and the supports of your language arts program, many pupils will continue to talk and think like their peers, and squelch their creative ideas before they are expressed. Further, because creative ideas and acts are often imperfect, many pupils will never have the courage to project themselves creatively without you. The fear of making a mistake (unless eliminated through the lessons that follow) could keep many students, even into their adult lives, from fashioning solutions and advancing their ideas through writing and speaking.

PUTTING THEORY INTO PRACTICE
HOW TO INCREASE STUDENTS' CREATIVITY

Before you implement the activities and lessons in this chapter you and your students may enjoy assessing your present level of creative thinking by taking the Remote Associations Test (Mednick & Mednick, 1967) that follows. You can also use the following items as a pre- and posttest for your students, but do not allow them to see correct answers until the posttest is taken.

Read the three words in each line and think of a fourth, that when added, gives new meaning to each of the words: e.g., river note   blood _____

This "associative" word answer is "bank." Now complete the five lines of the Remote Associations Test in the same fashion:

1. board   duck   dollar   + _____

2. file   head   toe   + _____

3. boiled   lid   flower   + _____

4. chicken   malaria   butter   + _____

5. class   stage   soccer   + _____

You should not check your answers until you have finished reading this chapter and learned how to mature you and your students' ingenuity. When you retake the Remote Associations Test, compare how much your creative abilities were enhanced by learning strategies of innovative thinking. If you answer all items correctly, you are among the top 10 percent of creative people. If you score four items correctly, you are among the top 25 percent of adults in your ability to generate new ideas. If you get 2 or 3 correct, you are normal in your creative capacity. If you get 0–1 correct, you are below average, but you can change that. (Answers on page 371.)

Once students have taken this pretest, there are several components of creative thinking, amenable to instruction, that you can teach:

I. Creative and Innovative Thinking Tools
    A. SCRAMBLIN'—the nine creative thinking processes
    B. Estimating
    C. Anticipating, forecasting, and predicting
    D. Taking a calculated risk
    E. Brainstorming and synthesizing
II. Generative Processes
    A. Generating hypotheses
    B. Planning
        1. Selecting strategies to fulfill a specific goal, product, or process by organizing time, materials, and effort
    C. Composing and building
III. Innovative Thinking
    A. Exploring a subject
    B. Mulling over a subject
    C. Making discoveries about form, rules, restrictions, values, and ideas

FIGURE 11-1
Steps in Brainstorming

NAME _____ DATE _____

1. *All ideas are welcomed.* No one says any idea is not good. No one needs to worry that their ideas are not good enough. All ideas help.
2. *Give as many ideas as you can.* The longer the list, the more likely it contains a number of workable ideas.
3. *Add to each other's ideas.* People can help each other.
4. *Think of crazy and new ideas.* One idea can trigger a useful idea for someone else. Problems are often seen in new ways as a result of a new thought.
5. *Record each idea and combine ideas at the end.* After all ideas have been given, combine and select the best.

INTRODUCING STUDENTS TO CREATIVE THINKING

Once you explain one of the above creativity components, create opportunities for students to initiate its use as they invent an idea alone and in groups. You can also alert them to the fact that the most consistent need for creative thinking is when impassess are reached. Approaching such tasks with a creative frame of mind and the processes of creative thinking often produce extremely successful solutions. Brainstorming, brainwriting, consensus building, humor, and problem definition are activities that prepare students for deeper applications of creative thought that are called upon in the more intensive lessons on pages 351–359.

Brainstorming. Brainstorming is *a thinking strategy to stimulate creative thinking by speaking or writing as many ideas as come to mind about a topic.* You teach brainstorming by asking students to follow the steps in Figure 11-1. Preschool through Grade 2 students can practice brainstorming by sharing their predictions about the ending of a book. To do so, select a book such as *Little Rabbit's Loose Tooth* by Lucy Bate to which students can easily relate, e.g., the little rabbit had a dilemma of not knowing what to do with her tooth after it had been pulled. You ask them to pay attention to how their minds work as they think and share as many ideas as they can about what the rabbit could do. After ideas have been listed, ask students to describe if they enjoyed thinking in this way and why. Also list their descriptions as of how creative thinking is different from simply remembering. Ask them when they likely will need to think creatively in their lives.

Continue instruction by brainstorming the endings of the books listed below that you read aloud on consecutive days. Also, when students begin to initiate creative thinking unprompted in other subjects acknowledge which of the eleven thinking processes they used (see p. 350) and praise them: *Animals Should Definitely Not Wear Clothing* (Jude Barrette); *The Very Busy Spider* (Eric Carle); *Little Polar Bear* (Hags de Beer); *The Day the Goose*

FIGURE 11-2
Additional Lessons for Brainstorming Skills

Divide the class into small groups of two or three students. A topic is chosen, e.g., *Candy, Fiber, Elephant,* etc. Each group is to answer the following questions concerning the topic.

1. What is it a kind of?
2. What are the kinds of it?
3. What is it a part of?
4. What are the parts of it?
5. What is it a stage of?
6. What are the stages of it?
7. What is it a product of?
8. What are the products of it?

All answers are acceptable. The purpose of the exercise is to require the students to think about the topic, approaching it from several different perspectives, and build brainstorming skills.

Created by and used by permission of Dr. P. Travis, Southwestern Oklahoma State University

Got Loose (Reeve Lindergh); *Oscar Mouse Finds a Home* (Moira Miller and Maria Majewska); *Obadiah Coffee and the Music Contest* (Valerie Poole); and *Stories to Solve* (George Shannon).

Third through eighth grade students can be taught the steps to brainstorming through the activities suggested in Figure 11-2. They can also learn ways in which brainstorming is used in the business world. Once students have used the process several times as a large class, ask them to brainstorm silently on their own for a few minutes, before they meet in small groups to combine brainstorming ideas. Inquire as to why pausing before important meetings to perform a mental brainstorm can be a valuable tool for them as adults.

Brainwriting.   Brainwriting is a modification of brainstorming (Rodriguez, 1983). In brainwriting, students are divided into small groups. Each student writes his/her ideas about a topic for which they wish to compose. When the group comes to a lull in brainwriting, one group member places his/her paper in the center of the table and takes another student's list, adding more ideas to that student's list. At the end of each brainwriting session, students return to their original brainwriting where classmates have assisted their thinking by adding their ideas.

Consensus Building.   As your students feel more comfortable with brainstorming, you model **consensus building** (*the ability to bring all members of a group to an agreed upon creative plan of action*). The cardinal principle of consensus building is that group members continue to generate plausible alternatives until a plan is satisfactory to every member. Exercises for consensus building require group members to agree on a short list of alternatives derived from the longer brainstorming list. Students practice trying to reach consensus as one of their group members takes field notes. Once agreement is reached, students list successful strategies they used to build consensus by referring to the field notes this member took concerning the consensus process. Then they generate principles that should be followed in the future whenever situations arise where a consensus must be reached.

Humor. The next activity that will enable students to become more comfortable with creative thinking is to introduce a study of humor, one of the purer forms of creative communication. Humor is defined as *a quality that appeals to a sense of the incongruous.* Students who understand types of humor and incongruities expand their ability to express their own creative ideas. After you have introduced the following types of incongruities, ask students to point them out in future classes when they appear in student writings and literature, or arise in discussions. You may also teach mini-lessons where students write or devise a spoken form of the following types of humorous incongruencies:

1. *Irony:* events turn out opposite from what is expected.
2. *Slapstick:* very physical comedy, such as having objects collide in strange ways.
3. *Contrast:* emphasizing differences between characters and events.
4. *Just desserts:* unusual things happen that result in wicked or foolish characters getting what they deserve.
5. *Exaggeration:* stretching the truth about someone or something.
6. *Word play:* using words in unusual or incorrect ways on purpose.

Problem Defining. Problem defining is *the generative processes of moving from disarray to order; and from misunderstanding to resolution* (Sternberg & Lubart, 1991). Students who learn to seek out and define problems become significantly stronger thinkers and communicators than students who are not taught problem defining skills (Collins, 1991a; Collins Block, in press b). An effective instructional strategy to present problem defining is to avoid telling students what problem they are going to solve and to refrain from offering suggestions. Rather, design a lesson where you ask students to share aspects of human behavior that they would like to better understand. At first students may not say anything as they may never have been asked to define problems for themselves. But as you wait, eventually, one student will speak up, and then another. With the ice broken, most students are anxious to contribute and to create a problem which they are curious to solve, e.g., Why do parents make us dress up on special occasions? Why do some siblings fight a lot while others don't? How do we choose our friends? With these problems defined you can teach the lessons on pages 354–363 to develop students' creative thinking about these problems they identified.

In brief, creative thinking is the sum of thinking processes that produce original ideas and products. It often requires constructive risk-taking, and thinking in new ways. There are many reasons to teach creativity, including the need for your students to (1) generate new ideas which will make a major contribution for their future professional success; and (2) learn creative thinking tools, such as innovative thinking processes. Brainstorming, brainwriting, consensus building, humor, and problem defining are instructional approaches that cultivate a positive climate for creativity. You can also test students' level of creative thinking.

In the next section of this chapter you will learn daily lessons that expand students' creative thinking: creative dramatics; puppetry; the nine innovative thinking processes (SCRAMBLIN'); and personal, direct, symbolic, and nature analogies.

STRATEGIES THAT TEACH
WAYS OF TEACHING CREATIVITY

Through the above approaches, students will feel more comfortable with the spontaneity and irregular pattern with which creative ideas emerge. With this comfort level in place, students can develop tools that make creativity more durable and resilient. The following lessons build these tools.

CREATING LESSONS FOR ELIMINATING BLOCKS TO CREATIVITY

M	T	W	Th	F

This lesson alerts students to the barriers that limit their creativity. It also provides methods by which they can overcome them.

Thinking Objective Presented to Students

Students will learn eight ways to increase their creativity and they will measure their success through comparisons of pre- and postinstructional drawings.

Dispelling Misconceptions

Teacher: You may believe that you are not creative, that you were born that way and you can never change it. Today you will learn that this is not really true—everyone can learn to be more creative. You will learn eight ways to do so and you can use these methods throughout your life.

Thinking Guide Instructions

Ask students to draw a piece of artwork and collect these pieces. Then read and discuss each element on Thinking Guide 11-1. With each thinking process cited on the guide, give an example of a time in your life when this process either increased or decreased your success. Then ask students to share illustrations from their lives. Classmates use the four thought processes at the bottom of Thinking Guide 11-1 to suggest what could have happened to make less successful outcomes more positive.

THINKING GUIDE 11-1
Eliminating Blocks to Creative Thinking

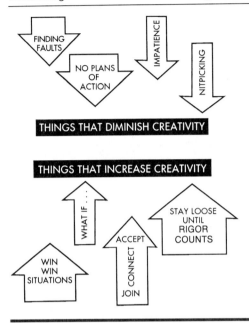

Students Complete the Objective

Students apply the four positive processes independently as they read and create chapter titles for *Jumanji* (Van Allsburg, 1985), *Sixth Grade Secrets* (Sachar, 1989), *Stranger at Winfield House* (Yeo, 1989), *The Tricksters* (Radin, 1956), *Fallen Angels* (Myers, 1988), *Call It Courage* (Sperry, 1940), and *Tuck Everlasting* (Babbitt, 1975). They compare titles in response groups and the creative processes they used in their constructions. Then, either in small groups or independently, students reorder and reconceptualize ideas using the four positive processes in Thinking Guide 11-1 to solve "two-minute mystery" stories. Finally, they produce a play using books whose endings they are not allowed to read. After the plays are presented to the class, students compare their renditions to those of the authors. Once these four lessons have been completed students draw a second picture without being told that they will compare it to their pre-lesson drawing. If students have grown in their levels of creative thinking, these processes will transfer to their drawings. Ask students to write comments relative to their growth in creativity that resulted from this lesson.

CREATING LESSONS THAT TEACH CREATIVE DRAMATICS

Creative dramatics is *the creation of a story based on experiences, literature, history, current events, content area knowledge, and/or children's imaginations. It is the acting out and revealing of one's imagination by becoming someone or some-*

thing else. Creative dramatics uses creative expression in movement and voice to enhance, extend, and deepen conceptual knowledge, and to empathize with character traits and objectives. It allows students to learn physically, kinesthetically, mentally, and emotionally. In addition it matures vocabulary, volume, tempo, pitch, and clarity in speech. Creative drama also integrates creativity, speaking, and listening with art. It can represent the human being's interpretation of life, expressed in a way that can be universally recognized and understood. At its best, creative drama can become students' innovations to depict real-world conflicts in life, and offer young players their first tastes of the magic and make-believe that their imaginations and the theater provide.

Creative dramatics, improvisations, role plays, and puppetry offer students the opportunity to step into someone else's shoes for a while and to imagine the motivations and feelings of others. This builds students' abilities to "people read" (Lundsteen, 1989), adjust their behaviors to others, and improve thinking and working in group settings.

Drama should also be used in your language program because it is therapeutic; it enables students to assume responsibility for group decisions, and is the most highly socialized art form we have (Creativity Book, 1990). It assists students to become proficient talkers and improves their spontaneous oral composition abilities (Lundsteen, 1989). While much has been said about the creative and critical thinking abilities drama stimulates, of equal importance is the opportunity it affords students to feel and release emotions. Because of this, emphasis should be placed upon the beauty of communicating, feeling, and thinking, with limited attention given to not forgetting even one word in a script (McCaslin, 1990).

Creative dramatics exists on a continuum from interpretive to improvisational activities, but it is *not* the memorization of someone else's script performed before an audience. You play an important role in providing opportunities for students' creativity and in supporting its components as they emerge. You encourage the evolution of each student's unique and most effective methods of creative expression, whether they surface through body language, vocal features, role plays, or acting.

The following activities provide a gradual progression of lessons that ease students into thinking dramatically with less difficulty. These lessons stretch imaginative thinking through pretending, and generative thinking through improvisations, role plays, and puppetry.

Imaginative Thinking and Improvisation.   The purpose of improvisations and imagination building is to mature students' ability to visually image unknowns, and to break away from accepted answers and trains of thought. Cultivating such abilities is important because it characterizes adults who think beyond usual parameters, and approach situations with unrestrained outlooks. Maurice Sendak (1989) stated it well: "The qualities that make for excellence in children's literature can be sweepingly summed up in a single word: imagination. And imagination as it relates to the child in my mind is synonymous with fantasy. Contrary to most of the propaganda in books for the young, childhood is only partly a time of innocence. It is, in my opinion, a time of seriousness, bewilderment, and a good deal of suffering. . . . Imagination for the child is a miraculous, free-wheeling device he uses to course his way through the problems of everyday life" (p. 3).

Providing opportunities for students to pretend they are book or historical characters they admire is a first step in developing imaginative thinking. To begin, students need to practice "mental computing," and "wondering," e.g., ask students to line up alphabetically by first name for lunch. To ponder things that happen that they don't understand ask students to complete:

> *A Past Event*
>   I wonder _____
> *A Present Event*
>   I wonder _____
> *A Future Event*
>   I wonder _____

Students continue to practice imaginative thinking by replicating actions in their minds of a character they've read. Then students imagine events they did not read that this character would have likely engaged. Such pretending is based on interpreting and inferencing from facts read. After they have invented their imaginary event, they describe it orally, in writing, or through **improvisations** (*opportunities to investigate possibilities through movement interacting with dialogue*, McCaslin, 1992). Students will rely upon their past experiences and judgment to orchestrate these make-believe worlds. They defend the logic behind their improvisations with you before they are shared in class. A book that works well for subsequent improvisations is Judith Viorst's, *If I Were In Charge of The World and Other Worries*. Students stimulate imaginative thinking as they emulate the changes Judith Viorst suggested and then add their own.

Students can also pretend they are people involved in important historical events. They reenact the event adding details not present in material studied.

THE CHALLENGE OF DIVERSITY

Gifted students often enjoy increasing the difficulty of this assignment. They engage in in-depth research concerning one historical figure who was (and was not) a contemporary to the historical figure other classmates study. These students then pretend conversations between their historical figures. They discuss their philosophies as related to problems other classmates submit. When these students ponder such "what if's" about life, they significantly augment their imaginative thinking.

Roleplay. Roleplay is a second step to develop generative thinking abilities. When students enact problematic events that could occur, their likelihood for success in such situations increases (Collins, 1991a; Collins Block, in press). You can reduce the risk-taking involved in roleplays by

FIGURE 11-3
Structure Students Can Follow to Create Their Own Dramas

Roles or identity; place or situation; focus or issue; which order? To help children create a workable drama, have them consider the three strands which combine to make the whole.		
1 ROLES or Identity the desire: People:	2 PLACE or Situation: in a place:	3 FOCUS or Issue: involved with others:
Who are you?	Where are you?	What are we concerned about?
A solider:	at a railway station:	becoming anxious because of the lateness of the train.
A farmer:	at a market:	complaining to others of the price of fertilizer.
Pirates:	on a ship:	lost.

pairing students. Pairs describe difficult situations they face, and roleplay one each member faces. To increase compassion and empathy, students can reverse roles and serve as one of their own adversaries. These reverse roleplays enable students to see an opponent's point of view more clearly, e.g., enact a conversation between parents and the student, with the student playing the role of the parent. For example, Ms. Cynthia Randolph, a middle school teacher, asked seventh graders to roleplay difficult interactions involving adults. She discovered that "When students play their parents (in roleplaying) they reveal the lack of respect they feel. According to their rendition, parents fail to ask questions; instead they jump to some incorrect conclusions. Through my students' roleplays I became a better parent and understood my own family better. As a teacher, roleplays enlightened me to my students' important points of view concerning family relationships" (C. Randolph, personal communication).

Students can also roleplay a piece of literature from the villains or minor character's point of view. Roleplay lessons increase in difficulty when students (1) roleplay actual past events or readings; (2) move this enactment into a current setting that involves unresolved issues in our society; and (3) recast the events into a probable future setting.

The structure in Figure 11-3 can guide students through the major strands they will orchestrate when they create original dramas. The two major purposes for producing a play are that it is one of the few activities that is likely to end in a celebrative experience (see Professional Portfolio (p. 372) for plays that students can create). Computers can also assist students' scriptwriting. *Play Write* (IBM) is a software package that provides a format for puppet and play scripts. This software enables students to easily set up a professional script. *Play Write* also assists students to understand spoken and written language. *Puppet Maker* (IBM) and *Puppet Plays* (IBM) are software that guide students to make their own puppets and provide hints for their productions.

Puppetry. Another type of drama is the use of puppets. Puppetry gives students a comfortable vehicle to project their creative expressions, images, and their imagination before others. Puppets are a powerful tool in providing flexible thinking as they enable students to be as creative or as structured as they desire. Young children enjoy talking through their puppets. These experiences enable them to understand the way authors "talk through words." Samples of puppets appear in Figure 11-4.

To implement this lesson, allow students to select a personal situation, idea from literature, or current issue they wish to improve through their imaginative thinking. Then they make their puppet of choice.

CREATING LESSONS TO TEACH SCRAMBLIN'
Nine Key Thinking Processes in Innovative Thinking

Many factors that are crucial to innovative performances have not yet been discovered (Adams, 1990). It has been proven, however, that the ability to sense problems is a critical ingredient, as is the ability to take care of needs and difficulties. Essentially, to be most ingenious, students must learn to "scramble" ideas, hence the title of this lesson, which is the acronym for the nine thinking processes of innovative thinking. You will teach these processes to students individually, even in nine separate lessons if you desire. Then you will introduce activities where students will self-initiate using the mnemonic aid of the acronym SCRMABLIN' to use the innovative thinking processes interactively. A description of these nine processes follows, as well as a sample method that students can use to elicit each process say:

1. *Substitute thinking processes:* Assists someone to reach a resolution by putting one idea in place of a first solution. A method of eliciting *substitute thinking* is to ask someone else's advice. In so doing, you will likely reason with their thinking pattern, which is likely to be different from yours. Another method is to think what a person you admire would do if he/she was in your situation. For example, you are not doing well on your weekly math tests, and you want to make good grades each week. You decide to *substitute* how you study by asking three people, who do well on their tests, what they do. You substitute their methods to see if that improves your test grades.

2. *Combine:* When new thoughts are not coming easily, combining two unlike objects, images, or events stimulate your *combining thinking processes*.

3. *Rearrange:* Rearranging thinking is to change sections of a process and reorder the steps in a previous solution or condition. Such rearranging

FIGURE 11-4
Types of Puppets

thinking is evident in the following problem situation: For example, pretend you have to sit beside someone who talks all the time in your mathematics class. You feel you have tried *everything* but that person keeps right on talking. You tried not listening, telling the person not to talk, and asking the teacher if you could move. You cannot be moved because you sit in alphabetical order. You just realized that you shouldn't waste time trying to rearrange things that you can't change, such as the other person, your naturally friendly nature, or the rule of having to sit in alphabetical order. But by using your *rearrangement* thinking with things you can change, you discover that you could change the direction in which the desks face in the room. If the chairs in the room were rearranged with two rows placed at the back of the room facing the front, and the remaining to the side by the windows, your class would remain in alphabetical order, but you would be across the room from the person disturbing you. You make this suggestion for rearrangement and your teacher agrees!

4. *Adapt:* Adaptive thinking is to change only one small detail about a first solution to improve it. For example, you want to become a better basketball player or to improve your hairstyle. You don't like the first solution you created: only to shoot the shots that you know you can make or to pull your hair back into a ponytail. If you *adapt* your thinking *slightly*, you add to this solution by practicing only one new position shot, alone, each week; or trimming to make bangs over your forehead. You can make several changes in simple steps, through adaptive thinking, until you are pleased with your results.

5. *Minimize:* You can change outcomes by making a produce smaller or by omitting something. This innovative thinking process assists you to identify disposable elements and to make things more compact. A method of initiating minimizing thinking is to ask yourself, "What is something in this idea that I can do without?"

6. *Bigger:* You can change outcomes by adding parts. You can think of ways to increase the size, strength, time, or frequency of actions to make them better. To magnify, students can write facts about a part of their problems to which they have not given adequate attention. Often this magnification involves reflecting on beliefs about the opposite side of an issue which adds important information that could have been depreciated by one's initial point of view. You ask yourself the following questions as well: (a) What else might be happening? (b) What other things are possible? (c) What if _____? (d) What ideas can I get about _____ by thinking about _____?

7. *Linking:* The principle upon which the innovative thinking process of linking is based is that the more responses produced, the greater the odds of producing a satisfactory solution. If you have twenty ideas to choose from, you have a greater probability of having a quality idea within that group than if you have only two ideas. Brainstorming is a demonstration of linking thinking. You initiate the linking thought process by asking yourself: (a) In what ways might I (we) _____? (b) Make a list of things that _____. (c) How many different examples (reasons, solutions, etc.) can I think of? (d) What comes to mind when you think of _____?

8. *Invent:* You teach students to turn their thoughts completely around. Often inventors use the inventive thinking process by making special but extreme case of rearrangements. You can initiate this type of thinking by turning objects upside down and all around. You can turn ideas "all around" by becoming your own "devil's advocate" by trying to think of all the reasons why it wouldn't work.

9. *Newness:* Originality is the creative thinking behavior that produces new or novel responses. You can invite a new idea by asking yourself: (a) What else, or what more? (b) What is a new, original way to _____? (c) Can I invent a new _____? (d) How can I change _____ to make _____?

Once students have been taught these processes, ask them to create a thinking guide of their own to remind them of methods that initiate each of these thinking processes. They then practice using these processes interactively by completing one of the following activities or solving a personal problem they face.

1. Identify a situation at school that annoys you. Suggest a change to eliminate this annoyance.
2. Think of a time in the past when you wished you would have used innovative thinking. Describe that time as if you were writing a short story. Only this time, change the ending by using innovative thinking. Describe which creative thinking process(es) you used to make this change.
3. Do you see a time in the near future when you could use your innovative thinking? Describe why this thinking might be necessary at that time, and how you will use it.
4. You have been told that too much of anything is not good. Use your innovative thinking to describe two situations in life when thinking creatively could be detrimental rather than valuable.
5. Your parents tell you that the family is going on a family vacation but the time conflicts with the most important party of the summer. What can you do?
6. Inventors take two objects and combine them to create solutions to difficult problems (e.g., taking away the difficulty of not having a washer and dryer in small apartments by putting small washers and dryers on top of one another; and taking away the discomfort of chairs and footstools by inventing Lazyboy chairs). Think of something that is uncomfortable in your life. Describe the process you would use to change this annoyance, and the end product of your inventive thinking. (See *Small Inventions That Make a Big Difference* by Donald Crump, National Geographic Publishers, 1984, for additional examples of inventions.)
7. Some people do not like something about their appearance. Improve something about your appearance or personality and describe the thinking you did to devise the plan.
8. Think of the last time you felt as if you had tried everything but failed. Knowing what you know now, what would you have done differently in that situation?

CREATING LESSONS THAT TEACH STUDENTS TO DRAW PERSONAL, DIRECT, SYMBOLIC, AND NATURE ANALOGIES

Gordon (1961) uses four analogies to strengthen creative thinking. *Personal analogy* thoughts find relationships between a person and some other phenomenon with which this person and others are familiar. Through such analogies students learn to express themselves more creatively and effectively. For example, suppose a student wants others to know how thin he is without giving a lengthy description. He may say "I'm as thin as a stick." *Direct analogy* is to find a relationship between two unlike phenomena or things that will explain your thoughts imaginatively and convincingly than is possible without the comparison, e.g., "John eats like a pig."

Symbolic Analogies are to compare something students wish to descibe to a symbol. For instance, if students want to describe someone as being dependable, strong, and consistent, they could draw a symbolic analogy and say that the person is like "the Rock of Gibraltar."

Nature Analogies are creative thinking processes that compare features of manmade problems to characteristics in nature. Through this comparison, students can reach solutions that are more successful and realistic than those created without such a natural reference. For example, most teenagers have difficulty solving the problem of pimples. You use this example to introduce how nature analogies can solve this and other problems. You do so by asking students what actions could eliminate parasites such as mistletoe and treebark mold from trees. Students might suggest that they can be broken off or cut off. You then report that such actions don't work because the roots of the mold are not removed, and they just grow back. Some might suggest that you just leave it alone and hope that it goes away. You add that such actions only cause the parasites to grow. Students may suggest that the parasites could be camouflaged, such as painting over the treebark mold. Such action causes the parasites to spread. Students may then suggest that a tree doctor be called. You then ask students to analyze what they've just learned about parasites to acne. They should realize that trying to remove individual blemishes, ignoring their problem, and covering them with heavy makeup only increases the problem. They must see a doctor and use medicine to cure their acne. Once this analogy is presented, students can suggest how other nature analogies can increase creative thinking during problem solving (e.g.,using characteristics of unstable air masses and their resulting thunderstorms to forecast family instabilities and correct them). Then students practice nature analogies by studying nature's phenomena that parallel features of problems they face at home or school. *The Hungry Leprechaun* can be used to introduce nature analogies to younger students; older students can use another strategy that builds nature analogous thinking. It is to use Mother Nature as a Mentor. Students watch how she changes seasons gradually and other ways she implements processes successfully. Students end this series of lessons by generating personal, direct, and symbolic analogies in reading response groups or writing centers.

CRITICAL THINKING ACTIVITY 11
Teaching Predictive Thinking

Recommended Grade Levels: Preschool Through Grade 8

Perhaps one of the most important survival skills in the twenty-first century will be the ability to predict. Predictive thinking is increasing in importance because of the speed with which students must adapt to conditions which change to accommodate the masses of new knowledge society creates. In the future, students must know how to select between several probable outcomes before they act. They can be taught to do so in the following ways.

Older students can learn the story of Milton Friedman, one of our country's best economists. Mr. Friedman recounts a happening in his life where he learned the value of, and how to do, predictive thinking. He vividly recalls how his *incomplete analysis to determine "how big an effect each change in present conditions would have upon a decision he would make for a future event"* (the thinking processes involved in predictive thinking) almost caused a company to go bankrupt. Tell students that they must learn to investigate all details, very carefully, before they predict. They are to think of what changes could occur in an environment, and how positive or negative each change would be upon a specific goal they want to reach. At this point in the lesson, older students can read *The Silver Whistle* and stop at several points to predict what Miguel is likely to do (or should do) next. Students diagram the positive and negative effects of each action Miguel could take. Students use these diagrams to explain to other members in their small groups why they made the predictions they did. After all students have explained their predictions, they read the next section of the book and discover the action the author led Miguel to take.

Younger students can be introduced to predictive thinking by describing how one has to attend to the positive and negative changes details affect upon outcomes. You also teach that it is important to withhold judgment until they feel they have explored enough details so that then their predictive thinking will be based on the maximum number of facts. Then you ask them to predict the title and picture that is likely to be beneath the construction paper that you taped over the cover of a book that you read aloud to them. Once younger students complete this activity as a whole class they can divide into small groups for a second practice session. In this session, you read a second book where students do not see any of the pictures, the cover, or the title, and do not read the ending. One small group predicts the cover picture; one the title; and the last predicts the ending. Each group shows their group's diagrammed analysis of predictive thinking and reasons for their prediction.

Following these activities, students can learn to make predictions relative to their lives. They begin by describing past incidents in the classroom and how one detail interacted with a second to produce the end result. Because these examples are based on events students actually experienced, they are likely to have the background necessary to understand why certain changes occurred. Once students feel comfortable, they elect to make creative and realistic predictions about events relative to their interest, e.g., sports, clothing trends, music, and technological advancements. They justify their predictions by showing how alternative predictions are inconsistent with existing evidence.

Each student then makes a prediction about something that is likely to occur by the end of the month in his/her life. This prediction is sealed in a dated envelope, opened, and reviewed at the end of the month, after the event is to have occurred. Students can elect to share their predictions and what they will do in the future to improve their predictive thinking.

THE CHALLENGE OF DIVERSITY

A more advanced activity enables gifted students to make *creative predictions*. In this activity gifted students are taught how to make predictions; then they work in small groups to make predictions about future events at the end of each chapter in *Jumanji, Sixth Grade Secrets, Two Minute Mysteries, Stranger at Winfield House, The Tricksters, Fallen Angels, Call It Courage, Tuck Everlasting, Jane Eyre,* or *King Bidgood's in the Bathtub.* With the second and subsequent predictions students make, the thinking difficulty is increased as they have to create a proverbial or metaphorical saying for their prediction. When each group has finished making predictions about their books, students write a proverb that states their opinion as to the author's reason for writing the book.

PROFESSIONAL DEVELOPMENT OPPORTUNITY
How You Cultivate Student Poets and Why It Is Important To Do So

A **poem** is defined as *an arrangement of words in verse, especially a rhythmical composition, sometimes rhymed, expressing facts, ideas, or emotions in a style more concentrated, imaginative and powerful than that of ordinary speech; some are in meter, some in free verse.* Poetry calls upon students to use high levels of selective and creative thinking, as well as to express their emotions. As a matter of fact, poetry is the only medium of expression where experience and emotions are captured simultaneously. McClure, Harrison, and Reed (1990) believe that people should hear fine poetry as well as attempt to write it because a poem read aloud unites cognitive and affective dimensions of the mind in new ways. It causes students to explore ideas rhymically until a unique communication evolves.

You may have never created a truly beautiful poem but you will have the opportunity to do so in FOR YOUR JOURNAL (p. 372). Creating a beautiful poem will enable you to show a model to students before you ask them to write poetically. The information in this chapter's Professional Development Opportunity will acquaint you with several poetic forms.

You can teach students to write poetry by allowing them to respond in poetic style after you have read several poems in class. One of the most successful ways of doing so is to make "personal poetry collections." On a regular basis, students bind their favorite poems and self-authored poems into a bound collection (see Figure 11-5). They can also use this anthology for choral readings, readers' theatre, and partner readings.

FIGURE 11-5
Students' Personal Poetry Collection

PERSONAL POETRY

On a regular basis, give students poems to keep in binders in their desks. Encourage students to add their own favorite poems and self-authored poems to the collection. Use this anthology for choral reading, readers' theatre, partner reading, and creative dramatics.

In addition to this book, model free expression types of poetic experiences, and teach the following types of poems, beginning with those of greatest interest to your students: lyrics, narrative, blank verse, diamante, cinquain, and Haiku. Definitions and examples of these types follow.

Couplet: Two-line stanza that usually rhymes and contains the same number of syllables.

Triplet: Three-line stanza that usually rhymes.

Quatrain: Four lines with several ways to rhyme (popular framework for poetry)

Five-Line Verse (not a limerick): *Sextet* (six lines); *Septet* (seven lines); *Octet* (eight lines). Each of these types of poetry can stand alone or become separate stanzas in a poem. For example, the first couplet was written as a poem in itself; the second is a stanza in a longer poem.

> Bladeskates glaze the sidewalk
> Taking me fast as a hawk.

> Rain comes down soft and steady,
> Making the world heavy,
> We put on our raincoats
> And march with raindrops as our notes.

Limerick: Five lines of humorous or nonsense verse with an "aa-bb-a" rhyming scheme.

Free Verse: The poet divides his/her lines according to the natural pauses in his/her thoughts, and is not concerned with rhyme.

Cinquain: A cinquain (pronounced *sinkane*) is a five-line poem. It assists students to choose more precise words that evoke the exact images they wish to represent. The cinquain pattern follows in a verse by Adelaide Crapsey, written in 1914, during the last year of her life. Her brief word etchings are similar to the Japanese tanka and haiku.

Pattern: 1st line: one word, giving the title;
2nd line: two words, describing the title;
3rd line: three words, expressing action;
4th line: four words, expressing a feeling;
5th line: another word for the title.

> Clouds
> Earth's roof
> Moving grey mists
> Gentle drops of rain
> Overcast

Diamante: Invented by Iris M. Tiedt, University of Santa Clara, Santa Clara, California. Diamante (dee-ah-mahn'-tay) follows a diamond shaped pattern:

———

————————

——————————————

————————————————————

——————————————

————————

———

This pattern produces a seven line contract poem following these specifications:

1 word:	subject noun	Winter
2 words:	adjectives	Cold Windy
3 words:	participles (-ing, -ed)	Chattering my teeth
4 words:	noun related to subject	My frozen red hands
3 words:	participles	Slapping my face
2 words:	adjectives	Warming soothing
1 word:	noun (opposite of subject)	Heat

Haiku: Japanese poetry that consists of seventeen syllables.

Pattern:	1st line: five syllables	Green leafy branches
	2nd line: seven syllables	in the wind wave greetings to
	3rd line: five syllables	the passing stranger

In the FOR YOUR JOURNAL activity (p. 372) you will have the opportunity to write one or more of these poems that expresses who you are and things you value. With your poem in hand, you will be ready to teach your

Pop-up Poetry is an extension activity that fosters imaging abilities by involving children in creating illustrations that capture the tone, mood, and images evoked by a set of poems (Roskos & Lenhart, 1992). As shown in the photo above, the result is a personally illustrated collection of poetry that can be shared and enjoyed for a long time.

students how to write poetically. You have the proof that they can. You did it. You will tell them from first-hand experience what they can expect to think and feel before, during, and after they create poems.

Poetry lessons you can implement with your students follow:

1. You can introduce three of the above types of poetry on one day, and three on the second day. Students practice writing each type and decide which type best matches the emotion they wish to express.

2. Write some cinquains on the board ahead of class (see the Portfolio p. 372 for books that contain these poems). Discuss their pattern and characteristics. Write the pattern on the board so the class will remember it. It's not important at this time if they don't follow the pattern exactly; only the message is important. Let them see that a cinquain briefly expresses an idea that grows and expands in the mind of the reader. Then read some cinquains to the class. Let them listen and think about them. Ask for comments and let them write some.

3. Exhibit a few choice Japanese prints. Create a central theme or scene on the bulletin board with Haikus the class made. Read a piece of Haiku chosen by you or a child. Let the children offer their interpretations. What things come to mind when they hear the poem?

4. Older students can write stories and poems for first graders. They need to use a basic word list. They can use the words from the first-grade reader or basic sight words from Chapter 4. If students have trouble writing poems, they may get some ideas of how to write poetry without rhyme.

NOTECARD 23: POETRY TO BUILD STUDENTS' CREATIVE THINKING AND WRITING ABILITIES

The Raucous Auk: A Menagerie of Poems by L. Hoberman

Pass the Poetry Please! by L. Hopkins

Poetry for Poetry Haters by Jane Moyer

Hey Bug! and Other Poems About Little Things by E. M. Itse

O Sliver of Liver, and Other Poems by M. C. Livingston

Where the Sidewalk Ends and other books by S. Silverstein

Let's Marry, Said the Cherry, and Other Nonsense Poems by N. M. Bodecker

Reflections on a Gift of Watermelon Pickles by Stephen Dunning

Morning, Noon, and Nighttime, Too by Lee Hopkins

Cricket Songs by H. Behn

Water Pennies and Other Poems by N. M. Bodecker

Casey at the Bat by E. Thayer

Children of Crisis by R. Cole

A Snail's a Failure Socially by E. Starbird

Out in the Dark and the Daylight by L. E. Fisher

Hailstones and Halibut Bones by Z. O'Neal

Hot Dog and Other Poems by K. Wright

Don't You Turn Back by Langston Hughes

Pick Me Up: A Book of Short Poems by J. Cole

Something Big Has Been Here by J. Prelutsky

If I Were in Charge of the World, and Other Worries by Judith Viorst

The Rose On My Cake by Karla Kuskin

Eats by Arnold Adoff

These Small Stones by Farber and M. Livingston

Favorite Poems Old and New by H. Ferris

Time for Poetry by M. H. Arbuthnot

It Doesn't Always Have to Rhyme by Eve Merriam

Of This World by R. Lewis

I Heard a Scream in the Streets ed. by N. Larrick

Laughing Time by W. J. Smith

(cont'd)

NOTECARD 23 (cont'd)

NURSERY RHYMES AND POETRY FOR KINDERGARTEN THROUGH SECOND GRADE STUDENTS

Mother Goose Rhymes by Arthur Rackham

Book of Nursery and Mother Goose Rhymes by Marguerite de Angeli

The Moon by Robert Louis Stevenson

Shoes by Elizabeth Winthrop

Fifty-One New Nursery Rhymes by R. Fyleman

The Book of Pigericks by Arnold Lobel

Poems Children Will Sit Still For: A Selection for the Primary Grades by DeRegniers, Moore, and White

Favorite Nursery Rhymes by R. Caldecott

All the Colors of the Race by Arnold Adoff

Blackberry Ink by Eve Merriam

Daydreamers by Eloise Greenfield

If You Are a Hunter of Fossils by B. Baylor

Poem Stew ed. by William Cole

The Tamarindo Puppy and Other Poems by Charlotte Pomerantz

Finger Rhymes, Hand Rhymes, Play Rhymes, and Party Rhymes by Marc Brown

TEACHER RESOURCE BOOKS FOR LESSON PLANNING

Rose Where Did You Get That Red?: Teaching Great Poetry to Children by K. Koch

The Haiku Handbook: How to Write, Share, and Teach Haiku by W. J. Higginson

Handbook of Poetic Forms by Ron Padgett

Moving Window: Evaluating the Poetry Children Write by Jack Collom

Wishes, Lies and Dreams: Teaching Children to Write Poetry by K. Koch

Using Poetry to Teach Reading and Language Arts by Richard J. Smith

Langston Hughes Curriculum Packet: Dig and Be Dug In Return by S. Danielson

STRATEGIES THAT TEACH

You can share poems from Eve Merriam's *It Doesn't Always Have to Rhyme* or Shel Silverstein's *Where the Sidewalk Ends*. Books from Notecards 23 and 24 also challenge students to express their reactions poetically. Books from Notecard 24 can also be used in many other activities in Chapter 11.

5. Parks and Parks (1992) and Craig (1992) recommend that you set poetry to music or let students use props to ignite their creative thinking. This activity assists students to understand the rhythm and sounds within the English language. Words have rhythms and these rhythms create

---

NOTECARD 24: BOOKS THAT SPUR CURIOSITY AND CREATIVE THINKING FOR STUDENTS

Stories to Solve: Folktales Around the World by G. Shannon

The Book of Think or How to Solve a Problem Twice Your Size by M. Burns

Friends Are Like That! Stories to Read to Yourself by Child Study Children's Association

Guinness Book of Phenomenal Happenings by McWhirter and McWhirter

Where Does the Sun Go at Night? by M. Ginsberg

Icebergs by R. Gans

Clocks and More Clocks by P. Hutchins

What's Hatching Out of That Egg? by P. Lauber

Greg's Microscope and other books by Selsam

Hear Your Heart and other books by P. Showers

The Invention of Ordinary Things by D. Wulffson

Model Buildings and How to Make Them by Weiss

The Cat Who Wished to be a Man by Alexander

Gildean: The Heroic Adventures of a Most Unusual Rabbit by E. Buchwald

Josephine's 'Magination by A. Dobrin

Getting Along with Your Friends by P. Naylor

Plants Do Amazing Things by H. Nusbaum

How You Were Born by J. Cole

Coast to Coast: Facts and Fun About the Fifty States by Black and Newberger

When Birds Change Their Feathers by J. Cole

Animal Fact-Animal Fable by S. Simon

Rain Puddle by A. Holl

The Wind Blew by P. Hutchins

Beyond Belief: Strange, True Mysteries of the Unknown by B. Steiger

---

thought which translates into meaning. Just as students become knowledgeable about (and use left-to-right directionality) by reading letters within words and words within sentences, they can develop their understanding that the modulation of sounds within the contexts of words and sentences affect meaning through poetry. They can use English rhythm to translate meaning into speech better when music is coupled with poetry as they read it.

6. Once students have experienced success with poetry, Roskos (1992) recommends "Free Response with a Sketch." This activity encourages high level thinking while developing mental imagery. *Procedure:*

- Preselect stops in a text. Make sure the stops are judiciously spaced so that the reader has an opportunity to build up adequate images.
- At the stops, ask the reader to jot responses to one or more of the following prompts (prompts may vary dependent on the type of text): I see . . .
    I hear . . .
    I smell . . .
    I feel . . .
- After reading the selection, encourage the reader to develop a sketch or series of sketches that depicts his/her sensations and thoughts in connection with the text and that he/she would share with the author.
- Have the reader evaluate his/her sketch(es) with the actual text, noting how the sketch captures the aesthetic feeling or gist of the selection.

- Provide an opportunity for sharing sketches through poetry as a means of retelling the text.

7. Students also enjoy learning how their favorite poets create their poetry. Through a nearby university, you may be able to invite a professional poet to class. This person can share the creative thought processes used to germinate ideas and mold poems. Many poets report that their first thoughts emanate from: (1) a fact or feeling they experience; (2) a verse or melody that appears in their consciousness; or (3) an image or picture that takes shape in their mind, as Theodore Weiss shares in videotape segment 8.

8. Once you have taught Critical Thinking Activity 8 (p. 268), introduce how important figurative language is to poets. Figurative language makes poems more intriguing, interesting, and vivid. Also, lead students to discover how their enjoyment is intensified when poems orchestrate figurative language to establish particular effects. Students then look at poems to determine exactly what the authors chose to compare; then they begin to analyze how this comparison helps them view the phenomena differently. Once students discuss how poets use figurative language they will begin experimenting with it themselves. As with all poetic devices, students will initially use the device rather literally, following a rule they construct (McClure, Harrison, & Reed, 1990).

As they practice they slowly begin to experiment with selecting just the right word and then to manipulate rhyme, lining, and phrasing so as to maintain the metaphor throughout the poem. For example, if students decide to compare tears to rain, you model how some words and similes work for *tears*, but not for *rain*. Thus they have to work hard to select and find the exact words that work for both. When problems arise as students write figuratively ask, "What are you trying to say in this poem?"

TRY IT

1. Post-test your level of creative thinking. Return to page 350, time yourself for three minutes as you take the Remote Associations Test. Has your reading of information concerning creative thinking increased your creative abilities? Why or why not? Administer the Remote Associations Test to your students before and after they have completed several activities in this chapter. What does the comparison of pre- and post-test scores indicate?

2. You may wish to begin a collection of sample student and adult poems to display as models for your students. Devise a plan whereby you can collect these samples. Also, make large decorative charts depicting the formulas for poetry types in this chapter that you can use in instruction.

3. Prepare the materials and a sample thinking guide to teach SCRAMBLIN'.

4. If you are teaching, you may wish to designate a group of students to plan the methods to make puppets for their classmates. This small group introduces and implements their plan and the class completes their puppets and puppet plays. If you are not yet teaching, decide upon and defend the proportion of time you feel should be spent in developing students' creative thinking. Should this proportion of time vary by grade levels? Why or why not? What are the differences between prose, poetry, and plays as far as the types of creative thinking they stimulate?

Answers to the Remote Associations Test are:

(l) *bill;* (2) *nail;* (3). *pot;* (4) *yellow;* (5) *coach.*

FOR YOUR JOURNAL

Once you've experienced the creativity poetry helps to release, you'll have an expressive tool few possess. If you lack confidence that you can become a poet, take a risk today. Read the following information: Select an important value in your life and one or more of the poetic formats in this chapter that appeal to you. Write one or more poems that express your values. These will become models for your students.

Journals can stimulate your students' creative and innovative abilities. Describe the benefits you experienced from writing poetically to your students. Share your poems with your students. If you aren't teaching, set a new goal to develop your creativity this week. Reassess it at the end of the week.

BUILDING YOUR PROFESSIONAL PORTFOLIO
References for Poetry and Plays

Poetry

Poetry Please! is a 13-tape, 15 minutes each, video series where three mice puppets interact with a poet and in the process they learn what poetry is. *Poetry Please!* is published by TV Ontario (143 W. Franklin Street, Suite 206, Chapel Hill, NC 27514).

Poetry Works is a kit of 75 posters and Idea Book for K–3. *Poetry Works* is published by Modern Curriculum Press (13900 Prospect Road, Cleveland, OH 44136).

Langston Hughes Curriculum Packet: Dig and Be Dug In Return by Susan Danielson, Oral History Program (5006 N.E. Mallory, Portland, Oregon).

Astro Poetry: Students Working As Poets by William Rakauskas and *Producing Award-Winning Student Poets: Tips from Successful Teachers* from the Illinois Association of Teachers of English are two books that provide ideas on teaching poetry.

Wishes, Lies, & Dreams: Teaching Children to Write Poetry; Rose Where Did You Get That Red?: Teaching Great Poetry to Children; and *Sleeping on the Wing: An Anthology of Modern Poetry with Essays on Reading and Writing.* The first two books were written by Kenneth Koch and the last by Kenneth Koch and Kate Farrell, available from Teachers and Writers Collaborative (5 Union Square West, New York, NY 10003).

The Haiku Handbook: How to Write, Share, and Teach Haiku by William J. Higginson, with Penny Harter, available from Teachers and Writers Collaborative.

Handbook of Poetry and *Poetic Forms: 10 Audio Programs* by Ron Padgett, available from Teachers and Writers Collaborative.

Here are some poetry books about teaching:

Moving Window: Evaluating the Poetry Children Write by Jack Collom;
Using Poetry to Teach Reading and Language Arts by Richard J. Smith;
It Doesn't Always Have to Rhyme by Eve Merriam;
Don't You Turn Back by Langston Hughes;
If I Were in Charge of the World, and Other Worries by Judith Viorst;
Poetry for Poetry Haters by Jane Moyer;
Where the Sidewalk Ends by Shel Silverstein;
Time for Poetry by May Hill Arbuthnot;
O Sliver of Liver, and Other Poems by Myra Cohn Livingston;
Morning, Noon, and Nighttime, Too by Lee Bennett Hopkins;
Let's Marry, Said the Cherry, and Other Nonsense Poems by N.M. Bodecker;
The Rose on My Cake by Karla Kuskin;
Eats by Arnold Adoff;
Reflections on a Gift of Watermelon Pickles by Stephen Dunning.

Plays

Holidays on Stage by Virginia Bradley. New York: Dodd, Mead and Company, 1981 (original plays for holidays);
Skits and Spoofs for Young Actors by Val R. Cheatham. Boston: Plays, Inc., 1977 (one act, royalty-free plays, skits, and spoofs for the amateur stage);
Easy Plays for Preschoolers to Third Graders by Amorie Havilan and Lyn Smith. Quail Ridge Press, 1985 (a collection of 12 plays for various holidays which can be read as a story, performed as a monologue with pantomime, or presented as a play);
Plays Children Love: A Treasury of Contemporary and Classical Plays for Children edited by C. A. Jennings and A. Harris. New York: Doubleday, 1981;
Plays From African Folktales by C. Korty. New York: Scribner, 1975;
Children's Plays from Beatrix Potter by R. Laurie. New York: F. Warne, 1980;
One Act Plays edited by A. Burnack. Boston: Plays, Inc., 1970;
Christmas Play Favorites for Young People: A Collection of Traditional and Modern One-Act, Royalty-Free Plays for Celebrating Christmas in Schools and Drama Groups edited by S. Kamerman. Boston: Plays, Inc., 1982;

STRATEGIES THAT TEACH

You might want to subscribe to *Plays, The Drama Magazine for Young People* available from Plays, Inc., 8 Arlington Street, Boston, MA 02116;

Speak Up, Edie by Judy Johnston. New York: Putnam, 1974 (Edie is the narrator for the class play and in the process she learns something about her incessant talking);

Mrs. Peloki's Class Play by Joanne Oppenheim. New York: Dodd, Mead, 1984 (Mrs. Peloki's second grade class has a disastrous dress rehearsal, but the play itself is a resounding success);

The Best Christmas Pageant Ever by Barbara Robinson, New York: Avon, 1972;

If you want to teach Shakespeare in new ways, contact *Shakespeare for Young People*, Swan Books, P.O. Box 2498, Fair Oaks, California 95628; (916) 961-8778. These books are 40-minute scripts with two optional announcers and stage directions.

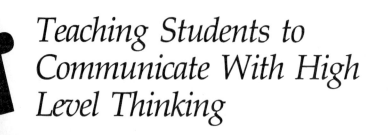

12 Teaching Students to Communicate With High Level Thinking

Once students have been taught group thinking processes they mediate, collaborate, and build consensus in pairs, groups of four, six, and eight until an agreed-upon three-page position paper concerning a current event has been negotiated.

The principal goal of education is to create men who are capable of doing new things, not simply of repeating what other generations have done—men who are creative, inventive discoverers. The second goal of education is to form minds which can be critical, can verify, and not accept everything they are offered.

—Jean Piaget

Once students risk creativity your student communication center can become home for still another kind of thinking, one characterized by breadth, objectivity, and reflection. You can teach students to think critically about their concerns and problems. They can learn to appreciate the strengths and limitations of their own knowledge, the methods and fallibility of rationality, as well as the generalizability and restraints of each communication medium (Hawes, 1990).

The purpose of this chapter is to demonstrate ways your communication center can increase students' critical thinking. You have already learned how lessons advance high level thinking and language abilities as students clarify their thinking by asking questions (Chapter 3); detect propaganda to become more objective (Chapter 4); recognize and use patterns to reason (Chapter 5); build semantic maps to understand global concepts (Chapter 6); use journal writing to solve problems (Chapter 7); employ idioms/figurative language/proverbs to increase depth and precision of thinking (Chapter 8); image to increase retention (Chapter 9); recognize the schema scientists follow to think like experts in content fields (Chapter 10); and call upon predictive thinking to enhance creativity (Chapter 11). In this chapter you will learn activities and lessons that expand seven of the eight dimensions of thought. The dimension omitted is creativity because it was treated separately in Chapter 11. By the end of the chapter you will know:

1. How to build students' critical thinking abilities metacognition, decision making skills, problem solving competencies, group work skills, and their abilities to think/work alone;

2. How to increase students' breadth/depth of thinking while reading, speaking, listening, and writing.

THEORETICAL FOUNDATION
THE NEED FOR STUDENTS TO THINK CRITICALLY

Many teachers want to advance their students' thinking. Reasons to do so were presented in Chapter 1. Moreover, research indicates that the information and lessons in this chapter not only strengthen students' cognitive and scholastic achievements but positively affect their self-esteem (Collins, 1991a; 1992b). While no one can accurately predict the problems our youth will face in their lives, we do know that teaching them to think (through the lessons in this chapter) will increase their cognitive repertoires. The number of tools they can use to conquer new challenges and open doors of opportunity will also expand.

Before we begin, it is important to note that lessons in this chapter are likely to increase your reflectivity as well. First, you will introduce content and use methods that you have not been taught. Planning such lessons will augment your thinking repertoire which will subsequently impact your students' cognitive abilities. As Frank Smith (1989) stated, the first action to improve the quality of thinking in our schools is to multiply the number of interactions students have with teachers who are high quality thinkers. He suggested how this intensification can occur:

> A serious problem is not so much demand for instant information or gratification as for instant decisions and comments. There is little tolerance for uncertainty and doubt, in others and in ourselves. The result of 30 second/three-paragraph news items and ten-minute debates encourage students to believe that they should be able to take an immediate position on any topic. The consequence is a readiness to respond with slogans rather than with reflection. To turn this around we, as teachers, must not be afraid of withholding judgment, of challenging the assertions of others, and of having our own ideas challenged in return (p. 129).

Second, as you teach the lessons in this chapter you will move students to work with thinking processes in opposition to habits that are inadvertently reinforced in society. As Onosko and Newmann (in press) state: "Higher-order thinking involves difficult mental work that can be personally unsettling, because it disrupts cognitive stability, order, and predictability. For many, it is psychologically more comfortable not to think too deeply about anything." The lessons in this chapter will teach students how to contemplate, resolve conflicts, tolerate uncertainty and ambiguity, engage in self-criticism and judge independence.

How your students acquire these abilities in your student communication center is discussed next.

PUTTING THEORY INTO PRACTICE
TEACHING STUDENTS TO COMMUNICATE WITH HIGH LEVEL THOUGHTS

There are eight dimensions of thinking that are amenable to instruction. You can introduce students to these components in several ways. First, you can describe all components and students select the ones that they want to learn to enhance their communication skills.

A second method of using the material in this chapter is to teach those thinking abilities your students most need. In this approach you describe to students how you diagnosed their needs. Once a new thinking process has been taught, students complete a sample to demonstrate the value of the thinking process they have learned. When one teacher applied this method in her class, one fifth grade boy described what the instruction did for him:

> When I look back [over the thinking lessons in Dimension 8 that I learned], I see how my poems used to be very basic in the beginning; they were all rhymed haiku because that was all I knew about. Then I experimented with going with the feelings or ideas . . . don't kill yourself going over the rhymes, go with what you feel. I did that for two months. Then I started compacting them, shortening them to make deeper meaning. I could see that it would make more of a point if I washed out the *the's* and *and's* and *if's*. Now that I learned the lessons about thinking processes, I am working on something different—the morals. If one day my mom's car broke down, I might write that night about how a fish got caught or the feeling of not being able to swim. I am not trying to write how I feel only, but metaphors (Wolf, Bixby, Glenn, and Gardener, 1991, p. 38).

A third method of using the material in this chapter is to ask students in what ways they would like to think better. You would begin instruction with the directions in which they prefer to advance their thinking skills. Regardless of the method you select to introduce the information in this chapter, your students will benefit from improving their skills in each of the following dimensions of thought.

ACTIVITIES THAT DEVELOP STUDENTS' HIGH LEVEL THINKING AND COMMUNICATION

The eight dimensions of thinking ability amenable to instruction are depicted in Chapter 1. Dimension 1 contains *basic thinking skills*, including the ability to clarify ideas, examine relationships, see errors, summarize, and remember. Dimension 2 includes *thinking processes* that call upon the interaction of more than one cognitive skill, including inferencing, interpreting, thinking like an expert, and making multiple comparisons. Dimension 3 is comprised of *decision making abilities* where one uses the decision making process, decision-making tools, and productive attitudes to select from competing alternatives. Dimension 4 consists of *abilities one uses to solve problems*, such as reasoning through perplexing situations, assessing the quality of ideas, eliminating biases, establishing criteria, and judging the credibility of sources.

Dimension 5 is *metacognitive thinking*, which includes assessing one's current knowledge relative to specific tasks, and identifying barriers that interfere with one's talents and goals. Dimension 6 contains the processes of *creative and innovative thinking*, such as shifting frames of reference; using models, risk-taking, humor, and curiosity; and forecasting to create new thoughts and products. Dimension 7 is comprised of the abilities one uses to *think effectively in groups*, such as exercising power/authority/influence appropriately; using talents interactively; and developing analytical listening abilities. Dimension 8 includes the *abilities to think effectively when alone*, such as setting goals, establishing redirection, taking action, and eliciting self-motivation to increase productivity.

In this section of the chapter 31 critical thinking processes will be introduced, as well as how these cognitive components can be taught. Instructional activities for each dimension will be presented separately.

Dimension 1: Basic Thinking Skills. These skills include the ability to translate, relate, and order sensory, literary, and imaginary input. Cognitive components of dimension 1 that are amenable to instruction are:

I. Basic Clarifying Skills
   A. Using, rehearsing, and repeating mnemonic lists (e.g., memory aids, imagery, semantic maps, examples)
   B. Refining and modifying impressions (e.g., using synonyms, ranges, contrasts, examples, nonexamples, specificity versus generality, connotations and denotations)
II. Accepting and Rejecting Incoming Information
   A. Based on factuality
   B. Acceptable beliefs, values
   C. Weighing opinion and merit
   D. Using the criteria of validity, reliability, and relevance
III. Advanced Clarifying Abilities—Organizing Thoughts
   A. By order
   B. By features (size, shape of argument, or position)
   C. By purpose or structure
   D. By degree of membership, as measured by how closely an item resembles a prototype
IV. Condensing, Summarizing, Expanding, and Revising
   A. Combining relevant points
   B. Most general to most specific
   C. Considering tangential relevant/nonrelevant positions
   D. Revising by attending to relevant outliers

The following activities teach these components of Dimension 1: Basic Thinking Skills.

1. You teach students Basic Clarifying Skills, such as to **avoid overgeneralization**, by requiring that they ask themselves the following questions when they receive new information: "Is this situation (data) just like that one?" and "What are some differences?" Through your modeling, students can learn to evaluate facts, draw conclusions, reason about a conclusion's attractiveness, and reflect upon what is true or best. In essence, you teach them to distinguish what they know from what they merely suspect to be true.

2. You teach students to accept and reject incoming information by requiring them to listen to and question those who think differently than they do. Through this requirement students will realize that others know things that they don't, and that together they can work interdependently to create new knowledge.

3. You teach condensing, summarizing, expanding, and revising by selecting two types of literature on the same topic. Through comparisons between the two selections and teaching summarizing and revising strategies (as described in Chapters 6 and 8) students refine many cognitive processes. For example, students better understand **fact and opinion** by learning how to verify authenticity through reading *Popcorn* by Millicent Selsam and *The Popcorn Book* by Tomie dePaola.

> **THE CHALLENGE OF DIVERSITY**
> More able students can compare and contrast qualities of villains as portrayed
> in literature (e.g., the foxes in *The Amazing Bone* by William Steig, and *Sylvester
> and the Magic Pebble*), and compare and contrast television sitcoms with reality.
> Such comparisons assist students to understand the complex relationship be-
> tween fiction and fact.

Through activities that build thinking skills in Dimension 1, students also
decrease their impulsivity and rigidity of thinking. Students will learn that
"critical thinking" is not merely offering critiques, but learning to examine
material to decide what they believe.

Dimension 2: Essential Thinking Processes.   These are complex
cognitive operations that require the interaction of more than one critical
thinking skill. These processes include the following:

I. Forming Concepts
   A. Labeling organized information
   B. Combining two or more sets of organized information
II. Recognizing Principles and Patterns
   A. Generating meaning from an ongoing barrage of data
   B. Interrelating features from different categories
   C. Noting similarities
III. Making Multiple Comparisons
   A. Aligning information for separate comparisons
   B. Diagramming overlapping classes and comparisons
   C. Using matrices to understand attributes and factors
   D. Analyzing contradictory information separately
IV. Applying and Inferring
   A. Recognizing suggestions
   B. Surmising purpose and tying it to a general theme
   C. Speculating what you would do in similar situations
   D. Determining if events are similar enough to your experiences
      that you can infer next events, causation, theme, and/or purpose
V. Translating and Interpreting
   A. Building deeper nuances and subtleties of meaning
   B. Noting inconsistencies and reason as to why they exist
   C. Interpreting negative statements and limited coverage
VI. Understanding Schema of Content Fields
   A. Learning how experts in science think
   B. Learning how experts in mathematics think
   C. Learning how experts in history and social science think
   D. Learning how experts in language arts think
   E. Learning how experts in fine arts think

You can teach students the cognitive components in Dimension 2,
Essential Thinking Processes, through the following activities:

1. You teach students how to **form concepts** by asking them to organize information, label it, and combine it with two or more sets of facts to create an example. Then, you present a list of items until students recognize a concept you are trying to depict. Once they recognize the concept, they describe, and you list the thoughts they used to create it. For example, you can list the following words on the board and ask what the next word could be:

ate	bite
cake	ice
eight	——

(Students should give a word with long /i/ sound as all words in first column are illustrations of the concept of "ways to spell the long /a/ sound." More able students could also suggest the word "eye.")

2. You can teach students to **make multiple comparisons** by diagramming how the thinking processes portrayed in a story would occur through similar events in students' lives.

3. You can teach **inference** by describing the components in an inference. With younger students, the components can be made more concrete by teaching through examples of inferences they have already made in their young lives, e.g., "If your mother or father told you to remember to take your umbrella to school, your brain will think of rain, although no one has said that word. The same thing happens when you read and listen. You add what you know about information in order to understand what is happening. You take what the author says plus what you know and end up with what was meant. For example, listen to this sentence: Nibbsie came running, with the stick in his mouth. You heard what I said and your brain just happened to add a few things—based on what you know. You came up with an entirely new thought, the author did not tell you Nibbsie was a dog, but you knew it, because there were clues that he was a dog. As you read and listen in the future look for clues and use more than one clue as you think. This is called inferencing."

Older students can be taught to inference by reflecting upon how they inferred specific traits of characters in books they read. To begin, describe how to inference and then model an inferred character trait. Model how writers convey these traits through relationships with other characters. Draw a semantic map to show how character traits evolved in a book you read aloud to the class. As students study the semantic web they realize that just as characters are developed by what the author tells them, their inferences are formed by what they read, know, or others tell them. Books that can be used in this lesson are *The Great Gilly Hopkins, Sarah Plain and Tall, The Eighteenth Emerging, Goodbye, Chicken Little, Julie of the Wolves, One-Eyed Cat, Sea Glass,* and *The Summer of the Swans.*

THE CHALLENGE OF DIVERSITY

Students who have limited English can learn the thinking skills in Dimension 1 and 2 by putting objects into categories and describing the thought process they used to do so. Then you present a second object and ask, "What would you have to do to build this?" The third step in this activity is to give them a piece of their writing or a taped reading they made and ask them to summarize it.

Dimension 3: Decision Making. Making effective decisions involves selecting from two or more competing, attractive alternatives that may or may not be obvious to the decision maker, or inventing a best option relative to specified criteria. You teach students that there are four components to making effective decisions: Using the decision making process correctly, employing decision making tools, having productive decision-making attitudes, and recognizing points at which making a decision will eliminate problems before they begin. Components of decisive thought follow.

I. The Decision-Making Process
    A. Establishing a Criteria
        1. Were the processes leading to the decision making point conducted correctly?
        2. Recognizing the personal filters of sensory input, psychological illusions, perceptions, and past inferences
    B. Deciding on an Action
        1. Defining the decision that needs to be made
        2. Forming alternative decisions
        3. Anticipating probable consequences of alternative actions before choosing among them
        4. Avoiding the influence of propaganda devices
        5. Selecting the best outside references
        6. Judging possible solutions as to how well each solution explains the evidence, is consistent with known facts, and is desirable
    C. Implementing and Monitoring the decision
II. Using Decision-Making Tools
    A. Barrier scanning and attribute listing
    B. Renewal, re-creation procedure
    C. Mentoring and modeling
    D. Debriefing and imaging
    E. Compromise through union of bests
    F. Research
    G. Maximum regret theory
III. Having Productive Decision-Making Attitudes
    A. Drives that increase chances for making correct decisions are devotion to truth, clarity, accuracy, fair-mindedness, and seeing the most central cause issue
    B. Personality traits that increase the chances for correct decision

FIGURE 12-1
Sample of First Grade Student's Lesson to Make Better Decisions

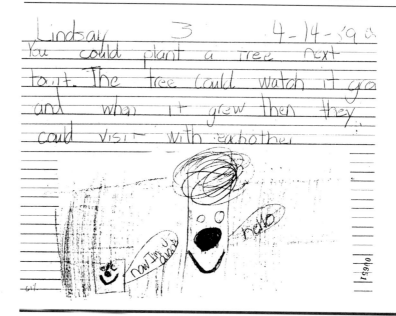

making are to listen to various points of view, seek evidence, recognize inconsistent applications of standards, and consider the well-being of those affected by decisions

IV. Recognizing Critical Points at Which Making a Decision Will Eliminate Problems Before They Begin

Activities that build decision-making abilities follow:

1. You can strengthen students' decision-making processes by introducing its subcomponents, described above. Then students write about a decision they do not know how to make; they follow the steps in Roman Numeral I above to make that decision. They report which steps in the decision-making process were most beneficial.

2. You can teach students to identify attitudes that increase the likelihood for success in decision making. For example, students in the first grade were taught how to anticipate probable consequences. Their teacher then read *The Giving Tree* by Shel Silverstein. Students met together to elect a decision that the tree and man could have employed to improve the outcome. Lindsay's group's decision is shown in Figure 12-1.

3. You can teach students how to have productive decision-making attitudes by instructing ways they can listen to various points of view and identify inconsistent aspects of an argument. Then students completed a point/counterpoint of a story. As they perform it, they analyze what thoughts entered into their decision making, and how they will better study the opposing sides of issues in real life. An example of such a point-

FIGURE 12-2
Example of Point/Counterpoint to Generate Alternatives in Decision Making

Table I

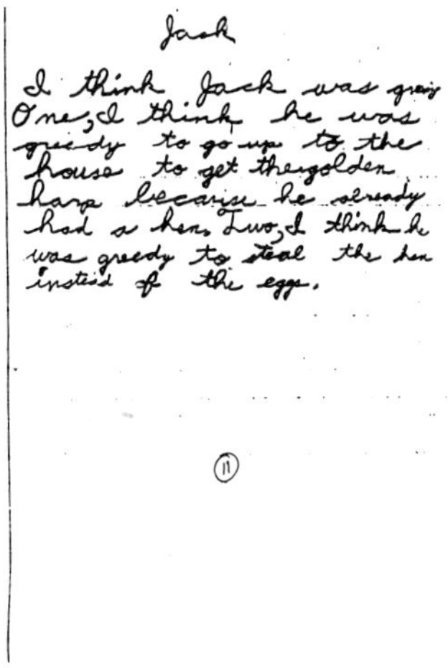
Jack
I think Jack was greedy. One, I think he was greedy to go up to the house to get the golden harp because he already had a hen. Two, I think he was greedy to steal the hen instead of the eggs.
(11)

Table II

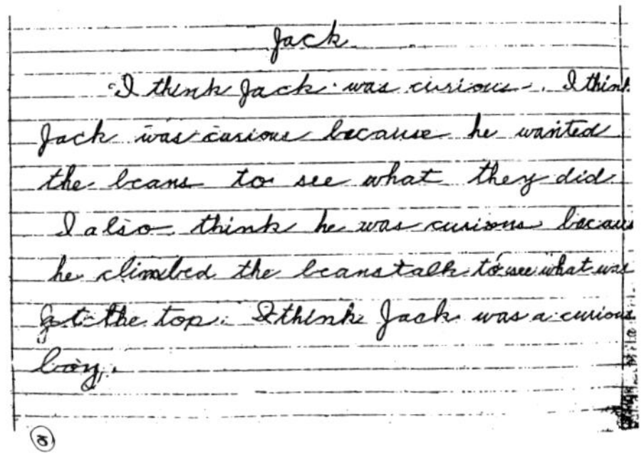
Jack
I think Jack was curious. I think Jack was curious because he wanted the beans to see what they did. I also think he was curious because he climbed the beanstalk to see what was at the top. I think Jack was a curious boy.
(8)

From *The Goal Critical Thinking from Educational Ideal to Educational Reality.* American Federation of Teachers, 555 New Jersey Ave. NW, Washington, D.C. 20001

counterpoint activity using *Jack and the Beanstalk* appears in Figure 12-2. Students were asked to formulate alternative reasons for Jack's decision to climb the beanstalk.

4. You can teach the decision-making tools described in Table 12-1. Once students feel comfortable with these tools they select two to use in their lives when decisions have to be made. They then apply these tools to a decision they face. Books that illustrate these decision-making tools are: *You Be the Jury* (Miller, 1987); *You Be the Jury II* (Miller, 1990); *The First Woman Doctor* (Baker, 1944); *Frederick Douglass Fights for Freedom* (Bontempo, 1959); *John F. Kennedy: America's 35th President* (Denenberg, 1988); *The Unfinished Stories for Facilitating Decision Making In the Elementary Classroom* (NEA Professional Library, P.O. Box 509, West Haven CT, 06516); and *Options: A Guide to Creative Decision Making* by Dianne Draze (Dandy Lion Publications, P.O. Box 190, San Luis Obispo, CA 93406).

Dimension 4: Problem Solving. Problem-solving thinking involves: (a) analyzing and resolving perplexing and difficult situations; (b) assessing the reasonableness and quality of ideas; (c) rejecting poor reasoning; (d) explicating assumptions; (e) suspending judgment; and (f) using problem-solving strategies.

The following activities build the components of problem-solving thinking.

FIGURE 12-3
Creative Problem-Solving Model

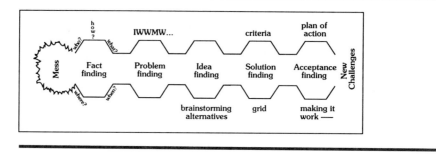

1. Creative Problem-Solving Process (CPS) was created by Alex Osborn and Sidney Parnes. In comparative studies of students who had and had not learned the *creative problem-solving process*, students with the course showed a statistically superior ability to produce good ideas (Osborn & Parnes, 1972). CPS assists students to devise a plan and a solution to a challenge while it develops task commitment skills. The process is described below and depicted in Figure 12-3.

Step 1: MESS-FINDING involves considering your goals, concerns, and personal orientation to determine the most important or immediate starting point for problem solving. Find facts, write, say, and think about the fuzzy statements that need to be explored before you can find the true problem.

Step 2: FACT-FINDING is turning facts into a problem-finding statement. State as many problems and subproblems as possible.

Step 3: PROBLEM-FINDING is to select the best problem statement.

Step 4: IDEA-FINDING is brainstorming alternative solutions and ideas. In Step 4, you apply all the decision-making tools and problem-solving strategies described previously in this chapter.

Step 5: SOLUTION-FINDING is to select criteria that will demonstrate a problem has been solved and not to yet think about possible solutions. Solution-finding is to write feelings and values relative to the problem in advance of selecting a solution.

Step 6: ACCEPTANCE-FINDING is to use the criteria in Step 5 to accept a best solution. Consider everything which will or won't work and stretch beyond first ideas.

Step 7: PLAN-OF-ACTION is to check progress in implementing the solution.

The following example uses the book *Grover Goes to School* (Duling, 1987) to teach CPS to younger students. By solving this character's problem, younger students can learn to apply CPS to their own problems. Before you read this book to students you would teach the above seven steps of CPS. Then, as you read the book students apply the steps Grover took. An example from a third grade class follows:

TABLE 12-1
Decision-Making Tools

Barrier Scanning or **Attribute Listing** is a decision-making tool whereby students list all the problems (barrier scanning) or all the positive of a situation (attribute listing). This tool helps clarify facts from opinions, and delineates factors that impact a decision at various points in the decision-making process.

Renewal, Re-creation Procedure is a decision-making tool whereby students recognize that they need to take a break from thinking, to re-create new thoughts or patterns. Recreation literally means to re-create, thus students are likely to make better decisions when they set aside time to rest and time to begin again. You can practice this at school by having a card labeled "5 minute break" whereby students are free to get the card, place it on their desk, and lie their heads down to "renew" for a few minutes when needed.

Debriefing and **Imagery** are two tools to use when alternatives are not evident. In debriefing, students are interviewed or conference with a teacher to explore why an impasse in thinking or writing occurred. Debriefing is also fueled through brainstorming and questions of clarification. Imagery was defined, and lessons to develop it appeared, in Critical Thinking Activity 9.

Compromise should be employed when two desirable, but opposing positions, unite to create a positive purpose. Compromise should not be used as a decision-making tool when items in a decision are unequal in weight. In these situations the weaker items forfeit their best attributes and succumb rather than unite to reach a decision.

Research should be used when students don't have alternative options. That is, students are taught that when they reach impasses their research should begin. You teach library research tools as well as interviewing strategies.

Maximum Regret Theory is a tool whereby students list all the regrets they would have if each alternative were set in action. Students then weigh each regret against the potential for positive gain that separate alternatives would cause. The best alternative would be the one that retained the highest level of positive gain once all possible negative effects had been subtracted.

Step 1: Mess-Finding—Grover was afraid he'd have no friends at his new school.

Step 2: Fact-Finding—We infer that Grover felt this way because no one from Sesame Street would be going to his school. He knew no one there.

Step 3: Problem-Statement—Grover did not act like himself. He cleaned up everybody's mess so he'd gain friends. He gave up his new crayon box, truck, and favorite sandwich, and played a game he disliked just to have a friend.

Step 4: Idea-Finding—Because he was not himself, he was unhappy.

Step 5: Solution-Finding—Be a helper and sharer, not a doormat.

Step 6: Acceptance-Finding—Grover may or may not have friends, but he'll like himself.

Step 7: Plan-of-Action—Grover can be friendly without doing anything against his will.

Another book that can be used to demonstrate CPS is *The Tale of Benjamin Bunny.*

TABLE 12-2
Problem-Solving Strategies

Setting three-part objectives was introduced in Chapter 1 and involves writing a goal or outcome desired with three parts. Students follow the declaration of their goal with one or two sentences that outline the action plan they will follow to reach it. Students then specify what they will see, feel, and experience to know that they have reached their goal. This specification also includes a predicted date when the goal is expected to be reached.

Bargaining and intermediate goals are strategies that students use when major changes are proving difficult. Bargaining and intermediate goals are temporary steps toward reaching larger, far-reaching goals.

Backward reasoning is the problem-solving strategy one should use when an end result is easy to visualize, but there are many paths one could take to reach it. Because the goal is clearer than the first step one should take, students think about the action that would probably occur right before the goal was reached. For example, if their goal is to run fast enough to become members of the school's relay team, they would use the backward reasoning strategy by picturing how fast they would have had to run the day the coach announced that they had qualified. Then, they ask the coach how fast that would be and they develop a day-by-day practice routine of timing themselves as they run.

Forward inferencing is the problem-solving strategy of drawing logical conclusions from given, verified information and premises. "Creating A Language Sandwich" is an activity to teach forward inferencing (Gauthier, 1992). In this activity, students turn to the middle of a book they have never read and read a passage. When finished, students use backward reasoning and forward inferencing to write paragraph(s) to describe things that could have happened before the passage they read. They compare their inferences to what actually occurred in the book. A few students volunteer to explain the thinking processes they used to inference and reason backward.

---

2. Older students can be taught one or more of the problem solving strategies in Table 12-2. After these strategies have been taught students can hold a trial and videotape it, so as to analyze aspects of their thinking that had the most positive impact on solving the problems, as shown on videotape segment 9.

For an example of the impact that teaching problem solving skills can have, see Figure 12-4. Christopher was a third grade student who was taught to use the strategies in Table 12-1. Prior to instruction he was asked what he would do if he had a problem (see #1 in Figure 12-4). Following instruction, Christopher was asked what he would do to solve problems (see #2 in Figure 12-4). Notice the improved reasoning evidenced.

Dimension 5: Developing Students' Metacognitive Thinking Abilities. Metacognitive thinking involves three components: self-knowledge, self-appraisal, and self-regulation. Paris and Wixson (1983) refer to metacognition as the *will* and *skill* to educate oneself. Students develop self-appraisal by reflecting upon and evaluating reasons for their beliefs. They learn to *not* (1) simply agree or disagree; (2) accept or reject conclusions on the basis

FIGURE 12-4
Sample of Student Self-Assessment Form for Group Work Skills

Sample 1: How Cristopher Would Solve His Problem Prior To Instruction

1. her mom had taxes.
2. she ran away.
3. sit on the couch, and wach t.v.

Sample 2: How Christopher Will Solve Problems After Instruction

1. make shure what the problem is.
2. find out all the infortion

---

of egocentric attachment or excessive desire; and (3) identify their errors by knowing why their reasons deviated from others. Students learn to self-regulate by using strategies that "repair" their thinking, and to overcome barriers that interfere with their talents, projects, and goals. They also analyze how, when, and why the tactics they create work.

Social interactions enable students to uncover their hidden metacognitive processes. Social interactions allow students to rework ideas vicariously as they watch others reshape performances.

1. A lesson that builds metacognition is called "You Be the Counselor." It builds metacognition by enabling students to walk in another person's shoes. Its purpose is to assist students to understand reasons for their beliefs by analyzing the metacognitive thoughts of main characters. You teach the following metacognitive processes prior to their reading: To assist others you must know a lot about yourself and the other person. You must pay attention to why you and they do things; you must understand which strengths and which weaknesses in your and in the other person's personal-

---

THE CHALLENGE OF DIVERSITY

Students with learning disabilities often need to be guided to see that many options are at their disposal during problem-solving. By asking them to practice more than one strategy when they are perplexed they learn to correct their own problems. You teach them to practice more than one strategy before asking for your help. This increases their chances for success and builds their self-esteem.

FIGURE 12-5
Sample of Analyzing the Metacognitive Thoughts of Main Characters in Children's Literature

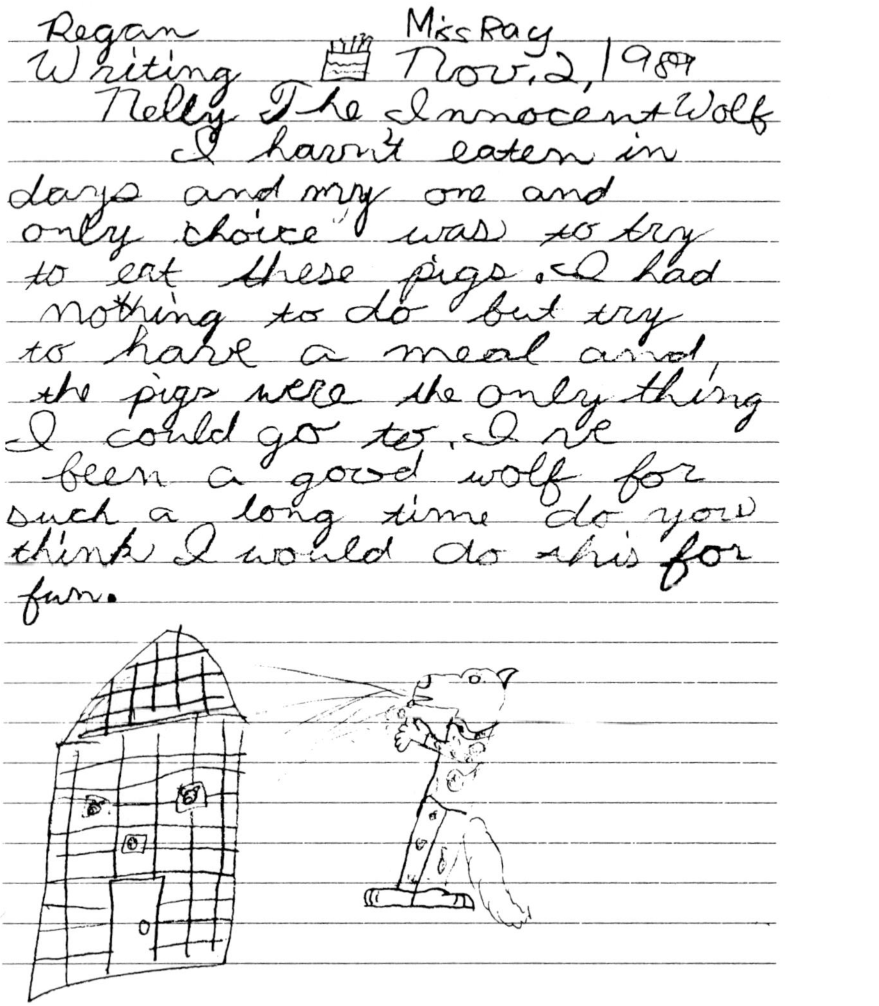

Regan   Miss Ray
Writing   Nov, 2, 1989
    Nelly The Innocent Wolf
    I haven't eaten in
days and my one and
only choice was to try
to eat these pigs. I had
nothing to do but try
to have a meal and,
the pigs were the only thing
I could go to. I've
been a good wolf for
such a long time do you
think I would do this for
fun.

ities led to the situation you and/or they face; you separate facts from your opinions, assumptions, and beliefs; and you question facts, beliefs, and assumptions others present that do not match what is expected or normal.

Then students select a book where character's conflict (such as the story of *The Three Little Pigs*), and where the author's metacognitions favor one side (e.g., the story of the three little pigs is told from the pigs' point of view). Students are then to use the metacognitive process you taught and write the likely metacognitions of the opposing character (the wolf). Figure 12-5 provides an example.

FIGURE 12-6
Students' Story Letters to Develop Metacognitive Thinking

Monday morning

Dear Reader,

An intriguing but not-much-used fictional device is storytelling by letter.

Because the technique is a little tricky, you might have students work on it in pairs. Each student will take one part in the correspondence. Also, make the first try an adaptation of a familiar story. For example, here's part of "The Three Little Pigs" retold as letters between the mothers of the characters.

Dear Mrs. Wolf,   July 9

My piglets have written me that your son has threatened to blow their houses down. Please talk to him about this.

Sincerely,

Mrs. Sow

Dear Mrs. Sow,   July 18

Your pigs are the trouble-makers. Tell them to stop calling my son names like "Big Bad Wolf."
I hate to cut this short but I'm making my son a sheep's costume for a Halloween party.

Sincerely,

Mrs. Wolf

Once students finish these metacognitive reports, they generate im-promptu metacognitions as if they were the wolf being interviewed. Students become the wolf they created and are asked questions by you and classmates. Sample questions are: "You will be brought to trial for harassing the pigs and for breaking and entering. What will you do if the jury decides to suspend punishment and place you on probation?" (Responses to this question in one second grade class ranged from "I will rebuild the three pigs' houses," "I will buy the material for them," and "I really didn't eat any of them, and actually the pigs learned a lesson about how to build their houses on account of me.") "If the city decided to give you a medal for reforming and rebuilding the pigs' houses, what will you think and how will you respond?" and "Why did you blow down the pigs' houses if you weren't intending to eat them?" (One second grade "wolf" answered this question by stating: "I thought it was unnatural for pigs to have houses.")

An extension of this activity was created by Fair, Melvin, Bantz, and Vause (1988). Students devise "story letters" as if they were the mothers/fathers of main characters in a story, e.g. wolf and the pigs (see Figure 12-6).

2. A second activity to develop metacognitive thinking gradually introduces students to metacognition by discovering what metacognition is and how it aids learning (Schmelzer, 1992). The activity begins by introducing the following symbols:

Ü - I know I know

☆ - I know I don't know

✓ - I don't know if I know

In this activity, students place one of the above symbols after each answer they write. If a student answers a question correctly and also places a Ü by a question, two points are given (for the correct answer and for knowing the answer was correct, indicating strong metacognition). If a student answers a question incorrectly and places a ☆ by the answer, points are *not* given for the incorrect answer but are given for the correct symbol because students used their metacognitive thinking correctly and acknowledged their uncertainty. No points are given for an incorrect answer followed by a ✓ . This symbol indicates that the student did not know if they were correct or not.

3. Students can also read a book and write five suggested metacognitions a main character could have used to improve his/her successes in the book.

Remember: you might think that a mistake has been made and that Dimension 6 was inadvertently omitted, as the discussion moves from Dimension 5 to Dimension 7. Dimension 6 is creativity thinking. Because it

"Man's greatest ability is the ability to care. If you *really do* care about the people around you, you will do the right things and make things happen."
—Bart Conner, Olympic Gymnast

was discussed in Chapter 11, this Chapter will now move directly to Dimension 7.

Dimension 7: Thinking More Effectively in Groups. Students who think more effectively in groups understand and depend upon the nature of thinking as it evolves in group settings and is influenced by group behavior. Components of group thinking that you can teach follow:

I. Mediation Abilities
   A. Interpreting the environment, formulating questions, holding positive attitudes, discouraging stereotypes, explaining how ideas are related, and visually representing problems
   B. Modeling their thinking processes by thinking aloud as a critical mediation strategy in group activities
   C. Mentoring, networking, and using group work tools such as the Nominal Technique and Delphi Procedure
   D. Using peer influence and authority appropriately
   E. Understanding the difference between winning an argument and being right
II. Adhering to and Knowing the Standards of Behavior Believed by the Group to be Important
III. Using Skills and Potential Interactively
   A. Creating effective, positive climates
   B. Following and forming logical arguments in discussions, writings, and in formal presentations

FIGURE 12-7
Sample of Student's Self-Assessment of Cooperative Groups

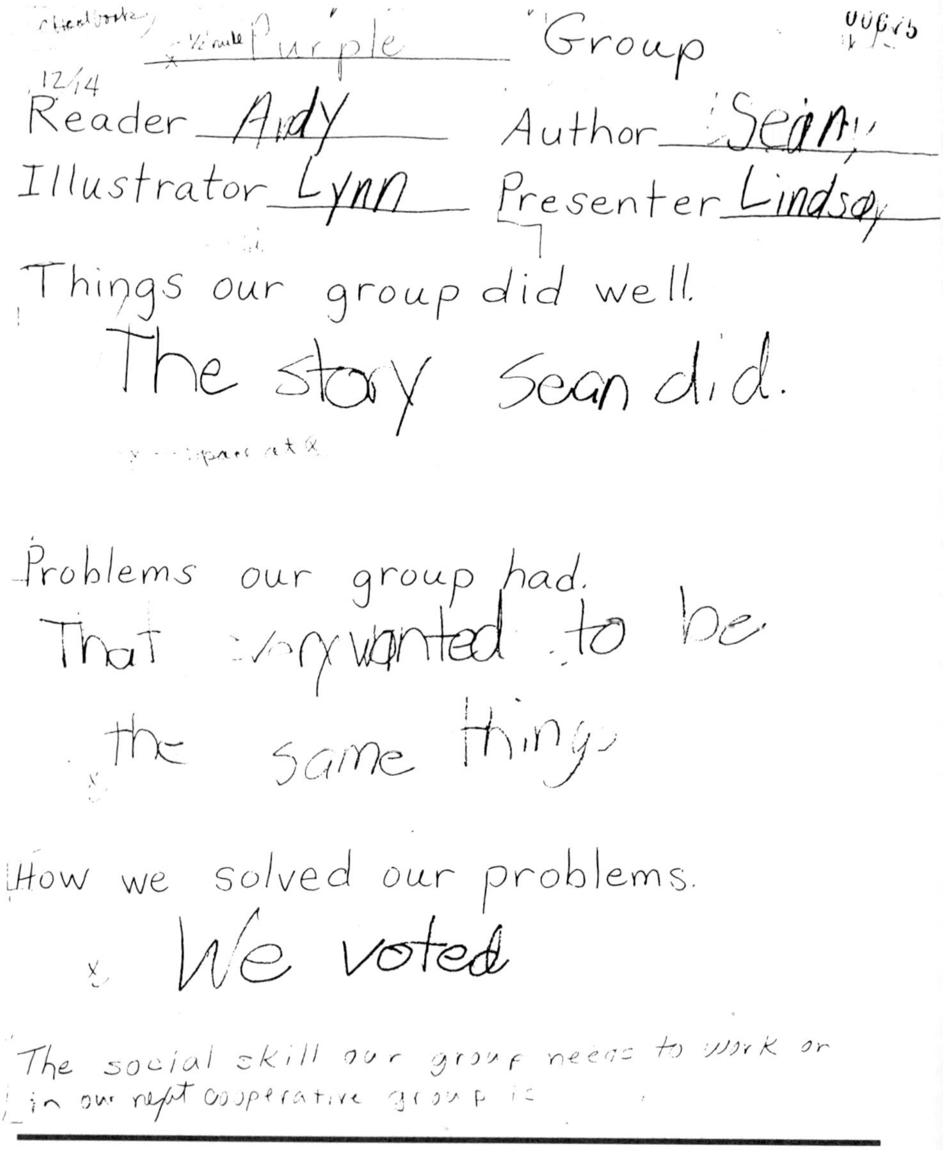

_____ Purple _____ "Group

12/14
Reader __Andy__   Author __Sean__
Illustrator __Lynn__   Presenter __Lindsay__

Things our group did well.
The story Sean did.

Problems our group had.
That everyone wanted to be
the same thing.

How we solved our problems.
We voted

The social skill our group needs to work on
in our next cooperative group is

    C. Perceiving where regards are given, which beliefs are held,
       and when and why values are stated
  IV. Thinking to Advance Others
    A. Setting and meeting challenging performance goals with
       others
    B. Using diverse talents collaboratively
    C. Analyzing actions of winners
    D. Exercising reciprocity

E. Eliminating blocks to group productivity

F. Listening carefully to other people's ideas

G. Being sensitive to the difference between the validity of a belief and the intensity with which it is held

H. Knowing how to take turns in discussions and how to ask better questions.

The following activity strenghtens such group work skills:

1. Once students have been taught the components of group thinking process, four-member groups read copies of the same selection of children's literature. Each member is assigned a different purpose: one student evaluates the quality of thinking/writing in the story; a second analyzes the main character's problem solving strategies; a third ties story events to the modern world, projecting when such events might occur in the future; and a fourth studies how characters increase or decrease their trustworthiness, relating this information as recommendations to classmates for successfully extending their trust to others. Each person shares what he/she learned with the group. Once groups are finished they evaluate their group thinking skills, using a form similar to Figure 12-7.

2. A second activity to build group thinking process is to teach students to make statements of appreciation and give compliments. Students are taught to offer the following statements when they work in groups: "I liked it when . . ."; "I felt good when you . . ."; "I admire you for . . ." The second step is to ask students to set the goal of making at least one statement of appreciation to each member of their group.

3. This activity teaches students to overcome peer pressure by learning about famous people in history who faced serious peer pressure (Myers, 1992). Introduce the books *Hey, Al* by Arthur Yorinks and *Gee, Wiz* by Linda Allison. Students analyze how characters in these books tried to discourage famous people. They complete a chart with these headings: *Peer Pressure and Its Consequences*. Students then list strategies other historical and fictitious figures used to overcome peer pressure by reading one of the following books: *Meaning Well* by Sheila Cole; *The Grass Pipe* by Robert Coles; *Amelia Quackenbush* by Sharloya Gold; *Trapped* by Roderic Jeffries; *Pickpocket Run* by Annabel and Edgar Johnson; *Cross-Country Runner* by Leon McClinton; *Edgar Allen* by John Neufeld; *The Girl from Nowhere* by Hertha Von Bebhardt; and "The Eye of Conscience" in *Perspectives* (Harcourt Brace Jovanovich, p. 92–101). After reading, they answer these questions:

1. How things might have been different if the people they read about had not used a strategy to overcome peer pressure.

2. Do they agree or disagree with the characters' actions?

3. What are some options the characters overlooked?

4. How will they respond if facing a similar situation?

Students then divide into groups and read, "The Bear and the Crow" from *Fables* by Arnold Lobel, and discuss their values about wearing the "right" clothes and being "in style." They answer the questions, "Who influences my decisions concerning what clothes I wear?" and "What are the consequences of my decisions?"

4. Another activity to develop group thinking skills is called *"We Goals."* Students develop class goals for thematic units in language arts, math, and science classes. Students identify important behaviors and thinking/ communication competencies they want to achieve by the end of the unit by asking questions such as: What is the best thinking we can do by the end of this unit? What talent do I have and want to contribute to help us reach our goals? Each student identifies a special contribution to make, which is written on a poster board, and assessed at the end of the unit.

Dimension 8: Ability to Think Effectively When Alone.   People differ in their ability and willingness to pursue and hold onto the power of their own ideas. You can increase students' willingness to "hold on" to their inventions by increasing the quality of thinking they use when working alone, such as being responsible for goals they set, directions they establish, and purposes they define. As Elbow (1981) stated: "The mark of the person who can actually make *progress* in thinking—who can sit down at 8:30 with one set of ideas and stand up at 11:00 with better ideas—is a willingness to notice and listen to those inconvenient little details, those annoying loose ends, those embarrassments or puzzles, instead of impatiently sweeping them under the rug (p. 131)." The components of these thinking processes that you can teach appear below.

  I. Setting personal priorities
    A. Holding rules and liberties in balance
    B. Dealing with marginal performances
    C. Stimulating one's own intellectual curiosity
    D. Planning one's best learning procedures
    E. Learning independently and having an abiding interest in doing so
 II. Affirming one's thinking by acting upon one's beliefs with a focused patterning, consistency, and repetition
    A. Arriving at a positive position and taking positive action
    B. Presenting ideas clearly
    C. Responding to diverse ideas
III. Balancing offering to, and accepting, offers of help
 IV. Completing work in a well-organized manner

1. A first method of teaching and modeling how to do each of the above thinking processes is to describe and show samples of the work of past students who were successful in completing self-initiated projects.

2. Ask the class to practice establishing weekly priorities for three weeks, and making journal entries each Friday concerning their growth in thinking when working alone. Then students create new strategies to use while reading, writing, and working alone for the coming week.

3. This activity is designed to increase students' self-initiated reflection. Students read a first person narrative from books such as: *Growing Up*

Adopted; The Diary of a Young Girl; If This Is Love, I'll Take Spaghetti; My Side of the Mountain; Boris; Little House in the Big Woods; A Year in the Life of Rosie Bernard; Roller Skates; Thimble Summer; All It Takes is Practice; On the Frontier with Mr. Audubon; Self-Portrait: Margot Zemach; Me and Willie and Pa; The Story of Abraham Lincoln and His Son Todd; and *Poor Richard in France.* Students do not see the title or any pictures as they read. They reason as to who the first person narrator is. They tell you and indicate the point in the story where they made an identification. Students write the rationale for their reasoning and continue to read the remainder of the selection. They may change their minds at any time. With each change, students describe weaknesses in their first reasoning process. After all have finished, the first students to identify the narrator correctly explain the thinking processes used to classmates. Students then make a journal entry to describe occasions in their life when they will increase their reflectivity by suspending judgments and attending to details.

4. A fourth method to build thinking processes used when alone is to designate a period of time in which students create their own strategy. Students benefit by hearing sample strategies successful people use, e.g., Orel Hershiser, the famous Los Angeles Dodgers' baseball player keeps a daily diary to plot conditions surrounding his success and plans for improvement. He told a radio announcer that his memory is too faulty and he cared too much about his professional baseball career not to develop a method for thinking better when working alone. Similarly, Sonny Rollins, the famous jazz musician, solves his problems by going outside to be alone and practicing his instrument uninterrupted.

Punctuate the importance of learning these abilities by telling students that The Power of Positive Students Program reports that 87 percent of people do not have goals. Of the 13 percent that set goals, only 3 percent write them down. These 3 percent of our population accomplish 50–125 times more than the others. Teach students to write their goals by asking them to set goals for the coming week, with a plan of action and a target date:

MY PERSONAL AND SCHOOL GOALS ARE **TARGET DATE**

1. _____ _____

   _____

2. _____ _____

   _____ etc.

5. A last activity is for students to identify thinking strategies peers and adults use to overcome problems they face when working alone. Students identify five people they judge to possess exceptional skill in one area of working alone. They survey these people and collapse their strategies into one that would meet their working style by using SCRAMBLIN' (p. 359). This activity aids students in planning strategies that repair their thinking relative to specific communication tasks.

To this point in the chapter you have learned strategies and activities that enhance students' thinking skills, processes, decision-making abilities, problem-solving skills, group work, and working alone strategies that will improve their abilities to read, write, speak, and listen. You also discovered that students' first step toward critical thinking is observing your modeling and subsequent descriptions of quality thinking.

STRATEGIES THAT TEACH

LESSONS THAT DEVELOP STUDENTS' HIGH LEVEL THINKING AND COMMUNICATION ABILITIES

You learned that there are several components within the seven dimensions of critical thinking that you can teach. You will now learn to construct lessons that foster students' abilities to (1) judge the credibility of sources; (2) make reliable comparisons and contrasts; (3) use the weighted characteristics test as a decision making tool; and (4) negotiate.

CREATING LESSONS THAT TEACH STUDENTS TO JUDGE THE CREDIBILITY OF SOURCES

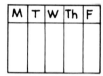

Recommended Grade Levels Are Grades 3–8

Open this lesson by presenting the objective to students. You describe that judging credibility involves applying details to the main point and using the thinking processes in Thinking Guide 12-1. You suggest that one way they will recognize that they have improved their ability to judge credibility is if they ascertain the verdict in a trial from *You Be the Jury*.

To dispel students' misconceptions you ask: "Has anyone ever called you "gullible"? Have you ever been embarrassed because you believed something that others knew wasn't true? When you learn the thinking and communication processes in our lesson today, you can avoid such situations in the future."

Ask students to read Thinking Guide 12-1 and describe how each person represents one quality of credibility. Read each quality and give an example of an incident when one student in the class exhibited each quality. Emphasize that when students use these qualities to judge the validity of new information, they will more likely select the most credible sections of that information (See Thinking Guide 12-1).

The lesson proceeds by providing the following examples of when students can use the Thinking Guide. You state: "One way you will use these qualities in real life, is when two friends come to you with conflicting stories and ask you to help resolve their differences. You will also find this skill helpful when people present information you know nothing about. When you become an adult, you may be called to serve on a jury. Using the information in Thinking Guide 12-1 will be important then and in your daily life."

THINKING GUIDE 12-1
How to Know Who Knows Best: Judging Credibility

Students then complete one of two objectives. First, they could meet in small groups, in pairs, or work alone as they use Thinking Guide 12-1 to determine the verdict in three stories from the books *You Be the Jury* and *You Be the Jury II*. As they read, they record points in the story where credibility of sources was indicated. When finished, they meet with you to present what they learned. Second, students could describe which of three reports of a current event is most credible. As they read they also record points in the accounts where credibility was built. They discuss their work with you when finished.

Students then rethink and reformulate their new thinking abilities by reading a mystery and determining the ending. Students indicate points in their reading where one of the qualities on Thinking Guide 12-1 was engaged to build credibility. [Students should identify five points in their reading where they recognize a quality or the absence of a quality of credibility. Five recorded incidents would earn the grade of "A," (4) a "B," (3) a "C," and (2) a "D." To integrate this lesson across the curriculum challenge students to (a) read a historical fiction and nonfiction book on the same topic and rate their credibility; (b) locate information on television and in printed sources that are not as credible as they could be; and (c) initiate qualities of credibility to resolve disputes that arise at school.

CREATING LESSONS THAT TEACH STUDENTS TO COMPARE AND CONTRAST

Recommended Grade Levels Are Preschool to Grade 2

To begin this lesson students select two books from the following list. Because most of these books were written by Steven Kellogg, advanced students can detect similarities and differences between writing styles of Steven Kellogg and Joanna Cole. They can also denote differences between Steven's books and analyze why such differences in writing style existed.

A Rose for Pinkerton, Steven Kellogg, Dial Press, 1981.

Aster Aardvark's Alphabet Adventures, Steven Kellogg, Morrow Junior Books, 1987.

Can I Keep Him? Steven Kellogg, Dial Press, 1971.

Dog's Body, Joanna Cole, Morrow and Co., 1986.

Much Bigger Than Martin, Steven Kellogg, Dial Press, 1976.

Pinkerton, Behave! Steven Kellogg, Dial Press, 1979.

Tallyho, Pinkerton! Steven Kellogg, Dial Press, 1982.

The Mysterious Tadpole, Steven Kellogg, Dial Press, 1977.

The Mystery of the Missing Red Mitten, Steven Kellogg, Dial Press, 1974.

Won't Somebody Play With Me? Steven Kellogg, Dial Press, 1972.

Present the objective of the lesson by stating: "Today we are going to become better speakers, listeners, readers, and writers by becoming better thinkers. You will learn to compare things that are similar and different. You will know that you can compare things when you are able to select two things that are alike and different in the books you selected for me to read." You dispel students' misconceptions by saying: "I know that sometimes you may think that it takes too much time to stop and compare things. When I go to the grocery store and if I'm in a hurry, then I don't compare prices to find out which one is the cheapest and I end up spending more money than I should. But when I go and take my time, I compare items and prices. This saves me a lot of money. Throughout life it will be important for you to learn how to compare things."

Teach students to compare things by using the Venn Diagram on Thinking Guide 12-2 as students hold and think about similarities and differences between the orange and apple that you placed on the table each small group is using. As each student suggests a way the fruits are alike, you ask them to do a think aloud as to the thought processes they used to detect the similarity, e.g., many will say that their senses assisted in recognizing common features. Then teach that comparing things means that one looks carefully at each part of objects, ideas, or events to determine sections that are like other objects, ideas, or events to which one can relate. By taking time to observe these relationships, one can learn and remember new information better.

After completing one large Thinking Guide 12-2 as a class, students choose one of the following activities to apply the Thinking Guide independently:

1. Go to the reading center and pick two books by Dr. Seuss. Look at each book and tell me how they are alike and how they are different. Write similarities and differences on Thinking Guide 12-2.
2. Go to the book center and pick any two books with a partner. Take these books to the listening center and record on the tape recorder how they are alike and how they are different.
3. Go to the art center with a partner. Each of you will draw a picture without showing each other the picture you drew until it is

THINKING GUIDE 12-2
Venn Diagram Strategy Sheet

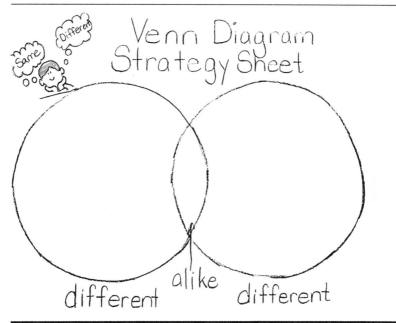

finished. Write as many ways as you can find that the two pictures are similar and different and write these on Thinking Guide 12-2.

4. Choose two favorite sports, television, or movie stars. Record how these two superstars are alike and different on Thinking Guide 12-2.

To grade the objective, students should record 10 features that are similar or different to earn maximum points. Once students' work has been graded, you challenge them to rethink and reformulate the compare and contrast thinking process by leading a discussion of how this type of thinking will increase their abilities to speak, listen, read, and write in the future.

CREATING LESSONS THAT TEACH STUDENTS TO USE THE WEIGHTED CHARACTERISTICS TEST TO SOLVE PROBLEMS

Recommended Grade Levels Are Grade 3 Through Grade 8

Introduce the objective of this lesson by saying: "Today you will learn a strategy to solve problems called The Weighted Characteristics Test. You will see several samples of it in practice and then use it to solve a problem in a book that a main character faces. You will know you have learned the strategy when you practice using it in a real world situation."

You can dispel students' misconceptions about the difficulty of this lesson by stating that the ability to solve problems is not as difficult to learn as they might expect. There are tools that can assist their thinking. The Weighted Characteristics Test is one such tool and you will learn how to use it today. Because you will be in situations throughout your life where you have to make choices to solve a problem, you will profit by using The Weighted Characteristics Test. It enables you to more clearly see both sides of the problem before you select an action that is best for you.

Then elicit students' thinking by asking them to recall a time in their lives when they had a very important problem to solve. Tell them that they should think about this problem as they learn a new tool they can use to help themselves when they have to solve such problems again.

Teach the Thinking Guide to students by saying: "The Weighted Characteristics Test was invented by Benjamin Franklin. Look at your Thinking Guide 12-3. Whenever you have a difficult problem to solve, list the choices you face on different sides of the balance scale. Below each choice, list every possible negative and positive consequence that could arise if you selected that choice. Once you've listed all consequences, count the total for both sides of the scale. For example, if the right side of the scale had six consequences and the left side had seven, you would have a total of 13 consequences. You would then use this total number to weigh each consequence. You assign a 13 to the most important consequence to you. It can be a positive consequence that you really want to occur or it can be a negative consequence that you really want to avoid. The second most important consequence receives a weight of 12, etc. Once all consequences are weighted, total both sides of the scale. The solution with the highest number of points is likely to be the decision that is best for you at this time."

You can use the following example to demonstrate how The Weighted Characteristics Test aids students to see both sides of a problem before determining a solution. Tell students that the principal has called for a faculty meeting this afternoon after school. He wants the teachers to help him decide whether or not we should continue having ice cream parties in the cafeteria. Recently, we have experienced groups of students fighting during this time. Ask students to help you decide what would be better for all involved. Hand out a simulated copy of Thinking Guide 12-3 and show how the principal and teachers listed weighed the consequences of holding and not holding ice cream parties.

Then students complete an objective using the Thinking Guide. They read a book and stop at the point where the main character has to solve a problem. Students are to place themselves in the main character's shoes and solve the problem using the weighted characteristics test. Students then compare their answer to the solution the main character drew. On the back of the Thinking Guide students describe why the main character's or their solutions were better and why. Books where the main character has several decisions to make are: *Grady the Great* by Judith Strommen; *Mississippi Bridge* by Mildred Taylor; *Danger in Tibet; Stage Door to Terror* by Robert Quackenbush; *Lost in the Amazon* by Robert Quackenbush; *Sherlock Holmes; The Adventure of Black Peter; The "Gloria Scott"; The Adventure of the Copper Beeches; The Redheaded League* by Murray Shaw; *The Tatooed Potato and Other*

THINKING GUIDE 12-3
The Weighted Characteristics Test

Clues by Ellen Raskin; *Choose Your Own Adventure—Journey Under the Sea* by R. A. Montgomery; *Ida and The Wool Smugglers* by Sue Ann Alderson and Ann Blades; and *The Courage of Sarah Noble* by Alice Dalgliesh.

You can integrate this lesson across the curriculum through the following activities:

1. Students identify a problem that exists in their school or community and use the weighted characteristics test to develop a possible solution.

2. Students divide into groups and use Thinking Guide 12-3 to effect a change in the lunchroom. They write a letter, that you approve, to the principal stating the proposed change and why they suggest that change.

3. Pretend you had a fight with a friend and you can't decide if you should (1) apologize and explain your side again; (2) go up and talk to your friend and pretend nothing happened; or (3) ignore your friend until he/she comes to you. What should you do and why? How did you decide what to do?

4. *Mathematics:* Read the books *If You Had A Million Dollars*, by David Schwartz, and *A Chair For My Mother*. Students use the weighted characteristics test to decide how to spend money the class has earned on a group project or money they have earned individually.

5. *Science:* Students complete a journal entry about Thomas Edison or a scientist of their choice. As they study the scientist, seek to discover how they solved problems and if they used the weighted characteristics test.

6. *Fine Arts:* Read the books *Great Painters* by Piero Ventura; *An Artist* by M. B. Goffstein; or *Marc Chagall* by M. B. Goffstein. Ask students to identify how these people solve problems.

CREATING LESSONS THAT TEACH HOW TO NEGOTIATE

Recommended Grade Levels Are Grade 4 Through Grade 8

Present a list of books that depict a wide range of cultural differences and negotiations that worked well. Samples of such books are:

1. *Ishi. Last of His Tribe* by Theodora Kroeber; Houghton/Parnassus Press. (Summary: story of last survivor of Yahi Indian Tribe.)
2. *Journey to Washington* by Daniel K. Inouye, with Lawrence Elliott; Prentice Hall. (Summary: autobiography of first Japanese-American to be elected to Congress.)
3. *The Story of My Life* by Helen Keller; Doubleday. (Summary: Helen Keller writes of her early life and education.)
4. *Martin Luther King, Jr.* by Jaqueline Harris; Watts. (Summary: Overview of the historic achievements of the civil rights movement and Dr. King.)
5. *My Family and Other Animals* by Gerald Durrell; Penguin Books. (Summary: As a boy, this British zoologist spent five years on an island with his family.)
6. *Just One Friend* by Lynn Hall; Scribner's. (Summary: A 16-year-old girl with learning difficulties deals with the loss of her best friend.)
7. *All Creatures Great and Small* by James Herriot; St. Martin's Press. (Summary: author tells of his life as a young veterinarian.)
8. *The Dog Who Wouldn't Be* by Farley Mowat; Little, Brown. (Summary: A dog's adventure.)
9. *Abe Lincoln Grows Up* by Carl Sandburg; Harcourt Brace Jovanovich. (Summary: Lincoln's early years up to age 19.)
10. *Amos Fortune, Free Man* by Elizabeth Yates; E. P. Dutton. (Summary: Biography of a slave from life in Africa to the U.S.)

Tell students that they will learn to improve their negotiating skills by following the steps you'll provide (which they can make into their own thinking guide). Tell students that they will know that they have been successful when, in the future, their group work has fewer disputes and misunderstandings. Dispel students' misconceptions by telling them that they are likely to enjoy the lesson, as students in other schools who completed it reported many benefits. For example, Jerry stated, "We liked learning to negotiate because it gives you a chance to get the point of views of your fellow classmates."

Keri stated, "The other day I was on the phone with a friend of mine. She said something and it made me mad, because I didn't know what she was trying to say. So I asked her what she meant by that and she told me.

But when she told what she meant by that it wasn't bad at all." The information in this lesson taught Keri how to resolve this potential misunderstanding.

To begin this lesson, students bring five objects or ideas about a way to improve the classroom or school. They must defend their positions and the point of view their five objectives and items represent. Before they begin their defense, teach the following attitudes and actions that lead to successful negotiations.

1. Negotiations occur more effectively when both people are:

calm	versus	angry
rational	versus	irrational
able to show care	versus	emotional
committed	versus	impulsive
can see other points of view	versus	unable to see other points of view

2. Students need to ask themselves the following questions before they enter a negotiation: (a) What things do they already know and what things do they need to know? (b) How should they present _____? (c) What or who can help them decide how well we've done or what we've missed?

3. During negotiations, the following rules should be in place: (a) Do forced "turn taking" if necessary to set up equality; (b) When there is a dispute one person goes first and a second person gets first choice next; (c) Set positive expectations for all consequences; (d) Do not be sidetracked by excuses; (e) At the end of each negotiating session implement one agreed-upon action immediately; (f) Avoid conflict by requiring both people in a dispute to generate two ways each that the issue could be resolved; (g) When an impasse has been reached, enact logical consequences which give participants choices; (h) Avoid side-tracking strategies and gain agreement by focusing on only one issue at a time; (i) Use "The All Around Strategy" which requires each person to take a turn to comment on an idea before anyone can make a second comment. All members have the right to say "I pass." If passing becomes a problem, go back and examine what you can do to make the climate safer.

Students give examples from their personal experiences where they have witnessed the positive effects of some of these negotiating strategies. Students videotape one of their small group meetings in a content area before and after this lesson to judge if their negotiating skills improved.

CRITICAL THINKING ACTIVITY 12
Developing Analytical Thinking Processes Through Fairy Tales

You can use the following lesson to develop and assess many of the higher level thinking abilities within this chapter. Bartelo (1992) also uses this activity to develop multicultural awarenesses. You begin by explaining that similar fairy and folk tales appear in many countries, e.g., there are over

900 versions of *Cinderella* (Rooth, 1951). You stop this lesson at any point, and ask students to analyze characteristics of the various cultures represented, the societal value the main character was designed to depict, the function magic served, and what the ending projects about the values that the people in that culture hold.

Begin this lesson by telling students that they can select what part of the books they wish to analyze. The objective of the lesson is to develop their abilites to infer and analyze purposes and values. Then read the "letter" to Cinderella in *The Jolly Postman* by Janet and Allan Ahlberg. This letter is to tell Cinderella about a book being published to celebrate her marriage to the prince. Continue the lesson with the book *Each Peach Pear Plum*, which catches Cinderella and other fairy tale characters in "Hide and Seek" situations. The stories of Cinderella by Perrault and the tale made famous by Walt Disney can also be read. A chart can then be drawn to contrast variant versions according to the categories students select. Students do think alouds as to the processes they used in the analyses.

Then students meet in response groups to discuss variant versions of Cinderella that they have read. Students can read from the following:

1. *Cinderella:* The old English version, also entitled *The Glass Slipper*, is typical of the well-known story line, except that Cinderella marries a lord. Her sisters also marry lords.
2. *Yeh-Shen:* The Chinese Cinderella meets the prince at a festival. The magic is provided by a fish. The stepmother and stepsisters are crushed to death by stones to end the story.
3. *The Egyptian Cinderella:* Phodopis is a Greek slave who loses a slipper which a falcon drops in the lap of the Pharaoh. The Pharaoh fears it is a sign from the gods and finds the girl to tell her he will marry her. Her eyes captivate him because "they are like the Nile."
4. *Konjee:* In this Korean version of Cinderella, she meets her prince at her uncle's wedding. A black cow and maid are the providers of magic. This story has at least three different versions. In one version, a stepsister tries to chase Konjee and dies by falling from a rope.
5. *Tatterhood:* This book presents a version where "Cinderella" is on equal terms with the man. In this version "Cinderella" takes an active role in shaping her own destiny.
6. *Sydneyrella and the Glass Slipper:* This modern version presents the man as the main character. It is particularly enjoyable because Sydneyrella is a football hero with glass sneakers, and a corporate executive in the end.
7. *The Paper Bag Princess:* In this modern version the princess rescues a prince who doesn't appreciate her efforts because she doesn't look "princesslike."
8. *Vasilisa the Beautiful* (T. Whitney, 1970): A Russian version of Cinderella in which Vasilisa, with the help of her magic doll, thwarts her stepmother and stepsisters.

9. *Princess Furball* and *Moss Gown* are two of the most recent versions.

To rethink and reformulate their analytical abilities, students fashion their own modern version of Cinderella, using values and unexplained phenomena they select to illustrate in their tale. Each group conceals the values and unexplained phenomena their version was designed to depict until it is presented to the class. Students compare and analyze their versions as to the common cultural values they exhibit.

Once these presentations are complete, books in Notecard 25 can be used in a wide variety of ways to strengthen analytical thinking. Notecard 25 lists variant versions of other fairy tales. Students can set their own analytical thinking and communication ability development objectives with these sets of books.

PROFESSIONAL DEVELOPMENT OPPORTUNITY
How to Build Thinking and Communication Abilities Through Autobiographies and Biographies

Students become more aware of their individual talents, thinking strengths, and metacognitions by reading about famous people born on their birthdate. Lists of famous people born on each day of the year appear in *126 Strategies That Build Language Arts Abilities* (Collins, 1992a). Students analyze characteristics of their selected person in the autobiography and biography they read. They compare these characteristics to their own personalities using a matrix, semantic map, or chart. Then they write or discuss what it would have been like to be the famous person's best friend. Each student identifies activities the two might enjoy in the student's community. Students also write an analysis of what made that person successful, in their opinion.

This activity culminates with students studying about and writing their own autobiography. They begin by stating the history of their name, through conferences with parents and books such as *Baby Names from Around the World* by Maxine Fields (Pocket Books, 1985); *American Surnames* by Elsdon C. Smith (Chilton Book Company, 1969); or *American Given Names* by George R. Stewart (Oxford University Press, 1979). Students then focus upon what they judge to be their strengths of character. Next, students pair with a friend and write a biography of their partner without conferring with him/her. Afterward students compare their autobiographies to the biography their partner wrote about them. They explain why differences in perceptions and self-perceptions exist. They report the differences that they have learned between the autobiographical and biographical genre. Then they describe the metacognitive thinking processes that this activity assisted them to develop.

References for autobiographies are *Exploring the Lives of Gifted People* by Kathy Balsamo (Good Apple, 1987) and six series of books from Scholastic entitled *Champions of Change, Spotlight on TV Stars, Spotlight on Movie Stars, Spotlight on Sports Stars, Superstars,* and *Superstars in Action.*

STRATEGIES THAT TEACH

NOTECARD 25: USING DIFFERENT VERSIONS OF FAIRY TALES TO BUILD COMPARATIVE, ANALYTICAL, AND EVALUATIVE THINKING ABILITIES

Share three different versions of the same fairy tale with students, then perform a think aloud of the comparative, analytical, and evaluative thought processes you used as you studied each version. Assign three versions of a different fairy tale to individuals, pairs, or cooperative groups. Students describe the thinking processes they used as they read and how they can use them again in their own lives.

The Three Little Pigs
Walt Disney's The Three Little Pigs by B. Brenner
The Three Little Pigs by Paul Galdone
The Three Little Hawaiian Pigs and the Magic Shark by
   Laird and Laird
The Three Little Pigs by Eric Blegvad
The True Story of The Three Little Pigs by J. Scieszka
The Three Little Pigs by M. Zemach

Little Red Riding Hood
Lon Po Po (Oriental Version) by Ed Young
Little Red Riding Hood by P. Galdone
Little Red Cap by J. Grimm
Little Red Riding Hood by J. Goodall
Little Red Riding Hood by J. Marshall

The Gingerbread Boy
The Runaway Pancake by A. Asbojornsen and J. Moe
The Bun: A Tale from Russia by M. Brown
The Gingerbread Boy by Paul Galdone
Johnny-Cake by J. Jacob
The Gingerbread Rabbit by R. Jarrel
The Pancake by A. Lobel
Journey Cake, Ho! by R. Sawyer

The Hare and the Tortoise
The Hare and the Tortoise by C. Castle
The Hare and the Tortoise by P. Galdone
The Tortoise and the Hare by J. Stevens
The Hare and the Tortoise by B. Wildsmith

(cont'd)

NOTECARD 25 (cont'd)

Jack and the Beanstalk
Jack and the Wonder Beans by J. Still
Jim and the Beanstalk by R. Briggs
Jack and the Beanstalk by Walter de la Mare
Jack and the Beanstalk by Joseph Jacobs
Jack and the Beanstalk by L. Cauley
Jack and the Beanstalk by B. deRegniers
Jack and the Bean Tree by G. Haley
Jack and the Beanstalk by D. W. Johnson

The Old Lady Who Swallowed a Fly
There Was an Old Woman by S. Kellog
I Know an Old Lady by A. Mills and R. Bonne
I Know an Old Lady Who Swallowed a Fly by E. Adams
I Know a Old Lady Who Swallowed a Fly by N. B.
   Westcott

Cinderella
Cinderella by M. Brown
Cinderella by A. Ehrlich
Cinderella by P. Galdone
Cinderella by J. Grimm
Cinderella by C. Perrault
The Paper Bag Princess by R. Munsch
Sydneyrella and the Glass Slipper by B. Myers
Yeh-Shen by A. Louie
The Egyptian Cinderella by S. Climo
Korean Cinderella by E. Adams
Princess Furball by C. Huck
Tatterhood and Other Tales by E. J. Phelps
Moss Gown by W. Hooks

Also see *The Upside Down Tale Series* published by Birch Lane Press/Ariel Books.

TRY IT

1. If you are teaching, select one activity from each dimension of thinking and teach it to your students. Ask them to assess what they've learned, as you analyze their strengths as well. If you are not teaching, prepare one lesson from each dimension of thinking by reading the literature that accompanies it and write lessons for the grade level you prefer to teach.

2. Pretend that you and your students are planning the following projects. State what thinking skills and which lessons you would teach so students have the language arts and thinking abilities necessary to be successful in each project.

a. Students want to work in groups on a science project. They want to decide who will be in their group, who will do each part of the project, and design a timeline for its completion.

b. Students want to plan a "quiet space" in the room where students can work uninterrupted and alone. The girls want it to be decorated; the boys want it to be at the windows.

c. Students want to plan a field trip. You want them to make all the necessary arrangements, plan which activities are to be included, and the types of language arts follow-up activities that will be necessary.

3. The following self-assessment statement was written by a fourth grade student after one of the activities in this chapter had been completed. What does his statement indicate about the component of thinking his teacher taught? Defend your answer.

> We solved mysteries in class together as a group and then alone. We solved mysteries like who stole the diamonds. It was really fun! I liked this lesson best. We learned to put all the conditions together to find one answer.

4. Read two or three different versions of fairy tales on Notecard 25. Identify analytical thinking and langauge arts objectives you will teach with the books you read. Describe why these fairy tales would foster competencies you selected.

FOR YOUR JOURNAL

Journals can be used for self-improvement. You and your students, if you are presently teaching, set a personal goal to learn more about one type of thinking. Students and you spend 15 minutes a day of class time reading and reflecting in your journal, as a learning log. At the end of the week, in small groups, students share what they have learned to improve their thinking.

BUILDING YOUR PROFESSIONAL PORTFOLIO Problem-Solving Competitions

You can contact the following agencies so your students can enter national problem-solving competitions, which refine and enhance many types of thinking abilities.

1. Silver Burdett and Ginn Invention Convention
   250 James Street
   Morristown, NJ 07960
   (Competition is for grades 1–6 and annual entry deadline is February 15)
2. Invent America!
   United States Patent Model Foundation
   510 King Street, Suite 420
   Alexandria, VA 22314
   (Competition is for grades K–8 and the annual entry deadline is April)

3. The *Weekly Reader* National Invention Contest
   245 Long Hill Road
   Middletown, CT 06457
   (Competition is for grades K–8 and the annual entry deadline is mid-December)
4. The Future Problem Solving Program
   St. Andrews College
   Laurinburg, NC 28352
   (Competition is for grades 4–12 and the annual entry deadline varies)
5. Odyssey of the Mind
   Odyssey of the Mind Association, Inc.
   P.O. Box 27
   Glassboro, NJ 08028
   (Team competition for grades K–12 and the annual entry deadline varies)
6. Cognetics
   National Talent Network
   c/o Educational Information and Resource Center
   700 Hollydell Ct.
   Sewell, NJ 08080
   (Competition is for grades K–12 and the annual entry deadline varies)
7. Young Creator's Contest
   National School Boards Association
   1680 Duke Street
   Alexandria, VA 22314-3493
   (More information about grade levels and annual entry deadlines can be obtained at the above address)
8. Young Publish-A-Book Contest
   and the Publish-A-Book Contest
   Raintree Publishers
   P.O. Box 518
   Milwaukee, WI 53201-0518
   (Competition is for grades 2–3 and grades 4–6 respectively and the deadlines for entries are March 1 and January 31 respectively)

Special Needs of Kindergartners and Middle School Students

Kindergarten and middle school language arts programs use learning centers to meet the special needs of these populations.

To understand children we must hear their words, follow their explanations, understand their frustrations, and listen to their logic.

—Ferreiro and Teberosky, 1982

Understanding the explanations, frustrations, logic, and language of pre-school and middle school students requires exceptional knowledge. It is exceptional because it requires a perception of the unique, developmentally driven forces that shape and motivate their communication and thinking. In this chapter you will learn how to use these forces to enlarge young children's and young adolescents' expressive and receptive language abilities.

In previous chapters you have learned strategies that expand elementary students' language and thinking competencies. In this chapter you will master strategies that support preschool and adolescent learning.

By the end of this chapter, you will:

1. Teach to the special needs of kindergarten and middle school students;

2. Know the developmental stages in young children's literacy;

3. Assist parents to reinforce their children's language and thinking development;

4. Understand the importance of play for young children and role play for middle school students;

5. Understand why the middle school years are the second most intricate developmental period in life, and what you can do to reduce its complexities;

6. Use mentors, on-the-spot instruction, language play, learning links, study skills, and learning centers to reinforce emergent literacy for students in preschool through eighth grade.

THEORETICAL FOUNDATION
KINDERGARTNERS AND MIDDLE SCHOOL STUDENTS' NEEDS

It was a glorious day! The kind of day when a giant thought suddenly surprises the rest of the mind, which had been peacefully plotting the daily routine. It was with that giant thought, on that kind of day, that this chapter began. The thought that launched this chapter was: (a) preschool and middle school students have added needs not yet discussed in this book; and (b) the needs of four- and five-year-olds and eleven- to fourteen-year-olds are more similar to each other than to the needs of elementary school age children.

The path middle school students follow to develop adult thinking patterns is analogous to kindergartners' progress toward literacy. Both are motivated by innate curiosities and quests for mastery of adult modes of communication and living. Similarly, young adolescents and kindergartners need extended periods of discussion, for its own sake, to advance their cognitive and communication competencies. Both need adult language/ thinking patterns; shared literacy experiences; supportive small group interactions; multiple exposures to complex concepts; and the freedom to explore language and cognitive problems for as long as nesessary if their learning needs are to be met. You will provide these experiences for kindergarteners in the ways discussed below.

SPECIAL NEEDS OF KINDERGARTEN AND PRESCHOOL STUDENTS

Emergent literacy is one of the most interesting and controversial topics in education and psychology today (Morrow, 1987; Teale & Sulzby, 1986). **Emergent literacy** is a *continuum of understandings that lead to a student's ability to read and write*. The reason "emergent literacy" replaced "reading readiness" as a description of preliterate behavior is because we now know that literacy is a continuous process; one that begins during the first months of life and continues through kindergarten and first grade (Adams, 1990). In Chapter 3 you discovered the depth of research presently underway to better understand the oral language acquisition processes a student must master. There are a comparable number of studies concerning emergent literacy, and how young children come to understand written language. A review of this research follows.

Research now indicates that children learn to read and write as early as two years of age; writing abilities often develop before reading; many students spell before they read; and reading and writing can be learned in conjunction with speaking. Most children enter preschools and kindergartens knowing 14 of 26 letters of the alphabet. Moreover, kindergarten children's literacy develops rapidly. For example, when a one-word label can no longer bear the weight of students' accumulated associations, they begin to use sentences and paragraphs. Most students, by five-and-a-half, have established their own writing style (Hilliker, 1986). By age five, most print in uppercase letters, and a few use both hands interchangeably for handwriting. Your responsibility, as a kindergarten teacher, is to develop hand dominance and fine motor skills, using the letters and words students write. If a student does not have hand dominance by the end of kindergarten, consult with school specialists/parents to ensure that slower evolving abilities are not misinterpreted as learning disabilities. Young children become easily frustrated because their motor skills cannot keep up with their speed in creating ideas they want to write. In such cases, invite older students into the room to scribe for them.

Kindergartners' Special Literacy Needs.   From the 1930s through the 1970s, educators believed that there was a "best time" to initiate reading and writing (and to some degree, speaking and listening) instruction. Educators believed that students had to reach a level of "readiness" before literacy concepts would "imprint" (Morphett & Washburne, 1931). This philosophical position, known as "reading readiness" or language readiness, followed a philosophy that children had to acquire a basic set of mental skills before instruction in reading and writing could begin. These competencies were believed to not be in place until students reached a mental age of six and one-half years for reading and nine years for writing instruction. During the early 1980s new research documented that students do not need a benchmark of accumulated life experiences before literacy instruction can begin.

The first six years of a child's life are extremely important since that is when most language is acquired. Linguists and psychologists have also found that emergent literacy follows a similar path regardless of the language a child is trying to learn. Signs of word recognition appear at about six to eight months of age. At approximately one year, children create their first scribbled words. Children join words together by the eighteenth month, and by four years of age most children have internalized the majority of basic rules that govern their written language. Approximately two years later, students master language to such an extent that they can speak and "write" sentences they never used before (Travers, 1982). What is even more amazing is that although children may have difficulties with other tasks during this six-year period, mastery of the language comes easily and naturally.

Language development parallels motor and cognitive abilities, and are connected to a child's biological makeup. For example, students' brains reach 90 percent of adult size by age five, and at approximately twelve or thirteen, discoveries about language diminish. It seems understanding the cognitive processes that underlie new ideas becomes more important to students than learning more complicated syntax.

Kindergarten Students' Special Language Needs. Research has demonstrated that children who are advanced in oral language tend to achieve better in literacy than those who have not used literary concepts prior to first grade. Studies also indicate that some children enter school with only 2–3 hours of print and text interaction while others have as many as 2,000–3,000 hours of such exposures (Teale, 1986). Research also suggests that this first group of students rarely recover from the disadvantage they carry into kindergarten (Adams, 1990). Because four- and five-year-olds talk to integrate subject matter, substantive conversations transform declarative into applied knowledge (Newmann, 1991).

Kindergarten Students' Special Cognitive Needs. Most students demonstrate many literary understandings in the preschool and kindergarten years. They evidence their awareness that writing has meaning when they *use the same mark repeatedly* (**the recurring principle**). When they realize that "real writing" is not made up of only one mark, but of various marks, they demonstrate the **generative principle**, *a small number of different marks used repeatedly*, but in various orders and directions.

As students become more aware of print conventions, they also realize that "adult writing" is ordered by the **linear principle** and *they place their* *letters horizontally*. At this point, however, they may not be clear as to the left-to-right principle of English. Therefore, while young children know their writing is to be written horizontally, they aren't sure where to begin. For this reason, you will notice that some students write backwards; they begin the first letter on the right and move across their page to the left or they do the "wrap-around" trick. Once students are aware of these principles, they turn their attention to individual letters. Students in this stage work to comprehend the **flexibility principle** in writing. Marie Clay (1975) reports that it takes students considerable time to fully *understand how to make each letter and which features distinguish one letter from another*. When they first begin to write, for example, children do not realize that "I" and "T" are different. When students realize that adding marks to letters can transform them to different letters, they wield the principle of literary flexibility.

As students begin to realize the flexibility of writing, they also *initiate contrasts between letters* or use the **contrastive principle**, e.g., students make comments such as an "a" and an "o" are a lot alike. The last developmental stage in emerging written literacy is when students intend their works to be read by others. They discover that others should be able to read back what they wrote. This stage has been identified as the **sign principle** (*writings are like signatures of thoughts*). An example of the sign principle appears in Figure 13-1.

FIGURE 13-1
Example of the Sign Principle

NOTECARD 26: ALPHABET BOOKS FOR YOUNGER READERS

Alfred's Alphabet by Victoria Chess
ABC of Cars and Trucks by A. Alexander
A is for Everything by K. Barry
A Folding Alphabet Book by M. Beisner
All Butterflies by M. Brown
A for the Ark by R. Duvoisin
Q is for Duck: An Alphabet Guessing Game by M. Elting and M. Folsom
Ed Emberley's ABC by E. Emberley
Jambo Means Hello: Swahili Alphabet Books by M. and T. Feelings
City Seen from A to Z by R. Isadora
Animal Alphabet by B. Kitchen
Lear Alphabet by Edward Lear
We Read: A to Z by D. Crews
On Market Street by A. Lobel
A for Angel: Beni Montresor's ABC Picture Stories by B. Montresor

Ashanti to Zulu: African Traditions by M. Musgrove
All About Arthur: An Absolutely Absurd Ape by Eric Carle
A Peaceable Kingdom: The Shaker ABECEDARIUS by A. Provensen and M. Provensen
Alligators All Around: An Alphabet Book by M. Sendak
A is for Annabelle by T. Tudor
All the Woodland Early: An ABC Book by J. Yolen
A to Z Picture Book by Gyo Fujikawa
An ABC in English and Spanish by R. Tallon
Have you ever seen . . . ? by Beau Gardner
Hey, Look at Me! by Sandy Grant

(cont'd)

NOTECARD 26 (cont'd)

Alphabears: An ABC Book by Kathleen Hague
Alphabatics by Susie MacDonald
Curious George Learns the Alphabet by H. A. Rey
Hosie's Alphabet by Tobias and Leonard Baskin
Computer Alphabet Book by Elizabeth Wall

Brian Wildsmith's ABC by Brian Wildsmith
A Beastly Circus by D. Parish
ABC of Monsters by D. Niland
I Unpacked My Grandmother's Trunk by S. Hoguet
What's Inside? The Alphabet Book by S. Kitamura
Humbug Potion: An A-B-C Cipher by L. Balian

Being an important part of children's discovery of literacy is exciting! As you may realize, you are needed not only to provide support and instruction during this important period of learning, but to express appreciation for the difficult task students undertake in decoding/encoding one of the most difficult languages in the world. You may now also realize why young children often elect to "play like they are reading" until their work with you breaks the "codes of English." Phonemic awareness can be acquired through the alphabet books in Notecard 26 or the Wordless picture books in Notecard 27, which develop students' concept of stories.

NOTECARD 27: WORDLESS BOOKS THAT CAN BE USED WITH STUDENTS OF ALL AGES IN A VARIETY OF WAYS

Airplane Ride by Douglas Florian
Anno's U.S.A. and other books by M. Anno
The Snowman by Raymond Briggs
Good Dog, Carl and other books by A. Day
The Hunter and the Animals by T. dePaola
In the Woods and other books by E. Cristini
Behind the Wheel by E. Koren
How to Hide a Butterfly and Other Insects (Series) by R. Heller
Here Comes Alex Pumpernickel and other books by F. Krahn
Humages and other books by M. Mariotti
Frog Goes to Dinner and other books by M. Mayer
What is New? What is Missing? What is Different? by P. Ruben

Look What I Can Do by J. Aruego
The Story of the Castle by J. Goodall
Charlie-Bob's Fan by W. B. Park
Up a Tree and other books by Ed Young
My Very First Book of Touch and other "Very First" books by E. Carle
If at First You Do Not See by R. Brown
Tall City, Wide Country by S. Chwast
Guess What? and other books by B. Gardner
Graham Oakley's Magical Changes by G. Oakley
Odd One OuT by R. Peppe
Nothing Ever Happens on My Block by E. Raskin
Look Again and other books by Tana Hoban

(cont'd)

NOTECARD 27 (cont'd)

Kitten for a Day and other books by E. Keats
Deep in the Forest by Brinton Turkle
Changes, Changes by P. Hutchins
Sunshine and other books by J. Ormerod

Lucky Puppy, Lucky Boy by T. Morris
Journey to the Moon by E. Fuchs
Dreams and other books by P. Spier
The Scribble Monster by Jack Kent
Family by E. Simmons

See Carolyn Lima's *A to Zoo: Subject Access to Children's Picture Books* for a listing by subject content of 4,400 picture books.

Concept Development.   Concept Development is enhanced when kindergartners copy words from buildings and signs on field trips and use them in the model buildings and plans they make in class. When you read aloud ask kindergartners to retell, predict outcomes, and list story elements.

such as characters, vocabulary words, and settings. Introduce vocabulary in some books by pointing to a word (and picture), and subsequently asking students to find the word on the page.

Students bring environmental print to the class for bulletin boards and charts, as shown on videotape segment 10. You and the class take "reading walks" where you have labeled objects by "planting" signs for them to read in the schoolyard and neighborhood. Ask students to look for environmental print and ask them, "What does it say?" (Sulzby, Teale, & Kamberelis, 1989). Dictation demonstrates the important link between thought, language, writing, and reading for many children as it allows you to offer alternative grammatical structures and elaborations upon thoughts. Moreover, Wuertenberg (1986) has evidence that dictations enable students to see that their language is valued and builds their courage to write something themselves. Students read their dictations. They write words using their own spelling, make-up games using magnetic letters, felt boards, and chalkboards, and compose messages to take home at least once a week. You also write messages to your class every week, following these principles: (1) Use shortest words and sentences possible; (2) Do not write paragraphs longer than three sentences; (3) Use large letters and large distances between words; (4) Write interesting things, using students' names when possible, but write simply; (5) Use only one thought per sentence; (6) Post a "dictionary" or chart of definitions of longer words you use, and add words to this "dictionary" throughout the year; (7) As much as possible, try your final draft writings out on a few students who arrive to the room early, before duplicating it or having the entire class read it (Lowe, 1992). A sample writing for the first day of school that illustrates these guidelines follows:

Hi! My name is _____ .
　　　　　　　　　　(your name)
What is your name? _____
　　　　　　　(Student puts name here, if possible)
We will have a great year!

Reading a small, traditional-sized book (or a big book) to children has proven to increase letter naming knowledge for them (Mason, Kerr, Santa, & McCormick, 1990). Using books with enlarged print allows small groups of children to approximate the visual intimacy of parent/child book sharing (Holdaway, 1979).

Pierson (1992) recommends that you appoint a committee of three students each week to generate a letter that the class can mail to all parents about what they learned that week. Students then add one sentence of their own concerning something special that they learned. You serve only as editor, assisting students to correct the letters they make, as when students take more and more responsibility for reporting what they learned, the quality of letters increases.

Assisting Parents to Help Their Children's Literacy and Cognitive Development.   When children come to parents for information, they seek affirmation of what they have assimilated. Many parents lack methods to assist their children to develop literacy, and they will request your help (Fitzgerald, Spiegel, & Cunningham, 1991; Morrow, 1983, 1987; Teale, 1986, 1987). Many parents will also ask how they can provide the best home environment for their children. The following references can aid the parents of your students:

David Elkind's *The Hurried Child* and *Parents Outreach Project* (2805 E. Tenth Street, Suite 150, Bloomington, IN 47408-2698) which publishes a pamphlet and tape series that has three read-along stories, with literacy activities for parents and their children. You can also duplicate the following list for your parents:

> *Laying the Foundations: A Parent-Child Literacy Training Kit*, Push Literacy Action Now, 1332 G. Street S.E., Washington, DC 20003
> *The Child's Concept of Story: Ages Two to Seventeen* by Arthur Applebee
> *Make Your Child a Lifelong Reader* by J. Gross
> *How Can I Prepare My Young Child for Reading?* by P. C. Grinnell
> *Helping Your Child Become a Reader* by N. Roser
> *The New Read-aloud Handbook* by J. Trelease
> *Young Children and Picture Books: Literature from Infancy to Six* by M. R. Jalongo
> *Comics to Classics: A Parent's Guide to Books for Teens and Preteens* by Arthea Reed
> *How to Help Your Child Become a Better Writer* by the National Council of Teachers of English
> *Beginning Literacy and Your Child* by S. B. Silvern and L. R. Silvern
> *Explorations in the Functions of Language* by M. A. K. Halliday
> *Rx for Reading: How the Schools Teach Your Child to Read and How You Can Help* by Barbara Fox
> *The First R: Fundamentals of Early Reading Instruction* by R. Baird Shuman
> *Emerging Literacy: Young Children Learn to Read and Write* by D. S. Strickland and L. M. Morrow

These home activities develop literacy and can be suggested to your students' parents as well:

1. When reading a newspaper, magazine, or other items, ask your child a question about what you have read. If your child is interested, point to the answer of the question as you read it aloud to the child.
2. When driving in the car, play tapes of children's books which can be checked out from the public library.
3. Right before your child goes to bed, read to him/her.
4. Let your children see you writing notes and letters so they associ-

ate writing with real-life functions. Read aloud some of their writing and see your children's reactions. Share letters from friends and relatives. Also, be alert to occasions when your child can assist in writing (e.g., adding to grocery lists, notes to letters, holiday cards).

5. Read and accept with enthusiasm your children's writings and attempts to read. The adoring audience your child most wants is you.

6. Find a special, quiet, well-lighted place for your children to read and write.

7. Be certain to hold meaningful conversations with your children daily. Three places where such conversations can be initiated are in the kitchen as they help with chores, in the yard as they "throw a ball" around, and at the dinner table.

To summarize, in the past kindergarten teachers did not spend as much time developing reading and writing competencies because a readiness for literacy was believed to be too difficult to achieve until children had reached a mental age of 6.5. It was assumed that children could not learn to write until they had learned to read.

MIDDLE SCHOOL STUDENTS' READINESS NEEDS ARE SIMILAR TO PRE-FIRST GRADERS IN MANY WAYS

Gathering evidence, forming initial hypotheses, and exploring ideas are psychological needs of young adolescents in much the same way as decoding/encoding are the principle needs of younger children. The purpose of this discussion is to demonstrate how middle school curriculum can enhance adolescents' thinking and refined applications of language. Middle school language arts curriculum should include methods similar to those in kindergarten programs.

There are five commonalities between the special cognitive and language needs of kindergartners and middle school students. First, aside from the kindergarten years, the middle school period is the most intricate developmental period in life, and the period in which high-level thinking most easily expands. Most middle school students are cradling their first abilities to think deeply, unaided (Collins, 1989a; Hahn, Dansberger, Lefkowitz, 1987). Without instruction, young adolescents' budding capacities to analyze their own thoughts will wither because they are aware of only a few thinking strategies. They need your help if their communication and thinking strategies are to expand.

Second, middle school students need special cognitive/language activities because they want to be taught to execute their first, often fragile, deep thoughts, just as they sought guidance in the difficult process of learning to walk. Without such support, many adolescents must continue to "crawl," avoiding deep thinking.

Equally important, ten- to fifteen-year-olds experience rapid changes physically, socially, emotionally, and intellectually. Adolescents need assistance to comprehend the complexities in each of these dimensions of their unfolding lives. This assistance can come through the instructional approaches in this chapter.

Moreover, like kindergarten students, middle schoolers have to reach responsible decisions earlier in our society than in the past. Instead of a "sweet sixteen and never been kissed" society (in which many of us lived as young adolescents), today's youth, by ages ten to fifteen, reach a point where they "have their last best chance to choose a path toward productive and fulfilled lives" (Carnegie, 1989, p. 20). In the process, they are tempted, if not pressured, to experiment with drugs and alcohol; they may live in neighborhoods where they are afraid to walk to school; and they experience sexual urges they do not understand (Brozo, 1990). Without developmental thinking activities many will make poor choices with harmful consequences (Carnegie, 1989).

In addition, a significant correlation exists between adolescents' inability to think on higher levels and their use of destructive means to fulfill a need for power and importance (Hahn, Dansberger & Lefkowitz, 1987). These destructive means serve a "release valve" function similar to preschool students' temper tantrums. It appears that unless we help middle school students learn to think, they may be forced to use identification with peers, emotional disengagement, and defense mechanisms as their only problem-solving strategies. We must develop a curriculum that assists our youth to think and to see the virtues of being a good thinker, and communicator. We can no longer afford to just "tell them to say no" or "say no to them." We must give them methods of building more effective standards, and of generating more successful solutions.

Finally, young adolescents, like kindergartners, have time to learn, and learn through leisure pursuits with peers. Today's adolescents spend 40–50 percent of their time in leisure activities (Csikszentmihalyi & Larsen, 1984; Worell & Danner, 1989). Not only is this percentage more than they will have later in life, but presently this time is not used most productively to build thinking/communication abilities. Because becoming a clear communicator, creator, and thinker takes time, and adolescents have time, we, as educators, need to examine what we can do to use this time more productively.

Before we consider making changes in kindergarten and middle school language arts programs, let's analyze their features and how young adolescents interact in presently existing middle school language arts classes.

PUTTING THEORY INTO PRACTICE
A TYPICAL DAY IN A MIDDLE SCHOOL LANGUAGE ARTS CLASS

To begin, as young adolescents prepare for school, they feel as if they are in perpetual motion and bombarded with change (Coles, 1989). One day, as they get ready for school, they have self-perceptions similar to sophisticated adults; the next morning they take their stuffed animals or wear their baseball caps to school as a security blanket. They are self-conscious, more so than people of other ages. Every cognitive development and classroom activity occurs in a "kaleidoscope of changing emotional states" (Csikszentmihalyi & Larsen, 1984, p. 211).

Psychologically, like kindergartners, they struggle to break their attachment to parents and have difficulty getting into a stimulus-free state of mind long enough to think. They have difficulty maintaining eye contact, making requests of others, and stating preferences and independent thoughts (Drash, 1980; Worrell & Danner, 1989). Presently, in school, they have two choices for dealing with problems. They can develop their own coping devices, without instruction; or become more sophisticated in use of strategies to avoid thinking and communicating. By the middle school years many will have developed a complex repertoire of such avoidance behaviors, as one student's statement illustrates: "I'm always scared the teacher is going to call on me. I'll fool around . . . and she tells me to shut up . . . you can do that or act sick or something to avoid having to think. Most of the time I just get the answer from Andrea" (Brozo, 1990, p. 324). Other avoidance strategies include "mock" participation, e.g., using appropriate head nodding and eye gaze to deceive teachers into believing that they are thinking (Johnston & Markle, 1986). They also purposely forget to bring materials to class, sit in the front row (to give the impression that they are interested), and become "a good listener" by knowing the teacher well enough to know when to pay attention.

Aside from maturational difficulties and lack of appropriate cognitive/communication instruction, young adolescents have another problem concerning their ability to communicate and think. Dorman and Lipsitz (1981) found that the quality of their language and thinking is significantly correlated to the types of lessons they are asked to complete. When asked what they want (and ultimately need) we will tell you that they want *less external supervision, intellectual stimulation, cognitive challenges, advanced information, positive thinking models, encouragement to commit to meaningful life goals, decision-making tools to build their responsibility, and a middle school environment that provides autonomy* (Collins, 1990a).

Best lessons include dense but sequenced information, such as small group discussions, and individual goal-setting activities that push them to exceed their past performances. Through such lessons, their enjoyment, personal engagement, energy, and idealism will rise above people at other age levels, and their communication and thinking abilities will develop rapidly (Collins, 1992b). Like preschoolers, when exposed to other types of lessons, such as when they *"have* to do uninteresting things" (Collins, 1990b), or listen to the teacher, young adolescents' minds wander to their insecurities, and little thinking occurs.

Young adolescents, like kindergartners, view learning to speak and read well as extremely important to their self-esteem. Because of this emphasis, many experience disproportionate fears about any inability to communicate and think. Such fears occur because of the emotional, physical, and social instabilities that exist in their lives. Because of these fears, when they become confused, they do not ask the teacher for help (as they often did in elementary school), or ask for help from parents/peers (as they will in high school). Instead, confusion builds into anxiety, worry, agitation, panic, and anger, e.g., "Listening to Mr. Molitor is causing me to 'go insane' " (Csikszentmihalyi & Larsen, 1984, p. 234). Similarly, their unstable self-concepts make it impossible to accurately evaluate their abilities. Therefore, they can *truly* panic over a homework assignment that, after great psychological effort, is begun, and once started, easily completed in only 20 minutes.

Equally devastating is when they are asked to work alone for long periods of time. In such classes, because they lack the thinking/communication strategies to gain and express knowledge, they mask their inabilities by either faking disinterest, or trying to convince their teachers that the information to be learned is "beneath them" (Collins, 1990b; Seigler, 1989).

They need language arts teachers who take a genuine interest in them and in language arts; ones who are intrinsically motivated and model their thinking and communication process so students realize that reasoning and planning are better than random activity and pleasure seeking. They need their teacher's adult judgments to learn to extend trust to other adults. Furthermore, when their teachers are the type of people that they want to become, adolescents are less likely to fear becoming adults themselves (Collins, 1989b). The best teachers teach how they developed their own hard-won thinking habits, and model mature decision-making abilities. They also provide cognitive work that develops the students' individual talents. They offer specific praises. With such intrinsic and extrinsic rewards, young adolescents experience the autonomy they need.

With these needs of middle school and kindergarten students in mind, you can better understand how important learning links, play, on-the-spot instruction, and learning to pay attention (study) are for both populations. Creative lessons that teach these strategies follow.

LESSONS THAT ADDRESS THE SPECIAL NEEDS OF KINDERGARTNERS AND MIDDLE SCHOOL STUDENTS

Because the needs of kindergarten children and middle school students are so similar, with slight variations, the following instructional strategies address the special needs of both populations.

CREATING LESSONS WITH LEARNING LINKS

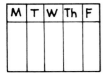

Both middle school and kindergarten students benefit from learning links. **Learning Links** *tie writing, reading, talking, drawing, imagining, and play to important events in children's and adolescents' lives.*

While elementary school students change rapidly from year to year, their growth is more steady and equally balanced than the physical, emotional, and cognitive spurts experienced by kindergarten and middle school students. For this latter group, the growth in one area is often so sudden and tumultuous that it overshadows the steady growth in the remaining areas. As a result, instruction for students in the kindergarten and middle school grades must be flexible and modifiable to support the rapid changes that are occurring. Learning links provide such flexibility.

One learning link is to place students as the heroes in their language experience stories or library books. After the class feels comfortable with such stories, single students can become a main character and a new story is created. After this story about the student is finished, that student writes a sequel about himself/ herself. You can also bring a camera and the student can go outside and select two different items. These items are included in a imaginative story which they will illustrate. Students can then read their stories to the class.

CREATING LESSONS THAT CAPITALIZE UPON THE VALUES OF "PLAY"

The importance of playful activity for preschoolers and middle school students can not be overemphasized. As Friedrich Schiller once said, "Man only plays when he is in the fullest sense of the word a human being; and he is only fully a human being when he plays." Through play, kindergartners and young adolescents learn to assume many new roles and responsibilities.

Play takes many forms. One end of the continuum is when children participate in games and sports that follow rules and rituals. The opposite end of the "play spectrum" occurs when children engage in dramas when they assume the roles of others. In play everything is possible. Children can shift from a game with rules to a world of fantasy, often stopping midway to give directions and explain actions, or answer questions. The dynamic phenomenon play has upon learning and thinking has fascinated philosophers, educators, psychologists, and anthropologists through the ages (Courtney, 1982). They posit that play is pivotal in developing spontaneity and exercises the opposite of habit (Blatner & Blatner, 1988). Spencer (1914) presented the notion that play is the result of surplus energy. Aristotle, on the other hand, believed that play can be a catharsis or safety valve for pent-up emotions. Huizenga (1955) argues that in the creating of a poetic phrase, a motif, and in the expression of a mood, play is always a part. Some advocate that through play, students discipline the imagination and enter the adult world of the arts and sciences (Hartley & Goldenson, 1975).

Among the most famous theorists concerning play's role in learning was Sigmund Freud. Freud's explanation of play is that it is a projection of wishes, and enables children to reenact conflicts so that they can master them. Physicians are also reporting the value of humor as a healing tool. Playing alleviates stress. Thus, designing playful creations is gaining importance in schools today. This natural impulse to play, if encouraged, can become a continuing way of learning throughout life. While it is tempting to believe that play is frivolous and unrelated to serious learning, Morrow and Rand (1991) cite several studies where "symbolic play" demands higher levels of cognitive involvement than serious cognitive tasks. Dramatic play has also shown to improve story comprehension and other literacy skills (see Morrow & Rand, 1991, for a review). Other teachers are striving to learn new ways of keeping "the play impulse alive" so it may enhance learning and enrich the lives of pupils throughout their lives.

Blatner and Blatner's research (1988) support the work of these educators. They found that young children's play benefits children's emotional, social, educational, and cultural lives in the following ways: Play enhances flexibility of mind, initiative, improvisation, humility, sense of humor, effective communication, inclusiveness, ability to interact and be at ease with others, questioning, looking for alternatives, solving problems, and learning new techniques. Kindergartners like to play, listen, and mimic. In playing, they "try out" many behaviors, language patterns/forms, and cognitive processes. In the process, they give those around them the opportunity to view their emerging hypotheses about the environment, words, and ideas. Through play, they develop their own curriculum and find answers they need. The following ideas incorporate play into kindergarten and middle school language arts programs.

Supporting Language Play.   You can support children's language play by valuing children's language inventions as they occur spontaneously. You can also encourage the effort of students to play with language by inventing fun words yourself each week. You may need to set aside and play with words a few moments each week.

Riddles, Limericks, and Tongue Twisters.   These forms of language encourage students to enjoy their own thinking and communication abilities. By adding dramatic expressions to the riddles students create, the value of play is increased.

Finger Plays.   Finger plays are among the favorite means of easing students into exploring learning through play in the classroom. Some of the best sources of finger plays include *Finger Rhymes* (Brown, 1980); *Hand Rhymes* (Brown, 1985); *Play Rhymes* (Brown, 1987); and *Finger Plays for Nursery and Kindergarten* (Poulsson, 1971). Examples appear in Figure 13-2.

Individual Lap Flannel Boards.   Jacobson (1989) recommends creating individual flannel boards for students. Children not only benefit from the playful atmosphere that is created in constructing their flannel boards, but they have a source of creating dramas and stories at home to be shared with family and at school.

At the middle school level, play occurs through role plays, and is equally important for all reasons stated previously.

Benefits of Drama (Play) and Role Plays.   Analogous to the kindergartner, middle school students need plays, dramas, and role plays to internalize society's messages and determine the roles they want to play in it. Because peers/respected adults are adolescents' main language models, role plays by peers/adults often cause middle school students to listen and learn more than from direct instruction. They learn to overcome thinking, reading, writing, speaking, and listening problems, when others, to whom they easily relate, demonstrate how they handle similar difficulties. Role play and drama also appear to provide a subtle escape from self that adolescents need in order to internalize values and think deeply.

Interestingly, as described in Chapter 11, plays and dramas benefit elementary school students in a different way. For elementary-age students, play and creative dramatics become important "celebrative events that bond them to each other and to school.

CREATING LESSONS THAT USE ON-THE-SPOT INSTRUCTION

Your responsibility during independent reading periods for kindergartners and young adolescents is different than it is for elementary-age students. In elementary school years, you will find that you take few notes during independent working periods. Most of your time is spent in one-to-one conferences, reading silently yourself, participating in a small group setting, or building individual student skills. However, in kindergarten and middle school grades, you will make *many* notes daily. Their growth is so rapid that you need these notes to "catch their moments of need," so you can plan for these the next day. In the middle school, students keep these daily notes. These records include their self-assessments of communication strengths, notes about books read, and strategies they used to support their speaking and listening during study periods. These notes provide specific, direct feedback middle school students need to internalize their value for communication and thinking. Daily notes motivate and direct kindergarten and middle school students in their independent areas of need.

FIGURE 13-2
Finger Plays

When using finger plays for any reason, remember to follow these basic guidelines:

1. Use motivating facial and verbal expressions.
2. Say the rhyme and show the accompanying action.
3. Repeat the rhyme, if necessary.
4. Say to the children: "Please help me say it while I do the motions."
5. Repeat the rhyme again with the children and invite them to join you in the finger action. They should now be ready to do so.

Little Jack *Horner*
Sat in the *corner*

Hickory, Dickory, *dock!*
The mouse ran up the *clock.*

Little Miss *Muffet*
Sat on a *tuffet.*

I know a little *girl*
Who had a little *curl.*

Little Boy Blue come blow your *horn;*
The sheep's in the meadow, the cow's in the *corn.*

Ding, dong *bell,*
The pussy's in the *well!*

Mary, *Mary,*
Quite *contrary.*

One, *two,*
Buckle my *shoe.*

Humpty-Dumpty sat on a *wall,*
Humpty-Dumpty had a great *fall.*

A dillar, a *dollar,*
A ten-o'clock *scholar.*

Then, move to activities where the children need to supply their own rhyming words in a familiar context:

I am thinking of a word.
It rhymes with *floor.*
It is kept closed in the winter.
What is it? (door)

It rhymes with *thing.*
It is worn on the finger.
What is it? (ring)

It rhymes with *dandy.*
It is good to eat.
What is it? (candy)

It rhymes with *sweater.*
It is something we write.
What is it? (letter)

Next, ask the children to supply the rhyming word to complete your sentences. For example:

An animal that rhymes with *hat* is _____ .
( ) (cat)

A little *mouse* ran into the _____ .
( ) (house)

My new *bed* was painted _____ .
( ) (red)

cont'd

FIGURE 13-2   (cont'd)

Finally, have the children generate the word that rhymes. Ask them to: Name a vegetable that rhymes with *born*; name a word that rhymes with *night*.

From: Makion, G. W. (1990). *The Sourcebook: Activities for Infants and Young Children*. Columbus, OH: Merrill.

CREATING LESSONS THAT TEACH STUDY SKILLS

Because middle school students have such depth of curiosity and breadth of elaboration, library skills and notetaking strategies are particularly valuable to this population. While study skills are not the exclusive domain of the language arts program, the following abilities should be introduced or reinforced in the most effective language arts programs.

Study skills to be emphasized include how to use encyclopedias and specialized reference books/sources such as atlases, almanacs, *Who's Who* reference books, *Contemporary Authors and Book of Junior Authors*, as well as *Bartlett's Familiar Quotations*, dictionaries, periodicals, computerized and noncomputerized card catalogs, and thesauruses. Study skills also include the use of study steps, learning logs, notetaking, and bibliographic reference systems. Students must also learn the Dewey Decimal System and the Library of Congress Classification System. Students can use a new computer program titled *Note Card Maker* to learn to make bibliographic references.

Study skills need to include strategies of previewing, to establish purposes, reading, reviewing, and taking notes from material studied. A number of such strategies (such as SQ3R, PQRST, POINT, and EVOKER) are available. Most important, students should be shown: (a) how to glance through material to determine the information it contains; (b) how to write the name of the source, author, and page numbers for each piece of information on separate notecard or to complete bibliographic information on a different sheet of paper; (c) how to write down only important facts and use their own words in doing so; and (d) if using authors' words, mark them with quotation marks and place the following information in parentheses after the quotation: author's last name, date of publication, and page number on which the quotation appeared.

When kindergarten and middle school students have completed these four lessons they will be able to work more independently. With this self-reliance intact they will profit from the introduction of Critical Thinking Activity 13.

CRITICAL THINKING ACTIVITY 13
How to Establish Successful Learning Centers

Learning Centers are one of the best instructional systems to introduce students to "new environments" and units of study. Kindergarten students need such centers because, for the first time in their lives, they are working in groups where they must establish their independence and group communication/thinking skills. They must maneuver the functions of language in their daily encounters; doing so in a small restricted area makes it easier. Similarly, middle school students need centers because they are entering a new school, and the adult world of responsibilities. Needs for identity, independence, displaying unique talents, and group communication/thinking abilities are important and can be more easily addressed in the small group learning center/cooperative group settings.

Through the following understanding and activities, you can create highly successful centers in your room. Laughter (1992) describes learning centers as an "organizational activity where students think, read, write, listen, speak, and role play as they acquire real information about their world and language" (p. 1). Learning centers integrate "learning about a topic" with "acquisition of language and thinking abilities." Laughter goes on to state that motivation for learning is intrinsic, in part because of student ability to select meaningful tasks, and because of the colorful designs, catchy titles, and "hands-on" nature of learning centers. Students report that they learn from their mistakes in learning centers. As one anonymous student stated, "I know immediately that I just missed something so I set a goal to do something about it."

Another objective of learning centers and cooperative groups is to promote feelings of belonging, acceptance, and support throughout the learning process. Students must feel that they are working toward a common goal in their groups, even as they strive to meet individual goals. While there are many types of cooperative groups and learning centers, all have two essential elements to be successful. First, the group goal must be important to the group, e.g., middle school students enjoy such topics as courage, immortality, modesty, shyness, heroes, imperishable beauty, leadership, and philosophical, ethical, and political issues. Second, there must be individual accountability as well as group accountability. All group members must see themselves as positively interdependent with other group members. When these conditions are met, group members can determine each other's level of mastery and provide support and assistance. Students must be taught the group thinking skills in Chapter 12 to promote maximum growth in communication and thinking competence.

Scott and Chavalier (1992) recommend that teachers introduce the following rules at the kindergarten level; such development focuses upon the new world of discovery that lies before them as they gain the "union card" to enter the "literacy club in our world" (Smith, 1986). At the middle school level, such development focuses upon the importance of self-selecting to enter the "literacy club" frequency, and to contribute to it, so that adults can benefit and appreciate their thoughts. This goal, while a part of the elementary program, is not the major objective during those years. At that time, teachers focus upon a more specific goal of teaching *how to read, write, speak, listen, and perform basic thinking processes.*

Organizing Learning Centers. Learning centers are organized differently in kindergarten and middle school level than in elementary school grades. In kindergarten and middle school programs, centers focus upon societal skills (e.g., homemaking, restaurant, architecture, and fine art centers in kindergarten; counseling, research, artistic illustrations, and small group discussion centers for middle school students). In the elementary school years, as explained in Chapter 6, centers focus on in-depth study of topics, such as poetry, intelligence, and editing. These topics are related to the content areas of reading, writing, speaking, and listening development.

Stombres (1992) suggests the following steps in creating a learning center:

1. Choose a theme that is related to important events in your students' lives.

2. Make center backdrop, three sheets hinged together. Hooks can be inserted in the peg holes to handle center ideas and forms. As an alternative, inexpensive, prefolded center boards are available from Showboards (Showboards Project Display Boards, 3725 Grace Street, Suite 305, Tampa, FL). These center boards can also be made into a shape that depicts the theme, such as a circle for pizza themes, a cookie jar, spider's web from yarn, or an apple box.

3. Create activities from Chapters 1–12 to be included in the center. For two examples, see the pictures of "popcorn" and "potatoes" units in kindergartens. In the center, place many trade-books and design group activities around these selections.

4. Students use a checklist attached to the front of their portfolios to guide themselves through the center. Students are free to select activities that are of greatest value to them, and to indicate why they made these choices, as well as why they elected to work alone or in groups.

5. Model how to use the center and establish a timeline, number of activities, and types of experiences students must have before they complete the center.

6. You have an active role in the center. After introducing it, you monitor the center often as students work. You can also allow sharing time at the end of each week while the center is in use. These times are designed to improve the center's materials, eliminate problems, and share individual student insights about the content.

The following centers can be created. In addition to these, Stombres (1992) has information about many other types of literature-based centers. These centers contain suggested selections of children's literature, 50 activities per unit, award stickers, bulletin board ideas, and recipes to match center themes.

Create a Writing Corner or Center: Students have a corner with many different things to write about and with. Allow students to create attendance charts, label belongings, lockers, class objects, and make class rules charts and class library books, using pictures for words they cannot yet write. As children develop, they can self-select to "rewrite" labels, removing the pictures.

Maintain a Listening Center: Students have music to use as background for writing poems and prose; records and tapes to transcribe words for the class; and tape-recorded messages from you concerning lists and notes they need to make as they listen to a specific story, song, or set of directions. The activities in the listening center also highlight role-playing once a week, where students can read recipes and cook, go to the corner-of-the-room "store" with a shopping list, or dress up as their favorite professional and write/read/say/listen/think the things that person would do during a day.

Alternatively, in kindergarten and middle school, most time is spent in teaching that there are many appropriate choices, as their environments are making students aware (so many centers from which to choose in kindergarten; and so many peers/activities to select between in middle schools). The centers and materials in Figure 13-3 can be used to develop kindergarten, elementary, and middle school students' creative and critical thinking and communication abilities in many different ways.

FIGURE 13-3
Materials to Develop Creative and Critical Thinking

Automobile Mechanic

used (and washed) motor
  parts, spark plugs, filters,
  carburetors, cable sets, and
  gears
tools: hammers, pliers, screw-
  drivers
oil funnel
empty oil cans

flashlight
wiring
air pump
windshield wipers
key carrier and keys
rags, old shirts, gloves
automobile supply catalogs
repair manuals

Beautician

mirror, curlers, hairpins,
  hairnets
dryers, combs, towels
aprons, magazines,
shampoo bottles
plastic basin
emery boards and manicure
  equipment
paper money
posters of hair styles and
  descriptions

wigs and wig stands
curling iron (with cord off for
  kindergarten centers)
appointment book
open/closed sign and schedule
  of hours
ribbons, barrettes, clips, bobby
  pins

cont'd

FIGURE 13-3   (cont'd)

Forest Ranger

canteen, flashlight, rope
mosquito netting, canvas for
    tent
grill, knapsack

food supplies, nature books
small logs, binoculars, maps

Plumber

piping: all lengths, widths, and
    shapes for fitting together
spigots
plungers
tools
hose and nozzles

spades
old shirts, caps
hardware supply catalogs
measuring devices
plumbing manual

Post Office

mailboxes (can use shoeboxes)
envelopes (all sizes)
stamps (can use Christmas
    seals)
pens, string, address labels

package seals, wrapping paper,
    tape, packages
scale, cash register, play money
posters about mailing
    procedures

Office

typewriter, calculator, business
    checkbook
clipboards, calendars, open/
    closed hours' signs
file cabinets for alphabetical
    ordering
index cards, business cards
post-its
address labels
paper, paper clips

notepads, scotch tape, stapler
telephone, message pads, hole
    punch
file folders
in/out trays
pens and pencils
envelopes
stamps, rubber stamps, stamp
    pad

Restaurant

tablecloth, napkins, tray
dishes, glasses, silverware
menus, order pads, and pencils
aprons for waitresses
vests for waiters

hats and aprons for chefs
cookbooks
blank recipe cards
play money

cont'd

FIGURE 13-3   (cont'd)

Fast Food Restaurant

menus
order pads
cash registers

specials of the day
recipes and list of flavors or
    products

Supermarket or Grocery Store

labeled shelves
cash register
shopping receipts
coupons

checkbooks
newspaper
advertisements

Grocery Store

grocery cart, food
grocery bags
marking pen
cash register, play money

price stickers
signs to make labels
plastic fruit and artificial foods

Airport

signs for departures and
    arrivals
tickets
boarding passes

luggage tags
magazines
name tags for flight attendants

Block Center

blocks
tinker toys
tape
scissors

popsicle sticks and straws
3″ × 5″ and 5″ × 7″ notecards
    for signs
paper, crayons for drawing
    maps

Travel Agency

travel posters
travel brochures
maps
airplane, train tickets

wallet with money and credit
    cards
cash register
suitcases

Veterinarian

white shirt/jacket
stuffed animals
cages (cardboard boxes)
medical bag
stethoscope

empty medicine bottles
prescription labels
bandages
popsicle stick splints
hypodermic syringe (play)

cont'd

FIGURE 13-3   (cont'd)

Library

children's books and magazines   sign for book fines
   (with card pockets and date   cash register
   due slips)   money
date stamp and stamp pad   library cards
book return box

Bank

teller window (use a puppet   money
   stage)   roll papers for coins
passbooks   deposit slips
checks   money bags

Scott (1992) and Chavalier (1992) recommend introducing the following rules to students prior to their first learning center/cooperative group experience. Once students have mastered the ones you taught, students select other rules they wish to add. A sample appears below:

Learning Center/Cooperative Group Rules

1. We take turns.
2. We listen to each other's ideas.
3. We help each other.
4. We check each other.
5. We encourage each other.
6. We only ask the teacher if everyone has the same question.
7. We listen without interrupting.
8. We use "I" and "We," not "You" statements.
9. We stay within time limits.
10. We paraphrase others' contributions.

Laughter (1992) uses task cards that contain the following items to manage learning centers:

Title and students' name of activity completed
Purpose or skill learned during the activity
Materials used
Steps to follow in completing the activity
Your evaluation

PROFESSIONAL DEVELOPMENT OPPORTUNITY
How to Use Mentors in the Student Communication Center

During kindergarten and middle school years, if a student is failing in school, the blame is most often viewed as lying outside the school. If kindergarten students cannot pay attention, parents and home environment are blamed. If middle school students exhibit delinquent behavior, parents and peer influences are viewed as the culprits. It seems that before and after the elementary school years, factors outside the school are believed to have more impact on students' lives. Whereas, if students fall behind peers during Grades 1–5, teachers and better instruction are most often blamed. The implications of these shifting views of responsibility are significant for language arts instruction. Parents and community resources should be used, such as guest speakers and parent aides. For example, cooking can be featured by inviting a nutritionist or local "TV celebrity chef" to class. After the visit, at the kindergarten level, the recipes are followed in rebus form, and in middle schools students create their own unique concoctions. Printed recipes can be found in *My First Cookbook: A Life-Size Guide to the Making of Fun Things to Eat* by Angela Wilkes (Knopf, 1989); *Vegetable Soup* by Jeanne Modesitt; *The Too-Great Bread and Bake Book* by Gail Gibbons; *A Birthday Cake for Little Bear* by Max Velthuijs (North-South, 1988); *Three Days on a River in a Red Canoe* by Vera B. Williams (Mulberry, 1981); and the *Please Touch Cookbook* (Silver Press, 1990).

Similarly, students develop the ability to find problems and reduce myopic perceptions when they design, implement, and evaluate projects for the community, such as helping the homeless and recycling lunchroom waste. For example, in San Francisco, during the summer of 1990, the schoolboard and teachers asked middle school students to assist in directing the summer school program. Students recruited/interviewed teachers, and made the content units for Grades K–3.

As demonstrated in Videotape Segment 11, children's authors and sports figures can become one of the most powerful "mentors" students can have. They are among the few people that have the capacity to become both "friend" and hero simultaneously. While the most obvious interaction between students and authors/sports figures is to invite a "live one" to class, two equally attractive options follow.

First, provide opportunities for students to read several autobiographies/biographies of famous children's authors and sports/movie star figures. Among them are *Writer's Voice* (Literacy Volunteers of New York City, Publishing Department, 121 Avenue of the Americas, New York, NY 10013) which features Bill Cosby, Carol Burnett, Kareem Abdul-Jabbar, and others; *Something About the Author: Autobiography Series; The Dictionary of Literary Biography: American Writers for Children Since 1960: Fiction; First Through Sixth Books of Junior Authors and Illustrators; Behind the Covers; Books Are By People: Interviews with 104 Authors and Illustrators of Books for Young Children; How Writers Write; How to Capture Live Authors and Bring Them to Your Schools; Something About the Author: Facts and Pictures About Authors and Illustrators of Books for Young People, Volumes 1–57; From Writers to Students: The Pleasures and Pains of Writing; The Pied Pipers: Interviews with the Influential Creators of Children's Literature;* and *Speaking for Ourselves: Autobiographical Sketches by Notable Authors of Books for Young Adults.* Students can also write to the United States Sports Teams listed in Figure 13-4.

FIGURE 13-4
ADDRESSES OF U.S. SPORTS TEAMS

FOOTBALL

National Football League, 410 Park Avenue, New York NY 14127 (Address updates for individual teams are available from the NFL.)

Chicago Bears
250 N. Washington Road
Lake Forest IL 60045

Buffalo Bills
One Bills
Orchard Park NY 14127

Cleveland Browns
Cleveland Stadium
Cleveland OH 44114

Dallas Cowboys
One Cowboy Parkway
Dallas TX

Atlanta Falcons
Suwanne Road
Suwanne GA 30174

Houston Oilers
6910 Fannin Street
Houston TX 77030

Los Angeles Raiders
332 Center Street
El Segundo CA 90245

New Orleans Saints
6928 Drive
Metairie LA 70003

Cincinnati Bengals
200 Riverfront Stadium
Cincinnati OH 44114

Denver Broncos
5700 Logan Street
Denver CO 80216

San Diego Chargers
San Diego Jack Murphy Stadium
P.O. Box 206666
San Diego CA 92120

Miami Dolphins
4770 Biscayne Boulevard
Suite 1440
Miami FL 33137

Detroit Lions
1200 Featherstone Road
Pontiac MI 48057

New England Patriots
Sullivan Stadium
Route 1
Foxboro MA 02035

Los Angeles Rams
2327 West Lincoln
Anaheim CA 92801

BASKETBALL

National Basketball Association, Olympic Tower, 645 Fifth Avenue, New York NY 10022

Chicago Bulls
980 N. Michigan Avenue
Chicago IL 60611

Boston Celtics
Boston Garden
Boston MA 12114

NY Knickerbockers
Madison Square Garden
Four Pennsylvania Plaza
New York NY 10001

Denver Nuggets
P.O. Box 4286
Denver CO 80204

Seattle Supersonics
Box C-900911
Seattle WA 98109

Cleveland Cavaliers
The Coliseum
Richfield OH 44286

Atlanta Hawks
The Omni
100 Techwood Drive N.W.
Atlanta GA 30303

Los Angeles Lakers
The Forum
P.O. Box 10
Los Angeles CA 90306

Detroit Pistons
Pontiac Silverdome
1200 Featherstone
Pontiac MI 48057

Second, invite mentors to school. Mentors are tutors who become friends and who share common aspirations. Clemens (1991) discovered that one of the reasons why mentoring impacts kindergarten students so much is that younger students need "hands-on communication competencies to express and receive the information of greatest interest to them." Instructors help apprentices by providing "big" words and "gigantic ideas and goals" that block and form dreams and abilities. Mentors learn cooperation and diplomacy. They feel increased self-worth and gratitude as they see what their ideas and work enable their partners to do and know. They know they alone contributed to that knowledge growth. Mentors also learn that it is tough to be a good role model but feel that it is important to do so. They see their apprentice's behavior improve as a result. Mentors and apprentices learn about responsibility and goal setting. They joke, sing, and walk through one segment of life "hand in hand," a type of celebration that will be remembered for life by both.

Developing a Mentor Program, by Walter W. Haeger and John F. Feldhusen (1989, D.O.K. Publishers, East Aurora, NY 14052), is an excellent reference of points to consider in establishing such a program between students and adults.

In summary, it is important to address the special language needs of kindergarten and middle school students. These students are similar in that their emotional, psychological, and social developmental needs are exceptionally high. You will use the levels of language acquisition of individual students to advance their confidence and skill in self-selected use of communication and thinking. You will also build middle school students' abilities to use the thoughts of others through attention to study and reference skills. In your pre-first grade and middle school language arts program you will attend to students who are particularly susceptible to falling behind their peers. With special attention such loss can be avoided by using books in Notecard 28.

TRY IT

1. Milner (1991) has reported that most young children tend to exaggerate, both when praised and when criticized. How will this impact your feedback to students? Describe three specific ways you can temper and increase the value of your feedback.

2. How would you respond to the following kindergartner's note if you were the teacher in the following scenario?

The teacher had been out sick for a few days. When she returned to school, her children smothered her with hugs and chatter. They had so much to tell her that she suggested that they sit right down and write her a letter or a note telling whatever they wanted. They were busily writing when one little boy whispered to her, "I forgot how to spell your name." The teacher whispered back, "It's right there on the wall near the door.

NOTECARD 28: POPULAR AUTHORS AND BOOKS FOR MIDDLE SCHOOL STUDENTS

POPULAR AUTHORS

Richard Adams	Susan Cooper	Jim Kjelgaard	Kin Platt
Lloyd Alexander	Barbara Corcoran	Madeleine L'Engle	Ellen Raskin
Mildren Ames	Robert Cormier	Ursula Le Guin	Wilson Rauls
Judi Angell	Paula Danziger	Robert Lipsyte	Willo Davis Roberts
Peter Beagle	Lois Duncan	Lois Lowry	Zilpha Snyder
Jay Bennett	Paul Gallico	Margaret Mahy	Mary Stewart
T. Ernesto Bethancourt	Jean George	Ann M. Martin	Mildred Taylor
	Barbara Girion	Harry Mazer	Theodore Taylor
Judy Blume	Bette Greene	Norma Fox Mazer	Crystal Thrasher
Frank Bonham	Lynn Hall	Jean Lowery Nixon	Stephanie Tolan
Betsy Byars	Harry Harrison	Scott O'Dell	Julian Thompson
Eleanor Cameron	S. E. Hinton	Zibby O'Neal	J. R. Tolkien
Joy Chant	Isabelle Holland	Katherine Paterson	Rosemary Wells
Agatha Christie	Irene Hunt	Richard Peck	Robert Westall
John Christopher	Judith Kerr	Robert N. Peck	Leonard Wibberley
Patricia Clapp	M. E. Kerr	Susan Beth Pfeffer	Paul Zindel
Ellen Conford	Gordon Korman	D. M. Pinkwater	

(cont'd)

NOTECARD 28 (cont'd)

POPULAR TITLES FOR YOUNGER READERS

Ira Sleeps Over by B. Waber
Alexander and the Terible, Horrible, No Good, Very Bad Day by J. Viorst
Where's Waldo? by M. Hanford
Is Your Mama a Llama? by D. Guarino
Clifford the Big Red Dog by N. Bridwell
The Messy Room by S. Berenstain and J. Berenstain

William's Doll by C. Zolotow
Days With Frog and Toad by A. Lobel
The Pain and the Great One by J. Blume
Arthur Goes to Camp by Marc Brown
Home Alone by J. Horowitz
Where the Wild Things Are by M. Sendak
Peter's Chair by Ezra J. Keats

POPULAR TITLES FOR OLDER READERS

The Great Gilly Hopkins by K. Paterson
My Side of the Mountain by Jean George
Sarah, Plain and Tall by Patricia MacLachlan
Tuck Everlasting by Natalie Babbitt
James and the Giant Peach by Roald Dahl
Cricket in Times Square by George Seldon
Ben and Me by Robert Lawson
Dear Mr. Henshaw by Beverly Cleary
Are You There God? It's Me, Margaret. by J. Blume
If I Were in Charge of the World by J. Viorst

There's a Boy in the Girl's Bathroom by L. Sachar
Superfudge by J. Blume
Black Stallion by Walter Farley
Summer of the Swans by Betsy Byars
The Lion, the Witch and the Wardrobe by C. S. Lewis
Skinny Bones by Barbara Park
Anne of Green Gables by L. M. Montgomery
The One-Eyed Cat by Paula Fox
Hank the Cowdog by J. R. Erickson

You can copy it." At the end of the day, the teacher read over the students' letters. She came to the paper of the little boy who hadn't known how to spell her name and read his note to her: "I love you, fire exit."

3. "When young children can't yet read, it is important that you do not require them to write." Defend your position in favor of or in opposition to this statement.

4. What principle(s) of emergent literacy does the following Valentine's Day activity, created by Manarino-Leggett (1992), employ? On experience chart paper print the following poem:

> 1,2 I love you.
> 3,4 I love you more.
> 5,6 Fiddlesticks.
> 7,8 I think you're great.
> 9,10 Say it again.

After reading the poem several times to the students, have them reread it with you. Students can increase their number recognition and learn the sight words "I" and "YOU." Students then make their own Valentine's card and decorate it. As they do, provide the words "I love you" which students can copy from the chart if they wish. Students also enjoy the idea that they are reading and they quickly memorize the poem.

FOR YOUR JOURNAL

Let's assume that it is the end of the school year. Your school district requires that you place a work sample from the end of the year's work in each student's portfolio which will be passed on to the child's next teacher. With each work sample the district requires that you make a comment relative to the child's strengths, growths, and talents that the sample illustrates; and one instructional suggestion to advance that student. The district also requires that all writing samples be from the same stimulus, so future teachers have a common referent in interpreting each child's work. The lesson upon which the samples are to be based is a whole class sharing of the wordless picture book entitled, *The Bear and the Fly.*

After the sharing, your kindergarten children elect to write, draw, or dictate a response to the book. The following two children elected to dictate the following stories to you. After reading each child's story, prepare the assessments that will accompany each child's sample in the cumulative folders. Place these statements in your journal.

Andrew asked you to scribe the following:

> The Three Bears were sitting down when suddenly a bee came buzzing along, so the Daddy Bear took the fly-swatter and tried to hit him. First, he hit the Mama Bear trying to hit him. Then, he hit the wee-wee Baby Bear. He hit him [the Baby Bear] so hard that he fell down. Written and Illustrated by Andrew.

And Andrew drew a picture on the bottom of the page.

Molly asked you to write:

> One evening when some bears were having dinner a fly came in the window. The daddy bear almost got the fly. "He Missed again," said the baby, "that hurts!" The dog said, "Do not do that again." "OK," said the daddy. "I'll do it to you," said the daddy. Soon the three bears' dinner would be finished. Now it was (Serebrin, 1986).

BUILDING YOUR PROFESSIONAL PORTFOLIO

Two very significant events occurred from 1986–1990 concerning literacy and young children. The first was the drafting of "A Joint Statement of Concerns about Present Practices in Pre-First Grade Reading Instruction and Recommendations for Improvement" by the seven professional organizations listed below. This statement was the first to provide guidelines upon which reading and language arts programs are constructed for preschool and kindergarten. The second event was the publication of a book by Marilyn Adams and the Center for the Study of Reading, which outlined the role of phonics instruction in emergent literacy. If you are interested in learning more about pre-first grade instructional guidelines, you might also enjoy *How Children Construct Literacy*, edited by Yetta Goodman and published in 1990 by the International Reading Association.

Joint Statement on Literacy Development and Pre-First Grade

A Joint Statement of Concerns about Present Practices in Pre-First Grade Reading Instruction and Recommendations for Improvement prepared by:
Association for Supervision and Curriculum Development
International Reading Association
National Association for the Education of Young Children
National Association of Elementary School Principals
National Council of Teachers of English

Presented by the Early Childhood and Literacy Development Committee of the International Reading Association

Objectives for a Pre-first Grade Reading Program

Literacy learning begins in infancy. Reading and writing experiences at school should permit children to build upon their already existing knowledge of oral and written language. Learning should take place in a supportive environment where children can build a positive attitude toward themselves and toward language and literacy. For optimal learning, teachers should involve children actively in many meaningful, functional language experiences, including *speaking, listening, writing,* and *reading.* Teachers of young children should be prepared in ways that acknowledge differences in language and cultural backgrounds and emphasize reading as an integral part of the language arts as well as of the total curriculum.

What Young Children Know About Oral and Written Language Before They Come to School

1. Children have had many experiences from which they are building their ideas about the functions and uses of oral language and written language.

STRATEGIES THAT TEACH

2. Children have a command of language, have internalized many of its rules, and have conceptualized processes for learning and using language.
3. Many children can differentiate between drawing and writing.
4. Many children are reading environmental print, such as road signs, grocery labels, and fast food signs.
5. Many children associate books with reading.
6. Children's knowledge about language and communication systems is influenced by their social and cultural backgrounds.
7. Many children expect that reading and writing will be sense-making activities.

Concerns

1. Many pre-first grade children are subjected to rigid, formal pre-reading programs with inappropriate expectations and experiences for their levels of development.
2. Little attention is given to individual development or individual learning styles.
3. The pressure of accelerated programs do not allow children to be risk-takers as they experiment with language and internalize concepts about how language operates.
4. Too much attention is focused upon isolated skill development or abstract parts of the reading process, rather than upon the integration of oral language, writing, and listening with reading.
5. Too little attention is placed upon reading for pleasure; therefore, children often do not associate reading with enjoyment.
6. Decisions related to reading programs are often based on political and economic considerations rather than on knowledge of how young children learn.
7. The pressure to achieve high scores on standardized tests that frequently are not appropriate for the kindergarten child has resulted in changes in the content of programs. Program content often does not attend to the child's social, emotional, and intellectual development. Consequently, inappropriate activities that deny curiosity, critical thinking, and creative expression occur all too frequently. Such activities foster negative attitudes toward communication skill activities.
8. As a result of declining enrollment and reduction in staff, individuals who have little or no knowledge of early childhood education are sometimes assigned to teach young children. Such teachers often select inappropriate methodologies.
9. Teachers of pre-first graders are conducting individualized programs without depending upon commercial readers and workbooks need to articulate for parents and other members of the public what they are doing and why.

Recommendations

1. Build instruction on what the child already knows about oral language, reading, and writing. Focus on meaningful experiences and meaningful language rather than merely on isolated skill development.
2. Respect the language the child brings to school, and use it as a base for language and literacy activities.
3. Ensure feelings of success for all children, helping them see themselves as people who can enjoy exploring oral and written language.
4. Provide reading experiences as an integrated part of the broader communication process, which includes speaking, listening, and writing, as well as other communication systems such as art, math, and music.
5. Encourage children's first attempts at writing without concern for the proper formation of letters or correct conventional spelling.
6. Encourage risk-taking in first attempts at reading and writing and accept what appear to be errors as part of children's natural patterns of growth and development.

14 Students With Special Language Needs: Meeting the Challenge of Diversity In the Classroom

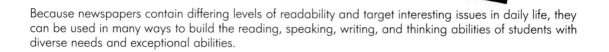

Because newspapers contain differing levels of readability and target interesting issues in daily life, they can be used in many ways to build the reading, speaking, writing, and thinking abilities of students with diverse needs and exceptional abilities.

If you treat individuals as they are, they will stay as they are, but if you treat them as if they were what they ought to be and could be, they will become what they ought to be and could be.

—Johann von Goethe

In this chapter you will learn how to teach students with special needs in speaking, listening, reading, writing, and thinking. When you better understand these needs, you can become a teacher that assists each student to reach his/her highest level of communication competency. You will learn characteristics of students with diverse needs, four lessons that address multiple learning needs, and how bibliotherapy, pen pals, and authorial studies can alleviate student problems.

By the end of this chapter you will know:

1. The principles that guide instruction for students who have differing language and cultural backgrounds from the majority of students in your room;

2. Strategies that assist students who have physical or behavioral problems that limit their thinking and communication abilities;

3. How to integrate bibliotherapy, reader's theatre, substituting, learning packages, narrow readings, authorial studies, and pen pals into your lessons to benefit students with special needs;

4. How to diagnose and instruct students who have multicultural disorientations, learn at a slow pace, suffer attention deficit disorders, lack behavior management skills, have emotional disabilities, and/or are more able than the majority of their peers.

THEORETICAL FOUNDATION
STUDENTS WHO NEED SPECIAL INSTRUCTION

You can profit by performing a mental activity before you work with students who have special needs. This activity helps you understand how such students feel and think. The activity begins by asking you to reflect for a moment upon the biggest problem you face in your life. As you think, recount the ways you have tried to solve this problem. When you have recalled four actions you've taken, read on.

Realizing that you have been unable to solve this problem alone, assume you could go to a teacher who promised to solve this problem with you. What would you want this teacher to say and do for you? Think of two things and then read on.

The last segment of this activity is to ask yourself: what two things must change before your problem is solved? Think of these two things before you read on.

Students with special langauge needs are likely to have tried many of the things you have tried, desire the same things from their teacher as you do, and realize that something has to change if their problem is to be solved. Like you, they probably have tried to avoid their problem or convince themselves that it does not exist. They may camouflage it so others don't think it exists; ask friends to help them; get depressed; get mad at themselves; and think that they are just "really stupid." Also, at some point in their past they are likely to have analyzed why everyone else in the world seems to be doing so well except them.

What they will likely want you, as their teacher, to do is: (1) "love them just the way they are" for who they are; (2) convince them that their problem can be solved; (3) listen to them; (4) give them courage and support; (5) expect them to succeed; (6) teach them *new* strategies that work and that they haven't tried before; (7) explain why certain of their actions are successful and others are not; (8) gradually let them set their own goals and keep track of their own progress so they can guide their own reading, speaking, listening, and writing in the future.

In brief, it is important to realize that most special needs students have tried many things to solve their problems before they work with you. They need your unending expectation that they can eliminate their problem; new language tools and back-up strategies; assistance in setting goals and evaluating their progress; and your instruction to identify which parts of each new strategy worked best for them.

PRINCIPLES FOR WORKING WITH SPECIAL NEEDS STUDENTS

You can address the needs of special students when the following principles guide your instruction:

Principle 1: Some educators profess that instruction for students who have special needs is the same as instruction for students without special language deficiencies, only slower, and less demanding. This is not true. Instruction for special need students is more complex and intense.   What you teach will often be in smaller steps, and it will be analogous to a doctor's use of penicillin. Through a thorough diagnosis, you can correct the student's problem. Your instructional intervention can diminish the "ailment" as quickly as physical ones are alleviated by proper physical treatment. When you have identified and addressed the specific communication problem a child faces, the problem can vanish almost instantly. For example, notice how the following teacher's diagnosis and implementation of a new decoding strategy alleviated Tom's reading problem almost immediately:

> After a few months in the Word Identification Program, an event occurred that proved to be the turning point in Tom's reading. While reading the predictable book *Night-time* by Joy Cowley (1988) . . . Tom came upon *stable*, a word he did not know. . . . Tom declared, "I know the 'pair'/'trast strategy [the new decoding strategy the teacher had taught]. I know *table*; this is *stable*!" This was the first time that Tom had used the compare/contrast strategy independently. . . . For the first time he viewed himself as a reader. The floodgates opened.

He wanted to share his reading with anyone who would listen. [Following this] Tom . . . read 100 books as part of his regular classroom's incentive program (Gaskins, Gaskins, & Gaskins, 1991, p. 221).

Principle 2: There are several types of learning disabilities. Through U.S. Congressional Law P.L. 94-142 (Education for All Handicapped Children Act), all types of students with learning disabilities must be given special instruction. Learning disability is defined in the *Federal Register* as:

> A disorder in one or more of the basic psychological processes involved in understanding or in using language spoken or written, which may manifest itself in an imperfect ability to listen, think, speak, read, write, spell, or to do mathematical calculations. The term includes such conditions as perceptual handicaps, brain injury, minimal brain disfunction, dyslexia, and developmental aphasia. The term does not include children who have learning problems which are primarily the result of visual, hearing, or motor handicaps, or mental retardation, or emotional disturbance, or of environmental, cultural, or economic disadvantage (*Federal Register*, August 23, 1977, p. 789).

According to the Education for All Handicapped Children Act (Sect. 619), learning disabled students are to be **mainstreamed,** *placed into classes where they can receive the best education possible in the least restrictive environment.* Mainstreaming is further explained:

1. All children who qualify for special services must receive them. There can be no waiting lists.
2. Children must receive individual evaluation, and the evaluation must consider the child's unique cultural and linguistic background. In some cases this means that the child must be evaluated in his or her native language. Each child must be reevaluated every three years.
3. Parents must consent to evaluations, approve the special education placement, and participate in designing the child's individual education program.
4. An individualized education plan (IEP), which includes the child's current performance and yearly goals, must be developed for the child.
5. The family has a right to disagree with the decisions concerning their child. They may have the child evaluated by a professional outside the school or seek legal help to settle their dispute.

Among the most common learning disabilities are: dyslexia, attention deficit disorder, and minimal brain disfunction or injury. Two primary behaviors that characterize the learning disabled student are indiscrimination and impulsiveness (Reynolds, 1991). While all students are indiscriminate and impulsive at times, those with learning disabilities exhibit these behaviors over prolonged periods. They are also less able to control these behaviors due to immature psychological or neural development. Indiscrimination manifests itself as an inability to note likenesses and differences in letters and sounds and to synthesize observations into meaning. It is important that you help learning disabled students identify one aspect of the language arts for which they are particularly skilled and areas of their talents. Such diagnoses not only promote self-esteem but lead less able students to use their most frutiful personal strengths to overcome their weaknesses.

Dyslexia. Cau yon raeb this seutenec? This is the way a sentence looks to more than 40 million Americans who have one type of learning disability called **dyslexia**. While educators do not agree upon the cause and treatment of dyslexia, it is defined as *a partial but severe inability to read, despite conventional instruction, adequate intelligence, and sociocultural opportunities, because of inborn factors.* A student with dyslexia may have numerous symptoms aside from reading and writing problems, including difficulty perceiving positions in space, size of objects, as well as level of brightness and color in natural and manmade creations.

In your class, mildly dyslexic students will benefit from multisensory instruction in writing, spelling, and reading. They also benefit from a flexible work schedule where they have significantly greater amounts of time to read, such as being allowed to read about a topic the night before it is introduced in class. For more serious cases of dyslexia, special instruction should be obtained in tutorial classes or special after-school programs. Many dyslexics also need alternative presentation and learning strategies in your student communication center. To receive updates concerning new instructional strategies, write to The Orton Dyslexia Society, 724 York Road, Baltimore, Maryland 21204; to Ms. Helen Irlen, Executive Director, Irlen Institute, 4425 Atlantic Avenue, a-14, Long Beach, CA 90807.

Attention Deficit Disorder (ADD). This is *the name given to the condition in children, teenagers, or adults when they show poor attention and impulsivity in their day to day behavior.* They may be hyperactive (overactive) or hypoactive (underactive), but they almost always have great difficulty organizing and completing their work. The needs of the ADD child are to have concrete versus abstract examples as well as physical models rather than verbal instructions. You can reduce the difficulties of students who have attention deficit disorders by giving clear, step-by-step directions. Being specific in phrasing directions and requests is helpful. If multiple directions must be given, praise the student for complying with the first step immediately.

Mental Retardation and Minimal Brain Disfunction. These students are defined as *"having significantly subaverage general intellectual functioning existing concurrently with deficits in adaptive behavior, and manifested during the developmental period (ages 0–18), which adversely affects a child's educational performance"* (*Federal Register*, August 23, 1977, p. 785). The educable mentally retarded (EMR) range in IQ from 55–70, their language and thinking abilities develop at only one-half to three-fourths the speed and depth of same-age peers, so that the mental capabilities of an average six-year-old EMR are equal to a child four-and one-half years old.

EMR students benefit from peer-tutors and repeated speaking, listening, reading, and writing opportunities. They also benefit, more than their classmates, from learning through molding words with clay, finger painting, and using flannel board displays. Because EMR students do not learn as easily through discovery methods, it is also important to state and relate objectives to personal experiences.

Emotional Disturbance. These students have *social and emotional disorders that interfere with learning. Emotionally disturbed students are unable to learn even though they have the intellectual, sensory, and health factors necessary for cognitive growth.* They are often unable to build and maintain interpersonal relationships with classmates and teachers, display appropriate behavior, and happy attitudes. They also have physical symptoms and fears associated with personal as well as school related problems (*Federal Register*, August 23, 1977, pp. 785–786).

Remedial readers, writers, and language users are students who are not as successful in language arts classes as they and you desire. They have the following problems:

- limited and inflexible learning strategies;
- disenchantment with school life;
- poor motivation toward improving their language abilities;
- pervasive and persistent inappropriate learning styles that interfere with their ability to spend enough time planning and thinking through problems, and checking their work and understandings;
- are overly anxious about making mistakes so they prefer to not commit themselves or perform in public;
- limited repertoire of cognitive skills;
- may perform with less precision in speaking, listening, reading and writing;
- spend a disproportionate amount of time failing to construct evolving wholes as they read, write, think, and listen, and struggle with aspects of literary discourse (Purcell-Gates, 1991; Gough, 1988; Kletzien, 1991; Englert, Raphael, Anderson, Anthony, & Stevens, 1991).

Principle 3: Gifted students are in equal need of your special attention. Gifted Students are *those who hold a capacity for high performance because of exceptional abilities.* They may be quite advanced in schoolwork, or may underachieve, fail tests, avoid homework, and daydream. Because of above-average abilities and task commitments, when gifted learners apply themselves, their thinking and communication progress at a rapid rate (Cassidy & Vukelich, 1980). As a general rule, gifted students have advanced language arts abilities, often have extensive vocabularies, use words in new and innovative contexts, and sprinkle complex sentences and complicated syntactical forms with accurate and creative expressions (Bonds & Bonds, 1984). They also have remarkable cognitive abilities: they perceive relationships, solve problems, and grasp abstract ideas quickly (Witty, 1971).

Such students, however, do not learn as well unaided as they can with your assistance (Cassidy, 1979; Moller, 1984). Among the types of assistance you will provide are the freedom to learn at a more rapid pace, engage in hypothetical reasoning, make higher order inferences, create interdisciplinary units, prepare in-depth studies in areas of talent and interest, and more in-depth instruction in thinking skill development. Gifted students also learn less through drill and routine (Labuda and James, 1985).

Gifted students can also experience social adjustment problems due to segregation by peers. As Don Herald stated, "The brighter you are, the more you have to learn." This is a challenge for you as the needs of the gifted are usually not as apparent as those of other students.

Principle 4: Special language needs arise for students who speak a second language or come from a minority cultural group.

You are likely to have students in your class who use English as a second language, since 90 percent of such students are taught in "English only" classrooms (Bonds & Bonds, 1984). Before World War I, English-speaking students met on Saturdays to learn languages other than English. Following the war, however, attitudes toward foreign languages changed and "English only" was mandated in schools. However, within the last thirty years, immigration to the United States and Canada has increased to the point where many schools are now mandated to provide education for students in languages that meet their educational needs (Lau v. Nichols). This ruling led to creation of thousands of bilingual and English-As-Second-Language (ESL) programs across the country.

The special language needs of second language students go beyond learning English. These students have cultural background differences from the American middle class, and norms of learning differ as well. Students whose first language, traditions, or values differ from those for whom our educational system was designed will encounter conflicts when asked to do apparently routine tasks such as: (1) compete for a grade; (2) earn points in a cooperative group; (3) bid for a turn to speak; or (4) demonstrate their knowledge before the class in a public forum (Moller, 1984). Such cultural differences, when misunderstood, can be interpreted as pupil withdrawal, indifference, and even incompetence (Cazden, 1988).

Another need of second language or minority culture students is to learn appropriate English syntax (Gunkel, 1991). "When people learn a second language, they are learning how to join a speech community. . . . Not only do the choices of sound, vocabulary, and syntax vary from speech community to speech community, but so do the ways of thinking about situations" (Edelsky, 1989, pp. 98–99). Research indicates that it takes seven years before non-native English speaking children gain the command of English necessary to perform successfully in language arts programs *which have not been modified to meet their language needs* (Sutton, 1989).

A fourth language need of minority culture students is to address the cultural discontinuity between their parents and teachers. These two sets of adults often create a conflict through dissimilar socialization patterns the student is expected to master. For example, Heath (1983) and Cazden (1988) found that when parents and teachers ask for even simple tasks such as to retell a story, significant contradictory messages are sent to the child. In some cultural groups, parents or teachers expect a literal account of what the child remembers, others want an explanation of reasons that underlie what occurred, and another encourages a child to embellish the story by adding people and actions that were not actually a part of the story. Further, if home cultural practices and values are not incorporated into your classroom, some second language parents will find that they are unable to support their children's academic pursuits, even when their fervent wish is to do so.

In summary, when you have minority cultural and/or second language students in your room, it is your responsibility to combine multiple sets of cultural values, and two (or multiple) speech communities so pupils' personal and cultural heritages are expressed. Essentially you have the responsibility to create a multicultural, democratic world in your classroom, a community in which students from many cultural, social, and ethnic backgrounds grow. One way to assume this responsibility is by adding parents and community resources from the neighborhood to your class. Additional ways you can honor and infuse student's cultural heritage into your student communication center will be described later in this chapter.

Teaching Specific Cultural Groups. As a general rule, nature is held in high esteem in the Native American Culture. Time is often of secondary importance, so that it is usually conceived in large blocks, such as morning, afternoon, and evening. Because of this, Native American students may have difficulty realizing the importance of completing assignments "by the time a 50 minute period is over." In addition, for many Navajo students, working in heterogeneous groups is against cultural values. They prefer same-sex, small groups or same-sex paired learning experiences.

As a general rule, African Americans value whole events as opposed to segmental steps. This culture appreciates approximations, as opposed to precision. It also values spontaneity, worth of people more than end products, kinship bonds, and having a keen sense of justice (Cazden, 1988; Heath, 1983). Freppon and Dahl (1991) taught vowels by incorporating values of African American into decoding instruction. They introduced letter sounds through saying and reading student names and physical movements, e.g., /e/ is taught by learning the word "Ethel" and /i/ by engaging in "itching."

Many African American students master nuances of intonation and connotations of individual words, and they value exaggeration in stories (Cazden, 1988). Most produce greater quantities of speech within peer groups than when teachers are group members. As a result, the speech they use in conversations with teachers will often be their simplest, least devoid of nuances and connotations, which is one of their language strengths. Their most complex speech occurs when classroom oral exchanges include participation and cooperation in a group rather than competition between groups or individuals. They also value electing their own group spokesperson and planning their oral, written presentations as an entire event, or "happening," rather than as daily, evaluated units less related to people and the social structure in their communication center (Collins, 1991b).

As a general rule, the Mexican American culture has a group-oriented, rather than individualistic focus. Many Mexican American students sacrifice to benefit classmates, judge others in terms of personal qualities rather than accomplishments, and relate more to recognition that validates them as a human being rather than their ability to produce products and material goods. Their pace of work is often more relaxed and slower than other cultural groups. Mexican American children tend to be motivated by (1) immediate feedback, and (2) person-centered rewards such as hugs, pats on the back, and verbal praise more than by grades (Rigg & Allen, 1989). When compared to the American middle class culture, Mexican American students tend to undervalue debating, expressing their own opinions, and critiquing others' opinions.

You can assist second language learners by describing on audiotape or videotape two language arts classes so second language learners (and their parents) can stop to ask questions about your procedures and tasks. In this tape, you can also list and define the terms you frequently use during instruction so students can study them at home.

Principle 5: The number of students who are language delayed and economically disadvantaged has increased. These students will expand the number of special language needs that need to be addressed in your class.   Many language delayed and economically disadvantaged students fall behind advantaged classmates because they have had limited environmental experiences with language outside of school hours (Reynolds, 1991).

Whether the cause for an individual student's language deficits is economic or physical, related to heredity, diet, or deprivation, these deficits often manifest themselves as emotional disturbances. While many students demonstrate emotional problems at times, emotionally disturbed students cannot move beyond their conditions. They are not willfully misbehaving but are unable to prioritize sensory messages. An emotionally disturbed student often cannot ignore "the footsteps in the hall, the light tumbling through the venetian blinds, the hand of his neighbor fixing her hair, the jangling earrings of his teacher" from learning stimuli (Smith, 1979, p. 16). They misunderstand oral directions, often hesitate or mispronounce words, and confuse word, letters, and sentences when reading. Those with emotional disturbances also have more good and bad days than other students; they do not finish work or do so carelessly and often lose their place easily. It is your responsibility to assist students to overcome (or compensate) for such psychological and temperamental variables that will interfere with their learning.

With your help, these students can learn to express frustrations appropriately, by using puppets (younger students) and journals to express feelings and thoughts. Art depictions of their feelings and bibliotherapy, as described in Creative Thinking Activity 14, are also especially valuable for these students.

There are four basic types of emotional disturbances. Each type demands special strategies to change the inappropriate behaviors associated with hyperactivity, power seeking, revenge seeking, and assumed disabilities. An extensive discussion of more than 50 of these strategies are contained in *The Acting Out Child* (Educational Research Dissemination).

Principle 6: Language problems do not happen indiscriminately. Language problems can be the result of a less than appropriate instructional plan for individual students. This "less than appropriate guidance" can arise from classroom and family demands that cause parents and teachers to become insensitive to students' learning strengths and weaknesses. Inadequate guidance is often accompanied by an absence of explanation as to reasons why the student experienced early difficulties with language, e.g., his/her long period of absences in second grade due to serious illnesses left large gaps in his/her knowledge of decoding strategies and writing conventions.

Misguidance also occurs because instruction does not consider the character of the knowledge students already possess and the role it plays in learning new information. For example, most students are unable to replace misconceptions with correct information without teacher or peer assistance. Indeed, most are not even aware of the misconceptions they hold—unless they are explicitly discussed and contrasted with accurate conceptions (Beck & Dole, 1992).

Principle 7: A large part of the success of your language arts program for special needs students rests upon your ability to manage movement. This is termed **classroom management**. Classroom management enables you to fashion periods of great concentration and sequences of productive discussion and movement. Effectively managed student communication centers have the following characteristics (Brophy, 1986; Collins, 1987; Kohn, 1991):

1. *Effective classroom managers have "clear behavioral expectations and install effective routines at the beginning of the year."* Procedures include students' knowing how and when to move and store materials; having clearly marked, color-coded areas where students turn in work, so time is not wasted collecting papers; and ending the day by arranging furniture for the next day's work. A special place is designated for students to elect to display their own work and messages.

2. *Students know procedures and rules for effective working conditions.* This includes: (a) moving from section to section in the room; (b) working in centers; (c) throwing trash away; (d) sharpening pencils; (e) leaving the room; and (f) raising or not raising hands during discussions. You build this knowledge by posing disruptive scenarios, such as, "What if I'm conferencing with a student and you need something, what do you do?" "What are the ways you can get help if I'm busy with other people?" "What must you do before going on to a new activity?" "How many children do you think can use the painting area at one time?" You also decide if the class will have class officers and/or group leaders, spend several days modeling and practicing these procedures, and point out features in practice sessions that went exceptionally well, as well as those that can be improved.

3. *Students know, enjoy, and often devise the "beginning of the day" ritual.* Such times help students acclimate to the day. Students know the signal to end activities and put materials away. Students anticipate and enjoy a pleasant and consistent closing routine, e.g., sharing important things they learned, relating something that someone else said or did that they appreciated, or hearing you read a chapter from a book.

4. *Students know and adhere to the discipline policy at their school.* You involve students in answering these questions: "What kind of person do I want to be?" "What do we want our classroom to be like?" For example:

> The realistic alternative is not for the teacher to abdicate responsibility for what happens in the classroom but rather to bring in (and guide) children so that they can play a role in making decisions about how their classroom is to be run and why, e.g., What is the best way for the class as a community to balance the principle of fairness and the spontaneity that encourages participation (Kohn, 1991, p. 504)?

5. *Model the following managerial attitudes.* (a) You know every child is behaving in the best way they can to meet their needs. Students who "act-out" in negative ways do not know how to satisfy their need to belong, ease their frustrations, receive help, or alleviate personal hurts through positive behavior. The class needs to reinforce an "acting out" student's positive behaviors (if this student is seeking attention) give reasons/written contracts for work to be done (if the student is angry and defies others), small tasks (if the student projects helpless), or assign a project (if the student hurts other's feelings or is revengeful). Additional strategies for assisting these four basic types of acting-out behavior is available in *The Acting Out Child*, (Educational Research Dissemination, P.O. Box 161354, Fort Worth, TX, 76161).

(b) Many times, students who disturb others need to know that others are willing to spend time caring about them. Because such students have personalities that may be difficult for you to understand, you can identify a talent these and all students can use to help others in the class. For example, Philip and Herbert were two students who repeatedly disrupted their fourth grade student communication communities. In one-on-one conferences with each boy, the teacher discovered that Philip "loved" projects with audiovisual equipment. He had a talent of attending to details. He was also an exceptionally bright and skilled orator. Herbert was equally bright, and he was a strong leader. But he could not read. The teacher identified a talent in both boys that they could contribute to the class.

The teacher asked Philip to use his special talents of organization and skill with audiovisual equipment to do something that would help the class: Philip prepared a narrated slide show using the slides the teacher had taken in Europe the previous summer (which she had dreaded putting together). The class enjoyed the presentation so much that they wanted Philip to operate all equipment in the future.

Herbert was asked to lead a group of four boys in creating a covered wagon from printed directions his teacher taught him to read from a book. Because the boys in his group were below grade level in reading and were not yet working effectively as a group, Herbert's leadership skills built group rapport. Herbert showed them that they too could learn how to read, and convinced them that it was important to do so. As a result of the tasks the teacher assigned to Herbert, the class began to value his leadership ability. Subsequently, Herbert was selected to play the leading role in the "Steadfast Tin Soldier." Because Philip's and Herbert's talents had been diagnosed and tapped to help others, their negative behaviors ceased.

With these principles in mind you can use the procedures and activities in the next section to further customize language arts instruction to address the needs of special students.

PUTTING THEORY INTO PRACTICE

TAILORING THE STUDENT COMMUNICATION CENTER FOR STUDENTS WITH SPECIAL NEEDS

In this section of the chapter, you will learn how performance-based activities, multicultural literature, picture files, Reading Recovery, and self-monitoring strategies can address special students' needs.

CUSTOMIZING INSTRUCTION FOR SECOND LANGUAGE LEARNERS

Second language and culturally different students should have activities in the language arts class that are performance-based and not language related, such as experiencing the joy of serving as a class officer, or telling important events in their lives in the language they prefer. Praise should be given for every appropriate use of English and for the knowledge that aspects of their language have been altered in English. You should also know the amount of English they speak, read, and write at home.

Second language learners can also use wordless picture books to tell stories, or write their own plots using magazine pictures as stimuli. Books written by authors from their own culture also assist second language learners as they are often more familiar with the content to be comprehended. They also especially benefit from Critical Thinking Activity 3 (p. 98) and *English Express*, a Macintosh software package that uses multimedia technology to teach English.

You can also ask adults or older students who speak both the student's native language and English to tutor the student. It is important to have many of the following books in your classroom or school library:

Multicultural Children's Literature
American Indian Stories (1991). New York: Raintree.

Anderson, D. (1988). *The Spanish Armada*. New York: Hampstead.

Anno, M. (1975). *Anno's Counting Book*. New York: Crowell.

Aoki, E. M. (1981). "Are You Chinese? Are You Japanese? Or Are You Just A Mixed-up Kid?" Using Asian American Children's Literature. *The Reading Teacher, 34*, 382–385.

Banchek, L. (1978). *Snake In, Snake Out*. New York: Crowell.

Bell-Villada, G. H. (1990). *Garcia Marquez: The Man and His Work*. Chapel Hill, NC: University of North Carolina Press.

Beller, J. (1984). *A-B-C-ing: An Action Alphabet*. New York: Crown.

Burningham, J. (1969). *Seasons*. Indianapolis: Bobbs-Merrill. (See also *Sniff, Shout* and other books about sounds by the author.)

Buttlar, L., and Lubomyr, W. (1977). *Building Ethnic Collections: An Annotated Guide for School Media Centers and Public Libraries*. Littleton, CO: Libraries Unlimited.

Cannon, A. E. (1990). *The Shadow Brothers*. New York: Delacorte.

Carlson, R. K. (1972). *Emerging Humanity: Multiethnic Literature for Children and Adolescents*. Dubuque, IA: Wm. C. Brown.

China and *Japan* (1991). New York: Raintree.

Cofer, J. O. (1990). *Silent Dancing: A Partial Remembrance of a Puerto Rican Childhood*. Houston, TX: Arte Publico Press.

Carle, E. (1974). *My Very First Book of Colors*. New York: Crowell. (See other concept books by same author.)

Conatty, M. (1987). *The Armada*. New York: Warwick.

Cox, J., and Wallis, B. S. (1982). Books for the Cajun Child: Lagniappe or a Little Something Extra for Multicultural Teaching. *The Reading Teacher, 36*, 263–266.

Crews, D. (1982). *Harbor*. New York: Greenwillow. (See other concept books by the same author.)

Delano, J. (1990). *Puerto Rico Mio: Four Decades of Change/Cuatro Decadas de Cambio*. Washington, DC: Smithsonian Institution Press.

Gibbons, G. (1981). *Trucks*. New York: Crowell. (See other concept books including *The Boat Book, Fire! Fire!* and *New Road* by the same author.)

Gilliland, H. (1982). A New View of Native Americans in Children's Books. *The Reading Teacher, 35*, 912–916.

Gilman, D. (1990). *Girl in Buckskin*. New York: Fawcett.

Goodwin, G. (1990). *Islamic Spain*. San Francisco, CA: Chronicle.

Goor, R., and Goor, N. (1983). *Signs*. New York: Crowell.

Hale, J. C. (1991). *The Owl's Song*. New York: Bantam.

Hauser, P. N. (1990). *Illegal Aliens (The Peoples of North America Series)*. New York: Chelsea House.

Hoban, T. (1982). *A, B, See*. New York: Greenwillow. (See *More than One, Over, Under and Through* by the same author.)

James, I. (1989). *Inside Spain*. New York: Franklin Watts.

Jones, J. C. (1991). *The American Indians in America* (Volume 2). Minneapolis, MN: Lerner.

Kemp, P. (1988). *The Campaign of the Spanish Armada*. New York: Facts on File.

Long, J. (1990). *Duel of Eagles: The Mexican and U. S. Fight for the Alamo*. New York: Morrow.

MacDonald, F. (1988). *Drake and the Armada*. New York: Hampstead.

MacDonald, P. A. (1990). *Pablo Picasso*. Englewood Cliffs, NJ: Silver Burdett.

Maestro, G. (1974). *One More and One Less*. New York: Crown.

May, J. P. (1983). To Think Anew: Native Americans In Children's Books. *The Reading Teacher, 33*, 790–794.

McIntyre, L. (1990). *Exploring South America*. New York: Clarkson N. Potter.

Milanich, J. T., and Milbrath, S. (Eds.) (1989). *First Encounters: Spanish Explorations in the Caribbean and the United States, 1492–1570*. Gainesville, FL: University of Florida Press.

Miller, A. (1989). *Spain*. New York: Chelsea House.

National Geographic Society (1990). *A Look at Native Americans* (Part 1 and 2). Washington, DC: National Geographic Society.

Oxenbury, H. (1981). *Dressing*. New York: Simon & Schuster. (See other basic concept books by the same author.)

Padfield, P. (1988). *Armada: A Celebration of the Four Hundredth Anniversary of the Defeat of the Spanish Armada, 1588–1988*. Annapolis, MD: Naval Institute Press.

Paulsen, G. (1990). *Canyons* and *The Night the White Deer Died*. New York: Delacorte.

Povsic, F. F. (1980, 1982). Czechoslovakia: Children's Fiction in English; Poland: Children's Fiction in English; The Ukraine: Children's Stories in English; Yugoslavia: An Annotated Guide to Children's Fiction in English. *The Reading Teacher, 33*, 686–691; and 806–815; *35*, 716–722; *33*, 559–566.

Robbins, K. (1981). *Trucks of Every Sort*. New York: Crown.

Rockwell, A. (1984). *Trucks*. New York: Dutton. (See *Cars* and other concept books by the same author.)

Rockwell, A., and Rockwell, H. (1972). *Machines*. New York: Macmillan. (See other concept books by these authors.)

Rockwell, H. (1975). *My Dentist*. New York: Greenwillow. (See *My Doctor* and other concept books by the same author.)

Smolan, R., and Cohen, D. (1988). *A Day in the Life of Spain*. New York: Collins.

Stensland, A. L. (1979). *Literature By and About the American Indian: An Annotated Bibliography* (Second Edition). Urbana, IL: National Council of Teachers of English.

Street-Porter, T. (1989). *Casa Mexicana*. New York: Stewart, Tabori and Chang.

Supraner, R. (1978). *Giggly-wiggly, Snickety-snick*. New York: Parents.

Wildsmith, B. (1962). *Brian Wildsmith's ABC*. New York: Watts. (See *Brian Wildsmith's Circus* and other concept books by the same author.)

Books in Spanish for Young Readers

Aula: Enciclopedia del Estudiante (*Aula: Students' Encyclopedia*). Barcelona: Editorial Planeta-De Agostini, 1988. 10 volumes. Grades 5–9. ISBN 84-395-0802-6. The purpose of this series is to interest young readers in the world in which they live. All titles include many illustrations and brief, easy-to-read descriptions. Each volume is translated by Javier Gomez (Grades 5–8).

Becklake, Sue. *El espacia: Estrellas, planetas y naves espaciales* (*Space: Stars, Planets, and Space Ships*). ISBN 84-7655-560-1.

Caselli, Giovanni. *Maravillas del mundo* (*Wonders of the World*). ISBN 84-7655-559-8.

Millard, Anne. *Como ha vivido la humanidad* (*How Humanity Has Lived*). ISBN 84-7655-639-X.

Parker, Steve. *Como es la tierra* (*How Is the Earth*). ISBN 84-7655-638-1. This series of books introduces young readers to astronomy, space and space exploration, the history of man and civilization, life in the oceans and seas, the effect of seasons on the Earth, and volcanoes and mountains. Each volume translated by Fernando Cano. Grades 4–7.

Elcielo (*The Sky*). ISBN 84-7417-086-9.

En el aire y en el espacia (*In the Air and in Space*). ISBN 84-7417-084-2.

Los hombres y lan civilizacion (*Men and Civilization*). ISBN 84-7417-091-5.

Los mare y los oceanos (*Seas and Oceans*). ISBN 84-7417-087-7.

Los paisajes y las estaciones (*Landscapes and Seasons*). ISBN 84-7417-085-1.

Los volcanes y las montanas (*Volcanoes and Mountains*). ISBN 84-7417-089-3.

Hernunes, Pollux. *Mitos, heroes y monstruos de la Espana antigua* (*Myths, Heroes and Monsters of Ancient Spain*). Grades 8 & up. ISBN 84-7525-496-9.

Kohler, Pierre. *La meteorologia, el tiempo y las estraciones* (*Meteorology, Weather and the Seasons*). Grades 5–9. ISBN 84-348-2572-4. This series of books introduces young readers to trees, birds, rivers and ponds, and butterflies. It contains close-up photographs, charts and drawings in color, and brief, clear descriptions. Each volume translated by Matia Puncel. Grades 4–8.

Burnie, David. *El arbol* (*Tree*). ISBN 84-372-3708-4.

Burnie, David. *El pajaro y su nido* (*Bird*). ISBN 84-372-2710-6.

Parker, Steve. *El rio y la laguna* (*Pond and River*). ISBN 84-372-2707-6.

Whalley, Paul. *De la oruga a la mariposa* (*Butterfly*). ISBN 84-372-2709-2.

Picture files can also be used to build background experiences for second language speakers (McClain, 1992). Using picture files for instruction helps to build the bridge from the known to the unknown. Small groups of second language learners and a few native English speakers can increase object name associations by mimicking actions, and pointing to objects where

---

NOTECARD 29: DUAL LANGUAGE BOOKS: CHILDREN'S LITERATURE PRINTED IN SPANISH AND ENGLISH

An ABC in English and Spanish by
  R. Tallon
Idalia's Project ABC—Proyecto ABC: An Urban Alphabet Book in English and Spanish by Idalia Rosario
Harry y el terrible quiensabeque (Harry and the Terrible Whatzit) by
  D. Gackenbach
Gato y perro (Cat and Dog) by
  E. H. Minarik
Como crecen los perritos (How Puppies Grow) by M. E. Selsam
Fievel y el nuevo mundo (An American Tail) by Judy Freudberg
La gallinita roja (The Little Red Hen) by
  L. McQueen

Arroz con leche (Popular Songs and Rhymes from Latin America) by
  L. Delacre
El premio del cuco (The Cuckoo's Reward) by A. Kouzel
El pirata sin cabeza (The Headless Pirate) and other books by J. Rohmer and
  R. Anchondo
Cuento de un cocodrilo (A Crocodile's Tale) by R. Aruego and A. Aruego
Clifford el gran perro colorado (Clifford the Big Red Dog) by N. Bridwell
El sandwich mas grande, jamas (The Biggest Sandwich Ever by R. G. Gelman
Los Dinosaurios Gigantes (Giant Dinosaurs) by E. Rowe

(cont'd)

NOTECARD 29   (cont'd)

Pollita Chiquita (Henny Penny) by
  S. Zimmerman
Donde esta Wally? (Where's Waldo?) by Handford
La historia de la Pollita (Little Chick's Story) by M. Kwitz
Mi mama, la cartera (My Mother, the Mail Carrier) by I. Maury
Los Espiritus de mi tia Otilia (My Aunt Otilia's Spirits) by R. Garcia
Ah! Belle Cite! (A Beautiful City ABC) by
  K. Poulin
Como es la tierra (What the Earth is Like) by J. Parker
El espacia: Estrellas, planetas y naves espaciales (Space, Stars, Planets, and Space Ships) by Becklake
Como ha vivido la humanidad (How Humanity Has Lived) by Anne Millard

Mitos, heroes y monstruos de la Espana antigua (Myths, Heroes and Monsters of Ancient Spain) by Pollux Hernunes
De la oruga a la mariposa (From the Caterpillar to the Butterfly) by Paul Whalley
Pinatas and Paper Flowers: Holidays for the Americas in English and Spanish by Alma Flor (Spanish version by Lila Perl)
El arbol (The Tree) by D. Burnie
Maravillas del mundo (Wonders of the World) by Giovanni Caselli
El rio y la laguna (The River and the Pond) by Steve Parker
La meteorologia, el tiempo y las estraciones (Meteorology, Weather and the Seasons) by Pierre Kohler
El pajaro y su nino (The Bird and Its Child) by David Burnie

---

nonnative speakers must give the English name. Books printed in both Spanish and English to assist in this activity appear in Notecard 29.

REMEDIAL READERS, REMEDIAL WRITERS, LANGUAGE DELAYED STUDENTS

Some teachers have the tendency to place a distance between themselves and less able students. They also give them less time to answer questions, pay less attention to them, call upon them less during discussions, seat them near the back of the room, and demand less from them. As an example, Willinsky (1990) reports:

> Interruptions [and correction] in [remedial] lessons for the low-achievement group were 20 times more frequent when compared to the better groups. It was the better group which controlled the pace of instruction in class as well. Much time was also lost to the "negotiations of embarrassment" by both teacher and student in the low group, in avoiding the task of reading out loud. . . . Children are living with what is in effect a caste system in which it is all too apparent that learning to read [write, and speak more reflectively] does not offer adequate compensation for the humiliation it can cause (p. 82).

Reading Recovery is an early intervention program designed to help low achieving readers. In 30 minutes of daily, intense, one-on-one instruction for 12–20 weeks, Reading Recovery teachers help students develop new strategies for effective reading. During lessons, students are taught to use their natural language, repeated reading, play, homework, predictable texts, and writing to learn to read/write (Clay, 1985).

SLOWER LEARNING (LEARNING DISABLED) STUDENTS

These students benefit from being told that their learning disability need not limit their capacity for success. It helps some slower learning students to also know that at one point in their lives the following people were also diagnosed as slower learning: Leonardo da Vinci, Woodrow Wilson, General George Patton, Winston Churchill, Nelson Rockefeller, and Albert Einstein.

Slower learning students also profit from special instruction in how to follow directions, as they often lack focusing skills. Picture directions, rebus directions, highlighting key words in the directions to focus attention, and audio recording are value strategies they can be taught to improve their focusing skills.

LaBuda and James (1985) also recommend giving the following clues during oral directions because they slow the direction-giving process: "Eyes on me. Now think through what you'll need. Are you ready? Concentrating? Good! Slow down. Organize your mind. We have time. Signal when you are ready for the next direction."

Students who have difficulty maintaining attention and concentrating need your instruction to learn a self-monitoring strategy for refocusing their attention when it is necessary. For example, you can teach them to respond to an established prompt, such as a bell. You can teach slower learning students to ask themselves a question each time the bell rings: "Am I thinking about the work I'm doing?" "Have I attended to my work better today than in prior days?" Some students also need to track how successfully they are paying attention every 30 minutes by marking a "yes" or "no" in a box on a sheet of paper taped to the corner of the desk.

GIFTED STUDENTS

Gifted students also benefit from challenges to publish their writings. A list of national publications that accept students' essays, editorials, poetry, narratives, graphics, photographs, and cartoons appear in *How to Help Students Publish in National Journals* (Educational Research Dissemination). Another method of meeting gifted needs is contracting. One of the benefits of contracting is that it is one of the most flexible teaching aids. Contracting involves student self-selection of activities from your predetermined options, or through discussions during conferences. Contracts can also vary in whether you or the students specify the deadline for completion and the criteria upon which success will be judged. Colangelo and Davis (1991) provide additional information concerning the special needs of gifted students. It is easy and enjoyable reading.

To sum up, each special needs student profits from a teacher who understands the characteristics they possess, as explained in this chapter. They need strategies, lessons, and instructional assistance that they have not had before if their language difficulties are to be overcome. The approaches described above and the lessons that follow provide such strategic knowledge.

STRATEGIES THAT TEACH
STUDENTS WITH SPECIAL NEEDS

Second language learners, remedial students, learning disabled, and gifted students benefit from learning packages, substituting, Reader's Theatre, and becoming class experts.

CREATING LESSONS THROUGH LEARNING PACKAGES

M	T	W	Th	F

Madden (1992) created and defined a **learning package** as *an instructional program which guides special needs students' reading, writing, speaking, and listening through a self-contained set of learning materials developed around selected children's books or stories*. Special needs students benefit from learning packages because they explain language arts processes more explicitly. They describe each strategy as separate parts. Each learning package focuses upon one language arts process and contains (1) an introduction and motivation device; (2) new words or ideas to be learned; (3) prereading, prelistening, prewriting, or prespeaking questions to guide students' thinking as they work; (4) oral reading and speaking activities; (5) reading and listening comprehension skills development activities; (6) vocabulary development; (7) word analysis skills; (8) enrichment; and (9) a student-teacher conference. You create learning packages in collaboration with special needs students.

CREATING LESSONS FOR SUBSTITUTING

This instructional strategy enables special needs students to work on a newly developing skill throughout the entire day. Substituting is to *give a tailor-made example in your teaching to meet a specific student's individual need. Its purpose is to call a special needs student's attention toward a skill being learned.* For example, a teacher asked students to write what they had learned at the end of a language lesson. In response to this request, one student wrote, "I learned about a farm." This same student was having trouble earlier in the day reading three-letter blends. His teacher came to his desk and read the above sentence. As the rest of the class continued to write, this teacher knelt beside the special needs student and employed substituting. She wrote two new sentences below the one he had written, and these sentences *substituted* words that contained three-letter blends for the word *farm*. The teacher then read these sentences aloud: "I learned about a school." "I learned about a string." Then the student exhuberantly read all the sentences too, and said: "String! String! I know how I done that. I said ring. Then I pick up ST and said 'string'" (Collins, 1991b). Through *substituting* in a single minute, this student learned a concept that had eluded him for the first four years of school.

Another way to use substituting is to write a framework where students only have to write words that represent the concept they are attempting to learn. This framework focuses students' attention directly, and requires attention toward one concept. For example, the writing substitution that follows was written for a bilingual student who was trying to learn time order and sequential clue words in writing. After the teacher had finished reading the last chapter of *A Wrinkle In Time* to the class, she wrote the following for this student to complete while the rest of the class wrote a free response to the book. As soon as the special needs student finished, that student initiated her own free response using the words "further," "in addition," and "in conclusion."

I think Meg in *A Wrinkle in Time* _____ self-reliant. I think this because _____ .
Further, _____ . In addition,
_____ .
In conclusion, _____
_____ .

CREATING LESSONS WITH READER'S THEATRE

Reader's Theatre is a form of drama in which participants read aloud from scripts and convey ideas and emotions through vocal expressions, and sometimes props. In Reader's Theatre a story/book/script is read and "enacted" before the class. Lines in Reader's Theatre are never memorized. All "actor-readers" are on the stage at all times. Characters not involved in a particular scene turn around or sit with their backs to the audience. When they turn forward, actors' entrances are marked. Costuming and staging are simple, with special needs students profiting by planning all aspects of preparing such props. The objective of these costumes, props, and staging are to suggest, not to replicate, reality. The practice that precedes a Reader's Theatre enables special needs students to provide their best performances before a group, enjoy participating and listening, increase speaking and reading speed, and make more thoughtful responses to literary events (Johnson & Louis, 1990).

The following books and publishers provide excellent scripts for Reader's Theatre:

1. D.O.K. Publishers, P.O. Box 605, East Aurora, NY 14052; distribute low-cost scripted Reader's Theatre for grades K–2 and 3–9.
2. Institute for Readers' Theater, P.O. Box 17193, San Diego, CA 92117; provide scripts and information about production.
3. Shirley Sloyer's book, *Readers Theater: Story Dramatization in the Classroom* (NCTE, 1982), and Caroline Feller Bauer's book, *Presenting Readers Theater* (NCTE, 1983), are handbooks of techniques that include suggestions for materials to use in Readers Theatre.
4. Reader's Theatre Script Service, P. O. Box 178333, San Diego, CA 92177; produce kits with parts written for different reading difficulty levels; (619) 961-8778.
5. The Economy Company, 1901 N. Walnut, Oklahoma City, OK 73125; produce kits with parts written at different reading difficulty levels.
6. *Reader's Theatre* by C. Georges and C. Cornett, Buffalo, New York: D.O.K. Publishers, 1990; contains 30 Readers Theatre scripts for various size casts.
7. *The Reader's Theatre* Series of Plays published by Curriculum Association.
8. *The Missing Prince, and Other Primary Plays for Oral Reading* by Ann R. Talbot.
9. *The Lost Cat, and Other Primary Plays for Oral Reading* by Ann R. Talbot.

THE CHALLENGE OF DIVERSITY

Gifted students as well as those who need to practice punctuation benefit by adapting children's literature for Readers Theater. John Warren Stewig (1990) recommends the following books, with the number of people needed in each production appearing in parentheses after each book: *Alphabet Soup* by Kate Banks (8); *How Joe the Bear and Sam the Mouse Got Together* by Beatrice Schenk de Regniers (2); *Iktomi and the Berries* by Paul Goble (variable number of speakers); *Kevin's Hat* by Isabelle Holland (7); *Lizzie's Invitation* by Holly Keller (5); *A Little Touch of Monster* by Emily Lampert (16); *It Wasn't My Fault* by Helen Lester (5); *What If?* by Else Holmelund Minarik (2); *Pancake Pie* by Sven Nordquist (3); *"Stand Back" Said the Elephant, "I'm Going to Sneeze!"* by Patricia Thomas (variable number of speakers); *"Not Me," Said the Monkey* by Colin West (5).

CREATING LESSONS USING CLASS EXPERTS

Students with special needs often are not among the most popular and sought-out members of the classroom community. When you identify an area of intense interest each has, you can assist them to receive special esteem and attention from peers by asking special needs students to become class experts on this topic they value. Not only will this request increase special needs students' desire to read, listen, write, think, and speak about that subject, but it creates valid reasons for others to come to them for advice and leadership. One special needs student reported about the benefits he received from a "class expert" lesson:

> "How is your story coming along?" the teacher asked.
> "Not too good," mumbled the student. "I don't know what to write about." The student braced himself for the lecture.
> "Tell me some more about medieval days. [The teacher knew this was the student's passion, as he had drawn several pictures of knights in tournaments during art lessons.] You know, I think you could become the class expert on that."
> The teacher let the student draw a picture and then they talked about it [so the student could begin his composition on tournaments].
> The student said, "You know, it was funny, but after we talked for a while I had a much better idea about what I wanted to write about. I got stuck on the spelling, but you told me just to write it the way I thought it should be spelled and that you would be able to read it. Any word I wanted help with I should underline. I read some more so I could tell the class specific things of interest" (Newman, 1987, pp. 167–168).

CRITICAL THINKING ACTIVITY 14
Narrow Readings, Writings, Speeches, and Listenings Through Authorial Studies

Critical Thinking Activity 14 advances special students' thinking skills through "saturation" both within and outside of your class. To implement Critical Thinking Activity 14, you will need to team teach or call upon another adult instructional partner. The benefits for your special needs students' higher level thinking competencies is worth the time you will spend in coordinating the activity with this person.

Narrow readings are *lessons in which students with special needs experience several works about a single topic or that are written by a single author.* Such narrow readings build students' schema and content knowledge of authors' writing styles so subsequent books relative to that topic are easier to comprehend. Thus, in a narrow readings activity, students can focus more directly on the plot, and add background and content knowledge gained from their previous books to discussions of second and subsequent readings. Freppon and Dahl (1991) describe one teacher who completes "narrow readings" by reading three or four stories each morning, writing the agenda of the day, talking about the words read, and showing how the words look like they sound.

Narrow readings can become even more powerful when the books students read/study in regular classrooms are coordinated with those they use in their resource room. Richek and Glick (1988) found that remedial readers who experienced narrow reading significantly outperformed control groups in their abilities to comprehend and they use fewer miscues during reading. Richek and Glick recommend the following books for narrow readings:

The *Curious George* Series: *Curious George, Curious George and the Dump Truck, Curious George Flies a Kite, Curious George Gets a Pizza, Curious George Goes to the Circus, Curious George Goes to the Hospital, Curious George Goes Sledding, Curious George Learns the Alphabet, Curious George Rides a Bike,* and *Curious George Takes a Job.*

The *Clifford* Series: *Clifford at the Circus, Clifford Gets a Job, Clifford Goes to Hollywood, Clifford's Good Deeds, Clifford Takes a Trip, Clifford, the Big Red Dog,* and *Clifford, the Small Red Puppy.*

The *Harry* Series: *Harry and the Lady Next Door, Harry by the Sea, Harry the Dirty Dog,* and *No Roses for Harry.*

Author studies can also center around animal themes, by including books by Beatrix Potter, Kenneth Grahame, Hugh Lofting, Walter de la Mare, Marie Hall Ets, Robert Lawson, E. B. White, and Louise Fatio. When students request more books by the same author, refer to *Developing Learning Skills Through Children's Literature: An Idea Book for K–5 Classrooms and Libraries* (1986) by M. K. Laughlin and L. S. Watt (The Oryx Press, Phoenix, AZ). This book includes 60 authorial studies.

THE CHALLENGE OF DIVERSITY

Older and gifted minority students benefit from narrow readings that identify ways in which the writings of the minority authors differ from majority culture authors, using authors such as: Arna Bontemps, Marguerite de Angeli, Mabel Leigh Hunt, Jesse Jackson, John Tunis, Dorothy Sterling, M. O'Moran, Eloise Jarvis McGraw, Laura Armer, Scott O'Dell, Ann Nolan Clark, Virginia Sorensen, Ellis Credle, and Jesse Stuart.

PROFESSIONAL DEVELOPMENT OPPORTUNITY
How to Use Pen Pals and Letter Writing to Meet Special Student Needs

Pen pals increase the responsibility students feel for writing and create many celebrative experiences as friendships deepen. Ollman (1992) also reported that her class wrote to an author to ask how much time he spent revising his writings. When the author wrote back to report that he spent 75 percent of his total time doing revisions, her reluctant and remedial writers significantly increased the amount of time they engaged in revising activities. Their attitudes toward their writing abilities changed as well. When they realized that even the most experienced writers labor over their writings, their patience with themselves increased.

Dear Sue. My birthday is april 23 im ficsin to be seren. Do you have a favorite book my'n is danyol and the lion's din. Your Friend, Chelsea

Pen pal letters truly meet the needs of special student population. By reading Chelsea's letter, you can identify some capitalization, punctuation, penmanship, spelling, and dialectical problems she may have.

Establishing a pen pal program brings authenticity to the task of teaching letter writing. To teach personal letter writing, put up model letters you and former students have written, as well as the basic letter format shown in Figure 14-1, on the bulletin board. Pen pals can be obtained by having students write to an upperclassman in another school, or to college students in a teacher education program. Lamb and Burk (1992), Cohen (1992), Busbroom (1992) and Collins (1992a) found that the latter program provides college students with an authentic experience to observe young writers' development; they learn developmental writing stages firsthand. College students then have "real-life" samples to discuss emergent literacy, writing process, and creating lessons that would advance their "pen pals" reading/ writing/thinking abilities. As Cohen (1992) stated:

> Recently one of my SUNY–Cortland undergraduate classes wrote to a first and third grade class during the same semester. They saw developmental differences within and across grades in spelling, handwriting, syntax, and writing interests. They also learned about students from many ethnic groups and social strata. The young children also learned what it was like to be in college, and studies their own teachers likely undertook to become their teachers. The pen pals began the first letters by writing about the books they enjoyed, and the program culminated with a joint picnic in the spring where pen pals met (p. 3).

FIGURE 14-1

Model Letter Format

St. John the Apostle Private School (Fort Worth, TX) developed a letter-writing program where students wrote to their "living heroes" or to their favorite authors using the suggestions in Figure 14-2. They asked why reading and writing were important to their heroes. A sample of the responses they received appears in Figure 14-3.

Another alternative is for students to write to peers with pets like theirs, or to write to peers who live overseas. A society of 5,000 elementary-age pen pals with pets can be obtained by sending two self-addressed, stamped letters of request to The World Wide Pet Lover's Society, P.O. Box 1166, Hurst, TX 76053. International pen pals can be obtained by writing to "Kids Meeting Kids Can Made a Difference," Box 8H, 380 Riverside Drive, New York, NY 10025; or World Pen Pals (a United Way affiliate), 1694 Como Ave., St. Paul, MN 55108. Students can also write to obtain free material from *Free Stuff for Kids*, Meadowbrook Publishing Co., Deephaven, MN 55391.

FIGURE 14-2

Suggestions to Follow in Writing to an Author

OPENING

Start by explaining that you are a seventh-grade student [at Grisham Middle School in Austin, Texas]. You have just finished reading [title of the book, underlined]. Comment that you found the book suspenseful, or enjoyable, or enlightening, etc. [if you did], and that you are writing to ask some questions.

QUESTIONS NOT TO ASK

(1) How much money does the author make? [not our business]
(2) Which book does the author like best? [The answer always is "All of them for different reasons." This question is like asking your mother which child she likes best. Better idea! Tell the author which book is your personal favorite and why.]
(3) Where do you get your ideas? [Too general. Be more specific. Is a particular character or setting based on your personal experiences?]

SUGGESTED QUESTIONS

(1) Characters: What motivated the character to make a certain decision? How would you have made a different decision? Talk about insights you gained from observing the character.
(2) Settings: Why did the author select this setting? Is it a real place or a combination of several places? Can you suggest a different setting?
(3) Plot: How did you feel about the ending? Why did events happen in a certain order? What did you learn from the book?
(4) Writing process: How long does it take to write a book such as the one you read? Did the author write the book all at once or a little each day? What kind of research did the author do? What kind of revision was involved?

As modified from Ollman, H. E. (1991/1992). The voice behind the print: Letters to an author. *Journal of Reading, 35*(4), 322–324.

TRY IT

1. The Daily Writing Sample (Figure 14-4) was prepared by a third grade student whose native language is Spanish. Analyze this writing sample based on what you have learned in this chapter, in Chapter 5 (Writing Instruction); Chapter 7 (Grammar); and Chapter 9 (Spelling). What would your next instructional goal and method be for Carlos?

2. Develop a program to meet the needs of your special students. One suggestion is that each six weeks you "adopt" a different student in each small group to nurture. This nurturing occurs on an individual basis and indirectly. That is, each day during the six-week period, every time students are working on small group assignments, your "adopted" student will be the first child with whom you will interact in that group. You meet a special need for that child before moving on to the next child.

3. Contact a nearby university to set up a program whereby one graduate or undergraduate student corresponds with individual, special needs students in your class. Your children can help the university student by

FIGURE 14-3
Sample Letter Received from Students' "Living Heroes"

Lee A Iacocca
Chairman of the Board
Chief Executive Officer

October 25, 1990

Master Chris Zacharia
St. John the Apostle
 Day School
7421 Glenview Drive
Fort Worth, TX 76180

Dear Chris:

Thank you for your letter and kind words.

Reading is an invaluable skill not only for the
vast knowledge it brings but for the sheer pleasure
as well. Books have a way of touching your heart
and inspiring adventure and success.

I learned to love reading at a young age. I read
everything I could get my hands on. I especially
liked the stories of John O'Hara. Master storytellers like Dickens, Hemingway, Fitzgerald, Crane
and O'Henry are old favorites of mine. I'm also a
big fan of mystery writers and have read a lot of
Robert Ludlum.

I'm enclosing the autographed photo you requested.
I hope you and your classmates enjoy it.

Best wishes for your future, and thanks again for
taking the time to write.

Sincerely,

Lee Iacocca

describing characteristics of "the best teachers" and the things they need and want in their language arts program. The university students can provide for the individualized instructional needs of your students. Alternatively, contact a local high school CEDTL program, Future Teachers of America Organization, or special parenting training classes. Students in such programs often can come to your room to work with students with special needs.

4. Develop a plan for evaluating the work special needs students do on an individual basis. Two ideas follow. You can list all individualized assignments each student completed in a specified period of time on one side of a paper. Include in the list the new ways you noticed that this student improved in his/her speaking, reading, writing and listening abilities, as well as in using strategies independently to meet his/her own special needs. After this list is complete, students turn the paper over and write about the

FIGURE 14-4

Daily Writing Sample from a Special Needs Student

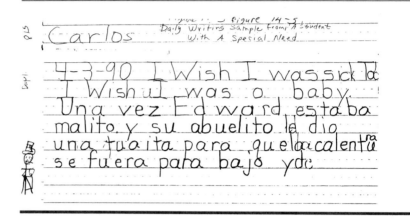

activities from which they learned the most as well as why these were successful. You and the student use this information as you plan new individualized assignments.

A second evaluation plan is to prepare a Tabulated Book of Growth for your class. This spiral notebook has one page for each student, marked by a tab with each student's name on it. To use the book, you and your students record anything someone else did that was especially appreciated, and improvements in communication abilities noticed about another person in the room. You also put your name on a page in the book. Each time a student or you make an entry in the Book of Growth, it is dated. Students can read comments about themselves at free moments throughout the week. No negative comments or suggestions for improvements can be made.

FOR YOUR JOURNAL

Bibliotherapy is the *use of books to influence a student's total development; a process of interaction between the reader and literature used for personality assessment, adjustment, and growth.* Bibliotherapy involves selecting reading materials that can have a therapeutic effect upon mental or physical ills of the reader. Bibliotherapy assists students to gain a greater insight into their problems, focus attention outside of self, realize that they are not alone in having a problem, and assist students to share problems with others. Bibliotherapy also gives students new insights into alternative solutions, and shows how others encounter anxieties, frustrations, hopes, disappointments, failures, and successes similar to their own.

Bibliotherapy can be used in conjunction with journal writing to prevent difficult situations from becoming big problems. To combine bibliotherapy and journal writing, the following guidelines will be helpful:

1. Plan carefully before implementing a bibliotherapy activity for the class or an individual student. Before introducing the topic, explain the

benefits of bibliotherapy to the class as well as how it is implemented in the journal writing time of the day. Select five books about different topics (see the Portfolio for a booklist) and mark passages from each that you will read aloud to stimulate discussion. You can lead students through a series of questions that (a) draw them into the main character's situation; (b) direct them to examine the actions the character took to overcome the problem; and (c) apply the story to problems that occur every day in their lives.

2. After bibliotherapy has been defined, students spend the first journal session writing about difficult situations they face. You can either read the journals and assist students to use bibliotherapy to overcome one of these situations, or establish a bibliotherapy unit whereby students spend several days reading books concerning one or more of their difficulties. When each book is finished students keep a daily diary in their journals in which they write the feelings and insights the book assisted them to apply to their own lives.

3. Involve parents in the bibliotherapy process if you desire. Allow students to select two or three books they wish to take home and discuss with their parents.

4. Pay special attention to any sudden behavior changes in students as this could signal that a problem outside of the classroom exists. In such incidents, maximize this student's participation in the bibliotherapic process by selecting a book jointly. Provide at least two books about the area of interest from which the student can choose.

5. You may wish to establish a permanent bibliotherapy section in your classroom library (Coleman, 1992). Such a section will enable students to discover books that deal with problems they face. Another advantage of a bibliotherapy section is that several students can select to read different books on the same problem and meet in response groups to evaluate how successfully each book resolved the problem. In this system, journals are used to record the groups' decisions. A recorder for the group writes a summary of their evaluations and places it inside each book for classmates' future reference.

6. It will be valuable for you to read a book and write a response in your journal. In this way you will have a model to provide when you introduce bibliotherapy to your students.

BUILDING YOUR PROFESSIONAL PORTFOLIO
Books to Use for Bibliotherapy

*Speech, Visual, or Hearing Problems

Arthur's Eyes by Marc Brown
The Silent Voice by Julia Cunningham
Follow My Leader by James Garfield
From Anna by Jean Little
I Have a Sister—My Sister is Deaf by Jean Peterson Whitehouse
Helen Keller by Micki Davidson

* Compiled by Ms. Mellie Goolsby, Texas Christian University.

STRATEGIES THAT TEACH

Amy, The Story of a Deaf Child by L. A. Walker
A Show of Hands: Say It In Sign Language by M. B. Sullivan
Keeping It Secret by P. Pollock
What Is the Sign for Friend? by J. E. Greenberg
Blind Outlaw by G. Rounds
See You Tomorrow by M. Cohen
The Half-a-Moon by P. Fleishman

Physical Disabilities

The Secret Garden by Frances H. Burnett
The Door in the Wall by Marguerite de Angeli
Darlene by Eloise Greenfield
Circle of Giving by Ellen Howard
Mine for Keeps by Jean Little
A Flowing by Joan Phipson
They Triumphed Over Their Handicaps by Joan Harris
Feeling Free by Mary Beth Sullivan
Someone Special, Just Like You by Tricia Brown
Like Me by Alan Brightman
How It Feels to Fight for Your Life by Jill Krementz
Where's Buddy? by R. Ray
Me and Einstein by R. Blue
Nick Joins In by J. Lasker
My Friend Leslie by M. B. Rosenberg
Our Teacher's in a Wheelchair by Mary Ellen Power
The Kids on the Block: A Troupe of Disabled and Non-Disabled Puppets,
     Kids on the Block, Inc., Columbia, Maryland (1-800-368-KIDS).

Learning Problems

Finding a Friend by Zilpha Booth
Summer of the Swans by Betsy Byars
He's My Brother by Joe Lasker
Take Wing by Jean Little
A Special Kind of Sister by Lucia B. Smith
Will the Real Gertrude Hollings Please Stand Up? by Sheila Greenwald

Gifted Children

Harriet the Spy by Louise Fitzhugh
Anastasia Krupnik by Lois Lowry
Alistar's Time Machine by Marilyn Sadler
Being Gifted: Because You're Special From the Rest
     by Sandra Warren

Appearance Problems

Obesity: In a Mirror by Mary Stolz; *Dinah and the Geen Fat Kindgom* by Isabele Holland; *There's a Bat in Bunk Five* by Paula Danziger; *Heads You Win, Tails I Lose* by Isabelle Holland; *Blubber* by Judy Blume
It's Not Easy Being Small by Mary K. Branson
The Twenty-One Mile Swim by Matti Christopher
The Ordinary Princess by M. M. Kaye

Personality and Behavior Problems

The Moves Make the Man by Bruce Brooks
The Hundred Dresses by Eleanor Estes
Meet the Austins by Madeleine L'Engle
Bridge to Terabithia by Katherine Paterson
Remembering the Good Times by Richard Peck
That Makes Me Mad! by S. Kroll
Sam, Bangs and Moonshine by E. Ness
The Ape Inside Me by K. Platt
The Temper Tantrum Book by E. M. Preston
Bear's House by M. Sachs
Tony and Me by A. Slote
The Bully of Barkham Street by M. Stolz
Let's Be Enemies by J. Udry
The Hurts of Childhood Series by Doris Sanford and Craci Evans

Death

Molly Make-Believe by Alice Bach
A Season In Between by Jan Greenberg
Run Softly, Go Fast by Barbara Wersba
Admission to the Feast by Gunnel Beckman
Annie and the Old One by Miska Miles
The Granny Project by Anne Fine
The Dead Bird by Margaret Wise Brown
My Grandpa Died Today by Joan Fassler
Charlotte's Web by E. B. White
A Taste of Blackberries by Doris Buchanan Smith
The Tenth Good Thing About Barney by Judith Viorst
Grandpa's Slide Show by Deborah Gould
That Dog! by Nanette Newman
When People Die by Joanne E. Bernstein and Steven V. Gullo
Loss by Joanne Bernstein
How It Feels When a Parent Dies by Jill Krementz
Learning to Say Good-bye by Eda LeShan
A Way of His Own by A. Dyer
Passing Through by C. Gerson

Listen for the Singing by J. Little
Season of Discovery by G. Goldreich
The Phoenix Child: A Story of Love by H. Vixcardi
Winners-Eight Special Young People by D. Siegel
A Special Kind of Courage: Profiles of Young Americans by G. Rivera

Love/Relationships

Forever by Judy Blume
Ring Around Her Finger by James Summers
Bargain Bride by Evelyn Lampman

Gangs and Violence

The Outsiders by S. E. Hinton
The Magician by Sol Stein
Durango Street by Frank Bonham
Headman by Kin Platt
Rumble Fish by S. E. Hinton

Alcoholism and Substance Abuse in Youth and Their Parents

A Look at Alcoholism by Rebecca Anders
The Cat Who Drank Too Much by LeClair Bissell and Richard Weath-
    erwax
A Hero Ain't Nothin' But a Sandwich by Alice Childress
My House Is Different by Kathe DiGiovanni
That Was Then, This Is Now by S. E. Hinton
Living With a Parent Who Drinks Too Much by Judith Seixas
Kids and Drinking by Anne Snyder
My Name Is Davy, I'm an Alcoholic by Anne Snyder
Are You Dying for a Drink? by Laurel Graeber
I Can Stop Any Time I Want by James Trivers
Tuned Out by Maia Wojciechowska
Teacup Full of Roses by Sharon Bell Mathis
The Peter Pan Bag by Lee Kingman

If one of your students is having problems with drugs, or knows some-one who is, they can call the Division of Substance Abuse Service, toll-free information line: 1-800-522-5353.

Divorce

It's Not the End of the World by Judy Blume
A Father Every Few Years by Alice Bach
Taking Sides by Norma Klein
Leap Before You Look by Mary Stolz
Win Me and You Lose by Phyllis Anderson Wood
The World of Ellen March by Jeannette Everly
Chloris and the Weirdos by Kin Platt

Love Is a Missing Person by M. E. Kerr
Sunday Father by John Neufeld
Don't Make Me Smile by B. Park
Dear Mr. Henshaw by Beverly Cleary
Aaron's Door by Miska Miles
The Great Gilly Hopkins by Katherine Paterson
Why Are We Getting a Divorce? by Peter Mayce
Dinosaur's Divorce by Lawrence Krasny Brown and Marc Brown
Surviving Your Parents' Divorce by Charles Bachman
Mommies at Work by Eve Merriam
A Month of Sundays by Rose Blue
My Dad Lives in a Downtown Hotel by Peggy Mann
A Family Failing by H. Arundel
A Month of Sundays by R. Blue
Where Is Daddy? by B. Goff
I'll Get There. It Better Be Worth The Trip by J. Donovan
Gus Lenny by H. Mazer
Mushy Eggs by F. Adams
The Boys and Girls Book About Divorce by R. S. Gardner
The Night Daddy by M. Gripe
I Won't Go Without a Father by M. Stanek
A Father Like That by C. Zolotow
Daddy by J. Caines
Where is Daddy? The Story of a Divorce by B. Goff

Single Parent Families

What's Best for You by Judie Angell
In Our House Scott Is My Brother by C. S. Alder
Daughters of the Law by Sandy Asher
Nuisance by Fredericka Berger
Notes for Another Life by Sue Ellen Bridgers
Storm in Her Heart by Betty Cavanna
The Divorce Express by Paula Danziger
Please Don't Kiss Me Now by Merrill Joan Gerber

Child Abuse

The Pinballs by Betsy Byars
Cinderella, Snow White, and *The Ugly Duckling* provide an opportunity
   to discuss how children should be treated.

Other Subjects

Let's Talk About Fighting by Joy Berry
My Name Is Not Dummy by Elizabeth Crary
My Mother's Getting Married by Joan Drescher

Tales of a Fourth-Grade Nothing by Judy Blume (younger sibling)
Sabrina by Martha Alexander (dislike of name)
Maggie Doesn't Want to Move by Elizabeth Lee O'Donnell
The Lonely, Only Mouse by W. Smith (only child)
The Very Worst Thing by B. Amoss (new student at school)
Nice New Neighbors by F. Brandenberg (adjusting to new neighbors)

Adoption

Here's a Penny by Carolyn Haywood
Foster Child by Loretta Holz
How it Feels to be Adopted by Jill Krementz

Dealing with New Baby

Nobody Asked Me if I Wanted a Baby Sister by Martha Alexander
Confessions of an Only Child by Norma Klein
Peter's Chair by Ezra Jack Keats
My Mama Needs Me by Mildred Potts Walker

Overcoming Fear

Frizzy the Fearful by Marjorie W. Sharmat
Maple Street by Nan Hayden Agle
There's a Nightmare in My Closet by Mercer Mayer

Finding of Self

Then Again, Maybe I Won't by Judy Blume
Are You There God? It's Me, Margaret by Judy Blume
Nikki 108 by Rose Blue
The Soul Brothers and Sister Lon by Kristin Hunter

For additional books, annotated by problem areas, reference *The Book-finder* by The American Guidance Council.

For additional books in Spanish for students contact the following publishers:

Aims International Books, Inc.
3216 Montana Avenue
P.O. Box 11496
Cincinnati, OH 45211

Bilingual Publications Co.
1966 Broadway
New York, NY 10023

Iaconi Book Imports
300 Pennsylvania Avenue
San Francisco, CA 94107

Hispanic Book Distributors, Inc.
1665 West Grant Road
Tucson, AZ 85745

Lectorum Publications, Inc.
137 West 14th Street
New York, NY 10011

15 Assessing Your Language Arts Program

When you put all of the pieces of the puzzle that you have learned together, you will create a language arts program to which you and your students will point with pride. There is only one puzzle piece left to complete. It is to learn how you can continuously evaluate yourself, your students, and your curriculum.

"The boundaries between assessment and instruction begin to dissolve when assessment occurs while students are actively engaged in usual classroom experiences."

—*Teaching and Learning Through Multiple Intelligences*, p. 199

Assessments in your language arts program are to provide a complete literacy description of each student's strengths and goals for improvement in speaking, listening, reading, writing, and thinking. Oddly enough, while evaluation is the last topic discussed in this book, it is among the first things you will plan as you design your language arts program. As you decide what types of documents you want to put forth as evidence of your students' learning, you sequence the types of instruction to include.

When you have finished this chapter, you can set your assessment guidelines, add your knowledge of assessment issues and tools to your instructional program, refine your teaching philosophy, and develop documents that provide complete literacy descriptions for all your students.

By the end of the chapter you will know:

1. How language arts assessments are changing;
2. How to select evaluation instruments to measure your students' success in reading, writing, grammar, spelling, speaking, listening, and thinking in an integrative manner;
3. How to use portfolios, anecdotal records, checklists, rating scales, student self-assessments, conferences, interviews, and group evaluations to document students' learning products and language/ thinking processes;
4. How to grade language arts products and processes;
5. How to create a full year's evaluation program that consists of weekly language arts' evaluation;
6. How to communicate basic measurement terms to parents and students;
7. How to evaluate the success of your instruction through an ongoing professional development program.

THEORETICAL FOUNDATION
STUDENTS' ASSESSMENT NEEDS

Language arts assessment is placed into practice in your room through eight types of measurement, weekly assessments, assigned grades, and annual language arts' program evaluations. It may take a full year of experimenting with the evaluation systems in this chapter before you discover the best adaptations of this material for your teaching philosophy and students' needs. Your pioneering experimentation will be worth the effort, as three teachers in Paradise's study reported (Paradise, 1991). Through developing a new assessment program, these teachers grew to know their students better, and assisted them to reach higher communication goals than they had ever accomplished before. Such a goal is possible for you and your students as we are entering a new era of language arts assessment.

This new era is based on the principles you will read in this section of the chapter and upon the conviction that you can use more authentic and performance-based measures than teachers had in the past (Brown 1989). Many school districts are developing such tests to replace paper-and-pencil language arts evaluations. These districts are constructing computer-based tests, videotaped evaluation, student-selected samples of in-class products, conference records, and students' self-assessments for judging the quality of their language abilities (Valeri, Gold, Olson, & Deming, 1991–1992).

In some school districts site-based principals may also ask you to assess students with a **standardized test** (*tests whose results are tabulated from criteria designed to compare students' performances one to the other*). Standardized tests differ from tests you compose because they compare students to large groups. They are either norm-referenced or criterion-referenced. Norm-referenced tests are constructed by administering items to large numbers of students in order to develop norms or a range of scores on the test from the sample of students who will be tested by this instrument. When your students take this test, their scores will be compared to those obtained by this sample of students.

Standardized tests are usually machine scorable instruments with scores reported in **norms** (*average performances as well as degrees of deviation above and below the average of a nationally based population sample*), **and percentiles** (*indicates where one student scores in relation to ninety-nine other students*). For example, a student who scored in the 97th percentile scored higher than 96 percent of the students in the normative sample population upon which the test was field-tested. Standardized tests also report **stanines** (*scores that range from 1 to 9 so that one-tenth of students' scores represent one stanine*). Stanine 1 designates the lowest 10 percent of all student scores; stanine 9 represents the highest 10 percent of student scores. Standardized test scores are also reported in **grade equivalencies** (*the performance of a student is equal to the average score of students in the fifth month of eighth grade if the score was 8.5*).

Criterion-referenced tests, on the other hand, are scored by totaling the number of items scored correctly. A score of 80 percent means that a student mastered 80 percent of the instructional objectives assessed by that testing instrument. The student is not compared to anyone else, and in most schools, all students are expected to reach a level of 75–80 percent proficiency on such tests. Reaching this level is judged to be evidence of satisfactory progress in the objectives measured.

THE CHALLENGE OF DIVERSITY

Hispanic children are able to express what they comprehend better through interviews than through standardized or teacher-made multiple choice tests. Hispanic children enrolled in the same classrooms as Anglo children and of the same socioeconomic level not only know less about the range of topics included on standardized tests but are unaccustomed to making the types of inferences needed to answer such scripturally implicit questions. The tendency of the low and average ability Hispanic students is to rely on a literal interpretation solely. Moreover, many Hispanic students require more time to finish tests than majority culture students.

ISSUES IN TEST ASSESSMENT

Within the last ten years standardized tests of language arts have been criticized and are being revised. Wooten and Spandel (1991) summarized these critiques when they stated that standardized tests of the past (a) did not promote student learning; (b) were poor predictors and indices of individual student performances; (c) contained content mismatched to individual teachers' classroom curriculum; (d) restricted the amount, depth, and breadth of material students were taught; (e) labeled students and placed them in programs beneath their capabilities; (f) were culturally and socially biased; and (g) measured superficial, nonauthentic, and limited ranges of students' knowledge. Moreover, there is growing impatience with student assessments that require and measure recall without assessing the thinking processes, creativity, and self-knowledge students use to answer questions and solve problems.

Wolf et al. (1991) argue that future language arts assessments must "be guided by a sense for the intent and meaning that develops over the long run of a discourse: to write or speak is to produce—to have ideas, to map them into chosen words, and to reflect on the power and accuracy of what you have produced . . . standard achievement tests offer no way to sample the wondering, investigation, data collection, or reflection that are essential to serious work well done" (p. 45).

On the other hand, Wolf et al. (1991) cautioned: "If the current interest in alternatives to standardized testing is to be anything but this decade's flurry, we have to be as tough-minded in designing new options as we are in critiquing available testing. Unless we analyze the workings of these alternatives and design them carefully, we may end up with a different, but perhaps no less blunt, set of assessment instruments" (p. 60). A summary of issues in language arts assessment that are being addressed through new evaluation instruments is presented in Figure 15-1. Educators are exploring ways in which these types of assessments can be used to meet the demands of institutional and national accountability. With these issues in mind, and by following the nine principles that follow, you can begin, to create better assessment tools for your students.

FIGURE 15-1

New Advancements in Language Arts Assessment

1. From paper and pencil testing:	To multiple types of assessment (observations, interviews, project performances)
2. From focusing on a limited range of abilities and talents:	To focusing on a range of abilities and talents:
*Cognitive	*Visual-spatial *Bodily-kinesthetic *Musical-rhythmical *Interpersonal *Intrapersonal *Logical-mathematical *Verbal-linguistic
3. From assessments of one or two dimensions of thinking:	To multidimensional levels of thinking:
*Recall *Inference	*Basic thinking skills *Complex cognitive processes *Decision making abilities *Problem solving skills *Metacognition *Creativity *Group process skills *Abilities to work alone
4. From measuring isolated skills:	To integrated assessment
5. From teacher directed:	To collaborative teacher/student/parent student assessment

Principle 1: Your assessments will become more authentic. Authentic assessment is evaluation that is expressed in discourses, conversations, performances, and products that make reasonably complete, integrated statements, and that reflect students' production of in-depth knowledge (Newmann, 1991). Assessments will use tasks, text materials, and contexts that students use in their lives outside of school. The focus of your assessments will be to prepare students to be learners/performers in the varying types of learning and working responsibilities they must accomplish in their lives.

You will include more than paper-and-pencil tests. Few asessments that expand thinking and integrate the language arts are possible when paper-and-pencil tests are the only evaluations used in your student communication center. More and more teachers are using oral, listening, and performance-based activities to assess language.

Principle 2: Your tests will scope a wider range of abilities and talents than in the past. Most former language assessments focused almost exclusively upon measuring language activities that occur only in the prefrontal cortex: governing students' verbal-linguistic knowledge and their abilities to be logical with, and manipulate, printed words. In the future, students' talents in auditory, kinesthetic, intrapersonal, interpersonal, gestalt, visual, and auditory dimensions of communication and contemplation will become a part of their literary profile. When these talents are assessed, such evaluations enable students to use their skills in visual/spatial, bodily-kinesthetic, musical-rhythmical, interpersonal, intrapersonal, logical-mathematical, and verbal-linguistic communication modalities (Gardner & Hatch, 1989).

Principle 3: You will no longer measure isolated language/thinking skills; rather, you will assess several student competencies simultaneously as these abilities work interactively to reach a measurable end product or process. Such tests also document students' planning abilities, and are essential if you are to obtain a complete picture of each student's capabilities. The need for this type of assessment was expressed as early as 1915, by William James, a father of our present educational reform movement:

> No elementary measurement, capable of being performed in a laboratory, can throw light on the actual efficiency of the subject; for the vital thing about him, his emotional and moral energy and doggedness, can be measured by no single experiment, and becomes known only by the total results in the long run . . . Be patient, then, and sympathetic with the type of mind that cuts a poor figure in examination. It may, in the long examination which life sets us, come out in the end in better shape than the glib and ready reproducer, its passions being deeper, its purposes more worthy, its combining power less commonplace, and its total mental output consequently more important (1915, pp. 135–136).

Principle 4: Your assessments will be less teacher-directed and provide for collaborative reflections between you and your students, as well as parents in some instances. Your assessments will be comprised of more student self-assessments than in the past. Students need the confidence and successful experiences of evaluating their own learning to be most successful in life. One of your assessment goals should be to help them internalize high standards and develop valid criteria for judging the quality of their work. As Levi (1990) stated, you can help students develop self-evaluative strategies, see their own new possibilities, and articulate their goals for their coming months' work. In doing so, you and they articulate targets for short and long periods of work, and fashion instructional/assessment instruments together.

Students hone their evaluative thinking through your guided practice in producing original conversations and writings for assessment, and through the repair and building of performances assessed with you. Such disciplined self-inquiry consist of three features: (1) self-selected use of their

When every student thinks this intensely on assessments you create, the evaluative component of your student communication center has attained its goal.

own knowledge bases; (2) in-depth demonstrations (rather than superficial, rote application) of information they have learned; and (3) production of new understandings in real, integrated forms that have intrinsic value to the students themselves (Newmann, 1991). Self-assessment also affords opportunity for students to ask and count upon the help of others in collaborative evaluations, which will occur more and more frequently as they enter their adult lives.

As more and more teachers guide students to become "co-responsible" for and co-owners of their learning, parents are becoming an important component in the assessment process. They provide distinctive information about their children's literary performances. As a matter of fact, the State Department of Education in Vermont includes a community component in its language arts assessment program. It asks schools to host assessment-report nights for citizens in a schools neighborhood to describe the language and thinking strengths and weaknesses that they have observed in the youth of their neighborhood (Allen, 1991).

Principle 5: Your assessment will demonstrate where students are in their own education and not where they are in comparison to a constantly changing peer population. Students' growth is measured relative to how much they have progressed since their last assessment. You assess them on how adeptly they are performing on goals they collaboratively established with you for themselves.

Principle 6: You will make planned and unplanned assessments. More and more of the evaluative component of language arts program will be made during, rather than after, instruction. Such assessments will document impromptu insights students have, how they transfer previous instruction to novel events, and how well they demonstrate a new communicative talent or skill for the first time. You will develop charts, inventories, and checklists where you record moments in your classroom community when individual members and groups demonstrate communication and thinking competencies at times when you had not planned to assess them.

You will also use the eight types of planned assessments to be described in the next section of this chapter. You will schedule them systematically so that you measure students' communication abilities approximately once a week.

Principle 7: New forms of statewide and national standardized testing are likely to continue and will be one component in your language arts program.   Statewide and national norm-referenced testing are likely to be the primary tools by which your school's total kindergarten through grade twelve language program will be measured. Your program will likely have to meet statewide, national, and international standards. In 1993, for example, each state has the option to participate in a new standardized test designed to rank statewide performances in language arts to international performance levels.

Principle 8: You will no longer view overnight grading as the most effective form of immediate feedback.   Presently many good teachers translate immediate feedback to mean quick, "overnight turn-around in grading written papers." Unfortunately, recent research suggests that nightly grading of daily papers not only violates some of the principles of best assessment presented above, but *does not provide immediate enough feedback to students so they can erase learning errors permanently.* Moreover, it may be impossible for you to accurately grade even one set of written work overnight. That is, if you have 25 students, you could only spend a total of seven-and-one-half minutes per paper in reading, grading, writing commentary, and recording a grade for each student's paper if you were to finish one set in three hours and twenty minutes! Even if you are able to complete such a feat, every night for 170 days a year, without illness or burnout, Linden and Whimbey (1990) found that many students do not know how to transfer your comments and grades to the new piece of work that they will do in class the next day. Most students are left to draw their own inferences about how the errors you marked can be corrected in new contexts. In addition, many students make the wrong inference about their grades. If they receive a "good grade," many are relieved and believe that they pleased you. They hope they are able, or lucky enough, to do so again. If they receive a "bad grade," many feel they are not smart and that they have disappointed and displeased you. Neither interpretation builds students' risk-taking behavior, confidence, self-assessment abilities, or thinking and language competencies.

A more effective method of providing immediate feedback is to disassociate it from assessment. You can give more immediate and effective feedback by providing detailed guidance on students' performances as they occur in class. This feedback enables students to correct the concept while it is forming, through the suggestions and strategies you offer in the immediately relevant context in which they are working. Such feedback will be as close as possible to the point in time when the communication was made, and within its same environment and context to effect lasting change for the student (Campione & Brown, in press; Linden & Whimbey, 1990). This type of feedback enables students to make a correct representation as soon as possible to a prior trial so students' full attention is centered upon that concept, e.g., an incorrect verb is written and you are watching the child write the sentence; you discuss a more appropriate alternative, watch the child write it, ask the child to read the altered sentence aloud, then ask, "How does this verb make your communication clearer?"

In brief, a comprehensive language arts evaluation provides a complete literacy description of each student's strengths and goals for improvement in speaking, listening, reading, writing, and thinking. Norm-referenced and criterion-referenced standardized tests will likely be one component of your language arts program. Several changes are occurring in language arts assessment. Among them are the use of fewer paper-and-pencil tests, and measuring language as students use it in the classroom. Students should learn to assess themselves. Ways in which these goals can be accomplished are to use the assessment tools described in the next section of this chapter: anecdotal records, portfolios, self-assessments, group work grades, rating scales, journals, retellings, debates, and outside evaluators. These can be administered on a weekly basis, as will be described in a subsequent section of this chapter.

PUTTING THEORY INTO PRACTICE
NEW ASSESSMENT TOOLS

There are eight new types of language arts assessments. As you read each description, you may profit from placing a checkmark to indicate the form of that assessment you prefer. After this section, you will have the opportunity to merge the tools you selected into a full year's evaluation program.

Anecdotal Records and Performance-Based Assessments. Anecdotal records are handwritten notes of student, small group, and class actions that indicate progress in communication and thinking. Although teachers for many years have made mental anecdotal records to guide their next day's instruction, more and more language arts teachers are using a formal, anecdotal record-keeping system to document their students' language progress. The first step in devising an anecdotal record-keeping system is to select a record-keeping form that is comfortable for you. Some teachers carry a clipboard throughout the day, and make notes about important occurrences constantly. Others use a spiral notebook, individual student notecards, or separate file folders to record information on different students at the close of each day. Others set aside a specific time at the end of the week to make anecdotal notes; and a few educators establish different categories of anecdotes and record information in each category on a different day. Regardless of the form you devise, the following guidelines increase the effectiveness of your anecdotal system:

1. Write the first thoughts you have as you document incidents with anecdotal descriptions. Your immediate reactions will be a more specific and less judgmental record of the salient features of that event. Observe specific dimensions of students' craftsmanship: (a) specific products/activities of (exactly) what an individual student (or class) is reading, writing, saying, listening, and thinking; (b) comments individual students (the class) make about their reading, writing, speaking, listening, and thinking processes they are using; (c) how individual students (the class) approach, execute, and complete reading, writing, speaking, listening, and thinking experiences; (d) accomplishments and products individual students (the class) make with notations of specific points they learned in the process; and (e) questions and concerns you and students seek to resolve in the future. For example:

> 8/31—Most of the children are struggling with their [descriptive] pieces. They want to write grand stories, but don't know enough about their topics to write well. They want to write fiction, and not personal narratives, which is what I think would make a difference for them (Paradise et al., 1991).

2. Make observations when students are working in an optimal educational environment.

3. Your records should be objective and nonemotional, capable of being shared with parents, principals, and other school administrators at all times.

4. You should set aside time each grading period to note individual/class performance patterns within your anecdotal records. It should take no longer than 20 minutes per grading period to note one or two patterns, which can become new instructional goals to guide students' learning during the next term.

5. You will consistently and faithfully uphold students' privacy, sharing records solely with individual students, excluding other class members (and their anecdotal records) during each sharing.

6. You can change the anecdotal record-keeping system you use in the course of a year, but it is important that each system remain in place for one full grading period.

7. When you begin to experience difficulties with your recording system, you may be trying to record too frequently (Paradise et al., 1991). By changing your system you can avoid one teacher's frustration:

> I was gung-ho on anecdotal records—got all organized, made about 3 entries per kid, then stopped on Sept. 28, for most of the kids (Paradise et al., 1991, p. 13).

To keep from derailing your best intentions, devise a record-keeping system that appeals to you. It must fit easily in the schedule of each week's activities, and you may use the following options to spur effective ways:

- Use blank mailing labels. Pils (1991) carries a stack of mailing labels in her pocket all day. When an important event occurs, she pauses and describes it on a mailing label. At the end of each day, she takes a few minutes to remove the backing from each label and adhere it to individual student pages, or to the full class's record, in her spiral notebook.
- Keep a daily log. A running record of daily events is made each day on a notebook pad. At the end of each day, the running record is read to the class and sections concerning individual student's progress is shared privately. Students know that any time you share something privately from the day's running record they are to record their interpretation and responses to what you discussed as an anecdotal record on their individual sheet in the anecdotal record keeping book. The sections read to the class are pasted in total in the front of the book so students and visitors alike can read about the class's growths from the first day of the year to present.
- Set aside fifteen minutes each week, while the class is working independently, to make whole class and individual student anecdotal entries. These entries document the class's and each student's most important accomplishment of the week, in your opinion. Setting aside this special time ensures that you make a specific, focused assessment of every student weekly.
- Schedule one hands-on performance experience each grading period for the explicit purpose of obtaining anecdotal records for students.
- Once the class has established the objectives to be studied for a grading period, you can create a form that delineates the types of performances students will accomplish to maximally achieve the objective. This form becomes the anecdotal record for that grading period. A form that can be used for this purpose appears in Figure 15-2.
- Create individual accountability contracts with students. These contracts establish a specific purpose for one grading period and the notes made on this progress contract become the anecdotal record for that grading period. For example, during the second six weeks the class decides that it is important for everyone to make a concerted effort to improve their creative thinking through self-initiated use of brainstorming, consensus building, problem defining, and scramblings. Each student then writes a contract to indicate specific ways in which you and they will know that they have acheived this goal.

Portfolios.   Portfolio assessment is a chronologically sequenced collection of students' work that represents their ability to make high level decisions; compare and contrast single entries of their work; and produce, perceive, as well as reflect upon their language and thinking competencies.

FIGURE 15-2

Summative Evaluation Based on Our Second Six-Week Objective in Reading

---

Student's Name: _____

Evaluation Period: from _____ to _____

Teacher-chosen criteria

To what extent do your entries indicate that you have:

- kept a complete record of the titles of each independent reading selection and the amount
  read?   /20

- included a number of personal responses to independent reading selections (at least three
  per week)?   /20

- looked back at previous entries and attempted
  to reflect on those experiences/opinions/emo-
  tions?   /25

- recorded questions/comments/observations
  for student/teacher conferences?   /10

Student-chosen criteria

To what extent have I:

- chosen and presented at least two read alouds
  to the class?   /10

- read to younger students as part of a buddy-
  reading project?   /10

- read a lot of different kinds of material for independent reading?   _____ /5

                                                              Total: ....../100

Comments:

_____

_____

_____

FIGURE 15-3

Samples of Record-Keeping Forms in a Student Portfolio

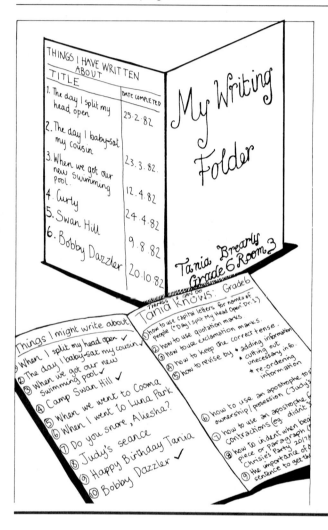

The portfolio focuses upon the students' growth over time, measures student effort, experimentation, and learning processes/products. Portfolios can become student/teacher/parent collaborative assessments, where students select entries. Students can express their opinions about what they want to include in their portfolios and how they want to measure their learning trails during each subsequent portfolio conference. As Fuhler (1990) reported, through such involvements students become more aware of the significant role their efforts play in their level of success, and that their opinions are valid. Samples of the types of items that can be included appear in Figures 15-3 and 15-4.

FIGURE 15-4
Sample of Criteria to Evaluate Students' Writing Ability Through
Portfolio Assessment

Continua of Descriptors		
Strong Performance		Needs Improvement
Versatility		
Wide variety of reading and writing across genre.	Some variety.	Little or no variety. Collection shows little breadth or depth.
Process		
Samples reveal discoveries or pivotal learning experiences.	Process illustrated in inflexible or mechanistic ways.	Minimal use of process to reflect on achievements.
Response		
Engaged with story. Discusses key issues. Evidence of critical questioning.	Personal reflection but focus is narrow.	Brief retelling of isolated events.
Self-Evaluations		
Multidimensional. Wide variety of observations.	Developing insights. Some specifics noted.	Single focus, global in nature.
Establishing meaningful goals.	Limited goal setting.	Goal setting too broad or non-existent.
Notes improvement.	Vague idea of improvement.	
Individual Pieces		
Strong control of a variety of elements: organization, cohesion, surface features, etc.	Growing command evidenced. Some flaws but major ideas are clear.	Needs to improve: sophistication of ideas, text features, and surface features.
Problem Solving		
Wrestles with problems using various resources. Enjoys problem solving and learning new ways.	Uses limited resources. Wants quick fix.	Seems helpless. Frustrated by problems.
Purposefulness/Uses		
Uses reading & writing to satisfy various goals including sharing with others.	Uses reading & writing to meet others' goals.	Apathetic, resistant.

As Uman (1991) states: "portfolio assessment positions students to learn about themselves at the same time as it places teachers in the position of being an assessment coach" (p. 105). Your students and you assess the connections between samples, patterns of growth, and the ability of students to plan new "thinking and learning trails."

If your school district does not have a portfolio program whereby portfolios are passed from one grade level teacher to the next, you can follow these procedures to begin such a program in your room, or school, if implemented by all teachers.

1. Designate a spot and a filing system where portfolios will be placed. This location will be accessible to students so they can store their work easily. Students will cull samples in their portfolios, and select their best at least once each grading period.

2. Decide upon the time when portfolio conferences will be held and the separate dimensions of literacy to be assessed during each conference.

3. Write a letter to parents to describe the portfolio program. In this letter also describe how the portfolio will be linked with other types of language arts assessments and why some student work samples are being held for the portfolio and not being sent home each week.

4. Introduce portfolio assessment to your class by showing portfolios from former students, or a portfolio you made of your work. Also describe (and show) how artists, models, writers, and other communication artists use portfolio assessments in their careers.

5. Make several options available as to the types of containers students can use for portfolios, e.g., artist's folders, pocket notebooks, manila folders, and compendium folders.

6. Explain that portfolios contain two types of documentations so that consistency from one student to another is ensured. The first documents are required work samples that meet criteria you and they set. These documents will be accompanied with student narratives that describe why each work sample was judged to demonstrate a new language growth, from that student's perspective. The second documents are those that you and the class agree to be representations of the learning objectives specified for the grading period. All class members will have one document for each learning objective. Therefore, in this system, one-half of each portfolio is personalized to each student's learning history and individual goals. The second half records each student's completion of goals the class established.

7. Students create a Table of Contents for their portfolio which is attached to the front cover. The Table of Contents lists "skills I can use," "things I want to learn," as well as the title and date of entry for each item in the portfolio sample. A sample follows.

Skills I Can Use, Things I Want to Learn, and Items in My Portfolio   Date Entered

1. _____   1. _____

2. _____   2. _____

3. _____   3. _____

8. You can allow parents to assist their children as they select their best work to be included in the portfolios.

9. Portfolios can be graded in several ways. First, as noted above, at the end of each grading period, students will sort through their documents and select those they wish to include. They will then state why they choose each piece, what it demonstrates that they learned, and their future goals relative to each document. Students can also develop a self-evaluation report which is submitted to the teacher during the portfolio assessment conference. Second, evaluation can be on the basis of only one or two pieces among the several that are stored in the portfolio that each student submits (Shuman, 1991). Third, you can use published, standardized portfolio programs and the assessment criteria they provide. Such commercially prepared portfolios are *The Riverside Integrated Literature and Language Arts Portfolio*, Psychological Corporation's *Integrated Language Arts Portfolio*, and portfolios published by Silver-Burdett and Ginn, D. C. Heath, Harcourt Brace Jovanovich, and Scott Foresman.

Fourth, you can evaluate portfolios by awarding points in more than one category of growth. For example, students and you can agree that portfolios will be graded on three criteria: degree of document variety (receiving from 1–5 points of weight); demonstrations of five major objectives taught during the grading period (receiving from 1–5 points of weight); and level of unique expressions of individual student's creativity, initiative, oral communication skill, group work competencies, and student-selected goal (receiving from 1–5 points of weight). Total points earned could then be multiplied by 6.67 to determine a portfolio grade on a 100-point scale.

Finally, parents can be involved in assessing portfolios. They can make written comments to the student/teacher, as demonstrated in Figure 15-5; review portfolios during parent conferences with teachers or at parents' nights at the school occasions; or complete suggestions for follow-up activities that can be carried out at home after a portfolio has been graded by you and the student in a collaborative conference.

A bulletin is now being published by Portfolio Assessment Clearinghouse, entitled "Portfolio News," to assist you in keeping abreast of advancements in portfolio assessment.

Student Self-Assessment. Self-assessments are opportunities for students to value, monitor, evaluate, and improve their own language and thinking. As Aristotle stated, "each man judges well the things he knows, and of these he is a good judge" (*Ethics* I:3). You begin this assessment system by selecting/adapting a self-assessment form such as the one on page 496. Then you complete a model form, as if you were a student, and illustrate how students can complete their self-assessment in the grading period specified.

In addition to the completion of written forms, students can assess their performances during evaluation interviews and conferences. Such assessments can occur by either awarding points for the number of questions completed or by being given a global score for quality of answers given on all questions. Example interview questions are:

FIGURE 15-5

Sample Parent Assessment

Childs name: _____

Date of last report: _____ Today's date: _____

The skills and attitudes you observed in your child on the last report have been recorded in the first column. Please place a check (✓) next to those items in the second column that you have observed in your child since the last report.

                My child

____   ____   1.   Reads from a wide variety of materials such as books, magazines, newspapers, etc.

____   ____   2.   Takes time during each day to read in a quiet place

____   ____   3.   Talks with family members about the things he/she is reading

____   ____   4.   Finds reading to be an exciting way to learn about the world

____   ____   5.   Brings home books and other reading materials from the school or public library

____   ____   6.   Seems to understand more of what he/she reads at home

____   ____   7.   Tries to discover new words and uses them in his/her conservations

____   ____   8.   Seems to have developed higher-level thinking skills

____   ____   9.   Uses study skills (e.g. notetaking, organizing time, etc.) regularly

____   ____   10.   Has shown improvement in his/her reading ability since the last report

My child would be a better if: _____

_____

_____

My child's greatest strength in reading is: _____

_____

_____

By the next report my child should learn: _____

_____

_____

From Fredericks, A. D. and Rasinski, T. V. (1990). Working with parents: Involving parents in the assessment process. *The Reading Teacher, 44*(4) p. 348.

1. List or describe what you can do now that you could not do earlier in the year.
2. What are your best works as a speaker, listener, reader, writer, and thinker? Why?
3. What were the most difficult concepts you have learned about writing, reading, speaking, listening, and thinking? Why were these difficult for you?
4. How have you changed as a reader, writer, speaker, listener, and thinker?
5. What would you like to do better as a reader, writer, speaker, listener, and thinker?
6. What do you do when you _____ [a specific objective taught during the grading period]?
7. Of the reading/writing/speaking/listening/thinking processes that we have studied lately, in which are you most confident?
8. What do you still not understand and how could I go about helping you to understand it?
9. Rate and defend how well you used your time [how well you learned] this grading period.
10. What do I need to ask for you to best demonstrate how much you've learned?

Students can also complete annotations which are attached to their report cards. In such annotations students also give themselves grades, after you explain the standards upon which you will grade them. An

FIGURE 15-6
Student Justifies the Grade She Should Receive in Language Arts

Mrs Lewis

Jennifer

I think something important to me about reading is I have been reading many books this year. Because I wrote a note to George Bush and he told me to read lots of books this year. I have read as many books as I can. And I think I'v learned that it is fun reading books.

How well you have learned to recognize new words _B_

How well you have learned to think while you read _A_

example of such a report card was presented by Judd (1989). Judd found that most students graded themselves much like the actual grades they actually earned. Judd also used these self-assessments as indicators for teachers/parents of students' levels of self-esteem, e.g., one student (Brian) wrote of himself: "Brian is doing well in his assignments but he has not been doing many independent activities. He's doing better in his reading group and he's writing in his journal a lot. P. S. I love his jokes" (Judd, 1989, p. 91). Samples of student self-assessments appear in Figures 15-6 and 15-7.

Evaluating Group Projects, Group Discussions, and Paired Assignments. Group grades can be given as individual member grades, total group grades, improvement scores, or as combined grades. The most frequently used assessments of group work include video and audio pre- and posttest replays, video and audio analyses, group self-assessments, and teacher-graded group work.

Paired learning sessions can be assessed through checklists, and by interviews completed by their partners, using questions such as the following:

FIGURE 15-7
Student Self-Assessment for Group Work During Consensus Building

Student Self Assessment for
Group Work during Consensus Building

Directions: Put an "x" on the continuum
at the point that best describes your
involvement today in your group
5 means "the whole time" and 1 means
"not at all."   5 4 3 2 1

① I offered my opinion to the group.   •—•—•—•—•

② I listened to others' opinions and   •—•—•—•
        statements.

③ I responded to anothers' statement   •—•—•—•
        or opinion.

④ I compromised on some of my   •—•—•—•
   opinions in order to reach a
   group decision.

⑤ I helped someone else add to the   •—•—•—•
   discussion by asking them for their
   opinion or statement.

⑥ I feel that I need to work on _____
   _____

⑦ A group skill I think I am good at is
   _____

⑧ Overall, the grade I think I deserve
   today is ____. ("0" for outstanding
              "5" for satisfactory
              "n" for ...)

1. What do you want to tell me about what you've learned relative
   to _____ ?
2. What was your favorite part?
3. What was the purpose of _____ ?
4. What was difficult about _____ ?

Partners can also tell each other something they do well. Other types
of paired assessment are long term in nature. For example, a group of fifth

FIGURE 15-8
Writing Checklist

Scale of 1 to 5 (high)
N.O. Not Observed

Name of child _____

Grade _____

School _____

Holistic Assessment

	Oct.	Jan.	May
Superior	—	—	—
Very Good	—	—	—
Good	—	—	—
Poor	—	—	—
Very Poor	—	—	—

Comments
List Titles of Writing Products
& Dates Completed

	Oct.	Jan.	May
UNDERSTANDING OF TASK			
1. Uses draft format			
2. Writes on topic			
SEMANTIC ORGANIZATION			
3. Organizes logically			
4. Uses a topic sentence			
5. Uses a support sentence			
6. Writes conclusions			
SENTENCE STRUCTURE			
7. Writes complete sentences			
8. Uses varied sentence structure			
9. Uses pronouns appropriately			
10. Uses tenses appropriately			
VOCABULARY & LANGUAGE			
11. Uses varied nouns and verbs			
12. Uses various adjectives			
MECHANICS			
13. Uses end punctuation			
14. Uses beginning capitals			
15. Uses proper name capitals			
16. Spells correctly			
PROOFREADING & IMPROVING (Teacher directed)			
17. Slots for adjectives			
18. Replaces with synonyms			
19. Combines into series or other forms			
20. Finds errors in capitalization			
21. Finds errors in end punctuation			
22. Finds errors in spelling			
FLUENCY			
23. Writes sufficient amount for the assignment			

graders participated in a cross-aged project with kindergarten children. The grade they received on the project came from the two books they completed at the end of the year. The first was written for parents of kindergarten students, entitled *The Favorite Books of Kindergarten Students at Our Elementary School*; the second was written for students/parents, entitled *How to be a Good Tutor*. Both were placed in the school's library.

Rating Scales. Rating scales are charts that indicate the degree to which specific traits or qualities have been achieved. Rating scales can be used as self-assessment instruments or as teacher-made tests. An example of a rating scale of writing abilities follows in Figure 15-8.

Assessing Integration of Language Arts and Thinking. About mid-year, evaluations of integrative uses of the language arts and thinking strategies should be taken. For example, you can give a student (or group

FIGURE 15-9
Sample of Assessing Student Thinking Skills

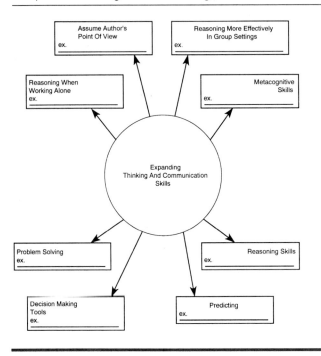

of students) a body of information and a simulated problem that they are to solve. Then you state the criteria upon which their work will be graded. An evaluation of thinking abilities appears in Figure 15-9. A second option is to ask students to provide three or more examples of their mastery of different language arts concepts relative to a single topic. For example, students can be divided into three groups. Each group prepares a written, oral, and thinking skill presentation relative to a body of knowledge upon which they will be assessed.

A third option is to give more than one grade to a performance or assign points to its aspects. For example, distinct assessments can be made of students' (1) preparation, (2) overall content, (3) presentation quality, and (4) documented language arts/thinking objectives learned, e.g.:

Performance Assessment Over Content Area Unit

1. Learning Log complete	1–5 points
2. Read five informational books on the topic	1–5 points
3. Helped the group to make a record and used one of the problem-solving strategies learned this grading period	1–15 points
4. Communicated effectively in the group presentation	1–15 points

cont'd

Performance Assessment Over Content Area Unit   (cont'd)

5. Made an original contribution to the class's body of
   knowledge   1–15 points
6. Written project was accurate and skillfully prepared,
   using objectives learned during this grading period   1–15 points
7. Group work skills improved   1–10 points
8. Documentation of insights gained into one's own
   communication and thinking abilities since last project
   grade   1–20 points
                                                                          0–100 points

Grading Journals and Other Writings.   Journals can be graded holistically (based upon overall impression of effectiveness in communication), by primary process assessment (focus upon a specific object, or trait of writing), or through a rubric (series of quality indicators). Each type adheres to the principle that assessment of student writing emphasizes the worth of each student's effort, and that every author has room for growth and improvement. Because journal writings are usually personal expressions where students have taken a risk to express their thoughts, acceptance and appreciation of these expressions should be evident in the evaluations given. For this reason, journal assessments must be planned as carefully as the instructional objectives they are designed to achieve.

The first step in journal evaluation is to make the evaluation criteria clear to students. You can emphasize different aspects of thinking and writing strengths at separate evaluation periods in the year. When journals are evaluated in this way, five aspects can be assessed:

1. *Thought:* The quality of thinking that underlies the ideas is rated: How rich are the ideas? Are any unique? Do the ideas evidence critical thinking? Any logical sequence?
2. *Authenticity:* Is the writing sincere? Does it represent a genuine (or convincing) experience? Do you hear the "voice" of the writer? Do readers become involved and can they relate the messages to their personal experiences easily?
3. *Power:* Is the language effective? Is the density, clarity, and breadth of writing power increasing?
4. *Growth:* Has the student improved since the last grading period, and to what degree? Is the student taking risks?
5. *Conventions:* Does the student use effective grammar, spelling, punctuation, and capitalization?

Student self-evaluation of their journals should be combined with your evaluation, as shown in Figures 15-10 and 15-11. After students have answered the four questions in Figure 15-10 you award points for the number of journal entries made, and award one to three points per journal entry for the correct use of writing conventions, one to three points per selection for quality of writing in that student used new objectives learned during this grading period, and one to sixteen points as a response to the quality of the student's self-assessment, completed in Figure 15-10. As you read each journal you will search for and note the next things this student is

FIGURE 15-10
Journal: Student Self Evaluation

Date: _____

Student's Name: _____ Grading Period:
1 2 3 4 5 6
(circle one)

I. Name four ways the quality of your Reading and Writing have improved in your journal entries this six weeks.

II. Name four ways that thoughts about things you have read are used in your journal entries this six weeks.

III. How have you improved in your ability to express your opinions, emotions, ideas, and experiences in your journal entries this six weeks?

IV. How have you met our previously set goals? How have you achieved the goals we set during our last conference?

Created in consultation with C. Brandt, L. Gore, S. Hatfield, S. Moore, and K. Oglesby, Texas Christian University, Fort Worth, TX, July 1991.

---

ready to learn to become a more effective writer. These notes are written at the bottom of Figure 15-11 and taken to your student-teacher conference. At that time you and the student set new objectives for the next grading period.

FIGURE 15-11
Journal: Teacher Evaluation

Date:_____

Student Name: _____ Grading Period

Criteria: _____ 1 2 3 4 5 6
(circle one)

A. Quantity: 12 Journal entries   12%
   (2 per week) re-
   quired each 6
   weeks. (One
   point per entry.)

   _____

B. Correct Use of Writing Con-   36%
   ventions (1–3 points per selection for grading period)
   1. Mechanics—Grammar
   2. Spelling/Punctuation/
      Capitalization
   3. Sentence Formation
      36 points—above av-
      erage
      24 points—average
      12 points—below av-
      erage

   _____

C. Quality: Using previously   36% (36 points
   stated objectives   maximum)
   1. Completely address the
      objectives learned this
      grading period (1–3
      points per selection)
   2. Quality and richness of
      language (1–3 points per
      selection)
   3. Express opinions, ideas,
      feelings (1–3 points per
      selection)

   _____

D. Grade on Self-Evaluation   16% (16 points
   (4 parts of 1–4 points each   maximum)
   from student self-evaluation
   form)

   _____

                               TOTAL POINTS
                               EARNED   _____

TEACHER & STUDENT CONFERENCE COMMENTS: (Set Goals for next grading period)

Created in consultation with C. Brandt, L. Gore, S. Hatfield, S. Moore, K. Oglesby, Texas Christian University, Fort Worth, Texas, July 1991.

FIGURE 15-12
Retellings and Debate Evaluation Form

Directions: Students assess peers or self; teacher grades their performances as well. Single points are awarded for:

1. Statements were short, clearly explained, and adequately supported.
2. Use of good facts.
3. Worded opinions effectively.
4. Good rebuttal pointed out poor explanation, faulty supports, or asked good questions about something left unsaid.
5. Listened to questions and demonstrated other critical listening skills.

TEAM A MEMBERS:

Names	OPENING	REBUTTAL	CLOSING	TOTAL POINTS
_____	1. _____			
_____	2. _____			
_____	3. _____			
_____	4. _____			
_____	5. _____			

TEAM B MEMBERS:

Names	OPENING	REBUTTAL	CLOSING	TOTAL POINTS
_____	1. _____			
_____	2. _____			
_____	3. _____			
_____	4. _____			
_____	5. _____			

After hearing the debate, I voted for team _____ **because**_____
_____ .

_____
DEBATE JUDGE

Retellings and Debates.   Retellings of readings, events, or uses of the thinking/communication process are valuable assessment tools. A retelling is where you analyze a students' free recall of an event, specific communication/thinking objectives taught, or reading/listening/writing experiences the student completed in the class, e.g., what types of inference did the student evidence, which parts of the event were most vividly remembered and why, and what did the retelling demonstrate about the student's growth as a communicator and thinker.

Figure 15-12 can be used in many ways to assess oral retellings and debates. All members of the class can award up to five points per speaker in debate teams, and debaters can sum these peer evaluations to improve their speaking abilities. Second, students can assess themselves by awarding points after a retelling or a debate. Third, you can use this form to assess students' retellings, debates, and other speeches, and change the directions section to include more advanced communication objectives, as students' abilities increase during the year.

Case Studies.   Special needs students profit from individual case study assessments. These assessments are usually completed in collaboration with the student, student's parent, and other professionals in your building who work with that student. The case study contains very specific weekly goals in each of the language arts, as well as targeted objectives for thinking development. Case studies are analyzed by professionals alone and then in consultation with the student.

Single or Multiple Outside Evaluators.   Your language arts program and students will benefit from outside evaluations of their work. Such evaluations can be over single samples, or of works in progress as evaluators observe the class engaged in normal activities.

In summary, as you read this section of the chapter, you may have selected new assessment tools you prefer. In the next section is a basic outline of a year-long language arts assessment program in which you can insert your selections. You will find that this basic program follows the principles outlined earlier, and can be modified to meet your students' needs.

STRATEGIES THAT TEACH
TRANSFERRING PRACTICES INTO GRADING PERIODS

Your language arts assessment program can be divided into six grading periods, with one assessment tool implemented each week. Through this program, you will record one language arts' grade per week, which is required in many states.

First Grading Period (Weeks 1–6 of the school year).   The focus of the first grading period is to teach students how to use each type of evaluation tool. You will also collect benchmark data for end-of-the-year comparisons. Assessments to be obtained during the first grading period follow:

Week 1: Describe the anecdotal record-keeping system you have designed. Collect one benchmark anecdotal record for the class as a whole, and one for each individual student.

Week 2: Describe the portfolio system you created for your room or one that will be used throughout the school. Create individual student portfolios, and allow students to select their first sample from their first two weeks' work. This choice will be graded and also becomes the benchmark to which students compare end-of-year samples.

Week 3: Describe the system the class will follow to write in and evaluate their journals. A benchmark entry is made in the journal and the grading system is modeled and implemented.

Week 4: Describe retellings, debates, oral/listening assessments, performance assessments, and rating scales. You and students develop objectives for the remaining two weeks for language arts and dimensions of thinking, and select one of these forms of assessment to evaluate these objectives. In your discussion, provide evidence of students' first-week levels of performance in speaking, reading, writing, listening, thinking processes, decision making, problem solving, creativity, metacognition, group skills, and abilities to work alone that you obtained from the diagnostic activities in Chapter 2 and from the first three weeks' evaluations described above.

Week 5: The process and purposes of self-assessment are explained. The first self-assessments in communication/thinking competencies are completed. Students either decide to design their own self-assessments or to select from three types you provide.

Week 6: Portfolio entries are selected, conferences are held and the second portfolio sample is taken (and graded). The evaluation form selected during the fourth week of the period is graded.

Second Grading Period (Weeks 7–12 of the school year).   The focus of the second grading period is to document students' rates of growth in each of the language arts, and to compare students' present achievements with their own performance-based learning history, which will be evidenced in works since the first week of school, or through references to prior years' performances if portfolios from past years are available. Also, it is during this grading period that standardized tests are often administered.

Week 7: Students compare and contrast the anecdotal entry you make this week both for the class and each student to the record made five weeks ago. Students discuss their growth and set a new goal for this grading period.

Week 8: Conduct conferences for the purpose of awarding grades concerning specific competencies in language arts and thinking development.

Week 9: Grade journal entries.

Week 10: Describe the purposes of and the types of group work skill assessments you and they can use. Collect a benchmark sample, and grade it using this instrument. Students select the instrument to be used from the choices you provide.

Week 11: Begin case studies for special needs students, and collect benchmark data for these studies in collaboration with these students. Students who are not involved in creation of case studies complete a self-assessment of this grading period's work, as compared to the last grading period.

Week 12: Portfolios and journals are assessed; individual student conferences are held.

Third Grading Period (Weeks 13–18 of the school year).   The focus of this grading period is to: (1) build students' goal-setting abilities; (2) guide them to understand the trail of progress they have accomplished in one-half year; and (3) assist them to increase their learning successes in the second half of the year.

Week 13: The anecdotal records from the first 13 weeks of school are analyzed for two patterns of strength per student, and for the class as a whole. Students improve the anecdotal record-keeping system and establish a new objective for their growth during this grading period. Students also complete Critical Thinking Activity 15 and evaluate their present language arts assessment program.

Week 14: Objectives for this grading period are established by all members of the student-centered community. Students also select an appropriate assessment for these objectives, e.g., retellings, debates, oral/listening assessments, group work skill assessment, or rating scales. The selected assessment is begun.

Week 15: Journals are analyzed for breadth and depth of communication/thinking strengths.

Week 16: Integrated assessments are explained and a benchmark assessment of students' abilities to integrate the language arts into content area instruction is taken.

Week 17: An external evaluator is invited to class to assess communication and thinking competencies; videotaped analyses of the class are shared with students, as the evaluator explains the growths noted.

Week 18: Mid-year portfolio and journal conferences are held; risk-taking, to expand communication/thinking competencies during the last half of the year, is encouraged.

Fourth Grading Period (Weeks 19–24 of the school year). The focus of this grading period is to award points on the basis of students' abilities to become more responsible for their own learning. Each weekly grade is based on students' collaborative evaluation and on their ability to set, implement, and judge the merits of their learning goals.

Week 19: Anecdotal records are taken and students reflect upon all that has been collected concerning their work throughout the year. Students set a goal to reach by the end of the year; they develop a plan of action; and a system by which they want to be assessed.

Week 20: Students self-assess their journals. Points are also awarded for students' abilities to set and reach new goals in their writing abilities by the last week of this recording period.

Week 21: Parents are invited to participate in the evaluation process, using a system that you and students create.

Week 22: The purposes of paired assessment are explained. The first paired assessment is administered and graded.

Week 23: The second integrated assessment is taken.

Week 24: Portfolios and journals are graded; individual conferences are held.

Fifth Grading Period (Weeks 25–30 of the school year). The focus of this grading period is to develop students' ability to design goals, methods, and evaluations that meet specific communication and thinking needs that they identify.

Week 25: Anecdotal records are examined. Students set a six to 12 week plan of action to improve in two communication and thinking competencies. Points are awarded for the identification of individual needs, problem solving skill, and the success of the plan created.

Week 26: A second outside evaluator provides information to you concerning specific objectives students have set for themselves. You and the outside evaluator consult to determine suggestions for each student's improvement.

Week 27: Journals become learning logs to document learning styles. Students do a self-assessment on one aspect of communication/thinking competence they have learned to date.

Week 28: A retelling, debate, or another speaking/listening activity is assessed.

Week 29: The third integrated assessment is made.

Week 30: Portfolios and journals are graded and conferences are held. Portfolios are graded based on students' ability to take risks and reach goals in each of the language arts and thinking competencies.

Sixth Grading Period (Weeks 31–36 of the school year). The focus of this grading period is to celebrate accomplishments! Students engage in comparisons of first six-week benchmarks to works completed during this grading period. A second, and equally important, purpose of this recording period is for students to design their own program for continued growth throughout the summer months.

Week 31: Students record their own anecdotal records and use their analysis of their year's record to prepare their "summer's learning plan."

Week 32: Taped readings are collected which are posttests of those administered during the first six weeks (see Critical Thinking Activity 2, p. 57). Students listen to their first of the year's reading and their last six week's reading. Analyses are made. Students also plan the way their reading, listening, speaking, writing, and thinking will be assessed this week.

Week 33: Journals are analyzed and students celebrate their trail of growth in writing ability for the year. They design the last goals for their journals, and how their journals will be continued throughout the summer months.

Week 34: The last integrated assessment is made and compared to previous ones. Acclaim is given for superior performances. Each student is exalted for one area of learning.

Week 35: A group, paired, debate, dramatic performance, or discussion grade is given. Oral improvement points are awarded. Tribute is given to each student for the area of most improvement in speaking, listening, and/ or thinking ability.

Week 36: Portfolios and journals are assessed by teacher, students, and parents. Students contribute something of value to the school on an individual basis or as a class.

CRITICAL THINKING ACTIVITY 15
How To Teach Students To Use Proactive and Evaluative Communication and Thinking Skills

The purpose of this critical thinking activity is to build students' abilities to evaluate communication and thinking processes throughout their lives. The activity used to develop these abilities is for students to establish and evaluate the assessment program they created for their language arts program. This is the activity you will implement on Week 13 of their school year (see page 504). To begin Critical Thinking Activity 15, ask students to create a hypothetical class at their grade level. Write their answers to the following questions:

1. What should students read, write, say, hear, and think in the course of the year to demonstrate their competence?
2. What should those students learn that they will use for the rest of their lives?
3. What attitudes about language arts and each other should they exhibit and value?
4. After you have explained and shown samples of the tools introduced in this chapter, ask "what should be used to document their progress and development?"
5. How could students demonstrate that they are self-directed learners and thinkers?
6. How should they be graded?
7. Do you want their parents involved in the planning and evaluation of their work? Why or why not?

Once these answers are obtained, students reflect upon how to improve their own evaluations that have been taken during their language arts classes. They can also make a chart with the following headings:

Outcomes Desired
Preparing for These Outcomes
Evaluations of the Outcomes

Once the class has selected the best types of evaluations for each outcome these are placed at points in the last half of the year when they will be implemented (see pages 503–506).

PROFESSIONAL DEVELOPMENT OPPORTUNITY
Mid-Year and End-of-Year Evaluation of Your Language Arts Program

At mid-year and at the end of the year assess your language arts program. Also, before you do so on the last day before winter vacation and on the last day of school, ask students to submit written suggestions for classroom improvement. Students cite the rationale and suggest methods of making the changes they suggest. Also ask what they would have liked to have learned that they have not yet learned, and how they would like to learn it. Read these suggestions and then complete the following evaluation before you leave for winter vacation and the summer. Commit to yourself that you will not turn off your classroom lights, or leave for your vacations each year until the following assessment of your language arts program has been completed. If your answer to any of the following questions is yes, you can spend the vacation period devising a plan to improve your student communications center.

Mid-Year and End-of-Year Program Evaluation

1. Have you unintentionally implemented a practice or schedule that doesn't create language learning (e.g., you have trouble disciplining students so you play records they bring to school and allow them to sing if they "behave" all week)? While reading lyrics can build reading vocabularies, singing random songs, unrelated to language and thinking developmental goals, is not within your master language arts plan. You would profit by improving your time and classroom management skills and eliminate this "Friday Reward" that does not help your students grow.

2. Are any of the students in your room not yet taking risks? Looking at each desk in the room, picture an incident where that child initiated a challenging language and thinking task for himself/herself. If you can't picture one, write that child's name on a piece of paper. Think about activities and grouping systems you can implement in January (or next year) to assist that child (or children similar to him/her) to become a more active, self-directed learner.

3. Recount the last week of instruction. As you recall each day's activities, were there any assignments where students spoke, read, wrote, listened, created, or thought in ways they will not do in the real world? What will you do to change these activities?

4. Look around the room to see if your instruction is student-centered. Count the number of items you asked students to perform, and the number of times students asked you to do a special project they wanted. How can you improve the ratio between these two numbers?

5. Have you avoided teaching a difficult concept? Do you have a student, colleague, or a parent-aide who could assist in making that instruction possible? How can you plan for it over the winter vacation/summer vacation?

6. Subconsciously, have you negotiated something with your students that doesn't build their language and thinking? For example, do they know that you really don't like for them to ask questions? Do they know they should agree with your points rather than disagreeing; do they know that if they are quiet and "just write the full period" that you will praise their writings even if their compositions aren't of quality?

7. Have you done a better job teaching thus far this year than ever before? If so, why and how do you plan to further improve? If not, what can you change to improve your teaching repertoire?

8. What have your students done better than any other group has ever done before?

9. Is something difficult or uncomfortable for you in the way you relate to a student? Will finding something that student does well or finding something that student can do to help you and the class strengthen the bond between you and this student? What is your first idea to change this difficult relationship? What can you do to accomplish it over the winter or summer vacation?

10. Are you taking more papers home to grade than you'd like? How can you alter this practice?

11. Have your students become lax in using effective classroom rules and procedures? Do they need to practice such things as moving from section to section in the room, working in centers, throwing trash away, sharpening pencils or leaving the room without disturbing others? Do you need to ask them questions about disruptive scenarios for them to answer, such as "What if I'm conferencing with a student and you need something, what do you do?"

12. Have you found yourself beginning class discussions without spending time preparing a variety of respondent-centered questions in advance of these discussions? (See Chapter 4 if you need to improve your questioning skills.)

13. Would you like more of your discussion periods to begin with questions students ask?

14. Would you like to make the following statements more frequently in your class: "Tell me another interpretation," "What do you think another reason might be," "I'd like to hear two viewpoints," and "I prefer that you think a moment before you respond to the next issue"?

15. Is the teacher-student-teacher turn-taking cycle evident in your room? Are you restating student responses, answering students' questions without using deliberate silence, or answering with another question? Do you want to increase the times you model how to ask questions for clarification?

16. Do you want to increase the number of times students make connections between concepts under discussion and information from their lives and previous discussions?

17. Do you want to increase the number of strategies you use to respond to students' incorrect answers, e.g., think again, give a relevant prompt, paraphrase, give an example, "Tell us your thinking," "Remember that . . ." "I'm going to return to you again today for that information," "That would have been correct if . . ."

18. Do you want to hold more exploratory, fishbowl, integrative, and paired discussions in your class?

19. Do you want to improve the *Individual Students' Oral Language Needs Monitor*, other diagnostic instruments in Chapter 2, or any evaluation or instructional tools used this year?

20. Your own question for this year is: _____ .

STRATEGIES THAT TEACH

TRY IT

1. Dr. Arthur Applebee (1991) made the following statement at the Annual Meeting of the National Reading Conference: In his opinion, future language arts teachers should not allow "eclecticism to run wild." What will you do to prevent this from occurring in your room?

2. Elizabeth Parillo (1991) stated: "I like questions now even better than answers." John Wooden stated: "It's what you learn after you know it all that counts." What is your response to these statements?

3. Ms. Sara Day, an elementary teacher, implemented an idea to advance language arts instruction in her school: "If I have an idea to work well, I write it up in a little note and post it in the lounge. That way, I'm not pushy or 'braggy' but I can help my other language arts teachers." What can you do to help your colleagues?

4. As we stated in Chapter 1, you must begin with an ideal and end with an ideal. Reflect upon how your philosophy of instruction and evaluation has changed in the course of reading this book. Note five changes in the ideal language arts program you now wish to implement.

FOR YOUR JOURNAL

Review your journal entries. Grade your journal. What did this experience do to improve your ability to grade your students' journals?

BUILDING YOUR PROFESSIONAL PORTFOLIO
Continuous Professional Development

This professional portfolio can be used to store many different tools you will use to assist your continuous growth as an educator. The following is a form you can use to assess the first videotape you make of yourself teaching your students. You can improve as a teacher if you videotape yourself for 15 minutes each year. If you store these segments on the same tape, you can see how you improve from year to year.

VIDEOTAPE ANALYSIS

Date _____ Grade Level _____ Subject _____
Goals (Improvements I Want to View):

What was one of the greatest instructional strengths I have gained since my last videotaping?

What were the most distracting elements in my teaching style, delivery, or lesson format/content that I want to eliminate before my next videotaping? How will I eliminate them?

What could I improve in my presentation style and my interactions with students?
   a. voice, tone, pitch, melody, speed, eliminate crutch words
   b. body movements, mannerisms, gestering, posture
   c. eye contact
   d. other:

CHAPTER 3

1. Answer to TRY IT, p. 103: **Verbs and phrases that refine thinking are:** *name, cite an example, explain, recall, cause-effect, compare and contrast, summarize, more specific, give us an illustration,* and *give us a non-example.*

Verbs and phrases that build elaborative thinking are: *predict, create, imagine, pretend, elaborate, justify, wonder, apply to your life,* and *infer.*

Verbs and phrases that both refine and build elaborative thinking, dependent upon the situation in which they are used are: *resolve,* and *analyze differences (strengths, weaknesses) between two kinds.*

CHAPTER 4

1. The answer to Figure 4-4 is "puppy."

CHAPTER 5

1. The answers to Figure 5-3 are:
   1. short
   2. long
   3. long, silent
   4. short, long, r-controlled vowel.
   5. i, e
   6. g, c; /j/ and /s/; /g/ and /k/
   7. k, p, silent
   8. w, silent
   9. ght, silent
   10. /f/
   11. schwa
   12. one sound
   13. vcv, vcve, cv
   14. vcv, vcv, -y, cv.

CHAPTER 9

1. The answer to the question of what to teach Susie about spelling (p. 289) follows. You should teach her that vce spells many words that have a medial long vowel sound. Once this rule is introduced, you might point to her two different spellings of the word "my" and ask her if she can create her own rule to remember the correct spelling.

ALPHABETICAL INDEX OF CHILDREN'S LITERATURE CITED IN TEXT: PAGE REFERENCES FOR SUGGESTED USES IN THE CLASSROOM

REFERENCES

Abartis, C. & Stallard, C. (1977). The Effects of instruction of writing and reading methodology upon college students' reading skills. *Journal of Reading, 23* (5), 408–415.

Adams, J. (1986). *Conceptual blockbusting: A guide to better ideas, 3rd Ed.* Reading, MA: Addison-Wesley.

Adams, M. J. (1990). *Beginning to read: Thinking and learning about print.* Cambridge, MA: MIT Press.

Adams, M. J. (1991). Beginning to read: A critique by literacy professionals and a response by Marilyn Jager Adams. *The Reading Teacher, 44* (6) 370–396.

Allen, J., Michalove, B., Shockley, B. & West, M. (1991). "I'm really worried about Joseph": Reducing the risks of literacy learning. *The Reading Teacher, 44* (7), 458–472.

Allen, D. (1991, November). Vermont's portfolio assessment goals statewide. *The Council Chronicle,* p. 6.

Anderson, J. R. (1985). *Cognitive psychology and its implications, Second edition.* New York: W. H. Freeman and Company.

Anderson, R. C. & Pearson, P. D. (1984). A schema-theoretic view of basis process in reading comprehension. In P. D. Pearson (Ed.), *Handbook of reading research* (pp. 255–292). New York: Longmans.

Anderson, R. C., Hiebert, E. H., Scott, J. A. & Wilkerson, I. A. G. (1985). *Becoming a nation of readers: The report of the Commission on Reading.* Washington, DC: National Institute of Education.

Applebee, A. M. (1991, December). *The future of literature instruction: Survey of effective teachers.* Paper presented at the Annual Meeting of the National Reading Conference, Austin, Texas.

Applebee, A., Langer, J. & Mullis, A. (1988). *Report on the national assessment of educational progress.* Princeton, NJ: Educational Testing Service.

Armitage, D. & Ratzlaff, H. (1985). The non-correlation of printing and writing skills. *Journal of educational research, 78,* 174–177.

Askov, E. N. & Peck, M. (1982). Handwriting. In *Encyclopedia of Educational Research,* (5th Edition), edited by Mitzel, H. E., Hardin, B., and Rabinowitz, W. New York: The Free Press.

Aulls, M. F. (1978). *Developmental and remedial reading in the middle grades.* Boston, MA: Allyn and Bacon.

Avery, J. (1989). Demonstration of internal monologues. In Newman, J. (1987) *Stories about language.* Portsmouth, NH: Heinemann, 283–289.

Balmuth, M. (1982). *The roots of phonics: A historical perspective.* New York, NY: Teachers College Press.

Baker, L. & Brown, A. L. (1984). Metacognitive skills and reading. In P. D. Pearson (Ed.), *Handbook of reading research* New York, NY: Longman, 491–572.

Bandura, A. & Schunk, D. H. (1981). Cultivating competence, self-efficacy, and intrinsic interest through proximal self-motivation. *Journal of Personality and Social Psychology, 41,* 586–598.

Barclay, K. (1992). Six ways lyrics assist students to improve their literacy. Unpublished manuscript. Macomb, IL: Western Illinois University.

Baron, J. & Sternberg, R. (1987). *Teaching thinking skills: Theory and practice.* New York: Freeman.

Barone, J. (1989). Young children's written response to literature: The relationship between written response and ortgographic knowledge. In McCormick, S. and Zutell, J. (Eds). *Thirty-Eight Yearbook of the National Reading Conference.* Chicago, IL: National Reading Conference, 371–379.

Barrell, J. (1991). *Teaching for thoughtfulness.* New York: Longman.

Bartelo, D. M. (1992). Oral language development. Unpublished Manuscript. Plymouth, New Hampshire. Plymouth State College.

Beach, R. & Marshall, J. (1991). *Teaching literature in the secondary school.* San Diego, CA: Harcourt, Brace Jovanovich.

Beary, M., Salvner, G. and Wesolowski, B. (1977). *Newscast: A simulation of a TV news team's coverage of present or historic events.* Lakeside, CA: Interact Company.

Beck, I., Perfetti, C. & McKeown, M. (1982). Effects of Long-term vocabulary instruction on lexical access and reading comprehension. *Journal of Educational Psychology, 74* (3), 506–521.

Beck, I. (1980). Topic Integration to improve comprehension. Paper presented at the Annual Meeting of the National Reading Conference, December, St. Petersburg, Fl.

Beck, I. (1989). Reading and reasoning. *The Reading Teacher, 42* (9), 676–684.

Beck, I. & Dole, J. (1992). Reading and thinking with history and science text. In C. Collins & J. Mangieri. (Eds), *Thinking development: An agenda for the Twenty-first century.* Hillsdale, NJ: Lawrence Ehrlbaum.

Bercik, J. (1992). Semantic Mapping. Unpublished manuscript. Chicago, IL: Northeastern Illinois University.

Berghoff, B. & Egawa, K. (1991). No more "rocks": Grouping to give students control of their learning. *The Reading Teacher, 44* (8), 536–542.

Berliner, D. C. & Tikunoff, W. J. (1976). The California beginning teacher evaluation study: Overview of the ethnographic study. *Journal of Teacher Education, 27,* 24–30.

Beyer, B. (1987). *Practical strategies for the teaching of thinking.* Boston, MA: Allyn & Bacon.

Bishop, D. (1992). Thinking through writing-focus journals and rhetorical stance exploration. Unpublished Manuscript. Highland Heights, Kentucky: Northern Kentucky University.

Bird, L. (1987). "What is whole language?" Paper presented at Whole Language Conference II. Lethbridge, Alberta, Canada, 1987.

Blachowicz, C. & Lee, J. (1991). Vocabulary development in the whole literacy classroom. *The Reading Teacher, 45* (3), 178–188.

Blatner, A. & Blatner, A. (1988). *The art of play.* New York, NY: Human Sciences Press.

Bloom, B. (1956). *Taxonomy of cognitive abilities.* New York, NY: Harper and Row.

Bloomfield, L. (1933). *Language.* New York: Holt, Rinehart and Winston.

Blout, N. (1973). Research on teaching literature, language and composition. In *Second Handbook of Research on Teaching,* R. Travers (Ed.), Chicago: Rand McNally, 692–744.

Bonds, C. W. & Bonds, L. T. (1984). Reading and the gifted student. *Roper Review, 5,* 4–6.

Boomer, G. (October, 1984). Literacy power, and the community. *Language Arts, 61,* 575–584.

Borick, G. (1979). Implications for developing teacher competencies from processes and procedure research. *Journal of Teacher Education, 30,* 77–86.

Brophy, J. & Evertson, C. (1974). *Process-product correlations in the Texas teacher effectiveness study.* Final Report No. 74-4. Austin: Research and Development. Center for Teacher Education, University of Texas.

Boyd, J. (1992). Reading wheels: Sustained silent reading records. Unpublished Manuscript. Jenkintown, PA: Manor Junior College.

Brackett, M. (1989). "The Super Storytree" Computer program, Pleasantville, NY: Sunburst Publishers.

Bridwell, L. S. (1980). Revising strategies in twelfth grade students' transactional writing. *Research in the teaching of English, 14,* 197–222.

Bromley, K. (1991). *Webbing with Literature.* Boston, MA: Allyn & Bacon.

Brophy, J. (1986). Classroom management techniques. *Education and Urban Society, 18* (2), 195–210.

Brown, J. (1992). Picture This! Unpublished Manuscript. Springfield, MO: South Western Missouri State University.

Brown, R. (1989). Testing and thoughtfulness. *Educational Leadership, 46,* 31–33.

Brown, A. L. & Palincsar, A. S. (1990). Reciprocal teaching of comprehension strategies. A natural history of one program for enhancing learning. In J. G. Borkowski & J. D. Day (Eds.), *Intelligence and cognition in special children: Comparative studies of giftedness, mental retardation, and learning disabilities.* NY: Ablex.

Brown, D. M. (1992). Integration through thematic units. Unpublished Manuscript. Tuscaloosa, AL: University of Alabama.

Brozo, W. G. (1990). Hiding out in secondary classrooms: Coping strategies of unsuccessful readers. *Journal of Reading, 33* (5), 324–328.

Bruner, J. (1986). *Actual minds, possible worlds.* Cambridge, MA: Harvard University Press.

Burke, J. (1992). What is a Thematic Unit? Unpublished Manuscript. Stephenville, TX: Tarleton State University.

Burley-Allen, M. (1982). *Listening: The forgotten skills*. New York: Wiley.

Busboom, J. (1992). Pairing special needs students with college students. Unpublished Manuscript. Mercer College.

Calkins, L. & Harwayne, S. (1987). *The writing workshop: A world of difference*. Portsmouth, NH: Heinemann Educational Books, Inc.

Calkins, L. M. (1986). *The art of teaching writing*. Portsmouth, NH: Heinemann.

Calkins, L. (1991). *Living between the lines*. Portsmouth, NH: Heinemann.

Campione, J. and Brown, A. (in press). Instant feedback in learning communities. *Educational researcher*.

Canady, R. J. (1977). Consistency of teachers' methods of teaching reading to specific learning theories. Unpublished Doctoral Dissertation, University of Arizona, Tucson.

Carnegie Council on Adolescent Development (1989). *Turning points: Preparing American youth for the twenty-first century*. New York: Carnegie Foundation.

Cassidy, J. & Vukelich. C. (1980). Do the gifted read early? *The Reading Teacher, 33*, 578–582.

Cassidy, J. (1979). What about the talented reader? *Teacher*, 76–80.

Castello, R. (1976). Listening guide—a first step toward notetaking and listening skills. *Journal of Reading, 19* (4), 289–90.

Cazden, C. B. (1988). *Classroom discourse: The language of teaching and learning*. Portsmouth, NH: Heinemann.

Cecil, N. L. (1989). *Freedom fighters: Affective teaching of the language arts*. Salem, WI: Sheffield Publishing Co.

Chall, J. S., Jacobs, V. A., & Baldwin, L. E. (1990). *The reading crisis: Why poor children fall behind*. Cambridge, MA: Harvard University Press.

Charters, J. & Gately, A. (1986). *Drama Any Time*. Australia: Primary English Association.

Chavalier, S. M. (1992). Learning Center/Cooperative Group Rules. Unpublished manuscript. Warrensburg, MO: Central Missouri State University.

Chomsky, C. (1969). *The acquisition of syntax in children 5–10*. Cambridge.

Chomsky, N. (1975). *Reflections on language*. New York: Random House.

Clark (1987). The writing process in my class. In Newman, J. (Ed). *Stories about language*. Portsmouth, NH: Heinemann.

Clay, M. (1975). *What did I write?: Beginning writing behavior*. Aukland, New Zealand: Heinemann.

Clay, M. (1979). *Observing young readers*. Portsmouth, NH: Heinemann Educational Books.

Clay, M. (1985). *The early detection of reading difficulties*. Portsmouth, NH: Heinemann.

Clemens, J. (1991). Mentoring. *Teacher*, 24–25.

Close, E. E. (1990). Seventh graders sharing literature: How did we get here? *Language Arts, 67* (8), 817–23.

Cohen, S. (1992). Teachers for the 21st Century: Project pen pal. Unpublished manuscript. Cortland, New York: State University College at Cortland.

Cohen, S. & Riel, B. (1989). The effect of Distant Audiences on Students' Writing. *American Educational Research Journal, 26* (2), 143–159.

Coleman, S. (1992). Bibliotherapic section in the library. Unpublished manuscript. Fort Worth, TX: Texas Christian University.

Colangelo, N. & Davis, G. A. *Handbook of Gifted Education*. Boston: Allyn and Bacon.

Cole, M. & Griffin, P. (1987). *Contextual factors in education*. Madison, WI: Wisconsin Center for Educational Research.

Coles, R. (1989). Grade eight students cope with today and get ready for tomorrow. In K. S. Goodman, Y. M., Goodman, K. & Hood, W. J. (Eds). *The whole language evaluation book*. Portsmouth, NH: Heinemann.

Collins, C. (1988). Principals: Taking the lead in Thinking Skills Development. *Reach: Volume III*. Austin, TX: Texas Education Agency.

Collins, C. (1992c). Thinking development through intervention. Middle school students come of age. In C. Collins & J. Mangieri (Eds.), *Thinking development: an agenda for the twenty-first century*. Hillsdale, NJ: Erlbaum.

Collins, C. (1987). *Time management for teachers*. Englewood Cliffs, NJ: Prentice Hall.

Collins, C. (1989b). *Bring out the talents & oral expression skills of shy students*. Fort Worth, TX: Educational Research Dissertation (P.O. Box 161354, zip code 76161).

Collins, C. (1991a). Diary of daily events in a non-segregated African-American school. Unpublished manuscript. Fort Worth, TX: Texas Christian University.

Collins, C. (1992a). *126 Strategies That Build the Language Arts*. Boston, MA: Allyn & Bacon.

Collins, C. (1990). Strategies for active engagement in reasoning: Vignettes that build a questioning mind. Paper presented at the annual meeting of the International Reading Association, Atlanta, Ga.

Collins, C. (1989a). Increasing thinking ability through middle school reading instruction. Paper presented at the Annual Meeting of the National Reading Conference.

Collins Block, C. (1993). History of reading instruction. In C. Collins Block. *Teaching the Language Arts: Annotated Instructors Edition*. Boston, MA: Allyn & Bacon.

Collins, C. (1992b). Improving reading and thinking: From teaching or not teaching skills to interactive interventions. In Pressley, M., Harris, K. & Guthrie, I. (Ed). *Promoting Academic Competence and Literacy In Schools*. San Diego, CA: Academic Press, 149–167.

Collins, C. & Mangieri, J. (Eds). *Thinking development: An agenda for the twenty-first century*. Hillsdale, NJ: Erlbaum.

Collins, C. (1991b). Audiotaped transcript of Tracy Boyd's Tutoring Session. Fort Worth, TX: Texas Christian University.

Collins Block, C. & Zinke, J. N. (in press). *Thoughts to begin students' day, k-2 and thoughts to begin students' day, 3–8*. Boston, MA: Allyn & Bacon.

Collins Block, C. (in press). A new lesson plan that builds reading and thinking ability. *Elementary School Journal*.

Collins Block, C. (in press b). Developing problem solving abilities. In Mangieri, J. & Collins Block, C. (Eds). *Advanced Educational Psychology: Creating Effective Schools & Powerful Thinkers*. Fort Worth, TX: Harcourt Brace Jovanovich.

Combs, W. E. (1975). Some further effects and implications of sentence-combining exercises for the secondary language arts curriculum. Unpublished doctoral dissertation, University of Minnesota.

Costa, A. L. & Lowery, L. F. (1989). *Techniques for teaching thinking*. Pacific Grove, CA: Midwest Publications.

Costa, A. (1990). When human beings behave intelligently. Presentation to the School of Education Faculty, Texas Christian University, Forth Worth, TX.

Craig, K. (1992). Using props to ignite creative thinking. Unpublished manuscript. Renesselaer, IN: St. Joseph College.

Courtney, R. (1982). *Re-Play*. Toronto: Ontario Institute for Studies in Education.

Cramer, E. (personal communication). Introducing mental imagery in your reading lessons.

Crosbey, M. & Hurely, B. (1960). *Adventuring with books*. Champaign, IL: National Council of Teachers of English.

Csikszentmihalji, M. & Larson, R. (1984). *Being adolescent: Conflict and growth in the teenage years*. New York: Basic Books.

Cullinan, B. (Ed.) (1987). *Children's literature in the reading program*. Newark, Delaware: International Reading Association.

Culyer, R. (1982). Practicing comprehension: A collaborative strategy. Unpublished Manuscript. Hartsville, South Carolina: Coker College.

Culyer, R. (1992). Word wizard. Unpublished Manuscript. Hartsville, SC: Coker College.

Cunningham, P. H. & Cunningham, J. W. (1987). Content area reading-writing. *The Reading Teacher*, 40 (6), 506–512.

Cunningham, P. H. (1980). Teaching "were," "with," "what," and other four letter words. *The Reading Teacher*, 34, 160–163.

Danielson, K. (1992). *Listening awareness activities*. Unpublished Manuscript. Omaha, Nebraska: University of Nebraska.

DeBono, E. (1970). *Lateral thinking*. New York: Harper & Row.

De Santi, R. (1992). *The Content Wedge*. Unpublished Manuscript. New Orleans, Louisiana: University of New Orleans.

Decker, B. C. (1985, November). Alteracy: What teachers can do to keep Johnny reading. Paper presented at the Annual Meeting of the Southwestern Regional Conference of the International Reading Association, Nashville, TN.

DeFord, D. E. (1981). Literacy: Reading, writing and other essentials. *Language Arts, 58* (6), 652–658.

DeHaven, E. (1988). *Teaching the language arts*. Glenview, IL: Scott Foresman.

De Mille, R. (1981). *Put your mother on the ceiling: children's imagination games*, Santa Barbara: Ross-Erickson.

Diederich, P. (1991). *Writing inservice guide for English language arts and TAAS.* Austin, TX: Texas Education Agency.

Donogue, P. (1990). Method to teach rationale behind silent consonants. Paper presented at the Annual Meeting of the International Reading Association. Atlanta, Georgia.

Dreyer, S. (1985). *The bookfinder.* Circle Pines, MN: American Guidance Service.

Drash, A. (1980). Variations in puberty development and the school system: A problem and a challenge. In D. Ster (Ed). *The emerging adolescent characteristics and educational implications.* Columbus, OH: National Middle School Association.

Duckworth, E. (1987). *The having of wonderful ideas and other essays on teaching and learning.* New York, NY: Teachers College Press.

Duffy, J. (1991). Business Partnerships For A Thinking Populist. In C. Collins and J. Mangieri (Eds.), *Teaching Thinking: An Agenda for The Twenty-first Century*, Hillsdale, NJ: Erlbaum.

Duffy, G. G. & Rohler, L. R. (1989). *Improving classroom reading instruction: A decision-making approach.* New York, NY: Random House.

Duling, M. (1987). *The magic of your mind.* Buffalo, NY: Bearly Limited.

Dunn, R. (1990). Rita Dunn answers questions on learning styles. *Educational Leadership, 48* (2), 15–21.

Durkin, D. (1978–79). What classroom observations reveal about reading comprehension. *Reading Research Quarterly, 14,* 481–533.

Durkin, M. J. & Biddle, B. J. (1974). *The study of teaching.* New York: Holt, Rinehart and Winston.

Duvall, B. (1986). Kindergarten performance for reading and matching four styles of handwriting. Government Document Number. CS 209 466.

Edelsky, C. (1989). Putting language variation to work for you. In P. Rigg and V. Allen (Eds.) *When they don't all speak English: Integrating the ESL student into the regular classroom* (pp. 96–107). Urbana, IL: National Council of Teachers of English.

Ehri, L. C. & Wilce, L. S. (1987). Does learning to spell help beginners learn to read words? *Reading Research Quarterly, 22* (1), 47–65.

Englert, C. S., Raphael, T. E., Anderson, L. M., Anthony, H. M. & Stevens, D. D. (1991). Making strategies and self-talk visible: Writing instruction in regular and special education classrooms. *American Educational Research Journal, 28* (2), 337–372.

Elbow, P. (1981). Unfocused & focused freewriting. Speech delivered at the Annual Meeting of the National Council of Teachers of English. Philadelphia, PA, November.

Fair, J., Melvin, M., Bantz, C. & Vause, K. (1988). *Kids Are Consumers, Too!: Real-world reading and language arts.* Menlo Park, CA: Addison-Wesley Publishing Co.

Fehring, H. & Thomas, V. (1985). *The teaching of spelling.* Victoria, Canada: Ministry of Education.

Ferreiro, E. & Teberosky, A. (1982). *Literacy before schooling.* Portsmouth, NH: Heinemann Educational Books.

Fitzgerald, J., Spiegel, D. L. & Cunningham, J. W. (1991). The relationship between parental literacy level and perceptions of emergent literacy. *Journal of Reading Behavior, XXIII* (2), 191–213.

Fitzgerald, J. & Markham, L. (1987). Teaching children about revision in writing. *Cognition and Instruction, 4,* 3–24.

Fitzsimmons, R. & Loomer, B. (1978). *Spelling: Learning and instruction.* Des Moines, Iowa: Iowa State Department of Public Instruction.

Fletcher, J. D., Havley, D. E., & Piele, P. K. (1990). Costs, effects, and utility of microcomputer assisted instruction in the classroom. *American Educational Research Journal, 27* (4), 783–806.

Flood, J. & Lapp, D. (1991). Using children's literature in content areas improves reading comprehension. Paper presented at the Annual Meeting of the International Reading Association, April, Las Vegas, NV.

Fowler, E. D. (1992). Charted response to articles as one method of integrating the language arts. Unpublished Manuscript. Austin, TX: University of Texas.

Fox, M. (1988). Speech. Teachers College Writing Project. Summer Institute. New York: July.

Fredericks, A. D. & Rasinski, T. V. (1990). Involving parents in the assessment process. *The Reading Teacher, 44* (4), 346–348.

Freeman, K. S. & Freeman, D. E. (1989). Evaluation of second language junior and senior high school students. In Goodman, K. S., Goodman, Y. M., Hood, W. J. (Eds). *The Whole Language Evaluation Book.* Portsmouth, NH, p. 149.

French, P. (1990). Computer assist in higher level thinking. *Chronicle of higher education.* 101, 5, 7–8, 11.

Freppon, P. S. & Dahl, K. L. (1991). Learning about phonics in a whole language classroom. *Language Arts, 68* (3), 190–198.

Fuhler, C. J. (1990). Let's move toward literature-based reading instruction. *The Reading Teacher, 43* (5), 312.

Gage, N. L. "The Yield of Research on Teaching." *Phi Delta Kappan, 60* (November 1978), 229–235.

Gambrell, L. B. & Bales, R. J. (1986). Mental imagery and the comprehension monitoring performance of fourth and fifth grade poor readers. *Reading Research Quarterly, XXI* (1), 460–462.

Gauthier, L. (1992). 1. Creating a Language Sandwich. 2. Developing Language: A Two Paragraph Strategy. Unpublished Manuscripts. Houston, Texas: University of Houston.

Gore, D. (1992). *Basic Word Approach and Spelling.* Unpublished Manuscript. Clarksville, Tennessee: Austin Peay State University.

Gardner, H. & Hatch, T. (1989). Multiple intelligences go to school: Educational implications of the theory of multiple intelligences. *Educational Researcher, 18* (8), 4–10.

Garner, R. (1987). *Metacognition and reading comprehension.* Norwood, NJ: Ablex.

Gaskins, R. W., Gaskins, J. C. & Gaskins, I. W. (1991). A decoding program for poor readers—and the rest of the class too! *Language Arts, 68* (3), 213–225.

Gaskins, I. W. (1992). Special Populations. In Feeley, D. S., Strickland, S. B., & Wepner, C. (Eds). *Reading and writing process: A literature based approach.* Portsmouth, NH: Heinemann.

Gauthier, L. R. (1992). Creating A Language Sandwich. Unpublished Manuscript. Houston, TX: University of Houston.

Gentry, J. R. (1982). An analysis of developmental spelling in GNYS AT WRK. *The Reading Teacher, 36* (November 1982), 192–200.

Gentry, J. R. (1992). A new look at grammar. Unpublished manuscript. Cullowhee, NC: Western Carolina University.

Ginott, Haim. (1972). *Teacher and Child.* New York: Macmillan.

Goa, J. P. (1973). Effects of individual goal-setting conferences on achievement, attitudes, and goal-setting behavior. *Journal of Experimental Education, 42,* 22–28.

Gordon, A. (196?). *Applied Imaginings.* NY: Wiley.

Good, T. & Grouws, D. (1975). *Process-product Relationships in 4th Grade Mathematics Classes.* Colombia: University of Missouri College Education, Doctoral dissertation.

Goodman, K. (1970). "Behind the eye: What happens in reading." In K. Goodman & O. Niles (Eds.). *Reading: Process and program.* National Council of Teacher of English. Urbana, IL: 3–38.

Goodman, Y. (1983). "Language, cognitive development and reading behavior." *Claremont Reading Conference Yearbook.* Claremont, CA: Claremont Graduate School, 10–16.

Goodman, K. S. (1987). Acquiring literacy is natural: Who killed Cock Robin? *Theory into Practice, 26,* 368–373.

Gore, D. A. (1992). Image Modeling. Unpublished manuscript. Clarksville, TN: Austin Peay State University.

Gough, P. (1988). Good versus poorer comprehension. Paper presented at the Annual Meeting of the International Reading Association, Toronto, Canada.

Gough, P. (1987). An Interview with William Glasser. *Phi Delta Kappan, 69* (7), 593–607.

Graham, S. & Stoddard, B. (1987). Teaching spelling to the learning disabled: Implications from research. *Illinois Schools Journal, 66,* 3–15.

Graves, D. H. (1975). "An Examination of the writing processes of seven year old children." *Research in the Teaching of English, 9,* 227–241.

Graves, D. H. (1977). Research update: Spelling texts and structural analysis methods. *Language Arts, 45,* 86–90.

Gregory, J. (1990). *Oral Discourse.* Cambridge, MA: Harvard University Press.

Greenlaw, J. M. (1987). Books in the classroom. *Horn Book, 63* (1), 108–110.

Gunkel, J. (1991). Please teach America: Keisuke's journey into a language community. *Language Arts, 68* (4), 303–310.

Hadaway, N. (1992). Integrating the language arts by "adopting countries." Unpublished manuscript. Arlington, TX: University of Texas: Arlington.

Hagerty, P. & Hiebert, E. (1989). A comparison of student outcomes in literature-based and conventional classrooms. Paper presented at the annual meeting of the American Educational Research Assoc., San Francisco, CA: March 1989.

Hall, D. P. & Cunningham, P. M. (1988). Context as a polysyllabic decoding strategy. *Reading Improvement, 25, 4,* 261–4.

Halliday, D. (1982). Children's oral language development. Paper presented at the Annual meeting of the National Council of Teachers of English, Nashville, TN.

Halliday, M. A. K. (1982). Relevant models of language. In Wade, B. (Ed). *Language perspectives.* Portsmouth, NH: Heinemann. Educational Books.

Hanna, P. R., Hanna, J. S., Hodges, R. E. & Rudorf, E. H. (1966). *Phoneme-grapheme correspondences as cues to spelling improvement.* Washington, D.C.: U.S. Department of Health, Education, and Welfare.

Hansen, J. (1989). *When writers read.* Portsmouth, NH: Heinemann.

Harste, J., Woodward, V. & Burke, C. (1984). *Language stories and literacy lessons.* Portsmouth, NH: Heinemann Books.

Harste, J. (1989). *New policy guidelines for reading.* Urbana, IL: National Council of Teachers of English.

Hartley, R. E. & Goldenson, R. M. (1975). *The complete book of children's play.* New York, NY: Cromwell.

Hawes, K. (1990). Understanding Critical Thinking. In Howard, V. A. (Ed). *Varieties of Thinking.* NY: Routledge, 32–61.

Hawisher, G. E. (1987). The effects of word processing on the revision strategies. *Research in the teaching of English, 21,* 145.

Heath, S. (1983). *Ways With Words.* London: Cambridge University Press.

Heimlich, J. E. & Pittleman, S. D. (1986). *Semantic mapping: Classroom applications.* Newark, DE: International Reading Association.

Hillerich, R. L. (1985). *Teaching children to write, K–8: A complete guide to developing writing skills.* Englewood Cliffs, NJ: Prentice Hall, Inc.

Hilliker, J. (1986). Labelling to beginning narrative. In N. Thomas and N. Atwell, *Understanding writing.* Portsmouth, NH: Heinemann.

Hodges, R. (1991). *Learning to spell.* Urbana, IL: National Council of Teachers of English.

Holdaway, D. (1990). *Independence in reading.* Portsmouth, NH: Heinemann.

Horn, T. D. (1947). The effect of the corrected test on learning to spell. *Elementary School Journal, 57,* 233–235, 246.

Horowitz, R. (1985). Text patterns: Part I. *Journal of Reading,* February, 448–454.

Howie, S. M. (1979). *A study of the effects of sentence combining and writing ability and reading level of ninth grade students.* Boulder, CO: Unpublished doctoral dissertation, University of Colorado.

Huizenga, J. (1955). *Homo Ludens: A Study of the Play Element in Culture.* Boston, MA: Beacon Press.

Irwin, J. W. (1991). *Teaching Reading Comprehension Processes, Second Edition.* Englewood Cliffs, NJ: Prentice Hall.

Jacobs, L. (1990). Listening to literature. *Teaching K–8, 20* (4), 34–38.

Jacobs, H. H. (1989). Interdisciplinary Curriculum Design & Implementation. Alexandria, VA: Association for Supervision and Curriculum Development.

Jacobson, J. M. (1989). Laptop flannel boards. *The Reading Teacher, 43* (2), 189.

James, W. (1915). *Talks to teachers.* New York: World Book.

Johnson, T. D. & Louis, D. R. (1990). *Bringing it all together: A program for literacy.* Portsmouth, NH: Heinemann.

Johnson, T. D., Langford, K. G. & Quorn, K. C. (1981). Characteristics of an effective spelling program. *Language Arts, 58,* 581–588.

Johnston, J. H. & Markle, G. C. (1986). *What research says to the middle level practitioner.* Columbus, OH: National Middle School Association.

Johnston, P. (1992). *Constructive evaluation in literacy.* White Plains, NY: Longman.

Jongsma, K. S. (1989). Reading recovery. *The Reading Teacher, 43,* 2, 184–185.

Judd, R. (1989). Students Self Assessment. In Cecil, N. L. (Ed.) *Freedom fights: Affective teaching of the language arts.* Salem, WI: Sheffield Publishing Co.

Keegan, S. & Shake, K. (1991). Literature study groups: An alternative to ability grouping. *The Reading Teacher, 44* (8), 542.

Keller, H. (1954). *The story of my life.* New York: Doubleday.

King, P. (1992). Reciprocal questioning. Paper presented at the annual meeting of the International Reading Association. Miami, FL: May.

Kletzien, L. (1991). Strategy use by good and poor comprehenders. *Reading Research Quarterly, XXVI* (1), 70–94.

Kohn, A. (1991). Group grade grubbing versus cooperation learning. *Educational leadership, 48* (5), 83.

Koval, C. (1992). From fact to fantasy—and back again. Saint Leo, FL: Saint Leo College.

Kozulin, A. (1990). *Vygotsky: A biological perspective.* Cambridge, MA: Harvard University Press.

Kutscher, R. E. (1989). Projections summary and emerging issues. *Monthly Labor Review, 112* (11), 66–74.

LaBuda, M. & James, H. J. (1985). Fostering creativity in children who differ. In M. LaBuda (Ed.), *Creative reading for gifted learners* (2nd ed). Newark, DE: International Reading Association.

Laib, N. K. (1989). Good writing cannot be taught effectively as an empty collection of rules. *The Chronicle of Higher Education,* July 5, 1989, 36.

Lamb, H. & Burk, J. (1992). *Pen Pal Program & Big Book Project.* Unpublished manuscript. Stephenville, Texas: Tarelton State University.

Langer, J. A. (1991). Literary understanding and literature instruction. Report Series 2.11. Albany, NY: Center for the Learning and Teaching of Literature.

Langer, J. A. & Applebee, A. N. (1987). *How writing shapes thinking: a study of teaching and learning.* Urbana, IL: National Council of Teachers of English.

Laughhter, M. Y. (1992). *Genuine Help During Language Arts Instruction.* Unpublished manuscript. Greenville, North Carolina: East Carolina University.

Lee, K. & Van Allen, R. (1963). *The language experience approach.* Newark, DE: International Reading Association.

Lehman, J. (1976). The value of good penmanship. Personal correspondence.

Linden, M. J. & Whimbey, A. (1990). *Why Johnny can't write.* Hillsdale: NJ: Lawrence Erlbaum Associates.

Lippman, M. (1988). Critical thinking: What it can be." *Congitare 2,* 4, 1–2.

Loban, W. (1976). Language development: Kindergarten through grade twelve. Urbana, IL: National Council of Teachers of English.

Lockhead, J. & Whimbey, A. (1987). Teaching analytic reasoning through thinking aloud pair problem solving. In S. Stice (Ed.), *Developing critical thinking and problem-solving abilities.* San Francisco, CA: Jossey-Bass.

Long, S. A., Winograd, P. N. & Bridge, C. A. (1989). The effects of reader and text characteristics on imagery reported during and after reading. *Reading Research Quarterly, XXIV* (3), 353–372.

Lowe, A. J. (1992). Cautions to consider while preparing whole language materials for the beginning readers. Unpublished Manuscript. Tampa, Florida: University of South Carolina.

Lundsteen, S. (1989). *Language arts: A problem-solving approach.* NY: Harper and Row.

Lundsteen, S. & Tunay, E. (1989). *Choose your own learning and teaching activities for language arts.* New York, New York: Harper and Row.

McCaslin, N. (1990). *Creative drama in the classroom* (Fifth Ed.). New York, New York: Longman.

Madden, L. (1992). Learning packages to meet the need of special students. Unpublished Manuscript. Fort Wayne, IN: Indiana—Purdue University.

Mager, R. (1977). *Behavioral Objectives.* N.Y., N.Y.: Wm Brown Publishers.

Manarino-Leggett, P. (1992). Fiddlesticks. Unpublished Manuscript. Fayetteville, NC: Fayetteville State University.

Many, Joyce E. (1991). The effects of stance and age level on children's literacy responses, *Journal of Reading Behavior XXIII* (1), 61–86.

Manzo, A. V. (1981). Using proverbs to teach reading and thinking; or come faceva mia nonna (The way my grandmother did it). *The Reading Teacher, 24* (2), 411–416.

Manzo, A. & Manzo, V. (1985). Expansion modules for the ReQuest, CAT, GRP, and REAP reading/study procedures. *Journal of Reading, 28* (4), 498–503.

Manzo, A. & Manzo, V. (1990). *Content area reading: a heuristic approach.* Columbus, OH: Merrill Publishing Co.

Manzo, A. V. (1992). Proverbs improve higher level thinking and inferrential comprehension. Unpublished Manuscript. Kansas City, MO: University of Missouri.

Manzo, A. V. (1969). The Request procedure. *Journal of Reading, 13,* 123–6.

Marguilies, N. (1991). *Mapping inner space: Learning & teaching mind mapping.* Tucson, AZ: Zepher Press.

Marley, B. & Marley, L. (1992). Shaped Books. Unpublished Manuscript. Oakland City, IN: Oakland City College.

Marsh, J. & Wilder, E. *Identify the effective instructor: A review of the Quantitative Studies, 1800–1952.* Research Bulletin No. AFPACTRC-CCC-TR-54-44. San Antonio, Texas: USAF Personnel Training research Center, 1954.

Marzano, R., Jones, B. F. & Brandt, R. (1988). *Dimensions of thinking.* Alexandria, VA: Association for Supervision and Curriculum.

Mason, J. M. & Au, K. (1990). *Reading instruction for today.* (2nd Edition). Glenview, IL: Scott, Foresman.

Mason, J. M., Kerr, B. M., Senha, S. & McCormick, C. (1990). Shared book reading in an early start program for at-risk children In Zuttrell, J. & McCormack, S. (Eds). *Literacy Theory and Research: Analyses from multiple paradigms.* Chicago, IL: National Reading Conference.

Maxim, G. W. (1990). *The sourcebook: Activities for infants and young children second edition.* Columbus, OH: Merrill.

Maynor, L. C. (1982). An investigation of the revising practices of college freshmen writers. Doctoral dissertation, Duke University, Durham, NC.

McCaslin, N. (1990). *Creative drama in the Classroom* (Fifth Ed.) New York, New York: Longman.

McClain, S. R. (1992). Picture files for second language background building. Unpublished manuscript. Canton, OH: Walsh College.

McClure, J. (1989). *Teaching Poetry.* Portsmouth, NH: Heinemann.

McClure, A., Harrison, P. & Reed, S. (1990). *Sunrises and songs: Reading and writing poetry in an elementary classroom.* Portsmouth, NH: Heinemann.

McIntyre, J. (1991). Phonics: Success In First Grade Speech. Delivered at Texas Christian University. Fort Worth, TX: April.

McNeil, J. D. (1980). How to teach reading successfully. Boston, MA: Little, Brown.

Medley, D. M. (1977). Teacher competence and teacher effectiveness: A review of process-product research. Washington, D.C.: American Association of College for Teacher Education.

Mednick, R. & Mednick, N. (1967). Remote Association Test. NY: Wiley.

Meltzer, L. & Solomon, B. (1988). *Educational prescriptions for the classroom for students with learning problems.* Cambridge, MS: Educators Publishing Service, Inc.

Mervar, K. & Hiebert, E. (1989). Student's self-selection abilities and amount of reading in literature-based and conventional classrooms. Paper presented at the Annual Meeting of the American Educational Research Association, San Francisco, CA.

Miles, B. (1990). When children write to authors. *Learning,* March 1990, pp. 80–82.

Milner, J. O. (1991). Suppositional style and teacher evaluation, *Phi Delta Kappan, 72* (6), 464–467.

Mize, G. J. (1992). The relationship between oral language and reading/writing ability. Unpublished Manuscript. Keene, NH. Keene State College.

Moffett, J. & Wagner, B. J. (1983). *Student-centered language arts and reading, k–13: A handbook for teachers.* Boston: Houghton Mifflin.

Moller, B. (1984). An instructional model for gifted advanced readers. *Journal of Reading, 27,* 323–327.

Moman, J. (1986). *Graciela: A Mexican-American child tells her story.* New York: Watts.

Morgan (1989). Ability grouping in reading instruction: research alternatives. (Fast Bib No. 21 RCS). Bloomington, IN: ERIC Clearinghouse on Reading and Communication Skills.

Morphett, M. V. & Washburne, C. (1931). When should children begin to read? *The elementary school journal, 31,* 496–503.

Morrow, L. M. (1987). Promoting inner city children's recreational reading. *The Reading Teacher, 41* (4), 266–274.

Morrow, L. M. (1983). Home and school correlates of early interest in literature. *Journal of Educational Research, 76,* 221–230.

Morrow, L. M. & Rand, M. K. (1991). Promoting literacy during play by designing early childhood classroom environments. *The Reading Teacher, 44* (6), 396–406.

Moss, J. F. (1984). *Focus units in literature: a handbook for elementary school teachers.* Urbana, IL: National Council of Teachers of English.

Murray, D. (1984). *Write to Learn*. New York: Holt, Rinehart and Winston.

Murray, D. (1982). Teaching the other self: the writer's first reader. *College Composition and Communication, 23*, 140–147.

Myers, C. (1992). Overcoming peer pressure: Teaching students to do so. Unpublished Manuscript. Forth Worth, TX: Texas Christian University.

Nagy, W., Anderson, R. C., Schommer, M., Scott, J. A. & Stallman, A. C. (1989). Morphological families in the internal lexicon. *Reading Research Quarterly, 24* (3), 262–81.

Neisser, V. (1976). *Cognition and reality*. San Francisco: Freeman.

Nessel, D. D. & Jones, M. B. (1981). *The language experience approach to reading: A handbook for teachers*. New York: Teachers College Press.

Neve, R. (1992). Daybooks. *Stories about language, Part 5*. In Newman, J. (Ed). Portsmouth, NH: Heinemann, 79–84.

Newman, J. (1987). *Stories about Language*. Portsmouth, NH: Heinemann.

Newmann, F. M. (1991). Linking Restructuring to Authentic Student Achievement. *Phi Delta Kappan, 72* (6), February, 458–464.

Norton, D. (1990). Teaching multicultural literature in the reading curriculum. *The Reading Teacher, 44* (1), 17–28.

Noyce, C. (1983). Effects of an integrated approach to grammar instructions on third graders reading and writing. *Elementary School Journal, 84*, 63–69.

Nystrand, M. (1991). On the negotiation of understanding between students and teachers: Towards a social-interactive model of school learning. Paper presented at the annual meeting of the American Educational Research Association, Chicago, IL, April.

Nystrand, D. (1989). Sharing Words: The effects of readers on developing writers. Invited address to the American Educational Research Association, Division C. San Francisco, CA: March, 1989.

Nystrand, M. & Gamoran, A. (in press). Instructional discourse student engagement, and literature achievement. *Research in the Teaching of English*.

O'Daly, E., Neiman, E. & Folds, T. (1988). *Adventures for readers*. Orlando, FL: HBJ.

O'Hare, F. (1973). *Sentence combining: Improving students writing without formal grammar instruction*. Urbana, IL: National Council for Teachers of English.

Obenchain, A. (1971). *Effectiveness of the precise essay question in programming the sequential development of written composition skills and the simultaneous development of critical reading skills*. Unpublished master's thesis. George Washington University.

Ogle, D. (in press). Developing problem-solving through language arts instruction in Collins, C. & Mangieri, J. (Eds). *Thinking Development: and agenda for the Twenty-first Century*. Hillsdale, N.J. Lawrence Erlbaum Associates.

Ogle, D. (1991). Problem Solving Through Reading. In Collins, C. & Mangieri, J. *Teaching Thinking: An Agenda For the Twenty-first Century*. Hillsdale, NJ: Erlbaum.

Ollman, H. E. (1991/1992). The voice behind the print: Letters to an author. *Journal of Reading, 35* (4), 322–324.

Osburg, B. J. (1989). The student-centered classroom: Speaking and listening in American literature. In Phetan, P. (Ed) *Talking to learn*. Urbana, IL: National Council of Teachers of English.

Onosko, J. & Newman, F. (in press). Establishing Thoughtful Classrooms. In Mangieri, J. & Collins Block, C. (Eds). *Advanced Educational Psychology: Creating effective schools and powerful thinkers*. Fort Worth, TX: Harcourt Brace Jovanovich.

Owens, R. (1984). *Language development*. Columbus, OH: Charles E. Merrill.

Page, W. D. & Pinnell, G. S. (1979). *Teaching reading comprehension*. Urbana, IL: National Council of Teachers of English.

Palinscar, A. S. & Klenz, L. (1992). Examining and influencing concepts for intentional literacy learning. In Collins, C. & Mangieri, J. (Eds) *Teaching thinking: An agenda for the 21st Century*. Hillsdale, NJ: Laurence Erlbaum.

Palardy, J. (1992). Unpublished Manuscript. Tuscaloosa, Alabama: University of Alabama.

Papalia, D. (1978). *Human development*. New York: McGraw Hill.

Paradis, E. E., Chatton, B., Boswell, A., Smith, M. & Yovich, S. (1991). Accountability: Assessing comprehension during literature discussion. *The Reading Teacher, 45* (1), 8–18.

Parillo, E. (1986). Safety. In Newell, J. (Ed) *Sto-*

ries about language. Portsmouth, NH: Heinemann, 216–219.

Parks, J. H. & Parks, J. E. (1992). Combining Music Instruction With Reading Instruction. Unpublished Manuscript. Topeka, Kansas: Washburn University.

Patullo, D. & Stacy, J. (1986). Skinny Books. *Teaching K–8*, 37.

Pauk, W. (1989). *How to Study in College.* Boston, MA: Houghton Mifflin.

Paul, R. (1990). *Critical thinking handbook: 4th, 6th Grades: A guide for remodeling lesson plans in language arts, social studies, and science.* Rehnert Park, CA: Sonoma State University: Center for Critical Thinking and Moral Critique.

Pearson, P. D. (1989). "Reading and the Whole language movement," *The Elementary School Journal*, 90 (2), 231–241.

Peck, M., Askov, E. N. & Fairchild, S. H. (1980). Another decade of research in handwriting: Progress and prospect in the 1970s, *Journal of Educational Research*, 73, 283–98.

Petelin, C. (1991). Bibliotherapy: A Study of Effects Upon Second Grade Students. Unpublished Manuscript. Fort Worth, TX: Texas Christian University.

Peterman, F. P. (1990). Successful Middle Level School and the Development. *NASSP Bulletin*, 74 (526), 62–65.

Peters, C. W. & Wixon, K. K. (1989). Smart new reading tests are coming. *Learning*, 17 (8), 43–44, 53.

Petry, A. K. (1991). "Data Retrieval Charts." Unpublished Manuscript. Providence, RI: Rhode Island College.

Pflaum, S. W. (1986). *The development of language and literacy in young children.* (3rd. ed.) Columbus, OH: Merrill.

Pflaumer, E. M. (1971). A definition of listening. In Diker, C. (Ed.) *Listening: Readings.* Metuchen, NJ: Scarecrow Press, 1971.

Pflomm, P. N. (1986). *Chalk in hand: The draw and tell book.* Metuchen, NJ: Scarecrow Press.

Piaget, J. (1963). *The origins of intelligence in children.* New York: W. W. Norton and Co., Inc.

Pierson, C. A. (1992). Letter-writing in Kindergarten. Unpublished manuscript. San Marcos, TX: Southwest Texas State University.

Pils, L. J. (1991). Soon anofe you tout me: Evaluation in a first-grade whole language classroom. *The Reading Teacher*, 45 (1), 46–50.

Pinnell, G. S., Fried, M. D. & Estice, R. M. (1990).

Reading recovery: learning how to make a difference. *The Reading Teacher*, 43 (4), 282–295.

Porter, A. & Brophy, J. (1988). Synthesis of research on good teaching. *Educational Leadership*, 45 (8), 74–85.

Powell, A. (1991). Rap and reading speech delivered at Texas Christian University. Fort Worth, TX. April.

Pressley, M., Johnson, C. J., Symons, S., McGoldrick, J. A. et al (1989). Strategies that improve children's memory and comprehension of text. *Elementary School Journal*, 90, 3–32.

Prawat, R. S. (1991). The value of ideas: The immension. *Educational Researcher*, 20 (2), 3–10 and 30.

Pressley, M., El-Dinary, P. B., Gaskins, I., Schuder, T., Bergman, J. L., Almasi, J. & Brown, R. (1991). Direct explanation done will: Transational instruction of reading comprehension strategies paper presents at Annual Meeting of the American Educational Research Association. Chicago, IL. April.

Pressley, M., Harris, K. R. & Marks, M. B. (1991). But strategy instructors are constructionists!! *Educational Psychologist*, 34 (4), 346–378.

Pressley, M., Harris, K. R. & Guthrie, J. (1992). (Eds). *Promoting Literacy and Cognitive.* San Diego, CA: Academic Press.

Pritchard, F. (1992). Concept Spin. Unpublished Manuscript. Salisbury, Maryland: Salisbury State University.

Purcell-Gates, V. (1991). On the outside looking in: A study of remedial readers' meaning-making while reading literature. *Journal of Reading Behavior*, XXIII (2), 235–253.

Purnele, K. N. & Solmon, R. T. (1991). The influence of technical illustrations on students' comprehension in geography. *Reading Research Quarterly*, XXVI, 3, 277–296.

Putnam, L., Bader, L. & Bean, R. (1988). Clinic directors share insights into effective strategies. *Journal of Clinical Reading*, 3, 16–20.

Quinn, C. E. (1988). Sight word spelling tricks. *Academic Therapy*, 23, 289–291.

Raines, S. C. & Canady, R. J. (1990). *The whole language kindergarten.* New York: Teachers College Press.

Raphael, T. E. (1984). Teaching learners about sources of information for answering comprehension questions. *Journal of Reading* 27, 303–311.

Rasinski, T. V. & Fredericks, A. D. (1991). The

Akron paired reading project. *The Reading Teacher, 44* (7), 514–515.

Read, C. (1975). *Children's categorization of speech sounds in English.* Urbana, IL: ERIC Clearinghouse of Reading and Communication Skills and National Council of Teachers of English, Arlington, VA: ERIC Clearinghouse on Languages and Linguistics, ED 112 426.

Reed, P. L., & Roller, C. M. (1991). Moving learners toward independence: The power of scaffolded instruction. *The Reading Teacher, 44* (9), 648–56.

Resnick, L. (1989). *Education and learning to think.* Washington, DC: National Academic Press.

Reynolds, A. J. (1991). Early schooling of children at risk. *American Educational Research Journal, 28* (2), 392–422.

Rhoten, L. & Yellin, D. (1992). Bookbinding: Promoting authorship in emerging readers. Unpublished manuscript. Stillwater, OK: Oklahoma State University.

Richek, M. A. & Glick, L. C. (1991). Coordinating a literacy support program with classroom instruction. *The reading teacher, 44* (7), 474–479.

Riddell, C. B. & Bartlett (1988). Towards a more active vocabulary. *English Journal, 77,* 50–51.

Rieth, H. & Everston, C. (1988). Variables related to the effective instruction of difficult-to-teach children. *Journal of Learning Disabilities, 35* (7), 3384–391.

Rigg, P. & Allen, V. (1989). *When they don't all speak English.* Urbana, IL; National Council of Teachers of English.

Riply, W. & Blair, T. (1991). *Teaching reading in the content area.* Fort Worth, TX: Harcourt Brace Jovanovich.

Rodriques, P. (1983). Brainstorming. Paper presented at the annual meeting of the International Reading Association. Miami, FL.

Rose, L. H. (1992). The writing cycle. Unpublished Manuscript. Mississippi State, MS: Mississippi State University.

Rosenblatt, L. M. (1978). *The reader, the text and the poem.* Carbondale, IL: Southern Illinois University Press.

Rosenshine, B. & Furst, N. "Research on teacher performance criteria." In B. O. (Ed). *Research in Teacher Education.* Englewood Cliffs, N.J.: Prentice-Hall.

Roskos, K. (1992). Free response with a sketch. Unpublished Manuscript. University Heights, Ohio: John Carroll University.

Rosswork, S. G. (1977). Goal setting: The effects on an academic task with varying magnitudes of incentive. *Journal of Educational Psychology, 69,* 710–715.

Ruddell, R. B. & Kern, M. (1986). Characteristics of the most effective teachers. Paper presented at the annual meeting of the American Educational Research Association, Chicago, IL.

Ruddell, R. B. & Haggard, M. R. (1985). Oral and written language acquisition and the reading process. In Singer, H. & Ruddell, R. B. (Eds). *Theoretical models and processes of reading* (3rd ed.) (pp. 63–80). Newark, DE: International Reading Association.

Ruddell, R. (1986). Vocabulary learning: A process model and criteria for evaluating instructional strategies. Paper presented at the annual meeting of the International Reading Association. New Orleans, LA.

Rumelhart, David. "Understanding understanding." In James Flood (Ed.) *Understanding Reading Comprehension.* Newark, DE: International Reading Association.

Rupley, W. H. & Blair, T. R. (1989). *Remedial diagnosis and remediation, third edition.* Columbus, OH: Merrill Publishing Co.

Sadler, W. A. & Whimmey, A. (1985). A holistic approach to improving thinking skills. *Phi Delta Kappan 67* (3), 199–203.

Samson, K. (1992). The interdependent relationship between reading and writing skills. Unpublished Manuscript. Chicago, Illinois: Chicago State University.

Schunk, D. H. (1983). Developing children's self-efficacy and skills: The roles of social comparative information and goal setting. *Contemporary Educational Psychology, 8,* 76–86.

Sadoski, M., Goetz, E. T., Olivarez, A., Lee, S., & Roberts, N. M. (1990). Imagination in story reading: The role of imagery, verbal recall, story analysis, and processing levels. *Journal of Reading Behavior, XXII* (1), 55–70.

Sagan, C. (1990). Science fiction: A personal view. In J. Williamson (Ed). *Teaching science fiction.* Philadelphia, PA: Owlswick Press, 71–83.

Saikey, J. & Fry, E. (1984). *3,000 instant words.* Providence, RI: Jamestown Publishers.

Sampson, M. R. (1986). *The pursuit of literacy: Early reading and writing.* Dubuque, IA: Kendall/Hunt.

Salinger, T. (1989). New directions in testing. Paper presented at the annual convention of the National Reading Conference, Austin, TX.

Santa, C. (1992). Finding main idea grid. *The Reading Teacher, 45* (4), 334–335.

Scott, L. (1992). Introducing classroom rules in kindergartens. Unpublished Manuscript. St. Cloud, MN: St. Cloud State University.

Schaffer, J. (1989). Improving discussion questions: Is anyone out there listening? *English Journal, 78* (4), 40–42.

Schmelzer, R. V. (1992). Teaching metacognitive thinking. Unpublished manuscript. Richmond, KY: Eastern Kentucky University.

Schunk, D. H. & Rice, J. M. (1989). Learning goals and children's reading comprehension. *Journal of reading behavior, 21* (3), 279–293.

Schunk, D. H. (1985). Participation in goal setting: Effects of self-efficacy and skills of learning-disabled children. *Journal of Special Education, 19,* 307–317.

Sebesta, S. & Calder, W. (1986). A canon of children's literature. Paper presented at the World Congress of the International Reading Association, London.

Sendak, M. (1989). Imagination. Videotape from Edwards Film Company. London, England.

Serebrin, W. (1986). Andrew and Molly. In Newman, J. (Ed). *Whole Language.* Portsmouth, NH: Heinemann, 36–43.

Shanklin, Nancy (1982). *Relating reading and writing: Developing a transactional model of the writing process.* Monographs in teaching and learning. Bloomington, IN: Indiana University School of Education.

Shapiro, Jon (1988). Quality of writing and topic choice in whole language classrooms. Paper presented at NRC. Tucson, AZ.

Shuman, R. B. (1991). A portfolio approach to evaluating student writing. *Educational Leadership, 48* (8), 77.

Siegler, R. S. (1989). Strategy diversity and cognitive assessment. *Educational Research, 18* (9), 15–19.

Silberman, A. (1989). *Growing up writing: Teaching children to write, think, and learn.* NY: Random House.

Sinatra, R. (1990). Semantic Mapping: A thinking strategy for improved reading and writing development: Part 1. *Teaching Thinking and Problem Solving, 12* (1), January-February 1990, 3–4.

Singer, H. & Ruddell, R. (1985b). *Theoretical models and processes of reading* (3rd ed.). Newark, DE: International Reading Association.

Skinner, B. J. (1957). *Verbal Behavior.* Boston, MA: Appleton-Century-Crofts.

Sloan, G. D. (1984). *The child As critic: Teaching literature in elementary and middle schools, Second Edition.* New York, NY: Teachers College Press.

Smith, F. (1988). *Insult to intelligence: the bureaucratic invasion of our classrooms.* Portsmouth, NH: Heinemann.

Smith, F. (1978). *Understanding reading.* New York; Holt, Rinehart, and Winston.

Smith, F. (1979). *Reading without nonsense.* New York: Teachers College Press.

Smith, P. (1992). Integrating reading & writing. Unpublished Manuscript. Houston, TX: University of Houston—Clear Lake City.

Smith, R. (1982). *Understanding reading (Third Edition).* New York, NY: Holt, Rinehart, and Winston.

Smith, F. (1988). *Joining the literacy club.* Portsmouth, NH: Heinemann Educational Books.

Smith, D. (1987). Talking with young children about their reading. *Australian Journal of Reading, 10,* 2, 120–123.

Sowers, C. (1986). Three responses in the writing conference. In N. Thomas & N. Atwell (Eds.). *Understanding writing.* Portsmouth, NH: Heinemann.

Spencer, H. (1914). *The principles of psychology.* New York, NY: Appleton and Co.

Sollon, K. (1983). Deliberate silence. Personal correspondence.

Spiegel, D. (1991). Instructional resources for poetry. *The Reading Teacher, 44* (6), Feb. 1991, 427–430.

Stafford, W. (1986). *You must revise your life.* Ann Arbor, MI: University of Michigan Press.

Stahl, S. A. & Fairbanks, M. M. (1986). The effects of vocabulary instruction: A model-based meta-analysis. *Review of Educational Research, 56,* 72–110.

Stombres, K. (1992). *Literature-based learning centers.* Elgin, IL: Judson College.

Statsky, C. (1989). Differences in search process between high school and college seniors, and a comparison with search process of students who have difficulty writing. Paper presented at the American Educational Research Association Annual Meeting, New Orleans, LA.

Stauffer, R. (1969). *Directed reading and thinking approach*. Urbana, IL: National Council of Teachers of English.

Sternberg, R. J. (1985). *Beyond IQ*. New York: Cambridge University Press.

Sternberg, R. J. (1991). Pushing what we know into the twenty-first century. In Collins, C. & Mangieri, J. (Ed). *Building the quality of thinking in and out of schools in the twenty-first century*. Hillsdale, NJ: Erlbaum.

Sternberg, R. J. & Lubant, T. (1991). Creativity reconsidered. *Educational Researcher, 20* (8), 4–14.

Stevens, R. J., Madden, N. A., Slavin, R. W. & Farnish, A. M. (1987). Cooperative integrated reading and composition: Two field experiments. *Reading Research Quarterly, XXII* (4), 433–454.

Stice, C. (1992). Children's literature that teaching letter names, shapes, temporal order, seasons, and basic natural phenomena. Tennessee State University.

Sticht, T. G., Beck, L. J., Hauke, R. N., Kleiman, G. M. & James, J. H. (1974). *Auding and reading: A developmental model*. Alexandria, VA: Human Research Organization.

Stotsky, S. L. (1989). Differences in search process between high school and college seniors, and a comparison with search process of students who have difficulty writing. Paper presented at the American Educational Research Association Annual Meeting, New Orleans, LA.

Stotsky, S. L. (1975). Sentence-combining as a curricular activity: Its effects on written language development and reading comprehension. *Research in the Teaching of English, 9*, 30–71.

Straw, S. B. & Schreiner, R. (1982). The effect of sentence manipulation of subsequent measures of reading and listening. *Reading research Quarterly, 17*, 339–352.

Strong, C. (1986). Creative approaches to sentence-combining. Urbana, IL: Eric clearing house on reading and communication skills and the National Council of Teachers of English.

Stuart, V. & Graves, D. (1987). *How to teach writing*. Urbana, IL: National Council of Teachers of English.

Suhor, C. (1987). Orthodoxies in language arts instruction. *Language Arts, 64*, 4, 416–420.

Sulzby, E., Teale, W. H. & Kamberelis, G. (1989). Emergent writing in the classroom: Home and school connections. In D. S. Strickland & L. M. Morrow (Eds.). *Emergent literacy: Young children learn to read and write*. Newark, D. E.: International Reading Association.

Sulzby, E. (in press). Computer writing instruction in early literacy. In Magieri, J. & Collins, Block C. (Eds.) *Advanced Educational Psychology: Creating effective schools and powerful thinkers*. Fort Worth, TX: Harcourt, Brace, Jovanovich.

Sumner, D. (1986). Time and the taking of it. In Newkirk, T. & Atwell, N. (Eds.). *Understanding writing*. Portsmouth, NH: Heinemann, 155–160.

Sutton, C. (1989). Helping the nonnative English speaker with reading. *The Reading Teacher, 42* (8), 684–688.

Swanson, C. H. (1986). Teachers as listeners: An exploration. ''Paper presented at the 7th Annual Convention of the International Listening Association,'' Philadelphia.

Taba, H. (1975). New Social Studies curriculum models. Paper presented at the National Council of Social Studies Teachers. Boston, MA.

Tang, B. (1992). Reading & writing instruction with the whole language perspective. Unpublished Manuscript. Ponce, Puerto Rico: Catholic University of Puerto Rico.

Teale, W. H. (1987). Emergent literacy: Reading and writing development in early childhood. In J. E. Readence and R. S. Baldwin (Eds.). *Research in literacy: Merging perspectives* (pp. 45–74). Thirty-sixth Yearbook of the National Reading Conference. Rochester, NY: National Reading Conference.

Teale, W. H. & Sulzby, E. (1986). *Emergent literacy: Writing and reading*. Norwood, NJ: Ablex Publishing Corporation.

Teale, W. H. (1986). Home background and young children's literacy development. In W. H. Teale, and E. Sulzby (Eds.). *Emergent literacy: Writing and reading* (pp. 173–206). Norwood, NJ: Ables.

Temple, C., Nathan, R. Burris, N. & Temple, F. (1988). *The Beginning of Writing*. Boston, MA: Allyn and Bacon.

Thurber, D. N. (1978). *D'Nealian handwriting*. Glenview, IL: Scott, Foresman.

Tierney, R. J., Readeance, J. E. & Dishner, E. K. (1990). *Reading strategies and practices, a compen-

dium, Third Edition. Boston, MA: Allyn and Bacon.

Tobiias, T. (1974). *Isamu Noguchi: The life of a sculptor.* New York: Crowell.

Tollefson, N., Tracy, D. B., Johnsen, E. P., Tarner, A. W. & Bueaning, M. (1984). Goal setting and personal responsibility training for LD adolescents. *Psychology in the schools, 21,* 224–233.

Tompkins, G. E. & Yaden, D. B. (1986). *Answering students' questions about words.* Urbana, IL: ERIC Clearinghouse on Reading and Communication Skills and National Council of Teachers of English, 1986.

Topping, P. (1987). Tutoring through computers. *The Reading Teacher, 41* (1), 113–117.

Torrance, E. P. (1979). The Torrance tests of creative thinking. Lexington, MA: Personal Press/Gunn.

Travers, R. (1982). *Essentials of learning: The new cognitive learning of students in education.* New York: Macmillan.

Travers, P. (1992). The importance of teaching creativity in our schools. Unpublished manuscript. Weatherford, OK: Southwestern Oklahoma State University.

Trelease, J. (1989). *The new read-aloud handbook.* New York: Penguin.

Tunnell, M. O. & Jacobs, J. S. (1989). Using "real" books: Research findings on literature based reading instruction. *The Reading Teacher, 42* (7), 470–477.

Valencia, S. & Pearson, P. D. (1987). Reading assessment: Time for a change. *The Reading teacher, 40,* 726–732.

Valeri-Gold, M., Olson, J. R. & Deming, M. P. (1991–1992). Portfolios: Collaborative authentic assessment opportunities for college development learners. *Journal of Reading, 35* (4), 298–304.

Van Allen, R. (1974). *Language experiences in reading: Teachers resource guide.* Chicago: Encyclopedia Brittanica Educational Corporation.

Vaughn, S. C. & Milligan, J. L. (1986). If they learn to read by reading, how do we get them started? Paper presented at the 7th Annual Transmountain Regional Conference of the International Reading Association, Vancouver, British Columbia, May 29–31.

Veatch, J. (1991). Individualized reading was the beginning of the whole language approach. Paper presented at the annual meeting of the International Reading Association. Las Vegas, NV, April.

Veatch, J. (1989). Individualization. Video tape. JV Productions, Tucson, Arizona.

Vygotsky, L. (1962). *Thought and language.* Cambridge: MIT Press.

Vygotsky, L. S. (1978). *Thought and language.* Translated by A. Kozulin. Cambridge, MA: MIT Press.

Walker, J. (1975). *Your reading.* Urbana, IL: National Council of Teachers of English.

Ward, G. (1988). *I've got a project on.* Rozell, Australia: Primary English Teaching Association.

Wardhaugh, R. (1971). Theories of language acquisition in relation to beginning reading instruction. In F. B. Davis (ed.). *The literature of research in reading with emphasis in models.* New York: McGraw Hill.

Washington, V. M. (1988a). Report writing: A practical application of semantic mapping. *The Teacher Educator, 24,* 1, 24–30.

Washington, V. M. (1988b). Semantic mapping: A heuristic for helping learning disabled students write reports. *Reading, writing, and learning disabilities, 4,* 17–25.

Wasik, B. A. & Slavin, R. E. (1990). *Preventing early reading failure with one-to-one tutoring: A best evidence synthesis.* Baltimore, MD: The Johns Hopkins University, Center for Research on Effective Schooling for Disadvantaged Students.

Watson, R. (1979). *Psychology of the child and adolescent.* New York: Macmillan.

Weaver, C. (1988). *Reading process and practice: From psycholinguistics to whole language.* Portsmouth, NH: Heinemann.

Weisberg, R. & Balajthy, E. (1991). Transfer effects of prior knowledge and use of graphic organizers on college development readers' summarization and comprehension of expository text. In Zutell, J. & S. McCormick (Eds.). *Literacy Theory and Research: Analysis from multiple paradigms.* Chicago, IL: National Reading Conference, 339–346.

Welker, W. A. (1991). Oral reading: Don't teach class without it. *Reading Today,* December 1990/January 1991, 24.

Wells, G. (1986). *The meaning makes: Children learning languages and using Languages to Learn.* Portsmouth, NH: Heinemann.

Wendler, D., Samuels, S. J. & Moore, V. K. (1989). Comprehension instruction of award-winning teachers, teachers with master's degrees, and other teachers. *Reading Research Quarterly, 24* (4), 382–401.

Wepner, S. (1992). How to help your child become a better writer. Unpublished Manuscript. Wayne, New Jersey: William Paterson College of New Jersey.

White, M. (1979). *High interest—easy reading lists.* Urbana, IL: National Council of Teachers of English.

White, T. G., Power, M. A. & White, S. (1989). Morphological analysis: Implications for teaching and understanding vocabulary growth. *Reading Research Quarterly, 24* (3), 283–304.

Wiesendanger, K. D. (1992). Using semantic mapping to integrate the reading and writing process. Unpublished manuscript. Alfred, NY: Alfred University.

Wiseman, D. L. (1992). Double entry diary. Unpublished manuscript. College Station, TX: Texas A&M University.

Wikstrom, M. (1992). Unpublished Manuscript. Storm Lake, Iowa: Buena Vista College.

Wilde, S. (1989a). Looking at invented spelling: A kidwatcher's guide to spelling, part 1. In Goodman, K. et al. (Ed.) *The whole language evaluation book.* Portsmouth, NH: Heinemann.

Wilde, S. (1989b). Understanding spelling strategies: A kidwatcher's guide to spelling, part 2. In Goodman, K. et al. (Ed.) *The whole language evaluation book.* Portsmouth, NH: Heinemann.

Williams, J. (1991). Phonics: Success in first grade. Speech. Texas Christian University. Fort Worth, TX. April.

Willinsky, J. (1990). *The New Literacy.* New York: Routledge.

Wisconsin Language Arts Curriculum Guide. (1987). *Wisconsin State Department of Education Curriculum Guides.* Madison, WI: State Department of Education.

Witty, P. A. (1971). *Reading for the gifted and creative student.* Newark, DE: International Reading Association.

Witty, P. A. (1985). Rationale for fostering creative reading in the gifted and the creative. In M. Labuda (ed.). *Creative learning for gifted learners (second edition).* Newark, DE: International Reading Association.

Wolf, D., Bixby, J., Glenn, J. & Gardner, H. (1991). To use their minds well: Investigating new forms of student assessment. In Grant, G. (Ed.). *Review of Research In Education, Volume 17,* pp. 31–75.

Wolven, A. D. & Coakley, C. G. (1979). Listening instructions (TRIP Booklet). Urbana, IL: ERIC Clearinghouse on Reading and communication Association.

Worell, J. & Danner, F. (1989). *The adolescent as decision maker: Applications to development and education.* San Diego, CA: Academic Press.

Wuertenberg, J. (1986). Conferencing with young authors. Paper presented at the Annual Bill Martin Literary Conference, East Texas State University, Commerce, TX.

Wyatt, F. (1992). Research beginnings. Unpublished Manuscript. Lawrence, Kansas: The University of Kansas.

Yochum, N. (1990). Children's learning informational text: The relationship between prior knowledge and text structure. *Journal of Reading Behavior, XXIII* (1), 87–104.

Young, T. (1992). Extending thinking about literature: The double entry diary. Unpublished Manuscript. Arlington, TX: University of Texas—Arlington.

Zabrucky, K. & Ratner, N. H. (1989). Effects of reading ability on children's comprehension evaluation and regulation. *Journal of Reading Behavior, 21,* 69–83.

ACKNOWLEDGMENTS

CHAPTER 3

TABLE 3-1   Adapted from Walter Loban, *LANGUAGE DEVELOPMENT: KINDERGARTEN THROUGH GRADE TWELVE* (Urbana, IL: National Council of Teachers of English, 1976) and Christine Pappas, Barbara Z. Keifer, and Linda S. Levotik, *An Integrated Language Perspective in the Elementary School* White Plaines, NY: Longman, 1990.

Figure 3-5   *Critical Thinking Handbook: 4th–6th Grades; A Guide for Remodeling Lesson Plans in Language Arts, Social Studies & Science,* Paul, Richard W., Binker, A. J. A., Jensen, Karen, Keklau, Heidi, c. 1990, Foundation for Critical Thinking, Santa Rosa, California.

CHAPTER 5

Figure 5-1   *3,000 Instant Words,* 2nd Edition, by Elizabeth Sakley and Edward Fry, Jamestown Publications, Providence, RI. 1984, reprinted by permission of author.

Figure 5-3   References used in compiling the list of phonic generalizations from: Hanna, P. R. et al. (1966). *Phoneme-Grapheme Correspondences as Cues to Spelling Improvement.* Washington, D.C.: US Department of Education: Clymer, T. (1963). "The Utility of Phonic Generalizations in The Primary Grades." *The Reading Teacher* 15(5), 252–258.

Figure 5-4   Total Reading, Los Angeles, CA, reprinted by permission of the publisher.

Figure 5-6   From Johnson D. and Pearson P. D. (1978). *Teaching Vocabulary.* Fort Worth, TX: Harcourt Brace Jovanovich.

Figure 5-8   From Levin, McCormick, Miller, Berry, Pressley, American Educational Research Association (1986), reprinted by permission of the publisher.

CHAPTER 6

Figure 6-2   Reprinted with permission from Constance Weaver, *Reading Process and Practice* (Heinemann Educational Books, Portsmouth, NH, 1988).

Figure 6-3   Reprinted with permission of Donna Ogle and the International Reading Association.

Figure 6-9   From *Kids, Kittens, and a Frog,* Hartley Courseware, Dimondale, MI.

Figure 6-10   Courtesy of Dr. Katherine D. Weisendanger, Alfred University, Alfred, NY.

Figure 6-11   "Mind Mapping to Improve Listening and Reading Comprehension," New Horizon Publishing Company, Yelm, WA.

"Guidelines for Judging and Selecting Elementary Language Arts Textbooks," from the NCTE Committee on Elementary Language Arts Textbooks, *Language Arts,* March 1991, by the National Council of Teachers of English. Reprinted with permission.

CHAPTER 7

Figure 7-7   Created by and courtesy of Dr. Terrell A. Young, University of Texas-Arlington, Arlington, TX.

CHAPTER 8

Figure 8-3   Taken from TCU Information Services Newsletter, 1989, Fort Worth, TX.

Figure 8-9   Courtesy of Dr. Rhonda Taylor, Marietta College, Marietta, OH.

Nancy © 1973 reprinted by permission of UFS, Inc.

From Language Arts: *Learning Processes and Teaching Practices,* 2nd Edition, by Charles Temple and Jean Wallace Gillet. Copyright © 1989, 1984 by Charles Temple and Jean Wallace Gillet. Reprinted by permission of HarperCollins Publishers.

CHAPTER 9

Picture 9-2   Courtesy of Dr. Bernard Bull, Carson-Newman College, Jefferson City, TN.

Figure 9-4   "Fat Cat Words," *Basic Goals in Spelling,* 5th ed., William Kottmeyer and Audrey Claus. Reproduced with permission of Macmillan/McGraw-Hill School Publishing Company, c. 1976.

Figure 9-6   *Handwriting: A Way to Self-Expression,* Copyright 1991. Zaner-Bloser Educational Publishers, Columbus, OH.

Figure 9-10   From *Phonics They Use; Words for Reading and Writing*, by Patricia M. Cummingham. Copyright 1991 by HarperCollins Publishers. Reprinted by permission.

CHAPTER 10

Picture 10-1   Courtesy of Dr. Sylvia Artmann, Dallas Baptist University, Dallas, TX, and Dr. Romaine Jesky-Smith, Geneva College, Beaver Falls, PA.

Picture 10-2   Courtesy of Dr. Allison Brennan, Director of Reading Programs in Louisville, KY.

CHAPTER 11

Picture 11-1   Courtesy of Dr. Sylvia Artmann, Dallas Baptist University, Dallas, TX, and Dr. Romaine Jesky-Smith, Geneva College, Beaver Falls, PA.

CHAPTER 12

Figure 12-6   Adapted from "Story Letters," Addison Wesley, Palo Alto, CA.

CHAPTER 13

Permission to reprint from the Whole Language Kindergarten Excerpts from the NAEYC Position Paper: Developmentally Appropriate Practice in Programs for 4- and 5-Year Olds.

Excerpted from: Moyer, J., Egertson, H., and Isenberg, J. (1987). The Child-Centered Kindergarten. *Childhood Education, 63*, 235–242. Reprinted by permission of the authors and the Association of Childhood Education International, Wheaton, MD. Copyright 1987 by the Association.

CHAPTER 14

Figure 14-2   "Writing to an author" from "The voice behind the print: Letters to an author," Hilda E. Ollman, *JOURNAL OF READING,* December 91/January 92, PP 322–324, reprinted with permission of the International Reading Association.

Figure 14-3   Reprinted with permission from Lee Iacocca, Chrysler Corporation, Highland Park, MI.

CHAPTER 15

Figure 15-2   Copyright Les Parsons from his book *Response Journals.* Reprinted with permission. Pembroke Publishers Limited, 528 Hood Road, Markham, Ontario L3R 3K9. Available in the US from Heinemann Educational Books.

Figure 15-3   From *An Integrated Language Perspective in The Elementary School: Theory Into Action*, by Christine C. Pappas, Barbara Z. Keifer, and Linda S. Levistik. Copyright c. 1990 by Longman Publishing Group.

Figure 15-4   Reprinted with permission, Christopher-Gordon Publishers, Inc., Norwood, MA.

Index